# ESSAYS IN NINETEENTH-CENTURY AMERICAN LEGAL HISTORY

# ESSAYS IN NINETEENTH-CENTURY AMERICAN LEGAL HISTORY

## EDITED BY WYTHE HOLT

**PROFESSOR OF LAW, UNIVERSITY OF ALABAMA, TUSCALOOSA**

*CONTRIBUTIONS IN AMERICAN HISTORY, NUMBER 60*

GREENWOOD PRESS
WESTPORT, CONNECTICUT • LONDON, ENGLAND

Library of Congress Cataloging in Publication Data

Main entry under title:

Essays in nineteenth-century American legal history.

(Contributions in American history ; no. 60)
Includes index.
1. Law—United States—History and criticism
—Addresses, essays, lectures. I. Holt, Wythe.
KF366.E8      340'.0973      76-27129
ISBN 0-8371-9285-4

Library of Congress Catalog Card Number: 76-27129
ISBN 0-8371-9285-4

First published in 1976

Greenwood Press, Inc.
51 Riverside Avenue, Westport, Connecticut 06880

Printed in the United States of America

Each of the articles in this volume has been reprinted here by express permission both of the holder of the copyright thereto and of all others concerned, as acknowledged below.
    *Now and Then: The Uncertain State of Nineteenth-Century American Legal Histoy* is reprinted with the permission of the Indiana Law Review and of Fred B. Rothman & Co.
    *The Law in United States History,* by Willard Hurst, was originally published in the Proceedings of the American Philosophical Society and is reprinted by permission of and payment to the American Philosophical Society, and with the permission of the author.
    The book review, by G. Edward White, is reprinted by permission of and payment to the Virginia Law Review, and with the permission of Fred B. Rothman & Co. and the author.

*This volume is from my teachers, for my students,
and to my friends: may the circles coincide.*

# CONTENTS

# PREFACE

## I

The last ten years have seen a burgeoning of interest in the area of American legal history. A large group of young scholars has made it a field of serious substantive endeavor. The production of articles and minor studies has reached measurable proportions, although it is by no means yet a flood, and a few major works have reached print. Deans are beset by requests to double or triple the number of course-offerings in this area. Law schools and departments of history in major universities have, sometimes severally, occasionally jointly, demonstrated an increasing level of interest. Law students, though ever wary of the demands and delimitations of bar examinations, are also showing signs of a collective increase in enthusiasm. Those major figures, such as George Haskins and Willard Hurst, who have labored in the legal history vineyards almost alone for decades at last have a growing fellowship of companions.

It is not yet clear whether this phenomenon is a fad or an awakening of real interest. For legal history to establish itself as a real and useful field, the traditional obscurantist pettinesses of dilettantism, antiquarianism, and production under the pressure to publish or perish must yield to a true spirit of inquiry devoted to education, to the uplifting of the human spirit, and to the betterment of the republic. Research and writing should be based upon solid philosophical grounds and should be devoted to the argumentation and explication of broad but definite sociophilosophical points of view.

However, the rise of interest in American legal history has come at a crucial moment of philosophical uncertainty. The bankruptcy of modern liberal thought, academically represented in its decadence by the chauvinistic, uncritical, and practically schizophrenic dispute-stifling of Cold War consensus pluralism, has been forcefully demonstrated by authors such as Roberto Unger (in his recent *Knowledge and Politics*). Liberalism itself has increasingly tended to be antiphilosophical, eschewing open reliance upon an articulate and systematic collection of beliefs in favor of a stated adherence to pragmatism. And so the confident multifariousness of liberalistic scholarly production at its zenith has begun to give way to a hasty and even frightened scramble to find new philosophical roots as liberalism crumbles.

These two sources of differing directions—confident liberalism and crumbling liberalism—are mirrored in the work now being produced in American legal history. A cross-section of the scholarly production in the field demonstrates a melange of interests, a potpourri of typologies, a variety of purposes. A useful and representative collection of essays in the area must, then, reflect this variegated uncertainty, and I have attempted to bring together the best examples of all of the widely differing styles, methodologies, and points of view now available. Every flavor of recently taken historiographical approach is included, in the form of a major statement where possible.

The introductory piece is a historiographical essay designed to give the reader a more thoroughgoing idea of the current state of the art. That is, specific themes, trends, and interconnections are dealt with in much greater detail therein. Those articles which I consider to be major statements of approach and theme by representatives of the primary schools of thought follow next. In order to give examples of these schools—and to include the many articles that do not fit neatly into any school—the remainder of the collection is rather loosely grouped under three headings: substance and procedure, constitutional issues, and the profession. Topics range from substantive fields of law to biography, to developments in a single county, from the study of cases to legal education to social theory.

Unfortunately I have not been able to include all I wished. Space has been limited, despite the publisher's generosity in this regard. The boundary dates are, very roughly, 1789 and 1900, the former because David Flaherty has put together an excellent collection of essays dealing with the legal history of our colonial and revolutionary periods (University of North Carolina Press, 1969), and the latter because of the relative dearth of good work concerned with the twentieth century. Where an essay was easily available in another collection, such as the 1971 volume of *Perspectives in American History* edited by Bernard Bailyn and Donald Fleming, I declined to reprint it here (with the exception of Morton Horwitz's seminal essay on the beginnings of instrumentalism, included because of its primary importance). The electroreproductory manner of publication has prevented both the inclusion of essays that have not previously appeared elsewhere and the reworking or correcting of the articles included.

Nevertheless this collection contains the best examples of the recent large increase in work in nineteenth-century American legal history. The general reader will find that there is a good deal of illumination cast by supposedly "legal" topics upon our social and political history. Those of a more academic bent will find more than enough to be utilized in courses in legal, social and political history. As all of us grow, and as present uncertainties dim while others emerge, many of these essays will take on new significance and utility.

## II

The debts one accumulates even in compiling a collection are enormous, and it is now my pleasure to attempt to acknowledge some of them. In concluding upon the present twenty-three essays, I have sifted through and filched from the syllabi and suggestions of many of my fellow American legal historians. Kitty Preyer, Willie Lee Rose, Joe Smith, George Priest, Steve Presser, Wex Malone, and Joseph Burke have gone out of their way to be kind and supportive. Stanley Kutler and my colleague at the University of Alabama School of Law, Timothy Hoff, offered helpful suggestions concerning the contents of the collection. For help in the tasks of assembling, organizing, and publishing the whole, I am indebted to the kind and generous assistance of David Flaherty, Stanley Katz, Harry Scheiber, Bill Nelson, James Ely, and particularly Max Bloomfield, who has offered moral support whenever it was needed and who has saved this idea from extinction on at least one occasion.

It has been my good fortune to have encountered three of the great people in my field, and to have been able to benefit from the depth and breadth of their visions, from their offerings of intellectual sustenance, and most of all from their encouragement, kindness, and generosity. Calvin Woodard, Willard Hurst, and Morty Horwitz have each consistently demonstrated an unselfish, lofty, and passionate spirit of academic and scholarly debate and enterprise. They are inspirational teachers.

To you all, many thanks.

WYTHE HOLT
Cambridge, Massachusetts
April 1, 1976

# A. INTRODUCTION

# 1

# NOW AND THEN: THE UNCERTAIN STATE OF NINETEENTH-CENTURY AMERICAN LEGAL HISTORY

*WYTHE HOLT*

VOLUME 7          1974          NUMBER 4

INDIANA LAW REVIEW

# NOW AND THEN: THE UNCERTAIN STATE OF NINETEENTH-CENTURY AMERICAN LEGAL HISTORY

WYTHE HOLT*

Two conclusions must be drawn by anyone who attempts a survey of nineteenth-century American legal history. First, there is no general agreement on what "legal history" is or what the utility of legal history research may be. Second, most legal historians either are sure they know what they are doing or are unconcerned with the problem. This is a deplorable state of affairs, but fortunately we are in our infancy and there is sufficient time and few enough practitioners of the art to allow for comprehensive appraisal and debate upon these problems. Hopefully this Article will help to focus the issues and stimulate such a debate.

## I. DEFINITIONS

We must constantly caution ourselves against going about the task of writing legal history from the standpoint that "law" is something studiable by itself. We have, perhaps, from the very existence of the legal profession and of schools in which "law" is "taught," but more likely from our own desire to be considered scholarly, the idea that there is a discipline, a practical subject-matter called "law," internally complete, which is recondite, complex, and difficult to fathom but which nevertheless can be "mastered" or even written about. Thus, we say to ourselves, it must have a history.

Such is not the case. While it is true that there is a great deal of detritus lying about law school libraries, attics of county courthouses, and storerooms in state legislatures, these are merely compilations of words. "Law" has no meaning unless we are attempting to investigate why a statute was passed, what forces and factors influenced any given court decision or administrative ruling, how legal education developed as it did, and why members of the bench and bar play the rigid roles they play. Legal history is only social history, political history, educational history, urban history, and labor history in a fashionable, mystical, and somewhat impenetrable and awesome disguise. Nothing could be less interesting and less useful than tracing how trespass grew into negli-

---

*Associate Professor of Law and Lecturer in History, University of Alabama. B.A., Amherst College, 1963; J.D., University of Virginia, 1966.

gence, unless one understands and operates from the assumption that legal doctrine grows and changes only to meet certain social needs.[1] Legal history, as Willard Hurst has for so long emphasized, deals both with the effect of social change upon "law" and with the ways in which men use "law" to effect social change.[2] Or, as Oliver Wendell Holmes put it, "[t]he law is the witness and external deposit of our moral life. Its history is the history of the moral development of the race."[3]

This is not to say that we are in no need of Holdsworths. Indeed, so long as our present-day Holdsworth understands that it is social change and not really the growth of doctrine that he is chronicling, he ought to be in much demand. We do not know much at all about the growth of most branches of substantive law during what is called the "formative era of American law,"[4] and the pioneering efforts of Lawrence Friedman,[5] Morton Horwitz,[6]

---

[1]*See* Gregory, *Trespass to Negligence to Absolute Liability*, 37 VA. L. REV. 359 (1951).

[2]*See, e.g.*, W. HURST, THE LEGITIMACY OF THE BUSINESS CORPORATION IN THE LAW OF THE UNITED STATES 1780-1970 (1970); W. HURST, LAW AND ECONOMIC GROWTH: THE LEGAL HISTORY OF THE LUMBER INDUSTRY IN WISCONSIN 1836-1915 (1964); W. HURST, JUSTICE HOLMES ON LEGAL HISTORY (1964); W. HURST, LAW AND THE CONDITIONS OF FREEDOM IN THE NINETEENTH-CENTURY UNITED STATES (1956); W. HURST, THE GROWTH OF AMERICAN LAW: THE LAW MAKERS (1950).

An excellent summary of Hurst's work and thought may be found in Murphy, *The Jurisprudence of Legal History: Willard Hurst as a Legal Historian*, 39 N.Y.U.L. REV. 900 (1964); most of his articles and reviews are also referred to in Flaherty, *An Approach to American History: Willard Hurst as Legal Historian*, 14 AM. J. LEGAL HIST. 222 (1970). My own criticism of Hurst's approach has been made at greater length elsewhere. *See* Holt, Book Review, 1971 WIS. L. REV. 982. For other useful criticism of Hurst, see Scheiber, *At the Borderland of Law and Economic History: The Contributions of Willard Hurst*, 75 AM. HIST. REV. 744 (1970); Woodard, Book Review, 19 LA. L. REV. 560 (1959).

[3]Holmes, *The Path of the Law*, 10 HARV. L. REV. 457, 459 (1897).

[4]This era was so called by Roscoe Pound, R. POUND, THE FORMATIVE ERA OF AMERICAN LAW (1938), and the concept has been enthusiastically accepted by many ever since. *See, e.g.*, A. CHROUST, THE RISE OF THE LEGAL PROFESSION IN AMERICA (1965).

[5]*See, e.g.*, L. FRIEDMAN, A HISTORY OF AMERICAN LAW (1973); Friedman, *Legal Rules and the Process of Social Change*, 19 STAN. L. REV. 786 (1967); Friedman, *The Dynastic Trust*, 73 YALE L.J. 547 (1964). *See also* Friedman & Ladinsky, *Social Change and the Law of Industrial Accidents*, 67 COLUM. L. REV. 50 (1967).

[6]*See* Horwitz, *The Transformation in the Conception of Property in American Law: 1780-1860*, 40 U. CHI. L. REV. 248 (1973); Horwitz, *The*

and Harry Scheiber,[7] to mention three outstanding scholars at work in doctrinal history, are most necessary and welcome.[8]

Moreover, since we are dealing with the history of social change in the United States, more attention must be paid to theory. As Hurst expresses it, "legal history research needs more philosophical dimension than it has typically shown, to put it into some context of theory about the working relations of legal processes to the overall structure and processes of American history."[9] Many of our nineteenth-century legal historians do attempt to set their work within a comprehensive theoretical scheme—Hurst and Calvin Woodard[10] being prime examples—but most of the work done so far lacks any sense of philosophy. To be most useful, legal history must attempt to trace the most important ways in which law has been utilized and acted upon in American society. Law and legal institutions have proven to be crucial in American history, and so legal historians, as demonstrated by Richard E. Ellis' valuable book on Jeffersonian times,[11] are dealing with issues and events fundamental to an understanding of American history. To grapple with such material, only a broad and deep theoretical approach will suffice.

The difficulty is that constructing a theory requires having a philosophy; the legal historian must make some hard choices about what has been and, indeed, what ought to be most valuable in the American experience. Only if the writer is capable of judging can he do his job. He must be aware of the broad range of moral choices open to the American people and must have a

---

*Historical Foundations of Modern Contract Law*, 87 HARV. L. REV. 917 (1974); Horwitz, "Damage Judgments, Legal Liability, and Economic Development Before the Civil War," to be published in the *American Journal of Legal History*.

[7]*See* Scheiber, *Property Law, Expropriation and Resource Allocation by the Government: the United States, 1789-1910*, 33 J. ECON. HIST. 232 (1973); Scheiber, *The Road to* Munn: *Eminent Domain and the Concept of Public Purpose in the State Courts*, 5 PERSPECTIVES AM. HIST. 329 (1971).

[8]*See* text accompanying notes 31-33, 74-79 *infra*.

[9]Letter from Willard Hurst to Wythe Holt, July 25, 1973.

[10]*See* Woodard, *History, Legal History and Legal Education*, 53 VA. L. REV. 89 (1967); Woodard, *Reality and Social Reform: The Transition from Laissez-Faire to the Welfare State*, 72 YALE L.J. 286 (1962).

[11]R. ELLIS, THE JEFFERSONIAN CRISIS: COURTS AND POLITICS IN THE YOUNG REPUBLIC (1971). This work is discussed in the text accompanying notes 69, 70 *infra*.

fairly complete notion of how and why certain paths were thought better than others or were thought about incompletely or not at all. He must also understand that much of history is not made through rational human choice. Holmes summed up the task confronting the legal historian:

> The way to gain a liberal view of your subject is . . . in the first place, to follow the existing body of dogma into its highest generalizations by the help of jurisprudence; next, to discover from history how it has come to be what it is; and, finally, so far as you can, to consider the ends which the several rules seek to accomplish, the reasons why those ends are desired, what is given up to gain them, and whether they are worth the price.[12]

The dangers inherent in this task are enormous. Foremost among them, because most prevalent, is the danger of supposed omniscience. The job of writing anything, but especially legal history, must be approached from a view of enlightened skepticism: there are no absolutes, other people will make other value choices, the universe is a formless and chaotic place. Given that one is unable to take into account all the factors and possibilities that occur randomly to one's active mind, or to put into words the multitude of thoughts which from time to time come to the surface of consciousness, one surely cannot comprehend the whole of the American past nor make all of the correct evaluations of it. People feel differently about things. Events occur that are beyond one's planning capabilities. Dogmatism should be furthest from the mind of someone writing the history of legal dogma, but unfortunately such is rarely the case. The necessary balance between the historian's task of making judgments and his awareness that he will not always make the right ones is precarious, frustrating, and productive in itself of intolerance and rigidity on a grand scale. But the best legal historians will maintain the balance and indeed will sharpen their judgmental acuity by doing so.

Even more dangerous is the probability—given the aversion that most people have to thinking in the ways delineated here, the limited nature of man's capacity to perceive, and the disorder of man's surroundings—that the work of the legal historian will be to no avail. This tends to discourage one from giving to the task the enormous amounts of time, energy, and concentrated seriousness that it requires. Nevertheless the task must be attempted. As Holmes wrote:

---

[12]Holmes, *supra* note 3, at 476.

> It does not follow, because we all are compelled to take
> on faith at second hand most of the rules on which we base
> our action and our thought, that each of us may not try to
> set some corner of his world in the order of reason, or that
> all of us collectively should not aspire to carry reason
> as far as it will go throughout the whole domain.[13]

This view is shared by Hurst: "[T]hough directed effort may
have only marginal effects, those effects are humanly important,
and . . . in any case our human dignity requires that we make the
effort."[14] The idea can be put more positively. Writing into the
teeth of chaos is cause for rejoicing rather than despair, because
it means that one is free to make mistakes without threat of
mysterious damnation, and because it gives rise to two of the
greatest joys it is possible to experience: the joy of engaging in
activity buoyed by the hope that it might prove useful and the
joy of attempting to communicate with and give aid to others.

It occurs to me that, having reached the end of a section entitled "Definitions," I may be thought to have failed to define
legal history. I can do no better than repeat the words of Calvin
Woodard:

> The true function of Legal History . . . is to help lawyers
> and legal scholars, who are essentially concerned with
> current problems, to be meaningfully aware of the past
> as a healthy check on our often overly-optimistic and un-
> founded hopes; to provide gentle redress in our moments
> of frustration and disappointment; to act as an indispens-
> able aid in drawing the ever-difficult distinction between
> the "temporal" and the "eternal," the changing and the
> unchanging; and, above all, to provide awareness and ap-
> preciation of the value and meaning of "civilization."[15]

## II.  WORK TO DATE

### A.  *Theme and Theory*

The nature and the amount of work currently being done in
the field of nineteenth-century American legal history is, on the
whole, disappointing, although the situation is improving. There

---

[13]*Id.* at 468.

[14]Letter from Willard Hurst to Wythe Holt, Feb. 22, 1971.

[15]Woodard, *History, Legal History and Legal Education*, 53 VA. L. REV.
89, 105-06 (1967).

are very few people working from guided theoretical approaches, attempting to delineate and explain important changes in American society. Many studies seem to be motivated by sheer personal interest, by the desire to be chic, or by the necessity of having to write something to get or maintain an academic degree or position. People, of course, should write about that which interests them; but to do so in the absence of a coherent theoretical perspective, without stated values, is wasteful. Those who frankly acknowledge their inadequacy to puzzle through and construct a theoretical approach ought to be content at least to work under some other person who does—to criticize and fill in the interstices of the theoretician's proposals with careful empirical studies, while bearing in mind the theory's philosophical and historical implications.

At least two men have approached the writing of nineteenth-century American legal history from a broad, original, and useful perspective—Willard Hurst of the University of Wisconsin and Calvin Woodard of the University of Virginia—and at least one other, Morton Horwitz[16] of Harvard, shows real promise. At least three others have produced a mature and useful body of work in the field—Harry Scheiber[17] of the history department at the University of California at San Diego, Lawrence Friedman[18] of the Stanford University Law School, and John Phillip Reid[19] at New York University School of Law. While his three-volume history of the United States from colonial times to the present

---

[16]In addition to the works cited in note 6 *supra*, see Horwitz, *The Conservative Tradition in the Writing of American Legal History*, 17 Am. J. Legal Hist. 275 (1973); Horwitz, *The Emergence of an Instrumental Conception of American Law: 1780-1820*, 5 Perspectives Am. Hist. 287 (1971).

[17]In addition to the works cited in note 7 *supra*, see H. Scheiber, Ohio Canal Era: A Case Study of Government and the Economy, 1820-1861 (1969); Scheiber, *Government and the Economy: Studies of the "Commonwealth" Policy in Nineteenth-Century America*, 3 J. Interdisciplinary Hist. 135 (1972); Scheiber, *On the New Economic History—and Its Limitations*, 41 Agricultural Hist. 385 (1967).

[18]In addition to the works cited in note 5 *supra*, see L. Friedman, Government and Slum Housing: A Century of Frustration (1968); L. Friedman, Contract Law in America (1965); Friedman, *Law Reform in Historical Perspective*, 13 St. Louis U.L.J. 351 (1969).

[19]*See* J. Reid, A Law of Blood: The Primitive Law of the Cherokee Nation (1971); J. Reid, An American Judge: Marmaduke Dent of West Virginia (1968); J. Reid, Chief Justice: The Judicial World of Charles Doe (1967).

cannot be said to be legal history, Daniel Boorstin[20] has much to say about the interaction between legal institutions and American history. Just coming into prominence are Maxwell Bloomfield,[21] a historian at the Catholic University, Phillip Paludan,[22] in the University of Kansas history department, Richard E. Ellis[23] of the history department at the University of Virginia, Gerald Gawalt,[24] a historian now at the Library of Congress, and William Nelson,[25] educated in both law and history and teaching at the University of Pennsylvania Law School. Working respectively in the colonial and the modern periods, but with significant contributions to a study of the nineteenth century, are Stanley Katz,[26] a historian teaching at the University of Chicago Law School, and Edward White,[27] educated in both law and history and teaching at the University of Virginia School of Law. Special mention must be made of Harold

---

[20]*See* D. BOORSTIN, THE AMERICANS (3 vols. 1958, 1963, 1973). Boorstin is a lawyer as well as a historian. *See also* Boorstin, *Tradition and Method in Legal History*, 54 HARV. L. REV. 424 (1941).

[21]*See* Bloomfield, *Lawyers and Public Criticism: Challenge and Response in Nineteenth-Century America*, 15 AM. J. LEGAL HIST. 269 (1971); Bloomfield, *Law vs. Politics: The Self-Image of the American Bar (1830-1860)*, 12 AM. J. LEGAL HIST. 306 (1968).

[22]*See* Paludan, *Law and the Failure of Reconstruction: The Case of Thomas Cooley*, 33 J. HIST. IDEAS 597 (1972); Paludan, *The American Civil War Considered as a Crisis in Law and Order*, 72 AM. HIST. REV. 1013 (1972).

[23]*See* note 11 *supra*.

[24]*See* Gawalt, *Massachusetts Legal Education in Transition: 1766-1840*, 17 AM. J. LEGAL HIST. 27 (1973); Gawalt, *Sources of Anti-Lawyer Sentiment in Massachusetts: 1740-1840*, 14 AM. J. LEGAL HIST. 283 (1970).

[25]*See* Nelson, *The Impact of the Antislavery Movement upon Styles of Judicial Reasoning in Nineteenth Century America*, 87 HARV. L. REV. 513 (1974); Nelson, *The Reform of Common Law Pleading in Massachusetts, 1760-1830: Judicial Activism as a Prelude to Legislation*, 122 U. PA. L. REV. 97 (1973); Nelson, *Changing Conceptions of Judicial Review: The Evolution of Constitutional Theory in the States: 1790-1860*, 120 U. PA. REV. 1166 (1972).

[26]*See* Katz, *The Politics of Law in Colonial America: Controversies over Chancery Courts and Equity Law in the Eighteenth Century*, 5 PERSPECTIVES AM. HIST. 485 (1971); Katz, *The Origins of American Constitutional Thought*, 3 PERSPECTIVES AM. HIST. 474 (1969).

[27]*See* White, *The Evolution of Reasoned Elaboration: Jurisprudential Criticism and Social Change*, 59 VA. L. REV. 279 (1973); White, *From Sociological Jurisprudence to Realism: Jurisprudence and Social Change in Early Twentieth-Century America*, 58 VA. L. REV. 999 (1972).

Hyman,[28] chairman of the history department at Rice University, both because of his large *oeuvre* and because of the relatively large group of graduate students he has attracted. Hurst, of course, has also achieved due fame for the large number of students and friends who have been inspired by his example and who have accepted his theoretical framework.

The theory and work of Hurst and his "school" clearly provide the most important and useful approach to our field, and so it is logical to begin there. The nineteenth century is viewed by the Hurst school of historians as a time during which Americans concentrated their attention on "release of creative energy"—the economic development of the country's resources by a large group of optimistic, busy, and pragmatic middle-class entrepreneurs who paid little attention to ideology. Law was one of the chief tools utilized to accelerate and cement growth by these bustling Americans, and in turn law and legal institutions were affected by their materialistic emphasis and their success. Hurst has produced an enormous well-researched, and detailed body of work in pursuit of his theory[29] and had the good fortune and magnetism to attract friends and students who write in the same vein and thus amplify in ancillary contexts Hurst's major theses.[30] The value of Hurst's work is immeasurably enhanced by his kindness, social concern, open-mindedness, gentleness, and serious-mindedness.

The most recent product of the "Hurst school" is Lawrence Friedman's *A History of American Law*,[31] which focuses primarily on the nineteenth century. It typifies many of the good and bad traits of the genre. Friedman's approach, while consistent with the tenets of legal realism and with the view that the study of law is an inquiry into the sources, nature, and results of social change, nevertheless follows Hurst in emphasizing economic history and economic problems to the exclusion of almost all other problems. There are two chapters on criminal law, another on the status of "wives, paupers, and slaves" in the Early American period, and

---

[28]*See* H. HYMAN, A MORE PERFECT UNION: THE IMPACT OF THE CIVIL WAR AND RECONSTRUCTION ON THE CONSTITUTION (1973); H. HYMAN, ERA OF THE OATH: NORTHERN LOYALTY TESTS DURING THE CIVIL WAR AND RECONSTRUCTION (1954).

[29]*See* note 2 *supra.*

[30]*See, e.g.,* Murphy, *supra* note 2, at 938-43. *Primus inter pares* in Hurst's "school" is Lawrence Friedman. *See* note 5 *supra.*

[31]L. FRIEDMAN, A HISTORY OF AMERICAN LAW (1973).

a fourth entitled "The Underdogs: 1847-1900," but as noted by Edward White in a recent review:

> [E]ven some of the major social issues of the nineteenth and twentieth centuries are seen to have an economic tinge: Friedman treats the legal problems of slavery primarily as a form of property holding; he views the philosophy of administrative regulation, an ideological innovation of the twentieth century, as a response to the emergence of giant business organizations.[32]

Friedman's book is in many ways encyclopedic in its study of the interaction between and among law, business, and the growth of American abundance. If, however, some chapters seem thin or overblown the reason lies partly in the lack of basic research in certain areas. As the bibliography demonstrates, Friedman has undertaken the enormous task of producing almost all of his own monographic study. Dissertation topics by the hundreds pounce upon the wary student from the pages and especially the footnotes of this book.

A far more serious problem is that Friedman's work pays little attention to ideology or jurisprudence or politics in the nineteenth century and, like Hurst's work, slights or ignores most intellectual trends and most other historians and their theories. It is consensus history, consciously but only slightly self-consciously so, which, while probably mirroring nineteenth-century majoritarian ideological attitudes, denigrates or at least infantilizes radicalism and dissent—although at times one senses that Friedman is helplessly sorry for the havoc that headlong and heartless growth wrought upon the humans who were crushed by it. This history is essentially incapable of dealing adequately with the enormous problems which have permeated the growth and development of middle-class capitalistic entrepreneurship. Hurst himself has been a bit more aware of, as he puts it, the problem of "the legitimacy of the business corporation."[33]

Most other major legal historians of our period seem to share many of Hurst's biases. Friendman belongs to the same "school," while the bulk of Harry Scheiber's excellent work deals with the

---

[32]White, Book Review, 59 VA. L. REV. 1130, 1136 (1973). *See also* Presser, Book Review, 122 U. PA. L. REV. 217 (1973).

[33]*See* W. HURST, THE LEGITIMACY OF THE BUSINESS CORPORATION IN THE LAW OF THE UNITED STATES 1780-1970, at 75-111 (1970). For an indication of Hurst's present research interests, see the text accompanying note 103 *infra*.

interrelation of law and economic development.[34] While voluminous, readable and important, Scheiber's contribution produces
conclusions essentially no different from those of Hurst. Leonard
Levy's one foray into our period—his good biography of Lemuel
Shaw—falls into an indistinguishable ideological mold.[35]

A fresh approach has been developing recently, chiefly from
the work of Morton Horwitz. His first, seminal article demonstrated
how judges began by about 1800 to see their job as one of making
law rather than declaring it.[36] Thus, "instrumentalist" judges as
conscious policy makers began to aid and abet the development of
America's economic resources. Later pieces show how the growth
of capitalism moved the substantive law of property and contracts
away from enlightenment and humanistic values.[37] Of course,
Hurst has always emphasized the connection between the "pragmatic" approach of American nineteenth-century lawmakers and
burgeoning economic growth, but his aim was to trace developments rather than to criticize changes in ideology. Horwitz does
not see nineteenth-century developments as uniformly benign. In
noting the darker side of the intimacy between instrumentalist
judges and entrepreneurs, he emphasizes that the law not only
facilitated but cemented and protected the enlargement of the
political power of the capitalist class. There was, he asserts in
another article, concomitantly the beginnings of a "politically conservative ideology of legalism" pervading the thought of legal
writers of all kinds.[38] In a way Horwitz has turned Hurst on his
head. Future studies should demonstrate the repression of a more
democratic, more radical set of legal alternatives, and indeed
the first publication by a Horwitz student, Stephen Presser's
excellent study of adoption law in America,[39] is an indication that
radical concern is and will be more for humanity than for im-

---

[34]_See_ notes 7, 17 _supra._

[35]L. LEVY, THE LAW OF THE COMMONWEALTH AND CHIEF JUSTICE SHAW:
THE EVOLUTION OF AMERICAN LAW 1830-1860 (1957).

[36]Horwitz, _The Emergence of an Instrumental Conception of American
Law: 1780-1820_, 5 PERSPECTIVES AM. HIST. 287 (1971).

[37]_See_ works cited note 6 _supra._ These essays and others will also be
published in a book dealing with the growth of American law from the
Revolution to the Civil War.

[38]Horwitz, _The Conservative Tradition in the Writing of American Legal
History_, 17 AM. J. LEGAL HIST. 275, 276 (1973).

[39]Presser, _The Historical Background of the American Law of Adoption_,
11 J. FAMILY L. 443 (1972).

personal economics.[40] It is America's value system, and not her economic system, that most needs scholarly investigation, elaboration, and discussion. These works will legitimize and spawn studies in American legal history upon topics now only the soft underbelly of consensus writing.

But, as William E. Nelson argues in another recent and excellent article, conservatives do not have to utilize the instrumentalist style of reasoning.[41] The bench, influenced in large part by many reasonably wealthy Northerners opposed to slavery and concerned that the "amoral" overtones of instrumentalism could be used, as they were in fact used in the *Dred Scott* case, to justify slavery on pragmatic nationalistic grounds, moved away from the antebellum judicial style in the years following the outbreak of war. The retreat to formalistic reasoning was subsequently put to able use by giant corporations to cement their political position.[42]

Finally, a seminal article by Calvin Woodard deserves attention, not only because of its depth, breadth, and humanity, but because it contains another attempt to establish a field theory for the nineteenth century.[43] For Woodard, the growth of economic productivity during the nineteenth century meant that for the first time in man's history it was conceivable to think in terms of a sufficiency of food and necessaries for every living human. This allowed and indeed demanded a change from laissez-faire thinking, which matured about 1800 and was the dominant philosophy of the period, to welfare-state thinking, a notion attaining general acceptance during the first part of this century. "Laissez-faire" meant utilizing every social means at hand, including the law, to enhance the economic opportunities of each individual. Founded upon the deplorable assumption that proverty was inevitable, justification was had on the moral grounds that the evil are poor, or at least the poor are evil and thus are providentially punished. Welfare-state thinking meant that poverty, having now metamorphosed from a moral necessity to an intolerable economic condition, had to be eradicated, and the state was the only handy

---

[40]*See* Thelen, *Collectivism, Economic and Political: Ben Lindsey Against Corporate Liberalism*, 1 REV. AM. HIST. 271 (1973).

[41]Nelson, *The Impact of the Antislavery Movement upon Styles of Judicial Reasoning in Nineteenth Century America*, 87 HARV. L. REV. 513 (1974).

[42]Nelson promises to trace this development in a series of **forthcoming** articles.

[43]*See* Woodard, *Reality and Social Reform: The Transition from Laissez-Faire to the Welfare State*, 72 YALE L.J. 286 (1962).

tool capable of accomplishing this result. Such an historical theory is as comprehensive as that of Hurst's, indeed more so, and ought to explain why radically-oriented people were not so attuned to human deprivations in 1800 as they were in 1950. But unfortunately Woodard has attracted no "school" and has now turned his attention to comparative legal philosophy, so we have no other literature to substantiate and proliferate this conceptual model. This abandonment is regrettable when it is realized that Woodard has many of the same attributes of greatness as Hurst, including an intellectual breadth and an open-minded vision tempered by a stabilizing sense that derives from the realization that all things are not possible. As Woodard has put it, "one way or another, society must come to terms with conduct or conditions, however deplorable, however repulsive, which man has no rational hope of abolishing."[44] This haunting realization, evaded by most, gives others the impetus for abandon or despair, but for Woodard and Hurst it provides reinforcement for inspiration.

### B. *Constitutional History*

There is a bit more to show for the efforts of historical scholarship in the field of constitutional law, but much of what has been done here is even more disappointing, replete with "persistent and uncompromising attention to lawyer's detail, to the exclusion of larger interpretive themes,"[45] and in many instances, too in awe of the judicial mystique or too imbued with consensus to be very critical. It serves no purpose to recapitulate the various histories of the Court or biographies of the Justices. Charles Warren's treatment is both uncritical and out of date.[46] I find Fred Rodell's *Nine Men* useful, if read with a clear understanding of the author's point of view, but it has passed out of print.[47] Desks are beginning to be weighted with the ponderous and seemingly definitive tomes eventually to constitute the Holmes Devise History of the Supreme Court, but the two volumes to appear so far, while comprehensive, are overflowing, pedantic, and tech-

---

[44]*Id.* at 286.

[45]Horwitz, Book Review, 85 HARV. L. REV. 1076, 1077 (1972). On the history of the writing of constitutional history, see Belz, *The Realist Critique of Constitutionalism in the Era of Reform*, 15 AM. J. LEGAL HIST. 288 (1971); Belz, *The Constitution in the Gilded Age: The Beginning of Constitutional Realism in American Scholarship*, 13 AM. J. LEGAL HIST. 110 (1969).

[46]*See* C. WARREN, THE SUPREME COURT IN UNITED STATES HISTORY (1922).

[47]F. RODELL, NINE MEN: A POLITICAL HISTORY OF THE SUPREME COURT OF THE UNITED STATES FROM 1790-1955 (1955).

nical.[48]  Also, insofar as they fail to take into account broader
historical and philosophical themes or to deal with the history of
the Court as an institution, they are incomplete. The four-volume
collective biography of all Supreme Court Justices in 1969, edited
by Leon Friedman and Fred Israel, is useful but uneven.[49] New
histories of the Court during various eras have begun to appear,
including Bernard Schwartz's treatment[50] of the period from 1835
to 1877 and Loren Beth's contribution to the usually well-done
New American Nation series dealing with the period from 1877
to 1917.[51] Beth's book is unfortunately almost too thin and diffuse
to be of much utility.

It seems, in the abstract, that perhaps a better way to integrate into Supreme Court studies a modicum of social context
would be to write the history of a famous case from its beginning
to its final doctrinal and social repercussions. An excellent model,
from twentieth-century legal history, has recently been provided
by Daniel Carter's monumental *Scottsboro* study.[52]  A series of
little volumes on important cases during the Marshall and Taney
regimes has also appeared. Each has its own merits: Richard
Morin's[53] comprehensive pamphlet on *Dartmouth College* is a
delightful reminiscence; Gerald Gunther,[54] in the midst of producing two volumes for the Holmes Devise, has discovered some
interesting evidence about *McCulloch v. Maryland;* Donald

---

[48]J. GOEBEL, HISTORY OF THE SUPREME COURT OF THE UNITED STATES:
I, ANTECEDENTS AND BEGINNINGS TO 1801 (1971), *reviewed*, Flaherty, 40
U. CHI L. REV. 460 (1973), and McDonald, 59 J. AM. HIST. 994 (1973); C.
FAIRMAN, HISTORY OF THE SUPREME COURT OF THE UNITED STATES: VI, RE-
CONSTRUCTION AND REUNION 1864-1888 (1971), *reviewed*, Casper, 73 COLUM.
L. REV. 913 (1973), and Keller, 85 HARV. L. REV. 1082 (1972).

[49]*See* L. FRIEDMAN & F. ISRAEL, THE JUSTICES OF THE UNITED STATES
SUPREME COURT, 1789-1969: THEIR LIVES AND MAJOR OPINIONS (1969), *reviewed*, Ireland, 15 AM. J. LEGAL HIST. 224 (1971).

[50]B. SCHWARTZ, FROM CONFEDERATION TO NATION: THE AMERICAN CON-
STITUTION 1835-1877 (1973).

[51]L. BETH, THE DEVELOPMENT OF THE AMERICAN CONSTITUTION, 1877-1917
(1971).

[52]*See* D. CARTER, SCOTTSBORO: A TRAGEDY OF THE AMERICAN SOUTH
(1969).

[53]R. MORIN, WILL TO RESIST: THE DARTMOUTH COLLEGE CASE (1969).

[54]G. GUNTHER, JOHN MARSHALL'S DEFENSE OF MCCULLOCH V. MARYLAND
(1969).

Dewey's[55] treatment of the background of *Marbury v. Madison* is eminently readable; and Peter Magrath[56] and Stanley Kutler[57] have produced major, though slight, tomes on *Fletcher v. Peck* and the *Charles River Bridge* case respectively.[58] All have flaws, some serious. A common fault occurs with the telling of the facts. None of the smaller books has the verve, comprehensiveness, or readability of *Scottsboro*, likely because none has the relevance and poignancy of the *Scottsboro* incident, but due in part to a relative dearth of source materials for the first half of the nineteenth century. A worse flaw is in interpretation of the law—even *Scottsboro* fails on some of the evidentiary technicalities. Most of the cases deal with points of law that are somewhat out of date, but there is no excuse for inaccuracy in explaining them. Finally, not a great deal of attention is paid to some of the broader theoretical implications of the cases. The best example lies in the most ambitious and thought-provoking volume, Kutler's *Privilege and Creative Destruction*.[59] The holding of the majority in *Charles River Bridge*[60] is actually a quite narrow statement that legislative charters for businesses will be read strictly; it is only in dicta that the Court speaks of "creative destruction."[61] It is also important to investigate, then, the gap between the popular interpretation that the Court approved entrepreneurial innovation and the true, narrow holding. One wonders why such gaps exist and whether they are perpetrated. Why do dicta, dissents, and "aura" mean more than a strict holding? What then is the function of the narrow holding? Basically, more time, thought, and care must be put into future studies of this type if they are to achieve maximum utility.

---

[55]D. DEWEY, MARSHALL VERSUS JEFFERSON: THE POLITICAL BACKGROUND OF MARBURY V. MADISON (1970).

[56]C. MAGRATH, YAZOO: LAW AND POLITICS IN THE NEW REPUBLIC, THE CASE OF FLETCHER V. PECK (1966).

[57]S. KUTLER, PRIVILEGE AND CREATIVE DESTRUCTION: THE CHARLES RIVER BRIDGE CASE (1971).

[58]*See also, e.g.*, M. BAXTER, THE STEAMBOAT MONOPOLY: GIBBONS V. OGDEN 1924 (1972); Scheiber, *The Road to* Munn: *Eminent Domain and the Concept of Public Purpose in the State Courts*, 5 PERSPECTIVE AM. HIST. 329 (1971).

[59]A good review of Kutler's book, a student work product from my seminar, is to be found at 24 ALA. L. REV. 249 (1971).

[60]36 U.S. (11 Pet.) 420 (1837).

[61]*Id.* at 546-47.

Special notice must be taken of two articles by Phillip Paludan. "Low and the Failure of Reconstruction"[62] is a thoughtful, provocative, and remarkably even-handed treatment of the interplay between jurisprudence and constitutional history. It shows in particular how Thomas Cooley, adhering strongly to belief in the negative state and fearing that large accretions to national power might threaten the stability of the union, was forced to neglect his Free Soil and Jacksonian Democratic roots in order to urge a restrictive interpretation of the privilege and immunities clause of the fourteenth amendment. The view that the Civil War can best be interpreted as "A Crisis in Law and Order" is developed in the second article,[63] resting on the thesis that nineteenth-century Americans believed law to be an expression of popular sentiment and were convinced that law and order must be maintained at all costs. These contain a fresh jurisprudential approach to the legal history of the period. Paludan is now at work upon a study of local courts and small community in the nineteenth-century United States a much-needed endeavor in an area in which almost nothing has been done.[64]

In an important essay William Nelson propounds the view that the doctrine of judicial review did not assume its present meaning and function until about 1820.[65] Prior to that time, state courts did not decide many questions concerning fundamental social issues, leaving such issues to legislatures and upholding legislative resolutions that seemed broadly supported. After 1820, courts acting under an increasingly instrumentalist theory of judicial decision-making found that minorities had to be protected from tyrannous majorities.

Two other monographic studies demonstrate what can be done in the area of constitutional history. Russel Nye has attempted to show how abolitionists both gathered crucial political

---

[62]Paludan, *Law and the Failure of Reconstruction: The Case of Thomas Cooley*, 33 J. HIST. IDEAS 597 (1972).

[63]Paludan, *The Civil War Considered as a Crisis in Law and Order*, 72 AM. HIST. REV. 1013 (1972).

[64]The only detailed study of the flow of business through a trial court of general jurisdiction is F. LAURENT, THE BUSINESS OF A TRIAL COURT: 100 YEARS OF CASES, A CENSUS OF ACTION IN THE CIRCUIT COURT FOR CHIPPEWA COUNTY, WISCONSIN, 1855-1954 (1959).

[65]Nelson, *Changing Conceptions of Judicial Review: The Evolution of Constitutional Theory in the States, 1790-1860*, 120 U. PA. L. REV. 1166 (1972).

support and added new meaning to the word "man" through their demonstration that those who advocated slavery threatened the civil liberties of white men as well as black.[66] Arnold Paul has ably demonstrated the degree of conservatism of the great bulk of the bar during the beginnings of social convulsion in the United States in the late 1880's and early 1890's.[67] Charles McCurdy, a student of Scheiber at the University of California at San Diego, is completing a dissertation on "Justice Field and the Jurisprudence of Government-Business Relations" from which he hopes to derive two studies, one on the judicial allocation of resources among competing groups in the Far West, and another, more jurisprudentially oriented, dealing with the interaction of the Supreme Court and the "changing role of government in promoting and regulating the economy."[68] Scheiber himself is at work on a study of American federalism, 1790 to the present.

One other book deserves extended attention. Richard E. Ellis, an immensely capable historian who refuses to be fit into any school of theoretical mold,[69] has written a monograph on the meaning of the election of Jefferson in 1800, which provides important insights into the nature and constitution of the nascent judicial system at both the state and federal levels. *The Jeffersonian Crisis*[70] ought to stimulate further investigation into eighteenth-century views regarding the task and nature of judging, the attitudes of judges and lawyers regarding the same topic, and the functioning and makeup of the bench from about 1750 to 1810, including the meaning at that time of such fundamental

---

[66]R. NYE, FETTERED FREEDOM: CIVIL LIBERTIES AND THE SLAVERY CONTROVERSY 1830-1860 (2d ed. 1963).

[67]A. PAUL, CONSERVATIVE CRISIS AND THE RULE OF LAW: ATTITUDES OF BAR AND BENCH 1887-1895 (1969). Equally well done is the study by B. TWISS, LAWYERS AND THE CONSTITUTION: HOW LAISSEZ-FAIRE CAME TO THE SUPREME COURT (1942).

[68]This, and all the other information concerning work currently in progress, results primarily from questionnaires sent by me to a small group of colleagues and friends in legal history, and to some of their students. The list of addresses was developed haphazardly and I apologize for the omissions which likely occurred. I am grateful for the warm, complete, and relatively quick responses received.

A more general listing of work in progress, still useful although unfortunately already out of date, is to be found in Bell, *Research in Progress in Legal History*, 17 AM. J. LEGAL HIST. 66 (1973).

[69]*But cf.* Holt, Book Review, 16 AM. J. LEGAL HIST. 197 (1972).

[70]R. ELLIS, *supra* note 11.

notions as judicial tenure. How, for instance, did the state of Georgia endure for its first half-century without a supreme court? Ellis is currently at work on a long article entitled "The Transformation of the States' Rights Argument, 1776-1833," which should prove equally stimulating.

### C. Substance and Procedure

Although until recently the most neglected aspect of nineteenth-century legal history, detailed and sophisticated treatments of various areas of substantive and procedural law are beginning to appear.[71] Hurst has been a pioneer here and his monumental study of the lumber industry in Wisconsin contains fairly thorough treatments of contract, tort, real property, and taxation.[72] Soon these areas will be accorded extensive coverage, which is really the *sine qua non* for establishing an intelligent lecture course syllabus in American legal history.

The field of property law has received, simultaneously, attention from two important legal historians. In "Property Law, Expropriation, and Resource Allocation of the Government,"[73] Harry Scheiber has written a thoroughly researched and important history of eminent domain during the nineteenth century. He has demonstrated, within the framework of his and Hurst's theoretical approaches, that expropriation was used throughout the period as a conscious instrument of resource allocation at the state level. Eminent domain was used to promote and even to subsidize some types of entrepreneurial enterprise at the expense of older "vested" interests, and there was widespread transfer of this important power by legislatures directly to elements of the private sector. Scheiber plans to publish a larger work dealing with property and regulation by state governments in the nineteenth century, incorporating this article and another on *Munn v. Illinois*.[74] He does not deal in detail with the interesting

---

[71] An excellent student note details the growth of admiralty jurisdiction in the nineteenth century. Note, *From Judicial Grant to Legislative Power: The Admiralty Clause in the Nineteenth Century*, 67 HARV. L. REV. (1954). *See also* Mark DeWolfe Howe's classic study of the growth of democracy in juries. Howe, *Juries as Judges of Criminal Law*, 52 HARV. L. REV. 582 (1939).

[72] W. HURST, LAW AND ECONOMIC GROWTH: THE LEGAL HISTORY OF THE LUMBER INDUSTRY IN WISCONSIN 1836-1915 (1964).

[73] *See* Scheiber, *Property Law, Expropriation, and Resource Allocation by the Government: The United States, 1789-1910*, 33 J. ECON. HIST. 232 (1973).

[74] Scheiber, *The Road to Munn: Eminent Domain and the Concept of Public Purpose in the State Courts*, 5 PERSPECTIVES AM. HIST. 329 (1971).

and crucial philosophical problem of why indirect and consequential damages of expropriation were not deemed compensable, but Morton Horwitz will soon favor us with a treatment of the growth of damages law in the nineteenth century.[75] Horwitz has already published a seminal work on the history of American property law during the same period,[76] and another article covers the growth of the law of contract.[77] All of these articles will be incorporated into a book on the changes in American law, from the Revolution to the Civil War, caused by the beginning of the Industrial Revolution. With respect to property, Horwitz demonstrates a development from a gentry-oriented concept of property emphasizing static and undisturbed enjoyment by the owner, to one of dynamism and instrumentalism, emphasizing "the newly paramount virtues of productive use and development."[78]

> At the beginning of the century, property law tended to encourage high risk investment through a doctrine of priority, which conferred exclusive property rights on the first developer. By the middle of the century, however, the law had shifted to a reasonable use or balancing test which allowed newer entrants to compete while destroying the claims that existing property owners had acquired under older legal doctrines.[79]

Horwitz' support for his view seems somewhat weak and will require some sublateral monographic aid, but the thesis is convincing.

Other, noneconomically-oriented areas of law are at last receiving some of their due. This is especially true with respect to criminal law and family law. Furthermore, no fewer than

---

[75]Horwitz, "Damage Judgments, Legal Liability, and Economic Development Before the Civil War," to be published in the *American Journal of Legal History.*

[76]Horwitz, *The Transformation in the Conception of Property in American Law, 1780-1860,* 40 U. CHI. L. REV. 248 (1973).

[77]Horwitz, *The Historical Foundations of Modern Contract Law,* 87 HARV. L. REV. 917 (1974).

[78]Horwitz, *supra* note 76, at 248.

[79]*Id.* at 290. For good treatment of portions of tort law, see FRIEDMAN & LADINSKY, *supra* note 5; Malone, *The Formative Era of Contributory Negligence,* 41 ILL. L. REV. 151 (1946). A good recent article concerning the history of labor legislation is Schreiber, *The Majority Preference Provisions in Early State Labor Arbitration Statutes: 1880-1900,* 15 AM. J. LEGAL HIST. 186 (1971).

three colleagues are currently at work on the law of slavery: Stanley Katz of the University of Chicago Law School, Daniel Flanigan of the University of Virginia's history department, and Robert Cover at Yale University Law School. A. E. Keir Nash, in a series of articles taken from his dissertation, has argued that blacks received a good deal of fair treatment by some judges on some ante-bellum Southern supreme courts,[80] while an excellent student note discusses the interaction between the conflict of laws and the question of slavery.[81] William Nelson has persuasively argued that the Revolution caused a significant shift in the function of criminal law, from the enforcement of morals to the protection of property and security.[82]

We need to know more about other aspects of criminal law in the nineteenth century, as well as about other legal ways in which people were accorded less than their full rights. More, for instance, ought to be known about Indian law, from both the white man's and the Indian's perspective. Wilcomb Washburn's *Red Man's Land/White Man's Law*[83] is an interesting starting effort that demonstrates the need for a comprehensive treatment of the broken treaties with the Indians, paternalistic treatment by the Government, and legal deprivation, as well as what legal alternatives might have existed for the parties involved. John Phillip Reid has recently completed the first volume of a multivolume treatment of Cherokee tribal law which is excellent and bodes well for the future.[84] A fine article by Joseph C. Burke deals with the difficult political problems presented by the Cherokee cases during the last years of Marshall on the Supreme Court.[85]

---

[80]*See* Nash, *Fairness and Formalism in the Trials of Blacks in the State Supreme Courts of the Old South*, 56 VA. L. REV. 64 (1971); Nash, *A More Equitable Past? Southern Supreme Courts and the Protection of the Antebellum Negro*, 48 N.C.L. REV. 197 (1970); Nash, *Negro Rights, Unionism, and Greatness on the South Carolina Court of Appeals: The Extraordinary Chief Justice John Bolton O'Neall*, 21 S.C.L. REV. 141 (1969).

[81]Note, *American Slavery and the Conflict of Laws*, 71 COLUM. L. REV. 74 (1971).

[82]Nelson, *Emerging Notions of Modern Criminal Law in the Revolutionary Era: An Historical Perspective*, 42 N.Y.U.L. REV. 450 (1967).

[83]W. WASHBURN, RED MAN'S LAND/WHITE MAN'S LAW (1971).

[84]J. REID, A LAW OF BLOOD: THE PRIMITIVE LAW OF THE CHEROKEE NATION (1971). The second volume of this work should be completed by the end of this year.

[85]Burke, *The Cherokee Cases: A Study in Law, Politics, and Morality*, 21 STAN. L. REV. 500 (1969).

In no small part due to the guidance of David Flaherty, a colonialist at the history department of the University of Western Ontario, several good monographs dealing with aspects of family law will soon appear. George Curtis is finishing a dissertation on the juvenile courts of the late nineteenth and early twentieth centuries in Virginia; Suzanne Williams is completing one on "Law and the Family: New York 1700-1850;" and James Deen, whose competence has already been demonstrated in his excellent article on "Patterns of Testation,"[86] is now at work with Stanley Katz on family law in New England from 1800 to 1850. Suzanne Lebsock, currently a graduate student at the University of Virginia, is at work upon the law of divorce and married women's property rights from 1865 to 1900, while Katz is also working on the legal status of women in the nineteenth century. Charlotte Rottier, studying under Bloomfield, is examining the rise of women lawyers in the District of Columbia in the late nineteenth and early twentieth centuries.

## D. Bench and Bar

While most previous work on the profession during this period has been anecdotal and thus primary rather than interpretive in nature, excellent histories and biographies are beginning to emerge. Premier work in judicial biography is presented by the studies of Joseph Story by Gerald Dunne,[87] of Lemuel Shaw by Leonard Levy,[88] and of Marmaduke Dent and Charles Doe by John Phillip Reid.[89] These thorough and thoughtful books establish a high standard and provide material that is excellent for classroom use. A similarly high mark for the biography of a practicing lawyer is earned by William Harbaugh with his recently published and first-rate biography of John W. Davis.[90] Since Harbaugh had the distinction of being granted access to Davis' files by his law firm, an opportunity usually not available to biographers of lawyers, this effort effectively portrays all facets of the busy

---

[86]Deen, *Patterns of Testation: Four Tidewater Counties in Colonial Virginia*, 16 AM. J. LEGAL HIST. 154 (1972).

[87]G. DUNNE, JUSTICE JOSEPH STORY AND THE RISE OF THE SUPREME COURT (1970). *But see* the excellent partially dissenting review, Bloomfield, *A Man for All Seasons*, 1 REV. AM. HIST. 213 (1973).

[88]L. LEVY, THE LAW OF THE COMMONWEALTH AND CHIEF JUSTICE SHAW (1957).

[89]J. REID, AN AMERICAN JUDGE: MARMADUKE DENT OF WEST VIRGINIA (1968); J. REID, CHIEF JUSTICE: THE JUDICIAL WORLD OF CHARLES DOE (1967).

[90]W. HARBAUGH, LAWYER'S LAWYER: THE LIFE OF JOHN W. DAVIS (1973).

and successful twentieth-century corporate lawyer and eminent appellate advocate working for both private and public profit. Maxwell Bloomfield is beginning work on a biography of the noted Jacksonian law teacher, David Hoffman, while James Ely is studying the career of the post-Revolutionary South Carolina jurist, John F. Grimke. Dorothy Hawkshawe, one of Bloomfield's students, is completing a biography of D. Augustus Straker, the noted Negro civil rights lawyer and text writer of the late nineteenth century.

Bloomfield has just finished a volume of essays dealing with the legal profession in the hundred years after the Revolution which, given the quality of his previously published articles, should prove to be incisive and useful. Bloomfield has aptly shown that the bar in Jacksonian times, in conscious response to the barrage of criticism it received, adopted a professionalistic image which it has retained to the present day and which has successfully masked the continuation of many of the attributes and practices vehemently criticized.[91] Another fine, but anonymous, student note argues that the real purpose of Story's _Swift v. Tyson_ decision was to protect the legal profession from popular demands, an argument which meshes well with Bloomfield's findings.[92] The sources collected by the late Perry Miller[93] for his sweeping essay on the ethos of the profession between the Revolution and the Civil War[94] are perhaps more useful than the essay itself.[95]

Gerald Gawalt has published two portions of his dissertation on the legal profession in Massachusetts from 1760 to 1840. In "Sources of Anti-Lawyer Sentiment"[96] Gawalt establishes the existence of a lawyer class and thus provides a basis for acceptance of contemporaneous criticism of the bar because of "general dis-

---

[91] The volume of essays will be entitled "The Power Brokers: American Lawyers and Social Change, 1776-1876." _See_ Bloomfield, _Lawyers and Public Criticism: Challenge and Response in Nineteenth-Century America_, 14 AM. J. LEGAL HIST. 269 (1971); Bloomfield, _Law vs. Politics: The Self-Image of the American Bar (1830-1860)_, 12 AM. J. LEGAL HIST. 306 (1968).

[92] Note, Swift v. Tyson _Exhumed_, 79 YALE L.J. 284 (1969).

[93] THE LEGAL MIND IN AMERICA (P. Miller ed. 1962).

[94] P. MILLER, THE LIFE OF THE MIND IN AMERICA: FROM THE REVOLUTION TO THE CIVIL WAR 99-265 (1965).

[95] _See_ Friedman, _Heart Against Head: Perry Miller and the Legal Mind_, 77 YALE L.J. 1244 (1968).

[96] Gawalt, _Sources of Anti-Lawyer Sentiment in Massachusetts: 1740-1840_, 14 AM. J. LEGAL HIST. 283 (1970).

satisfaction with the restrictive nature of a professional elite—an anomalous development during an era characterized by rising expectations for social, economic, and political democracy.[97] In "Massachusetts Legal Education in Transition"[98] Gawalt demonstrates that the relatively late appearance of the institution of law schools in the Bay State was the deliberate result of the bar's attempt, through fostering apprenticeship training, to regulate and restrict entrance into the profession, to maintain a high standard of quality, and to reduce competition. He concludes that "[t]his dual role of education and regulation led to the failure of both."[99]

## E. *Other Monographs and Studies*

Two model monographs indicate subject matter that should be diligently pursued by American legal history students: Robert Ireland's study of county courts in Kentucky to 1850,[100] and John Guice's treatment of the supreme courts of Colorado, Montana, and Wyoming during their territorial days.[101] Lawrence Friedman is presently at work on a comparison of two California trial courts during the period from 1890 to 1970 and will collaborate with Yale sociologist Stanton Wheeler to study the work of American appellate courts from 1870 to 1970. An interesting article by George Priest,[102] a student at the University of Chicago Law School, demonstrates the value of statistical and economic analysis of legal materials both to provide direct evidence for the use of economic, political, and social historians and to demonstrate the effectiveness of attempted legislative amelioration of social problems. Such a

---

[97]*Id.* at 283.

[98]Gawalt, *Massachusetts Legal Education in Transition: 1766-1840,* 17 AM. J. LEGAL HIST. 27 (1973).

[99]*Id.* at 28. For an extensive if uncritical history of American legal education, see Stevens, *Two Cheers for 1870: The American Law School,* 5 PERSPECTIVES AM. HIST. 405 (1971). *See also* A. REED, TRAINING FOR THE PUBLIC PROFESSION OF THE LAW (1921); Currie, *The Materials of Law Study,* 3 J. LEGAL ED. 331 (1951).

[100]R. IRELAND, THE COUNTY COURTS IN ANTE-BELLUM KENTUCKY (1972).

[101]J. GUICE, THE ROCKY MOUNTAIN BENCH: THE TERRITORIAL SUPREME COURTS OF COLORADO, MONTANA, AND WYOMING 1861-1890 (1972). For an article on some aspects of the functioning of the same courts, see Bakken, *Judicial Review in the Rocky Mountain Territorial Courts,* 15 AM. J. LEGAL HIST. 56 (1971).

[102]Priest, *Law and Economic Distress: Sangamon County, Illinois, 1837-1844,* 2 J. LEGAL STUDIES 469 (1973).

study of the judgments and executions in Songamon County, Illinois, in the period from 1837 to 1844, indicates the need for substantial revision of previous impressionistic judgments concerning the effects of both the depression of 1937 in Illinois and the attempts by the legislature to afford relief.

Several other important studies are under way which bode well. Willard Hurst, as mentioned above,[103] is devoting his attention to the growth and development of antitrust policy in an attempt to understand "what went on between about 1870 and 1920 in public policymaking to present us with pretty much of a *fait accompli* in economic concentration."[104] I expect that much will be learned therefrom concerning basic ideological and philosophical attitudes toward the proper place of business and economic growth in America. Richard E. Ellis will soon be undertaking a thorough study of the legal problems relating to the Panic of 1819, including relief legislation, usury laws, bankruptcy measures, imprisonment for debt, stay and replevin laws, and banking regulations. And, with the imminent completion of his dissertation entitled "The American Codification Movement: A Study in Ante-Bellum Legal Reform," Charles Cook, a student of Mary Berry at the University of Maryland, will present the first in-depth treatment of one of the topics in our period most in need of attention. Elizabeth Gaspar Brown has forcefully argued that, contrary to the commonly held view, the practice of law on the frontier, at least in Wayne County, Michigan Territory, was conducted in a professional, sophisticated, and competent manner.[105] Concomitantly, two investigations of the immediate post-Revolutionary experience in South Carolina, by James Ely[106] and Leigh Harrison,[107] conclude that a well-trained and conservative bench, bar, and legislature were unmoved by any spirit of revolt against English law on legal institutions. Ely's study of the legislation of the period is particularly imaginative and comprehensive. John Phillip Reid is currently at work

---

[103]*See* text accompanying note 33 *supra*.

[104]Letter from Willard Hurst to Wythe Holt, July 25, 1973.

[105]Brown, *Frontier Justice: Wayne County 1796-1836*, 16 AM. J. LEGAL HIST. 126 (1972); Brown, *The Bar on a Frontier: Wayne County, 1796-1836*, 14 AM. J. LEGAL HIST. 136 (1970). *See also* J. BALDWIN, THE FLUSH TIMES OF ALABAMA AND MISSISSIPPI (1957).

[106]Ely, *American Independence and the Law: A Study of Post-Revolutionary South Carolina Legislation*, 26 VAND. L. REV. 939 (1973).

[107]Harrison, *A Study of the Earliest Reported Decisions of the South Carolina Courts of Law*, 16 AM. J. LEGAL HIST. 51 (1972).

upon the law on our frontier, particularly the law of overland wagon trains and the law in California mining camps.

Harold Hyman has just published a study subtitled *The Impact of the Civil War and Reconstruction on the Constitution*[108] and is currently continuing his investigation of the legal history of government in the same period, while beginning research on a study of the legal history of American cities. Three of his students are at work upon related topics: Harold Platt is studying the "Legal History of Public Services in Houston, 1850 to the Present"; Edward Weisel has selected "City and State: The Development of Intergovernmental Relations in Nineteenth Century Texas"; and Louis Marchiafava is working on "A Comparative History of the New Orleans and Houston Police Departments."

### III.   Chto Nado Dyelat'?[109]

Activity is necessary on two fronts which together comprise the whole of our useful activity as scholars. Some remarks are pertinent concerning research activities that ought to be undertaken; and a large amount of thought and dialogue ought to be devoted to pedagogical methods and tools. We are valuable not only as creators of a relevant past but as transmitters of interesting, scholarly, high-minded, and serious work.

Even accepting my belief in the necessity of adopting a theoretical and philosophical schema, the opportunities for further research are practically limitless. An immediate need exists for Hurst-type studies in other regions of the country in order to test Scheiber's suggestion that the locale of much of the work of the Hurst school—Wisconsin—is not typical of the rest of the country.[110] Moreover, and this is especially true of the South which is severely understudied, other areas will have distinct economic problems which may at least fill out the contours of mainstream history.

Perhaps the most pressing need is for more monographs on a microcosmic level. Quantitative research would be quite helpful at this stage of historiographical development, and, as the Sanga-

---

[108]H. Hyman, A More Perfect Union: The Impact of the Civil War and Reconstruction on the Constitution (1973).

[109]*See* V. Lenin, *What is to be Done?*, in 1 Selected Works 123 (Moscow ed. 1960).

[110]*See* Scheiber, *At the Borderland of Law and Economic Thought: The Contributions of Willard Hurst*, 75 Am. Hist. Rev. 744, 753-56 (1970).

mon County, Illinois, study shows,[111] it is likely that this can only
be done at the local level. We need many studies of how local
government, and particularly county courts, functioned, both
juridically and politically. What did people at the basic level of
government perceive the function of their local courts to be? How
closely was the ideal followed? What sort of skewing effect did
the existence of a more or less organized professional bar have?
What substitutes have various segments of society evolved for
court-given justice and police-oriented law? How did law serve
locally to cement such institutions as the family, the church, or
public education? How did law and legal institutions react to
depression, war, or oppression?

Concomitantly, the device of biographical study needs to be
widely utilized. The Alderman Library at the University of Virginia, for example, has for approximately sixty years contained a
rather complete file of papers taken from the small town practice
of Allen Caperton Braxton, a brilliant Old Dominion attorney at
the end of the Victorian era. He has so far only been viewed as
a political figure, never as a practitioner. He was, I think, a rather
typical progressive in the mold of those portrayed by Wiebe:[112]
a young, well-organized, high-minded, hard-working man clearly
aware of the social disjunctions caused by the emergence and im-
morality of large corporations and willing to spend hundreds of
hours, as he did in the 1901-1902 Virginia Convention, drafting
the constitutional provisions for a state corporation commission
to combat this evil. Otherwise he was rather elitist and conservative in his approach to the "solution" of most contemporary
problems.[113] But his mode of attack was that of a lawyer, and
his chief and primary concerns arose from and were for his legal
practice; he and countless others like him, important in a plethora
of local and state issues throughout the nineteenth century, are
waiting to be discovered and brought to light. We need to know
their backgrounds, the nature of their educations and practices,
their impacts upon the community, the bar, and the practice of law
and, if possible, their jurisprudential and philosophical views. The

---

[111]Priest, *supra* note 102.

[112]*See* R. WIEBE, THE SEARCH FOR ORDER 1877-1920, at 111-63 (1967).

[113]The only treament of Braxton is to be found in V. Weathers, The
Political Career of Allen Caperton Braxton, April 22, 1956 (unpublished thesis
in Alderman Library, University of Virginia). My dissertation on the
Virginia Constitutional Convention of 1901-1902 will treat Braxton's contributions to that body at some length and will attempt to place him more
in perspective.

bench, as well as other functionaries, such as masters in chancery, sheriffs, clerks of the court, and members of administrative boards and commissions, should receive similar biographical treatment.

Meanwhile the history of the growth of legal doctrine must continue to receive attention. We especially need to know more about the origins of and changes in tort law and criminal law, and the fields of procedure and jurisdiction have not received the attention due. Specific types of law, such as the poor laws, deserve attention as well. Law during Jacksonian times and especially on the frontier needs more attention, and the period after the Civil War is almost a *tabula rasa* from any point of view. As one can see from the preceding section, it appears that work is currently under way in all of the indicated areas and directions.

What is not clear, however, is that work of a more philosophical and jurisprudential nature is proceeding. To iterate a point made by Hurst many times and defended here, "[l]egal history should be structured about some defensible theories of social structure and processes, so that it is to a substantial extent a sociological history of law and not a history of law as a self-contained field."[114] This implies that the study of legal ideas is important also. Edward White has indicated the direction that some such studies might take by the example of his recent work on legal philosophy in the twentieth century,[115] and Phillip Paludan's work also involves jurisprudential inquiry.[116] Horwitz' article on the conservative style and ideology of nineteenth-century legal writers should stimulate interest.[117] We need to know more about the history of thought, from within and without the profession, about the nature and function of being a lawyer or a judge. We need to know more about the concept and function of legal rules as contemporaneously conceived, for it is my observation that we are most blatantly present-minded in our thinking in this area.[118] We know almost nothing of the history of such an important concept as *stare decisis*, although the recent work of

---

[114]Section on Legal History, Association of American Law Schools, Report on the Teachings of Legal History in American Law Schools 58 (1973) [hereinafter cited as Legal History in American Law Schools].

[115]*See* note 27 *supra*.

[116]*See* notes 62, 63 *supra* & accompanying text.

[117]Horwitz, *supra* note 38.

[118]Woodward, *supra* note 43, gives a good warning about this kind of present-mindedness.

Horwitz and Nelson on instrumentalism provides a good starting point.[119] Exactly how did judges, lawyers, or the general populace know what the law was when there were no reports and no codes? Why was it so universally acceptable in colonial times for nonlawyers to sit on the bench, and why did this custom disappear rapidly and simultaneously with the appearance of reporters and with the emergence of the new nation? What, exactly, was a pettifogger? What is the history, at the state level, of the process of having one judge speak for "The Court" rather than allowing all to speak _seriatim_, and why did this change occur? How did the lessening of professional qualifications during Jacksonian times affect the practice of law? What is the relation of rulemaking and judicial rhetoric to the maintenance of the supremacy of the wealthy and the upper middle class? Exactly what ethics, mores, and political purposes were reflected in the adoption of formal codes of ethics at the end of our period? How did the introduction of the large corporate law firm change the lawyer's and the layman's conceptualizations of the task of practicing law? What is the sociology of the adoption of Story's and Langdell's pedagogical revolutions?

Even more attention needs to be given to the teaching of legal history, if only because it is rather abominably taught now. Woodard has ably stated the case.[120] In a forthcoming article I shall argue at greater length that the subjects which ought to be required in a law school's first-year curriculum comprise legal history, legal ethics, legal profession, jurisprudence, Constitutional history, legal bibliography and library usage, and case-parsing rather than the current and time-honored substantive law courses.[121] Legal history should be in the first rank, as it is of first importance in giving students some grasp of the social and ethical context of judicial decision-making, legislative activity, and counseling. Two perceptive comments from the results of the questionnaire submitted by Professor Smith, Chairman of the Section on Legal History of the AALS, are directly on point. According to Professor Opala of the University of Oklahoma, "the legal history teacher must be evangelistic in his approach to persuade students that their ability to use legal materials affords them a potent weapon in both trial and appellate advocacy"[122] and, according to

---

[119]Horwitz, _supra_ note 36; Nelson, _supra_ note 41.

[120]Woodward, _supra_ note 15.

[121]_Cf._ Bergin, _The Law Teacher: A Man Divided Against Himself,_ 54 VA. L. REV. 637 (1968).

[122]LEGAL HISTORY IN AMERICAN LAW SCHOOLS 59.

Professor Strickland at the University of Tulsa, legal history, by providing "an in-depth approach to a limited number of problems, interests the student because he can get his teeth into the real considerations of how real people resolved their legal problems."[123]

In developing materials, syllabi, and approaches, we should concentrate on the principles stated by Horwitz in his response to the AALS questionnaire. We should "avoid antiquarianism; use history to raise theoretical, philosophical, and jurisprudential questions; avoid tedious doctrinal or institutional explications; relate legal changes to more general social, economic, or philosophical changes."[124] As Hurst notes in the same source, we should build courses which

> [R]espond to the students' concern with the moral and political legitimacy of the uses of law in society. We seem to be in a generation of law students uncommonly disturbed about the morality of their discipline. Legal history, insofar as it bears on these legitimacy doubts, seems to strike a response in students, even though they may disagree sharply with the value-orientations in the subject as offered by the instructor.[125]

Students are quite interested, as Professor Wise from Wayne State University Law School points out, "in historical examples of the venality of the legal profession and the extent to which law and the lawyers have been the servants of vested interests."[126]

This calls for cross-pollination among legal historians, not only with regard to the introduction of approaches, techniques, evidence, and concerns from other disciplines, but also in the establishment of a clearinghouse whereby we can exchange bibliographies, syllabi, lecture notes and ideas, information concerning work in progress and recent publications, and the like. The newsletter of the American Society for Legal History, edited by Charles Cullen, is a step in the right direction, but it should be amplified and regularized. Further, pedagogy ought to be a regular topic at scholarly meetings, not only for the benefit of new teachers but for the, benefit of us all. We ought to talk seriously and at length about the merits of seminars versus those of lecture courses, about the

---

[123]*Id.* at 65.

[124]*Id.* at 58.

[125]*Id.* at 64.

[126]*Id.* at 66.

differences between law students and history students and between graduates and undergraduates, and about various pedagogical techniques that work or do not work. Professor Bridwell of the University of South Carolina, responding to the AALS questionnaire, said that "courses should be taught by persons with sufficient interest and commitment to develop a sound knowledge of the field and the literature pertaining to it."[127] We should not, however, be so selfishly concerned about the laziness of some colleagues, about privacy in matters of lecture notes and publication topics—in short, with competitiveness—that we act counterproductively with regard to our common field and enterprise. Academic selfishness is our worst communal disease and should be stamped out.

The availability of classroom materials is also a significant problem, but, as several teachers noted in the AALS questionnaire, so little has been done to solidify theory, philosophy, and historiography in American legal history, let alone for the nineteenth century, that it is unrealistic to expect wide acceptance of any book of "cases and materials." Friedman's *History of American Law*[128] is a good start towards a classroom text, but, frankly, I find it too idiosyncratic to be used as a basic theme book. I suggest the need for compilations of useful source material and of collections of useful articles patterned along the lines of the book Flaherty has edited for the colonial period.[129] A good substitute is good communication about materials inside our confraternity.

## IV. Conclusion

The study of legal history must be viewed as the study of the history of social change. The researcher and writer in this field must have a philosophy and a general field theory; he must also be deeply skeptical. A good deal of research is currently under way, and there has been recently a relative explosion of publications, but much more needs to be done, and it all needs to be done with more conscious organization. We need more conferences, exchanges, bibliographies, newsletters, and the like, to stimulate and continue the cross-pollination necessary to provide proper growth in our field. Pedagogy—classroom teaching—must be given a prime share of attention.

---

[127]*Id.* at 41.

[128]L. FRIEDMAN, *supra* note 31.

[129]*See* ESSAYS IN THE HISTORY OF EARLY AMERICAN LAW (D. Flaherty ed. 1969).

# B. SCHOOLS OF HISTORICAL THOUGHT

# 2
# THE LAW IN UNITED STATES HISTORY

*WILLARD HURST*

# THE LAW IN UNITED STATES HISTORY

WILLARD HURST

Professor of Law, University of Wisconsin

(*Read April 21, 1960*)

## 1.

NOT only the man in the street but also professional students of society hold very limited images of what "law" means. Most often they take it to mean simply the drama of criminal trials: Perry Mason on Saturday night television, the lurid promise of the murder yarns on drugstore racks. If they think of law in a little broader reference, probably it will be in terms of a remembered picture in a high school history text, of portly gentlemen in frock coats, striking attitudes: Webster replies to Hayne. If one presses them, the social scientists at least may concede there is more to law than this. Law, they will grant, states a great many doctrines which provide much of the vocabulary of public policy discussion. But this is, after all, largely formal stuff; sophisticated students know that reality lies in the substance, in operations, in getting behind the law's formalism to the hard facts of interest and practical maneuver. So much for law—and little wonder, then, if neither the man in the street nor the student of society shows much curiosity to learn what aspects of social events or social processes might be better illumined by knowing more about the law's contribution.

Criminal trials and constitutional debates are important. Important, too, in ways which to a distressing degree are not understood even by well-educated men, is the formality of legal process. But these aspects of legal order, however important, fall far short altogether of representing the significance of legal process in this society. A more adequate definition of the attributes of our legal order suggests that study of law in these terms—and in particular study of legal history in these terms—should contribute more to the understanding of the society than the lay stereotypes would indicate.

For studying social process, the most useful definitions of law are made in terms of social functions of law. What are the most distinctive and most important jobs we have asked the law to do in this society? This asks for a modest definition: not what is "law," anywhere, anytime, but what has law been in the development of this particular society. This modesty is appropriate to the limits of what we know about the social functions of legal order. It is appropriate also to a definition of law looked at historically, because history regards events, that is, looks at processes always in particular context. Moreover, this relativist definition of law is peculiarly appropriate to our situation. For we have taken as a central value the idea that legal order should find its warrant in serving men as they strive to realize the larger potential of being—which means that law must find its warrant in relation to particular experience.

Four functions have been specially important to defining law's roles in the growth of this society. (1) To law we assigned the legitimate monopoly of violence; normally only the policeman goes armed. As a corollary, to law we assigned ultimate scrutiny of the legitimacy of all forms of secular power developed within the society—that is, of all means by which some men may exercise compulsion over the wills of other men. Modes of competition and forms of private association thus exist subject to legal regulation to protect the public interest. (2) We used law to define and to implement an idea of constitutionalism as the norm of all secular power. This is an idea which with us had reference to all forms of secular power, not merely to official power. It meant, first, that we believed there should be no center of secular power which was not in some way subject to review by another center of such power. If there seems something paradoxical in this notion, the historic record nonetheless shows that we lived by it; for example, we used law to foster and protect the growth of private (that is, non-official) associations like the business corporation or religious, political and social associations, to build centers of energy and opinion which might provide counter weights to official power. Thus we sought to make all secular power responsible to power outside itself, for ends which it

VOL. 104, NO. 5, 1960]        THE LAW IN UNITED STATES HISTORY                519

alone did not define. But responsibility means nothing until we know, responsibility for what? The second and most distinctive aspect of our insistence that all secular power be responsible (constitutional) power, was that we held the final measure of responsibility to be in serving individual life. (3) We used law to promote formal definition of values and of appropriate means to implement values. In other words, this legal order was characterized by strong insistence on procedural regularity. (4) Finally, we assigned to legal process important roles in allocating scarce resources—of manpower and human talent, as well as of non-human sources of energy—for shaping the general course of economic development. This was an especially important use of law, in a society which believed that in economic creativity it held the means to fashion new standards of human dignity. At the outset government here held the unique asset of the public domain, which we spent to help build turnpikes, canals, and railroads and to create in the Mississippi Valley a republic of family farms. Likewise, we made bold use of taxing and spending powers of national, state, and local governments to help create the framework of economic growth. Resource allocation by law was the more striking in our history because we placed great reliance on broad dispersion of economic decision making into private hands through the market, implemented through the law of property and contract. We supplemented private energies in market by important delegations to non-official persons of powers of public concern. We gave railroads the right of eminent domain; we granted franchises to enterprisers to conduct public utilities and to charge toll for their services; by grant of limited liability to corporation stockholders and by contract, property and tort doctrines which in effect favored venture, we encouraged men to take the risks of action, letting losses lie where they fell unless someone who had been hurt showed compelling reason why the law should help shift the burden.

These uses of law mean that law wove itself into the organization and processes of this society in ways which should make the study of legal process—and in particular of legal history—important to social science. (1) Because it held the legitimate monopoly of force, and incident thereto the authority to call to account all other forms of secular power, law bore some relation to all types of association and all means for mustering collective will and feeling. The obverse of free religious association here, for example, was the legally embodied policy of separation of church and state. (2) Because North American legal order sought to give content to the idea that all power must be constitutional (responsible) power, law entered into the practical meaning that individuality had in this society. The constitutional character of this legal order likewise meant that law was actually or potentially part of the social structure and social process; there was no pattern of social organization, no procedure of social interaction whose significance could be appraised without taking into account the demands which an ideal of constitutional order either did in fact make on it, or should make on it. Thus, for example, we cannot tell the story of the status and roles of women in the United States without including the meaning which the movements for married women's property legislation and equal suffrage had for defining the condition of woman as an effective member of the society. Again, we cannot understand the social history of the business corporation without including the search for acceptable definitions in law of the grounds on which, first, the practical power of corporate owners, and, more recently, of corporate management may establish legitimacy. (3) Because this legal order emphasized procedural regularity—providing diverse organized means for bringing choices to definition and mustering evidence and reasoned argument for their resolution—law entered significantly into the process by which men created social goals and mobilized energies of mind and feeling to move toward their goals. Of course we must not exaggerate the rationality of the law, any more than of other institutions. Regard for procedures tends to create inertia or complacency with familiar ways; passion and prejudice color legal operations as they color any human operations where men feel deep concern about the stakes. Moreover, how men feel is at least as valid a part of their experience as what they achieve by reason; indeed, reason probably finds justification ultimately only as an instrument by which men achieve more subtle, more varied, and more shared emotion. So qualified, however, and always within the framework of a constitutional ordering of power, the increase in men's rational competence and the extension of more rationalized processes of human relations ranked high among the organizing values of this society. Legal process ranked with industrial technology and with organized science as a major means to enlarge the scope of rationalized behavior. In the second half of the twentieth century the trend of events seemed likely to give larger importance to the law's rationalizing role, in the interests of maintaining a vital constitutional tradition. The pressure of scientific and technical rationalization of social processes increased the scale and intricacy of social organization, the demands made in the name of organizational integrity and efficiency, and the inertia created by organization mass. Legal procedures in part had served and would continue to serve to provide a framework of reasonably assured expectations, backed by the force of the state, within which a complex social division of labor could work. More important, however, in our tradition legal procedure had the ultimate function of implementing the constitutional idea—that choices and the costs as well as gains of choices be brought to definition, that power holders be made to account for their use of power, and all this in last analysis that power be used to serve individual life. That growth proceeded along these lines was witnessed by the painful efforts to hammer out a law of labor relations within which management and labor might create a kind of due process and equal protection of law to govern the discipline of the modern factory. (4) Because we used law boldly as a means of resource allocation—with at least as great effect as we used the market—the history of legal process was woven closely into the general growth of the economy and of key relations of social and economic power in the United States. The terms on which we disposed of the public domain in the Mississippi Valley, for example, materially affected the development of a tradition of agrarian political revolt on the one hand, and on the other the growth of the political as well as business and social power of big corporations, of which the first models were the land-grant railroads. The public domain no longer offers government the unique leverage it afforded for nineteenth-century social planning—though current controversy over franchises for use of the air waves reminds us that social growth may bring new areas of public domain into policy significance. However, through its fiscal powers twentieth-century government plays as large a role in affecting the directions and content of the commonwealth as did nineteenth-century government through the public lands. Demands upon the resources-allocation functions of law continue to involve law in the main processes of social change and stability.

Finally, let me note that these social functions of law mean that legal processes produce uncommonly valuable raw materials for studying institutions, transactions, and events whose main focus lies outside law. Law's procedural emphasis —its provision of varied methods of bringing to definition and decision value choices of all degrees of importance—is at the bottom of the fact that law tends to build a storehouse of data for general social science. But it is the fact that law's procedures work for purposes set by the other three functions of legal order that produces the activity that fills the storehouse. Law scrutinizes the over-all dispositions of power in the society; it embodies and insists upon the constitutional idea that the uses of power show justification; it is used to reach decisions on resource allocation outside the market calculus. These functions mean that a great range of men's economic and social as well as their political objectives, tensions, and strivings are made more visible and are caused to leave more tangible evidences of their presence, through legal records. In constitutions, statutes, judgments, and executive and administrative orders, and in the enormous volume of statement and rationalization which surround these in recorded proceedings, in committee reports, in judicial and administrative opinions, as well as in petitions and bills and such routine forms as the income tax return—in all these we have one of the largest and perhaps on the whole the most ordered body of evidence that any of our institutions produces, to reflect many of our values and the troubles we have in bringing values to awareness and doing something about them. It is a sign of the too narrow ideas that the student as well as the man in the street has of law's functions, that both historical and current cross-sectional study of human relations have made limited use of the data afforded by legal process.

## 2.

However, if laymen draw less understanding than they might from legal materials, they may properly say that they have had little guidance from law men to do better. Aside from providing concepts and ordering judicial precedents for the immediate operating needs of bench and bar, legal research has a thin record of accomplishment over the past ninety years in which university law schools have grown to some stature. The defects are not primarily defects of method, though when we press more ambitious study of legal order we as

VOL. 104, NO. 5, 1960]　　THE LAW IN UNITED STATES HISTORY　　　521

soon encounter the hard limits of our present techniques as do students of other aspects of men's behavior. But at this stage the trouble lies much deeper than method. The fundamental defect is a want of philosophy. Legal research has moved within very limited borders, relative to its proper field, because it has not been grounded in ideas adequate to the intellectual challenge which the phenomena of legal order present.

This essay seeks to appraise United States legal history as a field of scholarship, in its promise and in its development to date. I need not, nor could I within this span, take stock of the whole reach of research in law. However, what can be said of the discipline of legal history applies in large measure to other types of legal research.

Research and writing in North American legal history show four major limitations. Implicit are limitations of conception which characterize most of the published work. Here criticism should move carefully. Where men have defined meaningful problems for study it is irrelevant as well as unfair to criticize the particular product because it does not deal with some different subject. Fair criticism may be made of the over-all allocation of energy, where work concentrates on a narrow range of problems to the neglect of others of equal or greater meaning. Fair criticism may be made where the over-all allocation of effort rests on express or implied rejection of other themes for whose development a good case can be made. Fair criticism may be made where particular work is done from a parochial point of view which omits effort to trace relations either to the larger issues of legal order or to the relations of legal to social order. There is much work that needs doing in the study of our legal history, and thus far there are too few able recruits for the work. Hence the most pertinent criticism may be not of particular jobs done, but of the failure of practicing legal historians to show the excitement inherent in the field with enough conviction to enlist more talent for the whole enterprise. Ordered learning is made from the building blocks fashioned by devoted study of particulars. There need be no parochialism in work on a limited subject, if the worker sees the subject in relation to a large context. But significant ordered learning does not consist in rubble, nor does it grow without the skill of master craftsmen who know how to fit building blocks together.

Four limitations of the general product attest the want of philosophy in the study of North American legal history. (1) Historians have exaggerated the work of courts and legal activity immediately related to litigation. (2) They have paid too little attention to the social functions of law. (3) They have not distributed their effort with adequate response to the facts of timing and the reality of major discontinuities in the country's growth in relation to the uses of law. (4) They have exaggerated areas of conscious conflict and deliberate action, at the expense of realistic account of the weight of social inertia and the momentum of social drift.

Anglo-American law men are by tradition and training biased toward equating law with what judges do, to the neglect not only of legislative, executive, and administrative activity, but also to the neglect even of the out-of-court impact of the work of lawyers, let alone the additions or subtractions made in legal order by lay attitudes and practices affecting legal norms. We early trained lawyers by apprenticeship which taught them court pleadings and client caretaking. When the principal revolution in legal education arrived in the 1870's, it was organized about the case method of instruction, which again emphasized the work of courts. Most of the business of the bar through the nineteenth century had to do with the property and contract affairs of clients, and most of the law of these fields was common (that is, judge-made) law, so that through the formative period of our main legal tradition the focus remained on the judicial process. Thus, first our treatise writing and later the writing done for legal journals dealt mainly with public policy as declared by courts. This bias of professional thinking was not affected by the fact that through the nineteenth century Congress and the state legislatures churned out large quantities of important legislation, or by the fact that in great areas of policy which did not lend themselves easily to common law development the framework of the law was erected mainly in statutes (as in the law of the public lands, public education, public utilities, highways, health and sanitation, or the organization of local government). From limited beginnings in the late nineteenth century, executive and administrative lawmaking grew to great proportions alongside statute law. Judicial law-making was never as exclusively important as the concentration of legal writing might seem to show. From the 1870's on, legislative, executive, and administrative processes definitely became the principal sources of formed policy. The course offerings of even the better law schools were slow to reflect this reality. But legal research was even slower, with legal historians badly lagging the field. Of course the work of the courts continues of great importance. In our time legal and non-legal institutions take on increasing size and there is growing readiness to accept demands made on individuals in the name of the security and operating efficiency of large social aggregates. In this context more than ever before the availability of independent courts and an independent class of professional advocates supported not by grace of the state but by private fees, represent basic elements of civil liberty. In the second half of the twentieth century the courts have distinctive importance because they are the forum in which individuals and small groups, of their own resources, can best call organized power to account. To recognize this, however, in no measure justifies the extent to which legal history writing, along with legal philosophy and other legal research, has treated the judicial process as if it were the whole of legal order. Symbolic is the fact, for example, that while twentieth-century scholarship has given us at least four large-scale treatises, a dozen substantial monographs and scores of essays in the law journals on the history of constitutional doctrine as it has been made by the Supreme Court of the United States, we lack a single first-rate modern work on the history of constitutional doctrine as it has been formed in the Congress.

The bulk of legal history writing has been about topics defined by legal categories. We have much writing about commerce clause doctrine, but little about the meaning of commerce clause doctrine for the development or operation of sectional or nationwide marketing organization, or about the impress which such business history may have made on constitutional principles. There is some rather formal history of property law, but little history of the significance of fee simple title for types of land use, for the private and social accounting of income and costs of alternative land uses, or for the political and social balance of power. There are some essays on the history of contract law, but little or no effort to define or appraise the meaning that contract law had for the functioning of the market, the provision of credit, or the allocation of gains and costs of business venture. There are scattered writings about the history of the mortgage, the corporate indenture, the receivership and tax law, but we lack the good studies we should have of the historic relations of

law to the growth and channeling of investment capital. There is a good deal in print about various aspects of the Bill of Rights, but no connected story of the implications of civil rights doctrines for the shifting balance of power among various kinds of groups and between the individual and official and private group power at different stages of the country's growth. Though better than a generation has gone by since we heard the call for a sociological jurisprudence, legal history writing has made little response, but continues content on the whole to let the formal headings of the law fix its subject matter. It is an ironic course of affairs, in a society whose tradition is so strongly constitutional, insisting that legal order is not an end in itself but gains legitimate meaning only in terms of its service to ends of life outside law.

In the total distribution of effort, there has been a disproportionate attention in legal history writing to beginnings—and to beginnings in their most obvious sense—at the expense of proper development of hypotheses concerning the main lines of growth through to our own time. Much attention has focused on colonial origins, on the period of constitutional experiment from 1776 to 1790, and on the successive frontier phases of national expansion. I do not quarrel with the worth of attending to such formative periods taken in themselves, but only with the tendency to fasten onto origins without equal curiosity to follow through, and with failure to see that in terms of law's relation to gathering issues of power and social function there were other less obvious periods of beginnings which should also be studied. First, as an example of the want of follow through, it is odd that for so many states we have writing which with care sometimes verging on antiquarian enthusiasm traces the beginnings of territorial and state courts (once again, the excessive preoccupation with judicial process), but little good writing on such basic themes as law's relation to the creation of transportation networks, the law's response to the business cycle, or the relation of tax policy to the fortunes of agriculture and other extractive industries. These omissions are, of course, part of the neglect of the social-function history of law which I have already noted. But they also represent a neglect of a familiar and important time sequence characteristic of the growth of these states, whose people normally established their basic legal institutions in the nineteenth century with some obvious impatience to get on to

VOL. 104, NO. 5, 1960]          THE LAW IN UNITED STATES HISTORY          523

their central care, which was the expansion of their economy.

Second, on the neglect of the less obvious beginnings, the most notable examples are the relative inattention to the sharp changes in direction and pace of social movement which came about in the 1830's, the 1870's, and the 1930's. The 1830's saw rapid development of markets and marketing emphasis in the public policy-making of one state after another, with reflection especially in the statute books, as we passed from relatively simple agrarian to more commercial and credit-centered economies. The 1870's saw the rapid cumulation of forces channeled or given new impetus by the new scale of organization of men and capital and the new techniques of public and private finance generated out of the North's war effort. Change here was far more drastic than in the 1830's and amounted to a major break in continuity. Due mainly to the shifts in the size of private industrial and financial organization and in the reach of markets which gathered force in the '70s, by the late '90s the United States was a qualitatively different society from what it had been before the Civil War. The strains and conflicts, the gains and losses attendant upon this rapid and major alteration of the country's power structure and modes of operation provide main themes for legal history which we have hardly begun to explore. The 1930's saw the cumulated impact of trends in social and economic interdependence which had been gathering force since World War I. The challenge of these themes is so large, indeed, that one may wonder whether more essays on territorial beginnings represent so much contributions to knowledge as refuges from more exacting studies.

Legal history research may be especially subject to a bias toward themes of conflict, or at least toward themes which emphasize conscious and debated decisions. Such a bias is favored by the emphasis of our legal order on formal procedures. So far as they are efficient, regular procedures for framing, deliberating, and adopting constitutions, statutes, executive orders and administrative rules work toward bringing choices to definition, aligning interested parties, promoting expression and energizing will. Lawsuits and court decisions work even more dramatically to these ends. Hence, so far as legal history research has tended toward exaggerated emphasis upon the judicial process, it has particularly strengthened a bias toward equating men's history with the record of their more or less conscious strivings. Yet, the broader

the reach of our hypotheses and the deeper our concern to study the social functions of legal order, the more we will learn to respect the relative influence of inertia and drift in affairs. The most realistic view of all aspects of man's history leads to the conclusion that most of what has happened to men has happened without their wanting it or striving for it or opposing it or—more important—without their being aware of the meaning of trends until patterns of structure and force have developed past points of revoking. This general judgment seems no less true of legal history in this country. There is peculiar irony in the fact, since it is the business of constitutional legal order to promote responsible control of events. No example is more instructive than the history of antitrust law, whose development both reflected and persistently lagged the imperious course of revolutions in industrial and financial organization. Aside from some efforts either to expound or refute Marxian styles of hypothesis,—and even here the institutional cast of language only thinly disguises villains or heroes felt to be working in the background—the writing of North American legal history has paid little attention to putting legal phenomena in due perspective relative to the massive weight of inertia or to the implacable movement of decisions taken by drift and default.

3.

If legal history research and writing in this country have moved within too narrow limits, the criticisms point to some positive prescriptions. (1) We need allocate more effort to studying legislative, executive, and administrative processes as well as the bar's contributions to these formal processes and to the informal social regulation that goes on through the market and through private association. Likewise we need more attention to ways in which lay attitudes toward law (including laymen's disregard of law or their mistaken images of it) have affected the creation of institutions of social order other than formal legal institutions. (2) Legal history should begin to contribute more to develop fact-based, fact-tested theories of social structure and social process. For example, we should have more legal history written in terms of law's operational significance for the institution of the market, studied in as wide a range of interplay of law and market as the wit and devotion of legal scholarship can compass. (3) Legal history writing should come to bear with greater emphasis upon the past one hundred years in the United States. Especially should there be substantial scholarly investment in study of the profound shifts in structure, process, and attitudes that occurred in the generations beginning about 1820 and 1861, and in the depression 1930's. Legal history has not been made only by quill pen and candlelight. (4) Not with despair but with realistic estimate of the odds against man's conscious contrivance and out of convicton that his distinctive quality lies in rebellion against the odds, legal history should treat as critical themes the impact of social inertia and social drift. Nor can we afford to take this direction with any moral complacency, weighing our own shrewdness against the blunders of our ancestors. If the more significant decisions regarding natural resources use were made by default in the nineteenth century, no less by default have been the twentieth-century decisions on metropolitan growth; if the nineteenth century allowed market demands for rail transport unduly to determine the course of public policy, no less has the twentieth century allowed the immediate conveniences, comforts, and social status markings of the automobile to determine a fantastic range of matters of public concern, from the safety of life to the location of commerce and industry. The physical size of this country, the invitations to large-scale economic effort posed by its natural resources and population growth, as well as deep-rooted, but little-calculated faith in the self-evident values of growth and movement and change (in intangible senses of status and accomplishment as well as by tangible measures of product and location)—such factors contributed to make provision of transport an element of uncommon influence on our public policy, and a good example in both nineteenth- and twentieth-century settings of the type of unplanned and largely undirected cumulation of events which had basic shaping effect upon what law was asked to do and how it did it.

There are many profitable directions in which a broader conception of legal history might take us. I have drawn specific prescriptions from four criticisms of limitations implicit in the bulk of work so far done. In addition let me note some more general developments that would be useful. Two concern the more effective study of legal institutions themselves. Two concern particularly critical kinds of meaning which the study

of legal history might have for better understanding the general course of this society.

First, as to legal institutions: (1) In times when social change moves fast, wide, and deep amid peril to the prized values of a constitutionally ordered community, we need more sophisticated knowledge of the potentials and the limits of the major agencies of law-making. If no other currents of events enforced this need, it would gain enough urgency because of the extent to which we depend upon public finance to sustain the momentum of the economy and upon foreign policy to maintain the national security. On the whole the organization, procedures, and working traditions of the legislative and executive branches represent responses to conditions which the fast pace of events has put far behind us. If there need be less concern for the adequacy of judicial organization, this is not because it lacks serious defects. However, the most important job for the courts in this highly organized modern society is not that of general policy-making but of insuring some minimum of decent procedural protection for individuals and small groups confronting large organized power. On the whole this is a task simpler enough than general policy-making so that it can be handled with what we have, if bench and bar apply their traditions with intelligence and courage. The situation is quite different as to the sufficiency of the legislature and executive before the daunting challenges of the times; the difference is reflected, for example, in contemporary controversies over the proper roles of legislative investigation, and over functions of the National Security Council or the Joint Chiefs of Staff, or in hearings and debates of the Congressional Joint Committee on the Economic Report of the President's Council of Economic Advisors. Types of public problems vary in distinctive character and challenge; types of public agency vary in distinctive capacities, whether born of formal structure and process or of tradition. Legal history should lend us more insight into the working character, promise, and limitations of formal agencies for making public decisions. (2) There is no more badly neglected area of legal research than that of sanctions, the comparative study of methods of implementing policy. Given life's infinite variety and the hard limits of social science research techniques so far available, the study of sanctions is an area in which we now stand to gain most from history. Nor should we view it as the study of factors of secondary importance. The more difficult the basic policy choices, the more surely must judgments of the promise and costs of implementation enter into the basic decisions. Moreover, we grow into some basic decisions out of experience of what we can expect to do. Sophisticated study of experience in enforcing public policy will require overleaping the limitations which have marked the bulk of legal historical writing—appraising the interplay of legislative and executive with judicial processes, relating law to the functional character of other social institutions on which it impinges, putting legal decisions and procedures into the proper perspective of the times in which they are made, weighing the positive investment of resources which the law must provide or direct to obtain desired results. It is a commentary on the failure of scholarship thus far to tackle many major problems, that, for example, in the 1960's when we confront the difficulties of building equal protection of the laws for Negroes in voting and schooling we have no studied body of experience for guidance in handling problems of large-scale hostility to public policy. If legal historians will set themselves to significant problems in legal sanctions, they will lack no longer for a more searching philosophy of their discipline; their problems will push them into philosophy.

Second, consider two respects in which a broader approach to legal history might yield insights of two types specially important to understanding the general life of the society.

(1) Because of the four key functions we have assigned to law—its scrutiny of all types of secular power, its constitutionalism, its emphasis on procedural regularity and its role in resource allocation—but especially because of law's formality (its attention to regular procedures for examining and taking decisions), law offers peculiarly important evidence of the values which give this society coherence and vitality. Of course this is not true in equal measure of all we find recorded in law; inertia and drift play their roles here, too, so that a prime job for legal history is to distinguish what has living force from what is dead or dying, deceptive or hypocritical. Granted this need of taking distinctions, legal history, just because of its relative formality, offers unusual evidence of the development of the values our people have held. Thus, study of legal history can make special contribution to the general history of ideas. The study of a people's

values has basic importance to understanding a society, for it is the sharing of values that provides the bond of lasting human relations, even where (as with the value we put on the competitive processes of the market) the shared values may express themselves in secondary conflict. Study of the growth of shared values has special importance not only for understanding this particular society, but for contributing to its strength. We have grown fast amid a great bustle of events and subject to major discontinuities in the emergence of new relations of power and process. We need to know ourselves in our strengths and failings much better than we do. There is evidence of this need in the uncertain allegiance which common opinion has shown under stress even to such traditional values as those of the Bill of Rights. A broader concern with legal history as an avenue to study of ideas will bring this discipline into relation to the most fundamental kinds of social analysis as well as into relation with the most critical living problems of our own generation.

(2) Because legal processes and legal records bulk large among ways in which we bring values to definition, a broadly conceived legal history could help us come to terms with the good and the bad features of the pragmatic attitudes that are so central in this culture. Our actions show that we have believed that within a framework of generalized values men must make meaning for themselves, in a universe whose baffling detail and sweep favor drift and inertia as the norm of men's experience. In this light the main theme of man's history is the cultivation of his awareness and of his capacities of mind and will to act upon his greater awareness of his situation. We need to strive to see, and to learn what our creative possibilities are by striving to act upon what we see. The experimental and activist bias of our culture rest upon these valid insights. On the other hand, our preoccupation with directed effort and what it teaches has led us also into a bias toward exalting the immediately practical—in the sense of knowledge which can be translated into immediate operations—at the expense of understanding larger causes and more remote chains of effects. Thus a valid pragmatism is constantly at war with an illegitimate pragmatism in our way of life. Because it brings so much focused effort to bear upon making choices and counting gains and costs, legal process offers rich tangible evidence of these

warring brands of pragmatism in our common life. For example, the history of our worship of the fee simple title to land—in its fruitful relation to the development of civil liberty on the one hand, and its unfortunate relation to the waste of natural resources on the other—could be told in ways to show how legal history might illuminate the sound growth and also the distortion of pragmatic values in this society. If the cultivation of awareness is the basic theme which expounds man's most distinctive life role, the most characteristic functions of our legal order— its scrutiny of the arrangements of power, its insistence on the responsibility (constitutional status) of legitimate power, and on procedural regularity, and its uses for resource allocation— point to the intimate relation which the imaginative study of legal history should have to the study of general history.

Implicit in what I have said in appraising some approaches to legal history is the notion that we should study history to learn more about realizing life's possibilities. History itself will teach us not to hold a naive faith that men readily learn from history. Moreover, the view I take of man means that there is no need to apologize for studying history partly because there is pleasure in the effort; the enjoyment lies precisely in man's nature, for his life consists most distinctively in his consciousness. But writing and reading history are more than aesthetic experiences. They are themselves kinds of activity which constitute man's distinctive being, which consists in his response to and rebellion against the challenges of an impersonal universe. It is in this sense that legal history research and writing stand under the functional command to serve the growth of our philosophy.

# 3
# BOOK REVIEW (OF A HISTORY OF LAW BY LAWRENCE M. FRIEDMAN)

*G. EDWARD WHITE*

# BOOK REVIEW

A HISTORY OF AMERICAN LAW. By Lawrence M. Friedman. New York, Simon & Schuster, 1973. Pp. 655. $14.95.

*Reviewed by G. Edward White**

It is too much to say that American legal history has come of age with the publication of Lawrence Friedman's *A History of American Law*, the first attempt "to do anything remotely like a general history"[1] of law and legal institutions in America. But the appearance of Friedman's work indicates that a sufficient amount of monographic literature in American legal history exists to allow some form of synthetic treatment. That in itself is an accomplishment, for American legal history has been one of the most unfortunate step-children of the academic profession, disdained by historians and lawyers alike, struggling to establish itself in curricula and to disengage itself from antiquarianism, largely bereft of distinctive or distinguished scholarship.

That Friedman has been the first to attempt a general treatment of American legal history is not without personal significance. He has been a pioneering and innovative contributor to the monographic literature of the field;[2] he has emphasized the historical antecedents of substantive areas of American law;[3] he has attempted to modernize the discipline of legal history by introducing to it the analytical techniques of the social sciences;[4] and he is a charter member of the school of thought currently dominant among American legal historians. His *History* illustrates his functions in each of these

---

* Assistant Professor of Law, University of Virginia. Member, District of Columbia Bar. B.A., 1963, Amherst College; M.A., 1964, Yale University; Ph.D., 1967, Yale University; J.D., 1970, Harvard Law School.

[1] L. FRIEDMAN, A HISTORY OF AMERICAN LAW 9 (1973). [Hereinafter cited as FRIEDMAN].

[2] *E.g.*, Friedman, *Law, Order, and History*, 16 S.D.L. REV. 242 (1971); Friedman, *On Legal Development*, 24 RUTGERS L. REV. 11 (1969); Friedman, *Legal Culture and Social Development*, 4 LAW & SOC'Y REV. 29 (1969); Friedman, *Law Reform in Historical Perspective*, 13 ST. LOUIS U.L.J. 351 (1969); Friedman, *Legal Rules and the Process of Social Change*, 19 STAN. L. REV. 786 (1967); Friedman, *Tenement House Legislation in Wisconsin*, 9 AM. J. LEGAL. HIST 41 (1965); Friedman, *Patterns of Testation in the 19th Century*, 8 AM. J. LEGAL HIST. 34 (1964); Friedman & Ladinsky, *Social Change and the Law of Industrial Accidents*, 67 COLUM. L. REV. 50 (1967).

[3] L. FRIEDMAN, CONTRACT LAW IN AMERICA (1965); L. FRIEDMAN, GOVERNMENT AND SLUM HOUSING: A CENTURY OF FRUSTRATION (1968).

[4] L. FRIEDMAN, LAW AND THE BEHAVIORAL SCIENCES (1969).

capacities. Accordingly, it provides a starting point for an analysis of the present state of American legal history.

\* \* \*

An outstanding characteristic of American legal history in the twentieth century has been the relative absence of scholarship. While American legal philosophy and jurisprudence were passing through at least four academic phases since 1900, complete with intellectual controversies and polemics,[5] and while other sub-branches of American history, such as economic history or social history, were exhibiting distinctive patterns of growth and change, American legal history before 1950 produced only isolated studies: treatments of historical periods[6] or particular institutions[7] reflecting the idiosyncratic interests of the scholars involved.

The sporadic nature of intellectual contributions to the discipline can be partially explained by its peculiar methodological problems. Analyzing legal source material requires the technical skills imparted by a legal education: the majority of historians are deterred from doing research in legal materials by their inability to read the relevant sources. Taking the time to acquire the necessary skills, for an historian, is in many instances far more costly than simply choosing a less formidable area of specialization. Other deterrents exist for American lawyers interested in legal history. The methodological techniques of the legal profession, perhaps because of their proven success in analyzing cases and statutes, tend to become the central focus of legal education: substance, on balance, is subordinated to methodology. But history is not so easily reduced to concrete problems of analysis: descriptions of the flow of change and syntheses of large masses of data are important in rendering it intelligible, and the standard techniques of legal analysis are less helpful in those tasks. Further, modern American legal education, with its emphasis on the contrary uses to which data can be put and the ambivalent nature of reality, may serve as a philosophical deterrent to historical scholarship, which until recently has been seen by its practitioners as an objective search for truth.[8]

These deterrents contributed to the depressed state of scholarly activity in American legal history during the first half of the twentieth century. The one major exception was study of the Supreme Court of the United States. In contrast to the reluctance with which nonlawyers approached most areas of legal research, historians and political scientists enthusiastically analyzed

[5] *See* White, *From Sociological Jurisprudence to Realism,* 58 Va. L. Rev. 999 (1972); White, *The Evolution of Reasoned Elaboration,* 59 Va. L. Rev. 279 (1973).

[6] *E.g.,* R. Pound, The Formative Era of American Law (1938).

[7] *E.g.,* C. Warren, The Supreme Court in United States History (1972).

[8] *See* White, *The Appellate Opinion as Historical Source Material,* 1 J. Interdisciplinary History 491 (1971).

the Supreme Court. However, the result was an unfortunate amalgam of diverse and sometimes opposing perspectives. Political scientists found an interest in the Court as an institution of American government, historians as a repository of socially significant issues. None of the concerns of one group particularly excited the other; indeed, basic assumptions about the proper way to study the Court remained unresolved. As a consequence the Court's work was over-evaluated but seldom illuminated.

Beginning in the 1950's a group of scholars, primarily lawyers some of whom were trained in the social sciences, began a reorientation of the focus of American legal history. Led by Willard Hurst, the most prolific legal historian of his generation, and using the University of Wisconsin as its common intellectual base, the group advocated a twofold shift in the primary concern of American legal historians: from national themes to predominantly local issues and from public (constitutional and administrative) to private (business and commercial) law. Hurst himself began a massive empirical study of the legal history of the lumber industry in Wisconsin, and on the basis of his exploratory research wrote essays[9] suggesting that fruitful connections could be drawn between the growth of private law in America and changing patterns of economic development.

Following Hurst, a "Wisconsin School" of legal historians embarked on a series of monographic studies involving the relationship of private law to economic development. As their focus came to coincide with one previously identified by economic and business historians, a measure of interdisciplinary cooperation began to emerge. At the same time the social sciences developed distinctive methodologies which gave more attention to analysis of empirical data; the Wisconsin School enthusiastically seized upon these methodologies. The result was both an outpouring of monographs and the advancement of a new set of generalizations about the development of law and legal institutions in America. The first was the observation that law in America had functioned not as a divine body of rules but as a "rational tool"[10] which interest groups used to secure particular goals. Private law was the creation of private parties and groups with distinct aims in mind; its purpose was to ensure certainty and predictability for these groups.

Following from this generalization was a second: since economic or commercial interest groups were relatively easy to identify, and since the ordinary function of law was to accomodate the needs of those groups, the central focus of scholarship in legal history should be on economic issues and their relationship to the normal workings of legal institutions. Issues in "high

---

[9] J. W. HURST, THE GROWTH OF AMERICAN LAW: THE LAW MAKERS (1950); J. W. HURST, LAW AND THE CONDITIONS OF FREEDOM IN THE NINETEENTH CENTURY UNITED STATES (1956); J. W. HURST, LAW AND SOCIAL PROGRESS IN UNITED STATES HISTORY (1960).

[10] FRIEDMAN, *supra* note 1 at 25.

politics," as Hurst called them,[11] were to be eschewed for the more mundane affairs of the free enterprise system and its legal appendages. Legal history came to be identified in economic terms: its phases were correlated to the waves of entrepreneurial innovation and consolidation that marked the nineteenth and early twentieth centuries in America.

Implicit in the economic and commercial orientation of the Wisconsin School was a deemphasis of the ideological themes of American legal history except insofar as they touched upon those particular areas. Although the school was responsive to the empirical innovations in social science methodology of the 1950's and sixties, it ignored the formation of an increasingly sophisticated vocabulary for addressing nonempirical data, such as the concepts of national myths, ideals, and symbols developed by the American Studies movement to analyze ideological developments. The result was a juxtaposition in the Wisconsin School of painstaking empirical research with unrefined and simplistic generalizations about historical trends.[12]

\* \* \*

Friedman is a product of the Wisconsin School and shares its assumptions. He cites the "work, personality, and spirit" of Hurst as a "major influence;" [13] he credits "the atmosphere of ferment" [14] at Wisconsin as generating his interest in legal history and the relation of law to the social sciences; he admits to having "surrendered [him]self wholeheartedly to some of the central insights of social science";[15] he emphasizes in his *History* "the separate histories of the law of the fifty states" and "the more mundane workings of the system" [16] rather than constitutional law and the Supreme Court. He sees law as "an instrument" used by "the people in power" to "push or pull toward some definite goal." [17] In short, he offers not so much a general history of American law as a history which attempts to "redress the balance" [18] by focusing on the particular levels of the American legal system that have received attention from the Wisconsin School. His work is ultimately an argument for the proposition that American legal history can derive its identity as a discipline from the concerns and assumptions of the Wisconsin scholars: that it can center its focus on the reaction of private law to economic trends.

---

[11] HURST, LAW AND SOCIAL PROCESS IN UNITED STATES HISTORY, *supra* note 9, at 18.

[12] *See, e.g.,* Hurst's chart of "shifts in time among principal and secondary preoccupations of public policy" from 1620 to 1900 in LAW AND THE CONDITIONS OF FREEDOM, *supra* note 9, at 40.

[13] FRIEDMAN, *supra* note 1, at 11.

[14] *Id.*

[15] *Id.* at 10.

[16] *Id.* at 11.

[17] *Id.* at 25.

[18] *Id.* at 10.

Friedman has deliberately deemphasized constitutional law and jurisprudence in his *History*. There is relatively little on the history of the Bill of Rights; the Alien and Sedition Acts receive only a cursory mention; Leonard Levy's recent study of the origins of the Fifth Amendment[19] is not cited; the relationship between religion and law in colonial America is not emphasized; the Zenger trial and free speech problems in the eighteenth century are not discussed. Nor do the major constitutional issues of the early nineteenth century receive much attention. Some of Marshall's decisions articulating the power of the national government in a federal system are alluded to, but others, such as *McCulloch v. Maryland*,[20] are not; the Taney Court's modification of Marshall's theories in such cases as *Cooley v. Board of Wardens*[21] is not mentioned. The early nineteenth-century constitutional cases that Friedman treats are those which have an impact on economic themes: *Dartmouth College*[22] and its effect on the status of corporations; *Charles River Bridge*[23] and its implications for state-supported economic expansion. With certain exceptions, such as a minor treatment of civil rights in the context of the Reconstruction Amendments,[24] the pattern after the Civil War is the same. The "main themes in the law" are the uses of land, the regulations of business, the emergent role of labor unions, changes in the law of corporations, and the interaction between social welfare legislation and the economic theory of laissez-faire.

Developments in jurisprudence receive a similar deemphasis. Friedman devotes some attention to the great treatise writers of the early nineteenth century, Kent, Story, Simon Greenleaf and Theophilus Parsons, and to their post-Civil War counterparts, Thomas Cooley, Christopher Tiedeman, and John Forrest Dillon, and brings the history of juristic scholarship into the twentieth century. He has a brief treatment of legal realism and its impact on twentieth-century legal education. But he ignores such developments as the influence of an "instrumentalist" conception of law on judicial decision-making in the early nineteenth century[25] and its manifestation in the opinions of such judges as Lemuel Shaw. Nor does he treat the rise of "mechanical jurisprudence," an artificial method of inductive reasoning common to the late nineteenth century by which judges reasoned syllogistically downward from initial premises to results. Similarly omitted is the counter-movement of sociological jurisprudence, conceived by Roscoe Pound and others

---

[19] L. LEVY, THE ORIGINS OF THE FIFTH AMENDMENT (1968).

[20] 17 U.S. (4 Wheat.) 316 (1819).

[21] 53 U.S. (12 How.) 299 (1851).

[22] Trustees of Dartmouth College v. Woodward, 17 U.S. (4 Wheat.) 518 (1819).

[23] Proprietors of the Charles River Bridge v. Proprietors of the Warren Bridge, 36 U.S. (11 Pet.) 420 (1837).

[24] FRIEDMAN, *supra* note 1 at 298-301.

[25] *Cf.* Horwitz, *The Emergence of an Instrumental Conception of American Law, 1780-1820*, in D. FLEMING AND B. BAILYN, 5 PERSPECTIVES IN AMERICAN HISTORY 287 (1971).

in the early twentieth century as a protest against the mechanical school; and the decline of realism in the years immediately preceding World War II, with the consequent rise of a new school of jurisprudence that emphasized the obligation of judges to give detailed and coherent reasons for the results they reached.[26]

In the face of his stated attempts to provide a "social history of American law" in which law is seen "not as a kingdom unto itself . . . but as a mirror of society,"[27] Friedman's failure to include these areas of American legal history is significant. Insofar as ideological change is an important facet of a civilization's development, this omission is a serious one. We have no help from Friedman in attempting to analyze such historical phenomena as the relationship between the social assumptions of the Enlightenment and the framing of the Constitution; the parallels between the early nineteenth century reform literature concept of an organic community and the emergence of a community welfare standard by which judges tested the validity of legislation; the connections between social Darwinism, a prevalent ideology of the late nineteenth century, and the doctrine of substantive due process, developed by judges after the Civil War; or the validity of the theory advanced by Alexander Bickel[28] that Warren Court activism was stimulated by early twentieth century assumptions about the inevitability of progress.

But all of this is not to say that there is not a good deal of interesting information and rewarding analysis in Friedman's *History*. He gives us an excellent guide to the development of substantive law in the states. We can determine the status of civil procedure in early nineteenth century North Carolina,[29] the division of the crime of murder into degrees in early nineteenth century Missouri[30] and the contrasting treatments of the insanity defense after the Civil War in Iowa and New Hampshire.[31] We can explore the status of married women as property holders in Mississippi in the 1830's;[32] the legal techniques employed by Illinois and Nebraska to regulate railroads during the late nineteenth century;[33] Michigan's treatment of mortgages at the turn of the last century;[34] the growth of the doctrine of charitable immunities in Massachusetts and Maryland;[35] or the gradual efforts to achieve uniformity in state laws governing sales and negotiable instruments.[36] These

---

26 *See* White, *supra* note 5.

27 FRIEDMAN, *supra* note 1, at 10.

28 *See generally* A. BICKEL, THE SUPREME COURT AND THE IDEA OF PROGRESS (1970).

29 FRIEDMAN, *supra* note 1, at 131.

30 *Id.* at 249.

31 *Id.* at 515.

32 *Id.* at 185-86.

33 *Id.* at 305-06.

34 *Id.* at 374.

35 *Id.* at 416.

36 *Id.* at 468-73.

pieces of information do more than satisfy an antiquarian curiosity. They provide us the antecedent reference points to which the law, in its process of change, is continually recurring and thereby help to explain its anomalies and irregularities. They lend persuasive weight to Friedman's thesis that law is inevitably "molded by economy and society." [37] Each of these local laws is a microcosm of social attitudes of a distinct time and place. The conception of women in antebellum Mississippi affects their very limited autonomy as property holders; agrarian hostility to the symbols of an advancing urban and industrial civilization helps generate the Granger legislation regulating railroads. In these examples we can see law in an instrumentalist capacity, as Friedman would like us to see it.

Friedman's work is also a full demonstration of the pervasive relationship in America between law and economic development. He documents, in a chapter on law and the economy from 1776 to 1847, the active role of government in promoting entrepreneurial ventures and the supervisory powers it enacted as a condition of its promoter role. Although this revisionist approach to a period in American economic history once inaccurately characterized as dominated by theories of laissez-faire is not new,[38] Friedman's is the first attempt to popularize it on a wide scale.

Other chapters pursue the same theme. One ties shifts in the legal doctrines governing the use of property and commercial transactions to the expanded meaning of property rights and the outgrowth of commerce in the early nineteenth century. Another deals with the modification of land use concepts in the face of the increasingly industrial character of post-Civil War America. Another traces the growth of regulation of business enterprise in the later nineteenth century, during which American government changed its stance toward business enterprise from sponsor to sometimes reluctant regulator and trustee. Another deals with the rise of the corporate form of business enterprise and the consequent growth of the law governing corporations. Even some of the major social issues of the nineteenth and twentieth centuries are seen to have an economic tinge: Friedman treats the legal problem of slavery primarily as a form of property holding; he views the philosophy of administrative regulation, an ideological innovation of the twentieth century, as a response to the emergence of giant business organizations.

In addition to his concern with state and local law and the adjustment of the legal system to economic change, Friedman is interested in the educational patterns, literary habits, and styles of practice of the legal profession. Hence we are shown the changes in legal education from the apprenticeship system of the eighteenth and early nineteenth centuries to the rise of law

---

[37] *Id.* at 10.

[38] It appeared in the 1940's in such works as Oscar and Mary Handlin's *Commonwealth* (1947) and Louis Hartz's *Economic Policy and Democratic Thought: Pennsylvania, 1776-1860* (1948).

schools with Joseph Story's appointment to Harvard as a fulltime professor in the 1830s to the eventual emergence of the law school as a necessary step in the process of being called to the bar. We are also given some indication of the curricular revolutions of American law schools. Friedman traces the lecture system, dominant in the early nineteenth century and not necessarily confined to legal subjects; the use of nonannotated casebooks and the Socratic method of classroom teaching under Langdell at Harvard in the 1870s; the reactions against the case method and the attempts to reintegrate law with other disciplines that have variously appeared, with mixed success, since the 1930s.

Friedman has also demonstrated the close relationship between the state of legal education and the production of technical literature. In general, the more autonomous the methodology of analyzing legal materials taught in the law schools, the less necessity for the appearance of treatises as academic tools. Thus the early nineteenth century, with its relatively short supply of lawbooks and rudimentary state of legal education, saw the appearance of the first great wave of treatises. With the advent of the case method after the Civil War, treatises and textbooks largely disappeared from the law schools, to reappear as practical guides to the practice of law. With the innovations of the twentieth century, the treatises came to take on a more academic character and even to represent jurisprudential points of view. Samuel Williston's *Contracts* was "fully armored against the intrusion of any ethical, economic, or social notions whatsoever;"[39] Arthur Corbin's *Contracts* attempted to describe the relation of legal doctrines to their social context.

Finally, Friedman gives us brief overviews of American legal history in the colonial period and in the twentieth century. His main themes in both chapters are the interplay between the diversity of economic and social conditions that has characterized life in America and the continual attempts to make our legal system uniform. This framework serves Friedman for discussions of twentieth century legal reform movements as well as for descriptions of the organization of colonial courts. It is a highly workable one. As numerous commentators on American civilization have pointed out, our history has been in large measure an effort to develop a unifying set of distinctively American social values out of an extraordinary diverse, multifaceted and polarized cultural experience. The major cultural crises of our civilization, from the Revolutionary War through the Civil War to the Vietnamese War, have been times when a surface consensus of values has disintegrated under pressure from competing groups who interpret its meaning in radically different ways. Against those episodes can be juxtaposed other periods, the 1830s, the post-Civil War generation, the 1950s, when American civiliza-

---

[39] FRIEDMAN, *supra* note 1, at 593.

tion seems to have achieved a certain surface unity, as manifested in the collective enshrinement of a national model of success: the self-made man, the captain of industry, or the organization man. In discussing legal institutions in the framework of a dialectic between homogeneity and cultural pluralism Friedman has found a rich and powerful theme.

\* \* \*

Throughout his discussion run Friedman's persistent organizing assumptions: the permanency of social change and the resultant "growth" of law; the "rational" use of the legal system to achieve particularistic economic ends; and the instrumentalist nature of historical change, in which nothing happens by accident, and "nothing is autonomous," but everything is "molded" [40] purposively by mankind in the rational pursuit of its goals. These assumptions require as much evaluation as Friedman's substantive emphases, for the two are inevitably linked.

On becoming fascinated with the remarkable *usefulness* of economic theory—its skill at assembling, synthesizing, and manipulating data, its reduction of obtuse phenomena to simple, workable concepts and systems, the kinetic energy of its methodology, in which one is constantly busy with the graph or the equation—one may be tempted to ignore the fact that it rests on unproven starting assumptions about behavior and that those assumptions, once accepted, clear away many nasty complexities for the sake of a manageable working model. The difficulty is that the very clearing away may ultimately hinder understanding instead of improve it; that too easy a transition from the model to the "real world" may be made. In that transition an admirably clear but perhaps overly simplistic and even wrongheaded description of social behavior may result. For example, the very act of assuming that individuals *make* history—that they develop institutions in their own image and use them for their own purposes, create events rather than react to them, "mould" rather than undergo "accidents"—may oversimplify at the outset.

To be sure, individuals aspire after power and status, elites are created, elites use their influence to achieve various parochial goals, and social change is affected by the pressures that elites generate. But that is not in any sense a complete description of the process of history. As in the lives of individuals, so in the life of a culture a series of random, disoriented, and inexplicable events occur. Persons react—not always "rationally" unless that term has lost its meaning—and their reactions make a difference, even though they cannot be said to have been thought out in advance. At any point in time there are a series of limitations on the capacity of a nation's citizens to perceive and think, a set of cultural blinders that prevent certain

---

[40] *Id.* at 10.

options from being entertained or even considered. And even within the cognizable framework resulting from the shared values of a nation at a moment in time, there are options which, with hindsight, seem culturally determined rather than truly chosen. One need only examine the process of decisionmaking in foreign affairs from 1950 to 1970 to see the extent to which all the decisionmakers, whatever their individual shades of disagreement, were prisoners of the mythologies of the cold war.

So perhaps the most fundamental difficulty with Friedman's view of American legal history is that he takes "nothing as historical accident." [41] If by that he means that law and legal institutions in America must necessarily reflect the goals and values of their contemporary social context, one can hardly quarrel. But to say that social institutions are "mirror[s] of society" [42] is a truism. If, however, he intends to inject a thoroughly purposive quality into the relation of social groups and the legal system, as if the latter is entirely created or used by the former so that it is the equivalent of "an instrument," [43] one is given pause. However attractive the notion of the law as an ongoing, functioning, purposive process[44] used reasonably by rational men in the pursuit of their common goals, it is surely more than that, and its history in America has embodied more than the pushing or pulling of "people in power . . . toward some definite goal." [45] Our legal institutions, over time, have been to an important extent repositories of the helplessness and prejudices of mankind and the disorderliness and absurdities of our experience.

But these are mainly matters of philosophy rather than historiography. At one level Friedman's *History* has succeeded admirably. It has demonstrated the coming maturity of the discipline of American legal history by building a synthesis—itself an argument for a particular point of view— from the growing monographic literature in the field. The important contributions of the Wisconsin School and its predecessors, the Handlins,[46] Hartz,[47] Levy,[48] Friedman and Ladinsky,[49] Goodrich,[50] Hurst,[51] Kimball,[52]

---

[41] *Id.*

[42] *Id.*

[43] *Id.* at 25.

[44] *Cf.* H. HART & A. SACKS, THE LEGAL PROCESS iii (tent. ed., 1958).

[45] FRIEDMAN, *supra* note 1, at 25.

[46] O. and M. Handlin, *supra* note 37.

[47] L. Hartz, *supra* note 37.

[48] L. LEVY, THE LAW OF THE COMMONWEALTH AND CHIEF JUSTICE SHAW (1957).

[49] Friedman and Ladinsky, *Social Change and the Law of Industrial Accidents, supra* note 2.

[50] C. GOODRICH, GOVERNMENT PROMOTION OF AMERICAN CANALS AND RAILROADS, (1960).

[51] J. W. HURST, LAW AND ECONOMIC GROWTH: THE LEGAL HISTORY OF THE LUMBER INDUSTRY IN WISCONSIN 1836-1915 (1964) and sources cited *supra*, note 9.

[52] S. KIMBALL, INSURANCE AND PUBLIC POLICY (1960).

Scheiber,[53] serve as foundations for Friedman's generalizations. Once isolated voices in the historical wilderness, those contributions are now seen
as part of an overall framework, and private law and economic development
have become central source materials of American legal history. There
are successes in Friedman's *History:* his work is an excellent reference for
the state of common law doctrine in a given locality at a particular time.
He has provided abundant leads for the student who wants further detail
on the topics Friedman has described. And, perhaps most importantly, he
has helped demonstrate the predominantly conflict-free nature of the legal
system in America. That system is intended to resolve conflict; at its heart,
the countless ordinary private transactions managed daily by practitioners
and their clients, it effectuates this resolution without undue stress or strain.
"Great" constitutional law cases give the system an appearance of turmoil
and conflict that is partially illusory; in ordinary and mundane ways, it
adapts and adjusts to changing conditions with relative ease, and an emphasis on private law transactions helps to illustrate its flexibility and re-
silience.

But Friedman's work cannot be called a full treatment of the history of
American law, only a redressing of a previous overemphasis on national and
public law themes. American legal history has been an interplay of the
ordinary workings of private actions with issues of high politics. In addition to patterns of economic and attendant legal change, it has contained
issues of profound ideological significance, such as the tension between
egalitarian and humanitarian ideals and the system of slavery, the pressure
placed upon historic notions of fairness and justice by sociopathic criminals,
the limits of the power of a government to invade the privacy of its citizens
in the name of the national interest, the rights of legislative majorities to
impose their collective social views on unwilling minorities.

Each of these issues raises questions of constitutional interpretation. Each
involves the area where law, politics, and ideology interact to define the social
values of a nation. None receives treatment in Friedman's work, yet they
are surely part of American legal history. Friedman might respond by
pointing out that these issues have received treatment in other places and
that no one-volume history can be all-inclusive. But even granting this
rejoinder, American legal history simultaneously occurs on a series of levels,
from the level of the daily work of the average practitioner, to the level
of the steady, changing flow of substantive doctrine from the law offices,
treatises, and courts, to the level of the large constitutional issues at the
Supreme Court. Thus there is a sense in which Friedman's *History* is like
a cathedral without a dome: its foundations are intact and a structure has
been built on them, but nothing caps it.

---

[53] H. SCHEIBER, OHIO CANAL ERA (1969).

Perhaps only when we have as rigorous a treatment of the ideological dimensions of American law as we have had of its "more mundane workings" [54] can such an intellectual edifice be constructed. Before such an effort is possible, there may be necessary as extensive a monographic investigation of particular problems in the relationship of ideas to law in America as the Wisconsin School has undertaken for economic subjects. This undertaking may be neither as attractive nor as successful. But in any case, Friedman's *History* should not be regarded as a stopping place, except for the conferral of some deserved praise.

---

[54] FRIEDMAN, *supra* note 1, at 11.

# 4

# REALITY AND SOCIAL REFORM: THE TRANSITION FROM LAISSEZ-FAIRE TO THE WELFARE STATE

*CALVIN WOODARD*

# REALITY AND SOCIAL REFORM: THE TRANSITION FROM LAISSEZ-FAIRE TO THE WELFARE STATE

## CALVIN WOODARD†

EVERY society has standards which render certain conduct and conditions intolerable. And each society endeavors, by pressure exerted through its various institutions, to abolish such conduct and conditions. One such institution is the state which acts through the law.

Two principles are of decisive significance in determining the nature and form of those standards: tradition and reality. Tradition—by which I mean the experience of the past crystallized into customary modes of looking at and responding to the world—comes down to man in countless conscious and unconscious ways. But perhaps its most powerful, if less conspicuous, influence is exerted on man's expectations. By so doing, tradition determines what he regards as normal or natural, good and worthwhile; and, thereby it gives direction to human activities and social aspirations.

Reality, meaning man's ability to control his environment to his own ends, is at least as determinative, for it limits the range and types of conduct and conditions which man and hence society can reasonably hope to abolish. No society can long live with standards which are completely and hopelessly unattainable; and, therefore, man's ability to abolish any given conduct or condition generally precedes society's acceptance of a standard condemning such conduct or condition. One way or another, society must come to terms with conduct or conditions, however deplorable, however repulsive, which man has no rational hope of abolishing. Thus, from time immemorial, societies (and men) have lived and died by standards which condemn pecadillos with grotesque harshness while leaving intact those factors which caused wholesale misery and suffering. Societies have, in short, had to be satisfied with changing the changeable and living with the rest.

Standards, then, are the means by which society strikes a balance between reality and tradition. They determine not only the conduct and conditions conceived to be intolerable: they also dictate the terms in which the problem is cast, the nature of the solutions sought and, hence, the forms of pressure demanded of its several social institutions.[1]

---

†Instructor in History and Research Associate in Law, Yale University.

1. As will be discussed more fully in the text, the terms in which a problem is cast are decisive in determining the relative significance of social institutions. Thus when problems are cast in supernatural terms, the Church must be the dominant institution, for the evils confronting society appear to have religious overtones (such as "sin") with which the Church alone can deal. Failure to perceive the significance of this fact—the relationship between man's point of view and the dominant social institution—has caused much unfair criticism of certain social institutions, and particularly of the Church for its failure to maintain, in the modern world, the central position it held during the Middle Ages. R. H. Taw-

History can thus be viewed as the chronicle of the rise and fall of various standards. And the most cataclyϑmic phases in the saga of any society, the so-called "water-shed" periods, are those in which fundamental standards are supplanted by new ones; standards which, by condemning conduct and conditions theretofore condoned, or vice versa, generate a new type of pressure either to reform the existing, or to devise new, social institutions. One of the greatest functions fulfilled by reformers is to sense that, in one way or another, for one reason or another, man's ability to control his environment has developed to a point where society can realistically aspire to abolish conduct or conditions theretofore conceived to be, and accepted as, unalterable. Hence, by agitation and ingenious resort to reason, they demand new patterns of social behavior which, by weakening the grip of tradition, bring expectations (and eventually standards) in line with reality.

In the last hundred years or so, western societies have gone through, and indeed are still going through, such a cataclysmic phase. We have been in the process of sloughing off an old, and adjusting to a new, set of standards. By an examination and analysis of the problem of poverty, I shall undertake to illustrate how changes in traditions and reality have wrought a change in social concern, a fundamental alteration in the type of conduct and conditions re-

---

ney, for example, bitterly condemned the Reformed Church for its "tacit denial of spiritual significance in the transaction of business and in the relationship of organised society." TAWNEY, RELIGION AND THE RISE OF CAPITALISM 188 (1929). And he, along with many reform-minded "social gospel" clergymen, fervently believed that the Church should be restored to its rightful place in the modern world: the center of society. But Tawney failed to see that the Church with its power over things spiritual, could not deal with the problems confronting modern society as it could in the past. For our problems are cast not in religious terms but in economic ones. Thus Tawney himself diagnosed poverty as being "not a problem of individual character and its waywardness, but a problem of economic and industrial organization." Quoted in YOUNG & ASHTON, BRITISH SOCIAL WORK IN THE 19TH CENTURY 67 (1956). Whereas the Church could do a great deal about the problem of wayward character, it can really do very little about industrial organization.

During the Middle Ages (to quote Father Jarrett) "the evils of trade were thought to spring from a wrong principle or motive on his part who entered it, that it was precisely the intention of the trades which had to be just right, and that therefore economics became a moral question to be solved only by moral answers." JARRETT, SOCIAL THEORIES OF THE MIDDLE AGES, 1200-1500, at 164 (1926). Accordingly, that which we now call economics was a part of moral theology, and the leading authority was Thomas Aquinas, whose *Summa Theologica* "remained the groundwork of all later writers [on economic matters] until the end of the 15th Century." O'BRIEN, AN ESSAY ON MEDIEVAL ECONOMIC TEACHING 18 (1920).

But in the modern world, as the quotation from Tawney indicates, we have increasingly appraised problems in non-religious, and particularly, economic terms. And, as we say, the Church cannot even purport to control the forces which govern the economy—rates of interest, business cycles, unemployment, depression of trade. Once the problems ceased to be cast in religious terms, the role of the Church could not continue to be central; and the more amoral or scientific the appraisal of those problems became, the more removed from the center of society the Church became. It could scarcely be otherwise. We shall discuss, in the text, the dynamics of this shift in point of view.

garded as "intolerable" and, consequently, in both the types of social action called for, and the chief social institutions called upon.

As regards the particular problem of poverty, I shall denominate the contemporary standard by the phrase, welfare state standard, and the old by the term, *laissez faire* standard. These phrases—*laissez faire standard* and welfare state *standard*—will be used henceforth as terms of art and will be defined presently.

Though the phrase, welfare state, is notoriously ambiguous,[2] it implies, in all its various interpretations and definitions, certain basic assumptions which, when taken together, adumbrate a standard regarding poverty. They may be stated as follows: poverty is an "economic" phenomenon that can, must, and should be abolished; the state is the sole social institution capable of dealing with the economic forces which give rise to that phenomenon; hence the chief responsibility for abolishing poverty rests on the state and the state must, in turn, exert its faculties towards that end.[3]

These assumptions, when taken together, constitute the welfare state standard toward poverty. But as trite and commonplace as they may seem to modern readers they are peculiar to the twentieth century and of themselves demarcate the difference between the past and present. Certainly, the widespread acceptance of the welfare state standard has brought about one of the greatest intellectual and moral upheavals in western history—one, indeed, analogous in import and ramifications to the Reformation of the sixteenth century. For it has vitiated the old *laissez-faire* standard (which dominated Anglo-American attitudes towards poverty throughout most of the nineteenth century) as ruthlessly and irrevocably as Luther and his confederates destroyed the authority of the Medieval Church; and, as a concommitant, its acceptance has occasioned a wholesale defrocking of old, and canonizing of new, values and virtues. Whereas men formerly prided themselves in the strength of their convictions, we are now at pains to purge ourselves of all "value judgments"; where men once glorified faith as the crowning virtue we now honor most the questioning mind which takes nothing for granted; and where men once strove to fulfill "duty" (Wordsworth's *Ode to Duty* was the favorite poem of T.H. Green, the idealist philosopher) we now find meaning in the struggle for human "rights." Throughout society, in every aspect of life, the changes have been felt; and such basic relationships as man and wife, father and son, debtor and creditor, employer and employee have all undergone radical change. Indeed, vices have become virtues, and virtues vices, at a pace comparable only to that of the sixteenth century and seventeenth century when the

---

2. For some of the interpretations, and misinterpretations, given the phrase, see Tit-
muss, Essays on "The Welfare State" 34-55 (1958).

3. The welfare state standard is, it seems to me, deducible from the Employment Act of 1946—a statute which has been of particular significance in our post-war history. For a full discussion of the importance of this statute, see E. V. Rostow, Planning For Freedom: The Public Law of American Capitalism 12-16 (1959); Bailey, Congress Makes A Law (1950).

"Protestant ethic" exalted and sanctified such quondam vices as usury, trade, and the accumulation of wealth (theretofore known as "cupidity").[4]

To explain this development through an examination of the problem of poverty, we must look to the deposed *laissez-faire* standard before turning to its modern counterpart. For the welfare state standard is the creation of those reformers who, in the face of the monumental changes in reality effected during the nineteenth century, reacted against the narrowness with which the *laissez-faire* standard defined the problem of poverty and dictated the orthodox methods of dealing with it. I shall attempt to show first, how in 1800 the *laissez-faire* standard represented a reasonable reconciliation of tradition with reality; secondly, the nature of the changes in reality that took place thereafter; thirdly, how those changes gave rise to a new mental outlook which inspired new demands and expectations incompatible with, and ultimately destructive of, the old standard; and how, as a consequence of these developments, the modern welfare state standard emerged, and is possibly undergoing modification itself at present.

## II

Although the term "laissez faire" is as ambiguous as the phrase "welfare state,"[5] still modern scholars seem to be in accord on one point: *whatever* it means, it was never anything more than a myth in English or American his-

---

4. From the time of Sombart, Weber and Tawney, everyone has been familiar with the idea that religious doctrine, and particularly Protestantism, was closely related to the rise of capitalism. That relationship has usually been thought to be a causal one: by reforming religious doctrine so as to sanction, and indeed encourage, certain economic traits and activities theretofore condemned, the Church, in effect, inspired the spirit of capitalism. There is, no doubt, much truth in this. But I am persuaded to agree with Robertson that the reforms of Church doctrine, the glorification of the doctrine of the "calling," was itself the result, the consequence of deeper causes. "All has gone to prove one point," he concluded, "the Churches, one and all, have had to accommodate themselves to an extraneous development of busy commercial spirit; that Capitalism has created, or found already existant, its own spirit, and set the Churches the tasks of assimilating it." ROBERTSON, THE RISE OF ECONOMIC INDIVIDUALISM 165 (1933). See also Gordon Walker, *Capitalism and the Reformation,* 8 ECO. HIST. REV. 1, 19 (1937).

One good reason for believing this is that in many commercial countries (*e.g.,* northern Italy and Holland) the Reformation did not destroy the Catholic Church. Yet—and this is the point—in such areas the doctrine of the Catholic Church was altered to sanction economic activity. Thus St. Antonius of Florence adapted Catholic doctrine to reality by condoning payments of interest—a "reform" not recognized in agrarian countries such as Ireland or even other parts of Italy. Conversely, in agrarian parts of Protestant countries— the American South is a classic example—Protestantism has become as rigid and dogmatic (though militantly anti-Catholic) as the medieval Catholic Church. And we should not forget Sombart's splendid conclusion that "Puritanism is Judaism." SOMBART, THE JEWS AND MODERN CAPITALISM 249 (Epstein transl. 1913).

5. For a discussion of the origin and history of the phrase *laissez-faire* see MACGREGOR, ECONOMIC THOUGHT AND POLICY ch. 3 (1949).

tory.[6] And this assertion is no doubt true so long as it simply means that the law was used and frequently used to attain economic ends during the nineteenth century.

But *laissez-faire* cannot be exorcised from history simply by showing that the law was so used in the past. Of course it was used in the past. To say no more than that begs the decisive question: whether the law was used in ways which clashed with the particular proscriptions of the *laissez-faire* doctrine. For *laissez-faire* was not merely a blanket injunction. To the contrary, as ex-

---

6.   Studies which have reached this conclusion are, for England, Brebner, *Laissez Faire and State Intervention in 19th Century Britain*, THE TASKS OF ECONOMIC HISTORY 59-93, Supplement to 8 J. ECON. HIST. (1948); MacDonagh, *The Nineteenth Century Revolution in Government*, 1 HIST. J. 52-67 (1958); and ROBERTS, VICTORIAN ORIGINS OF THE WELFARE STATE (1960). Studies reaching similar conclusions for the United States include HANDLIN, COMMONWEALTH MASSACHUSETTS, 1774-1861 (1947); HARTZ, ECONOMIC POLICY AND DEMOCRATIC THOUGHT: PENNSYLVANIA 1776-1860 (1948); and HURST, LAW AND THE CONDITION OF FREEDOM IN THE NINETEENTH CENTURY UNITED STATES (1956). From a rather different point of view, Lord Robbins reached the same conclusion in *The Theory of Economic Policy in English Classical Political Economy* (1952). He found that the classical political economists, those who were traditionally thought to be the champions of *laissez-faire*, were not so at all. "The invisible hand," he wrote, ". . . is not the hand of some God or some natural agency independent of human effort; it is the hand of the law giver . . . ." *Id.* at 56.

I cannot doubt the facts that these writers rely upon in concluding that *laissez-faire* was a myth in the nineteenth century: the law *was* used, very frequently and imaginatively in both England and America. But I do believe that in their efforts to "revise" history so as to weed out the *laissez-faire* predilections of earlier historians, modern historians are in danger of blinding themselves and their readers to vital distinctions between nineteenth and twentieth century attitudes towards, and uses of, the law. For example, in their enthusiasm to compensate for Dicey's personal (Utilitarian) bias, many authors seem prepared to dismiss his really splendid book, *Law and Public Opinion in England during the 19th Century* (1905), and its conclusion that the period 1825 to 1870 was the "Age of Benthamism or Individualism." See, *e.g.*, Stone, *The Myths of Planning and Laissez Faire: A Re-orientation*, 18 GEO. WASH. L. REV. 1, 15-23 (1949), reprinted in part in COHEN & COHEN, READINGS IN JURISPRUDENCE AND LEGAL PHILOSOPHY 773-79 (1951). In its place we are being presented with a picture of the nineteenth century that looks strikingly like the modern day—so much so that one can legitimately wonder if there was any difference at all. I think there was. And in this article I shall attempt to show that difference as regards the limited, but important, problem of poverty.

Forty years ago Dean Pound made the precise point—for quite the opposite reason—that I would stress. He said:

> In the last century legal history was written as a record of the unfolding of individual freedom, as a record of continually increasing recognition and securing of individual interests, through the pressure, as it were, of the individual will. But it would be quite as easy to write it in terms of a continually wider and broader recognition of securing of social interests, that is, of the claims and demands involved in the existence of civilized society, not the least of which is the social interest in the individual human life.

POUND, INTERPRETATIONS OF LEGAL HISTORY 163 (1923). Pound feared the social interests aspect of the past was being ignored by *laissez-faire* historians; I fear the individualist aspect of the past is being dismissed too cavalierly by those seeking the roots of the welfare state. The time has come, I think, when the history of the nineteenth century must be written in terms that account for *both,* not simply one or the other of these trends.

pounded by its most influential champions, many uses of the law were quite compatible with *laissez-faire*.[7] One nineteenth century commentator clearly perceived this:

> The importance of government, or the extent of the functions assigned it, is not measured by the amount of legislation which its law-making bodies turn off from year to year, but rather by the nature of the administrative duties imposed upon it, or by the extent of the power assigned to its courts. . . . It is especially the administrative function of government that the doctrine of Laissez Faire attacks.[8]

The advocates of *laissez-faire* were not so much intent upon hamstringing the state as they were upon increasing the economic opportunities of the individual. And insofar as the law could contribute to that end, the champions of *laissez-faire* were by no means loath to make use of it.[9]

7. I have considered this point—that the champions of *laissez-faire* sanctioned many uses of the law even as they advocated *laissez-faire*—in a review of HURST, *op. cit. supra* note 6, Woodard, Book Review, 19 LA. L. REV. 560 (1959).

8. H.C. ADAMS, RELATION OF THE STATE TO INDUSTRIAL ACTION IN ECONOMICS AND JURISPRUDENCE: TWO ESSAYS 116-17 (J. Dorfman ed. 1954).

9. Any attempt to define the *laissez-faire* doctrine (as distinguished from the *laissez-faire* standard regarding poverty) lies outside the scope of this article. Suffice it to say that that doctrine was frequently evoked to proscribe state action on the grounds that it tended to weaken the moral character of the poor. As Henry Fawcett said, the "crucial test" to be applied to all legislation designed to assist the poor was this: "does the remedy tend to raise or lower the spirit of self help?" STEPHEN, THE LIFE OF HENRY FAWCETT 161 (5th ed. 1886). All uses of the law that threatened the spirit of self-help were *verboten*. And most of the great issues involving *laissez-faire* in the nineteenth and twentieth centuries, those which give that doctrine much of its historical significance, have centered around that very test. Reformers urging old age pensions, child labor acts, unemployment insurance, national health programs, assistance for unwed mothers, and state regulation of hours and conditions of work have all, sooner or later, had to confront, and overcome, the charge that the proposed law would undermine the spirit of self-help. In the nineteenth century, that charge was rarely overcome.

But there was another side of the coin: if legislation which weakened self-help was *per se* bad, that which strengthened it was *per se* good. Thus we find the seeming paradox of many *laissez-faire* champions supporting and even advocating legislative action. David Ricardo, for example, did not hesitate in extolling the virtue of saving banks (because they were "calculated to improve the character of the poor") to demand that depositors should have a check on bank managers which "should be afforded by the legislature." 7 WORKS AND CORRESPONDENCE OF DAVID RICARDO 16 (Sraffa ed. 1952). And J. R. McCulloch (whom Carlyle caricatured as "McCrowdy," the quintessence of a dogmatic political economist) ended his *A Treatise on the Circumstances Which Determine the Rate of Wages* (1851) (wherein the phrase "wages fund" was first used) with this sentence; "[H]ence it appears that it is the duty of governments . . . to lend their aid to establish a really useful system of public instruction."

But more was required of the state than this. It also had to provide inducements and incentives to individuals. For men, not machines, were assumed to be the chief source of the nation's wealth. And as early as 1759, Adam Smith indicated the primary means of inducing men to work: "What is the reward most proper for encouraging industry, prudence and circumspection? Success in every sort of business." 1 A. SMITH, THE THEORY OF MORAL SENTIMENTS 296 (11th ed. 1792). And success, of course, required opportunities to ex-

As regards poverty a standard deriving from the *laissez-faire* doctrine dominated Anglo-American attitudes down to the end of the nineteenth century. The law was either used to assist the poor in ways compatible with that standard, *or,* when incompatible, such instances were regarded as "exceptions" to a still inviolate general rule. And the welfare state standard regarding poverty did not, and could not, come into existence until *laissez-faire* (and its derivative standard) ceased to dominate the aspirations of men and circumscribe the role of the state in dealing with the poor.

The *laissez-faire* doctrine was the product of a particular point of view: one which treated men as the center (and measure) of the universe. Under it, all of what we term "social" problems were conceived to be "moral" ones which reflected, one way or another, the conduct or character of men. And so long as this point of view prevailed, so long as men believed that "the proper study of mankind is man," the welfare state standard on poverty was not only unknown but inconceivable. For this approach inevitably subordinated amoral aspects of worldly phenonema (including economic causes and consequences) to their moral aspects (the imprudent conduct, the lack of virtue and bad character, of man). Poverty was thus a moral problem because it involved the moral character of the poor. As J. S. Mill said:

> It is most true that the rich have much to answer for in their conduct to the poor. But in the matter of their poverty, there is no way the rich *could* have helped them, but by inducing them to help themselves. . . .[10]

For, he continued, "if the whole income of the country were divided among them in wages or poor-rates, still, until there is a change in themselves there can be no lasting improvement in their outward condition."[11] The problem was, at bottom, a moral, rather than an economic one.

---

ploit one's talents to the utmost and to enjoy the fruits of one's labor to the fullest. James Mill stated it with characteristic clarity and vigor:

> To obtain all the objects of desire in the greatest possible quantity, we must obtain labour in the greatest possible quantity; and to obtain labour in the greatest possible quantity, we must raise to the greatest possible height the advantage attached to labour. It is impossible to attach to labour a greater degree of advantage than the whole of the product of labour. Why so? Because if you give more to one man than the produce of his labour, you can do so only by taking it away from the produce of some other man's labour. The greatest possible happiness of society is, therefore, attained by assuring to every man the greatest possible quantity of the produce of his labour.

J. MILL, ESSAY ON GOVERNMENT 4-5 (1820).

This passage brings together and unites the two aspects of *laissez-faire* we have been discussing: any legislation that would assist the poor without regard to their moral character would not only destroy their incentive to work, but also—by taking from the diligent—deprive them of the right to enjoy the fruits of their labor, thereby destroying their incentive to work.

Whatever else *laissez-faire* may have meant, I am convinced this is a vital part of it; and I am most certainly not convinced that this aspect of it was in any way mythical.

10.  2 J. S. MILL, DISSERTATIONS AND DISCUSSIONS 181, 199 (1859) (originally printed as *The Claims of Labour* published in the *Edinburgh Review* for 1845).

11.  *Id.* at 198.

Paradoxically enough, the *fin de siecle* champions of the welfare state standard berated Mill and his colleagues, the so-called Classical Political Economists, for their failure to recognize the moral aspects of the problem. Thus in 1893 Neville Keynes (the father of Maynard) wrote:

> . . . although in the past there may have been a tendency with a certain school of economists to attempt the solution of practical economic questions without adequate recognition of their ethical aspects, there is, at the present time, no such tendency discernible amongst economists who have any claim to speak with authority.[12]

To Keynes and his contemporaries, the "ethical aspects" of the problem did not involve the moral character of the poor. Rather they involved the "unjust" suffering of victims of economic forces beyond their power as individuals to control. Therefore, when I say the *laissez-faire* standard treated poverty as if it were a moral problem, I mean that it assumed the chief cause to be the moral failure of the poor; and when I say that the welfare state standard treats poverty as if it were an amoral problem, I mean it assumes the chief cause to be amoral economic forces.

To be sure, it is possible to use the word "moral" as Keynes did. Used thus, the welfare state standard is "moral" in that it refuses to lay the blame for poverty on innocent victims. And the *laissez-faire* standard appears, in retrospect, to have been "immoral" in that it laid the blame for poverty on individuals not really responsible for it. Indeed, modern readers are probably more likely to use the term "moral" in this latter sense. Nonetheless, in this paper, I will use it primarily in the former sense—to characterize a point of view that makes the character of man the measure of what we now call "social problems."

This moral point of view which permeated the *laissez-faire* doctrine, when applied to the problem of poverty, produced a standard composed of three separate tenets. These tenets, which taken together constituted the *laissez-faire* standard, may be stated as follows: first, poverty is an inevitable condition of human life; second, man's worldly condition is, by and large, a reflection of his own moral character; and, last, private voluntary charity is the proper source of relief for the legitimate needs of "the poor."[13] Each of these tenets was

---

12.  KEYNES, THE SCOPE AND METHOD OF POLITICAL ECONOMY 61 (3d rev. ed. 1904).

13.  A typical expression of the attitude underlying the *laissez-faire* standard appears in *The Original,* a weekly published in 1835, by Thomas Walker, a fellow of Trinity College, Cambridge. The weekly papers were subsequently bound into a single volume which, by 1838, had gone through four editions, and which, in 1870, was reissued under the editorship of Dr. W. A. Guy, a prominent *laissez-faire* reformer. Speaking of the Poor Laws and proposals to extend their benefits to aid more poverty stricken persons, Walker indicated the conditions which had to be met before he would approve of state action; and these conditions precedent gave rise to a rebuttable presumption against such action which was very similar in import to what I have called the *laissez-faire* standard:

> Till government, both general and local, should be put into the most efficient order, till every encouragement should be given to prudence, and till charity should be excited by all possible means, it would be too much to say that any other resources would be necessary; and recurring to any other resources prematurely would be to retard improvement in the right quarters.

THE ORIGINAL 306 (Walker ed. 1838).

deeply rooted in the tradition and eminently compatible with the reality of the late eighteenth century.

The first tenet, that poverty was inevitable, stemmed from the conviction that poverty was something more than an economic problem. To the moralistic minds of the eighteenth and nineteenth centuries it was similar in character, and closely allied to those other two scourges of humanity, "sin" and "evil." As such it simply could not be abolished and certainly not by the state.[14] For the root of the problem lay deep inside man, perhaps, indeed, in the nature of man. And a world without poverty was as inconceivable as a world without sin and evil.

Christ's celebrated dictum, "Ye have the poor always with you," echoed down through the ages, and had been reaffirmed by the experience of each subsequent generation. And the efficacy of this message was reinforced by the fate of those brave souls who, daring to believe otherwise, set out to abolish poverty: the grandiose dreams and quixotic schemes of sundry utopians had uniformly resulted in failure. Tradition thus taught that poverty was inevitable, and experience perpetuated tradition.

And the tenet was equally justified by reality for as of the late eighteenth century, man did not have sufficient command of the economic forces that caused poverty to abolish it. Economic poverty can be abolished only by two ways: increasing the total wealth available to society, thereby lifting it, as it were, *en masse* to a higher standard of living; or redistributing the existing wealth—taking from the rich to give to the poor—so as to elevate all persons and classes above a certain arbitrarily defined "poverty-line."[15]

---

14. Once the problem was appraised in "moral" (as opposed to "economic") terms it did not, by its nature, admit of solution by legislative action. Of course, as Patrick Colquhoun observed:

> The People are to the Legislature what a child is to a parent:—As the first care of the latter is to teach the love of virtue, and a dread of Punishment; so ought it to be the duty of the former to frame laws with an immediate view to the general improvement of morals.

Colquhoun, A Treatise on the Police of London 187 (1st American ed. 1798).

But as Colquhoun's friend, Jeremy Bentham, pointed out, the role of the state in dealing with problems involving personal ethics must be "indirect."

> All [the legislator] can hope to do, is to increase the efficacy of private ethics, by giving strength and direction to the influence of moral sanction. With what chance of success, for example, would a legislator go about to extirpate drunkenness and fornication by dint of legal punishment? Not all the torture which ingenuity could invent would compass it . . . .

Bentham, *An Introduction to the Principles of Morals and Legislation,* reprinted in A Fragment on Government and an Introduction to the Principles of Morals and Legislation 420 (Harrison ed. 1948).

Of course Bentham himself was extraordinarily ingenious in concocting schemes to induce the poor to improve their moral character. His "Panopticon" scheme became the basis of the much-hated "New Poor Laws"; and his proposals for teaching the public the cost of breaking the law, through the policy of deterrence, are alluded to below. See text accompanying note 58 *infra.*

15. The notion of a "Poverty-Line" did not come into being, as such, until the end of the nineteenth century when Charles Booth made his celebrated study of the slums of Lon-

As of the end of the eighteenth century society had a Hobson's choice: it could only choose to deal with poverty through some sort of redistribution of existing wealth and even that choice, implemented in the most radical fashion, could not eradicate poverty. It is true, of course, that deep changes had been wrought throughout the eighteenth century, changes inherent in the phrase, "industrial revolution," which could, and ultimately did, give society the power (and hope) of abolishing poverty through increased production. But those changes were not apparent until later in the nineteenth century. In 1800 England was, as regards

---

don. Even so we can get a good idea of the changing "Poverty-Line" by comparing a comment made by a philanthropist in 1868 with Booth's conclusions. According to C. B. P. Bosanquet the problem was the " 'sunken sixth'—a degraded class whom their fellow citizens are very apt to look on as a mere nuisance." BOSANQUET, LONDON : SOME ACCOUNT OF ITS GROWTH, CHARITABLE AGENCIES, AND WANTS 44-45 (1868). Twenty years later Booth shocked all England by showing, in a pioneering effort to collect primary data based on observed fact, that 13 per cent of the London population were "very poor" and 25 per cent were "poor." He explained his terms as follows: "My 'poor' may be described as living under a struggle to obtain the necessaries of life and make both ends meet; while the 'very poor' live in a state of chronic want." 1 BOOTH, LIFE AND LABOUR OF THE PEOPLE IN LONDON 33 (1889). A few years later, in 1901, B. Seebohm Rowntree, following Booth's methods, made a similar study of a provincial town (York) and reached similar conclusions: 9.91 per cent of the population were in "primary" poverty and 17.93 per cent in "secondary" poverty—a total of 27.84 per cent of the population living in "poverty." ROWNTREE, POVERTY : A STUDY OF TOWN LIFE 353 (1901). In the United States Robert Hunter, making a similar study in 1904, concluded that 10,000,000 people lived in poverty; and J. A. Ryan discovered in 1906, that at least 60 per cent of the adult male wage earners received less than $600 per year. For a discussion of both Hunter and Ryan, see BREMNER, FROM THE DEPTHS : THE DISCOVERY OF POVERTY IN THE UNITED STATES 151-54 (1956).

The effect of these several studies was to shift the attention of the public away from the "sunken sixth" to this much wider category of victims. And the modern problem—that with which the welfare state standard deals—is (to quote one of Roosevelt's better known phrases) the "ill-clad, ill-housed, and ill-fed" third of the nation. The "Poverty-Line" had, in short, been lifted as society's ability to cope with the economic forces giving rise to poverty had increased.

We need only add that at the time of the great transition from the "sunken sixth" to the "impoverished third" the need for more consumers of industrially produced wealth outweighed the need for more producers displaying the traditional wealth-producing virtues of thrift, diligence, temperance and sexual restraint. So the standard for relief became an economic one—need—and ceased being a moral one—desert. As reality was on the side of the reformers who led the way to the new standard, the conclusions they taught rang too true to be dismissed by logic or "proof." No one was bothered by the devastating criticism made of the methods used by the statisticians in reaching their conclusions. (Helen Bosanquet very effectively demolished Rowntree's conclusions in a painstaking critique, which impressed no one except those who opposed the emerging welfare state standard. Bosanquet, *The Poverty Line,* CHARITY ORGANISATION SOCIETY OCCASIONAL PAPERS, 3d ser., No. 11.) Nor did anyone heed the warnings of those who, clinging to the *laissez-faire* standard, insisted that the very idea of an economically defined "Poverty Line"—a notion which lumped "deserving" and "undeserving" poor together—was degrading to the former. The point is that reforms which comport with reality prevail irrespective of all the force reason and learning can muster. And those which clash with reality however bolstered by learning and reason cannot long survive.

industrialism, still in what W. W. Rostow has called its "take off" stage;[16] and any cause for optimism which we can read back into that period was buried deep beneath a flood of humanity, by the most precipitous increase in population in England's long history. (Between 1695 and 1801 the population increased by about two-thirds, the most rapid increases coming after 1750.)[17]

Thus in 1800 reality was not governed by the numerous industrial innovations of the preceding century. Rather it mirrored other economic activities, agriculture and foreign trade,[18] which were deeply influenced and largely governed by factors which man had little ability to control. For agricultural output was sharply conditioned by such factors as the quantity of arable land, the fertility of the soil, the length of the growing season, and meteorological conditions generally; and profits from foreign trade were contingent upon the

---

16. W. W. ROSTOW, THE STAGES OF ECONOMIC GROWTH (1960). Rostow contends that a nation becomes "industrialized" by going through three "stages" of development: (i) a "take-off" period, which he defines as "an industrial revolution, tied directly to radical changes in method of production having their decisive consequences over a relatively short period of time" (*id*. at 57) ; (ii) a period of "maturity" in which "an economy demonstrates the capacity to move beyond the original industries which powered its take-off and to absorb and to apply efficiently over a very wide range of its resources . . . the most advanced fruits of (then) modern technology" (*id*. at 10) ; and (iii) an "era of high mass consumption" where "the leading sectors (of the economy) shift towards durable consumers' goods and services" (*ibid.*).

According to Rostow, England's "take-off" began in 1782 with the construction of the first cotton mill; its "drive to maturity" was concluded in 1851; and it broke through to the "era of high mass consumption" only in the 1930's. For the United States, the dates of the same stages would be 1840, 1900, 1913—to date. *Id*. at xii.

Rostow's general theory of the "stages of economic growth" and its applicability to the various corners of the world has been received with mixed reaction. But as a description of the developments of two specific economies, that of England and the United States, it seems to me perfectly valid. I shall have occasion to allude to these "stages" from time to time and the reader is asked to hold them in mind.

17. ASHTON, AN ECONOMIC HISTORY OF ENGLAND: THE 18TH CENTURY 2 (1955). For a most enlightened discussion of the effect of population changes in the nineteenth century see G. KITSON CLARK, THE MAKING OF VICTORIAN ENGLAND ch. 3 (1961).

18. For the year 1812 Patrick Colquhoun estimated "the New Property Created Annually in Great Britain and Ireland" to be £ 430,500,000 derived from the following sources:

| | |
|---|---|
| Agriculture | £ 216,817,624 |
| Mines and Minerals | 9,000,000 |
| Manufacturers | 114,230,000 |
| Inland Trade | 31,500,000 |
| Foreign Commerce and Shipping | 46,373,748 |
| Other | 12,000,000 |

COLQUHOUN, TREATISE ON THE WEALTH, POWER, AND RESOURCES OF THE BRITISH EMPIRE 96 (1814).

If the value of the "manufacturers" item seems overstated, we might bear in mind Ashton's warning of the many uses of the word "manufacturer" in the eighteenth and early nineteenth centuries: "It related, on the one hand, to the man who employed several thousands of his fellows, and on the other, to the small craftsman who worked at the loom or the bench aided by a single apprentice or journeyman." ASHTON, *op. cit. supra* note 17, at 21.

mysteries of exchange rates (which, in turn, were affected by accidental discoveries of precious metal deposits), the whims of foreign governments with their power to impose tariffs and declare war, as well as the risks and hazards of long sea voyages. In short, the wealth of the nation was still governed by factors over which man had very limited control. So long as this was the case society had no rational hope of abolishing poverty by increasing wealth.

The only alternative was, as we have said, to effect some sort of redistribution of wealth so that the poor could share in the surplus of the rich. And for this purpose the notion that poverty was inevitable was highly convenient, for it realistically restrained the expectations of the poor, and limited the obligation of the rich. Given the economic reality of the times, nothing could have been more disastrous than to adopt a standard that encouraged people to expect the abolition of economic poverty; for expectations soon ripen into demands— demands which could not have been fulfilled, and which could be urged only with irreparable harm to the basic institutions and traditions of society. It made far more sense to come to terms with reality and adopt a standard that assumed poverty to be inevitable and regarded only the most extreme forms of economic deprivation as intolerable.

Thus we find in eighteenth and nineteenth century parlance a tendency to give poverty a very narrow meaning. As Edmund Burke wrote, in condemning the egalitarian principles of the French Revolution:

> Hitherto the name of 'poor' (in the sense that it excites compassion) has not been used for those who can, but for those who cannot labour—for the sick or infirm, or orphan infancy, for languishing and decrepid age . . . I do not call a healthy young man, cheerful in mind and vigorous in arms, I cannot call such a man poor.[19]

For, he added (with striking insight into the reality of the situation) to "affect to pity as poor those who must labour or the world cannot exist" is to "trifle with the condition of mankind."[20]

Fittingly enough resignation to the inevitable was extolled as a virtue. As the author of a widely-read series of "Sermons on the Doctrines and Duties of Christianity" proclaimed in 1803:

> It is the duty of the poor to be contented, and never to murmur at the dispensations of Providence. If we are perfectly convinced of this great truth, that all the events of life are directed by an all-wise and good God, who orders them in the way that is best for us, and will at last make all work together for good to those who love Him, we shall be ready to follow the example of Christ, and to say, "Not my will, but thine be done!"[21]

This, then, was one consequence of the moralistic outlook. Poverty was not reckoned to be simply an economic problem; and insofar as it was a moral

---

19. BURKE, THREE LETTERS ON A REGICIDE PEACE, reprinted in 6 THE WORKS OF BURKE 279-80 (World Classics ed. 1907).

20. *Id.* at 280.

21. SERMONS ON THE DOCTRINES AND DUTIES OF CHRISTIANITY 152-53 (Anon., 4th ed. 1803).

one, it could not be abolished by state action. In short, poverty was treated as an inevitable condition of human life.

The second tenet underlying the *laissez-faire* standard was that man's worldly condition was a reflection of his own moral character. And this tenet, which appears to be logically inconsistent with the notion that poverty is inevitable, was actually conjoined with it to form the conclusion that economic deprivation was, by and large, caused by the moral shortcomings of its victims. This conclusion was a by-product of the already mentioned tendency to identify poverty with those other great human and social imponderables, sin and evil. As these were reckoned to stem from the defects in the soul or character of man, so poverty was assumed to be caused by lack of virtue. And the cause, once determined, dictated the remedy. Thus the orthodox, and to a remarkable extent the unorthodox, eighteenth and nineteenth century solution to this great problem was to regenerate the moral character of man, and particularly of the lower classes.

Tradition lent credence to this tenet. From the time of the Reformation, if not before, the most influential teachers and preachers had decried those secular vices which contributed most to poverty: drunkenness, promiscuity, indolence, and lack of thrift. The great seventeenth century divine, Jeremy Taylor, devoted two chapters of his enormously influential *Rules and Exercises of Holy Living* to denouncing those vices;[22] and the "Reformation of Public Morals," a movement revived by John Wesley in 1763, became so effective that Dr. Radzinowicz devoted a chapter of his history of the English *criminal* law to these "Evangelical Police."[23] Tradition reeked with a concern for moral character rivaled only by the extent to which this tenet comported with reality.

As we have said, man could not, at the end of the eighteenth century, rationally entertain hopes of abolishing economic deprivation. For the wealth of the nation stemmed largely from economic activities, agriculture and foreign trade, which were governed, or greatly influenced, by factors beyond the control of man. But even so there was another very important source of wealth—the textile trade based on home manufacturing—over

---

22.  Jeremy Taylor's enormously influential *Rules and Exercises of Holy Living* begins with a "consideration of the general instruments and means serving to a holy life'"; and the first of three such instruments was "care of our time." God, he pointed out,

> provides the good things of the world to serve the needs of nature, by the labours of the ploughman, the skill and pains of the artisan, and the dangers and traffic of the merchant: these men are, in their callings, the ministers of the Divine Providence, and the stewards of creation, and servants of a great family of God, the world, in the employment of procuring necessaries for food and clothing, ornament and physic.

TAYLOR, RULES AND EXERCISES OF HOLY LIVING 5 (1682). And, he warns, that "time, which we spend in our idle talk as unprofitable discourse" is sin for which man is accountable. *Ibid.* In section I of Chapter 2 (on "Christian Sobriety") he emphasizes the virtues of temperance and chastity as well as thrift.

23.  For a discussion of this movement see 3 RADZINOWICZ, A HISTORY OF ENGLISH CRIMINAL LAW pt. III (3d ed. 1956).

which man could exercise a very significant degree of control. For man himself—the source of (human) labor—was, at this time, a decisive factor in determining the total quantity and quality of the output.

Hence in confronting the problem of poverty, men of the eighteenth century tended, quite reasonably, to concentrate on improving the one source of wealth that was alterable: the character of man. If, it was thought, the indolent and profligate, the intemperate and promiscuous could only be made to conduct themselves reasonably and prudently, a great deal of economic want and misery would disappear.

To this end, probably the greatest character building program of all times was launched:[24] church, educational institutions, the family, and the state joined together in exhorting men, and particularly the lower classes, to reform their moral character. By so doing, individuals would not only improve themselves economically; they would also augment the wealth of the nation. For in this period man's moral character was, literally, "affected with a public interest."[25]

This message was meaningful, for the moral qualities that were extolled so vigorously were decidedly secular in nature and economic in import. Although the abolition of poverty was by no means in sight there was manifest opportunity for economic advancement. As Professor T. S. Ashton stated (in referring to a writer who, in 1780, held that "every man has his fortune in his own hands") :

---

24. In 1704, Daniel Defoe stated this point quite clearly in a pamphlet, entitled *Giving Alms No Charity*. There he said:

> The poverty and exigence of the poor in England is plainly derived from one of these two particular causes,
>
> *Casualty or Crime.*
>
> By Casualty, I mean sickness of families, loss of limbs or sight . . . .
>
> The crimes of our people, and from whence their poverty derives, as the visible and direct fountains are:
>
> 1. Luxury
> 2. Sloth
> 3. Pride

Reprinted in ENGLISH ECONOMIC HISTORY: SELECT DOCUMENTS 649-50 (Bland, Brown & Tawney eds. 1914).

This pamphlet was often quoted and in the late nineteenth century it was reprinted by reformers who insisted (unsuccessfully) on clinging to the *laissez-faire* standard until the very end.

25. The phrase "affected with a public interest" was first used by Sir Matthew Hale in his book *De Portibus Maris*, published in the late seventeenth century to justify the regulation of certain types of private property, *viz.* public houses and common carriers. Two hundred years later, in 1877, the United States Supreme Court used this same phrase to justify the increased regulation of private property. See Munn v. Illinois, 94 U.S. 113 (1877). The point we are making, however, does not concern private property but human character. When moral·conduct is the most essential factor in the production of wealth it is a public, as well as a private, virtue. And it behooves society through the law, religion and learning, to use all its force to cultivate virtue as it did in the post-Reformation period. This, then, is what I mean when I say that, prior to the growth of industrialism, man and his moral character were "affected with public interest."

... anyone who looks closely at English Society in the mid and late 18th Century will understand how it was possible for it to be said, for at this time vertical mobility has reached a degree higher than that of any earlier, or perhaps any succeeding, age.[26]

Hence it seemed plausible to preach that moral improvement—the cultivation of frugality, diligence, temperance, and sexual restraint—would reap material gains.[27]

The third tenet of the *laissez-faire* standard was that private voluntary charity was the best means of ministering to the legitimate needs of the poor and was vastly superior to the Poor Law in principle and more effective in practice.[28] This tenet was also a natural concommitant of the moral outlook. As regards "the rich" it imposed a non-legal, moral obligation to assist their less fortunate fellow-men; as regards "the poor" this meant distinguishing between the "deserving" (the non-able bodily infirm, sick and children who were unable to take care of themselves) and the "non-deserving" (those who could, if they only would, provide for themselves).

The distinction between these two classes of the poor was important in determining the type of relief: the "deserving" were entitled to a full measure of sympathy and the most economic assistance possible; the "undeserving" were entitled to no sympathy at all (though they were frequently given moral advice). And for the purpose of recognizing this distinction, private voluntary charity was vastly superior to legal relief. As J. S. Mill observed:

> What the state may and should abandon to private charity, is the task of distinguishing between one case of real necessity and another. Private charity can give more to the more deserving. The state must act by general rules. It cannot undertake to discriminate between the deserving

26.  ASHTON, THE INDUSTRIAL REVOLUTION 1760-1830, at 17 (1948).

27.  The initial impact of industrialism was not to decrease the demand for human labor but to increase it by giving rise to new skills and new opportunities.

28.  The role of private voluntary charity, as opposed to the Poor Law, has been greatly neglected in studies dealing with social reform. Most historians have assumed that the Elizabethan Poor Law of 1601 shifted the burden of caring for the poor to the State. Yet W. K. Jordan has found, in his monumental study of philanthropy, that,

> ... the major responsibility continued to be borne by ever-expanding charitable endowments during the whole of our period, the great legislative undertakings having been regarded essentially as emergency measures to be employed when periods of economic crisis imposed greater burdens than private funds and voluntary institutions could assume.

JORDAN, PHILANTHROPY IN ENGLAND 1480-1660, at 98 (1959). Though there are no comparable studies of philanthropy during the period after 1660, there is (as I have pointed out) every reason to believe that the "charitable urge" became increasingly more pronounced through the eighteenth and nineteenth centuries.

Be that as it may, there was, at the end of the eighteenth century, a strong reaction against the Poor Law as a remedy to social problems. The failure of the Speenhamland experiment accounts for much of it. Nevertheless, the tradition that every man had a legal right to subsistence was deeply ingrained; and the most influential Poor Law commentators of the nineteenth century—men like Edwin Chadwick and Nassau Senior—were prepared to reform the Poor Law rather than to abolish it. Of course "reform" meant to limit it to the narrowest possible scope, to providing minimum assistance necessary for survival.

and the undeserving indigent. It owes no more than subsistance to the first, and can give no less to the last . . . . Private Charity can make these distinctions.[29] . . .

As in the case of the other two tenets, the faith in the efficacy of charity (which was a vital, if often overlooked, aspect of *laissez-faire*) was supported by both tradition and reality. The religious minded who gained their inspiration from the Gospel, Saints, and the Church Fathers were taught the virtue of Christian charity; and the more secular minded who looked to this world and its populace for their inspiration, were taught the virtue of militantly secular "Philanthropy."[30] But everyone learned, one way or another, that they were under obligation to the poor. Certainly, a most impressive pattern of private charity has been documented during the period 1480 to 1660,[31] and there is good reason to believe that the pattern continued throughout the eighteenth century—a period one commentator has called "The Age of Beneficence."[32]

---

29.  J. S. MILL, PRINCIPLES OF POLITICAL ECONOMY 585 (Peoples ed. 1865).
Today we are wont to take for granted that the state is capable of dealing deftly with complex social problems. But prior to the twentieth century, the state was reckoned to be a clumsy leviathan beast totally devoid of finesse and lacking in ability to discriminate between the deserving and non-deserving. That attitude is well illustrated by the following statement which was often quoted by social reformers of the last century:

> The bane of all pauper legislation has been the legislating for extreme cases. Every exception, every violation of the general rule to meet a real case of unusual hardship, lets in a whole class of fraudulent cases, by which that rule must in time be destroyed. Where cases of real hardship occur, the remedy must be applied by individual charity, a virtue for which no system of compulsory relief can be or ought to be a substitute.

POOR LAW COMMISSIONERS' REPORT OF 1834, at 263 (1905 ed.)
Given the inefficient and poorly organized government of the day, this attitude was quite reasonable. Indeed, when the Poor Law reformers of 1834 sought a precedent for their proposal to centralize the administration of the Poor Law under one commission, the sole precedent they could find was a statute which provided for a single barrister to examine the accounts of friendly societies. 3 STEPHEN, THE ENGLISH UTILITARIANS 169 (1900).

30.  The word "philanthropy" was first used, according to the *Oxford English Dictionary*, in 1607. And it is obviously a secularized version of "charity"—a term meaning (in contrast to the abstraction and complexities of the Christian doctrine) the love of man by God! Indeed "philanthropy" was the Reformation equivalent of charity; and Jordan found that, between 1480 and 1660, the purposes for which the rich gave their funds became as secular as the new word. Specifically, the contribution for purely religious purposes (such as cathedral building and soul saving) fell from about 53% at the earlier date to about 15 % later on. JORDAN, *op. cit. supra* note 28, at 247-48. The new purposes were for such secular undertakings as university scholarships, schools, and hospitals.
The only reason the distinction between charity and philanthropy did not continue to be significant was that the former as expounded by the Reformed Church became as secular in import as the latter. Thus Hannah More, who played such an important role in the great Sunday School movement of the eighteenth century, undertook this work because she believed it her calling to "train up the lower classes to habits of industry and Piety," an end that she was convinced could be accomplished only by teaching them the Gospel. 1 THOMPSON, THE LIFE OF HANNAH MORE 116 (1838).

31.  See generally JORDAN, *op. cit. supra* note 28.
32.  See M. G. JONES, THE CHARITY SCHOOL MOVEMENT 3-14 (1938).

Charity was compatible with reality for two reasons. First, it was marvellously flexible. The obligation of the rich to help the poor was not fixed but could and did differ with the circumstances.[33] Thus the amount of wealth actually redistributed, or transferred, from one class to another could vary as the need arose; in times of famine it could be increased; in times of feast it could be decreased. Such a method of relief was highly advantageous at a time when surplus wealth was not abundant enough to support large scale compulsory transfer of wealth from one class to another.

Secondly, charity permitted necessary redistributions of wealth under circumstances that maintained the social *status quo*.[34] For the relationship between donor and donee was such that the actual transfer of wealth, while increasing economic equality, actually perpetuated and enforced social inequality. And at a time when the supply of wealth was not sufficient to abolish poverty, charity fulfilled the great function of providing emergency means of redistributing wealth without creating expectations in the recipients incompatible with economic reality.[35]

---

33. The traditional inspiration for charity, and for Protestant philanthropy, was the salvation of the donor's soul. In fact the poor—the recipients of the assistance—were rather like third party beneficiaries to a contract between the rich and God. As Sir Thomas Browne wrote in 1643:

> I give no alms only to satisfy the hunger of my brother, but to fulfill and accomplish the will and command of my God; I draw not my purse for his sake that demands it, but His that enjoined it . . . .

2 WORKS OF SIR THOMAS BROWNE 417 (Wilkin ed. 1852).

34. From the very beginning charity implied social differences that were repugnant to social equality. Thus St. Thomas Aquinas wrote that "beneficence is an effect of love in so far as love moves the superior to watch over the inferior." SUMMA THEOLOGICA, pt. II, 2d pt., Q. 31, Art. 2. And this same air of condescension continued to permeate post-Reformation charity. For example, Highmore tells us that every person relieved by "The Lying in Charity for the Delivery of Poor Married Women at their Own Habitation" (established 1801) was "expected to return thanks to Almighty God at her usual place of worship, and to the governor who remembered her; and upon neglect, is refused any benefit from this charity for the future." HIGHMORE, PIETAS LONDINENSIS 387 (1810). Likewise the patients cured by the Eastern Dispensary (established 1782) were required to "return thanks" to the persons granting them letters of admission "on neglect of which they are excluded the future favour of the charity." *Id.* at 345.

In all these cases, as indeed in charity generally, a considerable redistribution of economic wealth was brought about under circumstances that maintained, and even strengthened, the social order and *status quo*. And it was this aspect of charity that came under fire at the end of the nineteenth century. For the stigma of "charity," like that of "pauperism," was abhorrent to the advocates of "social justice," who demanded equality. They urged compulsory (rather than voluntary) redistribution of wealth administered by the State, before whom all citizens were equal, in order to avoid the element of "giving" inherent in charity.

35. Many historians have failed to recognize that institutionally propagated or sanctioned checks on individual ambition *can* be socially desirable. Thus during the Middle Ages, there was (to quote W. J. Ashley) "such an absence of opportunities for productive investment as relatively to justify" restrictions on trade and usury. 1 ASHLEY, AN INTRODUCTION TO ENGLISH ECONOMIC HISTORY AND THEORY 156-57 (1888). And under such circumstances social institutions were, quite reasonably, concerned to restrain (or divert to the Other World), rather than stimulate, the ambition of society's members. Certainly the glorifica-

REALITY AND SOCIAL REFORM

This, then, was the *laissez-faire* standard—one which was well suited to the tradition and reality of the late eighteenth century. Cast in moral terms, it assumed poverty to be an inevitable condition of human life; and, as a result, it refused to consider economic want to be an intolerable condition *per se*. Rather it condemned only the moral causes and consequences: insofar as the poor were victims of circumstances acknowleged to be beyond their control they were deserving of assistance and the rich were morally obligated to assist them; insofar as the poor were able-bodied and capable of taking care of themselves, they were deemed to be victims of their own shortcomings and society could do nothing for them except to help them to help themselves through moral reform. Consequently, the role of the state in dealing with poverty could only be "indirect" (since the evil could not be abolished by legislation) and subordinate if not insignificant (for other social institutions, such as the Church, universities and the family were as well, if not better, suited to influence and build moral character).

## III

As of 1800, therefore, the *laissez-faire* standard was a reasonable approximation of both tradition and reality. Not the least reason for believing this is that the most effective reformers of the day—men like Bentham, Colquhoun, Bishop Shute Barrington, and Sir Thomas Bernard—spent their time and energy endeavoring to implement rather than undermine that standard. It was not until much later, in fact after 1870, that the most effective reformers were those (such as the Marxists,[36] the Single Taxers,[37] the Fabians and the

---

tion of poverty, comported more with reality than the glorification of wealth; and the widespread popularity of mendicant orders was, at least until reality reflected new needs and opportunities, in the best interests of society. Yet Lecky, for example, failing to see this, berated the medieval Church for propagating a policy which promoted mendicancy rather than "economic men." "The stigma [he says], which it is the highest interest of society to attach to mendicancy, it became a main object of theologians to remove." 2 LECKY, HISTORY OF EUROPEAN MORALS 40 (1911). And, I would add, for very good reason: reality in a static economy demanded a rigid social institution just as later (when Lecky wrote) reality in a dynamic (industrial) economy demanded flexible social institutions.

36. Marx, of course, wrote many books, and did much organizing, prior to 1870. But in England he was not widely known. As late as 1877 Charles Booth, who, as we have noted, conducted the epic-making survey of the London slums, referred to "Carl Marx (is that the name?) and the ultra set." BOOTH, CHARLES BOOTH: A MEMOIR 52 (1918). This is understandable, for *Capital* was not translated into French until 1873 and into English until 1886. And many of Marx's stoutest champions did not read it until the late 1870's. Indeed H. M. Hyndman, who paraphrased Marx's ideas in a book called *England for All* (published in 1881), read *Capital* in 1880 while on a tour of the United States. HYNDMAN, RECORD OF AN ADVENTUROUS LIFE 209 (1911). "And finally the day began to dawn in England also," wrote Marx's official biographer. MEHRING, KARL MARX: THE STORY OF HIS LIFE 525 (Fitzgerald trans. 1936).

37. The "Single Taxers" were the followers of the American Henry George. For an account of George's influence in England see LAWRENCE, HENRY GEORGE IN THE BRITISH ISLES (1957) and BARKER, HENRY GEORGE (1955). But for our purposes, the following com-

Socialists) who advocated measures which were not only incompatible with, but openly destructive of, the *laissez-faire* standard.

Even so, at the beginning of the nineteenth century, and indeed for some years before, great changes were at work which would ultimately transform reality so completely that the aforementioned tenets of the *laissez-faire* standard would become anachronistic. That change was, of course, the growth of industrialism.

Few terms are more frequently used today; and probably none—not even welfare state or *laissez-faire*—is more ambiguous. Whatever industrialism means,[38] it is certainly more than a mere source of wealth. For it not only subsumes the other (traditional) sources of wealth; land, labor, and capital: it destroys the distinctive features of each and refashions all in its own image. Thus, for example, land-based economies have been characterized by a relatively inexpandable output and a large serf-like class "wedded to the soil." But industry has completely destroyed these characteristics. Through various industrial and scientific innovations the unalterable conditions which made agricultural output inexpandable—conditions involving fertility and weather and knowledge of crops—have been brought more or less under man's control; and mechanical equipment has not only freed but alienated the agrarian classes from the soil. Therefore, the land-based sector of an industrial society bears the marks of the highly developed manufacturing sector and not those of the pre-industrial land-based society. This complete change in the character of a traditional source of wealth was a part of the Great Transformation, a change which converted land, labor and capital into commodities.[39]

Although we scarcely possess the perspective necessary to delineate the fundamental nature of industrialism, a number of characteristics and ten-

---

ment written at the end of the nineteenth century brilliantly demonstrates George's role in the demise of the *laissez-faire* standard:

> [W]hatever view may be taken of his ideas about land, the great conception he contributed to the thought of the 'eighties was that poverty was an evil preventable by State Action. That was criticism, and a damning criticism, of the economic doctrines then current, not perhaps amongst the economists themselves, but amongst politicians and social reformers. They held that poverty was caused by weakness of character, by indulgence in drink, by inefficiency, idleness, and want of thrift. The State, they thought, could not beneficially interfere except in certain well-accustomed ways . . . .
>
> Against this philosophy, comfortable enough for the possessing classes if they could persuade themselves to regard the sufferings of others with equanimity, *Progress and Poverty* burst like a bombshell.

KIRKUP, THE HISTORY OF SOCIALISM 369-70 (5th ed. 1913). See also PEASE, THE HISTORY OF THE FABIAN SOCIETY 21 (1925).

38.  For discussion, if not definition, of the term "industrialism," see 2 THE DICTIONARY OF POLITICAL ECONOMY 399-401 (Palgrave ed. 1900), and 8 ENCYCLOPEDIA OF SOCIAL SCIENCE 18-26 (1932).

39.  Karl Polanyi makes this point in his brilliant work, *The Great Transformation* (1944). His analysis is in terms of the rise, and acceptance, of the notion of a "Self-Regulating Market mechanism"—which I think was, rather, a reflection of economic reality in the early nineteenth century: a stage at which amoral industrialism was in the process of developing, but had not advanced far enough to provide sufficient output to warrant governmental policy being visibly shaped by the interest of consumers as well as producers.

dencies have emerged which appear particularly relevant to our analysis of the welfare state and *laissez-faire* standards regarding poverty. First, an industrial society appears theoretically capable of producing any desired quantity of material output; secondly, industrial processes are such that the quantity of human labor exerted plays a very small part in and has a minor bearing on the volume of output; and, thirdly, the high initial investment required for industrial enterprises, together with the economics of large scale and full capacity production, create incentives to attain and maintain high levels of output. Such levels are inherent in this process itself and abstractly determinable without reference to the particular characteristics (and certainly not the moral character) of the demand for its output.[40] Consequently a *sine qua non* for industrial prosperity is a large enough class of potential consumers to absorb the output produced when operating near the maximum capacity.

These are among the features which appear to distinguish an "industrial" economy. And taken together they create a reality that is utterly incompatible with each of the tenets of the *laissez-faire* standard. For the vast material output realizable by industrialism is inconsistent with the notion that poverty is inevitable; the decreasing role that human labor plays in the production of industrial wealth inevitably weakens the proposition that moral character is the decisive factor in determining man's economic well-being; and the minimum level of consumption which society must maintain to absorb output produced at the abstractly ascertainable optimal level of production cannot be guaranteed through the creation of new purchasing power by private voluntary charity. This method of creating new consumers is too dependent upon the caprice of the rich to meet the chronic (as opposed to occasional) need for increasing purchasing power. Furthermore, charity has social overtones abhorrent to the economic equality inherent in mass production. Thus industrialism demands a method of redistributing wealth that can be relied upon to provide an evergrowing minimum number of consumers free of the stigma of charity. The state, armed with the compulsion of the law, is eminently qualified to meet this need.

Thus reality, in an industrial society, is decidedly at odds with the *laissez-faire* standard. But—I would emphasize—the features discussed above represent deductions based on hindsight. While reasonably clear now, they were not so easily seen earlier. Rather, they appeared, to nineteenth century observers, only as poorly defined tendencies. Until those tendencies became pronounced enough to be recognized as inhering in the nature of industrialism itself, until society could be convinced that this was the reality with which it must learn to live, the *laissez-faire* standard, with its roots deep in tradition, con-

---

40.  This is not an attempt on my part to take issue with the proposition that profit is maximized when marginal cost equals marginal revenue. Rather, it is simply a statement which, translated into economic terms, means that the shape of the cost curve is to some extent ascertainable independently of considerations of demand; and that because of the high fixed costs of most industrial enterprises, the per unit cost will, subject to certain qualifications, tend to decrease as volume increases.

tinued to govern social policy. Deviations from that standard continued to be regarded as "exceptions" rather than the general rule.[41]

The *laissez-faire* standard itself was a delicately balanced reconciliation of two antithetical philosophical propositions: on the one hand, the notion that poverty was inevitable revealed a haunting strain of fatalism; and on the other hand, the conviction that man was morally responsible for his worldly condition revealed an equally deep belief in free will and the possibility of progress. The growth of industrialism did not immediately destroy the *laissez-faire* standard, but rather upset the balance between the two irreconcilables— fatalism and free will—by emphasizing the latter, thereby giving rise to a giddy optimism that led nineteenth century moralists to glorify the omnipotence of the individual. But extraneous circumstances, to be discussed presently, tended to conceal this effect down through the first decade or so of the nineteenth century. Indeed, those factors actually reinforced and perpetuated the fatalistic strain.

The changes in reality wrought by industrialization, and the corresponding effects on the *laissez-faire* standard, fall into three time periods: the first, when fatalism prevailed, was roughly down to the end of the Napoleonic Wars; the second was from 1814 down through the "Great Depression" (which continued off and on throughout the last quarter of the century); and the final one, during which *laissez-faire* fell and the welfare state standard arose, began at the turn of the century, give or take a decade either way, and is still going on. (In the United States, the latter stage did not reach fruition until the New Deal, some twenty years after the equivalent changes were effected in Great Britain.)

It is difficult to say when the so-called Industrial Revolution began. But we are not, in this article, so much concerned with the date of its inception as with the time at which its effects became palpable. For it would be at that time, and not at some more obscure, although more scholarly accurate, date that we would expect it to become a part of reality. To quote a leading economic historian:

> When Arnold Toynbee gave currency to the term "industrial revolution" he set the beginnings of the movement at 1760; and the tendency of

---

41. The orthodox nineteenth century attitude towards poverty focused attention on the "general rule"—circumstances under which man is morally responsible for his own economic well being. Other circumstances were "exceptions" which, by their nature, should not form the basis of social policy. This view was well expressed by Col. Robert Torrens:

> From all that has been said, it must be evident that the important power of increasing, or of diminishing, the reward of labour, is, by the essential order of society, placed in the hands of the labourers themselves. Irregularities in the seasons bringing on scarcity and famine, foreign incursions, or domestic commotions, destroying property, or suspending production by rendering it insecure, may sometimes occasion a depression of wages, which no prudence on the part of the labouring classes can avert or mitigate. But under all ordinary circumstances, when the usual course of nature is preserved, and when law and order are maintained, it depends upon the labouring classes themselves whether wages shall ascend to the ultimate maximum, or sink to the extreme minimum.

TORRENS, ON WAGES AND COMBINATIONS 26 (1834).

later scholars has been to seek an earlier *terminus a quo*. The roots of modern industrial society can be traced back indefinitely into the past, and each historian is at liberty to select his own starting point. If, however, what is meant by the industrial revolution is a sudden quickening of the pace of output we must move the date forward, and not backwards from 1760. After 1782 almost every statistical series of production shows a sharp upwards turn. More than half the growth in the shipment of coal and the mining of copper, more than three-quarters of the increase of broadcloths, four-fifths of that of printed cloth, and nine-tenths of the exports of cotton were concentrated in the last eighteen years of the century.[42]

Taking 1782 as the date at which industrialism made its first spectacular change in economic reality, at least two factors served to conceal the nature of the changes being introduced. First, the enormous increase in population led many thinkers, notably Malthus, to fear for the worst, despite changes in economic reality.[43] And, second, the war with France excited men's fears, and diverted their attention away from these profound economic developments. Those who did consider such matters did so with gloom and trepidation.[44]

Thus despite the fact that seminal innovations were introduced during the eighteenth century—innovations which included the steam engine, Crompton's mule, Arkwright's frame and developments in the techniques for mining coal and making steel—their potentialities were too dimly perceived and weakly felt to make reasonable men doubt that poverty was inevitable. Contemporaneous events only served to confirm the fatalistic aspect of the *laissez-faire* standard.

With the close of the Napoleonic Wars, industry burst forward at a pace that catapulted England to preeminence as a world power.[45] And America was not far behind. In some sectors of the economy such as textiles it caused

---

42. ASHTON, *op. cit. supra* note 17, at 125.

43. See generally Beales, *The Historical Context of the Essay on Population,* in INTRODUCTION TO MALTHUS 3-24 (Glass ed. 1953).

44. Thus so astute an observer as William Playfair, who was remarkably cognizant of the upswing in manufacturing and trade experienced towards the end of the eighteenth century, wrote in 1807:

> The increase of the trade of Britain to foreign parts, within these last fifteen years, though a very natural effect of the cause that have operated during that period, is not itself a natural increase, because the causes that produced it are uncommon, temporary, and unnatural.

PLAYFAIR, AN INQUIRY INTO THE PERMANENT CAUSES OF THE DECLINE AND FALL OF POWERFUL AND WEALTHY NATIONS 193 (1807). Accordingly he could only conclude, after a survey of England's situation: "There is something very gloomy in this view of national affairs, and yet there is no apparent method of making it more pleasing." *Id.* at 207.

45. The magnitude of the advance in industrialism in the period after the Napoleonic Wars is indicated by the quantity of raw materials imported by England's two leading staple industries, cotton and wool:

| | *1790* | *1816* | *1856* |
|---|---|---|---|
| Wool | 3,245,352 | 8,117,869 | 116,211,392 |
| Cotton | 30,574,374 | 94,140,330 | 1,023,886,304 |

URE, THE PHILOSOPHY OF MANUFACTURES 468 n. (3d ed. 1861).

enormously expanded output; in other sectors such as the iron and steel industries it created new demands for labor and those in turn provided the mean for further industrialization. Accordingly the belief grew that (as one writer in 1836 noted) "they had made the greatest advance in civilization that can be recorded in the annals of mankind."[46] The extent to which this optimism supplanted the gloom of the earlier generation is perhaps best illustrated by J.S. Mill's description of how he and his contemporaries received, and enlivened, the gloomy teachings of their elders:

> Malthus's population principle was quite as much a banner, and point of union among us, as any opinion belonging to Bentham. This great doctrine, originally brought forward as an argument against the indefinite improvability of human affairs, we took up with ardent zeal in the contrary sense, as indicating the sole means of realizing that improvability by securing full employment at high wages to the whole laboring population through a voluntary restriction of the increase of their numbers.[47]

This great optimism, this great opulence, effectively killed the fatalism which manifested itself in the tenet that held poverty to be inevitable. Increasingly as the nineteenth century progressed, reality taught men that poverty was not, and should not be considered inevitable.

But the weakening of this strand of fatalism did not immediately destroy the *laissez-faire* standard. Rather it simply shifted the emphasis, and brought to the fore, the free will strand that held man to be morally responsible for his economic well-being. The interim reasoning ran thus: if poverty is not inevitable; and if man is morally responsible for his economic well-being; then surely moral factors are the only deterrents to wealth unlimited. This reasoning accounts, I think, for both that extraordinary concern for moral character shared by all Victorians and the enthusiasm with which they sought "the Elevation of the Labouring Classes." Men of all professions, religions and backgrounds echoed William Ellery Channing's conclusion: "the great obstacles to the improvement of the labouring classes are in themselves, and may therefore be overcome."[48]

However, industrialism continued to grow, and the more it grew the more pronounced became its tendencies to reduce the significance of man as a producer and to increase his value as a consumer. The result was to intensify the conflict between this reality and the free will tenet of the laissez faire standard.

The conflict was concealed for a long time because industrialism created (during its early stages) demands for new skills and hence increased demands for human labor. Yet as early as 1836, a commentator could write:

> The vast improvement made during the last few years in the machinery applied to spinning has caused such an economy in the application of labour, that not one-half of the persons is now required for carrying

---

46. 1 PORTER, THE PROGRESS OF THE NATION 1 (1836).
47. J. S. MILL, AUTOBIOGRAPHY 88-89 (Laski ed. 1924).
48. WORKS OF WILLIAM ELLERY CHANNING 55 (Centennial ed. 1880).

forward the various manufacturing processes with a given weight of cotton, that were employed for producing an equal result thirty years ago.[49]

And, in the wool trade, which was the paradigm of home industry, the plight of the hand-loom weavers was notorious.[50]

How could these bald facts be reconciled with the notion that man is responsible for his economic well-being? The answer is that they could not be reconciled. But man lives with many unreconciled paradoxes and so it was in the nineteenth century. As an example, we may take the way society modified the *laissez-faire* standard in response to the innovations in the textile industry.

In consequence of the application of Adam Smith's division of labor principle, together with the widespread use of the power loom, the flying shuttle and other such mechanical devices, the demand for human labor was very substantially reduced. Yet in the face of this development, nineteenth century reformers did not draw what to us appears the obvious conclusion: that man's value as a producer had been permanently reduced and that therefore moral character could not be responsible for his economic condition. For industrialism had not at that time so completely altered reality as to support such a radical break with tradition. Indeed, as Clapham has pointed out, "no single British industry had passed through a complete technical revolution before 1830."[51]

Progressively, however, as the value of man as a producer decreased, and his value as a consumer increased, reformers have been able to press successfully for legislation which, in addition to humanitarian benefits, had the dual effect of withdrawing segments of the labor supply from the market and increasing the purchasing power of the working classes. Quite naturally this movement began with, and centered around, the plight of factory children.[52] It has progressed at

---

49.  1 PORTER, *op. cit. supra* note 46, at 230.

50.  Col. Torrens, an influential political economist of the Ricardo school, was moved by the plight of the hand-loom weavers to demand legislative relief for them. As would be expected, he believed the wider use of machinery was socially beneficial; as might not be expected, he held that "humanity and justice demand, that those who thus suffer for the public good should be relieved at the public expense." TORRENS, *op. cit. supra* note 41, at 44. See generally ROBBINS, ROBERT TORRENS AND THE EVOLUTION OF CLASSICAL ECONOMICS (1958).

51.  1 CLAPHAM, AN ECONOMIC HISTORY OF MODERN BRITAIN, THE EARLY RAILWAY AGE 1820-1850, at 143 (1939).

52.  It is round the occupation of children that the battle of the century has raged; and the great change that marks it is the gradual transference of children under fourteen from wage-earning to education. The transference is not yet complete. In 1901, 16.9 per cent of children from ten to fifteen were still returned as occupied (200,534 girls and 365,205 boys), and there were still 84,695 half-timers on the school registers in 1907; nevertheless the theory is now accepted that it is socially wrong and economically unsound to treat a child as an instrument of production. In all the great industries there has been a steady decline in the use of child labour. Yet in the first quarter of this century, of all those employed in cotton factories a half were under sixteen years of age, one in every six was under nine years of age; and there were

a pace that parallels precisely the stages of economic growth through a series of Factory Acts. In 1802, during the "take-off" period, the minimum age for employment was first set at eight; by 1844, when the "drive-to-maturity" was almost completed, the age was raised to nine; in 1874, after "maturity" had been attained, it was raised to ten. Again, during the same "stages" the number of hours "children" were permitted to work fell from twelve to nine to six and a half. And, at approximately the same pace, the benefits of factory legislation—including minimum wages, improved working conditions, and more effective enforcement of such provisions—were extended to new classes of workers: first to "young persons" (aged 13 to 18), then to women, and, in 1878, to all factory workers, irrespective of age, sex, or presumed moral responsibility. But —and this is the point—by concentrating their concern on children, nineteenth century reformers were able to vindicate the principle that "men" were morally responsible for their plight. *Laissez-faire,* in short, remained inviolate though an exception had been made for an ever widening group which was (all of a sudden) adjudged unable to take care of itself. Thus Lord Shaftesbury, who was the most conspicuous figure in pushing the important Factory Act of 1844 through Parliament, stipulated to the mill operatives as a condition for his support of the bill :

> . . . that there should be a careful abstinence from all approach to questions of wages and capital; [and] . . . the labour of children and young persons should alone be touched.[53]

This stipulation was necessary for the moralistic nineteenth century mind: the moral responsibility of the "able-bodied"—if not children—had to be affirmed if the values of the time (those of the *laissez-faire* standard) were to stand. Hence it was in a sense inevitable that, a few years later, Parliament would go out of its way to reaffirm the notion of man's moral responsibility. It did this in 1856 by defining the scope of an earlier factory act, which required guard rails to be put around machinery in factories employing children, to exclude those in which only able-bodied men worked. As the able-bodied could and should take care of themselves, the revised statute specifically provided :

> The said section 21 [which required the fencing of machinery] so far as the same refers to mill-gearing, shall apply only to those parts thereof with which children and young persons and women are liable to come in contact, either in passing, or in the ordinary occupation in the Factory.[54]

---

many hundreds employed much younger in factories and under the more terrible conditions of domestic workshops. PORTER, THE PROGRESS OF THE NATION 23-24 (Hirst ed. 1912).

53. As quoted in HODDER, THE LIFE AND WORK OF THE SEVENTH EARL OF SHAFTESBURY 85 (1892).

54. An Act for the further Amendment of the Laws relating to Labour in Factories, 1856, 19 & 20 Vict., c. 38 (pub.). Repealed, Factory and Workshop Act, 1878, 41 & 42 Vict., c. 16, § 107 (pub.).

Commenting on this act, Stanley Jevons said, "Adult males, then, were to be left to be crushed to death. . . ."[55] But he was writing some thirty years later—long after industrial maturity had been attained—at which time the inadequacy of this attempt to reconcile the *laissez-faire* standard with reality had become apparent. To the older generation, however, it had fulfilled the very important function of reaffirming a known truth that was rapidly ceasing to reflect economic reality.

In fact we can see, running throughout the statute books of the nineteenth century, similar attempts to affirm the notion of man's moral responsibility for his economic well-being, even as action inconsistent with that proposition was taken. Exception after exception has been piled on to the proposition that man is morally responsible for his economic well-being. And ultimately that proposition was to be virtually transformed by society's coming to equate the notion of "able-bodied" with one who is well-fed, decently clothed, medically attended, emotionally adjusted, adequately trained or educated, and provided with ample job opportunities as well as being physically strong.

From a twentieth century vantage point, these "exceptions" served two functions. First, these humanitarian reforms provided a rational scheme for gradually contracting the available labor supply at a time when technological unemployment made a contraction mandatory. And second, these exceptions expanded the class of the "deserving" poor—those whose plight resulted from circumstances which society *acknowledged* to be beyond their control—thereby progressively redefining the groups who were to share in the augmented wealth of the nation at a pace consonant with the changes in reality. In short, such humanitarian exceptions rationalized both the decreasing demand for human labor and the increasing need for consumers of the new industrial wealth.

## IV

Thus far we have spoken of the demise of the *laissez-faire* standard in terms of a clash with reality. But despite that clash, the welfare state standard itself was not a foregone conclusion. For it depended upon a frame of mind, a mental outlook, that was prepared to accept the proposition that poverty is an economic, not a moral phenomenon. And, as we have indicated, such an outlook was very rare indeed in the nineteenth century. Hence we must consider the changes in outlook that made this new standard possible.

That change came about largely through the teachings of the much abused classical political economists.[56] For they were the first to look at human (as opposed to natural) phenomena in the detached analytical manner of modern science. And it was through their works that the educated public became

---

55. JEVONS, THE STATE IN RELATION TO LABOUR 70 (3d ed. 1894).

56. By classical political economists I mean Adam Smith, David Ricardo, Jeremy Bentham, James Mill, Col. Robert Torrens, Nassau Senior, Archbishop Richard Whately, J. R. McCulloch, John Stuart Mill, J. E. Cairnes and Henry Fawcett.

acquainted with the application of science to man and society.[57] As such the classical political economists deserve to be remembered as pioneer social scientists.

Though the political economists differed among themselves on many issues including definition of terms, they were in accord on one vital point: political economy was the "science of wealth." They believed that wealth, like Newton's universe, was governed by abstract, autonomous laws—laws which, in sharp contrast to the teachings of clerics, philosophers and poets of the day, had no more to do with morals than earthquakes, floods and falling bodies.

To appreciate the novelty of this assertion we need only consider the intellectual milieu in which the classical political economists preached their message. When in 1798, John Bowdler called for a "thorough reform [which] would set all right, and restore, us to peace and happiness," he did not contemplate political reform; nor did he envision structural changes in the economy. Rather he demanded a moral regeneration of "all ranks of people throughout the kingdom."[58] What I have called the "moral" outlook determined the way society approached every "social problem" for it is only in this century that we have come to regard them as "social" rather than "moral". This approach applied equally to the despised criminal and the successful merchant, to failure and to success, in all their individual manifestations. Thus the notion of crime and punishment—even among such enlightened followers of Beccaria as Bentham, Patrick Colquhoun, and Sir Samuel Romiley—reflected an overwhelming preoccupation with the moral responsibility of the individual. Bentham, for example, urged that hangings should be made the occasion for teaching the public a hard lesson in the consequence of breaking the law—a lesson to be driven home by the use of black scaffolds, weird omens and appropriate background music.[59] This moral approach, which we call the theory of "deterrence," makes sense only if man is reckoned to be fully capable of governing, and hence responsible for, his own conduct. Granting those assumptions, it is quite logical to consider (as James Fitzjames Stephen did) criminal law to be "the organ of the moral indignation of mankind."[60]

---

57. The best example of the influence of the classical political economists involves Charles Darwin, who confessed in his autobiography that he derived his theory of the natural selection from a perusal of Malthus' *Essay on Population.* Likewise, however, the influence of the classical political economists can be gleaned from the following description of the impact of J.S. Mill's teachings, and particularly his *Principles of Political Economy,* at Oxford in the 1850's: ". . . to doubt or assail the doctrines of Mill was the *anathema maranatha,* the unpardonable heresy of my student days." Lord Goschen, Essays and Addresses on Economic Questions 330 (1905) ; and for a similar account of this influence in Cambridge, see Sidgwick, Henry Sidgwick: A Memoir 36 (1906). From a more practical point of view, the idealist philosopher Bernard Bosanquet advised his niece, who was about to start a career of social work, to read "the famous chapter upon the future of the working classes" in Mill's *Principles.*

58. Quoted in 3 Radzinowicz, *op. cit. supra* note 23, at 141.

59. Quoted in Radinowicz, *Changing Attitude Towards Crime and Punishment,* 75 Law Q. Rev. 381 (1959).

60. See Radzinowicz, Sir James Fitzjames Stephen, 1829-1894, at 39 (1957).

Attitudes toward "wealth" were governed by this preoccupation with man and his moral character and responsibility. To many persons this term was primarily an ethical one, denoting virtue, rather than an economic one referring solely to gold, silver and other things of material value. The words of Henry Venn, in his influential *Complete Duty of Man,* are indicative of the orthodox view of wealth in the eighteenth and early nineteenth centuries:

> . . . if [he wrote] whilst your heart is whole with him, he is pleased to make prosper whatever you do, your wealth is plainly his gift, as much as if it come to you by legacy or inheritance. It is the act of God to call you up to a higher station, who was content in your own, and to intrust you with *more* talents to improve for his glory.[61]

This was the state of public opinion in which the classical political economists proclaimed that wealth was a phenomenon that could be, through scientific analysis, reduced to quasi-natural laws. And from what has been said we can gather some idea of the magnitude of the innovation. Certainly, if wealth were governed by amoral laws (as they urged) the classical political economists were attaching a very important qualification to the proposition that man was morally responsible for his worldly condition. Indeed they implied though they did not assert, that wealth was completely unrelated to man's moral character. Hence we can readily understand the indignant reaction, and the violent criticism, evoked by the new science: many gentle, and sincere persons believed that the classical political economists were, by divorcing "wealth" from morality, glorifying an avaricious "economic man" who was driven by godless laws to a crass and virtueless accumulation of riches.[62] And, to such persons, this seemed nothing more than scientific Mammonism—a repulsive and disgusting mockery of all that was good and worthwhile in man and life.

At its inception, however, political economy was but a mere branch of moral philosophy, a "science" which, according to William Paley, "teaches men their

---

61. Venn, Complete Duty of Man 267 (1st Amer. ed. 1804).

62. Among the bitterest critics of the classical political economists were Ruskin and Dickens. And both perceived quite clearly the nature of the problem which had given rise to the science of wealth and the tendencies of that particular type of learning. Having blasted the mammonism of the classical political economists in *Unto This Last* and *Munera Pulveris,* Ruskin formed the Guild of St. George to "slay the dragon of Industrialism." Harrison, John Ruskin 171 (1902). And Dickens gave a brilliant parody of utilitarian education in his *Hard Times.* Indeed, one cannot read Bitzer's mechanical response, and coldly factual definition of a "horse," without feeling that the Gradgrinds have won: we cherish positive knowledge with the same ardor, and blindness, as Mr. Gradgrind himself. But Dickens, like Ruskin, became an ineffectual critic because he was unable to adjust to reality, and particularly the way of thinking inherent in an amoral source of wealth. Thus he remained morally-oriented to the end—though he placed moral responsibility for poverty not on the poor (as did most Victorians) but on the rich: his solution was to convert Bounderbys into Brothers Cheerable—a transformation that, as we saw in the case of Mr. Dombey, could be effected only through love. And when he turned his hand to a practical solution to the problem of the day, he took part in activities which we can only term peculiarly Victorian: starting a refuge to protect and succor fallen women like "Little Emily." See Collins, *Dickens as a Social Worker,* 15 Social Work 525 (1958).

duty and reason of it."[63] And Adam Smith, who is uniformly heralded as the father of English political economy, regarded his *Wealth of Nations* as a supplement to his earlier work, *The Theory of Moral Sentiment*. In his own mind political economy was not an independent subject but a part of a larger whole. (His lectures at the University of Glasgow, where he was Professor of Moral Philosophy, gave equal attention to police, natural religion, moral sentiments and political economy.)[64]

Despite its origins and affiliations with moral philosophy, political economy treated wealth as an economic phenomenon governed by amoral laws. And the aim of its expounders, and particularly the classical political economists, was to discover those "laws." Their discoveries reflected, quite accurately, the growth of amoral industrial wealth. Indeed the rise and growth of political economy itself paralleled to an astonishing degree the rise and growth of industrialism—so much so that we can correlate the discovery of new economic laws (including "pure theory") with changes which society was, in reality, undergoing at the time. Political economy, as such, came into existence almost at the exact moment that the effects of industrialism were first being felt. As J.R. McCullouch, who held the first university chair on the subject in England, wrote in 1825 :

> Political Economy is of very recent origin. Though various treatises of considerable merit have previously appeared on some of its destracted parts, it was not treated as a whole, or in scientific manner until after the middle of the last century.[65]

And we may observe, as a general rule, that the more pronounced industrialism became, the more abstract and scientific the laws of wealth became ; and the more mechanical the society's chief producers grew, the more important mathematics and statistics became. Thus, for example, the greatest single difference between Adam Smith and David Ricardo (who published his *Principles* in 1815) was that Smith, under the influence of the Physiocrats, was much more kindly disposed toward agriculture and landed wealth. Ricardo, on the other hand, dwelt upon the evils inherent in the law of diminishing returns ; and he did not hesitate to treat rent and *rentiers* as scourges of society. The change in economic theory, as expounded by these two writers, thus reflects a growing impatience with one of the traditional sources of wealth ; it also manifests an increasing confidence in, and recognition of, an alternative source of wealth. Industrialism had, in short, come into its own—in theory as well as in reality.[66]

---

63. 2 PALEY, WORKS 1 (1824).

64. A. SMITH, LECTURES ON JUSTICE, POLICE REVENUE AND ARMS xiii-xiv (Cannan ed. 1889). Professor D. W. Brogan has reminded me that Smith devoted the last years of his life to a manuscript which he ordered his executor to destroy after his death. The nature of the manuscript is not entirely clear though it was apparently a history of moral philosophy.

65. McCULLOCH, A DISCOURSE ON THE RISE, PROGRESS, PECULIAR OBJECTS AND IMPORTANCE OF POLITICAL ECONOMY 23-24 (1824).

66. If Ricardo propounded an economic theory that justified industrialism, it was not until several years later—after 1830—that industrialism acquired a philosophy. Then, at almost the same time, two such books were published. In 1832 Charles Babbage published his

This hand-in-hand growth of the new sources of wealth and the modification of the laws of wealth continued. J .S. Mill, who was raised on Ricardo's theory, supplied revisions to it in 1849. Under what he thought to be the influence of Harriet Taylor (and what I would consider, at least partially, that of this change in economic reality), Mill discovered that the laws of distribution, as propounded by Ricardo in 1815, were not iron-clad.[67] By so doing he effected a gentle shift in the emphasis of political economy from production as it had been under Smith and Ricardo to distribution. But it was not until later, after the industrial system had become fairly established as England's primary source of wealth that Jevons, Wicksteed, and Marshall developed the idea; and by so doing they turned the attention of theorists to consumption, an aspect of economic theory that, as Marshall noted in 1890, "until recently—has been somewhat neglected."[68] And the change, interestingly enough, was made, simultaneously, by several independent thinkers [69]— evidence, to my mind, that "pure theory" was a response to, and reflection of, a changing economic reality.

The pattern thus seems reasonably clear: when industrialism came into existence moral philosophy developed a secular branch, political economy; and that moral science provided first an intellectual justification for the new ways of production, and later a critical analysis of the characteristics of this novel system based not on human, but mechanical, labor. As the mechanical aspects became more prominent this branch of the moral sciences, which became progressively more "scientific" and less moralistic, grew quite as spectacularly as did amoral industry in the nineteenth century. So much so that in 1861 Sir Henry Maine noted that it was "the only department of moral inquiry which has made any considerable progress in our day."[70] By the end of the nineteenth century political economy was formally divorced from the moral sciences, had become simply economics—a subject far more statistical, than ethical, in approach (Marshall's *Principles of Economics,* published in 1890, was the first major treatise to drop the "Political" from the title).

In the twentieth century, as industrialism has come to dominate every aspect of economic activity, economics has become increasingly "a box of tools"[71]—

---

treatise *On the Economy of Machinery and Manufacturers,* a book which had gone through four editions by 1835. Again, in 1835 Andrew Ure published *The Philosophy of Manufacturers: or An Exposition of the Scientific, Moral and Commercial Economy of the Factory System,* a book which was enlarged and reissued posthumously under the editorship of P. L. Simmonds in 1861. The appearance, and enthusiastic acceptance of these books is evidence, I think, that industrialism was becoming a part, a significant part, of reality. Also it is noteworthy that F. W. Taylor's equally important study, *The Principles of Scientific Management,* did not appear until 1911 and in the U.S.A. rather than England, as the former was moving into its "Era of High Mass Consumption."

67.   See J. S. MILL, AUTOBIOGRAPHY 209 (Oxford ed. 1924).

68.   1 MARSHALL, PRINCIPLES OF ECONOMICS 142 (2d ed. 1891).

69.   "Nobody denies that, numerous differences in detail notwithstanding, Jevons, Menger, and Walras taught essentially the same doctrine." SCHUMPETER, HISTORY OF ECONOMIC ANALYSIS 952 (1954).

70.   MAINE, ANCIENT LAW 305 (10th ed. 1885).

71.   The phrase is Joan Robinson's, quoted in SCHUMPETER, *op. cit. supra* note 69, at 15.

tools being amoral, impersonal things ideally suited to deal with amoral impersonal concepts like "national income," "structural unemployment," and "economic poverty." Indeed it threatens to become purely econometrics, a subject as remote from morals as an indifference curve is to duty. Thus, the history of economic thought, from moral philosophy to econometrics, has paralleled, and reflected the stages of growth of industrial wealth. For the very reason that theory reflects reality, poverty did not become an *economic* problem in theory, until industry had grown to a point that its maximum levels of output could be attained, but not *maintained,* without more consumers. In England that was not until the Great Depression at the end of the nineteenth century and, in America, until the depression of the nineteen-thirties.

In considering the shift from the *laissez-faire* standard to the welfare state standard, it is important to realize that the scientific approach of the classical political economists was strictly confined to the amoral laws which governed the production of wealth. Everything else was, as Cairnes said, "simply out of the pale of Political Economy."[72] Poverty was not treated as a distinct analyzable economic phenomenon. Rather it was reckoned to be simply the negative reciprocal of wealth, so that the classical political economists assumed the increase of the one would automatically bring about the decrease of the other.[73] It remained for a later generation to show (as Henry George did so brilliantly) that "progress" did not necessarily diminish "poverty"; and it was left to subsequent theorists (such as Marshall, Pigou, and Keynes) to seek the laws of poverty with the same avidity that Smith, Ricardo and Mill had sought the laws of wealth. Despite all the jargon about "laws" and "science," however, the amoral laws of wealth expounded by classical political economists were, as regards poverty, moral in import. And in fact they all served to prove one basic proposition: individual regeneration was the only hope of the poor. The unanimity of the classical political economists on this score is well illustrated by comparing the attitudes of those celebrated disputants, Ricardo and Malthus. Ricardo differed with Malthus enough on theoretical matters to write a paragraph-by-paragraph critique of the latter's *Principles of Political Economy.*[74] When, however, Ricardo came to the passage in which Malthus held that "it is quite obvious . . . that the knowledge and prudence of the poor

72. CAIRNES, THE CHARACTER AND LOGICAL METHOD OF POLITICAL ECONOMY 67 n. (1857).

73. The automatic either/or reasoning runs throughout the thinking of the classical political economists: just as they believed the relationship between wages and profits, and wages and the size of the labor force, to be such that the increase of the one automatically brought about a decrease of the other, so they believed that an increase of wealth would automatically bring about a decrease of poverty. This approach was no doubt influenced by Bentham's "Bifurcate Mode" analysis by which everything was reduced to an either/or. See, especially, his *Philosophy of Economic Science* in 1 JEREMY BENTHAM'S ECONOMIC WRITINGS 88-89 (Stark ed. 1952).

74. *Notes on Malthus,* in 2 THE WORKS AND CORRESPONDENCE OF DAVID RICARDO (Sraffa ed. 1951).

themselves, are absolutely the only means by which any general and permanent improvement in their condition can be affected,"[75] he said:

> I am particularly pleased with your observation on the state of the poor— it cannot be too often stated to them that the most effective remedy for the inadequacy of their wages is in their hands.[76]

And this conclusion, which may appear to be unrelated to economic theory, was in fact subtly interwoven into the very foundation of classical political economics and the "laws" of wealth, and particularly the "wage fund theory," the "labor theory of value," and the orthodox account of the source and manner of accumulating capital.

The "wage fund theory" was nothing other than the economic counterpart of the Malthusian population principle. As adopted by the classical political economists the population principle included the highly important qualification made by Malthus in his second edition of the *Essay on Population:* that "moral restraint" as well as "positive checks" (such as war, disease and famine) could be effective "checks" on the growth of population.[77]

That population principle was incorporated in political economy's celebrated "wage fund" doctrine.[78] According to this doctrine, the level of wages was determined by the ratio between the number of wage-earners and the amount of capital available for wages. If, therefore, the wage earners would only exercise "moral restraints"—chastity, late marriages, and prudence—they could, by holding the supply of laborers below the demand, raise the level of wages. But without such "moral restraints" the increasing number of wage earners would spread misery and offset any new accumulation of capital. The hope for society therefore depended very much upon the moral character, and especially the chastity, of the working class.

Likewise the "labour theory of value" had its moral implications. While holding the "natural price" of wages to be the cost of the laborer's subsistence, Ricardo (following Col. Torrens) held that this was not a fixed price but one which "essentially depends on the habits and customs of the people."[79] If, therefore, the laboring classes would only adopt good habits and higher standards of living, the cost of their subsistence and hence their wages would rise. But this depended not on economic, but moral, factors.

And finally, the orthodox theories of classical political economy relating to the source and method of accumulating capital depended upon moral character. Thus Adam Smith wrote:

---

75. MALTHUS, PRINCIPLES OF POLITICAL ECONOMY 299 (2d ed. 1836).

76. 8 RICARDO, *op. cit. supra* note 74, at 183-84 and see also *2 id.* at 262.

77  1 MALTHUS, AN ESSAY ON POPULATION 14 *passim* (Everyman's ed. 1914).

78. For a discussion (and restatement—after the fact), of the Wages Fund doctrine see TAUSSIG, WAGES AND CAPITAL (1896).

79. 1 RICARDO, *op. cit. supra* note 74, at 96-97. Col. Torrens had stressed the same point with such vigor in his *Essay on the External Corn Trade* that he insisted that Ricardo give him credit for the idea. And in fact Ricardo grudgingly added a footnote in the second edition of his *Principles.*

Parsimony, and not industry, is the immediate cause of the increase of capital. . . . Capitals are increased by parsimony, and minimised by prodigality and misconduct.[80]

James Mill characteristically hammered down this conclusion in his *Elements of Political Economy* by pronouncing it to be "a proposition which excludes all exceptions."[81] And Nassau Senior went so far as to designate saving—or, to use his terminology, "abstinence"—a "Secondary Instrument of Production.[82] In other words, a moral quality, frugality, was a linch-pin in the system of classical political economy.

Thus, we see embodied in, or underlying, these several fundamental doctrines of classical political economy the assumption that the sciences of wealth (and its laws) could operate to the benefit of society only on the condition that people, and especially members of the working classes, conducted themselves morally and rationally, like, in short, economic men. All roads in political economy lead to this conclusion; and the message of these writers was that he who would alleviate the plight of the poor must improve their character.[83]

The initial, and most enduring, contribution of the classical political economists was to apply the amoral, detached approach of the natural sciences to man. By so doing, they became, if not the first, certainly the first widely influential social scientists. Even so, however, they strictly limited their scientific analysis to only one aspect of human activity, the production of wealth, and they left unchanged their traditional appraisal of poverty. Ironically, classical political economy was robbed of its authority by subsequent theorists who, adopting the "scientific outlook" of the classical political economists, refused to confine it to wealth and overran what the classical political economists would have deemed the sacrosanct "private preserves" of morality. But the initial poaching, if it may be so called, was done by one of their own, Malthus, who, in this respect, was far ahead of his times. The shifts in Malthus' thinking between 1798 and 1830 indicate both the direction of economic thought during the next hundred years and the growth of industrialism.

In 1798 Malthus stated, in his *Essay on Population,* that since the quantity of food increased arithmetically, and the number of mouths increased geometrically, starvation was, sooner or later, inevitable. Such, he said, was the law of nature. In the second edition, however, he modify his own law by admitting that man, through "moral restraints," might vitiate the inevitableness of this "law." And in the succeeding six editions (there were seven in all) he steadily

---

80. A. SMITH, THE WEALTH OF NATIONS 149 (McCulloch ed. 1863).
81. J. MILL, THE ELEMENTS OF POLITICAL ECONOMY 35 (1821).
82. SENIOR, POLITICAL ECONOMY 58 (Encyclopaedia Metropolitana series, 6th ed. 1872).
83. The laws of wealth, as expounded by the classical political economists, purported to be scientific and amoral. But those laws were, in fact, closely related to man and his moral character. The classical political economists were, in fact transitional figures: on the one hand they were innovators by seeking amoral laws of human affairs; on the other hand they were traditionalists in so far as their laws were, when shorn of jargon and affectation nothing more than moral imperatives.

retreated from his own inexorable principle, by adding embellishments and qualifications, which reveal an underlying dissatisfaction with his own premise that population must, in the long run, outstrip production.

This is understandable for reality was, as we have seen, materially changing during the period in which he wrote, a change that can be best described by adapting Malthusian terminology: whereas the demand for human labor was increasing arithmetically, the output per hour of such labor was increasing not geometrically but astronomically.[84] And Malthus showed himself to be sensitive to this development. In his *Principles of Political Economy* (first edition 1815 and under revision at the time of his death in 1834) he was preoccupied with the problem of "gluts"—excesses of production which, for one reason or another, could not be consumed. Ricardo, McCulloch, James Mill and the other classical political economists, following J. B. Say, believed such a situation was impossible but Malthus persisted in his enquiry, thereby shedding light on a problem that did not become critical until a later stage of economic development.

Despite his inexorable population principle, we can observe, in the works of Malthus, a gradually decreasing anxiety about demand inevitably outstripping supply and an increasing awareness of the possibility that supply might actually exceed demand. In his work more perhaps than any of his colleagues, we see most clearly the great change that industrialism was to make in the nature of economic crises: the problem would cease being "famine" (or inadequate supply) and become "gluts" (inadequate demand). Malthus' defeat in his own time on this score was so decisive and his ideas so ignored that Maynard Keynes lamented:

---

84. We get an excellent idea of the technological developments taking place at the time (1798) that Malthus wrote his celebrated *Essay* from the following comment by Porter:

> In the year 1800, the quantity of cotton imported for use into the United Kingdom was 56,010,732 pounds, having been only 31,447,605 pounds in 1790, and 17,992,882 pounds in 1785. The total value of manufactured cotton goods exported in 1800 was 5,406,501 £ having been 1,662,369 £ in 1790. At the earliest of these two dates, Sir Richard Arkwright's inventions had very recently been thrown open to the public by the setting aside of his patent in the Court of King's Bench. The first steam-engine constructed for a cotton-mill was made by Mr. Watt in 1785, and put to use at Papplewick in Nottinghamshire; it was four years later that the application of steam power to the same purpose was first made in Manchester. In the year 1800 the number of such engines in that town had increased to 32, the aggregate power of which was estimated as equal to the labour of 430 horses. This increase shows that a great impulse had been given to the manufacture, which already was considered to be a thing of great national importance. If, however, we measure its amount at that time in comparison with the extension which it has since received, the cotton trade of 1800 dwindles into insignificance. At that time the application of the improved machinery was confined to the production of yarn; for although Dr. Cartwright's power-loom was invented as early as 1787, the first practical application of his machine was not made until 1801, when a weaving factory was erected by Mr. Monteith, at Pollockshaws, near Glasgow, and furnished with 200 self-acting looms.

1 PORTER, *op. cit. supra* note 46, at 203-04.

> If only Malthus, instead of Ricardo had been the parent stem from which
> 19th Century economics proceeded, what a wiser and richer place the
> world would be today.[85]

But we should not forget: Keynes wrote in the twentieth century, after industrialism had long been firmly established; and Malthus wrote at the time
when that new source of wealth was still only partially developed. If Malthus
saw the latent tendencies of industrialism more clearly than Ricardo—the
tendencies that would, by Keynes' day, became patent—Ricardo firmly understood the nature of economic reality as of the time he wrote.

In the years following 1870—after, that is industrial maturity had been
fully attained—the character of economic crises changed. Increasingly the
problem ceased being the traditional one of "famine"—a dearth of supply—
and become one of "gluts"—a lack of effective demand. And the remedies for
the former problem could not suffice to solve the latter for the one needed
more producers, the other more consumers. And the _laissez-faire_ standard's preoccupation with the moral character of the poor was really calculated to increase the number of producers. Furthermore by perpetuating
the moral outlook, which distinguished so sharply between the deserving and
the non-deserving poor, it had the effect of limiting the number of potential consumers. That standard was, in short, unsuited to deal with the problem at
hand. For the attainment of its aims—the complete moral regeneration of
the laboring classes—would not suffice. Until more effective demand was
created, all the temperance, diligence, thrift and sexual restraint in the world
would not solve the problem.

Sensing this change in reality, economists began to turn their attention from
wealth toward poverty. For the first time they began to treat it as an independent economic problem that could be subjected to amoral analysis. "Now
at last," wrote Alfred Marshall, in the book that served as a Bible for a generation of economists, "we are setting ourselves seriously to inquire whether
it is necessary that there should be any so-called 'lower classes' at all."[86] And
in his inaugural lecture of 1885 while criticizing the morally oriented Ricardians, he indicated the direction of all subsequent economic theory regarding
poverty.

> Their most vital fault [he wrote] was that they did not see how liable to
> change are the habits and institutions of industry. In particular they did
> not see that the poverty of the poor is the chief cause of their poverty:
> they had not the faith that modern economists have in the possibility of
> a vast improvement in the condition of the working classes.[87]

Marshall and his successors thus concentrated on trying to understand "the
habits and institutions of industry." They have dismissed as irrelevant, or
ignored, those cardinal virtues which, from the time of the Reformation, have

---

85. KEYNES, ESSAYS IN BIOGRAPHY 120 (1951 ed.).

86. MARSHALL, _op. cit. supra_ note 68, at 3.

87. Quoted from Marshall's inaugural lecture at Cambridge in 1885, reprinted in
MEMORIALS OF ALFRED MARSHALL 155 (Pigou ed. 1925).

constituted the panacea to poverty, and which were cornerstones of the laws of classical political economy: temperance, sexual restraint, diligence, and thrift. The fate of these virtues embodies the patterns of change we have been tracing.

(a) *Temperance.* Drink was the bane of the classical political economists not only because besotted workers could not perform efficiently or earn higher wages, but also because such non-productive expenditure constituted a grievous dissipation of capital:

> It needs but the slightest knowledge of the fundamental principles of political economy to perceive that the increasing want of employment is the result of deficient or misexpended capital. Mr. John Stuart Mill states that "while, on the one hand, industry is limited by capital, so on the other, every increase of capital gives, or is capable of giving additional employment to industry: and this without assignable limits. But for the enormous waste of capital somewhere, there would exist in this country ample means of employment for all able to work. How this waste is occasioned is obvious to all. It is the universal passion for alcoholic liquors. . ."[88]

Such was the prevalent attitude among educated persons prior to 1870: drunkenness was a cause of poverty because it deterred the production of wealth.

The new economists rejected this view. Alcoholism became a physical rather than a moral shortcoming—a disease which disabled otherwise able-bodied workers. Its effect on the production of wealth became negligible. In 1912 when Pigou published his *Wealth and Welfare* he limited his discussion of this once vital factor to the following observation: "the drink bill is diminishing, while wages are rising . . . ."[89] And the implication of this remark was that drunkenness had been caused by low wages, not *vice versa.* A modern historian has taken the argument even further by suggesting that drunkenness in the nineteenth century was largely the consequence, not of poverty, but of wealth. "It was," he says, "at heart a crisis of new money wealth, the demands of new social standards and old consumption pattern."[90] Amid the confusion only one thing is clear: the economic significance of drunkenness has materially decreased.

(b) *Sexual restraint.* The economic ramification of promiscuity was of course over-population; and, to Malthus, this was the great threat to civilization. To the classical political economists all discussion of wages and profits and capital began with this principle. Yet after 1870 it ceased to be important. Indeed many books, such as Wicksteed's *Common Sense and Political Economy* (published in 1910) made no reference to the problem at all. One reason, no doubt, was that Charles Bradlaugh and Annie Bessant had popularized a solution to the population problem that was infinitely more effective than ex-

---

88. *Increased Pauperism and the Remedy,* 11 MELIORA: A QUARTERLY REVIEW OF SOCIAL SCIENCE 314 (1869).

89. PIGOU, WEALTH AND WELFARE 28 (1912).

90. Mathias, *The Brewing Industry, Temperance, and Politics,* 1 HIST. JOUR. 97, 110 (1958).

hortation in economic treatises. But Schumpeter gives an explanation more closely related to economic theory. Speaking of the classical political economists he notes that "hypotheses about actual and expected rates of increased population entered into their theorising. . ."[91] But, he adds:

> The essential point to grasp is that this ceased to be so during the period under survey [1870 to 1914]. No theorist writing in, say, 1890 would have thought of doing what [Nassau] Senior had done. And this was not primarily because, very obviously, there was no longer any reason for worrying about pressure of population: it was because the marginal utility system no longer depended upon a particular hypothesis on birth and death rates . . . Hence the population branch of general economics tended to wilt and in its place developed a special field, not necessarily cultivated by economists alone, of population studies.[92]

Promiscuity thus not only ceased to be an economic problem; it also was consigned by the scientific outlook to coldly statistical and amoral population studies.

(c) *Diligence.* To the Ricardians the economic problem was to make the laboring classes work harder and more efficiently—to develop, in short, the virtue of diligence. And the classical political economists never tired of praising it and condemning indolence. After 1890, however, reference to indolence in economic treatises became less and less common. In its place crops up the word "unemployment"—a term which G.M. Young reminds us did not come into common parlance until the 'eighties.[93] And "unemployment" is, of course, plain old "indolence" stripped of its moral connotations.[94] The vice of indolence became of little interest to economists, though their concern for amoral unemployment was enormous. The economic problem was why men were unable to work—not why they chose to remain idle.

(d) *Thrift.* This final virtue of classical political economy has lost its moral, if not economic, status. Frugality, to the political economists, was not only a moral virtue but the sole source of capital. In the hands of J.A. Hobson, and later, Keynes, the virtue of thrift became a vice: the villainous cause of deflation or gluts (as Malthus called them).

Thus we see that after 1870 the effect of the scientific outlook of the "new economists"[95] was to reduce to irrelevance the four cardinal virtues that were so important to classical political economy. And the operative causes of poverty, in the view of the most influential economists, became quite independent of the poor and their moral character. Theoretically, anyway, poverty was an economic and not a moral problem.

---

91. SCHUMPETER, *op. cit. supra note* 69, at 889.

92. *Id.* at 889-90.

93. G. M. YOUNG, VICTORIAN ENGLAND 46 n. (Anchor Book ed. 1954).

94. In 1910 A. C. Pigou read a paper before a Paris Conference on Unemployment entitled "The Problem of Involuntary Idleness"—a title that clearly indicates the point we are trying to make: that "Unemployment" is indolence minus the moral element. This speech is referred to in 34 J. ROYAL STAT. SOC. 72 (1910-11).

95. The allusion is to Marshall's paper "The Old Generation of Economists and the New," which was read in 1897. It is reprinted in *op. cit. supra* note 87, at 295.

Once concern for moral character disappeared the laissez faire standard was doomed. Once men were free to regard poverty as a purely economic phenomenon devoid of all moral overtones, the underlying tenets of that standard—that poverty is inevitable, that man's economic status is a reflection of moral character, and that private voluntary charity is the best means of relieving the poor—were in grave danger. And in fact each fell, being replaced by those which we said, at the outset, constituted the welfare state standard. Society had, once again, brought tradition and reality into line and struck a balance with the new source of wealth by formulating a new set of tenets that comprise the welfare state standard; poverty is intolerable; all "needy" persons (an economic test) are thought to be victims of circumstances beyond their control; and the state is reckoned to be capable of, and therefore obligated to, regulate these economic forces which conspire to cause poverty.

## V.

And so it was that the *laissez-faire* standard fell and the welfare state standard came into being: as the former ceased to reflect reality (though it comported admirably with tradition), it failed to restrain the expectations of men; and as the latter was based on reality (though it clashed violently with tradition) it could not be ignored for long. Tradition yielded, so much so that, today, the tenets of the welfare state standard have penetrated our thinking, our expectations and our point of view so deeply that we are scarcely conscious of them: we not only accept the notion that poverty is an "economic" problem— we can scarcely conceive of it being treated otherwise; we are so used to the idea that poverty is abolishable that the fatalism of the *laissez-faire* standard seems medieval in remoteness as well as in flavor; and we all take for granted so much governmental action that Sir William Harcourt's famous comment made at the turn of the century—that "we are *all* socialists now"—is far truer today than it was when he spoke.

The point we have been trying to make throughout this article is that no standard which ceases to reflect reality can endure. For the "reformers"— those sensitive individuals whose powers of perception and depth of feeling exceeds their ability to submit to the discipline of logic and theory—inevitably make demands which clash with, or go beyond, the "provable" by existing standards. Yet those demands come too close to reality to be ignored. Standards, not reality, yield. In the light of the fate of the *laissez-faire* standard it may be worthwhile to consider the extent to which the welfare state standard now comports with reality.

In this country, since 1900, tradition and reality have taught that human problems can, and indeed must, be solved by scientific analysis. Accordingly, the "scientific outlook" applied by the classical political economists to wealth, and by the "new economists" (as Marshall called them) to poverty, has gradually been extended to every phase of human life. Almost without exception the "social sciences," as academic disciplines, date back no further than 1870— sociology, political science, anthropology, psychology, psychoanalysis, eugenics, history (as a science) and the inductive approach ("the case method") to the study of law are all instances in point. And their rise—together with the lethal blow that Darwin dealt the notion that Man is a divine species created in the image of God—has destroyed forever the old-fashioned belief in human superiority as well as moral responsibility. Like the child who has discovered, and can never forget (however much he may try), that there is no Santa Claus, modern man is too knowledgeable, too clinical—yes, too amoral—to be morally oriented again. And so long as this scientific outlook obtains so will some variation of the welfare state standard. It is well that it should be so.

Nevertheless, there are straws in the wind that unmistakably indicate a certain divergence between prevailing standards and reality. And, in a curious way, "reforms" are being urged today that are strikingly similar to those advocated by the classical political economists during the first half of the nineteenth century. We may cite a few examples. First, competition—the mainspring of classical political economy—seems to be enjoying something of a revival. Certainly the fate of the Labour Party in England, and widespread reawakening of the "Conservative Conscience," as indicated by the extraordinary popularity of Senator Goldwater in this country, suggests a tacit affirmation of the vitality of some form of competition. Once again antitrust policy seems to be a rival to "planning" as a staple in government economic policy. Adam Smith and his friends would scarcely be dismayed by this turn of events.

Again, the greatest fear of the classical political economists, that which shrouded the works of Malthus and Ricardo with gloom, was the possibility of a "Stationary State"—for, as J.R. McCulloch warned, "should the national capital diminish the condition of the great body of the peoples would deteriorate; the wages of labour will be reduced; and pauperism with its attendant train of vice, misery, and crime, will spread its ravages through society."[96] Today we are confronted with the same fear expressed somewhat differently. The New Frontier stands for, and demands, new "programs of economic growth." But make no mistake, we have no more choice today than did Ricardo's readers. As a distinguished American scholar has noted, such programs are absolutely "indispensable, if we are to avoid having to choose . . . between totalitarianism and chaos."[97] In other words, the same urgent need for "progress," for moving ahead, seems to be back once again, just as it was in the early nineteenth century. And whether we call it a fear of the "Stationary State" or a need for "economic growth" the consequences are remarkably similar. Once again, the spectre of Malthus' population principle reappears— though of course we stake our hopes on amoral birth control rather than moral restraints. Again, the old fashioned virtue of thrift is coming back into prominence, not so much on an individual as on an institutional basis. Corporations are once again being reminded that their primary function is to make profits

---

96. McCulloch, The Principles of Political Economy 108 (4th ed. 1848).
97. E.V. Rostow, Planning for Freedom: The Public Law of American Capitalism 355 (1959).

for their stockholders, not to promote good public relations.[98] And of course the widely publicized Newburgh case,[99] the over-hauling of our welfare laws and the increased emphasis on getting those on welfare back in the labor force, suggests that, once again, indolence as well as unemployment, is being regarded as a fundamental problem.

These signs—the resurgence of faith in competition, a compulsive need for economic growth and the reaffirmation of the virtue of diligence and thrift and a fear of over-population—are similar enough to (though admittedly different from) the teachings of the early nineteenth century "reformers" to make us wonder if present day reality might somehow be analogous to that of the past. I think we can account for these phenomena in at least two ways: First, we, today, are moving into a new era, one still poorly defined and perceived, in which the source of wealth is as new to us as "industrialism" (as we have defined it) was to Ricardo and his contemporaries. One aspect of that change involves the development of a new type of energy which underlines our industrial order. For the shift from water power and charcoal in the eighteenth century, to coal, coke and steam in the nineteenth century, to hydroelectricity and petroleum in the twentieth century has not only paralleled the growth of industrialism but also provided the energy necessary to attain and sustain an ever-increasing maximum level of output. The revolutionary possibilities of nuclear energy bid fair to produce an equally new phase of industrialism. And technical innovations—notably the computer—are of equal import. Together they make our situation analogous to the growth period at the beginning of the nineteenth century: once again man's relevance as a producer of wealth is threatened in a variety of ways. (Indeed, scholarship itself is not immune to this obsolesence.) Man's place in the world must, in short, be reappraised and redefined.

Hence, as regards these new and still dimly felt phenomena, it may well be that we are in an era of growth—rather like the nineteenth century "take-off" period. And if this is so, it would not be surprising that we are experiencing a reaction to the consumer-oriented welfare state standard. For history seems to suggest that in growth periods (perhaps by definition) society places its foremost emphasis on production—sometimes to the neglect or detriment of the non-producer segment of society. Certainly the doctrine of *laissez-faire,* as preached by the classical political economists, was, whatever else it may have been, a philosophy of growth.

A second suggestion to be extracted from resurgence of *laissez-faire*-like reforms is that poverty, to mention but one of a variety of social problems, is being redefined in international terms. Our discussion of the welfare state

---

98.   See, for example, Dean Rostow's vigorous reassertion of the notion that "maximization of profits"—and not some more socially-oriented purpose—should still be the measure of corporate responsibility. E.V. Rostow, *To Whom and For What Ends is Corporate Management Responsible,* in THE CORPORATION IN MODERN SOCIETY 46-71 (Mason ed. 1959).

99.   See Raskin, *Newburgh's Lesson for the Nation,* N.Y. Times, Dec. 17, 1961, § 6 (magazine), p. 7.

standard has, thus far, been implicitly cast in national terms. But the artificiality of purely national boundaries becomes more apparent every day. Indeed the very existence of the United Nations, the growing interest in "international law," the agitation for the Common Market, the Kennedy administration's trade bill, the appeal of international communism are all manifestations of the fact that reality is, for the first time, genuinely international in scope. For all parts of the world contribute to, and increasingly are sharing in, the *same* source of wealth. And once we redefine the problem in international terms we inevitably revert to a situation in which the moral element is more important. For there are many areas of the world, and many parts of each country, in which reality still consists of agrarian (or something other than industrial) sources of wealth. And in those areas some type of moral reform seems quite necessary to remake the under-developed areas into industrial societies. With agriculture becoming increasingly industrialized even those areas of the world which produce raw materials do not need, and can ill afford, to have a large percentage of the population tied to the soil; and as more mechanically produced wealth spreads to those areas the need for consumers will increase.

    Blue collar to white collar has been the way of the West. But such cannot be the way of the rest of the world. For they must go, in many instances, from bareback or homespun to the equivalent of the white collar. The so-called "under-developed" countries are in fact fully developed in non-industrial (mainly agrarian) ways. And long tradition has taught those peoples not equality but deference, not freedom but discipline. We made our break from the stultifying limitations of a land-based economy in the sixteenth century when the growth of the wool trade, in particular, and the concommitant spread of home industry and new opportunity, gave rise to a new reality which could no longer be contained by land based feudal institutions. The result was that great moral upheaval to which we have already alluded. (It was more than a little symbolic that the "Divine Rights" of the Lord Paramount of all the lands of England should have been denied by a judge who sat on a wool sack.) But the new reality to which we adjusted was quite different from that to which underdeveloped countries must now adjust: we moved into a period during which *human* (not mechanical) labor was preeminent, one in which the moral (not the scientific) outlook predominated, one in which the ideas of Locke and Adam Smith (not Norbert Wiener and Paul Lazarsfeld) were vital, new and indigenous. And we must not expect any country, however undeveloped, to make in the twentieth century, the same transition that we did in the sixteenth and seventeenth centuries. Nor should we expect or demand that they accept our post-Reformation values. For those values have never been a part of their traditions, and are not now, a part of their reality. And, not infrequently the values which we want to extoll the loudest and insist upon most strongly are those which draw their greatest support from our tradition rather than from present day reality. Not the least among these is "individual freedom" an idea frequently used in a way to blind us to reality and which (as we say) runs squarely counter to the subservience and discipline inculcated in non-western societies by generations of all-pervading tradition.

Our hope for the future lies in discovering the values inherent in the new reality, for the spread of industrialism will, in time, provide the world with a reality common to all and not peculiar to the traditions of the West. Building on this reality, we have the firmest basis for international—or perhaps I should say uni-industrial—understanding in the history of mankind.

From the fall of the *laissez-faire* standard, we can learn a solemn lesson about the cost of clinging too long, and insisting too strenuously (I almost said self-righteously), to the tenets of a standard which has ceased to comport with reality. The footnotes of nineteenth century history are full of references to individuals and groups who made really splendid efforts to attain the ends of the *laissez-faire* standard. Many of them—such as Thomas Chalmers of Glasgow, Sir Charles Loch of the Charity Organization Society in London, Robert Treat Paine of the Associated Charities in Boston—accomplished untold good in a cold and cruel world. They are largely forgotten, even by many historians. Yet every schoolboy knows something about Robert Owen, Karl Marx, the Webbs, the Fabians, and the New Dealers. Why? Because they had the courage and vision to reject the *laissez-faire* standard at a time when it was out of step with reality.

Now we, who are confronted (apparently) with a changing reality, are dealing with a brand new problem, international poverty. And we must consider whether our ways of dealing with it are too traditional, whether we are not, *vis-à-vis* this particular problem, like those gentle souls in 1880 who insisted that only the "deserving" poor should be permitted to share in the wealth of the nation. And we have witnessed the fate of such reformers: the lower classes refused to be preached to; they simply would not be satisfied with a pittance when they could, as easily, demand more. For reality was on their side. During the last seventy or so years reform has all flowed in the same direction: towards creating new consumers, or consumers with higher purchasing potential through the destruction of class and caste lines. Those reformers who tried to turn the tide—however logical their reasoning, however powerful their precedents, however forceful their argument—are remembered principally for the futility of their efforts. They were guilty of committing history's one unpardonable and unforgivable sin: of being out of step with reality.

And we are, or may be, in a similar state as regards the underdeveloped countries. Our staunch insistence that only those nations which meet *our* moral standards (though cast in political terms)—those which are democratic, hold free elections, swear subservience to the United States—may be productive of more harm than good. For we are trying to dictate the terms upon which the amoral (and increasingly internationally) produced wealth can be distributed. And those terms which seem reasonable enough to us (as did the "Ideal of Charity" at the turn of the century to the rich)— appear to others calculated to perpetuate our superiority and their subservience. Reality demands equality.

We have a right, and duty, to protect our tradition. But we must also live with reality. We must decide which of our traditions are important enough, and in what ways they clash least with reality, before we commit ourselves irrevocably to them. In making these decisions we must pay more attention to the mere existence of "radical" agitation ("right" and "left") than to the logic of their arguments. For man can put any proposition logically. It is only those reflecting reality that he can translate into social policy.

# 5

## THE EMERGENCE OF AN INSTRUMENTAL CONCEPTION OF AMERICAN LAW, 1780-1820

*MORTON J. HORWITZ*

# THE EMERGENCE OF AN
# INSTRUMENTAL CONCEPTION
# OF AMERICAN LAW, 1780-1820

EVEN the most summary survey of developments in American law during the nineteenth century confirms Daniel Boorstin's view that it represented one of those truly "creative outbursts of modern legal history."[1] And while other historians have characterized the period as a "formative era" or "golden age" in American law,[2] it has never been entirely clear why at this particular time the legal system should have taken on such an innovative and transforming role. The most fundamental change undoubtedly involves the function of the common law. In eighteenth-century America, common law rules were not regarded as instruments of social change; whatever legal change took place generally was brought about through legislation. During this period, the common law was conceived of as a body of essentially fixed doctrine to be applied in order to achieve a fair result between private litigants in individual cases. Consequently, American judges before the nineteenth century rarely analyzed common law rules functionally or purposively, and they almost never self-consciously employed the common law as a creative instrument for directing men's energies towards social change.

What dramatically distinguished nineteenth-century law from its eighteenth-century counterpart is the extent to which common law judges came to play a central role in directing the course of social change. Especially during the period before the Civil War, the common law performed at least as great a role as legislation in

1. Daniel J. Boorstin, *The Americans: The National Experience* (New York, 1958), p. 35.
2. Roscoe Pound, *The Formative Era of American Law* (Boston, 1938); Charles Haar, ed., *The Golden Age of American Law* (New York, 1965).

underwriting and channelling economic development. In fact, common law judges regularly brought about the sort of far-reaching changes that would have been regarded earlier as entirely within the powers of the legislature. During the antebellum period, Mark DeWolfe Howe observed, "the legislative responsibility of lawyers and judges for establishing a rule of law was far more apparent than it was in later years. It was as clear to laymen as it was to lawyers that the nature of American institutions, whether economic, social, or political, was largely to be determined by the judges. In such a period questions of private law were seen and considered as questions of social policy."[3] Indeed, judges gradually began to shape common law doctrine with an increasing awareness that the impact of a decision extended far beyond the case before them and that their function had expanded beyond the necessity merely of doing justice in the individual case. Courts "appear[ed] to take the opportunity which each case afforded, not only of deciding that case, but of establishing rules of very general application."[4] In short, by 1820 the process of common-law decision-making had taken on many of the qualities of legislation. As judges began to conceive of common law adjudication as a process of making and not merely discovering legal rules, they were led to frame general doctrines based on a self-conscious consideration of social and economic policies.

During the last fifteen years of the eighteenth century, one can identify a gradual shift in the underlying assumptions about common law rules. For the first time, lawyers and judges can be found with some regularity to reason about the social consequences of particular legal rules. For example, it would have been very unusual a decade earlier to hear a lawyer argue, as the attorney-general of South Carolina did in 1796, that the state Supreme Court should not require compensation for land taken for road building because it would "thwart and counteract the public in the exercise of this all-important authority for the interest of the community."[5] Sim-

3. Mark DeWolfe Howe, "The Creative Period in the Law of Massachusetts, "*Proceedings of the Massachusetts Historical Society*, 69 (1947–1950), 237.
4. Theophilus Parsons, *Memoir of Theophilus Parsons* (Boston, 1859), p. 239.
5. Lindsay v. Commissioners, 2 Bay 38, 45 (S.C. 1796).

Horwitz : An Instrumental Conception of Law    289

ilarly, jurists began to frame legal arguments in terms of "the importance of the present decision to the commercial character of our country,"[6] or of the necessity of deciding whether adherence to a particular common law rule will result in "improvement in our commercial code."[7] By the first decade of the nineteenth century, it was common for judges to argue that "to admit a party to a negotiable note to come forward as a witness to impeach that note would greatly embarrass trade and commerce, and almost entirely prevent the circulation of this species of paper. . . ."[8]

One of the best instances of the emerging legal mentality occurred in the New York case of *Palmer* v. *Mulligan*, decided in 1805. There the court was called upon to decide whether the plaintiff, a downstream mill owner, could recover damages for obstruction of the flow of water by the defendant, who had erected his own upstream dam. Not only did the court refuse to apply the common law rule, which had always allowed a downstreamer to recover for any obstruction of the natural flow, but the judicial opinions were filled with functional analyses of the common law test. Under the common law, one judge observed, "he who could first build a dam or mill on any public or navigable river, would acquire an exclusive right, at least for some distance. . . ." The result of allowing the plaintiff to prevail would be that "the public, whose advantage is always to be regarded, would be deprived of the benefit which always attends competition and rivalry."[9]

This increasing preoccupation with using law as an instrument of policy is everywhere apparent in the early years of the nineteenth century. Two decades earlier it would have been impossible to find an American judge ready to analyze a private law question by agreeing "with Professor *Smith*, in his 'Wealth of Nations,' . . . that distributing the burthen of losses, among the greater number, to prevent the ruin of a few, or of an individual, is most conformable to the principles of insurance, and most conducive to the

6. Liebert v. The Emperor, Bee's Admir. Rep. 339, 343 (Pa. 1785).
7. Silva v. Low, 1 Johns. Cas. 184, 191 (N.Y. 1799).
8. Winston v. Saidler, 3 Johns. Cas. 185, 196 (N.Y. 1802).
9. 3 Cai. R. 307, 314 (1805). For the common law rule, see Merritt v. Parker, 1 Coxe L. Rep. 460 (N.J. 1795).

general prosperity of commerce."[10] It would have been equally improbable that a judge, as in the *Philadelphia Cordwainers Case* of 1806, would "consider the effect" that a labor conspiracy "would have upon the whole community" so that, as a result of conspiracy, no "man can calculate . . . at what price he may safely contract to deliver articles."[11]

In a whole variety of areas of law, ancient rules are reconsidered from a functional or purposive perspective, often before new or special economic or technological pressure for change in the law has emerged. Only in the nineteenth century, for example, do American judges begin to argue that the English law of waste "is inapplicable to a new, unsettled country" because of its restraint on improvement of land, even though the problem appears to have been central to eighteenth-century concerns as well.[12] Similarly, the English rule of allowing dower on unimproved lands was routinely followed by the Massachusetts court at the end of the eighteenth century, but rejected early in the nineteenth century because "it would operate as a clog upon estates, designed to be the subject of transfer." Yet, the goal of free alienation of land in order to encourage economic improvement was regarded as equally important by eighteenth-century Americans as it was by their successors.[13] It is only in the nineteenth century that American courts abandon the marine insurance rule of strict construction of warranties in deciding cases under fire insurance policies on the ground that it "would render them so inconvenient as wholly to prevent them."[14]

10. Thurston v. Koch, 4 Dall. 348, app. xxxiv (C.C.A. Pa. 1803).

11. Commonwealth v. Pullis (The Philadelphia Cordwainers Case) (1806) in John R. Commons *et al.*, eds., *A Documentary History of American Industrial Society* (Cleveland, 1910), III, 229–230.

12. Jackson v. Brownson, 7 Johns. 227 (N.Y. 1810) (Spencer, J.). See also Findlay v. Smith, 6 Munf. 134, 142 (Va. 1818).

13 Conner v. Shepard, 15 Mass. 164 (1818); Nash v. Boltwood (Mass, 1783) in William Cushing, "Notes of Cases in the Supreme Judicial Court of Massachusetts, 1772–1789" (MS in Treasure Room, Harvard Law School Library). In the eighteenth century the Massachusetts legislature had substantially reduced the period during which a mortgagor could recover the equity of redemption in his land so "that the improvement of real estates thus taken might not be delayed or lost to the mortgagee." James Sullivan, *The History of Land Titles in Massachusetts* (Boston, 1801), p. 102.

14. Stetson v. Massachusetts Mutual Fire Ins. Co., 4 Mass. 330 (1808).

In short, an instrumental perspective on law does not simply emerge as a response to new economic forces in the nineteenth century. Rather, judges begin to use law in order to encourage social change even in areas where they had previously refrained from doing so. Our task, then, is to explain why it was only in the nineteenth century that the common law took on its innovating and transforming role in American society. This in turn forces us to ask whether an explanation for this fundamental shift in the conception of law between 1780 and 1820 can be found in more general changes in the political theory of the period.

## 1. The Eighteenth-Century Conception of the Common Law

THE generation of Americans who made the American Revolution had little difficulty in conceiving of the common law as a known and determinate body of legal doctrine. After more than a decade of insistence by political writers that the "grand basis of the common law" was "the law of nature and its author,"[15] it is not surprising that the first Continental Congress in 1774 should maintain that Americans were "entitled to the common law" as well as to English statutes existing at the time of colonization.[16] In a similar move, the Virginia Convention of 1776 adopted as "the rule of decision" "the common law of England" as well as all English statutes "of a general nature" passed before 1607, while the New Jersey Constitution of the same year declared that "the common law of England as well as so much of the statute law, as have been heretofore practiced in this Colony, shall still remain in force."[17] Between 1776 and 1784, eleven out of the thirteen orig-

15. James Otis, *A Vindication of The British Colonies*, in Bernard Bailyn, ed. *Pamphlets of the American Revolution*, I (Cambridge, 1965), 563.

16. *Journals of The Continental Congress*, I (Washington, 1904), p. 69.

17. William W. Hening, ed., *The Statutes at Large; Being a Collection of all the Laws of Virginia*, IX (Richmond, 1821), 127; Francis N. Thorpe, ed., *Federal and State Constitutions, Colonial Charters and Other Organic Laws . . .* , V (Washington, 1809), 2598.

inal states adopted, directly or indirectly, some provisions for the reception of the common law as well as of limited classes of British statutes.[18]

In light of the attacks on the common law that began to appear within the next generation, it is remarkable that the revolutionary generation saw no difficulty in establishing the common law as the rule of decision in legal controversies. None of the persistent hostility to English legislation that prevailed throughout the colonial period seems to have influenced their commitment to common law doctrines. Nor do anti-British attitudes, which later were to take the form of opposition to the English common law, result in such opposition at the moment of the break from Great Britain. Although there was considerable fear of judicial discretion voiced both during and after the colonial period, there is nevertheless little evidence in the earlier period—unlike the later one—that this fear was identified with the uncertain nature of common law rules. For example, Massachusetts Chief Justice Hutchinson could declare in 1767 that "laws should be established, else Judges and Juries must go according to their Reason, that is, their Will." It was also imperative "that *the Judge* should never be the *Legislator*: Because, then the Will of the Judge would be the Law: and this tends to a State of Slavery." Unless the laws were "known" and "certain" so that "People may know how to act," he concluded, "they depend upon the arbitrary Opinion of Another." Nevertheless, he saw no contradiction in maintaining that where there was no statutory rule, "the Common Law of England is the Rule."[19] The great danger of judicial discretion for the colonists arose not from common law adjudication but in connection with judicial construction of statutes, "for whenever we leave Principles and clear and positive Laws," John Adams observed, "and wander after Constructions, one Construction or Consequence is piled up upon

18. Elizabeth Gaspar Brown, *British Statutes in American Law, 1776–1836* (Ann Arbor, 1964), p. 24. Rhode Island enacted a reception provision in 1798, while Connecticut waited until 1818.

19. "Charge to the Grand Jury," Quincy's Mass. Rep. 234–235 (1767) (emphasis in original).

Horwitz : An Instrumental Conception of Law    293

another until we get an immense distance from Fact, Truth and Nature."[20]

Hutchinson's statement illustrates the "inevitable and rapid reception of the body of English common law" in the colonies during the eighteenth century. The persistent appeals to the common law in the constitutional struggles leading up to the American Revolution "created a regard for its virtues that seems almost mystical." As a result, by the end of the eighteenth century, lawyers regarded the "concept of the common law as a body of principles," which "encouraged uninhibited use of English precedents by the legal profession in the federal courts."[21] And while Americans always insisted on the right to receive only those common law principles which accorded with colonial conditions, most of the basic departures were accomplished not by judicial decision but by local statute, so that by the time of the American Revolution one hears less and less about the unsuitability of common law principles to the American environment.

By contrast, the colonial attitude towards British statutes was summed up in the typical revolutionary constitutional or legislative provision confining statutory reception to the period before colonization or else limiting the force of British statutes to those previously adopted. Indeed, this sharp distinction between statute and common law serves to underline the fundamentally different conceptions that eighteenth-century jurists applied to the two bodies of law. Until around 1720, both colonial and English discussions of common law reception continued to be dominated by Sir Edward Coke's distinction between lands conquered from Christians and those taken from infidels.[22] Resisting the claim that the Amer-

20. *Legal Papers of John Adams*, ed. L. Kinvin Wroth and Hiller B. Zobel (Cambridge, 1965), II, 199.

21. *The Law Practice of Alexander Hamilton*, ed. Julius Goebel, Jr. (New York, 1964), I, 10, 11, 33.

22. The distinction appears in Calvin's Case, 7 Coke Rep. 1, 17 (1608). It is discussed in Joseph Henry Smith, *Appeals to the Privy Council From The American Plantations* (New York, 1950), pp. 466–469 and St. George Leakin Sioussat, *The English Statutes in Maryland* (Baltimore, 1903), p. 18. Coke's categories were expanded considerably by Chief Justice Holt who, in 1693, acknowledged that in "uninhabited" lands founded by Englishmen British law prevailed. He held, however, that Jamaica was a "conquered" land. Blankard v. Galdy, 2 Salk. 411.

ican plantations were "conquered" territory and, as such, not entitled to the benefits of English law, the colonists largely succeeded after 1720 in establishing the proposition that they carried the English common law with them.

Between 1712 and 1718, the legislatures of South Carolina and North Carolina, and Pennsylvania, as well as the Maryland proprietor, claimed the benefits of the common law but of only limited categories of British statutes.[23] And while Coke's dichotomy continued to influence the debate over the authority of British statutes right up to the Revolution, it largely dropped from view after 1720 on the question of common law reception. In that year, English Attorney General Richard West acknowledged that "the common law of England is the common law of the [American] plantations and all statutes in affirmance of the common law, passed in England antecedent to the settlement of a colony, are in force in that colony, unless there is some private act to the contrary; though no statutes, made since those settlements, are thus in force unless the colonists are particularly mentioned. Let an Englishman go where he will, he carries as much of law and liberty with him as the nature of things will bear."[24] Although there were occasional attempts before the American Revolution to deny the applicability of the common law to the colonies,[25] West's statement came to represent the overwhelming view as to the authority of common law rules,[26] and his formula, distinguishing between statutory and common law reception, was almost uniformly adopted by American legislatures at the time of the Revolution.

The fundamentally different conceptions of the sources of common and statute law in the eighteenth century can also be illustrated by the frequent contention of colonial lawyers that the retroactive application of statutes was illegitimate. "It is a general observation," Virginia Attorney General John Randolph argued in 1768, "that laws are unjust and unreasonable, when by retrospec-

23. Brown, *British Statutes*, p. 17; Sioussat, *The English Statutes*, pp. 25–27.

24. Sioussat, *The English Statutes*, p. 21.

25. Such was Blackstone's position. William Blackstone, *Commentaries on the Laws of England* (Oxford, 1765–1769), IV, 107.

26. Smith, *Appeals to the Privy Council*, pp. 482–487.

## Horwitz : An Instrumental Conception of Law     295

tion they attempt to direct those that were prior." To retroactively apply a statute limiting entails of slaves under the guise of merely clarifying a prior law, he urged, "would fall heavy on purchasers who understood the former law in the common sense, and who saw not the hidden meaning which the legislature have thought it necessary to unfold by a subsequent law. In criminal cases they have been branded with an infamy well merited; and why should the safety of our property stand on a basis less firm than that of our persons?"

While Randolph was voicing a familiar complaint about the retroactive application of a statute, there is no indication that any colonial lawyer expressed a similar concern about an equivalent application of common law rules. Randolph, himself, acknowledged that a different theory would apply to nonstatutory crimes, and presumably, to common law civil rules as well. He conceded, "that a law founded on the law of nature may be retrospective, because it always existed, and a breach of it was criminal, though not forbidden by any human law: but that an institution, merely arbitrary and political, if retrospective, is injurious, since, before it existed, it could not be broken nor could any person foresee that such an action would, at a future day, be made criminal."[27] In short, common law doctrines are derived from natural principles of justice, statutes are acts of will; common law rules are discovered, statutes are made.

An excellent manifestation of this conception appears in *Anderson v. Winston*, a Virginia case decided in 1736. In an action of debt on a Virginia statute barring usurious interest, the defendant maintained that since he had contracted with the plaintiff before the act was passed it was "against natural justice to punish any man for an action, innocent in itself with respect to human laws, by a law made *ex post facto*." But his argument did not conclude there, for he understood that if the statute was merely declaratory of natural law, it hardly mattered whether or not the statute applied to his case. It was therefore essential also to demonstrate at great length that "most of the writers upon the law of nature agree" that natural

27. Blackwell v. Wilkinson, Jefferson's Rep. 73, 77 (Va. 1768).

296            Perspectives in American History

law principles did not establish any preexisting bar against usury.[28]

Believing, as the elder Daniel Dulany wrote in 1728, "That the Common Law, takes in the Law of Nature, the Law of Reason and the revealed Law of God; which are equally binding, at All Times, in All Places, and to All Persons,"[29] Americans had little cause to fear judicial discretion or the retroactive application of legal doctrine in common law adjudication. Where common law rules were conceived of as *"founded in principles, that are permanent, uniform and* universal," and where common law and natural law were interchangeably defined as "the Law which every Man has implanted in him," jurists would be unlikely to think of the common law as deriving its legitimacy from the will of a lawmaker.[30] It was precisely this reasoning that encouraged the colonists to receive those English statutes merely declaratory of the common law while refusing to be bound by those that changed common law rules. If, for example, it could be shown that "the [English] Act of Settlement created no innovation of the ancient constitution" with respect to tenure of judges and that judicial independence "is not of a late date but part of the ancient constitution," it seemed to follow that such a doctrine was an "inseparably inherent" right of individuals. There would be no difficulty in retrospectively applying that rule, it was argued, for it would "introduce no new law" but was merely an "affirmance of the old law, that which was really law before."[31]

In much of the prerevolutionary legal writing about common

28. Anderson v. Winston, Jefferson's Rep. 24, 27 (Va. 1736).

29. "The Right of the Inhabitants of Maryland to the Benefit of the English Laws" (1728), in Sioussat, *The English Statutes* p. 82. Dulany, however, was unusual among his contemporaries in maintaining that protection of liberty required the reception of English statutes as well as the common law. These Acts, he argued, "have always been deemed, as essential a Part of the Security, of the Subject to his Rights and Privileges as the Common Law itself . . . ." *Ibid.*, at p. 99.

30. Josiah Quincy's argument for the defense in *Rex v. Wemms* (1770), quoting Blackstone's *Commentaries* IV, 3, in *Adams Legal Papers*, III, 160; Hutchinson, "Charge to the Grand Jury," Quincy's Mass. Rep. 113 (1765).

31. Joseph Galloway, "A Letter to the People of Pennsylvania" (Philadelphia, 1760), in Bailyn, *Pamphlets*, I, 266–267; William Brattle, in *The Works of John Adams*, ed. Charles Francis Adams, III (Boston, 1851), 518. See also Gordon S. Wood, *The Creation of the American Republic, 1776–1787* (Chapel Hill, 1969), pp. 294–295.

law, we see this identification of natural law principles with customary usage. The determinations of English courts "for so many ages past," one judge maintained, "shew, not only what the common law . . . is, but that these rules of the common law, are the result of the wisdom and experience of many ages." Indeed, John Adams was prepared to argue—contrary to his own political desires—that the common law had not provided for life tenure of judges because *"custom and nothing else prevails, and governs in all those cases."* "General customs," he declared, ". . . form the common law . . . ; they have been used time out of mind, or for a time whereof the memory of man runneth not to the contrary." Thus, the only question was whether a particular office provided for life tenure "by custom, that is, immemorial usage, or common law."[32]

The equation of common law with a fixed, customary standard meant that judges conceived of their role as merely that of discovering and applying preexisting legal rules. Because a "Usage had been uninterrupted," proclaimed the judges of the Massachusetts high court in 1765, "the Construction of the Law [is] thereby established" and they "therefore would make no Innovation." Are common law courts free to depart from the known rules of the common law, one judge asked. "No, surely, unless they take it upon them to be wiser than the Law." Should there be a discretion in Equity to modify the legal rule concerning jointly held property? No, a Virginia lawyer argued in 1737, for it would "overturn the most ancient and established Rules of Law" and "render Right and Property very precarious." "Instead of being determined by fixed and settled Rules and Principles," he concluded, "Law and Right [would] depend upon arbitrary Decisions which are ever fluctuating & contradicting one another."[33]

The result of all this was a strict conception of precedent. While lawyers would occasionally argue, as did James Otis, that it is "Better to observe the known Principles of Law than any one Prece-

---

32. Charge of Justice Edmund Trowbridge in Rex v. Wemms (1770), *Adams Legal Papers*, III, 288; *Works of John Adams*, III, 527, 540, 546 (emphasis in original).
33. Watts v. Hasey, Quincy's Mass. Rep. 194 (1765); Hooton v. Grout, Quincy's Mass. Rep. 343, 362, (1772); Robinson v. Armistead, Barradall's Rep. 223 (Va. 1737).

dent," the overwhelming fact about American law through most of the eighteenth century is the extent to which lawyers believed that English authority settled virtually all questions for which there was no legislative rule. In fact, this state of mind continued for a time after the American Revolution. Writing in 1786, the young James Kent continued to emphasize the colonial dichotomy between statute and common law. While he regarded any "Admission" that statutes enacted after settlement were binding as "subversive in Effect of our independent Rights," he continued to believe that the common law "can only be discovered & known by searching into the Decision of the English Courts" which "are regarded with us as *authentic Evidence* of the Common Law & therefore are cited as *Precedents binding* with us even down to the year 1776." Thus, the rule of strict precedent was derived from the very conception of the nature of common law principles as preexisting standards discoverable by judges. Since "Judges cannot make law," the younger Daniel Dulany maintained in 1767, ". . . if they take upon themselves to frame a regulation, *in prospect*, which is to govern in [the] future, and which they have so framed, not to determine a case existing before them, but for the determination of cases that may happen, they essentially assume a power legislative." Just as the framing of general rules to guide future conduct was conceived of as a legislative function, judicial innovation itself was regarded as an impermissible exercise of will. This fundamental distinction between the very bases of legitimacy of common law and legislation determined the modest role the former played in the process of social change. In short, for the jurist of the eighteenth century, it was important, as Supreme Court Justice James Iredell declared in 1793, "that the distinct boundaries of law and Legislation [not] be confounded," since "that would make Courts arbitrary, and in effect *makers of a new law*, instead of being (as certainly they alone ought to be) *expositors of an existing one.*"[34]

---

34. *Adams Legal Papers*, II, 127; Goebel, *The Law Practice of Alexander Hamilton*, I, 50n; West v. Stigar, 1 H. & McH. 247, 254 (Md. 1767); Chisholm v. Georgia, 2 Dall. 419, 448 (1793) (emphasis in original).

Horwitz : An Instrumental Conception of Law    299

## II. Common Law Crimes: The Breakdown of the Eighteenth-Century Conception of Law

ONE of the most interesting manifestations of the breakdown of a unitary conception of the common law is the remarkable attack on the doctrine of federal common law crimes that emerged in the last years of the eighteenth century. Unheard of before 1793 and, with one exception, uniformly rejected by American judges during the first two decades of the Republic, the opposition to common law crimes nevertheless prevailed when in 1812 the United States Supreme Court declared that it had "been long since settled in public opinion" that a person could not be convicted of a Federal crime without a statute.[35]

What was the nature of the attack on federal common law crimes? Basically, there were two arguments, the first deriving from states rights constitutional theories, the second reflecting a changing conception of the nature of law. Growing out of Jeffersonian hostility to criminal indictments of American citizens for pro-French activities,[36] the constitutional objection to common law crimes boiled down to the assertion that if the federal judiciary possessed jurisdiction to impose criminal sanctions without a statute it would be able to obliterate all constitutional limitations on the federal government. "[I]f the principle were to prevail," Thomas Jefferson wrote in 1800, "of a common law being in force in the United States" it would "possess . . . the general government at once of all the powers of the State Governments and reduce . . . us to a single consolidated government."[37]

35. United States v. Hudson & Goodwin, 7 Cranch 32 (1812). This view has prevailed even though several members of the Supreme Court were disposed to reconsider the case four years later. At that time, however, the United States Attorney General refused to argue that the *Hudson* case should be overturned, and as a result, the Supreme Court did not reconsider its decision. United States v. Coolidge, 1 Wheat. 415 (1816). For a learned discussion of the subject, see Peter S. DuPonceau, *A Dissertation on the Nature and Extent of the Jurisdiction of the Courts of the United States* (Philadelphia, 1824).

36. For the political background of the battle over federal common law crimes, see Charles Warren, *The Supreme Court in United States History* (Boston, 1922), I, 157–164.

37. *The Writings of Thomas Jefferson*, ed. Paul Leister Ford (New York, 1892–1899),

Although it was reiterated many times over, it is difficult to understand precisely what the Jeffersonian argument was all about. In spite of his Jeffersonian loyalties, James Sullivan of Massachusetts understood that the question of common law jurisdiction involved no special constitutional difficulties, for all that it required was that federal common law jurisdiction be limited to those substantive crimes over which Congress had legislative power.[38] In short, if Congress could not constitutionally make an activity criminal, the courts could not impose common law criminal sanctions. There would be no greater danger of a federal court punishing activity beyond the scope of federal power than of Congress passing a statute exceeding those same limits.

There are still greater mysteries associated with the Jeffersonian constitutional position on common law crimes. Most thoughtful representatives of that position agreed that Congress could legitimately confer common law power on the courts to punish activities within the reach of federal constitutional power.[39] All that

---

VII, 451. A year earlier Jefferson had written that "Of all the doctrines which have been broached by the federal government, the novel one, of the common law being in force & cognizable as an existing law in their courts, is to me the most formidable. . . . If this assumption be yielded to, the state courts may be shut up." *Ibid.*, VII, 383–384.

38. [James Sullivan], *A Dissertation upon the Constitutional Freedom of the Press* (Boston, 1801), pp. 31, 40–41, 48–54. In his opinion in *United States v. Coolidge* (1 Gall. 488 [C.C.A. Mass. 1813]), Mr. Justice Story denied that there was a threat of federal usurpation in the argument in favor of common law crimes. "I admit in the most explicit terms," he wrote, "that the Courts of the United States are Courts of limited jurisdiction, and cannot exercise any authorities which are not confided to them by the Constitution and laws made in pursuance thereof."

39. In *United States v. Hudson & Goodwin*, 7 Cranch 32 (1812), the Supreme Court declared that it was "unnecessary" to decide whether Congress could confer common law jurisdiction on the federal courts, since it was "enough that such jurisdiction has not been conferred by any legislative act." But one year later, the author of that opinion, Mr. Justice Johnson wrote: "We do not deny, nor we suppose was it ever denied—that if . . . Congress had by Law vested in this Court jurisdiction over all cases to which the punishing power of the United States might . . . be extended, it would then rest with this Court to decide (wild and devious as the track assigned them would be) to what cases that jurisdiction extended." *Trial of William Butler for Piracy (1813)* (n.d., n.p.), pp. 34–35. (The text of this unreported circuit court opinion appears in a pamphlet in the Treasure Room, Harvard Law School Library.) See also *Blackstone's Commentaries: With Notes of Reference to the Constitution and Laws of the Federal Government of the United States and of the Commonwealth of Virginia*, ed. St. George Tucker (Philadelphia, 1803), I, Part I, pp. 429–430.

Horwitz : An Instrumental Conception of Law    301

was lacking, they maintained, was that Congress in fact had not done so in the Judiciary Act of 1789.[40] Yet, they were thereby conceding that if Congress had passed an act similar to those enacted after the Revolution by state legislatures adopting the common law as the rule of decision, there would be no special constitutional problem. Indeed, this approach laid bare the proposition that there was no real issue concerning the proper allocation of powers between national and state governments, and, in fact, that the only respectable constitutional question involved the separation of powers between legislature and judiciary. And it was here that the campaign against common law crimes revealed the changing conception of the nature of law.

Beginning sometime in the 1780s and reaching a highpoint in the first decade of the nineteenth century, American jurists succeeded in dethroning the common law from the unchallenged place it had occupied in the jurisprudence of the revolutionary generation. It would be "in vain," St. George Tucker wrote in his famous 1803 edition of Blackstone, that we should "attempt, by a *general theory*, to establish an uniform authority and obligation in the common law of England, over the American colonies, at any period between the first migrations to this country, and that epoch, which annihilated the sovereignty of the crown of England over them." Emphasizing the differences between rules of the English common law and those of the American colonies as well as the diversity among the various colonies themselves, he argued that "it would require the talents of an Alfred to harmonize and digest into one system such opposite, discordant, and conflicting municipal institutions, as composed the codes of the several colonies of the period of the revolution."[41]

Tucker's attack on the conception of a unitary common law constituted the foundation of a more general assault on the uncertainty and unpredictability of common law adjudication. The di-

---

40. Modern scholarship has suggested that the Act did confer such jurisdiction on the federal courts. See Charles Warren "The History of the Federal Judiciary Act of 1789," *Harvard Law Review*, 37 (1923), 73.

41. *Blackstone's Commentaries*, I, Part I, p. 405.

versity of the past, he emphasized, threatened uncertainty in the future. If the common law did not represent a known and discoverable body of legal rules, how could it provide either for the liberty of the citizen or for the protection of property? Indeed, these jurisprudential concerns as much as any question of constitutional allocation of power led the Virginia General Assembly in 1800 to instruct its United States Senators that the assertion of federal common law criminal jurisdiction "opens a new code of sanguinary criminal law, both obsolete and unknown, and either wholly rejected or essentially modified in almost all its parts by State institutions. . . . It subjects the citizen to punishment, according to the judiciary will, when he is left in ignorance of what this law enjoins as a duty, or prohibits as a crime."[42]

Due to an excessive preoccupation with the political and constitutional dimensions of the struggle over common law crimes, historians have not fully appreciated the underlying change in the conception of law that laid the foundation for the constitutional struggle. For it is clear that the decline in the authority of the common law was neither coextensive with party loyalty nor with constitutional philosophy. For example, the leading target of Jeffersonian attacks of the judiciary, Federalist Justice Samuel Chase, was also the first federal judge to hold that there were no federal common law crimes. In *United States v. Worrall* (1798)—delivered one year before the question burst forth as a political issue—Chase declared that since "the whole of the common law of England has been no where introduced" in America and since "the common law . . . of one State, is not the common law of another," there could be no general common law of the United States. Dismissing a common law indictment for bribery of a federal official, he argued that it was "essential, that Congress should define the offenses to be tried, and apportion the punishments to be inflicted." Even if Congress had declared and defined the offense, he added, it would be "improper" for a judge to exercise discretion in prescribing punishments. Thus, even where there was no need to discover and

42. Printed in *ibid.*, p. 438.

Horwitz : An Instrumental Conception of Law     303

apply common law rules, Chase maintained that only legislative standards could legitimize judicial discretion.[43]

Although fear of judicial discretion had long been part of colonial political rhetoric, it is remarkable that before the last decade of the eighteenth century it was not associated with attacks on the common law jurisdiction of the judiciary. As late as 1786, Pennsylvania Admiralty Judge Francis Hopkinson attacked an amendment of the Commonwealth's penal laws on the ground that it conferred discretion on judges to impose punishments within certain limits. "This is," he protested, "in fact vesting them with legislative authority within those limits. It is a distinguishing mark of a free government, that the people shall know before hand, the penalty which the laws annex to every offense; and, therefore, such a system is called a government of laws, and not of men. But within the scope of the present bill, no offender can tell what his punishment is to be, till after conviction. The *quantum*, at least, is to be determined by the particular state of mind the judge happens to be in at the time of passing sentence." Nevertheless, even though he wrote two lengthy articles largely anticipating the challenge to common law crimes during the next decade, Hopkinson never so much as mentioned the problem of convicting an individual without a statute.[44] Common law standards, it appears, were just not conceived of as allowing a judge discretion.

Similarly, the eighteenth-century debates over the obligation of English statutes in the colonies invariably brought forth concern over judicial discretion. As early as 1701, an anonymous Virginian wrote that the doctrine that only those Acts of Parliament were binding "where the Reason is the same here, that it is in England" was opposed by some as "leaving too great a latitude to the Judge. . . ." Without some guide as to the authority of British statutes, he concluded, "we [are] left in the dark in one of the most considerable Points of our Rights, and the Case being so doubtful,

---

43. United States v. Worrall, 2 Dall. 384 (1798).
44. *The Miscellaneous Essays and Occasional Writings of Francis Hopkinson* (Philadelphia, 1792), II, 97.

we are too often obliged to depend upon the Crooked Cord of a Judge's Discretion in matters of the greatest moment and value."[45] Yet, there was no indication that the writer saw any problem of judicial discretion in applying common law as opposed to legislative rules. In spite of a continuing colonial preoccupation with the "uncertainty" of statutory rules, there is no evidence that before the Revolution Americans ever thought that the reception of common law principles endowed judges with the power to be arbitrary.

One of the few suggestions that colonials had any qualms about imposing criminal punishments without a statute occurs in a 1712 Connecticut case. After a trial of one Daniel Gard, the jury returned a special verdict. Finding certain facts true, the jury declared that "whether . . . Daniel Gard is guilty of murther or manslaughter we leave to the discretion of the court." The judges, in turn, adjourned the case and inquired of the Assembly whether they might determine the nature of the crime "by the rules of the common law, there being not so particular direction for the resolution of that point contained in our printed laws." In addition, if they should decide that the defendant had committed only manslaughter, they wished to know "what directions the Judges ought to have reference to in determining the punishment and giving sentence." The Assembly replied that the Judges might, "in the case above proposed, determine by the rules of the common law."[46]

It is, of course, quite difficult to make much out of this sparse record. Why did the judges see any difficulty in applying the common law? Was it that they anticipated some modern conception of the primary legitimacy of statute law? If indeed they did believe that the legislature was the only legitimate agency for defining punishments, it still does not seem that it was because they believed that "the rules of the common law" were uncertain or unascertainable. More likely, they were merely reflecting the burden under

45. *An Essay upon the Government of the English Plantations on the Continent of America*, ed. Louis B. Wright (San Marino, 1945), pp. 23, 39.

46. *The Superior Court Diary of William Samuel Johnson*, ed. John T. Farrell (Washington, 1942), p. xviii. In another Connecticut criminal case in 1743, the legislature told the court that since there was no statute the judge should prescribe a penalty "according to their best skill and judgment." *Ibid.*, p. xviii n. 3.

Horwitz : An Instrumental Conception of Law      305

which all colonial jurists labored in the early years of the eighteenth century: uncertainty as to whether they were entitled at all to use and apply common law rules in this newly settled land. It seems therefore that, at most, the judges were looking to the legislature for authority to impose common law standards in criminal cases. Whatever the judges thought, however, it is clear that the Connecticut Assembly had no difficulty in believing that a direction to "determine" the case "by the rules of the common law" conveyed a clear and intelligible guide. Indeed, after this legislative direction, the judges themselves were able to determine the appropriate level of guilt.

Whatever one makes of the Gard case, it is plain that the specific attack upon common law crimes emerges from a distinctively post-revolutionary conviction that the common law was both uncertain and unpredictable. For example, even before the issue was turned into a constitutional question at the national level it began to surface in the states as well shortly after the Revolution. In his "Dissertation on the Act Adopting the Common and Statute Laws of England" (1793), Vermont Chief Justice Nathaniel Chipman "lay[s] it down as an unalterable rule that no Court, in this State, ought ever to pronounce sentence of death upon the authority of a common law precedent, without the authority of a statute." And two years later, in his treatise on Connecticut law, Zepheniah Swift, soon to be that state's chief justice, indicated that he too was troubled by the doctrine "that every crime committed against the law of nature may be punished at the discretion of the judge, where the legislature has not appointed a particular punishment." Distinguishing between "crimes which are expressly defined by statute or common law" and those actions over which "courts of law have assumed a discretionary power of punishing," he warned that judges "ought to exercise [the latter] power with great circumspection and caution," since "the supreme excellency of a code of criminal laws consists in defining every act that is punishable with such certainty and accuracy, that no man shall be exposed to the danger of incurring a penalty without knowing it." It would be unjust, he continued, for "a man [to] do an act, which he knows

306                Perspectives in American History

has never been punished, and against which there is no law, yet upon a prosecution for it, the court may by a determination subsequent to the act, judge it to be a crime, and inflict on him a severe punishment." "This mode of proceeding," he concluded, "manifestly partakes of the odious nature of an *ex post facto* law."[47] While Swift clearly did not abandon the natural law framework within which common law crimes traditionally had been understood, he was no longer prepared to assume that even the first judicial pronouncement of a legal rule was merely a declaration of some known and preexisting standard of natural law. Indeed, his entire discussion assumed the inability of individuals to know their legal duties without some express legislative or judicial pronouncement. Though it was left to others to extend Swift's analysis to the whole of common law crimes, his preoccupation with the unfairness of administering a system of judge-made criminal law was a distinctly postrevolutionary phenomenon, reflecting a profound change in sensibility. For the inarticulate premise that lay behind Swift's warnings against the danger of judicial discretion was a growing perception that judges no longer merely discovered law; they also made it.

Even at the national level, the problem soon transcended the constitutional rhetoric with which it had first been associated. In 1813, the question arose whether without a statute a person could be punished in admiralty for murder on the high seas. What distinguished this case from its predecessors was that there was no doubt that the Constitution had conferred exclusive jurisdiction in admiralty on the federal courts; thus, unlike earlier cases, no question could be raised of the federal court's exceeding their constitutional powers. Even so, Supreme Court Justice William Johnson, on circuit, held that there could be no punishment. "[I]t was a favorite object" of the framers of the Constitution, he wrote, "to leave no one to search for the road of safety or the *Dii Limini* between crime and innocence, anywhere but in the Statute Book of the Legislative body they were about creating." In the colonies as

47. N. Chipman's Rep. 61, 67. Zephaniah Swift, *A System of the Laws of the State of Connecticut* (Windham, Conn., 1795–1796), II, 365–366.

## Horwitz : An Instrumental Conception of Law     307

well, he argued, "the adoption of the Common Law, depended upon the voluntary act of the legislative power of the several States . . ." and not, as had previously been assumed, on some inherent obligation deriving from natural law or custom. Denying that the whole of the common law had been received in any state before the Revolution, or that the use of common law terms in statutes gave any "more validity to the Common Law than use of terms peculiar to the Civil or Cannon [sic] Law would to the latter," he concluded that the recognition of common law crimes even in Admiralty would invite "judicial discretion." Such a system "would . . . increase the oddity of the state of things," since "the judiciary would have then to decide what system they would adopt as their guide on the Law of Nations, or be left at large to be governed by their own views on the Fitness of things."[48]

As the attack on common law crimes became more and more dissociated from its originally narrow constitutional basis, there appeared in 1819 a remarkable and influential book articulating the problem entirely in terms of a new conception of law. In *Historical Sketches of the Principles and Maxims of American Jurisprudence,* Ohio lawyer John Milton Goodenow inquired for the first time whether common law crimes could be in force even in an individual state. Beginning his inquiry with a general analysis of the nature of legal obligation, his initial axioms reveal how far many Americans had moved from eighteenth-century natural law assumptions:

[L]aws, which man creates from himself, in his social state, are not the emanations of Divine Will, nor yet the pure institutions of nature and reason; but changeable and arbitrary in their formation; they are necessarily of a *positive, local existence*; made, declared and *published* in a shape and character clear and unequivocal to all to whom they are directed; otherwise, they could never become obligatory: because they are not of intuition, discoverable by the eye of reason.

Confining the obligations of natural law entirely to "what may be called the right of conscience," and asserting that for violations of natural law man "is accountable for error in judgment to none but

48. *The Trial of William Butler for Piracy*, pp. 28, 21–25, 32.

308                    Perspectives in American History

his GOD," Goodenow concluded that the principles of natural law "may be disregarded and lie for ages buried beneath the rubbish of human invention."

Our ears are often saluted in our courts of justice, with a sort of text to all common law arguments, that "law is the perfection of reason—that a law against reason is void—that no man is bound to obey a municipal law which infringes the law of nature." If such a doctrine were in fact to prevail, the blood of half mankind would flow in its execution.

From these premises Goodenow moved on to argue that "all human laws for the punishment of crimes, are mere matters of social policy; diverse in different states as their political purposes, forms and ends of government, are diverse." Criminal laws depended "no more upon man's natural reason, no more consonant therewith, than the political shade and texture of the time in which they are made." It followed that the only legitimate authority that could impose criminal sanctions was the legislature by means of statutory enactment. "The judge . . . of a criminal tribunal," Goodenow concluded, "is *governed* himself by *positive* law, and executes and inforces the will of the supreme power, which is the will of THE PEOPLE."[49]

With Goodenow's *Historical Sketches* we see most clearly the always implicit relationship between the attack on common law crimes and more general changes in political theory and conceptions of the nature of law. Our task now is to see more precisely how these changes came about, and finally, to determine how these transformations in legal theory led ultimately to an instrumental conception of common law.

49. John Milton Goodenow, *Historical Sketches of the Principles and Maxims of American Jurisprudence in Contrast With the Doctrines of the English Common Law on the Subject of Crimes and Punishments* (Steubenville, Ohio, 1819), pp. 3–4, 6, 33. For a discussion of Goodenow's influence on Ohio law, see Alexander Hadden, *Why Are There No Common Law Crimes in Ohio?* (Cleveland, 1919). It is important to note, however, that despite his far-reaching attack on common law crimes, Goodenow expressly exempted common law civil actions from his analysis. "Civil actions," he wrote, "are founded in the private rights and private wrongs of the individuals; in which the legislative power of the civil state has nothing to do. Natural justice and right reason, are foundation of all our private rights." Goodenow, *Historical Sketches*, p. 36.

## iii. The Emergence of an Instrumental Conception of Law

BEFORE the American Revolution, we have seen, common law and statute law were conceived of as two separate bodies of law, and the authority of judges and legislators was justified in terms of the special category of law that they administered. This dichotomy between the nature of the two forms of law was itself a fairly recent creation, reflecting the beginnings of the modern conception of sovereignty.[50] For example, when Lord Coke, in deciding *Calvin's Case* in 1608, held that English law was not automatically received in conquered territories, there was no suggestion of a distinction between statute and common law, for statutes were still largely conceived of as an expression of custom. We begin to see a different treatment accorded to the two forms of law early in the eighteenth century as represented by Attorney General West's 1720 statement confining the problem of reception to parliamentary acts. As statutes begin to be understood as a command of the sovereign, the formula governing reception thus takes on a function entirely different from Coke's formulation, raising the question of the basis of obedience to rules not derived from natural law principles. Finally, as the principle of sovereignty emerges full-blown in English law by the second half of the century, Blackstone is again able to maintain, with an eye towards the emerging constitutional struggles in the colonies, that both statute and common law are not received in America.[51]

It is not generally appreciated to what extent the American experience after the Revolution recapitulated that of the English. As much as they attacked the Blackstonian conception of a single and indivisible sovereignty, Americans after the Revolution began widely to accept the modern theory of law underlying that conception. While they disputed the supremacy of parliament, they simultaneously argued that written constitutions were legitimate

50. Samuel E. Thorne, *A Discourse upon the . . . Statutes . . .* (San Marino, 1942); J. W. Gough, *Fundamental Law in English Constitutional History* (Oxford, 1955), pp. 117–122.
51. Blackstone, *Commentaries*, I, 108–109.

because they embodied the "will" of the people. And as they sought to redefine the basis of legal obligation in terms of popular sovereignty, they tended to assert the ultimate primacy of the legislature and of statute law. The result was that the original natural law foundation of common law rules began to disintegrate.

The demand for codification of all laws, based on the principle that "in republics, the very nature of the constitution requires the judges to follow the letter of the law," emerged with particular vigor after the Revolution. If judges "put such a construction on matters as they think most agreeable to the spirit and reason of the law," the author of *People the Best Governors* argued, "they assume what is in fact the prerogative of the legislature, for those that made the laws ought to give them a meaning when they are doubtful." In fact, courts "must take the law as it is," another commentator argued, "and by all due and proper means execute it, without any pretense to judge of its right or wrong."[52]

What underlay these demands for codification was a new conviction that much of the English common law itself was a product of the whim of judges. Of great importance was the reforming work of Lord Mansfield in England, which convinced many Americans that judges could not be depended on merely to apply existing law. More than any other factor, it appears, Mansfield's decisions convinced Thomas Jefferson that a check need be established on the common law powers of judges. While "the object of former judges ha[d] been to render the law more & more certain," Jefferson wrote in 1785, Mansfield had sought "to render it more uncertain under pretence of rendering it more reasonable. No period of English law of what ever length it be taken, can be produced wherein so many of it's [sic] settled rules have been reversed as during the time of this judge." As a result, he concluded, Mansfield's "accession to the bench should form the epoch, after which all recurrence to English decisions should be proscribed. . . ." In some of his work, in fact, Jefferson went even further. Reporting on the efforts of the Virginia codifiers, Jefferson declared that "the common law of England, by which is meant that part of the Eng-

52. Quoted in Wood, *The Creation of the American Republic*, pp. 301–302.

### Horwitz : An Instrumental Conception of Law       311

lish law which was anterior to the date of the oldest statutes extant," was "made the basis" of the code. He was thus prepared to
limit common law reception to rules existing in the thirteenth
century, if not before![53]

In the course of several decades, the destruction of a conception
of a fixed and determinate common law would lead to the position
ultimately articulated by Robert Rantoul in his famous plea for
codification in 1836. "Why," he asked, "is an *ex post facto* law,
passed by the legislature, unjust, unconstitutional, and void, while
judge-made law, which, from its nature, must always be *ex post
facto*, is not only to be obeyed, but applauded."[54] By the time Rantoul asked the question, judges and jurists had begun to rebuild the
old natural law justification of the common law on top of a newer
theory of precedent, a course of events that is beyond the scope of
this paper. In the immediate post-revolutionary period, however,
the defense of common law was far different, representing an effort
to find a unitary foundation for both statute and common law.

This special crisis of common law adjudication after the American Revolution can be seen most dramatically in Supreme Court
Justice James Wilson's "Lectures on Law" delivered in 1791. The
central purpose of these lectures, he pointed out, was to demonstrate that Blackstone's assertion that law is the will of a superior
was "an improper principle," since "the sole legitimate principle
of obedience to human laws is human consent." In the process,
however, Wilson revealed the extent to which he had come under
the spell of the modern conception of law as a sovereign command.
"It is agreed, on all hands," he acknowledged, "that, in every state,
there must be somewhere a power supreme, arbitrary, absolute,
uncontrollable." The only dispute concerned "where does this
power reside."

53. Jefferson, *Writings*, IV, 115; *Notes on the State of Virginia* (Richmond, 1853), p. 148.
On pre-revolutionary efforts to find a "pure" common law system in ancient English
law, see Bailyn, *Pamphlets*, I, 26–27; J. G. A. Pocock, *The Ancient Constitution and the
Feudal Law* (Cambridge, Eng., 1957). One of Jefferson's earliest efforts to put forth a
theory of an ancient common law appears in "Whether Christianity is Part of the Common Law," (1764?), *Writings*, I, 360.

54. "Oration at Scituate" (1836) in *Memoirs, Speechs and Writings of Robert Rantoul,
Jr.*, ed. Luther Hamilton (Boston, 1854), p. 278.

While Wilson continued to acknowledge the obligations derived from natural law, unlike his predecessors he reduced them to private questions of conscience. For the fundamental question was "whether a man can be bound by any human authority, except his own consent?"

Let us suppose, that one demands obedience from me to a certain injunction, which he calls a law. . . . I ask him, why am I obliged to obey it? He says it is just that I should do it. Justice, I tell him, is a part of the law of nature; give me a reason drawn from human authority . . . he assails me on a very different quarter; and softening his accents, represents how generous, nay how humane, it would be, to do as he desires. Humanity is a duty; generosity a virtue; but neither is to be referred to human authority.

Thus, the basis of obedience of law was set entirely within the modern framework of a will theory of law, however much Wilson argued over whose will ultimately legitimized legal commands. This definition of the basis of obligation in terms of popular will was a far cry from the eighteenth-century conception of obligation derived from the inherent rightness or justice of law.

The result was a distinctly postrevolutionary phenomenon: an attempt to reconstruct the legitimacy not simply of statutes, but of common law rules, on a consensual foundation. Wilson, for example, insisted that custom was "of itself, intrinsick evidence of consent."

How was a custom introduced? By voluntary adoption. How did it become general? By the instances of voluntary adoption being increased. How did it become lasting? By voluntary and satisfactory experience, which ratified and confirmed what voluntary adoption had introduced. In the introduction, in the extension, in the continuance of customary law, we find the operations of consent universally predominant.

Thus, he concluded, the "origin of [the] obligatory force" of the common law rested "on nothing else, but free and voluntary *consent*."[55]

That Wilson had gone a long way towards the Blackstonian position can be seen by contrasting his argument with that of St.

55. *The Works of James Wilson*, ed. Robert G. McCloskey, (Cambridge, 1967), I, 180; II, 506; I, 121–122; I, 353ff. Wood, *The Creation of the American Republic*, pp. 292–296.

Horwitz : An Instrumental Conception of Law    313

George Tucker, who was equally desirous of resisting Blackstone's propositions concerning sovereignty. While Blackstone "presupposes an act of the legislature in every case whatsoever," Tucker maintained that "there is more ingenuity than truth in the idea . . . that all the unwritten rules of law are founded upon some positive Statute, the memory of which has been lost." But as he moved further from Blackstone's definition of sovereignty, Tucker tended to emphasize "immemorial Custom, and Usage" as sources of legitimacy opposed to sovereignty. Though he succeeded to some extent in resisting the pressure of Blackstone, he exposed even more the vulnerability of a system of common law adjudication under a regime of popular sovereignty.[56]

The problem of fitting the common law into an emerging system of popular sovereignty became the central task of judges and jurists at the turn of the century. One response and one of the most subtle shifts in the theory underlying the legitimacy of common law rules can be seen in Jesse Root's short essays, "The Origin of Government and Laws in Connecticut" and "On the Common Law of Connecticut" published in 1798 as an introduction to the first volume of Root's Connecticut Reports. Root sought to expose the "ignorance of those who are clamorous for a new constitution" that would end the authority of English law, emphasizing the "mistake of those who suppose that the rules of the common law of England are the common law of Connecticut, until altered by a statute." Pointing to the feudal origins of English law, he insisted that the citizens of Connecticut had long followed their own indigenous common law. "Their common law," he declared, "was derived from the law of nature and revelation; those rules and maxims of immutable truth and justice, which arise from the eternal fitness of things, which need only to be understood, to be submitted to, as they are themselves the highest authority."

Not only does Root's analysis at this point seem highly traditional, but if that were all there were it would be quite remarkable. One just does not find Americans at the turn of the century who ultimately rest upon immutable natural law principles while insist-

56. *Blackstone's Commentaries*, I, Part I, p. 53 n. 10.

ing at the same time on a separate and distinct body of indigenous American legal rules. But true to form, Root also found it necessary to explain the American deviation by the unifying principle of consent. There was, he wrote, "another branch of common law . . . derived from certain usages and customs, universally assented to and adopted in practice by the citizens at large . . ." which "courts of justice take notice of . . . as rules of right, and as having the force of laws."

But how does custom become law? No longer able to equate custom with obligatory natural law, Root's answer demonstrated the impact of the Blackstonian will theory of law. "That these customs and usages must have existed immemorially, and have been compulsory, in order to their being recognized to be law; seems to involve some degree of absurdity—that is, they must have the compulsory force of laws, before they can be recognized to be laws, when they can have no compulsory force till the powers of government have communicated it to them by declaring them to be laws." It was not enough that customs became law as soon as their origins were forgotten; "this may be necessary in arbitrary governments, but in a free government like ours," Root continued, there was a "better reason." Just as statutes are binding because they have been enacted with the consent of the legislature, he concluded, "so these unwritten customs and regulations . . . have the sanction of universal consent and adoption in practice" and for that reason courts of justice may declare them to be obligatory. "The reasonableness and utility of their operation, and the universality of their adoption" were the best evidence "of their having the general consent and approbation." Before he had finished, therefore, Root was forced to retreat from the traditional natural law framework with which he had begun. By insisting that America had its own common law, he managed ultimately to justify the "compulsory force" both of statute and common law by the single legitimating principle of consent.[57]

While Root sought to save the common law by appealing to an indigenous body of common law principles to which the people of

57. 1 Root's Conn. Rep. iv, ix–xiii.

Horwitz : An Instrumental Conception of Law      315

Connecticut had consented, there were others, such as James Sullivan of Massachusetts, who attempted to rest the old conception of a universal law on a new foundation of popular sovereignty. While rules concerning real estate, Sullivan pointed out, had always rested on local statutes or customs, legal doctrines governing "personal estate [are] not fixed to any place or country, and contracts depend on the *jus gentium* (the general law of nations) for their origin and their expositions, rather than on any municipal regulations of particular countries. . . . As personal contracts are founded in commerce, they cannot rest on the particular laws of one country only; but ought to be the subject of those principles of the general law of nations, which are acknowledged by the world." But Sullivan was no longer content to rest his appeal to a universal law on an eighteenth-century trust in natural law principles. While these legal rules were "transfer[red] . . . with certainty from age to age" through the "written institutes" and "reports" of the common lawyers, "it may be asked, where do these books derive an authority to become the law of the land?" "The answer," Sullivan concluded, equating statute and common law, "is that the most solemn act of legislation is no more than an expression of the public will." These principles had been "received" as "principles, to which the people of the country have, for a long time together, submitted, considering them as proper and useful."

If this explanation still sounded too much like the mere submission to custom which Root had found prevalent "in arbitrary governments" Sullivan restated his conclusion in a somewhat different way. "[I]t may be inquired," he wrote, "how are the English institutes and reporters evidence of the will of the American nation, or of this Commonwealth? The answer is, that the will of the people is expressed in the constitution, which they have of their own authority established for their Commonwealth." Since "the voice of the people has established this [common law] system, so far only as it had been before adopted and practiced upon," it was "the judges . . . who [were] to decide . . . whether a principle, urged as law, had heretofore been in practice."[58]

58. James Sullivan, *Land Titles*, pp. 337–340.

316        Perspectives in American History

The result of this transformation in the underlying basis for the legitimacy of the common law was that jurists began to conceive of the common law as an instrument of will. Delivering his charge to the jury in the 1806 prosecution of the Philadelphia Cordwainers for common law conspiracy, Mayor's Court Judge Moses Levy declared that the jury was "bound to conform" to the common law rule "even though we do not comprehend the principle upon which it was founded."

We are not to reject it because we do not see the reason of it. It is enough, that it is the will of the majority. It is law because it is their will—if it is law, there may be good reasons for it though we cannot find them out.[59]

Nevertheless, this view of law was decidedly a two-edged sword. While nineteenth-century judges were satisfied to limit the discretion of juries by reminding them that "unwritten custom" and "written law . . . are both equally the act of the legislature," their own behavior reflected James Sullivan's view that they had been given a popular charter to mould legal doctrine according to broad conceptions of public policy. In their influential lectures at the Litchfield Law School, Judges Tapping Reeve and James Gould reflected this changed conception of law. By 1813, they were instructing students in the Blackstonian definition of municipal law as "a rule of civil conduct prescribed by the supreme power of the state commanding what is right and prohibiting what is wrong." Not only had all of the earlier qualifications of the Blackstonian argument that had preoccupied James Wilson and St. George Tucker completely disappeared, but with their disappearance came a candid recognition of the new basis of the common law. "Theoretical[ly] courts make no law," they declared, "but in point of fact they are legislators." And after citing cases where courts had made law, they inquired: "How then could these laws have been prescribed by a supreme power in a state? By the acquiescence of the legislature, they impliedly consented to these laws, and it is immaterial whether this consent be subsequent or antecedent to there [sic] birth." Finally, with a dash of irony, they laid to rest the old conception of law.

59. Commonwealth v. Pullis in Commons, _A Documentary History_, III, 233.

### Horwitz : An Instrumental Conception of Law    317

How can [common law rules] be said to have existed from time immemorial, when there [sic] origin is notorious. The Judges of the Courts of Judicature are considered as the depositories of the common law. Therefore when they lay down a new, and before unheard of rule of law, they are supposed to take from this repository, where it had laid dormant and unwanted from time immemorial.[60]

As judges began to conceive of themselves as legislators, the criteria by which they shaped legal doctrine began to change as well. The principle upon which judges ought to decide whether to adhere to a series of decisions, one jurist noted, "resolves *itself into a question of expediency*." "But what shall be the test of . . . error" in prior decisions? he asked. "*I know nothing but the mind that is to judge.*" As a result, during the first two decades of the nineteenth century judges begin to conceive of themselves as the leading agents of legal change. Since "a Legislature must establish a general unbending rule," Zephaniah Swift argued in 1810, while "courts possess a discretion of shaping their rules to every possible variety of circumstance," there "is a vital principle, inherent in the constitution of the judiciary . . . furnishing remedies according to the growing wants, and varying circumstances of men, . . . without waiting for the slow progress of Legislative interference."[61]

One of the most dramatic manifestations of the new role of courts is a Pennsylvania statute of 1807 empowering the judges of the Supreme Court to decide which English statutes were in force in the Commonwealth. While the delegation of so explicit and self-conscious a legislative function to judges would have been inconceivable even two decades earlier, it was completely in tune with newly emerging perception of law as will. Reflecting this

60. Hugh Henry Brackenridge, *Law Miscellanies* (Philadelphia, 1814), p. 84; Elisha D. Whittlesey, "Reeve & Gould's Lectures," (1813) I, 1 (Unpublished MS.4024, Treasure Room, Harvard Law School Library); "Reeve's Lectures" (n.d.), I, 4–5 (Unpublished MS.2013, Treasure Room, Harvard Law School Library). There is a similar, but much less detailed, discussion of the same point in the Whittlesey manuscript, above, I, 6–7, which suggests that these remarks were made around 1813. In another undated manuscript, reprinted in Joseph H. Smith, *Development of Legal Institutions* (St. Paul, 1965), pp. 479–481, Reeve declares that in new cases courts "to all intents make the law. . . ." On the basis of the latest English report cited in the manuscript, Smith dates it at 1802.

61. Brackenridge, *Law Miscellanies*, pp. 54, 52 (emphasis in original); Zephaniah Swift, *A Digest of the Law of Evidence* (Hartford, 1810), pp. v–vi.

change, Pennsylvania Supreme Court Justice Hugh Henry Brackenridge strongly argued in 1808 for the abolition of the common
law and the introduction of statutory codification. By 1814, however, he was prepared to deplore "the sullenness: or affected timidity of English judges, in the narrowness of their construction of
powers given." Judges bind themselves to precedent, he observed,
only because they have "a dread of innovation," while in fact "*departure* from rule can be justified only by *success*." The two greatest
obstacles to change were "attachment to decisions" and "timidity
of mind in effecting a reform." Judges, he insisted, are the archi-
tects of the legal system. The bulk of judges "trudge on through
the slough as Hodge did *even after the bridge was built*; so far are they
from attempting *to build a bridge*. Such may have the praise of being
what are *sound lawyers*; but they must be contented with this, and
cannot be called *great judges*." A great judge, he argued, "who has
traversed all space of legal science," can be a reformer if "such a
mind happened to be at the head of the highest court." While "no
one but a *skilful architect* . . . who can have the whole edifice in his
mind," ought to undertake the task of legal change, he concluded,
reform is preeminently the judge's task, for "the legislature can act
only in detail, and in particulars, whereas the able judge can remove at once, or alter, what was originally faulty or has become
disproportioned in the building."[62]

As Brackenridge's observations indicate, one of the most universal features of postrevolutionary American jurisprudence was
an attack on the colonial subservience to precedent. Even conservative jurists like Vermont Chief Justice Nathaniel Chipman complained that the legal profession had followed precedents "with
too great veneration." These precedents, he noted in his "Dissertation of the Act Adopting the Common and Statute Laws of England" in 1793, "were made at a time when the state of society, and
of property were very different from what they are at present."

---

62. For the report of the Judges declaring which English statutes were binding in
Pennsylvania, see 3 Bin. 595 (1808). [Hugh Henry Brackenridge], *Considerations on the
Jurisprudence of the State of Pennsylvania* (Philadelphia, 1808). Brackenridge, *Law Mis-
cellanies*, pp. 382, 469, 75 (emphasis in original).

## Horwitz : An Instrumental Conception of Law  319

Moreover, many common law doctrines were formulated "in an age when the minds of men were fettered in forms [and] when forms were held to be substances, and abstractions real entities." As a result, at common law "technical reasoning and unmeaning maxims . . . frequently supplied the place of principles." In America, he emphasized, substance is more important than form. Consequently, Blackstone's rule of strict adherence to precedent might suffice in England, where "by too easy departure, Judges might unwarily disturb property acquired on the faith of such precedents." But to follow "arbitrary rules," or "arbitrary decisions" without understanding that they "arose out of [a different] state of society" would be "certainly contrary to the principles of our government and the spirit of our laws."[63]

Chipman's "Dissertation" reflects the beginnings of a post-revolutionary functionalism in American law. His emphasis on "principle" and "reason" in law and his rejection of the "arbitrary" authority of customary rules were derived from a new conception of common law as a self-conscious instrument of social policy. "[I]nstead of entertaining a blind veneration for ancient rules, maxims, and precedents," he insisted, "we [sh]ould learn to distinguish between those which are founded on the principles of human nature in society, which are permanent and universal, and those which are dictated by the circumstances, policy, manners, morals and religion of the age." Similarly, the soon to be chief justice of Connecticut, Zephaniah Swift, argued in 1795 that since the settlers of that state were "unfettered by the shackles of forms, customs, and precedent," they "have attended to enlarged, and liberal views of policy." Though he acknowledged that most colonial changes had been brought about by statute, these laws established "a variety of legal principles" by which judges would guide their own conduct. Thus, courts were "not absolutely bound by the authority of precedents."

If a determination has been founded on mistaken principles, or the rule adopted by it be inconvenient, or repugnant to the general tenor of the law, a subsequent court assumes the power to vary from it or contradict it. In such

63. N. Chipman's Rep. 63–65.

cases they do not determine the prior decisions to be bad law; but that they are not law. Thus in the very nature of the institution, is a principle established which corrects all errors and rectifies mistakes.[64]

Swift thus came as close as any jurist of the age to maintaining that law is what courts say it is. While no judge of the period acknowledged himself to be free from the restraints of "reason" and "principle" in formulating legal doctrine, one cannot survey the judicial output of the period without seeing the new policy orientation that judges bring to their work. Swift himself acknowledged in his 1810 treatise on the law of evidence what no jurist would have perceived a quarter of a century earlier: that "the rules of evidence are of an artificial texture, not capable in all cases of being founded on abstract principles of justice. They are positive regulations founded on policy." In short, "reason" and "principle" came to be understood not as rules or doctrines to be discovered, not as customary norms to be applied through precedent, but as a body of prudential regulations framed, as Swift himself saw, from the perspective of "enlarged and liberal views of policy." The result is that by the turn of the century, judges often explain in functional terms why they are free to disregard the authority of prior cases. In a typical case involving marine insurance decided in 1799, for example, a New York Supreme Court judge declared that if courts rigidly adhere to precedent "we must hope of little improvement in our commercial code. A single decision, though founded on mistake, would become of binding force, and by repetition, error might be continued, or heaped on error, until the common sense of mankind, and the necessity of the case oblige us to return to first principles, and abandon precedents."[65]

As courts were declaring their freedom from strict eighteenth-century conceptions of precedent, they also began to see the problem of order and uniformity in the legal system in a new light. For the eighteenth-century American jurist, the problem of legal certainty was essentially defined in political terms. Without "known" and "certain" laws, Massachusetts Chief Justice Hutchinson argued

---

64. *Ibid.*, p. 66n; Swift, *Laws of Connecticut*, I, 46, 41.
65. Silva v. Low, 1 Johns. Cas. 184, 190 (N.Y. 1799).

Horwitz : An Instrumental Conception of Law    321

in 1767, "the Will of the Judge would be Law: and this tends to a State of Slavery," for citizens would come to "depend upon the arbitrary Opinion of another." In the nineteenth century, by contrast, legal certainty is conceived of as important primarily to the extent that it enables individuals to plan their affairs more rationally. Swift, for example, remarked on the relationship between "uniformity of decision" in England and "the immense wealth, and unparalleled commercial prosperity of that nation." On the other hand, as adherence to precedent began to be understood as just one of a number of techniques for allowing men to order their affairs with regularity, judges were thus prepared to abandon precedent in order to create substantive doctrines that would themselves assure greater predictability of legal consequences. For example, in *Lee* v. *Boardman*, (1807), the Massachusetts Supreme Court departed from the English rule that an insured party could not recover for total loss upon abandoning a captured ship. For the ship owner to await the outcome, Chief Justice Parker declared, would create "uncertainty," since it would be "out of the power of the assured to calculate with any certainty upon the extent of his funds: his commercial enterprise will be checked, and his plans embarrassed and defeated." In short, adherence to precedent was thought of as necessary only to the extent that it allowed private parties to calculate in advance on the consequences of particular courses of conduct. Even where a judge acknowledged that it would not be "materially disadvantageous to commerce" to settle a marine insurance question "in either way, contended for in this cause,"—an agnostic attitude itself inconceivable two decades earlier—it was "of utmost importance, that the point should be clearly decided and settled in one or the other way; that merchants may know, and accommodate their affairs to the decision." As common law rules are conceived of as made and not discovered, precedent is no longer regarded as a technique for assuring that judges will apply a preexisting law. Instead, courts begin to classify categories of legal rules in terms of the extent to which innovation will have "retrospective influence" on existing private arrangements. Thus, in a "question of commercial concern, the determination of which can have no retrospective influence, nor affect pre-existing rights," a court regarded itself as "less restrained by the authority of existing cases."[66]

The retreat from precedent went hand in hand with a new definition of the role of the judge in formulating legal rules. One of the most radical departures occurred in a series of cases at the beginning of the nineteenth century involving the deference owed to decisions of English admiralty courts. The facts were all essentially the same: suits by ship owners to recover under marine insurance policies for ships that had been seized by the British for supposed violations of neutrality. Since the policies invariably covered only neutral property, the question was whether American courts were bound by the decision of the British admiralty holding that the property was non-neutral. The deeper question which confronted American judges was whether the traditional conception of courts discovering and impartially applying a fixed law of nations could coexist with clashing national policies at a time when critics were maintaining that the law of nations suffers from "the same uncertainty, which is felt so oppressively in the uncertainty of the common law." In a path-breaking decision, the New York High Court of Errors in 1802 held that New York courts were not bound by prior English judgments. "[T]here is not any uniform law by which these [English] courts govern themselves," one judge declared. "They listen more to instructions from the sovereign, than to the injunctions of the law of nations." It was important that American courts not establish rules interpreting insurance contracts "that would tend to embarrass commerce, or injure the assured; but adopt such a construction as will most promote the important objects in view." Since there was no clear requirement in international law, "we are at liberty to adopt such a construction as shall most subserve the solid interests of this growing country." The perception by American courts that the English admiralty

66. "Charge to the Grand Jury by the Chief Justice," Quincy's Mass. Rep. 232, 234, (1767); Swift, *Law of Evidence*, p. vi; Lee v. Boardman, 3 Mass. 238, 247–248 (1807); Thurston v. Koch, 4 Dall. 348, app. xxxiv (C.C.A.Pa. 1803); Silva v. Low, 1 Johns, Cas. 190 (N.Y. 1799).

Horwitz : An Instrumental Conception of Law     323

courts were "governed . . . by ideas of political expediency" soon
led American judges to see that it was necessary to adopt legal doctrines which in turn best promoted their own "solid interests."[67]

One of the most important consequences of the increased instrumentalism of American law is the dramatic shift in the relationship between judge and jury that begins to emerge at the end of the
eighteenth century. Although colonial judges had developed various techniques for preventing juries from returning verdicts contrary to law, there remained a strong conviction that juries were
the ultimate judge of both law and facts.[68] And since the problem
of maintaining legal certainty before the Revolution was largely
identified with preventing political arbitrariness, juries were rarely
charged with contributing to the unpredictability or uncertainty
of the legal system. But as the question of certainty begins to be
conceived of in more instrumental terms, the issue of control of
juries takes on a new significance. To allow juries to interpret questions of law, one judge declared in 1792, "would vest the interpretation and declaring of laws, in bodies so constituted, without
permanences, or previous means of information, and thus render
laws, which ought to be an uniform rule of conduct, uncertain,
fluctuating with every change of passion and opinion of jurors, and
impossible to be known till pronounced." Where eighteenth-century judges often submitted a case to the jury without any directions or with contrary instructions from several judges trying the
case, nineteenth-century courts become preoccupied with submitting clear directions to juries. Indeed, only when the judge-jury
problem begins to emerge at the end of the eighteenth century do
Americans insist on published reports in order to relieve "the uncertainty and contradiction attending judicial decisions."[69]

67. William John Duane, *The Law of Nations, Investigated in a Popular Manner* (Philadelphia, 1809) p. 3; Vandenheuvel v. United Ins. Co., 1 Cai. R. 217, 285, 289 (N.Y.
1802); Ludlow v. Bowne, 1 Johns. 1, 7 (N.Y. 1806) Brackenridge, *Law Miscellanies*, p.
344; DuPonceau, *Dissertation on Jurisdiction*, pp. 124–125.

68. Jefferson, *Notes on Virginia*, p. 140; *Works of James Wilson*, II, 540; "Powers and
Rights of Juries," Quincy's Mass. Rep. 558–572.

69. Alexander Addison, *Charges to Grand Juries of the Counties of the Fifth Circuit in the
State of Pennsylvania* (Washington, 1800), p. 53. (This volume often appears as an appendix to Addison's Reports.) Kirby's Conn. Rep. iii.

324            Perspectives in American History

Only in the nineteenth century do judges regularly set aside jury verdicts as contrary to law. At the same time, courts begin to treat certain questions as "matters of law" for the first time. For example, at the turn of the century it was typical for a court in even a complicated marine insurance case to suggest a rule for measuring damages while conceding that "unless the defendant could shew a better rule, the Jury might adopt that, or such other as would do justice." By 1812, however, in a decision that expresses the attitude of nineteenth-century judges on the question of damages, Justice Story refused to allow a damage judgment on the ground that the jury took account of speculative factors that "would be in the highest degree unfavorable to the interests of the community" because commercial plans "would be involved in utter uncertainty." As part of this tendency, legislatures began to take the question of damages entirely away from juries in eminent domain proceedings on the ground that, as one canal company maintained, this mode of assessing damages was "injurious and expensive, and . . . justice requires some amelioration" of the law's provisions. Finally, as part of the expanding notion of what constituted a "question of law" courts for the first time order new trials on the ground that a jury verdict is contrary to the weight of the evidence, despite the protest that "not one instance . . . is to be met with" where courts had previously reevaluated a jury's assessment of conflicting testimony.[70]

If an increasingly instrumentalist view of law led courts to narrow the province of the jury, this trend in turn encouraged judges to conceive of law in still more substantive terms, for a sharp distinction between law and facts provides a necessary inducement for courts to think of law in functional terms. Consequently, one of the most important symptoms of the emerging instrumentalism

70. John H. Morison, *Life of Jeremiah Smith* (Boston, 1845), pp. 165–166, 173–174; [Horace Binney], *Bushrod Washington* (Philadelphia, 1858), pp. 21–22; Bentaloe v. Pratt, Wallace Cir. Rep. 58, 60 (E.D.Pa. 1801); The Schooner Lively, 15 Fed. Cas. 634–635 (1812) "Report of Phillip Schuyler for Board of Directors of the Western Inland Lock Navigation Co. to the New York Legislature," (1798) in Albert Gallatin, "Report on Roads and Canals," *American State Papers*, Class I, Misc. I, p. 779; N.Y. Stat. ch. 101 (1798) Silva v. Low, 1 Johns. Cas. 184, 199 (N.Y. 1799).

Horwitz : An Instrumental Conception of Law     325

of nineteenth-century law is the decline in the significance of technicalities in determining the outcome of cases. Following the lead
of Nathaniel Chipman and Zephaniah Swift who in the last decade
of the eighteenth century sought to rescue American law from
rules developed in "an age when the minds of men were fettered
in forms," courts began to show contempt for lawyers who relied
on technicalities to win cases. Formal pleading, the New York
Supreme Court declared in 1805, "ought to be discountenanced,
as being calculated to mislead magistrates, and involve proceedings . . . in all the technical niceties of special pleadings." In 1809,
Massachusetts Chief Justice Parsons accused a defendant's lawyer of
attempting to use his superior knowledge of pleading to evade
"the apparent merits of the case." "All needless refinements," he
concluded, "ought to be rejected, and all finesse intended to *ensnare*
should be avoided." An important result is the increasing frequency
with which courts allow plaintiffs to amend imperfect pleadings
instead of throwing them out of court.[71]

This reaction against form was part of a deeper change in thought.
Not only were lawyers and jurists far less likely to analyze problems in relation to a static system of common law writs, but they
were also led to think less and less in terms of self-contained analogies to inherent categories of the legal system. When a Massachusetts lawyer in 1810 successfully argued in favor of the unprecedented position that a corporation should be liable in tort, he no
longer relied primarily on analogy to existing common law actions.
Rather, he contended that "this form of action should be main-
tainable" because "corporations were anciently not common, and
the necessity did not exist." However, since "they are now mul-
tiplying among us beyond all former examples, . . . individuals
may frequently sustain injuries from their neglect." Similarly,
when in 1793 Nathaniel Chipman reflected on whether promissory
notes were negotiable, he freely conceded points that earlier lawyers had taken as decisive barriers to negotiability. Even though, he
acknowledged, negotiability did not exist at common law and

71. DuPonceau, *Dissertation*, pp. 115–116; Kline v. Halsted, 3 Cai. R. 275, 278 (N.Y.
1805); Spear v. Bicknell, 3 Mass. 125, 133 (1809).

326                 Perspectives in American History

Vermont had not received the English statute permitting negotiability, it could still "be maintained . . . on principles of right,
arising from the nature of the transaction itself." Once the actual
understanding and purpose of the parties to the transaction were
identified, he insisted, the legal system should provide the mechanism for enabling individuals to accomplish their own desires.
The ascendancy of substance over form had begun to emerge.[72]

By 1820 the legal landscape in America bears only the faintest
resemblance to what existed forty years earlier. While the words
are often the same, the structure of thought has dramatically
changed and with it the theory of law. Law is no longer conceived
of as an eternal set of principles expressed in custom and derived
from natural law. Nor is it regarded primarily as a body of rules
designed to achieve justice only in the individual case. Instead,
judges have come to think of the common law as equally responsible with legislation for governing society and promoting socially
desirable conduct. This emphasis on law as an instrument of policy
encouraged innovation and allowed judges to formulate legal doctrine with the self-conscious goal of bringing about social change.
And from this changed perspective, American law stood on the
verge of one of the great "creative outbursts of modern legal
history."

72. Riddle v. Proprietors of the Locks and Canals of Merrimack River, 7 Mass. 169,
180–181 (1810); "A Dissertation on the Negotiability of Notes," N. Chipman's Rep. 89,
95. Compare M'Cullough v. Houston, 1 Dall. 441 (Pa. 1789); Mackie's Exec. v. Davis,
2 Wash. 281 (Va. 1796).

# 6

# THE IMPACT OF THE ANTISLAVERY MOVEMENT UPON STYLES OF JUDICIAL REASONING IN NINETEENTH CENTURY AMERICA

*WILLIAM E. NELSON*

VOLUME 87        JANUARY 1974        NUMBER 3

# HARVARD LAW REVIEW

## THE IMPACT OF THE ANTISLAVERY MOVEMENT UPON STYLES OF JUDICIAL REASONING IN NINETEENTH CENTURY AMERICA

### William E. Nelson [*]

*In the early nineteenth century, American judges frequently and candidly decided cases on the grounds of the social policies effected by their decisions. By the end of the century this instrumental mode of reasoning had fallen into disuse, and even disrepute; it had been replaced by a formalistic deduction of results from first principles and past decisions. This dramatic shift in judicial reasoning style calls for historical explanation, which Professor Nelson finds in the jurisprudential impact of the antislavery movement.*

MANY of the nation's most gifted and respected legal theorists of the present century have argued that law is not a formalistic body of doctrine that resists judicial adaptation to changing social and economic objectives in a modern industrial state.[1] Yet the fact that theorists found it necessary to make this

---

[*] Assistant Professor of Law, University of Pennsylvania. A.B., Hamilton College, 1962; LL.B., New York University, 1965; Ph.D., Harvard University, 1971.

The author is indebted to Bruce Ackerman, Morton Horwitz, Paul Mishkin, Stephen Schulhofer, and Mark Spiegel for their comments and criticism, and to Alan Bulliner and Gregory Sandomirsky for their research assistance.

This essay is the first in a projected series that will study the impact of the antislavery movement and the Civil War upon the American legal system. Forthcoming essays will include a study of the impact of what I here label "antislavery jurisprudence" upon congressional debate of the Reconstruction Amendments; a study of the post-Civil War movement for civil service reform and its impact upon the development of the bureaucracy; and, to the extent that economic tools are adequate to the task, a study of the impact of the shift from instrumentalism to formalism portrayed in this essay upon nineteenth century economic growth. A final essay will attempt to trace why the business community and the lawyers representing it, most of whom were instrumentalists during the 1850's, had found a formalistic style of reasoning suited to their needs by the end of the century.

[1] *See, e.g.*, Home Bldg. & Loan Ass'n v. Blaisdell, 290 U.S. 398 (1934) (Hughes, C.J.); Edwards v. Habib, 397 F.2d 687 (D.C. Cir. 1968) (Wright, J.); Escola v. Coca Cola Bottling Co., 24 Cal. 2d 453, 150 P.2d 436 (1944) (Traynor, J., concurring); Jacob & Young's, Inc. v. Kent, 230 N.Y. 239, 129 N.E. 889 (1921) (Cardozo, J.); B. CARDOZO, THE NATURE OF THE JUDICIAL PROCESS 167–80 (1922); J. FRANK, LAW AND THE MODERN MIND 6–12 (1930); H. HART & A. SACKS, THE LEGAL PROCESS 420 (tent. ed. 1958); K. LLEWELLYN, THE COMMON LAW TRADITION:

argument is historically anomalous. Recent scholarship has indicated that between 1820 and 1850 much of the American legal profession similarly thought that courts should change the rules of law in order to effectuate socially desirable policies.[2] Judges of the period justified their decisions not on the basis of authority, but rather on the basis of "general expediency — public policy,"[3] by which, as Karl Llewellyn has suggested, they meant an explicit consideration of the "prospective consequences of the rule" being formulated.[4] By the early decades of the nineteenth century American judges had developed what Morton Horwitz has labeled "an instrumental conception of law"[5] — a conception of law as a means to the attainment of an end.[6] Although somewhat similar to legal thought of the mid-twentieth century, early nineteenth century instrumentalism also differed: whereas twentieth century legal theorists recognize that law can have many ends,[7] instrumentalism in the early nineteenth century focused primarily on the promotion of economic growth by deciding specific cases in a manner "most conducive to the general prosperity of commerce."[8]

After several decades as a vital intellectual force, however, instrumentalism went into decline, and by the end of the nineteenth century, a new, formalistic style of judicial reasoning became dominant. As Llewellyn has observed, judges in the closing decades of the century typically maintained that "the rules of law. . . decide[d] the cases";[9] policy was "for the legislature, not for the courts."[10] Results followed "in deductive form with an air or expression of single-line inevitability" from the mere ap-

---

DECIDING APPEALS 38–39 (1960); W. TWINING, KARL LLEWELLYN AND THE REALIST MOVEMENT *passim* (1973).

[2] *See* K. LLEWELLYN, *supra* note 1, at 36–37; W. Nelson, The Americanization of the Common Law during the Revolutionary Era: A Study of Legal Change in Massachusetts, 1760–1830, Apr. 1971, at 418 (unpublished Ph.D. dissertation in Harvard University Library); Horwitz, *The Emergence of an Instrumental Conception of American Law, 1780–1820*, 5 PERSPECTIVES IN AM. HIST. 285, 287 (1971).

[3] F. HILLIARD, THE ELEMENTS OF LAW; BEING A COMPREHENSIVE SUMMARY OF AMERICAN CIVIL JURISPRUDENCE vi (1835).

[4] K. LLEWELLYN, *supra* note 1, at 36.

[5] Horwitz, *supra* note 2, at 285.

[6] *Cf.* R. VON JHERING, LAW AS A MEANS TO AN END (I. Husik transl. 1913) (referring to similar conception of the Civil Law).

[7] *See, e.g.*, Friedman, *On Legal Development*, 24 RUTGERS L. REV. 11, 30 (1969); Seidman, *Law and Development: A General Model*, 6 L. & SOC'Y REV. 311 (1972); Trubek, *Toward a Social Theory of Law: An Essay on the Study of Law and Development*, 82 YALE L.J. 1, 5 (1972).

[8] Thurston v. Koch, 23 F. Cas. 1183, 1186 (No. 14,016) (C.C.D. Pa. 1805).

[9] K. LLEWELLYN, *supra* note 1, at 38.

[10] *Id.*

plication of existing doctrine.[11] In deciding individual cases, judges no longer saw their task as the promotion of the goal of economic development, but as the preservation of the logical structure of the rules and fundamental principles of the law. If judges in the closing decades of the nineteenth century in fact thought that decisions ought to serve substantive policy goals rather than merely preserve existing legal doctrine, they left those goals unarticulated.[12]

If, as Llewellyn contends, a judicial reasoning process like that in vogue in the first half of the nineteenth century is *"always* the best style,"[13] why then did American judges abandon it in the latter part of the century for a formalistic style? This Article will hazard a tentative and imperfect answer to that question. Before turning to that answer, however, we must attempt to define more precisely the nature of the shift. We must also consider briefly some alternative explanations for the shift from instrumentalism to formalism.

Instrumentalism, as we have seen, is a self-conscious attempt to use law as a means toward the attainment of some end. Law can be seen as a means to an end on two levels. On the first level, the entire legal system, in the sense of entire bodies of law like the law of contracts, can be seen as a means to an end; on the second level, the rulemaking that occurs in individual adjudications can be perceived as such a means.[14] In the early nineteenth

---

[11] *Id.*

[12] I do not contend that the shift from an instrumental to a formalistic reasoning style was determinative of the substantive outcome of any particular case. Almost any result can be justified in almost any case by use of either style. Nonetheless, it seems likely that reasoning style will have some impact on the outcome of most cases. A judge's substantive preconceptions will often be merged in his reasoning style and will impose patterns upon both his perception of problems and his resolution of them. *Cf.* J. RAWLS, A THEORY OF JUSTICE 25 (1971) (suggesting that teleological doctrines will differ according to their conception of the good). Thus, judges in the first half of the nineteenth century, who believed that law should promote economic growth and whose first question about any proposed legal rule was whether it did so, must have found it difficult to decide any particular case in a way that might have impeded growth. Similarly, judges in the latter part of the century who felt obliged to harmonize particular decisions with past precedents must have found it difficult simply to ignore those precedents. The impact of reasoning style upon substantive results is, however, a topic that must await further study on another occasion. This Article attempts only to confront the intriguing question of why judges, in what must seem a regressive step to most lawyers today, repudiated ways of thought which have become today's orthodoxy.

[13] K. LLEWELLYN, *supra* note 1, at 37.

[14] A related distinction is made in Rawls, *Two Concepts of Rules,* 64 PHIL. REV. 3 (1955), between practices or systems of rules, on the one hand, and particular applications of those practices or rules, on the other. Another distinction is made in R. WASSERSTROM, THE JUDICIAL DECISION: TOWARD A THEORY OF LEGAL JUSTIFICATION 118–37 (1961), between judicial formulation of rules on grounds of their

century, law was often perceived as a means to the end of economic development on both levels. It is unclear whether by the end of the nineteenth century the legal system as a whole was perceived as a means to an end: there is evidence both that it was and that it was not.[15] What is clear, however, is that the legal profession almost uniformly viewed the process of rule articulation in individual cases not as a means to some policy end, but as an elaboration of an existing body of doctrine.

In talking about a shift from instrumentalism to formalism, we are thus not considering whether American judges after the middle of the nineteenth century abandoned a belief that the legal system as a whole should serve the goal of promoting economic development in favor of a belief that the system as a whole need not have forward-looking policy goals.[16] Rather we are talking about a shift in the style of judicial reasoning in individual cases — a shift from a style in which judges explicitly asked themselves whether a proposed rule would promote economic growth to a style in which judges asked whether a proposed rule was consistent with an existing body of doctrine. It is this shift that must be explained.

One explanation, which presupposes that judges have an inherent preference for a formalistic reasoning style, is that instrumentalism was forced upon judges in the early nineteenth century by the dearth of published American precedents and by the various reception acts and constitutional provisions that required judges, before following English precedent, to make a policy judgment whether the English law was suited to American needs and circumstances.[17] According to this theory, judges reverted to formalistic reasoning as soon as American precedents became available in sufficient number during the latter part of the century.[18] This theory seems unpersuasive for two reasons. First,

---

social utility and judicial decision of specific cases by (nonutilitarian) application of those rules.

[15] *Compare* H. SIDGWICK, THE ELEMENTS OF POLITICS 33–36, 63–64, 89–90 (1891) (contending that the end of all law is the promotion of general happiness and justifying specific property and contract doctrines as stimuli to the production of useful things) *with* J. CARTER, LAW: ITS ORIGIN, GROWTH AND FUNCTION 120–31 (1907) (defining law as a mere codification of custom without any explicitly forward-looking ends). Of course, once it is assumed that law has no forward-looking ends, it may be superfluous to attempt the sort of two-level analysis that I have suggested in the text. *See* Dworkin, *Does Law Have a Function? A Comment on the Two-Level Theory of Decision*, 74 YALE L.J. 640 (1965).

[16] *Cf.* Dworkin, *supra* note 15.

[17] For a discussion of the reception acts and similar constitutional provisions, see E. BROWN, BRITISH STATUTES IN AMERICAN LAW, 1776–1836, at 21–45 (1964).

[18] *Cf.* Goebel, *The Common Law and the Constitution*, in W. JONES, CHIEF JUSTICE JOHN MARSHALL: A REAPPRAISAL 101, 121–23 (1956).

American judges did not in fact lack American precedent during the early decades of the nineteenth century. Eighteenth century American courts had decided many, if not most, of the issues faced by judges around 1800, and those earlier decisions were well known.[19] In large part, knowledge of them came from manuscript notes handed down from generation to generation,[20] but by the 1820's, when instrumentalism was first being confidently articulated, eighteenth century precedents were also being disseminated with increasing frequency in books such as Nathan Dane's eight-volume *General Abridgment and Digest of American Law*, published in 1823.[21] These precedents, however, were frequently ignored. Second, American judges in the latter part of the century turned with increasing frequency to English precedent. As will appear,[22] English precedents were often held dispositive in late nineteenth century American cases without any discussion of whether they were suited to American needs and circumstances, even when they were directly contrary to American authority. This shift to English precedent cannot, of course, be explained by the simplistic observation that judges have an in-

---

[19] *See, e.g.,* Harris v. Willard, Smith 63, 67 (N.H. 1804), *citing* Harper v. Meloon (N.H. 1803) (unpublished case); Kerlin's Lessee v. Bull, 1 Dall. 175, 178 (Pa. 1786), *citing* "one judicial determination thirteen years ago"; Lane v. Winthrop, 1 Bay 116, 118 (S.C. 1790), *citing* Bay v. Frazer, apparently published at a later date as Bay v. Freazer, 1 Bay 66 (S.C. 1789); Commonwealth v. Cherry, 2 Brock. Cas. 20, 23–24 (Va. 1815), *citing* "the general practice of the Courts of Virginia, from the earliest period to this day."

[20] For Massachusetts, at least, there existed eighteenth century law notes of John Adams, which have since been published as LEGAL PAPERS OF JOHN ADAMS (L. Wroth & H. Zobel eds. 1965), and of Josiah Quincy, which have since been published as REPORTS OF CASES ARGUED AND ADJUSTED IN THE SUPERIOR COURT OF JUDICATURE OF THE PROVINCE OF MASSACHUSETTS BAY, BETWEEN 1761 AND 1772 (S. Quincy ed. 1865). The Massachusetts Historical Society, Boston, Mass., also has in its possession the legal papers of Robert Treat Paine, a three-volume set of notes of trial testimony, arguments of counsel, and responses of judges covering the period from 1760 to 1789, as well as extensive trial notes of two judges of the Supreme Judicial Court — Increase Sumner, covering 1782–1794, and Francis Dana, covering 1788–1806; Dana's notes, for example, contain over 200 summaries of opinions delivered from the bench. The Harvard Law Library has in its possession the notes of William Cushing, a judge from 1772 to 1789 who recorded, in full, texts of important judicial opinions and jury charges, while the Essex Institute, Salem, Mass., has custody of the notes of Judge Nathaniel Peaslee Sargeant, covering the years 1777 to 1794. It seems probable that many similar sets of notes must have been lost since the beginning of the nineteenth century.

[21] One also finds unreported eighteenth century cases discussed in such books as AMERICAN PRECEDENTS OF DECLARATIONS (B. Perham ed. 1802); BLACKSTONE'S COMMENTARIES (St. G. Tucker ed. 1803); J. STORY, A SELECTION OF PLEADINGS IN CIVIL ACTIONS (1805); J. SULLIVAN, THE HISTORY OF LAND TITLES IN MASSACHUSETTS (1801); Z. SWIFT, A DIGEST OF THE LAW OF EVIDENCE IN CIVIL AND CRIMINAL CASES (1810), all of which were published in America for an American audience.

[22] *See* pp. 560–62 *infra*.

herent urge to decide cases in a formalistic style whenever they can do so.[23]

A second alternative explanation is that judges turned from instrumentalism to formalism when, in mid-century, the latter style appeared to promote economic growth more effectively than the former.[24] As early as *Charles River Bridge v. Warren Bridge*,[25] where the issue was whether the owners of a toll bridge built pursuant to a legislative charter could enjoin the construction of a free bridge to be operated by the state along a parallel and proximate route, judges were debating whether growth would be promoted by a judicial style that permitted pro-developmental modification of the rules of law or by a judicial style that rendered the rules stable and predictable and thereby made investments more secure.[26] In *Charles River Bridge* and in innumerable contemporary cases,[27] the judges chose to modify rules to promote de-

---

[23] A related theory is that American judges and lawyers would not be inclined to become formalists until treatises on American law established a tradition of technical analysis of legal issues and prospective lawyers began to receive their educations not in offices but in academic surroundings which taught that tradition. This theory is undercut, however, by the fact that treatises on American law began to be published in the early nineteenth century, *see, e.g.*, H. BRACKENRIDGE, LAW MISCELLANIES (1814); J. SULLIVAN, *supra* note 21; Z. SWIFT, *supra* note 21, and that a number of law schools and law professorships were established during the same period — long before formalism became the dominant style of judicial reasoning. *See* A. SUTHERLAND, THE LAW AT HARVARD 25–31 (1967). More important to the emergence of formalism than the rise of treatises and of academic legal education is the nineteenth century shift in their content — a shift from the instrumentalism of a writer like Sullivan to the formalism of a teacher like Langdell.

[24] Judges in the second half of the nineteenth century, of course, decided cases in favor of those forms of business enterprise which promised to contribute most substantially to the nation's economic growth no less frequently than they had at the century's outset. *See, e.g.*, Pollock v. Farmers' Loan & Trust Co., 158 U.S. 601 (1895) (invalidating federal income tax statute which at least one member of the Court had perceived as an "assault upon capital," 157 U.S. at 607 (opinion of Field, J.)); *In re* Debs, 158 U.S. 564 (1895) (affirming conviction of labor leader for disobeying antistrike injunction); Wabash, St. L. & Pac. Ry. v. Illinois, 118 U.S. 557 (1886) (prohibiting state regulation of interstate rail shipments); J. W. HURST, LAW & ECONOMIC GROWTH: THE LEGAL HISTORY OF THE LUMBER INDUSTRY IN WISCONSIN, 1836–1915, at 297–333 (1964); A. PAUL, CONSERVATIVE CRISIS AND THE RULE OF LAW: ATTITUDES OF BENCH AND BAR, 1887–1895, at 45–60, 107–30 (1960); Corwin, *The Extension of Judicial Review in New York: 1783–1905*, 15 MICH. L. REV. 281, 294–96, 303–06 (1917).

[25] 36 U.S. (11 Pet.) 420 (1837), *aff'g* 24 Mass. (7 Pick.) 344 (1829).

[26] For the opposing views of Chief Justice Taney and Justice Story, see 36 U.S. (11 Pet.) at 552–53, 608; for a similar contrast between Justices Morton and Putnam of the Massachusetts Supreme Judicial Court, see 24 Mass. (7 Pick.) at 458, 462, 503. *See also* W. Nelson, *supra* note 2, at 382–87. In theory, of course, either instrumental or formalistic reasoning can further economic development. *See* Kennedy, *Legal Formality*, 2 J. LEGAL STUDIES 351, 374–82 (1973); Trubek, *supra* note 7, at 6–8, 18–21.

[27] *See, e.g.*, Hollister v. Union Co., 9 Conn. 436 (1833); Lexington & O.R.R.

velopment rather than to have stable and predictable rules, and during the 1830's, 1840's, and 1850's that choice appeared sound, as the nation's economy grew at a spectacular rate.[28] While the mid-century economy might have grown even more rapidly if judges had opted for legal stability, the economic tools available at the time were incapable of answering that question.[29] Given the apparent success of the choice made in *Charles River Bridge,* there accordingly seemed no reason for a growth-conscious mid-century judge to turn back upon it.

Hence, it seems unlikely that the shift from an instrumental to a formalistic style of judicial reasoning occurred because of any increasing availability of American precedent or because of any clear judicial perception of the relation between judicial style and economic growth. The hypothesis of this Article, instead, is that the roots of the shift go back into the cataclysmic event of mid-nineteenth century American life — the crisis over slavery that culminated in the Civil War. After Part I of this Article has outlined the principal characteristics of pre-Civil War American instrumentalism, Part II will suggest how instrumentalism became an obstacle in the path of the antislavery movement and how advocates of antislavery developed alternative jurisprudential ideas in response. Part III will then discuss the conflict from 1840 to 1860 between the two jurisprudential views, while Part IV will examine the resolution of the conflict and the development during the second half of the century of a new formalistic style of judicial reasoning.

## I. The Era of Instrumentalism

Underlying all styles of judicial reasoning in nineteenth century America was the legal profession's perception that all law,

---

v. Applegate, 38 Ky. (8 Dana) 289 (1839); Stetson v. Massachusetts Mut. Fire Ins. Co., 4 Mass. 330 (1808); Lansing v. Smith, 8 Cow. 146 (N.Y. Sup. Ct. 1828); M'Clenachan v. Curwin, 3 Yeates 362 (Pa. 1802).

[28] *See* pp. 520–21 *infra.*

[29] Classical nineteenth century economic theory, based largely on the writings of Thomas Malthus and David Ricardo, assumed that available natural resources and the technology for exploiting them were static and hence that substantial, long term economic growth was impossible. *See* R. Heilbroner, The Worldly Philosophers 80–95 (1953); E. Heimann, History of Economic Doctrines: An Introduction to Economic Theory 81–107 (1945); E. Roll, A History of Economic Thought 175–96 (1938). Accordingly, classical theorists gave no consideration to the question of how best to promote development. Although new natural resources and changing technology were economic realities in nineteenth century America — realities which affected Americans' perception of the feasibility of development — nineteenth century American economic theory was merely a primitive version of classical theory. *See* E. Heimann, *supra,* at 123–26; A. Schlesinger, Jr., The Age of Jackson 117–18, 306–27 (1945).

whether promulgated by a court or a legislature, was essentially mutable and transitory in nature.[30] In the decades following the American Revolution, judges and lawyers had come to believe that even "the common law" was "perpetually fluctuating"; [31] law, they thought, "must necessarily vary with the varying tempers of ages and nations," [32] since "[t]he grand law of human life . . . [was]mutability." [33] Few continued to view laws as "the emanations of Divine Will, nor yet the pure institutions of nature and reason; but changeable and arbitrary in their formation; they are necessarily of a positive, local existence." [34] There could be no doubt, as the author of one treatise observed, that "[o]ur reports are our law, and the publication of reports is, in fact, the enactment of laws." [35]

By the 1820's most of the legal profession also shared a conviction that the law's capacity for change was an instrument to be harnessed to promote economic growth. Although economic growth had been important throughout American history, that growth reached especially spectacular proportions in the first half of the nineteenth century, as a predominantly agrarian economy substantially confined to the Atlantic coast began to develop into an industrialized economy of continental scope.[36] This economic

---

[30] *See also* p. 557 *infra.*

[31] T. SEDGWICK, A TREATISE ON THE RULES WHICH GOVERN THE INTERPRETATION AND APPLICATION OF STATUTORY AND CONSTITUTIONAL LAW 14 (1857).

[32] Review, 3 PORTICO 193 (1817); *see* D. HOFFMAN, A COURSE OF LAW STUDY: RESPECTFULLY ADDRESSED TO THE STUDENTS OF LAW IN THE UNITED STATES viii–ix, xix–xx (1817); W. SAMPSON, AN ANNIVERSARY DISCOURSE, DELIVERED BEFORE THE HISTORICAL SOCIETY OF NEW YORK, ON SATURDAY, DECEMBER 6, 1823; SHOWING THE ORIGIN, PROGRESS, ANTIQUITIES, CURIOSITIES, AND NATURE OF THE COMMON LAW 57 (1824); Gilpin, *Review of Edward Livingston's System of Penal Law,* 43 N. AM. REV. 295, 298–99 (1836); Sedgwick, *Review of William Sampson's An Anniversary Discourse Delivered before the Historical Society of New York, on Saturday, Dec. 6, 1823, Showing the Origin, Progress, Antiquities, Curiosities, and Nature of the Common Law,* 19 N. AM. REV. 411, 429 (1824); Story, *Review of David Hoffman's Course of Legal Study,* 6 N. AM. REV. 45, 49 (1817).

[33] H. SEDGWICK, THE ENGLISH PRACTICE: A STATEMENT SHOWING SOME OF THE EVILS AND ABSURDITIES OF THE PRACTICE OF THE ENGLISH COMMON LAW 12 (1822).

[34] J. GOODENOW, HISTORICAL SKETCHES OF THE PRINCIPLES AND MAXIMS OF AMERICAN JURISPRUDENCE IN CONTRAST WITH THE DOCTRINES OF THE ENGLISH COMMON LAW ON THE SUBJECT OF CRIMES AND PUNISHMENTS 3 (1819) (emphasis deleted). *See also* Bell v. State, 31 Tenn. 42, 43 (1851).

[35] T. SEDGWICK, *supra* note 31, at 141. Legislators concurred in this sentiment, for they required courts to publish their opinions so that the law they made would be made known to the people. *See* Willets v. Ridgeway, 9 Ind. 367 (1857); Baker v. Kerr, 13 Iowa 384 (1862); Act of Feb. 18, 1864, Iowa Laws of 1864, ch. 22.

[36] *See* A. FISHLOW, AMERICAN RAILROADS AND THE TRANSFORMATION OF THE ANTE-BELLUM ECONOMY 205–61 (1965); G. TAYLOR, THE TRANSPORTATION REVOLUTION, 1815–1860, at 207 (1951); Segal, *Canals & Economic Development,* in

transformation was effectuated with much conscious effort: during the 1820's economic success became the preoccupation of many Americans.[37] Not surprisingly, the urge for economic development infected the legal profession. Judges began to think that law should be "a practical system, adapted to the condition and business of society"[38] and "suit[ed to] the local condition and . . . exigencies of every people."[39] For the legal profession of the early nineteenth century, the true glory of the common law was that its rules were "continually expanding with the progress of society, and adapting themselves to the gradual changes of trade and commerce, and the mechanic arts, and the exigencies and usages of the country."[40]

The courts frequently implemented such a philosophy, rejecting ancient authorities and looking instead to "the circumstances of the country,"[41] to "improvement in our commercial code,"[42] or to a rule's "inconvenience to holders of commercial paper"[43] in order to justify their decisions.[44] In *Pynchon v. Stearns*,[45] for example, an 1846 Massachusetts court failed to consider eighteenth century American precedent[46] and held, con-

CANALS AND AMERICAN ECONOMIC DEVELOPMENT 216, 221–48 (C. Goodrich ed. 1961). *See generally* P. GATES, THE FARMER'S AGE: AGRICULTURE, 1815–1860 (1960); C. NETTELS, THE EMERGENCE OF A NATIONAL ECONOMY, 1775–1815 (1962); G. TAYLOR, *supra.*

[37] *See generally* C. GREEN, AMERICAN CITIES IN THE GROWTH OF THE NATION 9–14, 47–50, 62, 80–82 (1957); J. HURST, LAW AND THE CONDITIONS OF FREEDOM IN THE NINETEENTH-CENTURY UNITED STATES 3–70 (1956); M. MEYERS, THE JACKSONIAN PERSUASION: POLITICS AND BELIEF 121–41 (1957).

[38] Steele v. Curle, 34 Ky. (4 Dana) 381, 390 (1836).

[39] Allison v. McCune, 15 Ohio 726, 730 (1846).

[40] Pierce v. Proprietors of Swan Point Cemetery, 10 R.I. 227, 241 (1872). *See also* J. STORY, *Value and Importance of Legal Studies: A Discourse Pronounced at the Inauguration of the Author as Dane Professor of Law in Harvard University, Aug. 25, 1829,* in THE MISCELLANEOUS WRITINGS OF JOSEPH STORY 503, 526 (W. Story ed. 1852).

[41] Potter v. Hall, 20 Mass. (3 Pick.) 368, 373 (1825); *accord,* Palmer v. Mulligan, 3 Cai. R. 307, 314 (N.Y. Sup. Ct. 1805).

[42] Silva v. Low, 1 Johns. Cas. 184, 190 (N.Y. Sup. Ct. 1799); *accord,* Thurston v. Koch, 23 F. Cas. 1183, 1185 (No. 14,016) (C.C.D. Pa. 1803); Liebert v. The Emperor, Bee's Admiralty Rep. 339, 343 (Pa. 1785); Watkins v. Crouch & Co., 32 Va. (5 Leigh) 522, 530 (1834).

[43] McFarland v. Pico, 8 Cal. 626, 631 (1857); *accord,* Winton v. Saidler, 3 Johns. Cas. 185, 196 (N.Y. Sup. Ct. 1802).

[44] *See generally* K. LLEWELLYN, *supra* note 1, at 64–72. Early nineteenth century courts consistently searched for the policy reasons underlying rules; if a rule had a basis in policy, the courts would follow it, but if "the reason of the rule ha[d] ceased," then the courts would cease to follow the rule. Campbell v. Johnson, 11 Mass. 184, 187 (1814).

[45] 52 Mass. (11 Met.) 304 (1846).

[46] An arguably relevant eighteenth century case was Nash v. Boltwood (Mass. 1783), in W. Cushing, Notes of Cases Decided in the Superior and Supreme

trary to the English common law rule, that a life tenant's construction of a house and an entryway thereto did not constitute waste. The court cited only three cases in its opinion, all dealing with the essentially political question of the power of American courts to reject English decisions, and then rejected the English rule on the ground that "[t]he ancient doctrine of waste, if universally adopted in this country, would greatly impede the progress of improvement." [47] Similarly, in *M'Culloch v. Eagle Insurance Co.*,[48] an 1822 case which raised the question whether a contract arose when an acceptance and a revocation of an offer crossed in the mails, the court held that there was no contract, arguing that its holding was "reasonable in mercantile contracts, though it was decided otherwise in the [English] case of *Cooke v. Oxley*." [49] Courts likewise demonstrated greater interest in the prospective consequences of their decisions than in ancient rules when, in a series of cases, they abandoned the established English doctrine of ancient lights,[50] on the ground that the doctrine could not "be applied in the growing cities and villages of this country, without working the most mischievous consequences." [51] And in an analogous line of cases beginning with *Thurston v. Hancock*,[52] early nineteenth century courts undermined ancient property doctrine by rejecting the rule that neighbors must provide each other's buildings with lateral support, since that rule too was seen as a threat to the growth of the nation's cities.[53]

In implementing their instrumental style of reasoning, early nineteenth century judges not only refused to give effect to ancient English and American authorities; [54] they also rejected

Judicial Court of Massachusetts, 1772–1789, at folio 35a (1789) (unpublished ms. in Harvard Law School Library). The court in *Nash* ruled that improvements on virgin land were not a bar to a writ of dower. *Nash* had been cited in a previous opinion of the Massachusetts court. *See* Webb v. Townsend, 18 Mass. (1 Pick.) 21, 22 (1822).

[47] 52 Mass. (11 Met.) at 312; *accord*, Hastings v. Crunkleton, 3 Yeates 261, 262 (Pa. 1801); Findlay v. Smith, 20 Va. (6 Munf.) 134, 142 (1818); *cf.* Van Ness v. Pacard, 27 U.S. (2 Pet.) 137 (1829). *See generally* Horwitz, *The Transformation in the Conception of Property in American Law, 1780–1860*, 40 U. CHI. L. REV. 248, 279–84 (1973).

[48] 18 Mass. (1 Pick.) 277 (1822).

[49] *Id.* at 281. *M'Culloch* was never the majority rule in this country. *See* 1 S. WILLISTON, A TREATISE ON THE LAW OF CONTRACTS 266–67 n.4 (3d ed. 1957), and cases cited therein.

[50] *See* Horwitz, *supra* note 47, at 264–65.

[51] Parker v. Foote, 19 Wend. 309, 318 (N.Y. Sup. Ct. 1838); *accord*, Pierre v. Fernald, 26 Me. 436 (1847); Haverstick v. Sipe, 33 Pa. 368 (1859); Hubbard v. Town, 33 Vt. 295 (1860).

[52] 12 Mass. 220 (1815).

[53] *See* Lasala v. Holbrook, 4 Paige 169 (N.Y. Ch. 1833); Richardson v. Vermont Cent. R.R., 25 Vt. 465 (1853).

[54] For other examples of the rejection of established American authority, com-

arguments that sought to deduce results in a formalistic style
from fundamental premises about the inalienable rights of man.
The leading case in which an instrumental style of reasoning triumphed over arguments based upon concepts of inalienable human rights was *Charles River Bridge v. Warren Bridge*,[55] decided
by the Supreme Court in 1837. As we have seen, the issue in that
case was whether the owners of a toll bridge built pursuant to a
legislative charter could enjoin the construction of a free bridge
to be operated along a parallel, proximate route by the state.
Counsel for the plaintiff toll bridge spoke often of "natural
right[s]" and "fundamental principles," among them the rule
prohibiting the taking of "private property for public use, without
compensation." [56] In the lower court, one judge agreed that the
"fundamental principles . . . [on which plaintiff relied were] no
longer considered disputable," [57] while Justice Story dissenting in
the Supreme Court observed that those principles had long "been
held to be fundamental axioms in free governments like ours." [58]
But the majority of the Court, in an opinion by Chief Justice
Taney, took an instrumentalist approach and ruled in favor of
the new state bridge, since "in a country like ours, free, active and
enterprising, continually advancing in numbers and wealth, new
channels of communication are daily found necessary, both for
travel and trade." [59]

State courts in contracts cases similarly rejected arguments
premised upon an allegedly inalienable right not to be held to contractual liability to which one had not consented. For example,
insurers were held liable for risks, such as additions to insured
buildings, that they had never agreed to insure in order to encourage individuals to construct additions to buildings.[60] And

---

pare the decision of the Supreme Court in Proprietors of the Charles River
Bridge v. Proprietors of the Warren Bridge, 36 U.S. (11 Pet.) 420, 567 (McLean,
J., concurring); *id.* at 583, (Baldwin, J., concurring), (1837), and the decision of
the Supreme Judicial Court of Massachusetts in Phillips v. Earle, 25 Mass. (8
Pick.) 182, 184-85 (1829), with Chadwick v. The Proprietors of the Haverill
Bridge, 2 N. Dane, Abridgement and Digest of American Law 686 (1823) and
Legal Papers of John Adams, *supra* note 20, at 11, 16.

[55] 36 U.S. (11 Pet.) 420 (1837), *aff'g* 24 Mass. (7 Pick.) 344 (1829).

[56] *Id.* at 451-52.

[57] Proprietors of the Charles River Bridge v. Proprietors of the Warren Bridge,
24 Mass. (7 Pick.) 344, 508 (1829) (Parker, C. J., dissenting).

[58] Proprietors of the Charles River Bridge v. Proprietors of the Warren Bridge,
36 U.S. (11 Pet.) 420, 642 (1837).

[59] *Id.* at 547.

[60] *See* James v. Lycoming Ins. Co., 13 F. Cas. 309 (No. 7182) (C.C.D. Mass.
1824); Jolly v. Baltimore Equitable Soc'y, 1 Harris & Gill 295 (Md. 1827);
Stetson v. Massachusetts Mut. Fire Ins. Co., 4 Mass. 330 (1808); *cf.* Thorndike
v. Bordman, 21 Mass. (4 Pick.) 471 (1827) (deviation by merchant vessel from
route prescribed in marine insurance contract).

persons who had agreed to pay only for perfect performance of a contract were required to pay for substantial performance [61] — a doctrine that enabled contractors to do more work by not requiring them to do it perfectly.

Instrumentalist arguments directed toward the promotion of economic growth were triumphant between 1820 and 1850 in yet another line of cases, in which the Supreme Court discerned the importance of national economic unity in furthering economic growth.[62] In the first case in the series, *Gibbons v. Ogden*,[63] the Court in 1824 invalidated a New York grant of a monopoly over steamboat transportation on the Hudson River, since the monopoly threatened to obstruct the free flow of commerce among the states. As Chief Justice Marshall declared in his opinion, that free flow and the economic growth to which it would lead were "primary objects for which the people of America adopted their government"; [64] as Attorney General Wirt had argued, the free flow of commerce in a market potentially of continental scope provided a means "of exciting the energies of the people, of invoking the genius of invention, and of creating and diffusing the lights of science." [65] Wirt later argued that the Framers had perceived the power to regulate commerce as "a great source of national wealth and aggrandizement[;] . . . a great means of developing the agricultural and manufacturing resources of the country, and its general industry; . . . [and] an instrument by which the nation could be enriched." [66] When another lawyer argued some years later that a free national market could not exist unless federal courts had power to declare "the common mercantile law of the respective States," [67] the Supreme Court in *Swift v. Tyson* [68] agreed and promulgated a uniform rule of commercial law "for

---

[61] *See* Hayward v. Leonard, 24 Mass. (7 Pick.) 181 (1828); Britton v. Turner, 6 N.H. 481 (1834); Fenton v. Clark, 11 Vt. 557 (1839).

[62] Of course, the idea of national unity was more than a merely economic idea; it also involved assumptions about America's spiritual and libertarian mission. *See generally* F. MERK, MANIFEST DESTINY AND MISSION IN AMERICAN HISTORY: A REINTERPRETATION 24–60 (1963); P. NAGEL, ONE NATION INDIVISIBLE: THE UNION IN AMERICAN THOUGHT, 1776–1861, at 145–231 (1964). But, as many historians have recognized, the goals of national economic growth and national economic greatness were an important element in the broader idea of national unity. *See* J. McCLELLAN, JOSEPH STORY AND THE AMERICAN CONSTITUTION 252–61 (1971); P. NAGEL, *supra*, at 19–22, 168–70.

[63] 22 U.S. (9 Wheat.) 1 (1824).

[64] *Id.* at 190.

[65] *Id.* at 167 (argument of counsel).

[66] Brown v. Maryland, 25 U.S. (12 Wheat.) 419, 434 (1827) (argument of counsel).

[67] Swift v. Tyson, 41 U.S. (16 Pet.) 1, 9 (1842) (argument of counsel).

[68] 41 U.S. (16 Pet.) 1 (1842).

the benefit and convenience of the commercial world." [69] Still later, the Court in *Cooley v. Board of Wardens* [70] reaffirmed the economic importance of unified national economic controls, "which the experience of more than half a century has taught us to value so highly." [71]

During the period from 1820 to 1850, an instrumental style of reasoning directed toward the objective of national economic growth and a corollary objective of national economic unity thus was prevalent among American judges. Almost as soon as instrumentalism had become prevalent, however, its days were numbered, for it was about to come into conflict with the rising movement to free the nation's slaves.

## II. THE JURISPRUDENCE OF ANTISLAVERY

During the closing years of the eighteenth and opening years of the nineteenth century, America's first antislavery movement had enjoyed great success, bringing about abolition in seven of the original thirteen states. [72] But thereafter the movement lay dormant until the 1830's. [73] Then, when instrumentalism was at the height of its influence, antislavery was revivified, and with it there arose ideas about morality which had jurisprudential implications inconsistent with the premises of instrumentalism. The intellectual foundation for this antislavery jurisprudence was laid during the 1830's and 1840's by politicians and propagandists in legislative debates and periodical literature; but as will appear in Part III below, it was only during the late 1840's and 1850's that lawyers began with frequency to transpose antislavery arguments from political forums into the courts.

The jurisprudence of antislavery was an amalgam of three strands of American thought. One strand was religion, particularly radical evangelical religion. Religion's contribution to antislavery thought was the ancient notion that there exists a higher law in the form of ultimate principles of morality, from which all human law is derived and with which all human law must be consistent. Western religion, of course, rests upon faith in the existence of immutable moral principles, and when religious emotions are deep and strong, as in early nineteenth century America, [74] faith in

---

[69] *Id.* at 20.

[70] 53 U.S. (12 How.) 299 (1851).

[71] *Id.* at 317. *See also* United States v. Coombs, 37 U.S. (12 Pet.) 72 (1838); Willson v. Black Bird Creek Marsh Co., 27 U.S. (2 Pet.) 245 (1829).

[72] *See* W. JORDAN, WHITE OVER BLACK, AMERICAN ATTITUDES TOWARD THE NEGRO, 1550–1812, at 349 (1968) (Conn., Mass., N.H., N.J., N.Y., Pa., R.I.).

[73] *See id.* at 344.

[74] *See generally* P. MILLER, THE LIFE OF THE MIND IN AMERICA FROM THE REVOLUTION TO THE CIVIL WAR 3–95 (1965).

higher-than-human principles of right and wrong is likely to be
equally deep and strong. For example, the Reverend William
Ellery Channing, a leading Unitarian minister of the time, extolled the "lofty strength in moral principle which all the power
of the outward universe cannot overcome." [75] Theodore Parker,
another Boston minister and later an antislavery activist, urged
men to recognize "the eternal nature of Truth" [76] and to see that
"[w]hat is of absolute value never changes." [77] Addressing the
relationship between politics and higher law, Parker warned that
a "nation, like a man, is amenable to the law of God; suffers for
its sin, and must suffer till it ends the sin." [78] For many religious
enthusiasts, truth was a fixed, permanent law which a man accepted when God worked a revelation in his soul and "the spirit"
aroused his "conscience and [made] it pierce like an arrow." [79]
The man who so trusted in his own commission as the Creator's
agent knew "certainly that he . . . [was] right exactly, and that
all men . . . were wrong in proportion as they differ[ed] from
him." [80] He also knew that rules enacted by human institutions
which were not in accord with his understanding of eternal law
were not law, "for none but the Law-giver himself . . . [could]
make exceptions to his own laws." [81] For such men the sin of
slavery was not difficult to discern.[82]

A second strand of antislavery jurisprudence was American
transcendentalism. Like religious leaders, the transcendentalists

---

[75] Channing, *Likeness to God*, in THE TRANSCENDENTALISTS: AN ANTHOLOGY 24–25 (P. Miller ed. 1950).

[76] T. PARKER, THE PREVIOUS QUESTION BETWEEN MR. ANDREWS NORTON AND HIS ALUMNI 23 (1840).

[77] T. PARKER, A DISCOURSE ON THE TRANSIENT AND PERMANENT IN CHRISTIANITY 28 (2d ed. 1841).

[78] T. PARKER, *The Administration of President Polk*, in THE RIGHTS OF MAN IN AMERICA 48, 88 (F. Sanborn ed. 1911).

[79] C. FINNEY, SERMONS ON GOSPEL THEMES 252 (1876). *See also* 14 BAPTIST REGISTER 74 (1837), *quoted in* W. CROSS, THE BURNED-OVER DISTRICT 201 (1950).

[80] LETTERS OF THE REV. DR. BEECHER AND REV. MR. NETTLETON, ON THE "NEW MEASURES" IN CONDUCTING REVIVALS OF RELIGION 93 (1828).

[81] *Id.* at 90.

[82] One of them, Theodore Weld, an antislavery activist who served throughout New York and the Western Reserve of Ohio as a Presbyterian preacher, encapsulated the religious position against slavery:

> The cause we are wedded to is the cause of *changeless eternal right.* God has decreed its ultimate triumph, and if the signs of the times are not mockers, the victory shout will ring around the world before the generation that now is, goes to the dead.

Letter from Theodore Weld to Elizur Wright, Jr., Jan. 10, 1833, in 1 LETTERS OF THEODORE DWIGHT WELD, ANGELINA GRIMKÉ WELD AND SARAH GRIMKÉ, 1822–1844, at 100 (G. Barnes & D. Dumond eds. 1934). For a biography of Weld, see B. THOMAS, THEODORE WELD: CRUSADER FOR FREEDOM (1950).

rarely concerned themselves with questions of human law and jurisprudence. However, some of them did articulate a moral philosophy that was inconsistent with the premises of early nineteenth century instrumentalism and on occasion recognized the inconsistency. The transcendentalists objected to the world they saw around them, in which "[t]he Material predominate[d] over the Spiritual"; "[t]he great strife . . . [was] for temporal goods, fame or pleasure"; "Right yield[ed] to Expediency, and Duty . . . [was] measured by Utility." [83] They found regrettable the "tendency . . . among a great number of benevolent and philanthropic men . . . to forget the eternal distinctions of right and wrong, and to substitute in their place, as the criterion of actions . . . merely empirical considerations, derived from an exaggerated sense of public utility." [84] They denied that "utility [was] the sole and ultimate ground upon which . . . obligation rests"; the ultimate ground was "conformity to our moral relations" as perceived "by the moral faculty." [85] Many transcendentalists, believing in "universal truths" and "a law of moral rectitude," [86] wished America to enjoy not only "a perpetual increase of prosperity and glory" but also "an equal increase of intellectual prosperity and moral glory." [87] They sought, in short, a moral rebirth of America — a rebirth that would occur when men began to "obey no law less than the eternal law." [88]

Because both evangelical religion and transcendentalism had a substantial impact upon subsequent nineteenth century reform movements, particularly the antislavery movement, they infused law and politics with higher law principles. The impact occurred in several ways. First, a number of clergymen and transcendentalists became active leaders in the antislavery cause.[89] Second, religious and intellectual leaders often influenced political leaders. In the early 1840's, for example, Theodore Weld served as counselor and speechwriter for John Quincy Adams while that elder

---

[83] Brownson, *New Views of Christianity, Society, and the Church* (1836), in THE TRANSCENDENTALISTS: AN ANTHOLOGY 118 (P. Miller ed. 1950).

[84] Ripley, *James Mackintosh* (1833), in THE TRANSCENDENTALISTS: AN ANTHOLOGY 66 (P. Miller ed. 1950).

[85] *Id.* at 65.

[86] Marsh, *Preliminary Essay* (1829), in THE TRANSCENDENTALISTS: AN ANTHOLOGY 37 (P. Miller ed. 1950) (emphasis deleted).

[87] Hedge, *Progress of Society* (1834), in THE TRANSCENDENTALISTS: AN ANTHOLOGY 74 (P. Miller ed. 1950).

[88] Emerson, *Self-Reliance* (1838), in THE GOLDEN AGE OF AMERICAN LITERATURE 112 (P. Miller ed. 1959).

[89] *See* THE TRANSCENDENTALISTS: AN ANTHOLOGY 124, 449 (P. Miller ed. 1950); B. THOMAS, *supra* note 82, at 68–87; Sanborn, *Preface* to THE RIGHTS OF MAN IN AMERICA at iii–xxxviii (F. Sanborn ed. 1911).

statesman led the abolitionist fight on the floor of Congress.[90] Other prominent political advocates of higher law during the 1840's and 1850's were, like Adams, strongly and openly influenced by the clergy or by their own religious experiences. Charles Sumner, for one, was deeply moved by William Ellery Channing's "pleading trumpet-tongued for humanity, for right, for truth" and by a faith in "great principles of justice and charity." [91] John Hale, a New Hampshire Senator who, when confronted with moral questions such as slavery, would ask "what . . . Jesus [would] have done in precisely similar situations," [92] was likewise influenced by his clergyman, the Reverend John Parkman.[93] And Gerritt Smith, a New York philanthropist and antislavery reformer, "fell easily and thoughtlessly into the common modes of religious terminology" when discussing legal questions; [94] in the words of his biographer, Smith refused to recognize any "distinction between higher law and lower." [95] For Smith, "all law . . . had its seat in the bosom of God; all law was high; if low things, policies, expediencies, devices, utilities took the name of law, they usurped it." [96] Third, evangelicalism played a vital role in preparing the common man for the coming of later reform movements. Throughout the first third of the nineteenth century much of New England, upstate New York, and the Great Lakes states were burned over by evangelical revivals; it was precisely in localities where revivalism had had its greatest impact that antislavery would have its greatest strength.[97]

The third strand in the jurisprudence of antislavery is found in eighteenth century traditions about human rights.[98] According to those traditions, which had been particularly strong during and after the American Revolution,[99] all men possessed certain

---

[90] *See* B. THOMAS, *supra* note 82, at 191–214.

[91] C. Sumner & W. Channing, *quoted in* D. DONALD, CHARLES SUMNER AND THE COMING OF THE CIVIL WAR 100, 133 (1960).

[92] Letter from John P. Hale to Mrs. Hale, Apr. 18, 1843, in R. SEWELL, JOHN P. HALE AND THE POLITICS OF ABOLITION 33 (1965).

[93] *See* R. SEWELL, *supra* note 92, at 33–34.

[94] R. HARLOW, GERRIT SMITH, PHILANTHROPIST AND REFORMER 193 (1939).

[95] O. FROTHINGHAM, GERRIT SMITH 172–73 (1878).

[96] *Id.*

[97] *See* W. CROSS, THE BURNED-OVER DISTRICT 218–26 (1950); B. THOMAS, *supra* note 82, at 211.

[98] For the distinction between right-based political theories, like those of the eighteenth century American revolutionaries, and duty-based theories, like those based upon the law of God, see Dworkin, *The Original Position*, 40 U. CHI. L. REV. 500, 519–24 (1973). Dworkin distinguishes both from goal-based theories, like nineteenth century instrumentalism.

[99] *See generally* 1 B. BAILYN, PAMPHLETS OF THE AMERICAN REVOLUTION, 1750–1776, at 99–115 (1965); E. MORGAN, THE BIRTH OF THE REPUBLIC, 1763–

rights that neither government nor other men could infringe.[100]  In the area of criminal procedure, for example, post-Revolutionary courts grew increasingly concerned about "the legal rights of the subject" [101] and accordingly held that rules which had been "established in arbitrary times" and were "expedient under a government of prerogative, . . . [but] not suited to the spirit of our free institutions," would have to be changed.[102]  Human rights rhetoric had also been important in the post-Revolutionary abolition movement, which had resulted in the emancipation of slaves throughout the North.  As soon as the Revolution had begun, many Americans had recognized that slavery was inconsistent with the ideals of the Declaration of Independence.[103]  As early as 1777, one group of slaves in New Hampshire had noted that "the God of nature gave them life and freedom, upon the terms of the most perfect equality with other men" and that their freedom was "an inherent right of the human species, not to be surrendered, but by consent." [104]  When Massachusetts several years later held slavery inconsistent with its state constitution, its highest court in similar language declared [105]

> that all men are born free and equal; and that every subject is entitled to liberty, and to have it guarded by the laws as well as his life and property.  In short, without resorting to implication in construing the Constitution, slavery is as effectively abolished as it can be by the granting of rights and privileges wholly incompatible and repugnant to its existence.

Twenty years later, St. George Tucker, campaigning for emanci-

---

1789, at 62–77 (1956); G. Wood, The Creation of the American Republic, 1776–1787, at 259–305 (1969).

[100] Some antislavery thinkers contended that these rights were bestowed on man by the Creator, whereas others contended that they were inherent in the concept of man or were bestowed by nature.  *See* W. Jordan, *supra* note 72, at 292–94.

[101] Commonwealth v. White (Mass. Sup. Jud. Ct., Cumberland County 1787), in R. Paine, Criminal Trials: Minutes of the Attorney General, 1780–1789 (ms. in Massachusetts Historical Society, Boston, Mass.).

[102] Commonwealth v. Green, 17 Mass. 515, 517 (1822).  The increasing concern over procedural rights of defendants in criminal trials was also reflected in the courts of other states.  *See* State v. Ledford, 3 Mo. 75, 76–77 (1832) (holding based upon right of defendant not to be deprived of "life, liberty, and property, but by the law of the land"); *In re* Thorn, 4 City Hall Rec. 81, 86 (N.Y. Mayor's Ct. 1819) (holding confessions made under a promise of favor invalid and inadmissible as evidence at trial); State v. Hobbs, 2 Tyler 380 (Vt. 1803) (holding right against self-incrimination guaranteed in state criminal prosecutions).

[103] *See* W. Jordan, *supra* note 72, at 287–304.

[104] Petition of Negro Slaves, 1777, *quoted in* W. Jordan, *supra* note 72, at 291 (emphasis deleted).

[105] Commonwealth v. Jennison (Mass. 1783), in W. Cushing, *supra* note 46 (emphasis deleted).

pation in Virginia, similarly argued "that a people who have declared, 'That *all* men are by nature *equally free* and *independent*,' and have made this declaration the first article in the foundation of their government," could not tolerate slavery.[106]

A particularly important aspect of the human rights tradition was the legal profession's longstanding concern for individual property rights. James Kent, for example, long believed in the "natural, inherent and inalienable" rights of man [107] and in "natural equity or reason" as a legitimate basis for judicial construction of legislation [108] — beliefs that he implemented in a leading eminent domain case, in which he construed a statute so that it would not authorize a taking that would have violated the "clear principle of natural equity, that the individual, whose property is thus sacrificed, must be indemnified." [109] Similarly, Joseph Story maintained that the idea of private property was "consonant with the common sense of mankind and the maxims of eternal justice" [110] and that legislative interference with private property would violate "the principles of natural justice . . . [and] the fundamental laws of every free government." [111]

Kent's and Story's concerns were given effect in a line of early cases, most involving takings of property, which declared that courts could invalidate legislative acts which transgressed natural rights, even if the acts violated no written constitutional rule. The cases in which courts actually held that they possessed such power were not numerous,[112] but the courts frequently asserted the power in dictum and then further bolstered their attack on the particular legislation at hand with references to relevant constitutional provisions or judicial precedents.

The power of the judiciary to invalidate legislation without relying on an explicit constitutional provision was first adumbrated in the Supreme Court in *Calder v. Bull*.[113] In an opinion concurring in the disposition of the case, Justice Chase wrote that "[a]n act of the legislature (for I cannot call it a law), contrary to the great first principles of the social compact, cannot be considered a rightful exercise of legislative authority." [114] Less than two

---

[106] 2 Blackstone's Commentaries App. at 41–42 (St. G. Tucker ed. 1803).

[107] 2 J. Kent, Commentaries on American Law 1 (1826).

[108] 1 *id.* at 419.

[109] Gardner v. Village of Newburgh, 2 Johns. Ch. 162, 166 (N.Y. 1816).

[110] Terret v. Taylor, 13 U.S. (9 Cranch) 43, 50 (1815).

[111] *Id.* at 52.

[112] *See, e.g.,* Ellis v. Marshall, 2 Mass. 269 (1807); Gardner v. Village of Newburgh, 2 Johns. Ch. 162 (N.Y. 1816); Ham v. M'Claws, 1 Bay 93, 98 (S.C. 1789).

[113] 3 U.S. (3 Dall.) 386 (1798).

[114] *Id.* at 388.

decades later, in *Terret v. Taylor*,[115] the Court struck down Virginia legislation interfering with corporate property rights since violation of those rights would be "utterly inconsistent with a great and fundamental principle of a republican government" [116] and with "the spirit and the letter of the constitution of the United States, and . . . the decisions of most respectable judicial tribunals." [117] Still later, in *Wilkinson v. Leland*,[118] the Court explained itself more fully: [119]

> The fundamental maxims of a free government seem to require, that the rights of personal liberty and private property should be held sacred. At least no Court of Justice in this country would be warranted in assuming, that the power to violate and disregard them — a power so repugnant to the common principles of justice and civil liberty — lurked under any general grant of legislative authority, or ought to be implied from any general expressions of the will of the people. The people ought not to be presumed to part with rights so vital to their security and well-being . . . .

Similar themes were echoed in state court opinions. In *Taylor v. Porter*,[120] for instance, a New York court struck down legislation authorizing the laying out of private roads because it found a taking of private property for private purposes. After citing the language in *Wilkinson* quoted above but before turning to detailed examination of state constitutional provisions, the majority explained that "security of life, liberty and property [lay] at the foundation of the social compact." [121] The Supreme Court of Maryland, reluctant to rest solely on the constitutional provision against impairment of contractual obligations, also invalidated legislation in reliance on "a fundamental principle of right and justice, inherent in the nature and spirit of the social compact, (in this country at least) . . . that rises above and restrains and sets bounds to the power of legislation." [122] In the same vein, a Connecticut judge rejected the concept of legislative omnipotence and argued that the judiciary was obliged to guard against palpably unjust enactments violative of the social compact.[123] And the Vermont Supreme Court explained that legislative power was

---

[115] 13 U.S. (9 Cranch) 43 (1815).

[116] *Id.* at 50–51.

[117] *Id.* at 52.

[118] 27 U.S. (2 Pet.) 627 (1829).

[119] *Id.* at 657.

[120] 4 Hill 140 (N.Y. Sup. Ct. 1843).

[121] *Id.* at 145.

[122] Regents of the Univ. of Maryland v. Williams, 9 G. & J. 365, 408 (Md. 1838).

[123] Goshen v. Inhabitants of Stonington, 4 Conn. 209, 224–25 (1822).

confined both by the constitution and by limits "resulting from the nature and principles of right and wrong, which must stand as boundaries to the sphere of every legislative operation." [124]

But by the 1830's, the tradition that judges could invalidate legislation interfering with property rights on the ground that such legislation deprived men of their natural rights was waning. As the instrumental style of reasoning became increasingly dominant, it seemed increasingly clear to judges that there was "no paramount and supreme law which define[d] the law of nature, or settle[d] those great principles" of legislation from which property was derived.[125] The rise of antislavery, however, rescued the waning tradition,[126] for economic rights of property and contract probably ranked next to the right of personal liberty as the most important rights of which slaves were deprived. In fighting that deprivation, the advocates of antislavery argued that the old natural rights doctrines were inconsistent with slavery and, by giving those doctrines wide publicity, reinvigorated them.

The inconsistency between the natural rights foundation of the new Republic and slavery was not at first universally acknowledged. It was possible to argue, for example, from the eighteenth century concept of the right to own property and to dispose of it at will, to the right to own and dispose of slaves.[127] Indeed, some abolitionists believed that the Constitution itself encouraged slavery.[128] This ambiguity in the natural rights tradition may account in part for the resiliency of instrumentalism among the judiciary and prominent members of the legal profession in spite of the human rights concepts which were apparent in American thought as early as the 1830's. The resiliency of instrumentalism may also be explained by the fact that the law and the legal profession had become too secularized by the 1830's for religious leaders and

---

[124] Langdon v. Strong, 2 Vt. 234, 256 (1829). For further state cases supporting, at least in dictum, the inherent power in the judiciary, independent of constitutional provisions, to invalidate legislative enactments as contrary to fundamental principles of justice, see Varick v. Smith, 5 Paige 137 (N.Y. Ch. 1835); Rogers v. Bradshaw, 20 Johns. 735 (N.Y. Ct. Err. 1823); People v. Platt, 17 Johns. 195 (N.Y. Sup. Ct. 1819); Raleigh & G.R.R. v. Davis, 2 Dev. & Bat. 451 (N.C. 1837); Bradee v. Brownfield, 2 W. & S. 271, 278 (Pa. 1841); Hatch v. Vermont Cent. R.R., 25 Vt. 49 (1852); Lyman v. Mower, 2 Vt. 517, 519 (1830).

[125] Bennett v. Boggs, 3 F. Cas. 221, 227–28 (No. 1319) (C.C.D.N.J. 1830). See also T. SEDGWICK, *supra* note 31, at 180–87.

[126] See Wynehamer v. People, 13 N.Y. 378, 428–29 (1856) (Selden, J.); People v. Edmonds, 15 Barb. 529 (N.Y. Sup. Ct. 1853); Benson v. Mayor of New York, 10 Barb. 223 (N.Y. Sup. Ct. 1850); People *ex rel.* Fountain v. Board of Supervisors, 4 Barb. 64 (N.Y. Sup. Ct. 1848); Sharpless v. Mayor of Philadelphia, 21 Pa. 147, 164 (1853).

[127] See W. JORDAN, *supra* note 72, at 349–56.

[128] See A. KRADITOR, MEANS AND ENDS IN AMERICAN ABOLITIONISM 185–89 (1969); R. NYE, FETTERED FREEDOM: CIVIL LIBERTIES AND THE SLAVERY CONTROVERSY, 1830–1860, at 235–44 (1963).

intellectuals concerned with fundamental philosophical issues to be of direct, immediate influence.[129]

It was only when Southerners and their sympathizers in the 1830's and 1840's gagged congressional discussion of antislavery petitions,[130] barred the federal mails to abolitionists,[131] assaulted abolitionist editors, killing one of them,[132] annexed Texas to the Union, and brought about a war with Mexico seemingly for the purpose of extending slave territory[133] that many Northern citizens who feared the loss of their own civil liberties became aware of the inconsistency between slavery and the rights of man which had been secured during the Revolution. To men like John Quincy Adams, who had been raised in the human rights tradition of the Revolutionary era, the congressional resolutions of the 1830's prohibiting discussion of antislavery petitions were "a direct violation of the Constitution of the United States . . . and the rights of [his] constituents."[134] Other antislavery apologists feared that the gag placed upon petitions related to slavery could "hereafter be drawn into a precedent to justify attempts to suppress the popular voice on other subjects,"[135] and that, gathering strength, encroachment might continue "until it shall sweep away . . . all the guarantees of popular rights."[136] "The next step," explained Adams, would "be to inquire into the political beliefs of the petitioners."[137]

Identical values were at stake in the analogous controversy over the use of the mails. There, too "[t]he next step" would be

---

[129] *See* P. MILLER, *supra* note 74, at 182–87.

[130] The first gag rule, known as the Pinckney gag rule, was enacted for the duration of the current House session on May 26, 1836. *See* CONG. GLOBE, 24th Cong., 1st Sess. 505–06 (1836). In each of the next three years, the House voted for a session-long gag rule on slavery-related petitions, and in January 1840 it enacted the toughest gag rule of all as Standing Rule 21. *See* CONG. GLOBE, 25th Cong., 2d Sess. 45 (1837); CONG. GLOBE, 26th Cong., 1st Sess. 89 (1839); CONG. GLOBE, 26th Cong., 1st Sess. 150–51 (1840). This rule stood for five sessions of Congress, until the abolitionists, their friends, and other defenders of civil liberties gathered sufficient strength to repeal it. *See* CONG. GLOBE, 28th Cong., 2d Sess. 7 (1844).

[131] *See* G. BARNES, THE ANTISLAVERY IMPULSE, 1830–1844, at 100–01 (1933); R. NYE, *supra* note 128, at 67–70, 80–85.

[132] For typical accounts of these attacks, see R. NYE, *supra* note 128, at 117–218; G. BARNES, *supra* note 131, at 39.

[133] Such, at least, was the view of leading advocates of antislavery. *See* M. DUBERMAN, CHARLES FRANCIS ADAMS, 1807–1886, at 87–89, 110–12 (1961); F. MERK, *supra* note 62, at 21–22; R. NYE, *supra* note 128, at 296; R. SEWELL, *supra* note 92, at 47–48.

[134] *Quoted in* G. BARNES, *supra* note 131, at 110. *See also* CONG. GLOBE, 24th Cong., 1st Sess. 506 (1836).

[135] W. Slade, Speech on the Right of Petition, . . . Delivered in the House of Representatives, on the 18th and 20th January, 1840, at 4 (1840). *See also* Cincinnati Philanthropist, Jan. 1, 1836, at 3, col. 4; *id.*, Mar. 31, 1840, at 1, col. 2–3.

[136] W. Slade, *supra* note 135, at 4.

[137] *Quoted in* R. NYE, *supra* note 128, at 49.

"to stop the circulation of all antimasonic papers, then those that
are opposed to the administration"; ultimately, lynch laws would
"be enforced against any who dare to utter sentiments not in accordance with those of their masters." [138] The Constitution, the
abolitionists argued to other Northerners, could not "at the same
time secure liberty to you, and expose us to oppression — give
you freedom of speech, and lock our lips — respect your right of
petition, and treat ours with contempt." [139] Either "all [must]
be free, or all slaves together." [140]

Mob attacks on editors likewise brought many new converts
to the antislavery fold, among them Salmon P. Chase, the future
Chief Justice, who was convinced that "Freedom of the Press
and Constitutional Liberty must live or perish together." [141] Most
important, perhaps, the attacks on editors, which occurred almost
simultaneously with the imposition of the gag rule in the House
and the attempt to bar abolitionist publications from the mails,
left many Northerners without "any doubt that there exist[ed]
. . . a secret confederacy, whose bond of union [was] a covenant
to put down the liberty of the press and the freedom of speech." [142]
They feared that, if men let a public meeting "[t]oday . . .
declare . . . that you shall not discuss slavery," then another
meeting would "[t]omorrow . . . decide . . . it is against the
peace of society that the principle of popery be discussed." [143]
Next, "speaking against distilleries, dram shops, and drunkenness"
would be forbidden, "[a]nd so on to the end of the chapter." [144]
"[I]n the great trial now pending between LIBERTY and DES-
POTISM," [145] it appeared that, if men gave "ground a single inch,
there . . . [would be] no stopping place." [146]

There were thus two great elements in the jurisprudential attacks on slavery: ideas about the higher law of God or some such
transcendental force and ideas about principles of human rights

---

[138] Dayton Republican *quoted in* R. NYE, *supra* note 128, at 79–80.

[139] Cincinnati Philanthropist, July 8, 1836, at 4, col. 4.

[140] *Id.*

[141] Cincinnati Daily Gazette, Aug. 4, 1836, at 2, col. 3. Similarly, William Ellery
Channing, the New England divine, saw the abolitionists as "sufferers for liberty
of thought, speech, and the press," and believed that for "maintaining this liberty
amidst insult and violence, they deserve[d] a place among its most honored defenders." 2 W. CHANNING, WORKS 159 (1843).

[142] Cincinnati Daily Gazette, July 20, 1836, at 2, col. 6.

[143] St. Louis Observer, Nov. 5, 1835.

[144] *Id.*

[145] 5 MASSACHUSETTS ANTI-SLAVERY SOCIETY, ANNUAL REPORT OF THE BOARD
OF MANAGERS 6 (1837).

[146] St. Louis Observer, Nov. 5, 1835. For further expressions of such sentiments,
see Massachusetts Anti-Slavery Society, An Account of the Interviews Which Took
Place on the Fourth and Eighth of March, Between a Committee of the Massa-

either conferred by God or inherent in a republican form of government. The first was a product of the religious or transcendental faith of many early antislavery advocates. The second was a product of the struggle for human rights, particularly the constitutional liberties of speech and press.

These two elements were not at first conjoined. A number of antislavery spokesman stressed only the divine origins of human law and human liberty. They argued that law was "simply the rule, principle, obligation, or requirement of natural justice," [147] that human rights were "the gifts of God . . . inseparable from human nature," [148] and "that God ha[d] made no difference in this respect between the white and the black." [149] William Lloyd Garrison believed in the "self-evident truth, that the liberty of a people is a gift of God and nature," [150] while others argued that to destroy another's "right to enjoy liberty" was "to usurp the prerogative of Jehovah." [151] Others emphasized natural rights. The Michigan Anti-Slavery Society, for example, resolved that free men had "certain inalienable rights, which no being in the universe, not even God himself, can have a right to infringe, among which are life, liberty, and the pursuit of happiness." [152] The Declaration of Independence, in particular, assumed a central role in antislavery thought. Men argued that the Declaration "embodie[d] the fundamental elements and principles of American constitutional law" and was a "solemn deed of acquittance of all rightful power to violate the natural and inalienable rights of man." [153] "By the affirmation in it of 'the existence of certain great fundamental principles,' the people 'estopped themselves' from ever 'rightfully' trampling upon them." [154] Compared to the Declaration, the Constitution was merely a vehicle "for the adjustment and proper application of these great principles of constitutional law." [155]

---

chusetts Anti-Slavery Society, and the Committee of the Legislature 11 (1836); Cincinnati Philanthropist, Feb. 12, 1836.

[147] L. Spooner, *quoted in* J. tenBroek, The Antislavery Origins of the Fourteenth Amendment 54 n.17 (1951).

[148] W. Channing, Slavery 31 (1936).

[149] Address by William Swain to the People of North Carolina on the Evils of Slavery, *quoted in* R. Nye, *supra* note 128, at 224 (emphasis deleted).

[150] 1 W. Garrison & F. Garrison, William Lloyd Garrison 200 (1894).

[151] Statement by the American Anti-Slavery Society Convention, 1833, *quoted in* R. Nye, *supra* note 128, at 224.

[152] Anti-Slavery Bugle, Mar. 3, 1856.

[153] J. Q. Adams, *quoted in* J. tenBroek, *supra* note 147, at 62–63 n.20.

[154] J. Tiffany, *quoted in* J. tenBroek, *supra* note 147, at 62 n.20. *See also* W. Channing, Slavery 31 (1936).

[155] J. Q. Adams, *quoted in* J. tenBroek, *supra* note 147, at 62–63 n.20. Because it incorporated the principles stated in the Declaration, "the Constitution . . .

But ultimately the moral and political elements of antislavery thought did merge into a single antislavery jurisprudence. The merger occurred whenever men sought to spell out the relationship among higher law, human rights granted by God, and human rights derived from the very meaning of republicanism. They would then explain that the doctrine of "natural rights, derived . . . from the constitution of human nature and the code of Heaven, . . . the same in all ages, . . . and destined to no change, [had been] proclaimed by our fathers in the Declaration of Independence to be self-evident" and had been "reiterated in our state constitution as its fundamental axiom." [156] "Master and slave" were thus free and equal both "according to the principles of the Declaration of Independence, and by the law of nature," [157] and abolitionism itself was "embodied in the self-evident truths of the Declaration of Independence . . . and in the Golden Rule of the Gospel — nothing more, nothing less." [158] In the words of Theodore Parker, "the idea of freedom" rested "on the immutable laws of God . . . [and] the natural religion of mankind . . . . [and] demand[ed] a government after natural justice." [159]

By the time antislavery had become politically prominent in the mid-1840's, its advocates had gone beyond merely stating the premises on which their jurisprudence rested. They had also begun to list, albeit in an imprecise way, the core rights subsumed under their ideas. In large part, the core rights were defined by the characteristics of antislavery's adversary, the slave system; by the deprivations that antislavery leaders suffered during the course of their struggle; and by older, inherited definitions of human rights.

The foremost contention of antislavery advocates was that all men were entitled to personal liberty. Within the concept of personal liberty were included many of the liberties protected by the Bill of Rights and infringed during the abolitionists' struggle for civil liberties. Foremost among these were the rights to freedom of speech, press, and assembly. "Freedom of speech and the liberty of the press" were referred to as "the palladium of our rights." [160] William Cullen Bryant, for one, argued that "[t]he right to dis-

---

[was] a temple of liberty." Letter from Gerrit Smith to Salmon P. Chase, in *Albany Patriot*, Nov. 10, 1847.

[156] Argument by Salmon P. Chase in Matilda's Case, Court of Common Pleas of Hamilton County, Ohio, Mar. 11, 1837, *quoted in* J. tenBroek, *supra* note 147, at 39.

[157] Cong. Globe, 33d Cong., 1st Sess. 138 (App. 1854) (remarks of Sen. Chase of Ohio).

[158] National Anti-Slavery Standard, Feb. 21, 1857.

[159] T. Parker, *supra* note 76, at 363.

[160] W. Birney, James G. Birney and His Times 243 (1890) (emphasis deleted).

cuss freely and openly, by speech, by the press, by the pen, all
political questions, and to examine and animadvert upon all
political institutions, . . . [was] a right as clear and certain, so
interwoven with our other liberties, so necessary, in fact, to their
existence, that without it we must fall at once into despotism and
anarchy." [161] Among other constitutionally protected rights which
some advocates of antislavery included within the concept of
personal liberty were "religious liberty," [162] "trials by jury," [163]
and " 'the right of the people to be secure' . . . against 'unreasonable searches and seizures.' " [164]

But the key element of personal liberty was the right to protection of the laws; it was precisely this right that slaves were
denied. All antislavery advocates agreed that "[t]he slave should
be legally protected in life and limb — in his earnings, his family
and social relations, and his conscience"; [165] that "he who mur-
ders a black man shall be hanged; that he who robs the black man
of his liberty or his property shall be punished like other criminals." [166] Notions of legal protection inevitably led to notions of
legal equality. The antislavery position was "[t]hat the benefit
and protection of these just laws [should] be extended to all human beings *alike*, . . . and that all mankind [should] be allowed
the *same* legal rights and protection without regard to color or
other physical peculiarities." [167] All men, in short, should be given
"impartial legal protection." [168] In the words of William H.
Seward, the Republican party, the final political arm of antislavery, stood above all for "one idea . . . — the equality of all men
before human tribunals and human laws." [169]

Another set of rights to which antislavery thought gave great
attention were property and contract rights. Antislavery advocates urged that economic rights of property and contract be
extended to all men, including slaves. One of "[t]he primary
and essential rights of humanity [was] the right to occupy a
portion of the earth's surface." [170] Ownership of land, it was
argued, would turn the dependent poor, such as slaves, into in-

---

[161] N.Y. Evening Post, Nov. 18, 1837. *See also* Chicago Democrat, Nov. 5, 1860.

[162] The Emancipator, July 22, 1834, at 1, col. 4.

[163] H. STANTON, REMARKS IN THE REPRESENTATIVES HALL ON THE 23D AND 24TH
OF FEBRUARY, 1837, BEFORE THE COMM. OF THE HOUSE OF REPRESENTATIVES OF
MASSACHUSETTS 34 (5th ed. 1837).

[164] Letter from Gerrit Smith, *supra* note 155.

[165] H. STANTON, *supra* note 163, at 34.

[166] CONG. GLOBE, 35th Cong., 2d Sess. 346 (1859) (remarks of Sen. Giddings).

[167] C. Olcott, *quoted in* J. tenBroek, *supra* note 147, at 26.

[168] H. STANTON, *supra* note 163, at 34.

[169] 4 W. SEWARD, WORKS 302 (G. Baker ed. 1884).

[170] Call for the Macedon Convention (1847), *quoted in* J. tenBroek, *supra*
note 147, at 117 n.2.

dependent yeomen; "by giving them independent freeholds, [it would] incite them . . . to rear families in habits of industry and frugality, which form the real elements of national greatness and power." [171] To deny men land, on the other hand, was to keep them dependent, and "to be dependent . . . [was] to be degraded." [172]

Of course, the right to own land also included the "natural right to eat the bread" earned from the land "with [one's] own hands without asking leave of anyone else." [173] The right of property, that is, "include[d], of necessity, [the] right to the products of [a man's] own industry, and his consequent right to dispose of those products, by barter or sale." [174] All men were entitled to "the inalienable right of unrestricted free trade," [175] and hence "all commercial restrictions . . . except the wise and needful prohibition of immoral and criminal traffic" [176] and "[a]ll monopolies, class legislations, and exclusive privileges" were "unequal, unjust, morally wrong, and subversive of the ends of civil government." [177] And, just as it was inappropriate for government to regulate lawful commerce, so too it was wrong to regulate the conditions of labor; "[i]t emasculated people to be protected in this way," since they ought to "be used to protecting themselves." [178]

This listing of core rights to which all men were inherently entitled, together with the synthesis of higher law and human rights thought, rendered the jurisprudence of antislavery complete and readied it for its coming conflict with instrumentalism.

## III. INSTRUMENTALISM AND ANTISLAVERY JURISPRUDENCE IN CONFLICT

As slavery became the preeminent issue in national politics during the 1840's and 1850's, a series of nationally prominent cases brought instrumentalism and antislavery into open conflict. The advocates of antislavery lost nearly all these cases, for, as we shall see, judges steeped in the instrumental style of reasoning continued to give effect to the related objectives of economic

---

[171] Statement of Schuyler Colfax, *quoted in* O. HOLLISTER, LIFE OF SCHUYLER COLFAX 161 (1886).

[172] North Star, Sept. 22, 1848.

[173] 2 THE COLLECTED WORKS OF ABRAHAM LINCOLN 405 (R. Basler ed. 1953).

[174] Call for the Macedon Convention (1847), *quoted in* J. tenBroek, *supra* note 147, at 118 n.2.

[175] *Id.*

[176] *Id.*

[177] *Id.* at 117 n.2.

[178] LETTERS AND JOURNALS OF SAMUEL GRIDLEY HOWE 385 (L. Richards ed. 1909).

growth and national unity. But antislavery advocates were able
to set before the public at large a coherent critique of instrumentalism based upon the antislavery jurisprudence they had already
developed.

The first slavery decision to attain national prominence was
_Prigg v. Pennsylvania_,[179] in which the Supreme Court in 1842
upheld the constitutionality of the Fugitive Slave Act of 1793.[180]
The white appellant, Edward Prigg, had been indicted under a
state statute prohibiting the capture of any Negro in Pennsylvania
and his subsequent transportation across state lines into slavery.
The jury had found Prigg guilty as charged, but had simultaneously returned a special verdict that the Negro taken out of
Pennsylvania was a slave under Maryland law who had fled to
Pennsylvania several years earlier to escape from slavery. After
the highest court of Pennsylvania had affirmed the verdict,[181]
Prigg appealed to the Supreme Court. Justice Story, writing for
the majority of the Court, overturned Prigg's conviction.[182] Story's
opinion rested on an instrumentalist concern for national unity,[183]
which can best be seen in his depiction of the fugitive slave clause

---

[179] 41 U.S. (16 Pet.) 539 (1842).

[180] Act of Feb. 12, 1793, ch. 7, 1 Stat. 302.

[181] To facilitate review, the Pennsylvania court affirmed pro forma; the decision
was unreported. _See_ Prigg v. Pennsylvania, 41 U.S. (16 Pet.) 539, 558 (1842).

[182] In upholding Prigg's contentions, first, that the fugitive slave clause of the
Federal Constitution gave Congress exclusive power to legislate on the subject of
fugitive slaves; second, that even if legislative power in the area were concurrent,
Congress' exercise of the power displaced all state legislation; and third, that even
if state legislative power had not been displaced, the state statute was directly
inconsistent with the Fugitive Slave Act of 1793 and hence was void, Justice Story
was interested chiefly in gaining Southern support for his long held views on the
issues of preemption and the scope of federal legislative power. _See_ G. Dunne,
Justice Joseph Story and the Rise of the Supreme Court 398–402 (1970);
J. McClellan, _supra_ note 62, at 261–63.

[183] For examples of Story's instrumentalism and his concern for national unity
and economic growth, see Story, _supra_ notes 32 & 40. As two recent biographers
have noted, Story was "a firm advocate of growth and expansion" who "was
keenly desirous of encouraging commerce and trade," J. McClellan, _supra_ note
62, at 50, 252, by creating "a relevant and authentically American law of commerce." G. Dunne, _supra_ note 182, at 387. _See generally id._ at 101–02, 386–87;
J. McClellan, _supra_ note 62, at 50–52, 252–61. At the same time, Story was a
firm believer in natural law and in the inalienable rights of free men. _See_ p.
530 _supra_. _See generally_ J. McClellan, _supra_ note 62, at 61–117, 194–237.
Story's adherence to such seemingly inconsistent views of law raises a paradox
which cannot be explored fully in the present Article. A possible explanation may
be that Story died a mere two years after the decision of _Prigg_, so that he was
never forced to confront the inconsistency between instrumentalism and concepts
of higher law and human rights except, perhaps, in _Prigg_ itself. In cases like
_Charles River Bridge_, for example, the various styles of reasoning all could be made
to lead to consistent results. _See_ pp. 518–19, 523 _supra_.

*HARVARD LAW REVIEW*            [Vol. 87:513]

of the Constitution [184] as "so vital to the preservation of [the] . . .
domestic interests and institutions [of the South] that it cannot
be doubted that it constituted a fundamental article, without the
adoption of which the Union could not have been formed" and
could not continue to exist.[185]  Of course, as Story might have
added, preservation of the Union was vital to the central instrumentalist objective of "prosperity of the community." [186]

Shortly after the *Prigg* case, Chief Justice Lemuel Shaw of
Massachusetts was asked to grant a writ of habeas corpus to one
George Latimer, allegedly a fugitive slave from Virginia.[187] Latimer, who had been seized pursuant to the 1793 federal Act, had
sought the writ in order to obtain a trial of his status before a
state court jury, pursuant to Massachusetts' Personal Liberty Law
of 1837.[188] Shaw, however, relying on *Prigg*, held the state personal liberty law preempted by the 1793 federal Act insofar as it
applied to slaves and denied Latimer relief.[189] Shaw thought "the
duty of returning runaway slaves . . . imperative on the free
states, and . . . that on no other terms could a union have been
formed between the North and South . . .";[190] implicit in his
reasoning was a judgment that the Union could be preserved only
on the same terms. Because of his overriding concern with the
preservation of the Union, Shaw thought that Latimer's "was a
case in which an appeal to natural rights and the paramount law
of liberty was not pertinent." [191]

Several years later, in *Jones v. Van Zandt*,[192] the Supreme
Court again faced issues arising under the Fugitive Slave Act.
The action was one for a penalty under the Act for concealing and
harboring a fugitive slave; it came to the Court on numerous
technical grounds and on the issue of the constitutionality of the
Act. Reaffirming its recent holding in *Prigg*, the Court observed
that the fugitive slave clause "was undoubtedly introduced into
the constitution, as one of its compromises,"[193] without which the

---

[184] U.S. CONST. art. IV § 2.

[185] Prigg v. Pennsylvania, 41 U.S. (16 Pet.) 539, 611 (1842).

[186] Proprietors of the Charles River Bridge v. Proprietors of the Warren Bridge,
36 U.S. (11 Pet.) 420, 547 (1837); *see* p. 523 *supra.*

[187] The Latimer Case, 5 LAW REP. 481 (Mass. 1843).

[188] [1837] Laws of Mass., ch. 221. The act guaranteed to anyone "imprisoned,
restrained of his liberty, or held in duress" a "writ of personal replevin," unless such
detention was "in the cutody of some public officer . . . by force of a lawful warrant or other process . . . issued by a court of competent jurisdiction."

[189] *Cf.* note 182 *supra.* On Shaw's instrumentalism, see L. LEVY, THE LAW OF
THE COMMONWEALTH AND CHIEF JUSTICE SHAW 118–82 (1957).

[190] The Liberator, Nov. 4, 1842, at 175, col. 1.

[191] *Id.*

[192] 46 U.S. (5 How.) 215 (1847).

[193] *Id.* at 229.

Union could not endure. The Court, as it had in the past, thus directed its reasoning toward the vital objective of preserving national unity.

The advocates of antislavery, however, viewed the issue of the constitutionality of the Fugitive Slave Act differently. They labeled Story's decision in *Prigg* as "unjust and unreasonable" and one that "establish[ed] . . . horrid doctrines." [194] They particularly complained about "the manifest injustice of deciding whether a man is free or a slave . . . by . . . a summary process, and without the intervention of a jury." [195] They concluded that the decision was simply *"not law* — for the entire system of slavery [was] at war with the rights of man." [196] They accused Justice Story, along with Justice Shaw, "of using their offices to oppress their fellow men," [197] of "act[ing] the part of Pilate in the Crucifixion of the Son of God," [198] and of being as morally reprehensible as a "slave pirate on the African coast." [199] The antislavery commentators likewise condemned the *Van Zandt* Court as violating "[t]he law of the Creator, which invests every human being with an inalienable title to freedom," [200] and "[t]he provisions of the Constitution," which "were mainly designed to establish as written law certain great principles of natural right and justice." [201]

The debate over fugitive slaves became even more heated following the passage of the Fugitive Slave Act of 1850,[202] part of the Compromise of 1850. On the one hand, the advocates of antislavery argued that the new Fugitive Slave Act was "incompatible with the power of [free Negroes to enjoy,] in safety and tranquility, their natural rights" [203] and further "violate[d] the golden rule of Christianity, of doing unto others as we would have them do to us." [204] They condemned the Act as "revolting to our moral

---

[194] The Liberator, Mar. 18, 1842, at 41, col. 4.

[195] *Id.*

[196] *Id.* Mar. 11, 1842, at 39, col. 4.

[197] 5 Law Rep. 492 (1843).

[198] The Liberator, Nov. 4, 1842, at 175, col. 2.

[199] *Id.* For similar criticisms of these court decisions, see 16 Massachusetts Anti-Slavery Society, Annual Report of the Board of Managers 54–55 (1848); 12 *id.* at 4 (1844); 11 *id.* at 70–71 (1843); Emancipator and Free American, Nov. 3, 1842.

[200] J. Schuckers, The Life and Public Services of Salmon Portland Chase 63 (1874), *quoting* S. Chase's argument in *Van Zandt.*

[201] *Id.*; *see* 11 Massachusetts Anti-Slavery Society, Annual Report of the Board of Managers 76 (1843).

[202] Act of Sept. 18, 1850, ch. 60, 9 Stat. 462.

[203] 19 Massachusetts Anti-Slavery Society, Annual Report of the Board of Managers 42 (1851).

[204] *Id.* (emphasis deleted).

sense, and an outrage upon our feelings of justice and humanity, because it disregard[ed] all the securities which the Constitution and laws ha[d] thrown around personal liberty." [205] The Act, in short, was seen as contrary to "the higher law of every man's own conscience." [206] The judiciary, on the other hand, found enforcement of the Act essential to the continued preservation of the nation. Judges evinced concern for "the peace, prosperity, and happiness of the citizens of these United States" [207] and took the position that it was "well known that our Southern brethren would not have consented to become parties to a constitution under which the United States have enjoyed so much prosperity unless their property in slaves had been secured." [208] The fugitive slave clause of the Constitution was thus an "essential element" in the formation and preservation of the Union,[209] "necessary to the peace, happiness and highest prosperity of all the states." [210]

The line of fugitive slaves cases culminated in 1859 with *Ableman v. Booth*.[211] The case was a consolidation of two appeals by federal authorities from decisions of the Wisconsin Supreme Court. In the first of the two Wisconsin cases,[212] Booth, an antislavery agitator, had obtained a writ of habeas corpus from a judge of the state court after he had been charged before a United States Commissioner with aiding and abetting a fugitive slave to escape from a federal deputy marshal. In the second of the two cases,[213] the Wisconsin court had again released Booth on a writ of habeas corpus after he had been duly indicted and convicted of the offense charged.

The Wisconsin judges first analyzed the relation of the state and federal judiciaries in a manner consistent with the instrumental style.[214] But they then disclosed their antislavery beliefs in holding the Fugitive Slave Act of 1850 unconstitutional. They found particularly objectionable the provision of the 1850 act authorizing the return of alleged fugitives without any appearance in court. They thought that even "without the express guaranty of the Constitution," the right of a man to "his 'day in court' would be implied as a fundamental condition of all civil governments"; for the Wisconsin judges the Bill of Rights merely con-

[205] *Id.* at 45.
[206] United States v. Hanway, 26 F. Cas. 105, 111 (No. 15,299) (C.C.E.D. Pa. 1851) (referring to denunciations of the Act by antislavery conventions).
[207] *Id.* at 123.
[208] Oliver v. Kauffman, 18 F. Cas. 657, 659 (No. 10,497) (C.C.E.D. Pa. 1850).
[209] Sim's Case, 61 Mass. (7 Cush.) 285, 319 (1851); *see id.* at 311–19.
[210] *Id.* at 319.
[211] 62 U.S. (21 How.) 506 (1859).
[212] *In re* Booth, 3 Wis. 1 (1854).
[213] *In re* Booth, 3 Wis. 157 (1854).
[214] *See In re* Booth, 3 Wis. 1, 7–39.

firmed what was otherwise "in accordance with the first principles of natural law." [215] The Wisconsin judges were unimpressed by the Government's reliance on *Prigg v. Pennsylvania* as a controlling precedent; their position was that when "duty and obligation require a departure from such precedent and authority, in obedience to a paramount law — the *fundamental law*, to which each and all are equally bound," they were compelled so to depart.[216]

In reversing the Wisconsin court, Chief Justice Taney affirmed the constitutionality of the 1850 Act in less than one sentence and devoted the remainder of his opinion to an instrumentalist analysis [217] of the need for national unity. He argued that "no one . . . [would] suppose that a Government . . . preserving the union of the States, could have lasted a single year . . . if offenses against its laws could not have been punished without the consent of the State in which the culprit was found." [218] He found it "evident that anything short of this" would have been "inadequate to the main objects for which the Government was established," and that, "unless there was a common arbiter" between the states "armed with power enough to protect and guard the rights of all, by appropriate laws, to be carried into execution peacefully by its judicial tribunals," government and, indeed, all social order would fall prey to "local interests, local passions or prejudices" and "to acts of aggression and injustice by one State upon the rights of another, which would ultimately terminate in violence and force." [219]

Twentieth century historians have sometimes tended to view the conflict between proslavery and antislavery forces during the 1850's as an essentially political one fought over underlying economic objectives.[220] The fugitive slave cases suggest, however, that the conflict had another important dimension. Those cases could have been contested by both sides entirely upon instrumentalist, higher law, or natural rights grounds. The fact, however, is that the advocates of compromise with slavery rested their case upon instrumentalist arguments about what was politically wise and economically expedient, whereas opponents of slavery made essentially moralistic arguments about the law of God and the rights of man. At least in the courts, the conflict between slavery and antislavery was not only a struggle for political power,

---

[215] *Id.* at 41–42.

[216] *Id.* at 91.

[217] For a leading example of Chief Justice Taney's instrumentalist bent, see the majority opinion in *Charles River Bridge, discussed* p. 523 *supra.*

[218] *Ableman v. Booth,* 62 U.S. (21 How.) 506, 515 (1859).

[219] *Id.* at 517.

[220] For a summary of the views of such historians, see T. PRESSLY, AMERICANS INTERPRET THEIR CIVIL WAR 204–14, 257–92 (1954).

but also a conflict between men possessing differing views about the proper role of law and government — between men who believed that courts should explicitly pursue socially expedient policy goals and men who believed that courts should decide cases consistently with standards of what, in some ultimate sense, was right and wrong.

This conflict came to a head in the 1857 case of *Scott v. Sandford*,[221] in which the Supreme Court held that Congress lacked power to bar slavery from the territories. The plaintiff, Dred Scott, claiming to be a citizen of Missouri, had brought suit in a federal circuit court for an assault upon himself, his wife, and his children. The defendant, John Sandford, a citizen of New York, claimed first, that since Scott was a Negro, he could not be a citizen of a state for the purpose of conferring diversity jurisdiction [222] and second, that the assaults were justified since Scott and his family were Sandford's slaves.[223] Scott replied that free Negroes were citizens and that he had become free when a previous master had taken him first to Illinois and subsequently to Fort Snelling in the territory of Upper Louisiana, which had been declared free territory by the Missouri Compromise of 1820.[224]

The Court, in an opinion by Chief Justice Taney, rejected Scott's replication. First, Taney held that Scott was not a citizen of Missouri for diversity purposes. Missouri did not recognize Scott as a citizen, and Taney, citing both precedent and legislative history, held that the Federal Constitution did not make him a citizen either. Although couched in historical terms, Taney's rationale reflected his concern for national unity. Taney would not presume that slaveholding states regarded Negroes as citizens because a contrary holding might throw Southern society into turmoil and force the South to leave the Union.[225] The Court also rejected Scott's claim that he had been made free by virtue of his sojourn either in Illinois or in the territory of Upper Louisiana. To support its rejection of the claim concerning the effect of Scott's stay in Illinois, the Court relied on its earlier decision in *Strader v. Graham*,[226] in which it had held that a temporary residence in a free state did not make a slave free if the law of the state to which he subsequently returned still deemed him a slave. While the Court might have used analogous reasoning to reject Scott's claim of freedom based on a stay in Upper Louisiana, it instead reached the much broader conclusion that the Missouri

---

[221] 60 U.S. (19 How.) 393 (1857).
[222] *Id.* at 396–97.
[223] *Id.* at 397.
[224] *Id.* at 431.
[225] *Id.* at 416–17.
[226] 51 U.S. (10 How.) 82 (1850).

Compromise of 1820,[227] which had declared Upper Louisiana free, was unconstitutional. Rejecting the argument that the provision in the Northwest Ordinance of 1787 [228] prohibiting slavery provided a precedent for congressional prohibition of slavery in other territories, the Court held that Congress had a constitutional obligation to keep all territories open for settlement and development by citizens of all states, including slaveowners. While there is no evidence that the Court expected its decision to promote directly the economic development of the territories, it clearly expected its appeasement of the South to promote national unity by preserving "the peace and harmony of the country" through "the settlement . . . by judicial decision" of the sectional crisis.[229]

The decision infuriated many Northerners. Antislavery leaders regarded the denial of Scott's citizenship as "a violation of the sacred principles announced in our Declaration of Independence, [and] hostile to the spirit of our institutions." [230] More disturbing was the holding that the Missouri Compromise was unconstitutional. Like the holding that a sojourn in a free state did not make a slave free, the invalidation of the Missouri Compromise was "contrary to . . . the fundamental principle . . . that every man has an inalienable right to his liberty, and that it can only be taken from him by a statute of the State in which he lives." [231] Liberty, according to the advocates of antislavery, was the natural state of man, while slavery could occur only when local police regulations altered that natural state. The very point of this argument was that, since Congress could not take away liberty without due process of law, Congress could not enact any law protective of slavery. The Court, however, had undercut that argument, holding, in effect, that the federal government was obliged to protect not liberty but slavery. As a result, antislavery advocates began to fear that slavery would be made legal throughout the nation — "that some future decision of the Pro-Slavery majority of the Supreme Court will authorize a slave driver, as threatened by the devotees of Slavery, to call the roll of his manacled gang at the foot of the monument on Bunker Hill, reared and consecrated to freedom." [232] They feared that nothing could stop a proslavery Supreme Court, unconcerned with the rights of

---

[227] Act of Mar. 6, 1820, ch. 22, § 8, 3 Stat. 548.

[228] "An Ordinance for the Government of the Territory of the United States north-west of the river Ohio," July 13, 1787, art. 6, 1 Stat. 51n., *reenacted as* Act of Aug. 7, 1789, ch. 8, 1 Stat. 50.

[229] 60 U.S. (19 How.) at 455 (Wayne, J., concurring).

[230] Report to the N.Y. Senate and Assembly, Apr. 9th, 1857, in CASE OF DRED SCOTT 102 (1857).

[231] *Id.*

[232] *Id.*

man, from legalizing slavery in the North.

The worst apprehensions of the advocates of antislavery were aroused by the case of *Lemmon v. People*,[233] a case decided by the New York Court of Appeals early in 1860 and pending on appeal to the Supreme Court during the fall elections of that year. The case arose when Mrs. Lemmon, in transit by sea from Virginia to Texas, disembarked with her slaves briefly in New York City to change vessels; immediately a writ of habeas corpus was taken out to obtain freedom for Mrs. Lemmon's slaves on the ground that they had been brought into a free state. The lower New York courts granted the writ, and in March 1860, the New York Court of Appeals, with three judges dissenting, affirmed.

The argument for granting the writ was based upon the principle that "[t]he state of slavery [was] contrary to natural right" and that "[t]he law of slavery [was] local, and [did] not operate beyond the territory of the State where it [was] established."[234] Thus, unless the Federal Constitution required New York to give extraterritorial effect to Virginia's slavery law, the slaves had become free as soon as they set foot on New York soil. Counsel for the state argued that the Constitution gave no such extraterritorial effect to Southern slavery and, indeed, that slavery was "inconsistent with the principle that lies at the foundation of our government . . . [and] in contradiction to the Declaration of Independence, and to the preamble to the Constitution."[235]

Judge Wright, speaking for himself and three of the other four judges in the Court of Appeals majority, agreed that "slavery [was] repugnant to natural justice and right . . . [and was] antagonistic to the genius and spirit of republican government."[236] Wright also ruled that there was "no grant of power to the Federal Government, and no provision of the Constitution from which any can be implied, over the subject of slavery in the States, except in the single case of a fugitive from service."[237]

Counsel for Mrs. Lemmon, on the other hand, took a typically instrumentalist approach to the case. He argued that the Federal Constitution's commerce and interstate privileges and immunities clauses protected the property rights of slaveowners who temporarily brought their slaves into free states and that, unless those "guaranties of the Federal Constitution" were "enforced, in the form and to the extent which we demand, the unbridled sovereignty of our smallest State . . . will hold in its hand the power

[233] 20 N.Y. 562 (1860).
[234] *Id.* at 584–85.
[235] *Id.* at 590.
[236] *Id.* at 617.
[237] *Id.* at 628.

of dissolving our whole social system." [238] Counsel added that "[e]vil passions or some new fanaticism might at any moment set that power in motion." [239]

Judge Clerke in dissent agreed with Mrs. Lemmon's counsel. In Clerke's opinion, the Constitution had sought to create "one nation, not only in its character as a member of the great family of nations, but also in the internal, moral, social and political effect of the Union upon the people themselves." [240] He thought it "essential to this grand design that there should be . . . free and . . . uninterrupted . . . intercommunication between the inhabitants and citizens of the different States." [241] Of course, such intercommunication would be facilitated if Southerners could bring their slaves with them to the North.

Although this instrumentalist point of view lost in the New York courts, the advocates of antislavery feared greatly that it would prevail before the Supreme Court of the United States. Within a year of *Scott*, Lincoln had warned that the Court's next step would be to decide that a state could not exclude slavery from its borders,[242] while Horace Greeley's *New York Tribune* was predicting that New Yorkers would soon "see men buying slaves for the New York market" with "no legal power to prevent it." [243] The accuracy of these prophecies, however, was never tested, for the appeal of Mrs. Lemmon, which was expected to be argued before the Supreme Court during the December 1860 Term, was never heard.[244]

## IV. THE NEW AMERICAN FORMALISM

The conflict between instrumentalism and antislavery jurisprudence was not, of course, brought to a resolution through intellectual analysis. On the contrary, the conflict was resolved through manipulation of the mechanisms of power when, beginning with the election of 1860, the forces of antislavery gained control of the political branches of the federal government [245] and later,

---

[238] *Id.* at 582–83; *see id.* at 570.

[239] *Id.* at 583.

[240] *Id.* at 634.

[241] *Id.*

[242] V. HOPKINS, DRED SCOTT'S CASE 172 (1951).

[243] N.Y. Tribune, Mar. 11, 1857, at 4, col. 3.

[244] 2 C. WARREN, THE SUPREME COURT IN UNITED STATES HISTORY 360–67 (rev. ed. 1922).

[245] Not only the radicals, but most moderate and conservative Republicans had strong antislavery convictions. *See* E. FONER, FREE SOIL, FREE LABOR, FREE MEN: THE IDEOLOGY OF THE REPUBLICAN PARTY BEFORE THE CIVIL WAR 186–225 (1970). The Republican party, of course, won every national election during the 1860's and the majority of national elections during the remainder of the nineteenth century.

through the appointment process, obtained control of the judiciary. The outcome upon the battlefields of the Civil War served to consolidate antislavery's electoral victories.

As a result of the association of instrumentalism with proslavery forces before the war and the political defeat of those forces during the 1860's, instrumentalism became discredited as a style of judicial reasoning, thereby creating a void that had to be filled. That void, as will appear, was ultimately filled by American formalism, which was an amalgam of antislavery ideas and ideas associated with the late nineteenth century conception of law as a science. What the two sets of ideas had in common was the notion that judges could reason logically and deductively — either from first principles of morality or from empirical data which no one could question. Formalism thereby enabled judges to avoid engaging in the sort of utilitarian and political reasoning that had been commonplace to instrumentalism.

Nonetheless, instrumentalism did not disappear entirely from American judicial opinions. One postwar judge, for example, adhered to precedents permitting a suit for anticipatory breach of a contract for the delivery of goods, because those cases "rest[ed] on strong grounds of convenience, however difficult it may be to reconcile them with the strictest logic." [246] Likewise, a New York judge refused to adopt the *Rylands v. Fletcher* [247] rule of strict liability, on the ground that the natural right to exclusive possession of property must be modified to conform to the exigencies of "factories, machinery, dams, canals and railroads," which are "demanded by the manifold wants of mankind" and lie "at the basis of all our civilization." [248] An equally clear statement of the old instrumentalism came from another New York judge: [249]

> Society has an interest in the cultivation and improvement of lands, and in the reclamation of waste lands. It is also for the public interest that improvements shall be made, and that towns and cities shall be built. To adopt the principle that the law of nature must be observed in respect to surface drainage, would, we think, place undue restriction upon industry, and enterprise . . . . [T]he question should, we think, be determined largely upon considerations of public policy, and general utility.

Arguments of this sort, however, were unusual. Instrumentalism and the judges associated with it emerged from the Civil War in disrepute. The Supreme Court, in particular, was exposed "to

---

[246] Dingley v. Oler, 11 F. 372, 373 (C.C.D. Me. 1881).
[247] L.R. 3 H.L. 330 (1868), *aff'g* L.R. 1 Ex. 265 (1866).
[248] Losee v. Buchanan, 51 N.Y. 476, 484 (1873).
[249] Barkley v. Wilcox, 86 N.Y. 140, 148 (1881).

popular derision and even contempt" [250] and had a "loss of influence and dignity inflicted on it by the Dred Scott decision and
the events of the war." [251] The newly triumphant forces of antislavery did not deride the Taney Court for its ultimate objectives
of economic growth and national unity, for antislavery forces also
valued those objectives highly. Their criticism, rather, was directed at the Taney Court's style of reasoning. Taney, for instance, was censured because he had "not hesitate[d] to embody
his political principles in judicial decisions," [252] while his Court
was criticized for forgetting "the maxim, 'Judicis est jus dicere,
non dare,' " and for "declaring . . . rule[s] of government"
rather than "rule[s] of law." [253] As one Senator noted, it was not
surprising that the Supreme Court should give effect to its own
views of policy rather than the rules of law, since men were appointed to the Court not "because they [were] lawyers, but
rather because they [were] not lawyers," and because they
"entertained sound views on . . . transcendent [political] question[s]." [254] For the remainder of the nineteenth century, the
reputation of the Taney Court remained clouded by the charge
that, as a result "of political appointments to the bench," its decisions "read like a collection of old stump speeches." [255]

The Supreme Court was not alone in being held in low esteem
during the 1860's and 1870's; the derision extended to other
courts as well. One writer wondered whether Americans would
"go on forever . . . distrusting our judges and judicial systems." [256] Leading members of the legal profession had a "contemptuous way . . . of speaking of Courts and Judges — not
simply those of the day, but the men of the past whom the profession [had] look[ed] up to as its great ornaments." [257] Indeed,
it was said that the great majority of "American Judges 'did not
know what they were talking about' . . . [and] were illogical,
inconsistent and unreasonable," [258] because they "did not treat

---

[250] 2 C. WARREN, *supra* note 244, at 324, *quoting* an editorial in the *New York Tribune*.

[251] Nation, Dec. 23, 1869, *quoted in* 2 C. WARREN, *supra* note 244, at 506.
Indeed, one member of the Court "lost the interest and pride [he had] once felt
in the tribunal." 2 C. WARREN, *supra*, at 321, *quoting* a writing of Justice McLean.

[252] *Roger Brooke Taney*, 15 ATLANTIC MO. 151, 153, 155 (1865).

[253] *Id.* at 153–55.

[254] CONG. GLOBE, 38th Cong., 2d Sess. 1013 (1865) (remarks of Sen. Hale).

[255] W. SUMNER, ANDREW JACKSON 427 (1900).

[256] J. WRIGHT, HOW TO GET GOOD JUDGES 2 (1892).

[257] Letter from Ephraim W. Gurney, Dean of the Faculty at Harvard, to
Charles W. Eliot, President of Harvard, Spring 1883, in A. SUTHERLAND, THE
LAW AT HARVARD 188 (1967) (referring to the teaching methods of Dean Langdell
and Prof. Ames).

[258] Letter from Louis D. Brandeis to his cousin Otto A. Wehle, Nov. 12, 1876,

this or that question as a philosophical [judge] . . . building up a coherent system would have done." [259]

But, while courts in the postwar era were discredited, men nonetheless remained aware of their importance. Writers observed that courts were "frequently called upon to decide questions in which, not individuals merely, but the whole people, take an interest, and in regard to which prejudices have become excited and passions inflamed." [260] They likewise recognized that "[t]here must be an arbiter somewhere, to decide such questions, which will command respect, or they will be brought to the arbitrament of force." [261] It seemed clear that the "dignity and usefulness" of the judiciary as the arbiter of such questions could only "be promoted by extreme caution" on its part.[262] The Civil War, Reconstruction, and subsequent crises, notably a series of labor disputes, had made men aware that economic and political disagreements often escalated into violence. Thus, the temper of the age required courts to deduce their decisions from first principles and to demonstrate that their judgments were in some ultimate sense "right" rather than merely politically wise or economically expedient.[263] In the last three decades of the nineteenth century, it was obvious that antebellum instrumentalism with its elevation of expediency over legal principle would no longer dominate the American bench. To what, however, would the postbellum era turn?

One important element in the legal method of the late nineteenth century was the jurisprudence of antislavery, whose moralistic tone kept it from being discredited, as instrumentalism had been, as a purely political mode of analysis. As advocates of antislavery began to fill both state and federal judicial posts, ideas associated with antislavery jurisprudence began to surface in innumerable judicial opinions. This phenomenon can be observed in some states as early as the late 1840's, when a few judges began again to speak about "natural right and justice" and about

---

in 1 LETTERS OF LOUIS D. BRANDEIS 10 (M. Urofsky & D. Levy eds. 1971) (referring to the viewpoint of Prof. Ames).

[259] Letter from Ephraim W. Gurney, *supra* note 257.

[260] Green, *Stare Decisis*, 14 AM. L. REV. 609, 639 (1880).

[261] *Id.*

[262] HARPER'S WEEKLY, Apr. 16, 1870, *quoted in* 2 C. WARREN, *supra* note 244, at 521. A careful student of the work of the New York courts during the nineteenth century has noted that "the period following the Dred Scott Decision" was one "of judicial modesty." Corwin, *The Extension of Judicial Review in New York: 1783–1905*, 15 MICH. L. REV. 281, 295 n.63 (1917).

[263] For examples of arguments that judges should base their decisions on rules and principles, see J. BISHOP, FIRST BOOK OF THE LAW §§ 80–126 (1868); Carter, *The Ideal and the Actual in the Law*, 24 AM. L. REV. 752 (1890); Rihani, *Stare Decisis*, 57 ALBANY L.J. 392 (1898). *See generally* Green, *supra* note 260.

"[p]rotection to life, liberty, and property" as the great duty of
all governments.[264] Courts of law, according to these judges, were
"no place for the doctrine of EXPEDIENCY" and ought not shape
"their decisions with reference to predicted consequences"; [265]
the duty of courts was merely "to follow the . . . law as it is
written, regardless of consequences." [266] Particularly in constitutional litigation, when property rights allegedly were being infringed by a legislative enactment, some judges in the 1850's
argued that courts ought not give effect to their own "speculative
opinions in regard to the wisdom of the act, or the beneficial results likely to flow from it"; [267] decisions in such cases should give
effect to those "rights fully recognized as inherent and indefeasible
in man, . . . which human government can neither grant nor
abolish, alter nor abridge." [268] Even in litigation between private
parties, some judges at mid-century referred to "elementary principle[s] in reference to private rights." [269]

The phenomenon of antislavery advocates ascending the bench
and then giving effect to antislavery ideas is best illustrated by
the careers of Justices Bradley and Field. Bradley since his college days had believed that men could "NEVER consent to relinquish those rights which NATURE ha[d] given" them [270] and

---

[264] People v. Board of Supervisors, 4 Barb. 64, 71 (N.Y. Sup. Ct. 1848); see
cases cited *supra* note 126.

[265] Thorne v. Cramer, 15 Barb. 112, 120 (N.Y. Sup. Ct. 1851).

[266] Oakley v. Aspinwall, 3 N.Y. 547, 568 (1850).

[267] Wynehamer v. People, 13 N.Y. 378, 428 (1856) (opinion of Selden, J.).
While the quoted language indicates the influence of higher law and human rights
concepts, acceptance of antislavery jurisprudence was far from universal in Northern courts during the 1850's. In *Wynehamer*, Judge Comstock, while agreeing with
Judge Selden in holding the statute in question void, noted "the danger . . . when
theories, alleged to be founded in natural reason or inalienable rights, but subversive of the just and necessary powers of government, attract the belief of considerable classes of men . . . ." *Id.* at 391–92. Several of the judges, including
Selden, disavowed the theory that a legislative act could be voided even if the act
violated no express constitutional provision. The Supreme Court of Pennsylvania
rejected higher law arguments in two contemporary cases. *See* Sharpless v. Mayor
of Philadelphia, 21 Pa. 147 (1853); Passmore Williamson's Case, 26 Pa. 9 (1855).
Concurring in the latter case, Justice Lowrie observed that "there can be no
organized authority superior to government itself . . . . In civil matters there can
be no moral principle of higher importance than . . . the principle of social
order." *Id.* at 30. For similar approaches rejecting higher law arguments, see
United States v. Hanway, 26 F. Cas. 105 (No. 15,299) (C.C.E.D. Pa. 1851);
Oliver v. Kauffman, 18 F. Cas. 657 (No. 10,497) (C.C.E.D. Pa. 1850); Sim's Case,
61 Mass. (7 Cush.) 285 (1851).

[268] People v. Gallagher, 4 Mich. 244, 266 (1856) (dissenting opinion).

[269] Hay v. Cohoes Co., 2 N.Y. 159, 160 (1849).

[270] Argument by Joseph P. Bradley before the Board of Trustees of Rutgers
College, New Brunswick, N.J., *circa* 1836, *quoted in* Fairman, *The Education of*

had long believed that all men were entitled to "the enjoyment of all the natural liberty compatible with mutual security."[271] Moreover, in the years before the outbreak of the Civil War Bradley had been a staunch Republican in New Jersey, the strongest Democratic state in the North.[272] Although a Democrat, Justice Field, the other prominent exponent of antislavery jurisprudence on the Supreme Court after the war, had also been a strong exponent of antislavery and its jurisprudence before the war. In an 1858 opinion delivered when he was a judge in California, Field had referred to Christianity as "the basis of our civilization" and had considered its infusion into the nation's law "as natural as that the national sentiment of liberty should find expression in the legislation of the country."[273] Field had also written that the nation would not be free until the infamous *Scott* decision was set aside and had been one of the first men in California to side with the Union once the Civil War had broken out.[274] Finally, he had always remained close to his brother, David Dudley Field, a longtime abolitionist and an organizer of the Republican Party.[275] Nor were Bradley and Field unique. Other less prominent judicial advocates of antislavery jurisprudence in the post-Civil War era, such as Justice Brewer of the Supreme Court and Chief Justice Doe of New Hampshire, had also been politically active opponents of slavery before the war and had been infuriated by the decision in *Scott*.[276]

It was natural for such judges to revert to notions of higher law and human rights once they ascended the bench. It was especially natural for antislavery ideas to proliferate in opinions dealing with enforcement of the Civil War amendments and the federal legislation enacted pursuant thereto. In one case, for ex-

---

*a Justice: Justice Bradley and Some of his Colleagues*, 1 STAN. L. REV. 217, 229 (1949).

[271] Address by Joseph P. Bradley at Newark, N.J., July 4, 1848, *quoted in* Fairman, *Mr. Justice Bradley*, in MR. JUSTICE 69, 78 (A. Dunham & P. Kurland eds. 1956).

[272] *See* Fairman, *What Makes A Great Justice? Mr. Justice Bradley and the Supreme Court, 1870–1892*, 30 B.U. L. REV. 49, 58 (1950). New Jersey was the only free state in which the Republicans did not win all the electoral votes in the election of 1860. *See* J. RANDALL & D. DONALD, THE CIVIL WAR AND RECONSTRUCTION 134 (2d ed. 1961).

[273] *Ex parte* Newman, 9 Cal. 502, 523–24 (1858) (dissenting opinion).

[274] *See* C. SWISHER, STEPHEN J. FIELD: CRAFTSMAN OF THE LAW 110–11 (1930).

[275] *See id.* at 116.

[276] *See* J. REID, CHIEF JUSTICE: THE JUDICIAL WORLD OF CHARLES DOE 66–69 (1967); Fairman, *supra* note 270, at 244–45. For brief biographies of several other post-Civil War judges having strong antislavery backgrounds, see 2 THE JUSTICES OF THE SUPREME COURT 1789–1969, THEIR LIVES & MAJOR OPINIONS 990, 1046, 1114–16, 1221, 1381 (L. Friedman & F. Israel eds. 1969) (Justices Swayne & Davis, Chief Justice Chase, Justices Hunt & Gray).

ample, involving defendants who had been indicted for attempting to prevent some freedmen from exercising their right peaceably to assemble, a federal circuit court held that freedom of speech and the right peaceably to assemble were among the privileges and immunities of citizens protected by section one of the fourteenth amendment.[277] The court reasoned that the amendment protected all rights "which may be denominated fundamental; which belong of right to the citizens of all free states . . . ."[278] The court also alluded to the higher law origin of those rights when it reported that "[i]t is not claimed by counsel . . . that freedom of speech and the right peaceably to assemble are rights granted by the constitution, but . . . [only] that they are rights recognized and secured."[279]

Similarly, Justice Field, riding on circuit, invoked a combination of Christian ideals, and the inalienable rights of man regarding criminal procedure, both of which had been important strands in antislavery thought, in holding unconstitutional California leglislation requiring that the hair of all persons imprisoned upon failure to pay fines be cut to a length of one inch.[280] Field emphasized that the purpose of the ordinance was to authorize the state to cut the queues of Chinese convicts who did not pay their fines. The state had argued that only the prospect of the loss of his queue, which for a Chinese entailed disgrace among his countrymen and a constant dread of misfortune and suffering after death, would induce a Chinese defendant to pay his fine. But Field responded that "[p]robably the bastinado, or the knout, or the thumbscrew, or the rack, would accomplish the same end,"[281] and concluded that it would "always be the duty of the judiciary to declare and enforce the paramount law of the nation" against such legislation, which was "unworthy of a brave and manly people."[282] It was simply "not creditable to the humanity and civilization of our people, much less to their Christianity, that an ordinance of this character was possible,"[283] and he accordingly ruled that the fourteenth amendment, codifying the nation's humanity, civilization, and Christianity, made it impossible.

Ideas about civil rights associated with the antislavery movement appeared in other cases as well. In *Leeper v. Texas*,[284] Chief

---

[277] United States v. Hall, 26 F. Cas. 79 (No. 15,282) (C.C.S.D. Ala. 1871).

[278] *Id.* at 81.

[279] *Id.* at 80.

[280] Ho Ah Kow v. Nunan, 12 F. Cas. 252 (No. 6546) (C.C.D. Cal. 1879).

[281] *Id.* at 265.

[282] *Id.* at 256–57.

[283] *Id.* at 255.

[284] 139 U.S. 462 (1891).

Justice Fuller confirmed that states could deal freely with criminals within their borders, provided they did not subject "the individual to the arbitrary exercise of the powers of government unrestrained by the established principles of private right and distributive justice." [285] Similarly, Justice Field spoke in *Ex parte Jackson* [286] of "the great principle embodied in the fourth amendment of the Constitution." [287] Most explicit of all was Justice Brewer, who in a state court opinion authored before his appointment to the Supreme Court referred to bills of rights as "those essential truths, those axioms of civil and political liberty upon which all free governments are founded . . . ." [288] In similar language, a Louisiana state judge viewed bills of rights as "declaratory of the general principles of republican government, and of the fundamental rights of the citizen, rights usually of so fundamental a character, that, while such express declarations may serve to guard and protect them, they are not essential to the creation of such rights, which exist independent of constitutional provisions." [289]

The antislavery ideal of equality was also commonplace in post-Civil War judicial opinions. Thus, when a railroad argued before the Supreme Court in the 1870's that a common carrier had a right to make a contract disclaiming its common law liability on the principle that all men were "permitted to make their own agreements," Justice Bradley responded for the Court that "[t]he carrier and his customer [did] not stand on a footing of equality." [290] Bradley thus refused to protect the railroad's liberty of contract with the same rigor he would have applied to protect similar individual freedom, since protection of the railroad's contract rights would not secure liberty and equality for all men. Likewise, the Supreme Court of Mississippi refused to recognize an alleged property right of a railroad to be exempt from taxation, for the claim was thought to be inconsistent with that "[e]quality in bearing a common burden, which is natural [and] right [and was] secured alike to the corporation and to the citizen." [291]

Finally, the antislavery concern with according special pro-

---

[285] *Id.* at 468.

[286] 96 U.S. 727 (1877).

[287] *Id.* at 733.

[288] State *ex rel.* St. Joseph & D.C.R.R. v. Nemaha County, 7 Kan. 542, 555 (1871) (dissenting opinion).

[289] State *ex rel.* Liversey v. Judge of Civil Dist. Court, 34 La. 741, 743 (1882).

[290] Railroad Co. v. Lockwood, 84 U.S. (17 Wall.) 357, 378–79 (1873).

[291] Adams v. Yazoo & M.V.R.R., 77 Miss. 194, 277, 24 So. 200, 216 (1898) (language reported in Southern Reporter slightly different from language quoted in text).

tection to property and contract rights was an important element in many postbellum cases, most notably the *Slaughter House Cases*.[292] Plaintiffs had challenged the constitutionality of state legislation conferring upon a corporation of seventeen persons the right to build the only plant for slaughter of animals in the city of New Orleans and requiring all butchers to use that plant. On circuit, Justice Bradley upheld the challenge, holding that the right to follow a lawful industrial pursuit, the right to hold property, and the right to equal protection of the laws were among the privileges and immunities of citizens of the United States. Bradley declared:[293]

> [A]ny government which deprives its citizens of the right to engage in any lawful pursuit, subject only to reasonable restrictions, or at least subject only to such restrictions as are reasonably within the power of government to impose, — is tyrannical and unrepublican. And if to enforce arbitrary restrictions made for the benefit of a favored few, it takes away and destroys the citizen's property without trial or condemnation, it is guilty of violating . . . one of the fundamental principles of free government.

The Supreme Court disagreed with him by a vote of 5–4, but Bradley adhered to his views. In a dissent to the Court's opinion, Bradley wrote that citizenship in a free nation carried with it "certain incidental rights, privileges and immunities of the greatest importance," and "a sure and undoubted title to equal rights in any and every State in this Union." [294] Certain rights, in short, inhered in the very nature of republican government. Justice Field, even more explicitly, wrote that the fourteenth amendment "was intended to give practical effect to the declaration of 1776 of inalienable rights, rights which are the gift of the Creator; which the law does not confer, but only recognizes," among them the rights to pursue an occupation and to acquire and hold property.[295] These companion dissents of Justices Bradley and Field would provide the foundation for the doctrine of substantive due process adopted by the majority of the Court at the turn of the century.

Other opinions and arguments continuing the antislavery traditions with respect to property and contract rights reasoned, for example, that regulatory laws could "not conflict with any

---

[292] 83 U.S. (16 Wall.) 36 (1873).

[293] Live-Stock Dealers' & Butchers' Ass'n v. Crescent City Live-Stock Landing & Slaughter-House Co., 15 F. Cas. 649, 652 (No. 8408) (C.C.D. La. 1870).

[294] Slaughter House Cases, 83 U.S. (16 Wall.) 36, 113, 116 (1873).

[295] *Id.* at 105. *See also* 83 U.S. (16 Wall.) at 115–16 (Bradley, J., dissenting).

. . . natural right" [296] and that "one of the fundamental objects of all civilized government was the preservation of the rights of private property" since those rights were "the very keystone in the arch upon which all civilized government rest[ed]." [297]  Mr. Justice Harlan stated that private property was "founded in natural equity, and . . . laid down by jurists as a principle of universal law. Indeed, in a free government, almost all other rights would become worthless if the government possessed an uncontrollable power over the private fortune of every citizen." [298] "[T]he demands of absolute and eternal justice" thus prohibited "private property, legally acquired or legally held," from being "spoliated or destroyed in the interests of public health, morals or welfare without compensation." [299]

As before the Civil War, the right to use and dispose of property was viewed as a necessary consequence of the right to acquire and hold it. Every man, that is, had a "natural right to sell or keep his commodities as best suit[ed] his own purpose." [300]  This concept of freedom of contract embraced not only the right to use and dispose of property, but also "the right of every man to be free in the use of his powers and faculties, and to adopt and pursue such avocation or calling as he may choose . . . ." [301] Judges spoke often of "the natural right to gain a livelihood by intelligence, honesty, and industry in the arts, the sciences, the professions, or other vocations"; [302] they added that "[a]mong [the] inalienable rights" proclaimed in the Declaration of Independence was "the right to pursue any lawful business or vocation." [303]

Judges put these antislavery notions of freedom of contract to use in a series of cases during the mid-1890's enjoining strikes and other activities by labor unions. Although a few judges and commentators thought that to enjoin a strike was "tantamount

---

[296] Butchers' Union Co. v. Crescent City Co., 111 U.S. 746, 754 (1884) (Field, J., concurring).

[297] Pollock v. Farmer's Loan & Trust Co., 157 U.S. 429, 534 (1895) (Joseph H. Choate, argument for Appellant).

[298] Chicago B. & Q.R.R. v. Chicago, 166 U.S. 226, 236 (1897).

[299] 10 RY. & CORP. L.J. 281 (1891). For similar statements on taxation and appropriation of private property, see Monongahela Navigation Co. v. United States, 148 U.S. 312, 324 (1893); Loan Ass'n v. Topeka, 87 U.S. (20 Wall.) 655, 664 (1874); People ex rel. Detroit & H.R.R. v. Salem, 20 Mich. 452, 473 (1870); Boston C. & M.R.R. v. State, 60 N.H. 87, 94 (1880); Morrison v. Manchester, 58 N.H. 538, 539 (1879) (argument for Plaintiff).

[300] Brief for Plaintiff in Error at 2–3, Walker v. Sauvinet, 92 U.S. 90 (1876).

[301] Braceville Coal Co. v. People, 147 Ill. 66, 71, 35 N.E. 62, 63 (1893).

[302] *In re* Leach, 134 Ind. 665, 668, 34 N.E. 641, 642 (1893).

[303] Butchers' Union Co. v. Crescent City Co., 111 U.S. 746, 757 (1884) (Field, J., concurring).

to decreeing a specific performance of a contract of service, which [would result] in a state of *slavery*"[304] and "an invasion of one's natural liberty,[305] others feared that many union activities would lead to "the obliteration of legal and natural rights."[306] One such right, in the words of William Howard Taft, the future President and Chief Justice, was the worker's "inalienable right to bestow his labor where he will."[307] Another was the right of "every owner of property" to "work it as he will, by whom he pleases, at such wages, and upon such terms as he can make . . . ."[308] These rights, particularly the right of the individual to bestow his labor as he pleased, were, it will be recalled, among the very rights for which the Civil War had been fought. Hence, even in granting injunctions against unions that had not called strikes, but merely sought to "coerce" or "vex" workmen,[309] judges who had received their education or begun their professional careers during the Civil War era were reasoning in a manner that was consistent with the values that had emerged triumphantly from the war. It was, they observed, simply "preposterous" that unions should take the place of former slave-drivers and "attempt to issue orders that free men are bound to obey . . . ."[310]

Antislavery ideas appeared in the scholarship as well as in the judicial opinions of the late nineteenth century. Some writers stressed the higher law basis which had characterized much antislavery thought. For instance, Joel Bishop, a leading scholar of the criminal law, wrote that "the rules of right, and of rightful association, given by God to man, are . . . portions of the 'authority' which binds our tribunals . . . ."[311] He continued that all legal institutions performed their labors "in subjection to one great, immutable, pre-existent law."[312] For Bishop law was thus not the product of man's will, but of eternal standards of justice

---

[304] Note, 28 AM. L. REV. 269 (1894).

[305] Arthur v. Oakes, 63 F. 310, 317 (7th Cir. 1894).

[306] Farmers' Loan & Trust Co. v. Northern Pac. R.R., 60 F. 803, 822 (C.C.E.D. Wis. 1894).

[307] Toledo, A.A. & N.M. Ry. v. Pennsylvania Co., 54 F. 730, 737 (C.C.N.D. Ohio 1893); *accord*, Coeur d'Alene Consol. & Mining Co. v. Miners' Union, 51 F. 260, 263 (C.C.D. Idaho 1892).

[308] Coeur d'Alene Consol. & Mining Co. v. Miners' Union, 51 F. 260, 263 (C.C.D. Idaho 1892).

[309] Old Dominion S.S. Co. v. McKenna, 30 F. 48, 50 (C.C.S.D.N.Y. 1887); *accord*, Farmers' Loan & Trust Co. v. Northern Pac. R.R., 60 F. 803, 820-21 (C.C.E.D. Wis. 1894); Casey v. Typographical Union No. 3, 45 F. 135, 143 (C.C.S.D. Ohio 1891).

[310] *In re* Higgins, 27 F. 443, 445 (C.C.N.D. Tex. 1886).

[311] J. BISHOP, *supra* note 263, at § 87.

[312] *Id.* at § 88.

and morality. Other commentators agreed that it was neither "possible, or, if it were, . . . desirable, to separate dogmatically the domain of law from that of ethics." [313] They thought that judges, when formulating law, were "rightfully, because necessarily, within the domain of ethics"; [314] that, although "lawyers must discriminate law from morality, and . . . keep separate and distinct their respective provinces, . . . these provinces always adjoin each other"; [315] and that "ethical considerations can no more be excluded from the administration of justice, which is the end and purpose of all civil laws, than one can exclude the vital air from his room and live." [316]

Other more secular writers placed primary emphasis on fundamental principles of republican government as a source of American law. One, for example, thought that "law should be the sanctuary of liberty" and that, if it did not so remain, "this glorious and grand country will be converted into a monarchy clothed in the garb of a republic." [317] Another writer thought that "[t]he distinctive and characteristic feature of the American system is equality before the law" — that the foundation of American law was "a government of equality of rights, equality of duties and equality of burdens." [318] Most explicit of all was Thomas M. Cooley, who in his book, *Constitutional Limitations*, spoke of rights which "may well be regarded as 'absolutely necessary to preserve the advantages of liberty, and to maintain a free government'"; [319] in particular, he wrote that "[t]he right of the people peaceably to assemble, and to petition the government for a redress of grievances, is one which 'would seem unnecessary to be expressly provided for in a republican government, since it results from the very nature and structure of its institutions.'" [320]

But, while the language of antislavery jurisprudence continued to be used frequently during the three closing decades of the nineteenth century, it never became the sole source of American law. At least two explanations suggest themselves. In the first place, a dogged adherence to immutable "higher law" precepts of antislavery jurisprudence would have been embarrassing in the many cases in which judges continued to change human law by

---

[313] J. DILLON, LAWS AND JURISPRUDENCE OF ENGLAND AND AMERICA 19 (1895).

[314] *Id.* at 13 n.1.

[315] *Id.* at 17.

[316] *Id.*

[317] Rihani, *supra* note 263, at 396.

[318] W. GUTHRIE, LECTURES ON THE FOURTEENTH ARTICLE OF AMENDMENT TO THE CONSTITUTION OF THE UNITED STATES 106 (1898).

[319] T. COOLEY, TREATISE ON THE CONSTITUTIONAL LIMITATIONS 378 (4th ed. 1874).

[320] *Id.* at 432.

overruling prior decisions.[321] "It [was] not an uncommon occurrence for the highest [court] . . . of the land, avowedly to reverse
its prior decisions," sometimes "to the intense astonishment of
the public"; [322] the *Legal Tender* cases, in which the appointment
of two new Justices resulted in the Supreme Court's overruling
its year-old decision that had declared the paper money issued
during the Civil War unconstitutional when used in payment of
pre-existing debts,[323] were only the most notorious examples. State
court precedents also were "frequently departed from, when such
adjudication[s] . . . [were] found to be wrong." [324] Although
some fluctuations in human law might have been explained away
as results of the varying abilities of men to ascertain higher-than-
human legal principles, the present author knows of no judge or
legal writer of the period who adopted such a rationale. Rather,
the courts in many cases continued to recognize that the rules of
law could not remain forever fixed by immutable moral principles
and that "the life of the common law system . . . consist[ed]
largely in its power of adaptation to . . . the requirements of
an ever advancing civilization." [325] Perhaps the best examples
of late nineteenth century judges' appreciation of *Realpolitik*
even when it flew in the face of their higher principles were the
*Civil Rights Cases* [326] and *Plessy v. Ferguson.*[327]

A second explanation is that the jurisprudential precepts of a
movement that had essentially one goal — freeing the slaves —
were of a limited usefulness which could not encompass all the
demands placed on the legal system of the late nineteenth century.
Human rights concepts provide courts a handle only in the narrow
range of cases in which human rights are at stake; such concepts
are of no help in deciding the great mass of cases in which two

---

[321] *See, e.g.,* Board of Comm'rs v. State *ex rel.* Shields, 155 Ind. 604, 58 N.E.
1037 (1900); Board of Comm'rs v. Allman, 142 Ind. 573, 42 N.E. 206 (1895);
Greencastle S. Turnpike Co. v. State *ex rel.* Malot, 28 Ind. 382 (1867); Remey v.
Iowa Cent. Ry., 116 Iowa 133, 89 N.W. 218 (1902); Adams v. Yazoo & M.V.R.R.,
77 Miss. 194, 24 So. 200 (1898); Storrie v. Cortes, 90 Tex. 283, 38 S.W. 154
(1896); Willis v. Owen, 43 Tex. 41 (1875); Burks v. Hinton, 77 Va. 1 (1883).
The courts hesitated to overrule prior decisions which protected property and
contract rights, however. *See, e.g., In re* House Resolutions Concerning St.
Improvements, 15 Colo. 598, 26 P. 323 (1891); Lindsay v. Lindsay, 47 Ind. 283
(1874); Rockhill v. Nelson, 24 Ind. 422 (1865); Grubbs v. State, 24 Ind. 295
(1865); Long v. Long, 79 Mo. 644 (1883); Roof v. Railroad Co., 4 S.C. 61
(1872); State *ex rel.* Gaines v. Whitworth, 76 Tenn. 594 (1881).
[322] Tiedeman, *The Doctrine of Stare Decisis,* 3 UNIV. L. REV. 11, 12–13 (1896).
[323] Legal Tender Cases, 79 U.S. (12 Wall.) 457 (1871), *overruling* Hepburn v.
Griswold, 75 U.S. (8 Wall.) 603 (1870).
[324] Bird v. Sellers, 122 Mo. 23, 32, 26 S.W. 668, 670 (1894).
[325] Parsons v. State, 81 Ala. 577, 584, 2 So. 854, 858 (1887).
[326] 109 U.S. 3 (1883).
[327] 163 U.S. 537 (1896).

or more possible results are equally consistent with men's enjoyment of their "natural rights."

For these reasons, judges and lawyers of the postbellum era were forced inevitably to supplement the jurisprudential ideas of their antislavery traditions with ideas derived from other sources. Despite its checkered reputation, instrumentalism itself, as we have seen,[328] sometimes provided the rationale for postwar judicial decisions. A more important input into the jurisprudence of the late nineteenth century was provided by that period's growing preoccupation with the scientific method. Within a few years of the publication of Charles Darwin's *Origin of the Species* in 1859, science, as a process of reasoning, had become a dominant force in American intellectual circles.[329] For reasons the analysis of which is beyond the scope of this Article, intellectuals in most fields of endeavor began to follow the "method of modern science" — "[t]he classification of facts and the formation . . . upon the basis of this classification . . . [of] judgments independent of the idiosyncrasies of the individual mind."[330] The extent to which the new scientific method permeated American intellectual circles emerges most clearly, perhaps, in the efforts not only of natural scientists and the newly emerging social scientists, but of students of history and of *belles lettres* as well, to organize their disciplines on a scientific basis and require prospective entrants to undergo rigorous scientific training culminating in the writing of a doctoral dissertation.[331]

The scientific ideal also became an aspiration of the legal profession.[332] In the words of one professor at the Yale Law

---

[328] See pp. 547–48 *supra.*

[329] See G. FREDRICKSON, THE INNER CIVIL WAR: NORTHERN INTELLECTUALS AND THE CRISIS OF THE UNION 199–216 (1965); M. HOWE, JUSTICE OLIVER WENDELL HOLMES: THE SHAPING YEARS, 1841–1870, at 208–22 (1957); R. WIEBE, THE SEARCH FOR ORDER, 1877–1920, at 147 (1967).

[330] K. PEARSON, THE GRAMMAR OF SCIENCE 7 (1895). This concept of science, which Pearson believed to be applicable to the social as well as the physical sciences, see id. at 6–7, was picked up by William Graham Sumner, perhaps the leading sociologist of the day. See W. SUMNER, *The Scientific Attitude of Mind,* in SUMNER TODAY: SELECTED ESSAYS OF WILLIAM GRAHAM SUMNER WITH COMMENTS BY AMERICAN LEADERS 127 (M. Davie ed. 1940). Although scientists today are beginning increasingly to view their discipline as involving a dynamic and ultimately personal process of theory formulation, followed by experiments seeking empirical verification of theory, which are followed, in turn, by a reformulation of theory, a leading historian of science maintains that, until recently, science was almost uniformly viewed as a series of techniques for gathering data, together with the logical operations employed in classifying and organizing that data into coherent, nonidiosyncratic scientific laws. See T. KUHN, THE STRUCTURE OF SCIENTIFIC REVOLUTIONS 1–5 (2d ed. 1962).

[331] See H. GOOD, A HISTORY OF AMERICAN EDUCATION 470–72 (2d ed. 1962).

[332] Of course, lawyers in the first half of the century had also been influenced

School, "the law [was], after all, the science of justice." [333] "Law, considered as a science, consist[ed] of certain principles or doctrines," the mastery of which so "as to be able to apply them with constant . . . certainty . . . [was] what constitute[d] a true lawyer." [334] As it had in other disciplines, the scientific ideal led to a revolution in legal education — the introduction of the case system, which "proceed[ed] on the theory that law is a science" and that "only by regarding [it] as a science [could] one . . . justify its being taught in a university." [335] "The whole tendency of the [case] system would be, to build up a great school of law as an exact science . . . ." [336]

The concept of law as science led to a very different analysis of precedents than the analysis in which the instrumentalists of the first half of the century had engaged. When presented with an alleged precedent, instrumentalist lawyers and judges first asked whether the precedent furthered a policy, such as economic development, which the law ought to further. If it did, then they

---

by concepts of science and had, on occasion, spoken of law as a science. *See* Gawalt, *Massachusetts Legal Education in Transition, 1766–1840*, 17 AM. J. LEGAL HIST. 27, 37–38, 42–43 (1973). In Horwitz, *The Conservative Tradition in the Writing of Legal History*, 17 AM. J. LEG. HIST. 275, 282 (1973), it is urged that the scientific ideal was used by the legal profession throughout the nineteenth century to demonstrate that law was distinct from the realms of power and politics. While it may be that the scientific ideal had its roots early in the nineteenth century, it is the mid-century crisis over slavery which, by weakening the courts, made the disassociation of law from politics particularly urgent.

[333] Phelps, *quoted in Methods of Legal Education*, 1 YALE L.J. 139, 142 (1892).

[334] C. LANGDELL, A SELECTION OF CASES ON THE LAW OF CONTRACTS viii (2d ed. 1879).

[335] Keener, *quoted in Methods of Legal Education*, 1 YALE L.J. 139, 144 (1892).

[336] Letter from Ephraim W. Gurney, *supra* note 257. Given these intellectual trends in the closing years of the century, one might have expected judges to have turned to principles associated with Social Darwinism. But, although the judges may have had Darwinian notions about the survival of the fittest in their minds, *see* Lochner v. New York, 198 U.S. 45, 74–76 (1905) (Holmes, J., dissenting), they do not appear to have given expression to them in their opinions. The present writer, at least, has found no opinion in which judges expressed Darwinian as distinguished from merely laissez-faire ideas that rested, in turn, upon antislavery ideas about the rights of the individual. The closest I have come to finding Darwinian language is in State v. Goodwill, 33 W. Va. 179, 10 S.E. 285 (1889), where the court observed that "[t]he natural law of supply and demand is the best law of trade." *Id.* at 184, 10 S.E. at 287. This language, however, is not truly Darwinian; rather it reflects the influence of classical economic theory, which was related to but nonetheless distinct from and antecedent to Social Darwinism. *See* R. HOFSTADTER, SOCIAL DARWINISM IN AMERICAN THOUGHT, 1860–1915, at 121–24 (1945). The quoted language, moreover, is merely a single sentence in an eight-page opinion that discusses at great length the rights of individuals in a free and republican society. For a discussion of Social Darwinism, see *id.*

followed the precedent, often with little discussion of the policy itself or of other arguably relevant but conflicting lines of authority. However, if the precedent did not further the desired policy, then the courts usually rejected it, arguing that they did not have to follow English cases since American constitutions adopted the common law only when it furthered American needs, or that their own precedents could be jettisoned when the needs of society had changed and the consent of the people to a new rule of law could be presumed.[337] For pre-Civil War courts, precedents were convenient justifications for results, since they had the sanction of the reception acts, but no precedent was conclusive if it did not further society's current needs.

For the legal scientists of the closing decades of the nineteenth century, precedents had a very different significance. "Adjudged cases [were] to juridical science what ascertained facts and experiments [were] to the natural sciences";[338] the law library was to lawyers "all that the laboratories of the university [were] to the chemists and physicists, all that the museum of natural history [was] to the zoologists, all that the botanical garden [was] to the botanists."[339] Just as the task of the natural scientist was "[t]he classification of facts" and the formulation of conclusions on the basis of those facts,[340] so too the task of the legal scientist was "to select, classify, and arrange all the cases which . . . contributed . . . [to the] establishment of any of its essential doctrines."[341] Normally, the legal scientists of the late nineteenth century expected all precedents to be consistent, but if they were not, then the scientist had to reconcile the seeming contradictions. "To believe two contradictory propositions at the same time . . . [was] no part of the duty of a legal writer."[342] His task was to "search for a principle which shall reconcile all the authorities, or, if this is out of the question, a principle which shall reconcile as large a part of them as possible . . . ."[343] If the cases could not be reconciled, then the final task of the scientist was to "determine which represent[ed] the main principle, and which the anomaly, the exception, and to do this he should look at the past . . . ."[344] Looking to the past meant, as a prac-

---

[337] Cf. Horwitz, supra note 2, at 311–16.

[338] Hover, Stare Decisis, 52 ALBANY L.J. 73 (1895).

[339] Address by C. Langdell to the Harvard Law School Association, 1886, in A. SUTHERLAND, THE LAW AT HARVARD 175 (1967); see Keener, supra note 335, at 144.

[340] K. PEARSON, supra note 330, at 7.

[341] C. LANGDELL, supra note 334, at ix.

[342] Gray, Remoteness of Charitable Gifts, 7 HARV. L. REV. 406, 414 (1894).

[343] Lowell, The Status of Our New Possessions — A Third View, 13 HARV. L. REV. 155 (1899).

[344] Gray, supra note 342, at 414.

tical matter, looking to England, as did most casebook authors like Langdell, who included over ninety percent English cases in his 1871 edition.[345] Whatever cases could be shown to "have no foundation in English jurisprudence" and "to be at variance with an unbroken line of precedents in the English books"[346] were simply viewed as "depart[ing] from the rule of the common law."[347] While it may be that the legal scientists refused to follow precedents as often as the instrumentalists had done, they did so on different grounds — on grounds of intellectual consistency rather than on grounds of policy.

Together with the higher law jurisprudence made popular by the antislavery movement's battlefield and electoral victories, the new scientific ideal reshaped the reasoning processes of both lawyers and courts. Whereas a typical antebellum case like *M'Culloch v. Eagle Insurance Co.*[348] had held that no contract arose when an acceptance of an offer crossed a revocation of the offer in the mails, on the ground that such a rule would be "reasonable in mercantile contracts,"[349] Langdell's *Summary of the Law of Contracts*,[350] published in 1879, took a very different approach. Taking note of an argument "that the purposes of substantial justice, and the interests of the contracting parties as understood by themselves . . . [would] be best served by holding that the contract [was] complete the moment the letter of acceptance

---

[345] 1–8 C. LANGDELL, A SELECTION OF CASES ON THE LAW OF CONTRACTS (1871). Counting only primary cases, the precise distribution is 92% British, 8% American. Other casebooks of the late nineteenth century, while rarely so extreme, also rely heavily on British cases: 1–2 J. AMES & J. SMITH, A SELECTION OF CASES ON THE LAW OF TORTS (1893) (50% British); M. BIGELOW, LEADING CASES ON THE LAW OF TORTS DETERMINED BY THE COURTS OF AMERICA AND ENGLAND (1875) (50% British); 1–6 J. GRAY, SELECT CASES AND OTHER AUTHORITIES ON THE LAW OF PROPERTY (1888–1892) (70% British); 2 S. WILLISTON, A SELECTION OF CASES ON THE LAW OF CONTRACTS (1894) (41% British — note however that this book was designed as a supplement to C. LANGDELL, *supra*). By comparison, typical modern casebooks contain only a smattering of British cases: L. FULLER & M. EISENBERG, BASIC CONTRACT LAW (3d ed. 1972) (16% British); C. GREGORY & H. KALVEN, CASES AND MATERIALS ON TORTS (1959) (15% British); F. KESSLER & G. GILMORE, CONTRACTS: CASES AND MATERIALS (2d ed. 1970) (14% British); W. PROSSER & Y. SMITH, CASES AND MATERIALS ON TORTS (4th ed. 1967) (7% British). In addition, the *American Law Revivew*, described as "probably the most important" American legal periodical of its day, was "as much concerned with developments in the law of England as with the current American scene." M. HOWE, *supra* note 329, at 264.

[346] J. Hare, Notes of a Course of Lectures on Contracts Delivered in the Law Department of the University of Pennsylvania, 1882, at 131–32 (Biddle Law Library, University of Pennsylvania).

[347] *Id.* at 133.

[348] 18 Mass. (1 Pick.) 278 (1822). For discussion of this case, see pp. 521–22 *supra*.

[349] 18 Mass. (1 Pick.) at 281.

[350] C. LANGDELL, *supra* note 334, at 985.

[was] mailed," Langdell responded that "[t]he true answer to this argument is, that it is irrelevant," [351] noting later that it was the obligation of a court in deciding a case "to support the decision upon principle." [352]  The same shift in legal reasoning was evidenced in cases dealing with the ancient law of waste. *Pynchon v. Stearns* [353] had rejected the English rule that construction of a house and an entry way on a life estate would constitute waste, since such a rule, if "universally adopted in this country, would greatly impede the progress of improvement," [354] *Gaines v. Green Pond Iron Mining Co.*,[355] an 1881 New Jersey case, reached an analogous result, holding that a life tenant could continue to extract ore from existing veins of a mine without committing waste. But it arrived at that result on very different grounds. It carefully analyzed twenty-one cases, the majority of them English, and concluded that the English rule permitted the extraction of ore from existing veins and that the American rule was at least as broad.[356]

---

[351] *Id.* at 20–21.

[352] *Id.* at 97.

[353] 52 Mass. (11 Met.) 304 (1846).

[354] *Id.* at 312.

[355] 33 N.J.Eq. 603 (E. & A. 1881).

[356] The legal scientists' predilection for reconciling inconsistent cases was also apparent in the efforts of late nineteenth century courts and commentators to harmonize a line of Massachusetts cases dealing with the duties between neighbors. By the early 1870's, Massachusetts had been left with a body of case law holding that a landowner could undermine his neighbor's cellar, *see* Thurston v. Hancock, 12 Mass. 220 (1815), but that a municipality could not flood it, *see* Wilson v. City of New Bedford, 102 Mass. 261 (1871); that one neighbor could deprive another of well water, *see* Greenleaf v. Francis, 35 Mass. (18 Pick.) 117 (1836), but could not pollute it, *see* Ball v. Nye, 99 Mass. 582 (1868); and that one man could injure his neighbor with a cane, as long as he struck him unintentionally, *see* Brown v. Kendall, 60 Mass. (6 Cush.) 292 (1850), but that he could not injure him with snow falling from his roof, even though he had taken every possible precaution to keep the snow from falling, *see* Shipley v. Fifty Associates, 106 Mass. 194 (1870). Thomas M. Cooley, the Michigan law professor and judge, made a number of attempts at harmonization. Focusing on *Ball* and *Greenleaf*, he reasoned in Upjohn v. Board of Health, 46 Mich. 542, 9 N.W. 845 (1881), that the law required a landowner to take whatever precautions were "practicable" not to injure his neighbor; he implied that, while it might be practicable to keep filth within a vault, it might not be practicable to drill a well without interfering with the water supply of a neighboring well, since the course of underground streams was often unknown. *Id.* at 549, 9 N.W. at 848. But, as Cooley himself realized, this distinction was not a persuasive one. *Id.* at 549–50, 9 N.W. at 848. He had made a far more comprehensive attempt at harmonization in his 1879 *A Treatise on the Law of Torts*. In part, he achieved apparent harmonization by the way in which he classified the cases: *Brown v. Kendall* was discussed under "Accidental Injuries," *id.* at 80 n.2, *Thurston v. Hancock* was discussed under "Removing Lateral Support," *id.* at 549 n.6, and the other four cases were discussed in sections dealing with nuisances caused by

The notion of science thus contributed importantly to the jurisprudence of the postbellum era. It was able to do so because, like antislavery jurisprudence, it enabled judges to avoid discussing questions of policy and expediency, questions which, in essence, were viewed as legislative. In most cases, either law as a science or higher law principles provided judges with a point of reference unalterable by any act of judicial will, from which the legal reasoning process could proceed by accepted modes of analysis. Men like Thomas Cooley and John Dillon thus drew both upon higher law ideas that had been a prominent part of antislavery jurisprudence [357] and upon concepts of scientific legal analysis [358] to synthesize a new jurisprudence of formalism.

In doing so, they and other judges sometimes adopted as their initial point of reference some principle of human rights that was fundamental to a republican form of government; the existence of such a reference point would justify a judge in refusing to promulgate a rule that would endanger such rights. But if, as was frequently true, concepts of human rights only limited and did not entirely eliminate the range of judicial choice, judges could then turn to another reference point — past judicial decisions — from which they could extract principles with which to decide cases. Although the courts could "extend the application of the principles of common law" by applying old principles to new cases [359] and, as new cases accumulated over the course of time, thereby transform the principles, no act of judicial will, not even overruling, could erase past decisions from the historical record. Moreover, the act of extracting principles from the decisions was not thought to be an act of will. On the contrary, the extraction of principles was an intellectual exercise; it required lawyers to reconcile and harmonize as many past decisions

---

water, *id.* at 567–75. Even *Greenleaf* was discussed some ten pages away from the principal discussion of the three post-Civil War cases, under the heading, "Subterranean Waters," *id.* at 581 n.1, thus making direct comparison of the cases unnecessary. To the extent, however, that a wary reader himself made the comparison, Cooley provided him with a principle of harmonization, for he discussed *Ball, Shipley,* and *Wilson* together with *Rylands v. Fletcher,* upon which all three had relied, in sections of the book devoted to the liability of property owners who gathered objects, such as filth, water or snow, on their premises. *Id.* at 567–75. *Brown, Thurston,* and *Greenleaf* were, of course, all distinguishable, since they involved no such gathering.

[357] For examples of higher law language used by Cooley and Dillon, see People *ex rel.* Detroit & H.R.R. v. Salem, 20 Mich. 452, 473 (1870); A. PAUL, *supra* note 24, at 79–81.

[358] For examples of scientific analysis by Cooley and Dillon, see T. COOLEY, A TREATISE ON THE LAW OF TORTS (1879); J. DILLON, TREATISE ON THE LAW OF MUNICIPAL CORPORATIONS (1872).

[359] Roberson v. Rochester Folding Box Co., 171 N.Y. 538, 561, 64 N.E. 442, 449 (1902) (dissenting opinion).

as possible and to reject only those that did not fit into the mainstream of case development. The process was one of sustained research and close analysis of the judicial record bequeathed by the past rather than one of determining desirable social policies for the future.

Judges in the last third of the nineteenth century, in the words of Oliver Wendell Holmes, Jr., did "not like to discuss questions of policy," for "[v]iews of policy [were] taught by experience of the interests of life," and "[t]hose interests [were] fields of battle." [360] Americans had just come from those fields and had no desire to return. Thus American judges sought to clothe their decisions in the language of formal "logical deduction" and to reason either from "general propositions" [361] about the essential meaning of republicanism or from the immutable records of the English common law. They sought to make "legal reasoning seem like mathematics" [362] and to convince themselves that, if men differed over a question of law, "it meant simply that one side or the other were not doing their sums right, and, if they would take more trouble, agreement inevitably would come." [363]

Formalism — the notion that social controversies could be resolved by deductions drawn from first principles on which all men agreed or by inductions drawn from the "evidence" of past decisions — thus became the common denominator of late nineteenth century American jurisprudence. The new jurisprudence of "logical method and form flatter[ed] that longing for certainty and for repose" [364] that arose out of the fratricidal strife of the middle and the seeming social chaos of the end of the century. But as Holmes foresaw when the old century was ending and a new one beginning, "certainty . . . and repose" would not be "the destiny" of American law in the years to come.[365]

---

[360] Holmes, *Privilege, Malice, and Intent*, 8 HARV. L. REV. 1, 7 (1894).

[361] *Id.* at 3.

[362] *Id.* at 7.

[363] Holmes, *The Path of the Law*, 10 HARV. L. REV. 457, 465 (1897); *see* J. BISHOP, *supra* note 263, at § 85–86.

[364] Holmes, *supra* note 363, at 466.

[365] *Id.* at 466.

# C. SUBSTANTIVE AND PROCEDURAL LAW

# 7
# THE HISTORICAL FOUNDATIONS OF MODERN CONTRACT LAW

*MORTON J. HORWITZ*

VOLUME 87        MARCH 1974        NUMBER 5

# HARVARD LAW REVIEW

## THE HISTORICAL FOUNDATIONS OF MODERN CONTRACT LAW

### Morton J. Horwitz *

*It has long been assumed that the development of modern contract law was complete once English judges had declared late in the sixteenth century that "a promise on a promise will maintain an action upon the case." Professor Horwitz argues to the contrary that the modern will theory of contract did not appear until the late eighteenth and early nineteenth centuries, when the spread of markets forced jurists to attack equitable conceptions of exchange as inimical to emerging contract principles such as those allowing recovery of expectation damages.*

MODERN contract law is fundamentally a creature of the nineteenth century. It arose in both England and America as a reaction to and criticism of the medieval tradition of substantive justice that, surprisingly, had remained a vital part of eighteenth century legal thought, especially in America. Only in the nineteenth century did judges and jurists finally reject the longstanding belief that the justification of contractual obligation is derived from the inherent justice or fairness of an exchange. In its place, they asserted for the first time that the source of the obligation of contract is the convergence of the wills of the contracting parties.

Beginning with the first English treatise on contract, Powell's *Essay Upon the Law of Contracts and Agreements* (1790), a major feature of contract writing has been its denunciation of equitable conceptions of substantive justice as undermining the "rule of law." [1] "[I]t is absolutely necessary for the advantage of the public at large," Powell wrote, "that the rights of the subject should . . . depend upon certain and fixed principles of law, and not upon rules and constructions of equity, which when applied . . . , must be arbitrary and uncertain, depending, in the extent of their application, upon the will and caprice of the

---

* Assistant Professor of Law, Harvard Law School. B.A., C.C.N.Y., 1959; Ph.D., Harvard, 1964; LL.B., 1967.

I wish to express my gratitude to Duncan Kennedy and Alfred S. Konefsky for many valuable suggestions.

[1] *See also* writings described in subsection II.*B.*, p. 946, *infra.*

judge."[2] The reason why equity "must be arbitrary and uncertain," Powell maintained, was that there could be no principles of substantive justice. A court of equity, for example, should not be permitted to refuse to enforce an agreement for simple "exorbitancy of price" because "it is the consent of parties alone, that fixes the just price of any thing, without reference to the nature of things themselves, or to their intrinsic value . . . . [T]herefore," he concluded, "a man is obliged in conscience to perform a contract which he has entered into, although it be a hard one . . . ."[3] The entire conceptual apparatus of modern contract doctrine — rules dealing with offer and acceptance, the evidentiary function of consideration, and especially canons of interpretation — arose to express this will theory of contract.

Powell's argument against conceptions of intrinsic value and just price reflects major changes in thought associated with the emergence of a market economy. It appears that it was only during the second half of the eighteenth century that national commodities markets began to develop in England. From that time on, "the price of grain was no longer local, but regional; this presupposed [for the first time] the almost general use of money and a wide marketability of goods."[4] In America, widespread markets in government securities arose shortly after the Revolutionary War, and an extensive internal commodities market developed around 1815.[5] The impact of these developments on both English and American contract law was profound. In a market, goods came to be thought of as fungible; the function of contracts correspondingly shifted from that of simply transferring title to a specific item to that of ensuring an expected return. Executory contracts, rare during the eighteenth century,[6] became important as instruments for "futures" agreements; formerly, the economic system had rested on immediate sale and delivery of specific property. And, most importantly, in a society in which value came to be regarded as entirely subjective and in which the only basis for assigning value was the concurrence of arbitrary individual desire, principles of substantive justice were inevitably seen as entailing an "arbitrary and uncertain" standard of value. Substantive justice, according to the earlier view, existed in order to prevent men from using the legal system in order to exploit each other. But where things have no "intrinsic value," there can be

---

[2] 1 J. POWELL, ESSAY UPON THE LAW OF CONTRACTS AND AGREEMENTS x (1790).

[3] 2 *id.* at 229.

[4] K. POLANYI, THE GREAT TRANSFORMATION: THE POLITICAL AND ECONOMIC ORIGINS OF OUR TIME 115 (Beacon Press ed. 1957).

[5] *See* pp. 937–41 *infra.*

[6] *See* p. 930 & note 71 *infra.*

no substantive measure of exploitation and the parties are, by definition, equal. Modern contract law was thus born staunchly proclaiming that all men are equal because all measures of inequality are illusory.

This Article will elaborate the view of the development of modern contract law outlined above. The first Section will describe the distinguishing features of the equitable conception of contract which dominated eighteenth century courts. The second Section will detail the late eighteenth and early nineteenth century disintegration of the equitable conception and the coalescence of new doctrine into the modern will theory of contract.

## I. The Equitable Conception of Contract in the Eighteenth Century

The development of contract, it often has been observed, can be divided into three stages, which correspond to the history of economic and legal institutions of exchange.[7] In the first stage, all exchange is instantaneous and therefore "involves nothing corresponding to 'contract' in the Anglo-American sense of the term. Each party becomes the owner of a new thing, and his rights rest, not on a promise, but on property."[8] In a second stage, "[e]xchange first assumes a contractual aspect when it is left half-completed, so that [only] an obligation on one side remains."[9] The "third and final stage in the development occurs when the executory exchange becomes enforceable."[10] According to orthodox legal history, when English judges declare at the end of the sixteenth century that "every contract executory is an assumpsit in itself," and that "a promise against a promise will maintain an action upon the case,"[11] the conception of contract as mutual promises has triumphed and, according to Plucknett, "the process is complete and the result clear . . . ."[12] "Damages were soon assessed," Ames added, "not upon the theory of reimbursement for the loss of the thing given for the promise, but upon the principle of compensation for the failure to obtain the thing promised."[13]

---

[7] *See, e.g.,* L. Fuller & M. Eisenberg, Basic Contract Law 121–22 (1972); F. Kessler & G. Gilmore, Contracts 27–28 (1970); T. Plucknett, A Concise History of the Common Law 643–44 (5th ed. 1956).

[8] L. Fuller & M. Eisenberg, *supra* note 7, at 121.

[9] *Id.*

[10] *Id.* at 122.

[11] T. Plucknett, *supra* note 7, at 643–44.

[12] *Id.* at 644.

[13] J. Ames, Lectures on Legal History 144–45 (1913). *See also* 3 W. Holdsworth, A History of English Law 452 (3d ed. 1923).

It is the purpose of this Section to demonstrate that, contrary to the orthodox view, the process was not complete at the end of the sixteenth century. Instead, one finds that as late as the eighteenth century contract law was still dominated by a title theory of exchange and damages were set under equitable doctrines that ultimately were to be rejected by modern contract law.

To modern eyes, the most distinctive feature of eighteenth century contract law is the subordination of contract to the law of property. In Blackstone's *Commentaries* contract appears for the first time in Book II, which is devoted entirely to the law of property. Contract is classified among such subjects as descent, purchase, and occupancy as one of the many modes of transferring title to a specific thing.[14] Contract appears for the second and last time in a chapter entitled, "Of Injuries to Personal Property." [15] In all, Blackstone's extraordinarily confused treatment of contract ideas [16] occupies only forty pages of his four volume work.

As a result of the subordination of contract to property, eighteenth century jurists endorsed a title theory of contractual exchange according to which a contract functioned to transfer title to the specific thing contracted for. Thus, Blackstone wrote that where a seller fails to deliver goods on an executory contract, "the vendee may seize the goods, or have an action against the vendor for detaining them." [17] Similarly, in the first English treatise on contract, Powell wrote of the remedy for failure to deliver stock on an executory contract as being one for specific performance.[18]

The title theory of exchange was suited to an eighteenth century society in which no extensive markets existed, and goods, therefore, were usually not thought of as being fungible. Exchange was not conceived of in terms of future monetary return, and as a result one finds that expectation damages were not recog-

---

[14] 2 W. BLACKSTONE, COMMENTARIES *440–70.

[15] 3 *id.* *154–66.

[16] *See* note 72 *infra.*

[17] 2 W. BLACKSTONE, COMMENTARIES *448. The title conception also appears in 1 Z. SWIFT, A SYSTEM OF THE LAWS OF THE STATE OF CONNECTICUT 380–81 (1796).

[18] 2 J. POWELL, *supra* note 2, at 232–33. The last important appearance of the title theory in American contract law occurred in Chancellor Kent's *Commentaries*. His treatment of contracts still focused entirely upon the question of when title passes by delivery, and there was as yet no trace of a discussion of damage remedies for breach of contract. *See* 2 J. KENT, COMMENTARIES ON AMERICAN LAW *449–57 (1827). In a world in which markets and speculation were becoming everyday events, *see* pp. 937–41 *infra*, Kent's treatment represented the final expression of the eighteenth century view of contract as simply one mode of transferring specific property.

nized by eighteenth century courts. Only two reported eighteenth century English cases touch on the question of expectation damages for breach of contract. *Flureau v. Thornhill* [19] (1776) seems to have confronted the question of damages for the loss of a bargain. A purchaser of a lease, who sued for failure to deliver because of a defect in title, sought to recover not only his deposit, but also damages sustained as a result of the lost bargain. The report of the case does not disclose whether the plaintiff attempted to recover the increased value of the lease, or, rather, the loss he had suffered from selling stock to finance the payment. In any event, the court refused to allow him more than restitution of his payment, one judge contemptuously noting that he could not "be entitled to any damages for the fancied goodness of the bargain, which he supposes he has lost." [20]

A second English case involving the damage issue is *Dutch v. Warren* [21] (1720). The case would be irrelevant were it not for the fact that it was regularly cited by later jurists ransacking the English reports for early instances of the recognition of expectation damages.[22] The case represented a buyer's action for restitution of money paid on a stock purchase contract, the price of the stock having fallen by the time delivery was due. Although the court said the case was "well brought; not for the whole money paid, but the damages in not transferring the stock at that time," [23] the case obviously does not establish the modern rule that one may recover expectation damages in excess of the purchase price for failure to deliver stock in a rising market.

---

[19] 2 Black. W. 1078, 96 Eng. Rep. 635 (C.P. 1776). The decision in *Flureau v. Thornhill* may have been responsible for the widespread adoption in America during the first quarter of the nineteenth century of the rule that for breach of warranty of good title only the purchase price and not expectation damages was recoverable. *See* Horwitz, *The Transformation in the Conception of Property in American Law, 1780–1860*, 40 U. CHI. L. REV. 248, 285–88 (1973). Although the American decisions adopting this rule may reflect deeper issues concerning the relations between speculative buyers and sellers of land, they also represent the continuing influence of an eighteenth century view of contract that had not yet developed a conception of expectation damages.

[20] 2 Black, W. at 1078, 96 Eng. Rep. at 635. I have been able to find only one buyer's action for nondelivery of goods on an executory contract in the English reports of the eighteenth century, and that case did not deal with the measure of damages. In Clayton v. Andrews, 4 Burr. 2101, 98 Eng. Rep. 96 (K.B. 1767), a buyer's action for nondelivery of corn, Lord Mansfield held that the statute of frauds did not apply to executory contracts.

[21] 1 Strange 406, 93 Eng. Rep. 598 (K.B. 1760). For a more complete discussion of the case, see Moses v. Macferlan, 2 Burr. 1005, 1010–11, 97 Eng. Rep. 676, 680 (K.B. 1760) (Mansfield, J.).

[22] *See, e.g.*, Shepherd v. Johnson, 2 East. 211, 102 Eng. Rep. 350 (K.B. 1802). *See also* 1 J. POWELL, *supra* note 2, at 137–38.

[23] 1 Strange at 406, 93 Eng. Rep. at 598.

Indeed, Lord Mansfield referred to it not as establishing a rule for damages, but as illustrating the equitable nature of the action for money had and received.[24]

One of the handful of executory contracts in America before the Revolution appeared in *Boehm v. Engle* [25] (1767), in which two sellers sued a buyer who, alleging bad title, had refused to accept a deed for land. Since Pennsylvania had no equity court in which a seller could have sued for specific performance,[26] Boehm brought "a special action on the case for the consideration money" [27] or contract price, not, it should be emphasized, for the value of the lost bargain. He was thereby suing, in effect, for specific performance and not for the change in value of the land. The suit was therefore consistent with Blackstone's title theory: the contract had transferred title from seller to buyer and all that remained was an action for the price.

To appreciate the radical difference between eighteenth century and modern contract law, consider a case decided during a period in which the demise of the title theory was becoming plain. *Sands v. Taylor* [28] was an 1810 New York suit against a buyer who had received a part shipment of wheat but had refused to receive the remainder contracted for. Under the old title theory, sellers were apparently required to hold the goods until they received the contract price from the buyer. But in *Sands v. Taylor* the sellers immediately "covered" by selling the wheat in the market and thereafter suing the buyer for the difference between market and contract price. While acknowledging that there were "no adjudications in the books, which either establish or deny the rule adopted in this case," [29] the court ratified the seller's decision to "cover" and allowed him to sue for the difference. "It is a much fitter rule," it declared, "than to require . . . [the seller] to suffer the property to perish, as a condition on which his right to damages is to depend." [30] In reaching this result the court was forced to fundamentally transform the title theory. The sellers, it said, "were, by necessity . . . thus constituted trustees or agents, for the defendants . . . " [31] The trust theory was thus

---

[24] *See* Moses v. Macferlan, 2 Burr, 1005, 1011–12, 97 Eng. Rep. 676, 680 (K.B. 1760). *See also* Clark v. Pinney, 7 Cow. 681, 688–89 (N.Y. 1827) (*Dutch v. Warren* "most manifestly decides nothing which has a bearing upon the question of damages where the action is brought *upon the contract itself*, and not to recover back the money paid . . . .").

[25] 1 Dall. 15 (Pa. 1767).

[26] A. LAUSSAT, AN ESSAY ON EQUITY IN PENNSYLVANIA 19–27 (1826).

[27] 1 Dall. at 15.

[28] 5 Johns. 395 (N.Y. 1810).

[29] *Id.* at 406.

[30] *Id.*

[31] *Id.* at 405.

created in order to overcome a result which, though inherent in eighteenth century contract conceptions, was becoming increasingly anomalous in a nineteenth century market economy. Under an economic system in which contract was becoming regularly employed for the purpose of speculating on the price of fungible goods, the old title theory of contract, conceived of as creating a property interest in specific goods, had outlived its usefulness. As we shall see in the succeeding Section, the demise of the title theory roughly corresponded to the beginnings of organized markets and the transformation of an economic system that had used contract as simply one means of transferring specific property.

The most important aspect of the eighteenth century conception of exchange is an equitable limitation on contractual obligation. Under the modern will theory, the extent of contractual obligation depends upon the convergence of individual desires. The equitable theory, by contrast, limited and sometimes denied contractual obligation by reference to the fairness of the underlying exchange.

The most direct expression of the eighteenth century theory was the well-established doctrine that equity courts would refuse specific enforcement of any contract in which they determined that the consideration was inadequate.[32] The rule was stated by South Carolina's Chancellor Desaussure as late as 1817:[33]

> [I]t would be a great mischief to the community, and a reproach to the justice of the country, if contracts of very great inequality, obtained by fraud, or surprise, or the skillful management of intelligent men, from weakness, or inexperience, or necessity could not be examined into, and set aside.

Four years later, the Chief Justice of New York noted the still widespread opinion of American judges that equity courts would refuse to enforce a contract where the consideration was inadequate.[34]

---

[32] See, e.g., Carberry v. Tannehill, 1 Har. & J. 224 (Md. 1801); Campbell v. Spencer, 2 Binn. 129, 133 (Pa. 1809); Clitherall v. Ogilvie, 1 Des. 250, 257 (S.C. Eq. 1792); Ward v. Webber, 1 Va. (1 Wash.) 354 (1794). On the other hand, Swift stated that "[i]nadequacy of price, abstracted from all other considerations, seems of itself to furnish no ground on which a court of equity can set aside or relieve a party to a contract." 2 Z. SWIFT, supra note 17, at 447–48. Swift, however, acknowledged that when inadequacy existed, together with other circumstances, a "court may conclude that the consent of the party was not free, or was conditional, thro [sic] mistake, fear, or misrepresentation, or under the impulse of distress, known to the other party . . . ." Id. at 448. In short, even according to Swift, inadequacy of consideration could lead to refusal to enforce a contract without a finding of fraud.

[33] Desaussure made this remark as an unnumbered footnote to his report of a case, Clitherall v. Ogilvie, 1 Des. 250, 259 n. (S.C. Eq. 1792).

[34] Seymour v. Delancey, 3 Cow. 445, 447 (N.Y. 1824) (Savage, C.J.).

Supervision of the fairness of contracts was not confined to courts of equity. The same function was performed at law by a substantive doctrine of consideration which allowed the jury to take into account not only whether there was consideration, but also whether it was adequate, before awarding damages. The prevailing legal theory of consideration was expressed by Chancellor Kent as late as 1822, on the very eve of the demise of the doctrine that equity would not enforce unfair bargains.[35] In contract actions at law, he wrote, where a jury determined damages for breach of contract, "relief can be afforded in damages, with a moderation agreeable to equity and good conscience, and . . . the claims and pretensions of each party can be duly attended to, and be admitted to govern the assessment." [36]

Eighteenth century American reports amply support Kent's statement. In Pennsylvania, for example, where no equity court sat,[37] eighteenth century judges instructed juries in actions on bonds that they "ought to presume every thing *to have been paid*, which . . . in equity and good conscience, *ought not to be paid*." [38] Without an equity court, Chief Justice McKean declared, courts were obliged to turn to juries for "an equitable and conscientious interpretation of the agreement of the parties." [39] As a result, Pennsylvania lawyers often argued that a plaintiff's claim on a contract "should be both legal and equitable before he can call on a jury to execute the agreement," [40] and that "[i]nadequacy of price, known to the other party, is a ground to set aside a contract."[41]

In Massachusetts, the eighteenth century rule was that a defendant in an ordinary contract case could offer evidence of inadequacy of consideration in order to reduce his damages. At three separate points in his student notes, written around 1759, John Adams indicated that "sufficient Consideration" was necessary to sustain a contract action.[42] "No Consideration, or an insufficient Consideration, a good Cause of Motion in Arrest of Judgment," Adams noted in one of these entries.[43] In *Pynchon*

---

[35] Kent refused to specifically enforce a contract on the grounds of the unfairness of the bargain, but he was to be overruled on appeal. Seymour v. Delancey, 3 Cow. 445 (N.Y. 1824), *rev'g* 6 Johns. Ch. 222 (N.Y. Ch. 1822).

[36] Seymour v. Delancy, 6 Johns. Ch. 222, 232 (N.Y. Ch. 1822).

[37] *See* note 26 *supra.*

[38] Holingsworth v. Ogle, 1 Dall. 257, 260 (Pa. 1788).

[39] Wharton v. Morris, 1 Dall. 125, 126 (Pa. 1785). *See also* Conrad v. Conrad, 4 Dall. 130 (Pa. 1793).

[40] Gilchreest v. Pollock, 2 Yeates 18, 19 (Pa. 1795) (argument of counsel).

[41] Armstrong v. McGhee, Addis. 261 (Pa. C.P. 1795) (argument of counsel).

[42] 1 LEGAL PAPERS OF JOHN ADAMS 9 (L. Wroth & H. Zobel eds. 1965). *See also id.* at 12, 15.

[43] *Id.* at 9. Pondering the implications of the conception of objective value

*v. Brewster* [44] (1766), Chief Justice Hutchinson instructed the jury in an action for a fixed price that they "might . . . if they thought it reasonable, lessen the Charges in the [plaintiff's] Account." [45] One year later Hutchinson observed that "[i]t seems hard that an Inquiring into the Consideration should be denied, and that Evidence should be refused in Diminution of Damages." [46]

Another indication of the equitable nature of damage judgments in the eighteenth century was the almost universal failure of American courts either to instruct juries in strict damage rules or else to reverse damage judgments with which they disagreed. As a result, the community's sense of fairness was often the dominant standard in contracts cases. A commentator, referring to a 1789 Connecticut commercial case, noted that "[t]he jury were the proper judges, not only of the fact but of the law that was necessarily involved in the issue . . . ." [47] Whatever they believed about the proper allocation between judge and jury on matters of law, most judges were prepared to leave the damage question to the jury. For example, in a 1786 lawsuit in which the jury's award was lower than the agreed contract price, the South

---

that lay at the foundation of these rules, Adams was finally undecided whether their "Inconvenience to Trade" was greater than "the Injustice" of enforcing unequal bargains.

> It is a natural, immutable Law, that the Buyer ought not to take Advantage of the sellers Necessity, to purchase at too low a Price. Suppose Money was very scarce, and a Man was under a Necessity of procuring a £ 100 within 2 Hours to satisfy an Execution, or else go to Goal. He has Quantity of Goods worth £ 500 that he would sell. He finds a Buyer who would give him £ 100 for them all, and no more. The poor Man is constrained to sell £ 500s worth for £ 100. Here the seller is wronged, tho he sell voluntarily in one sense. Yet, the Injustice, that may be done by some Mens availing them selves of their Neighbours Necessities, is not so Great as the Inconvenience to Trade would be if all Contracts were to be void which were made upon insufficient Considerations. But Q. What Damage to Trade, what Inconvenience, if all Contracts made upon insufficient Considerations were void.

1 DIARY AND AUTOBIOGRAPHY OF JOHN ADAMS 112 (L. Butterfield ed. 1961). In recognizing the inconvenience to trade, Adams had presaged later attacks on the substantive doctrine of consideration. *See* pp. 941-45 *infra*.

[44] Quincy 224 (Mass. 1766).

[45] *Id.* at 225 (emphasis deleted).

[46] Noble v. Smith, Quincy 254, 255 (Mass. 1767). The case held, by a 3-2 vote, that evidence of inadequate consideration could not be admitted in an action on a promissory note brought by the promisee against the promisor. But it is clear from the case that the court treated notes as an exception to the general rule governing contracts. Indeed, promissory notes soon became the leading example emphasized by those who wished to destroy the doctrine of consideration itself. *See* pp. 941-43 *infra*. Although Hutchinson voted to exclude evidence of inadequacy of consideration, his statement does acknowledge the general rule, which he did not contest.

[47] 1 Z. SWIFT, *supra* note 17, at 410, *referring to* Hamlin v. Fitch (Conn. Sup. Ct. Err. 1789).

Carolina Supreme Court refused to grant a new trial since "this is a case sounding in damages, and . . . the jury have thought proper to give a kind of equitable verdict between the parties . . . ."[48] Likewise, the Virginia General Court appeared to adopt the position that excessive damages were not sufficient cause for a new trial.[49] Where "positive law, and judicial precedents, [are] totally silent on the subject [of damages]," Pennsylvania's Chief Justice McKean remarked, "the principles of morality, equity, and good conscience, would furnish an adequate rule to influence and direct our judgment."[50] And it was entirely clear that it was the jury's sense of equity that would prevail. While trying a case in the United States Circuit Court, Supreme Court Justice Washington found that, by awarding a lesser judgment, the jury had ignored his instruction that the plaintiff was entitled to recover the full amount of the contract. Asked to award a new trial, Washington refused on the ground that "the question of damages . . . belonged so peculiarly to the jury, that he could not allow himself to invade their province . . . ."[51]

Further support for the existence of a substantive doctrine of consideration in the eighteenth century is found in American courts' enforcement of the rule that "a sound price warrants a sound commodity."[52] While there is no direct evidence of a substantive doctrine of consideration in eighteenth century England, several unreported trial decisions supported the "sound price" rule,[53] and as late as 1792 Blackstone's successor in the

---

[48] Pledger v. Wade, 1 Bay 35, 37 (S.C. 1786). *See also* Bourke v. Bulow, 1 Bay 49 (S.C. 1787).

[49] Waugh v. Bagg (Va. 1731), *reported in* 1 VIRGINIA COLONIAL DECISIONS, R77, R78 (R. Barton ed. 1909).

[50] Perit v. Wallis, 2 Dall. 252, 255 (Pa. 1796).

[51] Walker v. Smith, 4 Dall. 389, 391 (C.C.D. Pa. 1804).

[52] *See, e.g.*, Dean v. Mason, 4 Conn. 428, 434 (1822) (Chapman, J.); Baker v. Frobisher, Quincy 4 (Mass. 1762); Garretsie v. Van Ness, 1 Penning. 20, 27–29 (N.J. 1806) (Rossell, J.) (dictum); Toris v. Long, Tayl. 17 (N.C. Super. Ct. 1799); Whitefield v. McLeod, 2 Bay 380 (S.C. 1801); Mackie's Ex'r v. Davis, 2 Va. (2 Wash.) 219, 232 (1796); Waddill v. Chamberlayne (Va. 1735), *reported in* 2 VIRGINIA COLONIAL DECISIONS, *supra* note 49, at B45; 1 Z. SWIFT, *supra* note 17, at 384; *cf.* Rench v. Hile, 4 Har. & McH. 495 (Md. 1766). *See also* Z. SWIFT, DIGEST OF THE LAW OF EVIDENCE IN CIVIL AND CRIMINAL CASES AND A TREATISE ON BILLS OF EXCHANGE AND PROMISSORY NOTES 341 (1810) ("as in all other cases of the sale of personal property, our law implies a warranty"). W. Wyche's treatise on New York procedure contains an index entry," "Assumpsit for implied warranties." W. WYCHE, TREATISE ON THE PRACTICE OF THE SUPREME COURT OF JUDICATURE OF THE STATE OF NEW-YORK IN CIVIL ACTIONS 339 (1794). The text notes that the action "for deceit in selling unsound horses, or the like" was "especially of late years, usually *declared upon in assumpsit* . . . ." *Id.* at 23.

[53] *See* Parkinson v. Lee, 2 East. 314, 322, 102 Eng. Rep. 389, 392 (K.B. 1802) (Grose, J.); W. STORY, A TREATISE ON THE LAW OF CONTRACTS NOT UNDER SEAL 333 (1844); G. VERPLANCK, AN ESSAY ON THE DOCTRINE OF CONTRACTS: BEING

Vinerian Chair at Oxford, Richard Wooddeson, proclaimed the sound price doctrine to be good law.[54] Thus, one may conclude that in both England and America, when the selling price was greater than the supposed objective value of the thing bought, juries were permitted to reduce the damages in an action by the seller, and courts would enforce an implied warranty in actions by the buyer.

What we have seen of eighteenth century doctrines suggests that contract law was essentially antagonistic to the interests of commercial classes. The law did not assure a businessman the express value of his bargain, but at most its specific performance. Courts and juries did not honor business agreements on their face, but scrutinized them for the substantive equality of the exchange.

For our purposes, the most important consequence of this hostility was that contract law was insulated from the purposes of commercial transactions. Businessmen settled disputes informally among themselves when they could, referred them to a more formal process of arbitration when they could not, and relied on merchant juries to ameliorate common law rules.[55] And, finally, they endeavored to find legal forms of agreement with which to conduct business transactions free from the equalizing tendencies of courts and juries. Of these forms, the most important was the penal bond.

---

AN INQUIRY HOW CONTRACTS ARE AFFECTED IN LAW AND MORALS 28–29 (1825). *But see* 2 W. BLACKSTONE, COMMENTARIES *451 (warranties of good title, but not of soundness, are implied by law). An early English manuscript contract treatise had declared that an action lies on an implied warranty of merchantability, "for the party [seller] ought to make them Merchantable goods & see them well delivered without any special provision in the contract . . . ." "Of Contracts" (c. 1720) (Hargrave Ms. 265, British Museum). I am grateful to Professor John Langbein of the University of Chicago Law School for calling the manuscript to my attention. Professor Langbein believes that the eminent British lawyer, Baron Gilbert, wrote the treatise around 1720.

[54] 2 R. WOODDESON, A SYSTEMATICAL VIEW OF THE LAWS OF ENGLAND 415 (1792). On the basis of a doubtfully reported seventeenth century case, Chandelor v. Lopus, Cro. Jac. 4, 79 Eng. Rep. 3 (Ex. 1603), *noted in* 8 HARV. L. REV. 282 (1894), it was supposed by later courts that English law had never allowed an action on an implied warranty. *See, e.g.,* Seixas v. Woods, 2 Cai. R. 48 (N.Y. Sup. Ct. 1804). Let, like so many other early decisions in English legal history, the court's ruling seems to have been more the product of narrow considerations of pleading than of any direct confrontation with issues of substantive policy. *See* Hamilton, *The Ancient Maxim Caveat Emptor,* 40 YALE L.J. 1133, 1166–68 (1931); *Implied Warranty on Sale of Personal Chattels,* 12 AM. JUR. 311, 315–16 (1834). *See also* 8 W. HOLDSWORTH, *supra* note 13, at 68–70; McClain, *Implied Warranties in Sales,* 7 HARV. L. REV. 213 (1893).

[55] Various practices involving extrajudicial settlement of commercial disputes during the eighteenth century will be examined in a forthcoming book by the author.

The great advantage of the penal bond or sealed instrument was that at common law it precluded all inquiry into the adequacy of consideration for an exchange. In the medieval legal system, the use of "penal bonds with conditional defeasance," as they were called, enabled individuals to impose unlimited penalties on parties who had failed to perform agreed upon conditions.[56] The use of penal bonds declined somewhat in England during the seventeenth and eighteenth centuries as first equity, then common law courts undertook to relieve against the penal feature — the recovery of the entire sum stipulated because of even a minor breach of a specified condition.[57] Although American courts appear to have followed the English and also "chancered" these bonds,[58] virtually all large business transactions in America until the beginning of the nineteenth century took the form of two independent bonds, each of which stipulated damages for failure to perform the agreed act.[59]

Despite the practice of "chancering," the use of bonds may still have avoided an equitable inquiry into the fairness of the exchange in most cases. From the beginning of the eighteenth century English judges had begun to distinguish between penalties — which they would relieve against — and liquidated damages — which the parties were free to stipulate without the interference of courts.[60] By the time Lord Mansfield ascended to the bench, the English courts were predisposed to regard most damage provisions in bonds as liquidated and hence enforceable. "[W]here the covenant is 'to pay a particular liquidated sum,' " Mansfield declared, "a Court of Equity can not make a new covenant for a man . . . ."[61] And summing up developments during the preceding century, Lord Eldon declared in 1801 that he could "not but lament" any supposed principle that even an "enormous and excessive" damage provision, to which the parties had agreed, should be voided as a penalty.[62] "[I]t appears to me extremely difficult to apply, with propriety, the word 'excessive' to the terms in which parties choose to contract with each other. . . . It

---

[56] Simpson, *The Penal Bond with Conditional Defeasance*, 82 L.Q. Rev. 392, 411–12 (1966).

[57] *Id.* at 415–21.

[58] *See* Wroth & Zobel, *Introduction* to 1 Legal Papers of John Adams, *supra* note 42, at xliii n.38.

[59] *See, e.g.*, Thompson v. Musser, 1 Dall. 458 (Pa. 1789); Cummings v. Lynn, 1 Dall. 444 (Pa. 1789); Wharton v. Morris, 1 Dall. 124 (Pa. 1785).

[60] 6 W. Holdsworth, *supra* note 13, at 663 ("already equity had begun to limit . . . relief to cases in which the sum promised was clearly out of proportion to the loss incurred").

[61] Lowe v. Peers, 4 Burr. 2225, 2228, 98 Eng. Rep. 160, 162 (K.B. 1768).

[62] Astley v. Weldon, 2 B. & P. 346, 351, 126 Eng. Rep. 1318, 1321 (C.P. 1801).

has been held . . . that mere inequality is not a ground of relief . . . ." [63]

It is impossible to determine from court records whether American courts also distinguished penalties from liquidated damages. If juries were simply instructed to ignore stipulated damages in a bond and to return verdicts for actual damages, bonds could not have represented an important device for avoiding the jury's equitable inquiry into the nature of a transaction. However, it appears that even as late as the last decade of the eighteenth century the number of bonds used to effect business transactions still vastly exceeded the number of ordinary contracts containing mutual promises; this suggests that courts did not have unlimited discretion in cases involving bonds.

The late use of bonds, the absence of widespread markets, and the equitable conception of contract law conspired to retard the development of a law of executory contracts. Indeed, the primitive state of eighteenth century American contract law is underscored by the surprising fact that some American courts did not enforce executory contracts where there had been no part performance. For example, in *Muir v. Key*,[64] a Virginia case decided in 1787, a buyer of tobacco brought an action for nondelivery on a bond containing mutual promises. In the same action, the seller sued for the price. The jury returned a verdict for the buyer, which the court reversed on the ground that unless the plaintiff had paid in advance he could not sue on the contract. Thus, as late as 1787 in Virginia, there could be no buyer's action on a contract without prepayment. Nor, according to one of the judges, could the seller sue without delivery of the tobacco.[65]

---

[63] *Id.*

[64] St. George Tucker, Notes of Cases in the General Court, District Court & Court of Appeals in Virginia, 1786–1811, Apr. 18 & Oct. 15, 1787 (ms. in Tucker-Coleman Collection, Swen Library, College of William & Mary).

[65] Some of the language of the judges in the case may allow for other interpretations. Judge Tazewell, for example, seems to allow for enforcement of executory contracts without part performance when he states "that in an action upon mutual promise the parties may maintain reciprocal Actions . . . ." Tucker, *supra* note 64. He also may be recognizing expectation damages when he states that the jury "ought to have assessed Damages according to the differences of price, or any other *Special Damage* which plt. could have proved but here no special Damage appears: the plt. has failed in proving that he paid the whole money. The Damages therefore are excessive & a new Trial must be granted." *Id.*

At the new trial, Tucker reports, John Marshall for the defendant "submitted to the court whether the plt. must not prove paymt. on his part, in order to maintain the present Action." *Id.* The court, with Judge Tazewell dissenting, decided that he must. Thus, it is clear that enforcement of executory contracts in which there was no part performance did not yet exist in Virginia as late as 1787. Whether the requirement of payment was regarded simply as a necessary

The view that part performance was required for contractual obligation seems to have been held elsewhere in eighteenth century America as well. In his study of Massachusetts law, William Nelson states that "[a]s a general rule . . . executory contracts were not enforced . . . in pre-Revolutionary Massachusetts unless the plaintiff pleaded his own performance of his part of the bargain." [66] Thus, in his "Commonplace Book" [67] (1759) John Adams insisted that in "executory Agreements . . . the Performance of the Act is a Condition precedent [sic] to the Payment." [68] For example, if two men agree on a sale of a horse, Adams wrote, "yet there is no reason that [the seller] should have an Action for the Money before the Horse is deliverd." [69] And even as late as 1795, Zephaniah Swift of Connecticut wavered between the view that performance is unnecessary for an action on a contract and the view that without either payment or delivery, "the bargain is considered of no force and does not bind either [party]." [70] It is not difficult to understand why some courts did not enforce executory contracts without part performance. The pressure to enforce such contracts would not be great in a pre-market economy where contracts for future delivery were rare, [71] and where merchants

---

formality or whether buyers' actions were still conceived of as simply for restitution of money paid is not entirely clear.

[66] W. Nelson, The Americanization of the Common Law During the Revolutionary Era, ch. 4 at 26 (ms. of forthcoming book in author's possession).

[67] 1 Legal Papers of John Adams, *supra* note 42, at 4.

[68] *Id.* A modern lawyer would, of course, observe that the condition could be satisfied if the seller had tendered the horse. But in America, the first legal writer explicitly to use the concept of tender for this purpose was Daniel Chipman. *See* D. Chipman, An Essay on the Law of Contracts for the Payment of Specifick Articles 31–40 (1822).

[69] 1 Legal Papers of John Adams, *supra* note 42, at 4.

[70] 1 Z. Swift, *supra* note 17, at 380–81. In Gilchreest v. Pollock, 2 Yeates 18 (Pa. 1795), defendant's counsel reiterated the eighteenth century view that part performance was "a condition precedent to the payment, and the party who is to pay shall not be compelled to part with his money till the thing be performed for which he is to pay." *Id.* at 20. But by enforcing one of the early executory stock contracts the court rejected this view.

[71] Given the colonial economy, the only conceivable subject of futures contracts would have been agricultural commodities. However, "[t]he lack of a wide market for farm products was a fundamental characteristic of northern agriculture in the colonial period." P. Bidwell & J. Falconer, History of Agriculture in the Northern United States, 1620–1860, at 133 (1941). Lewis Cecil Gray states that there were "occasional instances of future-selling" in colonial Virginia. 1 L. Gray, History of Agriculture in the Southern United States to 1860, at 426 (1941). He offers only one example, a contract entered into by George Washington with Alexandria merchants for the sale of his wheat at a uniform price over a period of seven years. And he offers no instances of futures contracts in international trade, which provided the major market for commodities during the

framed most executory transactions that did arise in terms of independent covenants through the use of bonds.

Even where executory contracts were enforced without part performance, the infrequency with which they arose slowed the development of precise legal rules for dealing with them.[72] Eighteenth century courts were regularly confronted instead with commercial cases framed in terms of penal bonds. The legal categories required to enforce independent covenants were radically different from a conception of contracts depending on mutual promises. There was no need to inquire into questions of offer and acceptance to determine whether there had been "a meeting of minds." Nor was there any reason to develop rules for regulating "order of performance" or tender where each covenant was treated as independent.[73] Finally, because of its liquidated damage provision, the bond delayed until the nineteenth century any detailed inquiry into precise rules of damages.[74]

The use of bonds seems to have substantially declined in both England and America during the early decades of the nineteenth century. If, in fact, bonds were still an important vehicle for avoiding inquiry into the fairness of an exchange during the eighteenth century, they became increasingly unnecessary as judges took control of the rules for measuring damages. Furthermore,

---

colonial period. Nor is any mention made of futures contracts in any other southern colonies. *See id.* at 409–33. In addition, the widespread use of bills of exchange in commercial transactions made executory contracts unnecessary. A 1791 Virginia case noted "that it was the general custom of the English merchants, who solicited tobacco consignments, to appoint agents in this country for that purpose, with power to make advances to the planters, and to draw bills [of exchange] on their principals . . . ." Hooe v. Oxley, 1 Va. (1 Wash.) 19, 23 (1791).

[72] Blackstone's confused account of assumpsit demonstrates that English lawyers had little occasion to think through the rules governing executory contracts of sale. First, he seemed to deny that executory contracts could be enforced without part performance when he wrote: "If a man agrees with another for goods at a certain price, he may not carry them away before he hath paid for them; for it is no sale without payment, unless the contrary be expressly agreed." 2 W. BLACKSTONE, COMMENTARIES *447. Order of performance and contractual obligation, it appears, are confounded. "[I]f neither the money be paid, nor the goods delivered, nor tender made, nor any subsequent agreement be entered into, it is no contract . . . ." *Id.* Here Blackstone seems to waver between part performance as a necessary requisite for contractual obligation and a conception of executory contracts made enforceable simply through tender but not delivery.

[73] The problem of order of performance, inseparably linked to the idea of executory contracts, had not been worked out until the late eighteenth century. *See* Kingston v. Preston (K.B. 1773) (Mansfield, C.J.), *summarized in* Jones v. Barkley, 2 Doug. 685, 689–92, 99 Eng. Rep. 434, 437–38 (K.B. 1781). Even after Mansfield's resolution, the problem continued to confuse American courts for another generation. *See, e.g.,* Havens v. Bush, 2 Johns. 387 (N.Y. 1807); Seers v. Fowler, 2 Johns. 272 (N.Y. 1807).

[74] *See* p. 940 & note 124 *infra.*

liquidated damage provisions were not well suited to predicting market fluctuations in an increasingly speculative economy.[75] The result was that the executory contract came gradually to supersede the bond for most nineteenth century business transactions.

Before turning to outright reversals of eighteenth century law, however, it is important to note that there was a period of uneasy compromise between the old learning and the new. The transitional nature of the late eighteenth and early nineteenth centuries is revealed most explicitly in the confused relationship between the common counts, which by the end of the eighteenth century had emancipated the law of contract from the tyranny of the older forms of action, and Blackstone's 1768 division of the field of contract law into express and implied contracts.[76]

By highlighting the express agreement, Blackstone's division was an early indication of a tendency away from an equitable and toward a will theory of contract law. It also represented an effort to create a theoretical framework as a substitute for the older forms of action. However, Blackstone himself placed the common counts in the category of implied contracts,[77] which had the significant effect of identifying them with the still dominant equitable conception of contract. Implied contracts, Blackstone wrote, "are such as reason and justice dictate, and which therefore the law presumes that every man has contracted to perform . . . ." [78] For one of the common counts — indebitatus assumpsit for money had and received — Blackstone cited Lord Mansfield's then recent path-breaking decision in *Moses v. Macferlan*,[79] in which the Chief Justice declared: "In one word, the gist of this kind of action is, that the defendant, upon the circum-

---

[75] *See* Graham v. Bickham, 2 Yeates 32 (Pa. 1795) (recovery allowed on a bond in excess of penalty where there had been a sharp market fluctuation).

[76] 3 W. BLACKSTONE, COMMENTARIES *154–64. Blackstone's discussion of express contracts was brief and essentially uninformative. Its most important break with the past lies in his assertion that, except for the seal, ordinary promises were "absolutely the same" as sealed instruments. 3 W. BLACKSTONE, COMMENTARIES *157. Thus, we see the beginnings of a generic conception of contracts united by common principles that transcended the particular form of action under which suits on contracts were brought. But we have yet to see any detailed elaboration of the major categories of nineteenth century contract law: offer and acceptance, consideration, and, most important, rules of contract interpretation.

[77] 3 W. BLACKSTONE, COMMENTARIES *161. He divided implied contracts into two main headings. The first group consisted of obligations imposed by courts or statutes, which arose, Blackstone thought, from an original social contract. *Id.* at *158–59. A second class, including all of the common counts, arose, he explained, "from natural reason, and the just construction of law." *Id.* at *161. In the latter class, the law assumed "that every man hath engaged to perform what his duty or justice requires." *Id.*

[78] *Id.* at *158.

[79] 2 Burr. 1005, 97 Eng. Rep. 676 (K.B. 1760).

stances of the case, is obliged by the ties of natural justice and equity to refund the money." [80]

As a result of this unrestrained identification of contract with "natural justice and equity," the triumph of the common counts threatened to reinforce the equitable conceptions which Blackstone's distinction between express and implied contracts had appeared to displace as the unifying principle of contract. This persistence of an equitable tradition in English contract law also influenced American courts. *Palfrey v. Palfrey* [81] (1772), for example, involved an action in contract by children against their mother for improper occupation of a house they had inherited on their father's death. Rejecting the defendant's argument that the proper form of action was in trespass, the Massachusetts Superior Court held that the contract action would lie. In a long and elaborate opinion, the normally form-bound and technically oriented Judge Edmund Trowbridge maintained that there was an implied contract by the defendant to pay. Judge Trowbridge noted that "it [was] necessary to know what is at this day intended by an implied contract . . . because . . . 'many of the old cases are strange & absurd, the strictness has been relaxed & is melting down in common sense of late times.' " [82] Since the plaintiffs were "clearly entitled to recover upon the merits & must in another action if not in this," the judges "ought to use [their] utmost sagacity to give them judgment . . . ." [83] Judge Trowbridge concluded, using language borrowed from Blackstone and Mansfield: [84]

> [I]t seems to be settled that implied contracts are such as reason & justice dictate; Therefore if one is under obligation from the ties of natural justice to pay another money and neglects to do it, the law gives the sufferer an action upon the case, in nature of a bill in equity to recover it; and that mere justice & equity is a sufficient foundation for this kind of equitable action.

Blackstone's interpretation of the common counts as implied contracts did not ultimately secure the dominance of the equitable conception of contract, however, because of unresolved confusions in the pleading system. It appears that the common

---

[80] *Id.* at 1012, 97 Eng. Rep. at 681.

[81] *Reported in* W. Cushing, Notes of Cases Decided in the Superior and Supreme Judicial Courts of Massachusetts, 1772–1789, at 1–2 & App. 1–7 (unpublished ms. in Harvard Law School Library).

[82] *Id.*, App. at 3.

[83] *Id.*, App. at 5.

[84] *Id.*, App. at 6–7. In Griffin v. Lee (Va. 1792), *reported in* Tucker, *supra* note 64, Judge Tucker protested that the common counts had been "extended far beyond the limits which appear to be reasonable" and "need[ed] no Extending."

count of indebitatus assumpsit was variously used both for suing on an express contract price and for suing on an implied contract. When it was used to sue on an express contract, another common count, quantum meruit, was employed to sue on an implied contract. "[I]n an action for work done," a mid-eighteenth century English commentator noted, "it is the best way to lay a Quantum Meruit with an Indebitatus Assumpsit. For if you fail in the proof of an express price agreed, you will recover the value." [85] As late as the turn of the century, it was also the prevailing practice in America to sue in indebitatus assumpsit for an express contract and for counts in both indebitatus and quantum meruit to be "usually joined in the declaration; so that on failure of proof of an express debt or price, the Plf. may resort ad debitum equitatis," [86] that is, to an equitable action in quantum meruit.

The transitional nature of the late eighteenth century is thus revealed in the failure of eighteenth century lawyers to perceive any latent theoretical contradictions involved in joining counts on express and implied contract.[87] Their failure to do so undoubtedly resulted from the theoretical confusions underlying the common counts themselves. Two very different conceptions of contract were submerged within actions on the common counts. One was based on an express bargain between the parties; the other derived contractual obligation from "natural justice and equity." But in the eighteenth century there was little occasion to see the two doctrinal strands as contradictory. Contract had not yet become a major subject of common law adjudication. The existence of mercantile arbitration, on one hand, and the predominance of bills of exchange, bonds, and sealed instruments in business dealings, on the other, meant that few of the legal problems that a modern lawyer would identify as contractual entered the common law courts.[88]

---

[85] T. Wood, An Institute of the Laws of England 555–56 (9th ed. 1763), *quoted in* C. Fifoot, History and Sources of the Common Law: Tort and Contract 363 (1949).

[86] American Precedents of Declarations 95 (B. Perham ed. 1802). In Cone v. Wetmore (Mass. 1794). (F. Dana papers, Box 16, "Court Cases A–L," Mass. Historical Society), for example, the plaintiff sued in indebitatus assumpsit for cattle sold and delivered. The Supreme Judicial Court declared that "the Deft may have every advantage of the special [express] agreement in this action which he could have had if it had been special declared on. He might show the appraised value was less than plt. demanded . . . ." *Id.* The case thus supports the proposition that a suit on the common counts could be maintained even though an express agreement existed. *Cf.* pp. 935–36 *infra.*

[87] In the nineteenth century the practice of joining counts on express and implied contracts began to be perceived as contradictory, and the rule was ultimately laid down that the existence of an express agreement precludes recovery in quantum meruit. *See* p. 952 *infra.*

[88] *See* pp. 927–31 *supra.*

In eighteenth century America, the equitable tradition in the common counts was tied not only to a general theory of natural justice but also to an economic system often based on customary prices. The striking existence of this remnant of the medieval just price theory of value can be seen in two Massachusetts colonial cases. In *Tyler v. Richards* [89] (1765), the plaintiff brought indebitatus assumpsit for boarding and schooling the defendant's son. The defendant argued that indebitatus "will not lye; they ought to have brought a *Quantum Meruit.*" [90] For the plaintiffs, John Adams and Samuel Quincy argued that "[i]t ha[d] always been the Custom of this Court, to allow" the action "if the Services alledged were proved to have been done. As every Man is supposed to assume to pay the customary Price. Assumpsit is always brought for Work done by Tradesmen, and is always allowed. The Price for Boarding and Schooling is as much settled in the Country, as it is in the Town for a Yard of Cloth, or a Day's Work by a Carpenter." [91] Adams and Quincy were thus attempting to convince the court that if the value of goods or services was "settled" and bore a "customary Price," there was no difference between this action and indebitatus for a "sum certain." The defendant, however, argued that "[i]f this Proof is admitted, there will be an End of any Distinction between *Indebitatus Assumpsit* and a *Quantum meruit.*" [92] The court accepted the defendant's argument and dismissed the action.

In *Pynchon v. Brewster* [93] (1766), the plaintiff brought indebitatus "upon a long Doctor's Bill for Medicines, Travel into the Country and Attendance." [94] This time, Adams, for the defendant, argued on the authority of *Tyler v. Richards* that indebitatus would not lie. The Chief Justice, however, distinguished *Tyler* on the ground that "Travel for Physicians, their Drugs and Attendance, had as fixed a Price as Goods sold by a Shopkeeper, and that it would be a great Hardship upon Physicians to oblige them to lay a *Quantum Meruit.*" [95]

What emerges from these cases is that in America suits in indebitatus were sometimes based on a system of fixed and customary prices. Though the *Richards* court denied the analogy between the price of schooling and the "settled" price for a yard of cloth, it never challenged Adams' premise that the prices of most goods and services were conceived of as "settled." Similarly,

[89] Quincy 195 (Mass. 1765).
[90] *Id.*
[91] *Id.* at 195–96.
[92] *Id.* at 196.
[93] Quincy 224 (Mass. 1766).
[94] *Id.*
[95] *Id.*

while acknowledging the "uncertain" price of schooling, Chief Justice Hutchinson had no doubt that the price of a doctor's medicine and services "had as fixed a Price as Goods sold by a Shopkeeper." [96]

Of course, there could not have been a customary rate for every exchange that might be entered into and sued upon; the jury's power to set a reasonable price in quantum meruit was necessary to fill in the gaps. Indeed, it appears that the jury had discretion to mitigate or enlarge the damages even in indebitatus actions.[97] But the concept of customary prices formed the necessary foundation for a legal system which awarded contract damages according to measures of fairness independent of the terms agreed to by the contracting parties. By the end of the eighteenth century, however, the development of extensive markets undermined this system of customary prices and radically transformed the role of contract in an increasingly commercial society.

## II. The Rise of a Market Economy and the Development of the Will Theory of Contract

### A. Early Attacks on Eighteenth Century Contract Doctrine

For a variety of reasons, it is appropriate to correlate the emergence of the modern law of contract with the first recognition of expectation damages. Executory sales contracts assume a central place in the economic system only when they begin to be used as instruments for "futures" agreements; to accommodate the market function of such agreements the law must grant the contracting parties their expected return. Thus, the recognition of expectation damages marks the rise of the executory contract as an important part of English and American law. Furthermore, the moment at which courts focus on expectation damages, rather

---

[96] In *Pynchon*, Hutchinson also remarked that it was not the practice in England to allow an indebitatus for a customary price. Quincy at 224.

[97] *See* Pynchon v. Brewster, Quincy 224, 225 (Mass. 1766) (Hutchinson, C.J.); 1 Legal Papers of John Adams, *supra* note 42, at 16. This concession to jury discretion may not, however, mean that courts had eroded every practical difference between quantum meruit and indebitatus assumpsit. It was one thing to acknowledge a complete jury power to set "reasonable" prices in quantum meruit; it was another to place a special burden on the jury to modify a fixed price that the court had established as the standard measuring rod for actions in indebitatus assumpsit. In any case, all of this home-grown lawmaking was swept aside in Glover v. LeTestue, Quincy 225 n.1 (Mass. 1770), where the Massachusetts court, after hearing extensive citations of English authority, held that only quantum meruit and not indebitatus assumpsit would lie for "Visits, Bleeding [or] Medicines" by a doctor. *Id.* at 226. *Cf.* note 96 *supra*.

than restitution or specific performance to give a remedy for non-delivery, is precisely the time at which contract law begins to separate itself from property. It is at this point that contract begins to be understood not as transferring the title of particular property, but as creating an expected return. Contract then becomes an instrument for protecting against changes in supply and price in a market economy.

The first recognition of expectation damages appeared after 1790 in both England and America in cases involving speculation in stock. Jurists initially attempted to encompass these cases within traditional legal categories. Thus, Lord Mansfield in 1770 referred to a speculative interest in stock as "a new species of property, arisen within the compass of a few years." [98] In 1789 the Connecticut Supreme Court of Errors held that recovery of expectation damages on a contract of stock speculation would be usurious.[99] And as late as 1790, John Powell concluded that specific performance, and not an action for damages, was the proper remedy for failure to deliver stock on a rising market.[100]

These efforts to encompass contracts of stock speculation within the old title theory were soon to be abandoned, however. Between 1799 and 1810 a number of English cases applied the rule of expectation damages for failure to deliver stock on a rising market.[101] In America the transformation occurred a decade earlier, in response to an active "futures" market for speculation in state securities which rapidly developed after the Revolutionary War in anticipation of the assumption of state debts by the new national government. The earliest cases allowing expectation damages on contracts of stock speculation appeared in South Carolina, Virginia, and Pennsylvania.

In South Carolina, three cases between 1790 and 1794 established the rule of expectation damages in stock cases. The first case, *Davis v. Richardson* [102] (1790), involved a "short sale" of South Carolina indents, or government stock. The defendant had borrowed the stock, promising its return with interest at a future

---

[98] Nightingal v. Devisme, 5 Burr. 2589, 2592, 98 Eng. Rep. 361, 363 (K.B. 1770).

[99] Fitch v. Hamlin (Conn. Sup. Ct. Err. 1789), *reported in* 1 Z. SWIFT, *supra* note 17, at 410–12.

[100] 2 J. POWELL, *supra* note 2, at 232–33.

[101] The leading case is Shepherd v. Johnson, 2 East. 211, 102 Eng. Rep. 349 (K.B. 1802). *See also* M'Arthur v. Seaforth, 2 Taunt. 257, 127 Eng. Rep. 1076 (C.P. 1810); Payne v. Burke (C.P. 1799), *discussed at* 2 East. 212 n.(a), 102 Eng. Rep. 350 n.(a). While these cases deal explicitly with the question of whether damages should be measured as of the promised date of delivery or as of the date of trial, they are nevertheless also the first cases that recognize any measure of expectation damages.

[102] 1 Bay 105 (S.C. 1790).

time. "[I]n consequence of the prospect of the adoption of the funding system by Congress," the value of the stock increased and the defendant could only "cover" at a substantially higher price.[103] The South Carolina Supreme Court made no effort to conceal the significance of the damage question before it. "[I]t is of extensive importance to the community, that the principle should *now be settled and ascertained with precision,*"[104] the court declared. "A great number of contracts in every part of the state, depend upon the determination of this question: and it is fortunate, that so respectable a jury are convened for the purpose of fixing a standard for future decisions."[105] And with the aid of advice from a "respectable" merchant jury, the court announced its holding: "Whenever a contract is entered into for the delivery of a specific article, the value of that article, at the time fixed for delivery, is the sum a plaintiff ought to recover."[106]

It is entirely possible, of course, that the defendant in *Davis v. Richardson* was not the stock speculator that I have supposed him to be. In specie-scarce postrevolutionary South Carolina, where bonds and securities were regularly used for money, he may simply have been treating the indents as currency. As a result, he may have been one of the earliest casualties of the almost instant creation of a speculative market for state securities after the establishment of the national government. Prevailing economic and legal conceptions about the true nature of stock transactions were in a state of flux. Twice in the next four years, lawsuits [107] involving expectation damages on stock were carried to the Supreme Court of South Carolina in an attempt to reverse the ruling in *Davis v. Richardson*. The major argument put forth by Charles Pinckney, the leader of the South Carolina bar, was that the allowance of expectation damages was nothing more than the allowance of usury.[108] In *Atkinson v. Scott* [109] (1793), where the disputed securities had appreciated by 850% in one year, the Supreme Court admitted that such contracts "must strike every mind at the first blush" as "evidently usurious."[110] If, Pinckney argued, South Carolina stock was to be treated as money, the borrower could only be expected to pay the value at the time of the contract plus interest. But in a world in which a "respect-

---

[103] *Id.*

[104] *Id.* at 106.

[105] *Id.*

[106] *Id.*

[107] Wiggs v. Garden, 1 Bay 357 (S.C. 1794); Atkinson v. Scott, 1 Bay 307 (S.C. 1793).

[108] Atkinson v. Scott, 1 Bay 307 (S.C. 1793) (argument of counsel).

[109] 1 Bay 307 (S.C. 1793).

[110] *Id.* at 309. *Cf.* p. 937 & note 99 *supra.*

able" jury of merchants had recognized that stocks were traded on speculation, it made no sense for courts to deny the speculative purpose of the transaction. The result was that Pinckney's argument was rejected, and by 1794, the South Carolina legal system applied the rule of expectation damages to what appear to be the first organized markets that had developed in that state.[111]

In Virginia, the transformation of legal conceptions took an identical path. In *Groves v. Graves*[112] (1790), the rule of expectation damages arose in connection with a buyer's action for securities. After a jury had awarded the plaintiff expectation damages, however, Chancellor Wythe, still reflecting eighteenth century moral and legal conceptions, enjoined the enforcement of the judgment on the grounds that the transaction "appeared to have been designed to secure unconscionable profit . . . and to have been obtained from one whom he had cause to believe at that time to be needy . . . ."[113] He allowed damages only to the extent of the original value plus interest.[114] But the Virginia Court of Appeals reversed his decree, holding that "the contract was neither usurious, or so unconscionable as to be set aside . . . ."[115] And, in marked contrast to the earlier practice of not reviewing jury damage awards,[116] the court held that the jury erred in measuring damages as of the time of trial and not as of the time of delivery.[117] The case thus suggests that judicial supervision of juries' damage awards may have arisen simultaneously with the recognition of expectation damages.

The first published opinion in Pennsylvania allowing expectation damages for failure to deliver stock certificates on a rising market was decided in 1791.[118] The rule was elaborated in a 1795 case, *Gilchreest v. Pollock*,[119] where a seller of stock sued the buyer's surety for failure to accept the transfer of United States securities that had fallen in price after the contract was made.

---

[111] *See* cases cited note 107 *supra.*

[112] 1 Va. (1 Wash.) 1 (1790).

[113] *Id.* at 3 (recitation of chancellor's opinion).

[114] *Id.*

[115] *Id.*

[116] *See* pp. 925–26 *supra.*

[117] 1 Va. (1 Wash.) at 4. This issue remained unsettled ten years later. In Kirtley v. Banks (Va. 1800), *reported in* Tucker, *supra* note 64 (Dec. 9, 1800), a suit for failure to deliver securities, the court instructed the jury that it "may take the price at either period, but not any higher price at any intermediate period." *Id.* The jury selected the time of delivery as its standard.

[118] Marshall v. Campbell, 1 Yeates 36 (Pa. 1791).

[119] 2 Yeates 18 (Pa. 1795). Two other cases also granted expectation damages to enforce contracts for the sale of United States securities. *See* Livingston v. Swanwick, 2 Dall. 300 (C.C.D. Pa. 1793); Graham v. Bickham, 4 Dall. 149 (Pa. 1796).

While the merchant jury in South Carolina had had no difficulty in reaching their result, the Pennsylvania court felt compelled to charge its lay jurors that "[t]he sale of stock is neither unlawful nor immoral. It is confessed, that an inordinate spirit of speculation approaches to gaming and tends to corrupt the morals of the people. When the public mind is thus affected, it becomes the legislature to interpose."[120]

The early Pennsylvania case is somewhat anomalous in that it rested on an unpublished opinion, rendered in 1786, which recognized a market price for wheat and announced that "[t]he rule or measure of damages in such cases is to give the difference between the price contracted for and the price at the time of delivery."[121] With this one exception, however, the evidence appears to indicate that the rule for expectation damages first arose in connection with stock speculation both in England and in America.[122] In England the principle of expectation damages was not generalized in cases dealing with sales of commodities until 1825,[123] and Chitty's treatise on contracts, published in 1826, is the first to announce a general rule of expectation damages for failure to deliver goods.[124]

---

[120] 2 Yeates at 21.

[121] Lewis v. Carradan (Pa. 1786), *cited in* 1 Yeates at 37.

[122] The first reported case in Massachusetts involving the measure of damages for nondelivery is also a securities case. Gray v. Portland Bank, 3 Mass. 364, 382, 390–91 (1807).

[123] Greening v. Wilkinson, 1 Car. & P. 625, 171 Eng. Rep. 1344 (K.B. 1825); Gainsford v. Carroll, 2 B. & C. 624, 107 Eng. Rep. 516 (K.B. 1824); Leigh v. Paterson, 8 Taunt. 540, 129 Eng. Rep. 493 (C.P. 1818).

[124] J. CHITTY, A PRACTICAL TREATISE ON THE LAW OF CONTRACTS, NOT UNDER SEAL 132 (1826). Powell's *Essay Upon the Law of Contracts* (1790) does not appear to deal with sales. His only recognition of the effect of changes in the market on contracts of sale is his statement that if, after a contract for delivery of corn, the price *falls* to 5 pounds, the buyer "will be entitled either to . . . [the] corn, or five pounds." 1 J. POWELL, *supra* note 2, at 409. He also states the rule that "if one of the parties fail in his part of the agreement, he shall pay the other party such damages as he has sustained by such neglect or refusal." *Id.* at 137. Powell cited the famous case of Dutch v. Warren, 1 Strange 406, 93 Eng. Rep. 598 (K.B. 1720), which, as we have seen, was simply an action for restitution. *See* pp. 921–22 *supra*.

In Samuel Comyn's *Treatise on Contracts*, an entire chapter is devoted to contracts for the sale of goods. While Comyn does recognize executory contracts, most of the discussion is devoted either to formation of binding contracts or to sellers' remedies for breach. In his very brief reference to buyers' actions for nondelivery, Comyn concluded only that if the buyer tenders payment, he "may take and recover the things." 2 S. COMYN, TREATISE ON CONTRACTS 212 (1807). For this conclusion he cites only an obscure early seventeenth century treatise. Indeed, this discussion is more in line with Blackstone's title theory analysis of contract as one mode of transfer of property than with a nineteenth century market approach.

Finally, with Joseph Chitty's *Treatise on Contracts*, the rule of expectation

In America the application of expectation damages to commodities contracts correlates with the development of extensive internal commodities markets around 1815. The leading case is *Shepherd v. Hampton*[125] (1818), in which the Supreme Court held that the measure of damages for failure to deliver cotton was the difference between the contract price and the market price at the time of delivery. Within the next decade a number of courts worked out the problems of computing expectation damages for commodities contracts,[126] one of them noting that "[m]ost of the [prior] cases in which this principle has been adopted, have grown out of contracts for the delivery and replacing of stock . . . ."[127]

The absorption of commodities transactions into contract law is a major step in the development of a modern law of contracts. As a result of the growth of extensive markets, "futures" contracts became a normal device either to insure against fluctuations in supply and price or simply to speculate. And as a consequence, judges and jurists began to reject eighteenth century legal rules which reflected an underlying conception of contract as fair exchange.

It has already been noted that in the eighteenth century, commercial classes endeavored to cast their transactions in legal forms which avoided the equalizing tendencies of early contract doctrine. Not surprisingly, the first direct assault upon the equitable conception of contract appeared in adjudications involving one of these forms, the negotiable instrument.

During the second half of the eighteenth century, a movement developed to eliminate the substantive significance of the doctrine of consideration in cases involving negotiable instruments. In

---

damages is announced: "In an action of assumpsit, for not delivering goods upon a given day, the measure of damages is the difference between the contract price, and that which goods of a similar quality and description, bore on or about the day, when the goods ought to have been delivered." J. CHITTY, *supra*, at 131–32. Interestingly, he cites only two cases decided in the previous five years.

The chapters on damages in the treatises of Powell, Comyn, and Chitty do not mention the problem of expectation damages. Rather, they address themselves exclusively to the problem of how to distinguish penal clauses from clauses providing for liquidated damages. This emphasis reveals the extent to which commercial transactions were still far more dependent on the use of bonds than on contracts. *See* pp. 927–29 *supra*.

[125] 16 U.S. (3 Wheat.) 200 (1818). McAllister v. Douglass & Mandeville, 15 F. Cas. 1203 (No. 8657) (C.C.D.D.C. 1805), *aff'd*, 7 U.S. (3 Cranch) 298 (1806), superficially resembles *Shepherd*, but there was no agreed upon contract price.

[126] *See, e.g.*, West v. Wentworth, 3 Cow. 82 (N.Y. Sup. Ct. 1824) (salt); Merryman v. Criddle, 18 Va. (4 Muni.) 542 (1815) (corn).

[127] Clark v. Pinney, 7 Cow. 681, 687 (N.Y. Sup. Ct. 1827). One earlier case involving a commodity was Sands v. Taylor, 5 Johns. 395 (N.Y. Sup. Ct. 1810), *discussed* pp. 922–23 *supra*.

1767, the Massachusetts Superior Court held by a 3–2 vote that even in an action between the original parties to a promissory note, the promisor could not offer evidence of inadequate consideration in mitigation of damages.[128] "People," Chief Justice Hutchinson declared, "think themselves quite safe in taking a Note for the Sum due, and reasonably suppose all Necessity of keeping the Evidence of the Consideration at an End; it would be big with Mischief to oblige People to stand always prepared to contest Evidence that might be offered to the Sufficiency of the Consideration. This would be doubly strong in Favour of an Indorsee."[129]

It was one thing to argue that in order to make notes negotiable a subsequent indorsee would be allowed to recover on a note regardless of the consideration between the original parties. This argument, of course, itself entailed a sacrifice of judicial control over bargains that commercial convenience was beginning to demand. It was, however, quite a different matter to exclude evidence of consideration between the original parties to the note, as the Massachusetts court decided. With this decision, it became possible for merchants to exclude the question of the equality of a bargain by transacting their business through promissory notes.

The Massachusetts decision was handed down two years after Lord Mansfield's dramatic but unsuccessful attempt to destroy the doctrine of consideration in the case of *Pillans v. Van Mierop*,[130] a case between merchants involving a promise to accept a bill of exchange. "I take it," Mansfield declared in dictum, "that the ancient notion about the want of consideration was for the sake of evidence only; for when it is reduced into writing, as in covenants, specialties, bonds, etc., there was no objection to the want of consideration."[131] While it is impossible to know from this pronouncement whether Mansfield's *ratio decidendi* was that consideration was unnecessary for all written instruments or merely for those between merchants, two conclusions are clear. First, by explaining the requirement of consideration exclusively in terms of its evidentiary value in proving the existence of a contract, Mansfield had cut the heart out of the traditional equalizing function of consideration. Second, whether or not upon reflection Mansfield would have extended these views to cover all written

---

[128] Noble v. Smith, Quincy 254 (Mass. 1767).

[129] *Id.* at 255.

[130] 3 Burr. 1663, 97 Eng. Rep. 1035 (K.B. 1765). There is no citation of this case in *Noble v. Smith*. The third volume of Burrow's reports was first published in 1771, four years after *Noble v. Smith* was decided.

[131] *Id.* at 1669, 97 Eng. Rep. at 1038.

instruments — where the writing was itself sufficient evidence of a contract — he at least meant to apply the rule to negotiable instruments. Indeed, as Mansfield's decision was being announced, the second volume of Blackstone's *Commentaries* was at the press, also propounding the rule that evidence of lack of consideration would not be admitted in an action on a negotiable instrument.[132] For thirteen years, English law stood thus on the verge of rejecting the ancient requirement of consideration. But in *Rann v. Hughes* [133] (1778), the House of Lords reaffirmed the requirement of consideration for written instruments.

The views of Mansfield and Blackstone were to have a greater effect than the decision by the House of Lords, however. The report of that decision was unpublished until 1800, and was unknown by American judges before the early years of the nineteenth century.[134] Thus, even after Mansfield's opinion was overruled we find Zephaniah Swift, the first American treatise writer, stating that the principle that had emerged from negotiable instruments law — he cited Blackstone — "clearly destroys all distinction between sealed and unsealed contracts." [135] The result, he concluded, was that a written contract "precludes an enquiry into the consideration." [136] A more important factor than the accident of reporting, however, was the congeniality of Mansfield's and Blackstone's views to American judges, whose own opinions were gradually inclining towards a conception of contract as a sacred bargain between private parties.

The most persistent American advocate of the Mansfield position was the able judge of the New York Supreme Court, Brockholst Livingston, whose commercial law practice before he ascended to the bench was probably second only to that of Alexander Hamilton. In 1804, Livingston reiterated the position that as between even the original parties to a negotiable instrument, the failure of consideration could not be shown. "It is not necessary, as in other simple contracts, to state a consideration in the declaration; the instrument itself imports one, and in this respect

---

[132] 2 W. BLACKSTONE, COMMENTARIES *446.

[133] 7 T.R. 350 n.1, 101 Eng. Rep. 1014 n.1 (1778).

[134] In the typically chaotic fashion of law reporting of the time, the decision was casually included as a footnote to the report of another case, Mitchinson v. Hewson, 7 T.R. 350, 101 Eng. Rep. 1014 (1797). The earliest recognition of the House of Lords decision in America that I am aware of is St. George Tucker's citation in his 1803 edition of Blackstone. 3 BLACKSTONE'S COMMENTARIES *446 n.1 (St. G. Tucker ed. 1803). In 1804, William Cranch acknowledged that he just learned of the decision as he was about to publish his elaborate essay on negotiable instruments. 5 U.S. (1 Cranch) 445 n.1.

[135] 1 Z. SWIFT, *supra* note 17, at 373.

[136] *Id. See also* Z. SWIFT, DIGEST, *supra* note 52, at 339.

partakes of the quality of a speciality [sealed instrument]." [137] Livingston extended the argument to cover simple contracts in a case decided one year later. In *Lansing v. McKillip*,[138] he dissented from the court's opinion requiring that consideration be proved by the plaintiff before he could recover on a contract. At first, he urged only that the traditional burden of proof be altered so that a defendant who wished to negate a contract be required to show lack of consideration.[139] In the process, however, he was moved to attack the very requirement of consideration itself. Ridiculing a rule of consideration that "does not demand an absolute equivalent, but is satisfied, in many cases, with the most trifling ground that can be imagined," he urged the court to "be content in point of evidence, with a declaration . . . that he has received a *valuable one*, without indulging the useless curiosity of prying further into the transaction." [140] Livingston was fully aware that his opinion directly attacked the traditional equalizing function of consideration. "Why," he asked, is a court "so very careful of a defendant's rights as not to suppose him capable of judging for himself, what was an adequate value for his promise? Would it not be more just, and better promote the ends of justice, that one, who had signed an instrument of this kind, should, without further proof, be compelled to perform it, unless he could impeach the validity on other grounds?" [141]

Like Mansfield's earlier effort, this attack on consideration initially failed, but in its most important respect it ultimately succeeded. It was part of a movement, which had begun in England during Mansfield's tenure and continued throughout the nineteenth century, toward overthrowing the traditional role of courts in regulating the equity of agreements. The underlying logic of the attack on a substantive doctrine of consideration came to fruition in America with the great New York case of *Seymour v. Delancy* [142] (1824), in which a sharply divided High Court of Errors reversed a decision of Chancellor Kent, who had refused to specifically enforce a land contract on the ground of gross inadequacy of consideration between the parties. "Every member of this Court," the majority opinion noted, "must be well aware how much property is held by contract; that purchases are constantly made upon speculation; that the value of real estate

---

[137] Livingston v. Hastie, 2 Cai. R. 246, 247 (N.Y. Sup. Ct. 1804).

[138] 3 Cai. R. 286 (N.Y. Sup. Ct. 1805).

[139] *Id.* at 289–91 (Livingston, J., dissenting). This position was also adopted by another judge, William Cranch. *See* 1 Cranch 445.

[140] 3 Cai. R. at 290.

[141] *Id.*

[142] 3 Cow. 445 (N.Y. 1824), *rev'g* 6 Johns. Ch. 222 (N.Y. Ch. 1822).

is fluctuating . . . ."[143] The result was that there "exists an honest difference of opinion in regard to any bargain, as to its being a beneficial one, or not."[144] The court held that only where the inadequacy of price was itself evidence of fraud would it interfere with the execution of private contracts.[145]

The nineteenth century departure from the equitable conception of contract is particularly obvious in the rapid adoption of the doctrine of caveat emptor. It has already been noted that, despite the supposed ancient lineage of caveat emptor, eighteenth century English and American courts embraced the doctrine that "a sound price warrants a sound commodity."[146] It was only after Lord Mansfield declared in 1778, in one of those casual asides that seem to have been so influential in forging the history of the common law, that the only basis for an action for breach of warranty was an express contract,[147] that the foundation was laid for reconsidering whether an action for breach of an implied warranty would lie. In 1802 the English courts finally considered the policies behind such an action, deciding that no suit on an implied warranty would be allowed.[148] Two years later, in the leading American case of *Seixas v. Woods*,[149] the New York Supreme Court, relying on a doubtfully reported seventeenth century English case,[150] also held that there could be no recovery against a merchant who could not be proved knowingly to have sold defective goods. Other American jurisdictions quickly fell into line.[151]

While the rule of caveat emptor established in *Seixas v. Woods* seems to be the result of one of those frequent accidents of historical misunderstanding, this is hardly sufficient to account for the widespread acceptance of the doctrine of caveat emptor elsewhere

---

[143] *Id.* at 533.

[144] *Id.*

[145] *Id.* The year before *Seymour v. Delancey* was decided, Nathan Dane had already anticipated its main thrust. *See* p. 950 *infra*.

[146] *See* pp. 926–27 *supra*.

[147] Stuart v. Wilkins, 1 Doug. 18, 20, 99 Eng. Rep. 15, 16 (K.B. 1778). Though Mansfield was laying the foundation for the subsequent rejection of the sound price doctrine, his purpose was not clearly understood. Nathan Dane, for one, misread the case as upholding the doctrine and, therefore, attempted in 1823 to show that it was "contrary to most of the settled cases in the books . . . ." 2 N. DANE, A GENERAL ABRIDGEMENT AND DIGEST OF AMERICAN LAW 542 (1823).

[148] Parkinson v. Lee, 2 East. 314, 102 Eng. Rep. 389 (K.B. 1802).

[149] 2 Cai. R. 48 (N.Y. Sup. Ct. 1804).

[150] The case relied upon was Chandelor v. Lopus, Cro. Jac. 4, 79 Eng. Rep. 3 (Ex. 1603); *see* note 54 *supra*.

[151] *See, e.g.*, The Monte Allegre, 22 U.S. (9 Wheat.) 616 (1824); Dean v. Mason, 4 Conn. 428 (1822); Bradford v. Manly, 13 Mass. 139 (1816); Curcier v. Pennock, 14 S. & R. 51 (Pa. 1826); Wilson v. Shackleford, 25 Va. (4 Rand.) 5 (1826).

in America. Nor are the demands of a market economy a sufficient cause. Although the sound price doctrine was attacked on the ground that there "is no standard to determine whether the vendee has paid a *sound* price,"[152] the most consistent legal theorist of the market economy, Gulian Verplanck, devoted his impressive analytical talents to an elaborate critique of the doctrine of caveat emptor.[153] The sudden and complete substitution of caveat emptor in place of the sound price doctrine must therefore be understood as a dramatic overthrow of an important element of the eighteenth century's equitable conception of contract.[154]

### B. The Synthesis of the Will Theory of Contract

The development of extensive markets at the turn of the century contributed to a substantial erosion of belief in theories of objective value and just price. Markets for future delivery of goods

---

[152] Dean v. Mason, 4 Conn. 428, 434–35 (1822) (Chapman, J.).

[153] *See* p. 948 *infra*. I have not meant to assert that caveat emptor is more conducive to a market economy than the contrary doctrine of caveat venditor, though this might be independently demonstrated. Rather, I have argued that the importance of caveat emptor lies in its overthrow of both the sound price doctrine and the latter's underlying conception of objective value.

[154] We can best see the nature of the attack on the "sound price" doctrine in South Carolina, the only state in which it persisted well into the nineteenth century. Urging reversal of the sound price doctrine and adoption in its place of a rule of caveat emptor, the Attorney General of South Carolina argued in 1802 that "[s]uch a doctrine . . . if once admitted in the formation of contracts, would leave no room for the exercise of judgment or discretion, but would destroy all free agency; every transaction between man and man must be weighed in the balance like the precious metals, and if found wanting in . . . adequacy, must be made good to the uttermost farthing . . . ." Whitefield v. McLeod, 2 Bay 380, 382 (S.C. 1802) (argument of counsel). If a court should refuse to enforce a contract made by a man who has had "an equal knowledge of all the circumstances" as well as "an opportunity of informing himself, and the means of procuring information . . . ," he maintained, "good faith and mutual confidence would be at an end. . . . To suffer such a man to get rid of such a contract, under all these circumstances," he concluded, "would establish a principle which would undermine and blow up every contract . . . ." *Id.* at 383. According to South Carolina lawyer Hugh Legaré, the rule of caveat emptor was desirable because it rejected the "refined equity" of the civil law in favor of "the policy of society." Though there was "something captivating in the equity of the principle, that a sound price implies a warranty of the soundness of the commodity," he was "certain that this rule is productive of great practical inconveniences . . . ." 2 WRITINGS OF HUGH SWINTON LEGARÉ 110 (M. Legaré ed. 1845). In South Carolina, he noted, "where we have had ample opportunity to witness its operation, there are very few experienced lawyers but would gladly expunge from our books the case which first introduced it here." *Id. See also* Barnard v. Yates, 1 N. & McC. 142, 146 (S.C. 1818) (noting "the perversion and abuse of [the] rule" which many "thought to have opened a door for endless litigation" in those cases where "the contracting parties had not placed themselves upon a perfect footing of equality in point of value").

were difficult to explain within a theory of exchange based on giving and receiving equivalents in value. Futures contracts for
fungible commodities could only be understood in terms of a
fluctuating conception of expected value radically different from
the static notion that lay behind contracts for specific goods;
a regime of markets and speculation was simply incompatible
with a socially imposed standard of value. The rise of a modern
law of contract, then, was an outgrowth of an essentially procom-
mercial attack on the theory of objective value which lay at the
foundation of the eighteenth century's equitable idea of contract.

   We have seen, however, that there was a period during
which vestiges of the eighteenth century conception of contract
coexisted with the emerging will theory.[155] It was not until
after 1820 that attacks on the equitable conception began to
be generalized to include all aspects of contract law. If value is
subjective, nineteenth century contracts theorists reasoned, the
function of exchange is to maximize the conflicting and otherwise
incommensurable desires of individuals. The role of contract law
was not to assure the equity of agreements but simply to enforce
only those willed transactions that parties to a contract believed
to be to their mutual advantage. The result was a major tendency
toward submerging the dominant equitable theory of contract in
a conception of contractual obligation based exclusively on express
bargains. In his *Essay on the Law of Contracts* (1822), for example, Daniel Chipman criticized the Vermont system of assigning customary values to goods that were used to pay contract
debts. Only the market could establish a fair basis for exchange,
Chipman urged. "[L]et money be the sole standard in making
all contracts," for "[i]f, therefore, it were possible for courts in
the administration of justice, to take this ideal high price as a
standard of valuation, every consideration of policy, and a regard
for the good of the people would forbid it." [156]

   We will see that Nathan Dane's *Abridgment* (1823) and
Joseph Story's *Equity Jurisprudence* (1836) also contributed to
the demise of the old equitable conceptions. But nowhere were
the underlying bases of contract law more brilliantly and systematically rethought than in Gulian C. Verplanck's *An Essay on the
Doctrine of Contracts* (1825).

   Verplanck was the first English or American writer to see in
the "different parts of the system" of contract law "clashing and
wholly incongruous" doctrines.[157] He emphasized "the singular
incongruity" of a legal system that "obstinately refuses redress

---

[155] *See* note 18 & pp. 923, 924, 932–34 *supra*.
[156] D. CHIPMAN, *supra* note 68, at 109–11.
[157] G. VERPLANCK, *supra* note 53, at 57.

in so many, and such marked instances of unfairly obtained advantages" and yet "occasionally permit[s] contracts to be set aside upon the ground of inadequacy of price . . . ." [158] There were, he asserted, many "difficulties and contradictions" to be found in existing legal doctrine over "the question of the nature and degree of equality required in contracts of mutual interest,"[159] as well as over the standards of "inadequacy of price" and "inequality of knowledge." "Where," he asked, "shall we draw the line of fair and unfair, of equal and unequal contracts?" [160]

Verplanck's *Essay* was written as an attack on the doctrine of caveat emptor, which had then only recently been adopted by the United States Supreme Court in *Laidlaw v. Organ* [161] (1817), one of the first cases to come before the Court involving a contract for future delivery of a commodity. The case, Verplanck wrote, raised "the important and difficult question of the nature and degree of equality in compensation, in skill or in knowledge, required between the parties to any contract . . . in order to make it valid in law, or just and right in private conscience." [162] He attacked caveat emptor on the ground that it should be fraudulent to withhold "any fact . . . necessarily and materially affecting the common estimate which fixes the present market value of the thing sold . . . ." [163]

In refusing to separate law and morals,[164] Verplanck was boldly independent of other theorists of the market economy.[165] But at its deepest level, Verplanck's *Essay* marks the triumph of a subjective theory of value in a market economy. Wishing to base legal doctrine on "the plainer truths of political economy," [166] he insisted that although just price doctrines bore "the impression of a high and pure morality," [167] they were "mixed with error"

---

[158] *Id.* at 199.

[159] *Id.* at 14 (emphasis deleted).

[160] *Id.* at 10.

[161] 15 U.S. (2 Wheat.) 178 (1817). The case grew out of a futures contract for sale of tobacco purchased by a merchant who had advance knowledge that the United States and England had signed a peace treaty ending the War of 1812. "The question in this case," Chief Justice Marshall wrote, "is, whether the intelligence of extrinsic circumstances, which might influence the price of the commodity, and which was exclusively within the knowledge of the vendee, ought to have been communicated by him to the vendor?" *Id.* at 195. The Chief Justice held that there was no duty to communicate the information, since "[i]t would be difficult to circumscribe the contrary doctrine within proper limits . . . ." *Id.*

[162] G. VERPLANCK, *supra* note 53, at 5.

[163] *Id.* at 125–26.

[164] Verplanck referred to the issue of fraud as "the [only] purely ethical part of the question . . . ." *Id.* at 117.

[165] *See, e.g.*, pp. 949–50 *infra* (N. Dane).

[166] G. VERPLANCK, *supra* note 53, at 106.

[167] *Id.* at 96.

and arose "from the introduction of a false metaphysic in relation to equality . . . ." [168] Thus, he disputed the view of "[l]awyers and divines . . . that all bargains are made under the idea of giving and receiving equivalents in value." [169] There could be no "such thing in the literal sense of the words, as adequacy of price [or] equality or inequality of compensation," since "from the very nature of the thing, price depends solely upon the agreement of the parties, being created by it alone. Mere inequality of price, or rather what appears so in the judgment of a third person, cannot, without reference to something else, be any objection to the validity of a sale, or of an agreement to sell." [170]

Verplanck's *Essay* represents an important stage in the process of adapting contract law to the realities of a market economy. Verplanck saw that if value is solely determined by the clash of subjective desire, there can be no objective measure of the fairness of a bargain. Since only "facts" are objective, fairness can never be measured in terms of substantive equality. The law can only assure that each party to a bargain is given "full knowledge of all material facts." [171] Significantly, Verplanck defined "material facts" so as not to include "peculiar advantages of skill, shrewdness, and experience, regarding which . . . no one has a right to call upon us to abandon. Here, justice permits us to use our superiority freely." [172] Thus, while he refused in theory to separate law and morality, Verplanck confined fraud to a range sufficiently narrow to permit the contract system to reinforce existing social and economic inequalities.

Though Verplanck's reconsideration of the philosophical foundations of contract law was by far the most penetrating among the American treatise writers, Nathan Dane and Joseph Story were more influential in contributing to the overthrow of an equitable conception of contract. In the very first chapter of his nine volume work, Dane elaborated some of the principles of contract law. One of his most important themes involved the "[d]ifference between morality and law." [173] He explained that while "in some special cases the *law of the land* and *morality* are the same," they

---

[168] *Id.* at 104.

[169] *Id.* at 8.

[170] *Id.* at 115. *See also id.* at 133.

[171] *Id.* at 225.

[172] *Id.* at 135.

All know what a wide difference exists among men in these points, and whatever advantage may result from that inequality, is silently conceded in the very fact of making a bargain. It is a superiority on one side — an inferiority on the other, perhaps very great, but they are allowed. This must be so; the business of life could not go on were it otherwise.

*Id.* at 120.

[173] 1 N. DANE, *supra* note 147, at 100 (emphasis deleted).

differ in most cases, "when policy, or arbitrary rules must, also, be regarded." [174] " 'Virtue is alone the object of morality,' " he continued, but "law has, . . . often, for its object, the peace of society, and what is practicable: Hence, though every . . . undue advantage in a bargain, to the hurt of another party, practised by one, is an act of injustice in the eyes of *morality*; yet it is not the mean [*sic*] of restitution in the eyes of the *law*; because [it is] often, impracticable *in every minute degree*." [175]

Dane also attacked all conceptions of a substantive theory of exchange. Equity decisions, Dane exclaimed, had become "trash" since they were "the productions of inferior lawyers" and "ignorant and indolent judges" who offered "no rule of property or conduct . . . ." [176] "Inadequate price in a bargain," he wrote, "does not defeat it, merely because inadequate . . . ." [177] But Dane remained willing to regard an unequal bargain as evidence that a "person did not understand the bargain he made, or was so oppressed, that he thought it best to make it . . . ." [178] Indeed, in his characteristic style, he continued to repeat the substance of the old learning while contributing to its overthrow. "[W]hen an agreement appears very unequal, and affords any ground to suspect any imposition, unfairness, or undue power or command, the courts will seize any very slight circumstances to avoid enforcing it." [179]

Dane was still reflecting an eighteenth century world view in which unequal bargaining power was conceived of as an illegitimate form of duress and in which lack of understanding was not yet identified only with mental disability. And yet in the world of speculation and futures markets, in which all value must simply turn on "an honest difference of opinion," [180] legal doctrine eventually renounced all claims to make judgments about oppression. With the publication of Joseph Story's *Equity Jurisprudence* (1836), American law finally yielded up the ancient notion that the substantive value of an exchange could provide an appropriate measure of the justice of a transaction. "Inadequacy of consideration," Story wrote, "is not then, of itself, a distinct principle of relief in Equity. The Common Law knows no such principle . . . . The value of a thing . . . must be in its nature fluctuating, and will depend upon ten thousand different circumstances . . . . If Courts of Equity were to unravel all these

[174] *Id.*
[175] *Id.*
[176] *Id.* at 107–08.
[177] *Id.* at 661.
[178] *Id.*
[179] *Id.*
[180] Seymour v. Delancey, 3 Cow. 445, 533 (N.Y. 1824).

transactions, they would throw every thing into confusion, and set afloat the contracts of mankind." [181]

The replacement of the equitable conception of contract with the will theory can be seen in Dane's assault on the eighteenth century practice of suing on a theory of implied contract where there had been a express agreement. In a long and unusually polemical technical discussion, Dane argued that once there is an express contract there could be no quantum meruit recovery off the contract on a theory of natural justice and equity.[182] Dane's attack on quantum meruit becomes comprehensible only as an effort to destroy an equitable conception of exchange in light of a newly emerging theory of value based on the subjective desires of contracting parties. Without a socially imposed standard of value, implied contracts make no sense. Where "there is no fixed or unchangeable comparative value between one price of property and another" and all value "depends on the wants and opinions of men," [183] it becomes impossible to measure damages by reference to customary value. The only basis for measuring contractual obligation, then, derives from the "will" of parties, and the crucial legal issue shifts to whether there has been a "meeting of minds."

The victory of the emerging will theory of contractual obligation was not at first complete. When Theron Metcalf delivered his lectures on contracts in 1828 he still reflected the tension between the old learning and the new.[184] Implied contracts, he wrote, were "inferred from the conduct, situation, or mutual relations of the parties, and enforced by the law on the ground of justice; to compel the performance of a legal and moral duty . . . ." [185] In support of this, he cited Chief Justice Marshall's statement that implied contracts "grow out of the acts of the parties. In such cases, the parties are supposed to have made those stipulations which, as honest, fair, and just men, they ought

---

[181] 1 J. STORY, COMMENTARIES ON EQUITY JURISPRUDENCE 249-50 (1836).

[182] 1 N. DANE, *supra* note 147, at 223-29.

[183] G. VERPLANCK, *supra* note 53, at 133.

[184] Metcalf's lectures were first published between 1839 and 1841, although they were first delivered in 1828 at a law school he had founded in Dedham, Massachusetts. *See* 1 U.S. L. INTELL. & REV. 142 (1829). When, in 1867, Metcalf published his *Principles of the Law of Contracts*, he acknowledged that "[t]he first manuscript of the . . . work was prepared, in the years 1827 and 1828" and was published in *American Jurist* between 1839 and 1841. T. METCALF, PRINCIPLES OF THE LAW OF CONTRACTS iii (1867) [hereinafter cited as LAW OF CONTRACTS]. "That publication," he wrote, "has recently been revised and enlarged by reference to reports and treatises published since 1828; but no change has been made in the original arrangement." *Id.*

[185] LAW OF CONTRACTS 4; 20 AM. JUR. 5 (1838).

to have made." [186]  Though both Metcalf and Marshall were beginning to pretend that contractual obligation derives only from the will of the parties, their predominant form of expression continued to recognize standards of justice external to the parties. Indeed, Metcalf still maintained that "[i]n sound sense, divested of fiction and technicality, the only true ground, on which an action upon what is called an implied contract can be maintained, is that of justice, duty, and legal obligation." [187]

By the time William W. Story's *Treatise on the Law of Contracts* appeared in 1844, however, the tension between the two theories had dissolved. "Every contract," he wrote, "is founded upon the mutual agreement of the parties . . . ." [188]  Both express and implied contracts were "equally founded upon the actual agreement of the parties, and the only distinction between them is in regard to the mode of proof, and belongs to the law of evidence." [189]  For implied contracts, he concluded, "the law only supplies that which, although not stated, must be presumed to have been the agreement intended by the parties." [190]  Since the only basis for the contractual obligation was the will of the parties, Story now maintained, implied promises "only supply omissions, and do not alter express stipulations"; he was thus prepared to announce the "general rule" that there could be no implied contract where an express agreement already existed.[191]

With Story's announcement of the "general rule," the victory of the will theory of contractual obligation was complete. The entire conceptual apparatus of modern contract doctrine — rules dealing with offer and acceptance, the evidentiary function of consideration, and canons of construction and interpretation — arose to articulate the will theory with which American doctrinal writers expressed the ideology of a market economy in the early nineteenth century.

---

[186] Ogden v. Saunders, 25 U.S. (12 Wheat.) 341 (1827); *see* LAW OF CONTRACTS 4 n.(b); 20 AM. JUR. at 5 n.1.

[187] LAW OF CONTRACTS 5–6. This passage does not appear in *American Jurist*, though Metcalf did write that "it is manifestly only by a fiction, that a contract or promise is implied. And, indeed, the whole doctrine of implied contracts, in all their varieties, seems to be merely artificial and imaginary." 20 AM. JUR. at 9.

[188] W. STORY, *supra* note 53, at 4.

[189] *Id.*

[190] *Id. See also* 2 S. GREENLEAF, A TREATISE ON THE LAW OF EVIDENCE 87 (1850) ("The distinction between general or *implied contracts* and special or *express contracts* lies not in the nature of the undertaking, but in the mode of proof").

[191] W. STORY, *supra* note 53, at 6. *Cf.* pp. 933–34 *supra*.

## C. The Application of the Will Theory of Contract to Labor Contracts

Thus far, we have seen the changes in contract law which were necessary to meet the needs of the newly emerging market economies in England and America. There is evidence, however, that the change from the eighteenth to the nineteenth century also involved a pervasive shift in the sympathies of the courts. In the eighteenth century the subjection of individual bargains to the extensive supervisory powers of courts and juries expressed the legal and ethical culture of the small town, of the farmer, and of the small trader. In the nineteenth century, the will theory of contract was part of a more general process whereby courts came to reflect commercial interests. The changing alliances are painfully obvious in nineteenth century courts' discriminatory application of the recently discovered chasm between express and implied contracts.

The most important class of cases to which this distinction applied was labor contracts in which the employee had agreed to work for a period of time — often a year — for wages that he would receive at the end of his term. If he left his employment before the end of the term, jurists reasoned, the employee could receive nothing for the labor he had already expended. The contract, they maintained, was an "entire" one, and therefore it could not be conceived of as a series of smaller agreements. Since the breach of any part was therefore a breach of the whole, there was no basis for allowing the employee to recover "on the contract." Finally, citing the new orthodoxy proclaimed by the treatise writers, judges were led to pronounce the inevitable result: where there was an express agreement between the parties, it would be an act of usurpation to "rewrite" the contract and allow the employee to recover in quantum meruit for the "reasonable" value of his labor.[192]

Courts in fact seemed driven to resolve all ambiguity in contracts in favor of the employer's contention that they were "entire." It made no "difference . . . whether the wages are estimated at a gross sum, or are to be calculated according to a certain rate per week or month, or are payable at certain stipulated times, provided the servant agree for a definite and whole term . . . ."[193] Under these circumstances, it should be emphasized, the assumption that the agreement was "for a definite and whole term" was simply a judicial construction not required by the terms of the agreement. Moreover, it did not "make any

---

[192] *See* Annot., 19 Am. Dec. 268, 272 (1880).
[193] 1 T. Parsons, The Law of Contracts 522 n.(1) (1853).

difference, that the plaintiff ceased laboring for his employer, under the belief that, according to the legal method of computing time, under similar contracts, he had continued laboring as long as could be required of him." [194] Nor did it matter that the "employer, during the term, has from time to time made payments to the plaintiff for his labor." [195] The result of the cases was that any employee not shrewd or independent enough to demand immediate payment for his work risked losing everything if he should leave before the end of the contract period. The employer, in turn, had every inducement to create conditions near the end of the term that would encourage the laborer to quit.

The disposition of courts ruthlessly to follow conceptualism in the labor cases was not, however, quite matched in cases involving building contracts. Building contracts are similar to labor agreements in that there is no way of restoring the status quo after partial performance. Nevertheless, nineteenth century courts allowed builders to recover "off the contract" when they had committed some breach of their express obligation. The leading case is *Hayward v. Leonard* [196] (1828), in which the Supreme Judicial Court of Massachusetts held that a builder could recover in quantum meruit "where the contract is performed, but, without intention, some of the particulars of the contract are deviated from." [197] If there was "an honest intention to go by the contract, and a substantive execution of it," [198] the court held, it would not decree a forfeiture. It should be noted that the Massachusetts court in *Hayward v. Leonard* expressly rejected Dane's view that the existence of an express contract barred recovery in quantum meruit. There was, Chief Justice Parker declared, "a great array of authorities on both sides, from which it appears very clearly that different judges and different courts have held different doctrines, and sometimes the same court at different times." [199] The result was that in Massachusetts and in most other states two separate lines of cases were developed, one dealing with service contracts, for which recovery in quantum meruit was barred, and another applying to building contracts, for which recovery "off the contract" of the reasonable value of the performance was permitted.

Few courts attempted to rationalize what Theophilus Parsons was later to call these "very conflicting" decisions. [200] The leading

---

[194] *Id.*

[195] *Id.*

[196] 24 Mass. (7 Pick.) 181 (1828), *annotated*, 19 Am. Dec. 268 (1880).

[197] 24 Mass. (7 Pick.) at 186.

[198] *Id.* at 187.

[199] *Id.* at 184.

[200] 2 T. Parsons, *supra* note 193, at 35 & n.(d). There were two exceptions in this trend. The New York courts applied the express contract theory to building

explanation came from *Hayward v. Leonard* itself. In the labor cases the employee usually broke his contract "voluntarily" and "without fault" of his employer. Breach of building contracts was often "without intention" and compatible with an "honest intention" to fulfill the contract.[201] Thus, it was not that courts had abandoned an underlying moral conception of contracts, but that the morality had fundamentally changed. The focus had shifted from an emphasis on the role of quantum meruit in preventing "unjust enrichment." The express contract had become paramount; denial of quantum meruit recovery was now employed to enforce the contract system. It was now regarded as just for the employer to retain the unpaid benefits of his employee's labor as a deterrent to voluntary breach of contract. But it was still unjust for the beneficiary of a building contract to enrich himself because of an honest mistake in performing the contract.[202]

While the judges who adhered to the distinction between labor and building contracts never acknowledged an economic or social policy behind the distinction, it seems to be an important example of class bias. A penal conception of contractual obligation could have deterred economic growth by limiting investment in high risk enterprise. Just as the building trade was beginning to require major capital investment during the second quarter of the nineteenth century, courts were prepared to bestow upon it that special solicitude which American courts have reserved for infant industry. Penal provisions in labor contracts, by contrast, have only redistributional consequences, since they can hardly be expected to deter the laboring classes from selling their services in a subsistence economy.

Although nineteenth century courts and doctrinal writers did not succeed in entirely destroying the ancient connection between contracts and natural justice, they were able to elaborate a system that allowed judges to pick and choose among those groups in

---

as well as to labor contracts. Smith v. Brady, 17 N.Y. 173, 187 (1858). The second exception is the solitary challenge in New Hampshire to the doctrine against quantum meruit recovery in labor cases. *See* Britton v. Turner, 6 N.H. 481 (1834).

[201] 24 Mass. (7 Pick.) at 185.

[202] Even when courts modified in building contracts cases the dominant view of the treatise writers that express contracts barred all recovery on an implied contract, they shared at a deeper level the treatise writers' basic assumption about the relationship between express and implied agreements. The contract price, all agreed, set the limit on recovery in quantum meruit. *See, e.g.*, Hayward v. Leonard, 24 Mass. (7 Pick.) 181, 187 (1828). Similarly, in the great case of Britton v. Turner, 6 N.H. 481 (1834), where New Hampshire Chief Justice Joel Parker stood almost alone in resisting the orthodox view barring quantum meruit recovery on labor contracts, he permitted the employer to deduct from recovery "any damage which has been sustained by reason of the nonfulfillment of the contract." *Id.* at 494.

the population that would be its beneficiaries. And, above all, they succeeded in creating a great intellectual divide between a system of formal rules — which they managed to identify exclusively with the "rule of law" — and those ancient precepts of morality and equity, which they were able to render suspect as subversive of "the rule of law" itself.

# 8

# PROPERTY LAW, EXPROPRIATION, AND RESOURCE ALLOCATION BY GOVERNMENT: THE UNITED STATES, 1789-1910

*HARRY N. SCHEIBER*

Reprinted from THE JOURNAL OF ECONOMIC HISTORY
Volume XXXIII, March 1973, Number 1

# Property Law, Expropriation, and Resource Allocation by Government: the United States, 1789-1910

EXPROPRIATION of private property by government is seldom found on the list of policies which have influenced the course of economic development in American history. To be sure, the once-vigorous myth of antebellum *laisser-faire* has been discarded; and it is no longer taken as a startling proposition that governmental interventions to promote and regulate the economy occurred regularly throughout the nineteenth century.[1] But for two reasons, I think, expropriation as an instrument of conscious resource allocation has failed to receive from historians the attention it deserves.

In the first place, the whole notion of property takings on an involuntary basis by means of eminent domain law—what Corwin termed that "most invidious branch of governmental authority"— runs against the broad tendency to stress the stability of property rights in the American legal order.[2] When the "institutional environment" of U.S. economic development is analyzed, the legal system is usually portrayed as one "in which property received extreme protection"; and the doctrinal concern of lawmakers for vested property rights is cited as "the basic doctrine of American constitutional law."[3]

This study derives from a larger research project undertaken with generous support from the John Simon Guggenheim Memorial Foundation, the Center for Advanced Study in the Behavioral Sciences at Stanford, and the University of California. Charles McCurdy provided excellent assistance.

[1] Harry N. Scheiber, "Government and the Economy: Studies of the 'Commonwealth' Policy in 19th Century America," *Journal of Interdisciplinary History*, III (Summer 1972), pp. 135-151; James Willard Hurst, *Law and the Conditions of Freedom in the Nineteenth-Century United States* (1956, reprinted Madison: University of Wisconsin Press, 1964); James H. Soltow, "American Institutional Studies: Present Knowledge and Past Trends," THE JOURNAL OF ECONOMIC HISTORY, XXI (March 1971), pp. 87-105; Allan G. Bogue, "To Shape a Western State: Some Dimensions of the Kansas Search for Capital, 1865-1893," *The Frontier Challenge: Responses to the Trans-Mississippi West*, ed. John G. Clark (Lawrence: University of Kansas Press, 1971), pp. 203-234.

[2] Edward S. Corwin, *American Constitutional History: Essays*, eds. A. T. Mason and G. Garvey (New York: Harper & Row, 1964), p. 50.

[3] Francis S. Philbrick, "Changing Conceptions of Property in Law," *University of Pennsylvania Law Review*, LXXXVI (May 1938), p. 723; Corwin, "The Basic Doctrine of American Constitutional Law," *Michigan Law Review*, XII (1914), pp. 247-276.

## *Property Law*          233

Even when historians examine the police power of government, it is often on the assumption (which I have argued elsewhere is flatly wrong) that only with the Supreme Court's decision of the Granger Cases in 1877 did the common-law doctrine of "property affected with a public interest" establish the "ground rules" necessary to validate far-reaching regulative interventions.[4] Presumably, up to that time the legal system had operated largely to strengthen the bulwarks of vested rights; the "liberty" rather than the "duties" or "public obligations" of property, as Commons asserted, was ascendent in the law; and entrepreneurs had to acquire the property they needed for their undertakings through market transactions, while "vested rights" doctrines served to protect established interests in property.[5]

The second reason why expropriation gains little scholarly attention is that it lacked the visibility a policy issue of this sort would gain by its debate and definitive resolution in Congress. Professor Kuznets has written that each decade of nineteenth-century U. S. growth "marked some decision by the [government]—on currency, on tariffs, on internal improvements, on land, on immigration—and each one was reached after explicit discussion in which its importance for the country's economic growth was realized."[6] Unlike the policy decisions on Kuznets' list, the law of eminent domain was the product of policy-making at the state level, and there were striking differences of policy from one state to another. Moreover, many issues that centered on expropriation policy were resolved by the

---

[4] Lance E. Davis and Douglass C. North, *Institutional Change and American Economic Growth* (Cambridge: Cambridge University Press, 1971), p. 75. The conventional interpretation of the Granger Cases and the doctrine of property "affected with a public interest" are considered at length and critically examined in Harry N. Scheiber, "The Road to *Munn*: Eminent Domain and the Concept of Public Purpose in the State Courts," *Perspectives in American History*, V (1971), pp. 329-402. Extensive documentation is there available for some of the themes treated in this essay.

[5] John R. Commons, *Legal Foundations of Capitalism* (1924, reprinted 1959, Madison: University of Wisconsin Press), p. 328. Two Massachusetts studies provide a more accurate perspective on the police power before 1861: Oscar and Mary F. Handlin, *Commonwealth: . . . Massachusetts, 1774-1861* (revised edition, Cambridge: Harvard University Press, 1969), *passim*; and Leonard W. Levy, *The Law of the Commonwealth and Chief Justice Shaw* (Cambridge: Harvard University Press, 1957), pp. 229-281. The numerous valuable studies of Willard Hurst on this and related themes are considered in Scheiber, "At the Borderland of Law and Economic History: The Contributions of Willard Hurst," *American Historical Review*, LXXV (Feb. 1970), pp. 744-756.

[6] Simon Kuznets, *Economic Growth and Structure: Selected Essays* (New York: W. W. Norton, 1965), p. 108.

state courts, not constitutional conventions or even legislatures; and
there was significant variation in the timing, as well as outcome, of
decisions. Not until 1848 did the federal Supreme Court hand down
a decision directly on the eminent domain power of state governments. Both then and subsequently, its role was mainly a validating
one, supportive of state autonomy and tolerant of substantial diversity.[7]

From what one scholar has termed the "massive body of case law,
irreconcilable in its inconsistency, confusing in its detail and defiant
of all attempts at classification,"[8] one can still identify some coherent
policy patterns that indicate the place of expropriation in the larger
fabric of "institutional environment," the "decision rules" of the legal
system, and the spectrum of policy instruments by which government
allocated resources.[9] The following discussion attempts to illuminate
these themes and to offer both a conceptual and a narrative framework for historical study of expropriation in the United States to
1910. No measurements are offered concerning the redistributive
effects of eminent domain policies. But an effort is made to identify
the directions in which expropriation was purposefully used to allocate resources, to influence the structure of entrepreneurial opportunity, and even to provide effective subsidies for favored types of
business enterprise, often at high cost to "vested rights" in property.

I

In the colonial period, the provincial legislatures had authorized
the taking of land for highways and other transport facilities, while
mill-dam laws and (to some extent) fisheries regulations had "qualified" property rights in a manner that validated coercive takings.[10]
Even so, few of the early state constitutions contained explicit defini-

---

[7] See text at notes 29-32, below.

[8] Note, "Public Use Limitations on Eminent Domain," *Yale Law Journal,* LVI
(1949), pp. 605-606.

[9] No single monograph, even in the literature of legal history, provides a de-
pendable discussion of eminent domain law, accurate and in a conceptual framework
useful for analysis in economic history. Uniquely useful is Willard Hurst's case study
of public economic policy, *Law and Economic Growth: The Legal History of the
Lumber Industry in Wisconsin, 1836-1915* (Cambridge: Harvard University Press,
1964), pp. 181ff. *et passim;* see also J. M. Cormack, "Legal Concepts in Cases of
Eminent Domain," *Yale Law Journal,* XLI (1931), pp. 221-261; and Levy, *Law of
the Commonwealth,* pp. 118-135.

[10] Levy, *Law of the Commonwealth,* pp. 255-258; Joseph K. Angell, *A Treatise on
the Law of Watercourses* (5th edition, Boston, 1854), pp. 547-565; anon., "The Law
of Water Privilege," *American Jurist and Law Magazine,* II (1829), pp. 25-38.

tions of the eminent domain power or its limitations. It therefore fell largely to the courts to develop the fundamental doctrines of eminent domain law.

The state judiciaries proved uniformly disposed to derive from natural law, civil law, and common law three basic concepts which by the early 1820's had become firmly engrafted onto the constitutional law of the states. These concepts were: (1) that the eminent domain power was an inherent attribute of sovereignty, so that private property was held subject to takings by the state; (2) that this power could be legitimately exercised by the state only for a "public use" or "public purpose"; and (3) that when property was so taken, the injured private owner must be paid a "just" or "fair" compensation. Taken at face value, these three doctrines comprised a legal fortress behind which property would be secure from arbitrary or uncompensated expropriation. They expressed a theory that the cost of public undertakings would be "socialized" rather than left to fall upon those individual property owners who happened to stand directly in the path of improvements.[11]

The "public use" limitation did not arouse substantial controversy, so far as projects built and operated by government itself were concerned; a public road or state canal project was clearly a public use. But the courts went further than mere validation of coercive property takings in such cases. They also formulated a series of *expediting doctrines* to complement the basic expropriation concepts. These doctrines found their justification in the extraordinary public importance of such projects (for example, the Erie Canal—termed by Chancellor Kent "a great public object, calculated to intimidate by its novelty, its expense, and its magnitude"[12]); and the expediting doctrines were designed to render the power of the state consistent with the magnitude of such undertakings. Hence the antebellum state courts generally ruled that a private property owner who wanted to challenge state officials engaged in eminent-domain takings was restricted exclusively to statutory remedies; he was fore-

---

[11] Development of the limiting concepts in early jurisprudence is treated in J. A. C. Grant, "The 'Higher Law' Background of Eminent Domain," *Wisconsin Law Review*, VI (1931), pp. 67-85. See also Philip Nichols, Jr., "The Meaning of Public Use in the Law of Eminent Domain," *Boston University Law Review*, XX (1940), pp. 615-641. On the philosophical foundations of eminent domain, see Joseph L. Sax, "Takings and the Police Power," *Yale Law Journal*, LXXIV (1964), pp. 36-76; and Sax, "Takings, Private Property and Public Rights," *Yale Law Journal*, LXXXI (1971), pp. 149-186.

[12] Rogers v. Bradshaw, 20 John. R. 735 (N.Y. 1823) at 740.

closed from resorting to the traditional equitable remedies, such as nuisance, trespass, and damage suits.[13]

Another important expediting doctrine limited the right to compensation only to property that was physically taken. Indirect or consequential damages were not deemed compensable. One landmark decision, by the Massachusetts court in 1823, ruled that a house owner had no right to compensation when the city re-graded the street, exposing the house's foundations and destroying accessibility. "Every one who purchases a lot upon the summit or on the decline of a hill," the court declared, "is presumed to foresee the changes which public necessity or convenience may require."[14] One is left to ponder whether John Winthrop, when he announced the building of "a citty upon a hill," should have appended a *caveat emptor!* Pennsylvania's court, in a similar ruling, admitted that such a rule left an individual to "be made involuntarily to contribute much more than his proportion to the public conveniences"—precisely what eminent domain law was designed to avert—but offered plaintiffs the solace that they had "at least the miserable good luck to know that they have companions in misfortune."[15] Finally the federal Supreme Court, in 1857, upheld this devastating interpretation of the compensation requirement on the broad grounds that "private interests must yield to public accommodation. . . ."[16]

A third expediting doctrine related to procedure. So long as a statute provided specific procedures by which damages were appraised, could be appealed, and would be paid, there was no constitutional requirement that a jury trial should be permitted or the like.[17] Finally, most state courts permitted legislatures to mandate that benefits to the remaining property of an owner who lost only part of it under eminent domain takings should be "offset" against the appraisal of damages. This offsetting doctrine held down the state's costs, and it provided the basis for a potentially large involuntary subsidy for the projects being undertaken. Though a precise

13 Hurst, *Law and Economic Growth*, pp. 181-182; Scheiber, "Road to *Munn*," p. 361. Prof. Morton Horwitz has in progress a full-scale study of pre-1860 damage law and liability; I am indebted to him for useful suggestions and comments.

14 Parker, J. (per cur.), Callendar v. Marsh, 1 Pick. 417 (Mass. 1823) at 430.

15 Monongahela Navig. Co. v. Coons, 6 Watts & S. 101 (Penn., 1843) at 115.

16 Smith v. Corp. of Washington, 20 How. 135 (U.S. 1857) at 147-149.

17 The bias of juries in favor of small property owners suffering damages from takings can safely be assumed, I think. Corroborative evidence is in Wex S. Malone, "The Formative Era of Contributory Negligence," *Illinois Law Review*, XLI (1946), pp. 155-160.

quantitative estimate of that subsidy cannot be calculated,[18] the frequent references to the offsetting doctrine's effects in court records and other sources suggest that the subsidy was a considerable one.

## II

To validate a set of cost-reducing expediting doctrines, all in the name of great public works, owned and operated by the government, was one thing. But the most important single development in early nineteenth century eminent domain law probably was the wholesale transfer of these doctrines over to the private sector, in aid of incorporated companies on which legislatures devolved the power of eminent domain. That was something else again.

Devolution of the eminent-domain power upon turnpike, bridge, canal, and railroad companies was done in every state.[19] Indeed, if such companies had lacked the power to take property coercively for rights-of-way, they would have been left at the mercy of any individual landowner disposed to be stubborn or extortionate. Once a state legislature decided to vest its eminent domain power in a private corporation, the courts would generally rule that this carried with it all the expediting doctrines originally conceived to support the sovereign exercise of governmental power by the state itself. Hence in some states railroad companies were enabled to acquire land at virtually no cost, on grounds that the benefits to landowners' remaining property entirely offset the value of property taken. In Ohio, for example, railroads were notoriously successful in obtaining appointment by the courts of friendly appraisers, who would assess benefits as equal to all the damages; and in Illinois, railroad takings frequently resulted in assessment of damages of one dollar. In New York, Vermont, Massachusetts, and other states, subsidization of railroads through offsetting had become common by the 1850's.[20]

[18] Apart from the staggering problem of evaluating the available data as to damages awarded *versus* market value of property taken, there is the troublesome question of transaction costs: even if property owners arrived at negotiated settlement of damages, when did they do so because the offer made them was fair and when because the costs of litigation (the only alternative) and time considerations were so dear?

[19] For a brief period of time after 1840, New Hampshire suspended devolution policy. See Edward Chase Kirkland, *Men, Cities and Transportation: A Study in New England History, 1820-1900* (2 vols., Cambridge: Harvard University Press, 1948), I, 163-164.

[20] Scheiber, *Ohio Canal Era: A Case Study of Government and the Economy, 1820-1861* (Athens: Ohio University Press, 1969), pp. 277-278. Frequent damage

238                            *Scheiber*

Similarly, the courts afforded to both private transport-project promoters and mill-dam builders the same immunity to actions for nuisance, trespass, and torts as had been granted earlier to state officials. The property owner who dared seek a common-law injunction against such private promoters was put down with a heavy hand by the courts. And so long as some (almost any) procedure was specified in statutes for compensation of owners who lost land to companies exercising the eminent domain power through devolution, equitable remedies were foreclosed.[21]

The courts also authorized a corporation, once vested with the eminent domain power, to exercise that power repeatedly to expedite alterations or enlargements of the project within the broad terms of its state charter; and so abutting landowners stood in constant jeopardy. Justifying this interpretation of eminent-domain devolution, the Illinois court stated flatly that a railroad company must be able to lay its hands on whatever it might need "for its own convenience or the public accommodation." Similarly, in Massachusetts the high court validated property-takings beyond what was originally expropriated by a railroad on grounds that "these works are comparatively new, and improvements are constantly making in the structure and management of the works, and thus companies may profit by their own experience and that of others." Besides, the corporation's own officials could best judge the extent of its needs, "and their decision therefore must be definitive"![22]

Judges spun a fine web of doctrine to justify such devolutions of power on private companies. One thread was theoretical: it was for the legislature, in its exercise of the majestic powers of sovereignty, to decide where to place the expropriation power and how to wield it, "not only where the safety, but also where the interest or even

awards of one dollar, after offsetting had been figured, occurred in Illinois, as considered in a seminar paper (MS., 1972) by Mark Van Ausdal, University of Chicago Law School. Much later, awards of six cents, after offsetting, became a *cause celebre* in New York. See New York, Constitutional Convention of 1894, *Revised Record* (Albany, 1900), pp. 633-635, 651-653. "Oppression" of landowners through damage judgements is discussed in *American Jurist*, II (1829), p. 33; and, later in the railroad era, offsetting of benefits was singled out as the source of great "loss and wrong" in a polemical pamphlet, *Eminent Domain and Rail Road Corporations: Some Thoughts on the Subject—By a Farmer* (n.p., Philadelphia, 1873), p. 9 (copy in Eleutherian Mills Historical Library). Cf. J. B. Thayer, "The Right of Eminent Domain," *Monthly Law Reporter*, new series, IX (1856), pp. 307-312.

[21] Newcomb v. Smith, 2 Pinn. 131 (Wisc. 1849) at 138; Angell, *Watercourses*, chap. xii.

[22] Railroad Co. v. Wilson, 17 Illinois 123 at 127 (1856); Brainerd v. Clapp, 10 Cush. 6 (Mass. 1852) at 10-11; cf. Childs v. N.J. Centr. Railroad Co., 33 N.J.L. 323.

## *Property Law*        **239**

the expediency of the state is concerned." Jurists who were reluctant to adopt so sweeping a formal validating doctrine might instead insist that the legislature had a free hand in devolving the eminent domain power "for some necessary and useful purposes."[23] Another doctrinal thread was unwound from the common law: in many states, courts cited the common-law concept of riparian property that was not strictly private but rather *publici juris*—under special obligations, or a "servitude," to the public. Expropriation was justified for privately financed canals and railroads, in these courts, because like navigable rivers or highways they would have to be kept open to the public, or (like turnpikes) their proprietors were "compellable to permit the public to use them, on paying toll."[24]

Courts also drew upon long-standing legislative precedents afforded by the mill-dam acts. In many states, because of the importance of gristmills to a farming community the legislatures had extended special privileges to millers. Among these privileges was the power to overflow neighboring lands in order to create a mill-pond or reservoir for waterpower. To compensate owners of the land overflowed, the mill-dam statutes had provided for either annual assessment by commissioners of the income loss incurred, or else a once-for-all damage judgement.[25]

Beginning in the mid-1830's and continuing through the next three decades, numerous states greatly extended the mill-dam principle by devolving the expropriation power upon manufacturing firms in quest of waterpower sites for purposes other than grinding grain. The New Jersey court was the first to adjudicate a case challenging this dramatic enlargement of eminent domain doctrines. When that state's legislature authorized a private corporation to expropriate land for the development of some seventy mill sites along a six-mile stretch of the Delaware River, lawyers resisting the project termed it a blatant attempt to "take private property for private use"—a legal innovation that would render worthless the "public use" limitation on the eminent domain power. But the court upheld

[23] Beekman v. Railroad Co., 3 Paige 45 (N.Y. Ch., 1831) at 73; Boston etc. Mill Dam Co. v. Newman, 12 Pick. 467 (Mass., 1832) at 480.

[24] On similar grounds, many states had permitted expropriation for building wharves and basins, establishing ferries, draining marshes and swamps, and conveying water to towns. See Scheiber, "Road to *Munn*," pp. 367-368; and Thayer, "Right of Eminent Domain," *passim*.

[25] Boston etc. v. Newman, 12 Pick. 467 (Mass., 1832); Murdock v. Stickney, 8 Cush. 113 (Mass. 1851); Glover v. Powell, 2 Stock. 211 (N.J. Ch., 1854).

the statute. Even though the corporation's primary purpose was private profit, the court said, "The ever varying condition of society is constantly presenting new objects of public importance and utility; and what shall be considered a public use or benefit, must depend somewhat on the situation and wants of the community for the time being."[26]

Massachusetts followed suit soon afterward, its high court ruling that a tide-dam corporation given the expropriation power, "although commenced with a view to the private advantage of the stockholders, promised to be of immense and certain utility to the state."[27] Although New York, Georgia and Alabama courts refused to permit expansion of the "public use" concept to validate expropriation for general manufacturing purposes, the enthusiasm spread widely to other states. By 1870 such laws had been upheld in Maine, Connecticut, New Hampshire, Wisconsin, Indiana, and Tennessee. The most pragmatic sort of validating doctrine was adopted in all these states: that if waterpower development "would largely conduce to the prosperity of the state," as one critic phrased it, then expropriation of land at dam sites was constitutional.[28]

In effect these states gave to certain manufacturing firms the status of public utilities. But this was done only to justify arming them with power to expropriate some of America's choicest waterpower sites, such as those on the Connecticut River, the Delaware, and the Merrimac. Needless to say, legislatures that were so anxious to attract manufacturing investment did not seek to *regulate* such enterprises as public-utilities doctrine might have justified. The manufacturers had the best of both worlds.

## III

Before turning to the period after 1870, brief observations are warranted as to three subsidiary questions that entered into the history prior to that time.

In the first place, there was substantial opposition by some lawyers, jurists and political leaders who regarded the successive expansions of eminent domain doctrines as dangerous. For many con-

[26] Scudder v. Trenton Del. Falls Co., 1 N.J. Eq. 694 (1832). "The landholders adjacent to the Company's works held the key to its prosperity, and a perfect control over it." Trenton Delaware Falls Co., *Second Annual Report* (n.p., 1833), p. 12.
[27] Boston etc. v. Newman, 12 Pick. 467 (Mass., 1832) at 481.
[28] Cooley, C.J. (per cur.), Ryerson v. Brown, 35 Mich. 334 (1877) at 337.

# *Property Law*      241

servative figures, such as Daniel Webster and Joseph Story, the focus of their concern was a position taken by several state courts in the 1840's, holding that even corporation franchises could be taken under eminent domain. Such a doctrine, Webster contended, would destroy the climate of investment which had favored economic progress, and in the hands of "ultra" legislative radicals could lead to an "unlimited despotism."[29] But when the issue finally came before the Supreme Court in 1848, the Court found that a state could authorize the taking of a chartered company's bridge and its conversion to a public way, upon payment of compensation to the company. The eminent domain power, the Court declared, was "paramount to all private rights vested under the government."[30]

Others who opposed the eminent domain power's extension were men on the other side of the political spectrum. Suspicious of monopoly and privileged corporations, they denounced "offsetting" and other expediting techniques as instruments to exploit the little man, the simple farmer or householder who was subjected to loss of property to a favored business enterprise without truly just compensation.[31] But this group obtained no more support from the Supreme Court than did the property-minded conservatives. For in 1850 the Court ruled that even if the facts showed that a governmental taking blatantly violated both the "public use" and "fair compensation" requirements of a state constitution, "it rests with the State legislatures and State courts to protect their citizens from injustice and oppression of this description."[32] Beginning in the 1850's, however, opponents of the extended eminent domain power had begun to push through some reforms in state constitutional conventions. In language widely copied later by other state conventions, Ohio's constitution writers in 1851 wrote a provision that if a corporation took property under eminent domain, it must provide prior payment to the injured property owner, with compensation to be determined "irrespective of any benefit from any improvement proposed by such corporation, . . . by a jury of twelve men." Iowa followed suit in 1857, and the 1859 Kansas constitution included a provision nearly identi-

---

[29] West River Bridge v. Dix, 6 How. 507 (U.S. 1848), on which see Scheiber, "Road to *Munn*," pp. 376-380.

[30] *Ibid.*; the taking of a franchise was considered again in Richmond etc. Railroad v. Louisa Railroad, 13 How. 71 (U.S. 1852).

[31] See sources cited in note 20, above.

[32] Mills v. St. Clair County, 8 How. 569 (1850) at 584.

242                         *Scheiber*

cal. Over the next thirty years, other states adopted the Ohio model for constitutional reform on these lines.[33]

A second important feature of pre-1870 eminent domain law was the wide application, in state courts, of the "fair compensation" requirement as a *negative check* on the police power. Courts invoked the compensation doctrine, in other words, to require government to indemnify property-owners for some types of damage that resulted from regulatory statutes. Cases of this sort proved especially important as they influenced governmental efforts to allocate resources on internal waterways: they raised a host of questions about the legitimate reach of regulatory laws to protect public fishing rights, about mill-dam and log-boom franchises on rivers, and about the protection of navigational rights on streams deemed "under servitude to the public."[34]

Finally, it is noteworthy that by the 1850's the doctrine of "public use" developed in eminent-domain litigation was having major spillover effects in taxation law and in the law of nuisances. The extensive state aid and local assistance given private railroad corporations, beginning in the 1850's, was justified by the courts on the same grounds as had legitimated devolution of the eminent domain power.[35] As to the law of nuisances, the doctrine that certain types of business enterprise were so vital as to justify eminent-domain devolution could also be turned to their advantage by immunizing such enterprises from nuisance-damage liability. Thus the courts afforded to railroads a sweeping immunity from common-law suits against smoke or noise pollution. And in Pennsylvania and other states where the importance of mining as a "leading industrial interest" had been invoked by the courts to validate takings of property to build strictly private roads into mines, the same courts held that

[33] Ohio State Constitutional Convention of 1850, *Reports and Debates* (2 vols., Columbus, 1851), 883-893; Cormack, "Legal Concepts," pp. 244-246 (on the Illinois convention of 1870, debate on consequential damages); Charles T. McCormick, "The Measure of Compensation in Eminent Domain," *Minnesota Law Review,* XVII (1933), pp. 492-493 (on Iowa, etc.); New York Constitutional Convention of 1867-68, *Proceedings* (Albany, 1868), pp. 3247-3256.

[34] See, for example, Perry v. Wilson, 7 Mass. 393 (1811) on log-boom franchises; Anon., "Rights of the Public in Fresh Water Rivers," *American Law Magazine,* V (1845), pp. 267-281, on Connecticut and Pennsylvania doctrines; Commonwealth v. Chapin, 5 Pick. 199 (Mass. 1827), on rights in fisheries; and Holyoke Co. v. Lyman, 15 Wall. 500 (82 U.S. 133) (1873), retrospectively, on the same; State v. Tyre Glen, 7 Jones 321 (N.C. 1859); and Scheiber, "Road to *Munn,*" pp. 373-376.

[35] See Charles Fairman, *Reconstruction and Reunion, 1864-88* (Oliver Wendell Holmes Devise History of the Supreme Court, Vol. VI, Part i) (New York: Macmillan, 1971), pp. 918-1116, an exhaustive analysis of railroad bond-aid litigation.

## Property Law        243

mining companies were not liable for damages resulting to down-stream proprietors from their pollution of streams. "The necessities of a great public industry, which although in the hands of a private corporation, subserves a great public interest," the Pennsylvania court declared, justified such "trifling inconveniences to particular persons" as the contamination of a house owner's domestic water supply! Thus, in nuisance law, as in the jurisprudence of expropriation, "the rough outline of natural right or natural liberty," as an Alabama judge averred, "must submit to the chisel of the mason, that it enter symmetrically into the social structure"![36]

### IV

The heyday of expropriation as an instrument of public policy designed to subsidize private enterprise can probably be dated as beginning in the 1870's and lasting until about 1910. During that era of alleged *laisser-faire* (which in fact was a period of broad-ranging public subsidies for business), all the constitutional stops were pulled out.

No longer did judges or framers of state constitutions rely so much upon sophistries about "public use." Instead, they now merely paused to assert prescriptively that one private interest or another—mining, irrigation, lumbering or manufacturing—was so vitally necessary to the common weal as to be a public use by inference. In some of the western states, they went beyond that; without verbal evasion, they simply declared certain types of private enterprises to be "public" in their constitutions. All this was done, moreover, despite the availability of the federal Fourteenth Amendment—an instrument which the courts readily used when they sought to invalidate state laws to regulate private enterprise.[37]

By the time this period of eminent domain law had begun, the legal doctrines forged in the east had already provided a sufficient foundation for newer states to break through the cake of legal custom. Indeed, two of the most frequently cited precedents in this

[36] Penn. Coal Co. v. Sanderson, 113 Pa. 126 (1886) at 149; quotation from Hughes v. Anderson, 68 Ala. 280, in *ibid.*, at 139. On railroad immunity from nuisance, compare Penn. Railroad Co. v. Marchant, 119 Pa. 541 (1888), and see generally Lewis Orgel, *Valuation under the Law of Eminent Domain* (2nd edition, 2 vols., Charlottesville: Michie Co., 1953), I, pp. 37-38.

[37] On such Fourteenth-Amendment applications, see John P. Roche, "Entre-preneurial Liberty and the Fourteenth Amendment," *Labor History,* IV (1963), pp. 3-31.

# 244                          *Scheiber*

period came from New England. One was the case of *Talbot v. Hudson,* a Massachusetts decision of 1860 which declared:

It has never been deemed essential that the entire community or any considerable portion of it should directly enjoy or participate in an improvement or enterprise, in order to constitute a public use. . . . [E]verything which tends to enlarge the resources, increase the energies, and promote the productive power of any considerable number of the inhabitants of a section of the State, or which leads to the growth of towns and the creation of new sources of private capital and labor, indirectly contributes to the general welfare and to the prosperity of the whole community.[38]

A New Hampshire case of 1867, *Great Falls Manufacturing Company v. Fernald,* stressed the need to adapt law to the realities of topography and climate. Validating as constitutional an act that authorized a general manufacturing firm to overflow neighboring lands to create a reservoir for waterpower, the court stated: "Nature has denied us the fertile soil and genial climate of other lands, but by way of compensation has endowed us with unrivaled opportunities of turning our streams of water to practical account." It was legitimate, the court declared, to make the law bend to the dictates of nature and comport with "the character of our business and the natural productions and resources" of the state.[39]

Little wonder that these doctrines should have proved attractive to jurists in the far western states in ensuing years. For there, the hardships of life in arid lands and mountain fastnesses, the nature of the resource base, vast distances, and, above all, men's impatience to force the pace of economic development, all seemed to overwhelm the remaining bulwarks of legal-constitutional structure.

Colorado blazed the path of eminent domain law for the west. That state's constitutional convention of 1875-76 adopted a provision that private property might be taken for *private use* "for private ways of necessity, . . . reservoirs, drains, flumes, or ditches on or across the lands of others, for mining, milling, domestic, or sanitary purposes."[40] Other Rocky Mountain states followed this model

[38] Talbot v. Hudson, 82 Mass. 417 (1860) at 425. Interestingly, the case involved a challenge to the state's condemnation of a dam originally built under the expropriation power by a private canal company.

[39] 47 N.H. 444 (1867) at 461.

[40] Colorado, 1876 Const., Art. II, sec. xiv; cf. D. W. Hensel, "History of the Colorado Constitution in the Nineteenth Century" (Ph.D. diss., University of Colorado, 1957), pp. 167-174, esp. p. 169 on Colorado delegates' reference to drainage-works provisions for eminent domain devolution in Missouri and Illinois constitutions.

## Property Law                               245

closely.[41] In the Idaho constitutional convention of 1889, the debate over expropriation produced a sharp clash of farming interests against miners. Neither interest group stood for an abstraction that can be termed "vested rights"; rather, each wanted the upper hand in the rivalry to exploit common resources. The bitter debate over what one delegate termed "a doctrine that is anti-republican in every respect, . . . contrary to the right to hold property . . . or to pursue happiness" ended in a compromise.[42] Idaho's constitution thus declared as a "public use" all uses of land for irrigation and drainage purposes, for the draining and working of mines including "the working thereof, by means of roads, railroads, tramways, cuts, tunnels, shafts, hoisting works, dumps or other necessary means to their complete development, or any other use necessary to the complete development of the material resources of the state." For these purposes might private property be expropriated upon payment of compensation.[43]

To the state courts that subsequently reviewed statutes enacted under these western constitutions, doctrinal support for such elevation of "private uses" to an exalted constitutional status derived as well from a landmark Nevada territorial decision of 1876. Upholding an act of 1875 authorizing expropriation of land, lumber and other construction materials by mining companies, the court distinguished between two types of business enterprises. On the one hand, there were ordinary businesses that could be conducted without regard to a specific site location, and this type was ineligible for eminent-domain devolution. On the other hand, there were businesses like mining which were tied to a particular resource site; for this type of enterprise, a clear necessity for eminent-domain devolution existed.[44] This Nevada decision was widely cited in other western states. But interestingly enough, it was almost always for its blanket declaration that "an interest of great public benefit to the community" warranted expropriation for private use. Emblematic of the spirit which prevailed in the western courts was the fact that

[41] John D. Hicks, *The Constitutions of the Northwest States* (Lincoln, Neb.: University Studies, XXIII, 1923), p. 146 *et passim*. Gordon M. Bakken, "The Impact of the Colorado State Constitution on Rocky Mountain Constitution Making," *Colorado Magazine of History*, XLVII (1970), pp. 152-175 treats eminent domain debates.

[42] *Proceedings and Debates of the Constitutional Convention of Idaho, 1889* (Caldwell: Caxton, 1912), p. 304.

[43] Idaho Const. of 1889, Art. I, sec. xiv.

[44] Dayton Gold & Silv. Min. Co. v. Seawell, 11 Nev. 394 (1876) at 400-401, 411.

246                          *Scheiber*

the "site necessity" argument—a more impressive one by far—was left in the background.[45]

Given western terrain and the distribution of mineral resources, it was inescapable that the exigencies of site, or location, should often be controlling. This was highlighted in a Montana case of 1895, in which a railroad company sought to block the expropriation of part of its right-of-way (not actually in use for track) and repeated crossing of its tracks by a second railroad, then under construction, building into the Butte Hill mining area. The court ruled that if the Anaconda, the Wake Up Jim, the Buffalo, the Moscow and other mines in this region were to be benefitted by the second railroad, then the "publicity" (that is, "public use") of the enterprise was "too obvious to require more extended comment." For in that locality, mining was "the all-important pursuit" and so "benefits to the public" deriving from benefits to the mining companies could hardly be doubted.[46] In the scramble for development in this country where men dug ore out of mountains, the niceties of eminent domain limitations—which even in the more genteel eastern states had been treated with some sophistry—thus gave way without "extended comment."

In Idaho, the legislature enacted a law in 1887 for devolution of the eminent domain power which, after revision in 1903, embraced the following: "wharves, docks, piers, chutes, booms, ferries; bridges, toll-roads, by-roads, plank and turnpike roads; steam, electric, and horse railroads; reservoirs, canals, ditches, flumes, aqueducts, and pipes; [projects] for public transportation, supplying mines and farming neighborhoods with water, and draining and reclaiming lands," and for storing logs.[47] Reviewing this statute in 1906, the Idaho court found little in the state's constitution that could fault such a law, for unless the eminent domain power was so broad as this, "a complete development of the material resources of our young state could not be made."[48] On similar grounds, the courts of Nevada, Montana, Colorado, Idaho, Washington, New Mexico, and Arizona upheld laws permitting expropriation of property when necessary for purposes of running an irrigation canal or ditch across

---

[45] See, e.g., Highland Boy Gold Mining Co. v. Strickley, 78 Pac. 298 (Utah, 1904).

[46] Butte, A. & P. Railroad Co. v. M. U. Railroad Co., 16 Mont. 504 (1895).

[47] Stat. quoted in Potlatch Lumber Co. v. Peterson, 88 Pac 430 (Idaho 1906).

[48] *Ibid.* at 431.

## Property Law 247

private land. For as the Arizona territorial court insisted, a legislature must be permitted to use (or devolve) the power of eminent domain so that local "advantages and resources may receive the fullest development for the general welfare."[49] Elsewhere the public utilities doctrine was invoked to validate takings for private irrigated farming: so long as water companies could be regulated, they could be vested with eminent domain power.[50]

A vital part of the constitutional context was, of course, the response of the Supreme Court when the western states' doctrines were challenged. In a word, the Supreme Court largely upheld local practices. As early as 1871 the Court had begun to tighten the requirements for "just compensation" by ruling that certain kinds of consequential, or indirect, damages constituted a "taking" of property.[51] And in 1897 the Court expressly ruled that the Fourteenth Amendment in effect applied the federal Fifth Amendment's "just compensation" requirement to all state-sanctioned eminent domain proceedings.[52] But when the legitimacy of the broad expropriation power for explicitly "private use" in the western states came before the Court, there was no comparable will to intervene. California's laws permitting water companies to condemn private land for irrigation purposes were tested before the Court in 1896 and were upheld. Eight years later, in the case of *Clark v. Nash*, the Court validated a Utah statute authorizing an individual to condemn a neighbor's land in order to convey water to his own. If the taking "be essential or material for the prosperity of the community," the Court declared, it was valid.[53] Such statutes must be adjudged by a standard of con-

---

[49] Oury v. Goodwin, 26 Pac. 376 (Ariz. 1891) at 382 *et passim*. This topic is a main theme of analysis in Samuel C. Wiel, *Water Rights in the Western States* (3rd edition, 2 vols., San Francisco: Bancroft-Whitney Co., 1911), esp. chap. 8.

[50] *Ibid.*, I, pp. 148-157 *et passim*. Unlike western states which followed the Colorado-Idaho liberal line on private use, California and Oregon courts placed strict limitations upon expansion of the public-use doctrine to support strictly private interests. Cf. Gilmer v. Lime Point, 18 Cal. 229 (1861), and, *inter alia*, Wiel, *Water Rights*. In 1894 the New York constitution was revised to include a provision declaring agricultural drainage to be a "public use," so as to permit construction of drainage lines across private property on payment of "just compensation." But the high court of New York State promptly declared the new provision to be in violation of the U.S. Constitution. (New York, 1894 Constitutional Convention, *Revised Record*, p. 1061; Matter of Tuthill, 163 N.Y. 133, [1900, 79 Am. St. Rep. 574].)

[51] Pumpelly v. Green Bay, 13 Wall. 166 (1872).

[52] C.B. & Q. Railroad Co. v. Chicago, 166 U.S. 226 (1897).

[53] Clark v. Nash, 198 U.S. 361 (1904); Fallbrook Irrigation District v. Bradley, 164 U.S. 112 (1896).

stitutionality, said that Court, that takes account of "peculiar condition[s] of the soil or climate":

The validity . . . may sometimes depend upon many different facts, the existence of which would make a public use, even by an individual, where, in the absence of such facts, the use would clearly be private. . . . [The State's own courts] understand the situation which led to the demand for the enactment of the statute, and they also appreciate the results upon the growth and prosperity of the State. . . . The Court must recognize the difference of climate and soil, which render necessary these different laws in the States so situated.[54]

No doubt the Supreme Court may well have been moved to leave such broad discretion with the arid-land states out of sympathy, too, for efforts to prevent "water monopoly" from blocking new settlement or leaving latecomers at the mercy of men who had already established title to lands along the region's streams.[55] But its solicitude reached beyond the concerns of small farmers to embrace mining corporations, lumber companies, and railroad interests as well; and in 1907 the Court upheld an eastern railroad's taking of property to construct a spur track which would serve the factory warehouse of a large shipper and relieve congestion at the company's existing terminal and yards. The Court recalled that it had consistently upheld state courts' positions on what constituted a "public use" in expropriation cases, and it reaffirmed that it would give sympathetic consideration not only to evidence as to "the resources" and "the capacity of the soil" but also as to "the relative importance of industries to the general public welfare, and the long-established methods and habits of the people."[56]

V

By about 1910, the configuration of expropriation law had begun to change markedly in the United States. As mentioned earlier, many states adopted changes in their constitutions, such as requir-

[54] Clark v. Nash, 198 U.S. 367ff.
[55] On which problem cf. Hensel, "Colorado Constitution," pp. 298-300.
[56] Hairston v. Danville & W. Railroad Co., 208 U.S. 598 (1907) at 605. The Court also upheld statutes which specifically required offsetting of estimated benefits in appraising damages under eminent-domain takings; cf. Bauman v. Ross, 167 U.S. 548 (1897). On the other side of the same coin, however, the Court reaffirmed and somewhat widened its requirement that consequential damages, when they utterly destroyed "the use and value" of property, must be compensated; cf. United States v. Lynah, 188 U.S. 445 (1903).

## Property Law                                                   249

ing jury trials in cases of takings by private corporations, narrowing the range of permissible "offsetting" procedures, and requiring prior payment in cases of expropriation. In addition, numerous state constitutions were amended to require compensation not only when property was "taken" but also when "damaged."[57] By this time, moreover, eminent domain powers were being employed as an instrument of city planning and improvement; and the practice of "excess condemnation" was becoming a central issue, much debated, in legislatures and in courtroom litigation.[58] Later in the twentieth century, especially with the beginnings of massive regional development in the Tennessee Valley and with dramatic expansion of the federal urban-renewal and highway programs, the main focus of eminent domain law has shifted to government projects and their social consequences. As the checkered history of the urban and highway programs amply attests, however, the interpenetration of private business interests and governmental programs justifying expropriation continues to be a central problem of public policy. Nor has the expropriation power proved to be a policy instrument less fearsome in the hands of governmental authorities than it had been in the heyday of "private use." Witness the uses of eminent domain in recent decades to obliterate black urban neighborhoods or to cut broad highways through treasured landscapes at such high cost to our ecological heritage.[59] Hence perhaps the most important continuity in public debate over expropriation, coming down to our own day, is the widely shared sense that the appalling technical complexities of eminent domain law, troublesome enough in themselves, are but the surface manifestation of serious social inequities associated with it. To be sure, there has lately been a radical cutback in sovereign tort immunities, so that many issues which in 1910 would have reached the courts as eminent domain cases do so instead to-

[57] Orgel, *Valuation*, I, pp. 35-38. Many of the same western states as adopted the broadest definitions of public use also were early in the movement to reform compensation law; hence it is all the more difficult to put a dollar value on the subsidy effects of expanded eminent-domain law in the West. What is indisputable is the *strategic* importance of the expanded doctrine of public use—enterprises were given powerful instruments to set themselves going, and without those instruments would probably have foundered altogether.

[58] Robert E. Cushman, *Excess Condemnation* (New York: Appleton, 1917) covers the subject thoroughly for that period. See also Flavel Shurtleff, *Carrying out the City Plan* (New York: Survey Association, 1914).

[59] The best single source of analysis and documentation is Charles M. Haar, *Land-Use Planning: A Casebook on the Use, Misuse, and Re-use of Urban Land* (2nd edition, Boston: Little Brown, 1971).

250                          *Scheiber*

day as tort suits against the government.[60] But genuinely searching reappraisal and reform of expropriation law are probably only commencing.

To understand expropriation policy in the present era requires an appreciation of how that policy functioned in that earlier period of American economic history, which has been our concern here. If nothing else, closer study of our own history may offer a perspective from which to appraise such policy documents as one of last winter, issued by the White House and disarmingly entitled "Economic Assistance and Investment Security in Developing Nations." This fascinating contribution to the Pax Americana warns the developing nations that "the wisdom of any expropriation is questionable, even when adequate compensation is paid." It goes on to specify sanctions that the U.S. government will impose against nations that violate three American requirements in cases of expropriation: "That any taking of American property will be non-discriminatory; that it will be for a public purpose; and that [our] citizens will receive prompt, adequate compensation."[61] It would be a salutary thing, perhaps, to ponder that a doctrine of public use "depend[ing] somewhat on the situation and wants of the community for the time being" was expounded by a respected American court more than a century before Fidel Castro offered his own variant of it—or to consider what place "prompt, adequate compensation" has had in our own country's historic law of property taking.[62]

Another purpose to be served by reappraisal of expropriation as an American policy instrument is one more narrowly the profession's, concerned as we are with understanding the legal rules by which American capitalism flourished in the nineteenth century. It is to look anew at the standard notions of stability of property rights, and to reconsider the simplistic definitions of "vested rights" and interpretations of how those rights were treated in the law. In short, we ought to test through empirical study Professor Hurst's

[60] Allison Dunham, "Griggs v. Allegheny County in Perspective," *Supreme Court Review, 1962* (Chicago: University of Chicago Press, 1963), p. 82.

[61] Mimeographed, The White House, January 19, 1972.

[62] See text at n. 26, above. The White House policy document discussed above is squarely within the tradition of imposing what are supposed to be American values and institutions "on less fortunate countries," but particularly when American investment interests are served, a topic discussed in Robert B. Zevin, "An Interpretation of American Imperialism," THE JOURNAL OF ECONOMIC HISTORY, XXXII (March 1972), pp. 359-360.

## Property Law                                                251

contention (so ably documented in his own pioneering scholarship) that how the nineteenth-century American legal system functioned "in the name of vested rights had less to do with protecting *holdings* than it had to do with protecting *ventures*."[63]

HARRY N. SCHEIBER, *University of California, San Diego*

[63] Hurst, *Law and the Conditions of Freedom,* p. 24 (italics added).

# 9

# THE FORMATIVE ERA OF CONTRIBUTORY NEGLIGENCE

*WEX S. MALONE*

Reprinted from the ILLINOIS LAW REVIEW of Northwestern University
Vol. 41, No. 2, July-August, 1946

# The Formative Era of Contributory Negligence

## Wex S. Malone*

THE concise opinions of Bayley and Lord Ellenborough in *Butterfield v. Forrester* (1809)[1] afford no indication that either of those judges felt at the time that he was charting new paths for the law. Bayley's opinion, which could be wired at night letter rate without extra charge, might easily have been explained on several different grounds,[2] while Ellenborough's remark that one person being at fault will not dispense with another's using ordinary care, was entirely too casual to have compelled respect if his successors on the bench had not been friendly inclined toward the idea. But friendly they were, and from Ellenborough's observation has stemmed the now established rule that a delinquent plaintiff cannot recover irrespective of the fault of the defendant.

In America the idea of contributory negligence lay virtually dormant until about the middle of the last century; then suddenly it sprang to life and found its way into virtually every piece of litigation over a negligent injury to person or property. Even in Louisiana, whose Civil Code fairly interpreted would deny the notion, the court seized eagerly upon the contributory negligence of the plaintiff as a bar to his action.[3] In most cases everywhere it became much more than simply a new legal issue; it tended to overshadow all other contentions and become the central theme of dispute. As a result, the response to the issue of the plaintiff's fault usually determined the outcome of the case.

How to explain this sudden rise to prominence of contributory negligence? The story, it is believed, is one of the impact

---

* Associate Professor of Law, Louisiana State University.
[1] 11 East 59, 103 Eng. Rep. 926.
[2] For an explanation of these see Pollock, The Law of Torts (13th ed. 1929) 482 and 1 Street, The Foundation of Legal Liability (1906) c. 9.
[3] I have attempted to describe and account for this anomalous situation in Malone, Comparative Negligence—Louisiana's Forgotten Heritage (1945) 6 La. L. Rev. 125.

of a newer civilization upon our traditional judge-jury set up. It is a story of the newly emerging mass transportation system — an enterprise whose activities brought about a vast increase in the quantity of torts litigation, and radically transformed the entire complexion of torts controversies. The basis for the deciding of cases suddenly shifted from personal and moral considerations to the formulation of broad economic policies and the determination of group interests. It is an account of the breakdown of the jury as an effective arm of administration because the jurymen were unable to adjust their ways of thinking to legalistic conceptions of fair play, and of the consequent efforts of judges to take matters into their own hands.

The stage on which the story unfolds is, of course, nationwide, but little can be gained from a random sampling of cases from diverse jurisdictions. Each state has developed something of its own pattern, although the general outline is about the same everywhere. A more comprehensible picture can be gained from a compact study of a single jurisdiction where a graspable segment of material can be dealt with, where conflicts of positions and views can be focused, and where entanglements with previous decisions can be observed. The decisions of the appellate courts of New York seem to afford a fairly representative cross section of judicial experience for our purposes. New York was one of the first jurisdictions to deal extensively with railroad injuries. Shortly after 1840 steel rails were reaching westward from the Hudson more than halfway across the state, and by 1850 Albany and Buffalo were connected, and another line, the Erie, was approaching Dunkirk on Lake Erie. Thus New York became a fountainhead of American railroad law. Its courts were forced to pioneer from the start, and the early New York decisions contain a surprisingly small amount of borrowed doctrine. Second, the fact that New York City was isolated by water made it an unsuitable place for early railroad experimentation. Thus the initial railway experience of this state was gained in the rural areas in the vicinity of Albany, and the first expansions extended from there into the wilderness. For this reason the early decisions are almost entirely of rural origin. The accidents occurred and the cases were tried in an atmosphere fairly typical of pioneer America at that time. Later, urban accidents afforded a variety in material, but did not perceptibly affect the basic starting points of the law on the subject. The following pages sketch the period from the first cases in the 1850's through the last half of the century. It was during these years that the doctrine of contributory negligence received its formative development.

## The Doctrine Emerges to Dominate the Scene

TWENTY years elapsed after *Butterfield v. Forrester* before a court of record in New York directed its attention to the contributory negligence doctrine. In the case of *Burckle and Burckle v. New York Dry Dock Company* (1829) [4] the Superior Court of New York City was faced with a simple fact situation which was strikingly like that of the *Butterfield* case. The lessee of a drydock sought to recover against his lessor for damages to his vessel which burned in a fire that was occasioned in part by an accumulation of combustible rubble on the ground below. The plaintiff's own agents had set the flame by careless operation in repairing the boat. A refusal of recovery was to be expected and could have been justified on a number of grounds. The choice of contributory negligence as an explanation was probably entirely fortuitous. It is doubtful that the decision was regarded as being of much importance and only scant reference to it has been made in later opinions.

The two decades after 1829 produced only four cases of record that may fairly be said to involve contributory negligence.[5] Of these, three arose out of accidents in the operation of vehicles.[6] This paucity of reference to the doctrine at that time may seem strange in view of the fact that the period between 1800 and 1840 witnessed a prodigious growth in stagecoach traffic. Early in the century nearly all the principal cities as far west as Pittsburgh were connected by several lines of stage carriers. An eager public, dispersed in isolation throughout America, was clamoring for speedier and more efficient transportation, and, within the means then available, was getting it.[7] But there were many limitations, which, although they hopelessly retarded the schedules of traffic, nevertheless made for a comparatively high degree of safety. Foremost was the condition of the roads. Mud prevailed everywhere and the

---

[4] 2 Hall 151, 2 N.Y. Super. 170 (1829). The court cited Butterfield v. Forrester and the earlier New York decision of Bush v. Brainard, 1 Cow. 78 (N.Y. 1823), which dealt only with the right of an owner of a trespassing cow to recover for injuries suffered by the animal from drinking a quantity of maple syrup.

[5] Rathbun & West v. Payne, 19 Wend. 399 (N.Y. 1839); Hartfield v. Roper & Newell, 21 Wend. 615 (N.Y. 1839); Brownell v. Flagler, 5 Hill 282 (N.Y. 1843); Burdick v. Worrall, 4 Barb. 596 (N.Y. 1848).

[6] Rathbun & West v. Payne, Hartfield v. Roper & Newell, and Burdick v. Worrall, cited *supra* note 5.

[7] 3 Dunbar, A History of Travel in America (1915) c. 34.

stages often were able to move only through the combined
effort of horses, driver, and passengers.  One literary-minded
traveler observed concerning the inland roads: "If the mud
does not quite get over your boottops when you hit the saddle
they call it a middling good road."[8]  Under these conditions,
when travel from Albany to Rochester consumed six days and
seven nights, it is clear that the bystander was comparatively
safe, while passengers, although jolted and uncomfortable, usually arrived at their destination without major mishap. Minor
accidents, of course, were constantly taking place in the operation of the stages, and bruises and shakeups were not uncommon, but seldom was there a serious threat to life or limb.

The first street railway car in New York City, operated by
the newly chartered New York and Harlem Railroad Company,
made its initial trip on November 26, 1832, and steam was
adopted for motive power two years later.  The full length of
the track extended three-quarters of a mile from Fourteenth
Street southward.[9]  A few years earlier, in 1831, a small locomotive, the De Witt-Clinton, had been placed in operation on
a stretch of wooden track, topped with iron stripping, running
from Albany to Schenectady, seventeen miles away.[10]  It is doubtful, however, that these toylike beginnings of our modern
transportation system were to impose any substantial threat to
the safety of the populace for at least a decade.  The short
distances covered and the slow speed which the rudimentary
engines were able to develop made an extensive casualty list a
virtual impossibility in those times.

In 1840 the total track mileage in America was less than
three thousand; but at about that time the period of expansion
set in, and the growth thereafter was prodigious.  The miles of
steel rails leaped by geometric progression from one decade
to the next.  By 1850 there were over nine thousand miles.
This increased to thirty thousand in 1860, and, despite the civil
war, the year 1870 found America with a rail network of fifty-
two thousand miles of track.[11]  This, in turn, was nearly doubled by 1880.

---

[8] From Christopher Schultz, Travels on an Inland Voyage, as quoted
in 3 Dunbar, op. cit. supra note 7 at 755.
[9] Carman, The Street Surface Railway Franchises of New York
City (Studies in History, Economics and Public Law, Columbia University, vol. 88, no. 1, 1919) 17-24.
[10] Reck, The Romance of American Transportation (1938) 88.
[11] Reck, op. cit. supra note 10, at c. 10, where the growth of the
system in New York and elsewhere along the Atlantic seaboard is
graphically portrayed in charts.  See also Dana, Federal Restraints
upon State Regulation of Railroad Rates of Fare and Freight (1895)
9 Harv. L. Rev. 324.

Outstripping even the rate of expansion of American railways in these years was the enormous increase in personal injury litigation against the carriers. The great bulk of the cases arose out of crossing accidents. Equally impressive was the change in complexion of the decisions. The doctrine of contributory negligence gained a sudden and eager recognition by the courts. From the beginning it was apparent that this rule was to dominate virtually every torts case involving a railroad defendant. First came the inadequately reported case of *Spencer v. The Utica and Schenectady Railroad Company*[12] in the closing year of the forties. But this merely foreshadowed a beginning, for the doctrine was not put into substantial usage until the latter part of the next decade. The period from 1850 to 1860 witnessed twelve reported contributory negligence cases involving railroads, nine of which were after 1855. Even this, it will be noted, was three times the product of the preceding two decades. During the succeeding ten years, the total leaped to thirty-one, and the 1870's produced for the appellate courts no less than fifty-eight actions against railroads in which the negligence of the plaintiff was regarded as of controlling importance. How can we account for this sudden rise to domination?

### The Breakdown of Trial by Jury

UPPERMOST in the minds of both judges and lawyers of the time was a seething, although somewhat covert, dissatisfaction over the part they felt the jury was destined to play in these cases against corporate defendants. The simple disputes between neighbors which had characterized the torts litigation of the past epoch had been both easily and fairly disposed of through the homely agency of the jurymen. The guiding considerations in such cases were both personal and ethical, and commonsense notions of fair play were about all that were required so long as both plaintiff and defendant were in approximately the same economic sphere. Whatever shortcomings might have been attributable to the jury institution with respect to the way in which it blundered through cases of complicated commercial transactions, yet dramatic disputes involving physical action were still regarded as being within the jury's special province and were well adapted to its peculiar talents. The institution had been nurtured as a political safe-

[12] 5 Barb. 337 (N.Y. 1849).

guard against despotism and was rooted deep in the thought-ways of an aggressive, democratic people.[13]

Of course those now familiar devices for dispensing with the participation of the jury — the involuntary nonsuit and the practice of setting aside the verdict — were by no means unknown procedures to the New York courts of the middle 1800's.[14] In those early years, however, such powers seem to have been sparingly used in cases where the only disputed point was the sufficiency of the evidence to support the verdict.[15]

With the intrusion of the railway upon the scene came a marked change in the frame of mind of the average juryman. He quickly adopted the attitude that has characterized him ever since in claims against corporate defendants. He became distinctly and, at least for a time, incurably, plaintiff-minded.

It is hardly conceivable that it could have been otherwise. The mental makeup of the pioneer, the sudden shift in social and economic values, and the drama of the courtroom all combined to turn his mind in that direction. First should be remembered the provincial character of isolated peoples and their hostile suspicion of the outlander. The unproved stranger is seldom given the benefit of the doubt in such a community, and if his intrusion bodes ill for the safety of the vicinage and introduces hitherto unknown dangers for the homefolk, he can hardly expect a tender ministration at the hands of the local jury.

This feeling against the remote corporate defendant was sharpened by the novel character of the accidents that followed in the wake of the intrusion. Professor Vold, in discussing the doctrine of *Rylands v. Fletcher,* has aptly observed that where there is no reciprocity of risk, even judge-made standards become rigid, and absolute liability is apt to follow.

[13] See the opinion of Kent in People v. Croswell, 3 Johnson's Cases 337, 363 (N.Y. 1804). See generally Farley, Instructions to Juries—Their Role in the Judicial Process (1932) 42 Yale L.J. 194.

[14] An instance of the involuntary nonsuit where the evidence offered by the plaintiff was not sufficient to support his action is found as early as 1816 in Pratt v. Hull, 13 Johns. 334 (N.Y. 1816); and in Stuart v. Simpson, 1 Wend. 376, 379 (N.Y. 1828), Savage, C. J., remarked: ". . . it is a matter of common practice to set aside verdicts as against evidence, and sometimes because they are against the weight of evidence." Smith, The Power of the Judge to Direct a Verdict: Section 457-a of the New York Civil Practice Act (1924) 24 Col. L. Rev. 111. See generally, Thayer, A Preliminary Treatise on Evidence at the Common Law (1898) 45-182.

[15] "The fact of [contributory] negligence is very seldom established by such direct and positive evidence that it can be taken from the consideration of the jury and pronounced upon as a matter of law." Johnson, J., in Ireland v. Oswego, Hannibal and Sterling Plank Road Co., 13 N.Y. 526, 533 (1856).

"Another thread, common to cases where the law of strict liability has been applied in the one-sidedness of the risk of the activity. Perhaps the most effective way to express this element is to point out that in the standard situation where the law of negligence as a matter of course has come to be applied, two persons are by their activity mutually exposing each other to the risk of accident. It is submitted that this mutuality of risk is one of the great foundation stones on which the main structure of the law of negligence has been erected, and that without it the negligence doctrine loses its attraction as being inherently fair."[16]

This applies fairly to a typical injury at a railway crossing. The risk in such a case falls entirely upon the wayfarer whose unlucky path leads him across the iron rails. There is no threat moving the other way. The interjection of a new and unusual activity into a community which is greatly imperilled by it and which is entirely the passive recipient of the danger creates a state of things that sets the temper of the mind against the intruder. It will be recalled that similar considerations impelled the English courts to formulate the notion of absolute liability for ultra-hazardous activities and to draw that perhaps cryptic distinction between natural and non-natural user. Less articulate, but equally compelling, was the instinct of the jurymen to demand reparation of the intruding railway which created dangers but was not exposed to the perils of its own making.

Mention of other factors which still color the deliberations of juries is hardly necessary. The substitution of the bloodless and impersonal corporate defendant for the neighbor whose individual circumstances were known to the jurymen, and the deep pockets of the railroad companies whose new business was thriving and which could meet their judgments with no apparent inconvenience, all added up to an attitude of complete indifference to any persuasive claims that the defendants could muster.

The available evidence indicates that the jury tended to break down as an effective administrative arm in the railroad crossing cases. Although the jurymen shared, as members of the public, the advantages of present or anticipated railroad conveniences and benefits, nevertheless consistency of attitude was no more characteristic of lay opinion at that time than it is

---

16 Vold, West and Wolf, Aircraft Operator's Liability for Ground Damage and Passenger Injury (1935) 13 Neb. L. Bull. 373, 380.

now.  There is no feeling of professional loyalty on the part of jurymen, no awareness that individual verdicts all add up and exert together a sizable effect upon the economy of the enterprise.  There is only the desire of the juryman to express in his loose general verdict, the impulse that controls him and which, at the time, seems fair enough.[17]

### The Search for an Effective Means of Jury Control

JUST how ineffective the jury actually became in the administration of the railroad injury cases must remain, perhaps, a matter of conjecture.  What is important for our purposes is that most of the judges of the time had become thoroughly converted to the idea that the jury could not be depended on to handle these cases fairly according to standards that were acceptable to the courts.  As to the existence of such a belief there can be no doubt.  The decisions from the period between 1855 to 1870 are replete with expressions on the subject.  In each instance the courts were urged to exercise an increasing control over the deliberataions of the jury and to foreclose the case by nonsuit or otherwise.

"We can not shut our eyes to the fact that in certain controversies between the weak and the strong — between an humble individual and a gigantic corporation, the sympathies of the human mind naturally, honestly, and generously, run to the assistance and support of the feeble, and apparently oppressed; and that compassion will sometimes exercise over the deliberations of a jury, an influence which, however honorable to them as philanthropists, is wholly inconsistent with the principles of law and the ends of justice.  There is, therefore, a manifest propriety in withdrawing from the consideration of the jury, those cases in which the plaintiff failed to show a right of recovery."[18]

Particularly noteworthy is the opinion of Smith, in _Ernst v. Hudson River Railroad Company_.[19]  The learned justice made

---

[17] Over three hundred appellate cases arising from railroad accidents were read in the preparation of this article, and in only one instance was there an appeal from a verdict against the plaintiff.  This perhaps is not conclusive in view of the fact that defendants are much more given to appeal than are their adversaries.  It may be mentioned in passing, however, that there was no apparent reluctance on the part of plaintiffs to appeal from nonsuits or dismissals of their complaints. More persuasive evidence of the tendency of jurymen to ignore the contributory negligence of plaintiff has been presented elsewhere by the writer.  Malone, Contributory Negligence and the Landowner Cases (1945) 29 Minn. L. Rev. 61.

[18] Barculo, J., in Haring v. New York and Erie R. R., 13 Barb. 2, 15 (N.Y. 1853).

[19] 24 How. Prac. 97 (N.Y. 1862).

little effort to conceal either his impatience with the jury or his conviction concerning the supremacy of the court:

"It is not the *jury*, but the *courts* which administer justice. The duty and responsibility of seeing that equal and impartial justice is meted out to all men, devolves, under the constitution, by the common law, upon the *judges of the courts*. Juries are mere *assistants* of the courts, whose province it is to aid them in the decision of disputed questions of fact. If there is no real *dispute* in a case, the court gives judgment."[20]

After commending the jury as a most valuable adjunct in the decision of cases, he continued

"Aside from the difference in capacity to decide correctly, arising from professional education and practice, and judicial experience, the judges act and decide deliberately, after patient and careful investigation, and give the reasons for their decisions, which are open to the careful scrutiny of the parties, and the vigilant criticism of an educated and enlightened bar, and of the public.

"Juries will certainly act and decide more or less hastily, without time, in most instances, for much reflection, and also act and decide in secret; and from this consideration, and their large number, they certainly act under much less personal and individual responsibility than the judges; and besides, common observation and experience show that they are far more liable to be swayed by passion and excitement, and other undue influences. Their verdicts are therefore notoriously many times founded upon mistakes, misconceptions and other errors, which make it indispensable, to secure to this mode of trial the public confidence, that a power of supervision and review of the verdicts should exist in the courts, and should be exercised with fidelity and firmness."[21]

Most opinions of the time, although more restrained in tone, make clear the fact that the court was determined to exercise

---

[20] *Id.* at 105.

[21] *Id.* at 106. Another example typical of the prevailing attitude is found in Mackey v. New York Cent. R. R., 27 Barb. 528 (N.Y. 1858). "If this was not a suit against a railroad company in behalf of a widow woman whose husband had been killed by the casualty which was the subject of investigation, I should suppose that the positive affirmative testimony of the defendant, on the question of sounding the whistle and ringing the bell, was much more to be relied on and would rather be credited by a jury, than the mere negative uncertain testimony of the plaintiff's witnesses." (*Id.* at 539).

"I cannot see how such a finding can be sustained. It is directly *against the evidence*, and we cannot uphold it or refuse to set it aside, unless we adopt the rule which is, I fear, quite prevalent in the jury box, the same measure of justice is not to be meted out to a railroad corporation which is meted out to natural persons." (*Id.* at 541).

a rigid power in control of the jury. Thus began an earnest quest for the easiest, most direct, and least embarrassing means of attaining this end, a means which would successfully avoid conflict with all democratic ritual concerning the sacrosanct character of the jury.

### Jury Control Through the Negligence Issue

NO reader of the decisions of the middle 1800's can fail to be impressed with the monotonous similarity of the railroad crossing situations confronting the courts during that period. The pattern was virtually the same everywhere — the railroad was charged with a failure to give the crossing signals by bell or whistle, while the plaintiff had a good or middling view of the track and failed to watch out for himself. The facts were nearly always sharply disputed, and the alignment of witnesses was about the same in each instance. If the victim survived, he testified for himself; otherwise some bystander was produced. According to the plaintiff's testimony, the signal was never given; the victim had always looked out most carefully for himself. Aligned against these witnesses were the employees of the railroad, who unvaryingly swore that the requisite signal was given in ample time and that the deceased or injured plunged heedlessly onto the track.[22]

It is hornbook law that the court should nonsuit the plaintiff if he fails to make a plausible showing on any of the elements of the case which he must establish. This suggests that a shortcoming in proof with respect to the defendant's alleged negligence might be seized on readily by the court as a means of laying a controlling hand on the dispute. Such, however, was virtually never the case. Although there are numerous instances where the defendant seriously urged that proof of negligence had failed, yet when the case came up for consideration on appeal the negligence issue more often than not was either side-stepped completely or mentioned only in passing to add weight to the opinion.

The reason was that the negligence issue does not permit of the type of flexibility that was needed. We have previously observed that usually the only default chargeable against the

---

[22] The testimony of passengers seldom figures prominently. Their testimony is relatively useless. One judge remarked: "It is my own belief, founded on some experience and observation, that it is very rare, if indeed ever, that a passenger can hear the bell upon the engine when the train is under ordinary headway, and the doors and windows of the car are closed." Steves v. Oswego & Syracuse R. R., 18 N.Y. 422, 425 (1858).

railroad in the early cases was its failure to give the crossing signal. In fact, there was almost no other safety measure available to the defendant. All accounts of early railway travel mention the complete inadequacy of the braking system used in those times.

"Down to the year 1868 the brake system remained very much as it was in 1830 when railways were first adapted to commercial operation. Even though detailed improvements covering structural items had been incorporated, the essential principles were the same. Those in charge of the locomotive had no direct control over the brake manipulation on the vehicles comprising the train. Communications between the engineman on the locomotive who senses the danger and the brakeman in the cars who drew up the cables was effected by whistle signals in case of sudden emergency. The first action was to signal danger and to this signal the train crew was instructed to respond with all celerity. Each operation required time and every second of time represented many feet of space."[23]

The modern air brake, although it was invented by Westinghouse in 1868, was not in general usage until after 1880.[24] The device met with considerable skepticism on the part of railway management and even after it had gained adoption it was by no means the efficient mechanism we know today.

The lack of adequate brakes not only deprived the management of a means to control, it likewise deprived the element of speed of much of the significance as a danger factor it acquired in later years. What is the difference in terms of safety between ten and twenty-five miles per hour if the vehicle cannot be effectively controlled or brought to a prompt halt at the lower speed? It was only in cases arising in congested areas or in later years after the airbrake came into common usage that plaintiffs attempted to make serious capital of the speed of the defendant.[25] It is noteworthy also that in most cases where the

[23] Silcox, Safety in Early American Railway Operations: 1853-1871 (1936).
[24] Reck, *op. cit. supra* note 10, at 154-159. The use of the air brake was not made mandatory by law in New York until 1884 N.Y. Laws (1884) c. 439 §6. The first decision that the writer found indicating that an automatic brake was in use is Smith v. New York Cent. & Hudson River R. R., 11 N.Y. St. 795 (1887). *Cf.* Costello v. Syracuse, Binghamton & N. Y. Ry., 65 Barb. 92 (N.Y. 1873).
[25] During the period from 1850-1870 only six of 31 cases arising out of railroad crossing accidents were treated by the appellate court as involving some act or omission on the part of the defendant other than its failure to sound the crossing signal. These were Bernhardt v. Ren-

defendant was guilty of excessive speed in urban areas there was little urge to nonsuit the plaintiff because of his carelessness since the court was content to submit the controversy to the jury.[26]

Although little could be done by the companies at first to so operate their trains as to minimize the likelihood of crossing accidents, they nevertheless could afford a warning of their approach. The necessity of signals must have been prominently in mind from the start, for in 1850 the first general railroad law of the state imposed the duty of ringing the locomotive bell continuously beginning at a distance of eighty rods from the crossing.[27] Each violation subjected the offender to a penalty of twenty dollars, half of which might be claimed by the informer. Most important for our purpose was a clause, "and said corporation shall be liable for all damages sustained by any person by reason of such neglect." This law remained in effect substantially unimpaired from 1850[28] until it was repealed, probably through inadvertence, in 1886.[29]

Thus during all that period the element of fault was frozen by the legislature and there was little room for evaluation of the picture on that score by either court or jury. The only function remaining in the administration of the case on the negligence issue was to decide the question whether or not the signal was given at the prescribed distance and maintained without interruption. With the evidence on this nearly always in hopeless conflict, there was little the appellate courts could do. On a few occasions they were able to remand the case for petty, meaningless errors in the instructions, hoping (usually in vain) for a different verdict next time.[30] They brought into

---

selaer and Saratoga R. R., 18 How. Prac. 427 (N.Y. 1859); 19 How. Prac. 199, 32 Barb. 165 (N.Y. 1860); 1 Abb. App. Dec. 131 (N.Y. 1860); Johnson v. Hudson River R. R., 20 N.Y. 65 (1859); Owen and Lugar v. Hudson River R. R., 20 N.Y. Super. 329 (1860); Keller v. New York Cent. R. R., 24 How. Prac. 172 (N.Y. 1861); Brown v. Buffalo & State Line R. R., 22 N.Y. 191 (1863); Wilds v. Hudson River R. R., 29 N.Y. 315 (N.Y. 1864). In all the cases listed above except Owen v. Hudson River R. R., the accident happened in a congested area, and in each instance the verdict below for the plaintiff was affirmed on appeal.

[26] P. 25 of ms., *infra.*

[27] N.Y. Laws (1850) 232, c. 140, §39.

[28] In 1854 the act was amended so as to add the requirement that the whistle be sounded, and modifications were made to adopt the requirements to urban situations. All penalties were retained with slight modification. N.Y. Laws (1854) 611, c. 282, §7.

[29] Reference here is to an omnibus repealer which accompanied a revision of the criminal laws of this state. N.Y. Laws (1886) c. 592, §29. *Cf.* Lewis v. New York, Lake Erie and Western R. R., 123 N.Y. 496, 26 N.E. 357 (1890).

[30] Farley, *supra* note 13.

play rules of evidence that would tend to extricate the defendant. Sometimes the testimony of the sole or key witness for the plaintiff was suppressed on appeal because the record was barren of proof that he was affirmatively advertent for the sound of the signal. On a few occasions this resulted in nonsuit,[31] but the device was fortuitous by nature and did not offer a means of jury control that could be depended upon whenever needed by the court.

## Jury Control Through the Causation Issue

I T was incumbent upon the plaintiff to show that the failure to give the statutory signal played a substantial part in producing the injury or death. Probably a feeling on the part of the court that this element had not been satisfactorily established was in most instances the impelling reason for reversal. This shows through the opinions only indirectly, however; and in not more than a few of the New York decisions on crossing injuries does the court announce that a nonsuit should have been directed because of shortcomings in the proof on causation.[32]

Cause in fact is an issue which seldom lends itself to an unequivocal yes or no. Particularly is this true when the default is the failure to give the required signal. In most instances a court would be bold indeed to announce openly as a matter of law that the victim would have disregarded the warning even if it had been given and would have rushed forewarned to his doom. It would be equally difficult usually to assume that the signal would not have been heard if it had been sounded. Such determinations are by tradition too peculiarly within the province of the jury to permit of arbitrary actions by the court (particularly when the surrounding facts are in

[31] Culhane v. New York Cent. & Hudson River R. R., 60 N.Y. 133 (1875); Chapman v. New York Cent. & Hudson River R. R., 14 Hun. 484 (N.Y. 1878); McKeever v. New York Cent. & Hudson River R. R., 88 N.Y. 667 (1882); Tolman v. Syracuse, Binghamton & New York R. R., 27 Hun. 325 (N.Y. 1882).

[32] Haring v. New York & Erie R. R., 13 Barb. 2 (N.Y. 1852) (Evidence indicated plaintiff must have been aware of approach of the train, despite absence of signals. For this reason, the trial court entered a nonsuit. On appeal, however, the general term of the supreme court affirmed the nonsuit solely on the ground of contributory negligence.); Daniels v. Staten Island Rapid Transit Co., 7 N.Y.S. 725 (1889), reversed 125 N.Y. 407, 26 N.E. 466 (1891) (facts similar); Pakalinsky v. New York Cent. & Hudson River R. R., 82 N.Y. 424 (1880) (plaintiff's foot caught in track; no last chance available to defendant, and only alleged negligence was failure to give signal); Chrystal v. Troy & Boston R. R., 105 N.Y. 164, 11 N.E. 380 (1887), on second appeal 124 N.Y. 519, 26 N.E. 1103 (1891) (infant less than two years of age on tracks; signals would have been meaningless).

hot dispute). Hence the causation issue, like the issue of negligence, furnishes a poor implement for dispensing with the jury in this type of case except under unusual circumstances.

### Jury Control Through the Contributory Negligence Issue

THUS far we have sought only to show that neither the issue of negligence nor the issue of causation could be effectively used for controlling jury action in the crossing cases. In order to understand the character of the device required by the courts it is first necessary to inquire as to the reasons that demanded a tight judicial rein. In becoming more closely acquainted with the need we can appraise more accurately the characteristics of the implement that was adopted to fill that need. In view of the fact that the crossing signal was about the only precautionary means available to prevent railroad crossing accidents in those times it is apparent that the court was dealing primarily with a single requirement which, in New York at least, was statutory in form. What was the purpose of the statutory signal; what kind of accidents was it designed to prevent; and what victims were within the protective ambit of the rule that demands the giving of the signal?[33]

Certainly the legislature of 1850 did not feel that by enacting a crossing statute it was affording a panacea for all crossing hazards. The hope was to protect *some* persons under *some* circumstances, not *all* persons under *all* circumstances. The sorting of the cases, the determination of the fits and the misfits — these were jobs which, in the absence of some specific direction from the legislature, must be performed by the courts in the administration of the cases as they arose.

When effective means for preventing or controlling danger are at hand, the affording of warning plays a subordinate role. In these days when automobiles have adequate brakes and lights, horns are seldom sounded by motorists. In some municipalities their use is even prohibited. An emphasis on compulsory warning suggests a confession of inability to offer anything that is really effective. In ancient times the incurable leper carried his rattle and more recently the noisy and uncontrollable horseless buggy was preceded in many communities by a man on horseback with his red flag of danger. As

---

[33] The problem of defining the limits of protection is one with which courts are faced constantly in almost every type of litigation. Usually it is attacked through indirection. The great variety of forms that the problem may assume are discussed by Dean Green in The Rationale of Proximate Cause (1927) c. 1, §3, c. 2 and 3.

means of control were developed the warning retreated to the background or disappeared altogether.

The sounding of an alarm requires cooperation as an essential condition of success. There must be both a giver and a receiver of the warning and each must do his part. An alertness to danger on the part of the recipient is indispensable if the scheme is to succeed. In this respect the affording of warnings differs materially from all other precautionary measures. It follows that the benefit of a crossing signal statute can be made available only to those who show by their conduct immediately prior to the moment of danger that they can be alerted by the sound of the whistle or the bell. All other persons may well be regarded as outside the protective ambit of the rule. The focal point in the crossing cases, therefore, is the determination of whether the victim has entitled himself to protection, whether he has manifested sufficient indicia of cooperation that the warning scheme shows promise that it would have worked if the defendant had done his part.

For this reason the plaintiff's own conduct and the physical circumstances attendant upon the accident are inextricably woven into the fabric of the case. Notions of plaintiff fault, causation, duty, and negligence become hopelessly intervolved at this point, and any device that will be of real service in dispensing successfully with jury participation must be a weapon that affords a broadside attack upon the entire context of the problem involved and offers a means of suggesting in a single adroit but homely phrase the multifarious nature of the inquiry. At the same time it must afford a means of expression that will make possible a considerable degree of latitude for decision either way. Judged by these considerations, the contributory negligence issue was admirably suited to the need.

Even before the railroad cases, the doctrine of contributory negligence had been given a turn that made it particularly useful for the new purpose. The court had already alluded somewhat vaguely to the now familiar New York rule that the plaintiff must affirmatively show his freedom from carelessness.[34] In the early railroad crossing cases that position was unequivocally affirmed,[35] and contributory negligence was thus

---

[34] Burdick v. Worrall, 4 Barb. 596 (N.Y. 1848).

[35] In Spencer v. Utica & Schnectady R. R., 5 Barb. 337 (N.Y. 1849), the first railroad crossing case involving contributory negligence, the court said with assurance: "It was equally necessary for the plaintiff to establish the proposition that he himself was without negligence and without fault. This is a stern and unbending rule, which has been settled by a long series of adjudged cases, which we cannot overrule if we

firmly established as a ready means of justifying a nonsuit. In no other way could the doctrine have been made really serviceable, for if the onus of establishing the plaintiff's fault were cast upon the defendant, how could the plaintiff be deprived of access to the jury on account of shortcomings in his own proof in this respect? The position adopted comported nicely with accepted theory, and it is still defended stoutly in several quarters.[36] At that time the same procedure was in effect in many jurisdictions,[37] probably for the same reason that caused it to be adopted in New York.

The requirement respecting the burden of proof, like most legal rules of practical importance, ushered in a retinue of exceptions and ameliorating devices that enabled the court to sustain the plaintiff's position or reject it with comparative freedom. Without embarrassment it could be said that proof of freedom from fault might be gathered from the attendant circumstances alone without positive testimony on the subject, particularly where the defendants' negligence was clear.[38] It was also open to the court to find that the exercise of care by

would." (5 Barb. at 338.)  See also Haring v. New-York & Erie R. R., 13 Barb. 2 (N.Y. 1852). Since then the rule has been reaffirmed many times. Lee v. Troy Citizens' Gas-Light Co., 98 N.Y. 115 (1885).

[36] See, for example, 1 Shearman and Redfield, Negligence (rev. ed. 1941) §124.

[37] *Illinois*: Chicago, Burlington and Quincy R. R. v. Levy, 160 Ill. 385, 43 N.E. 357 (1895); Calumet Iron and Steel Co. v. Martin, 115 Ill. 358, 3 N.E. 456 (1885); *Indiana*: Toledo, W. & W. Ry. v. Brannagan, 75 Ind. 490 (1881); *Iowa*: Way v. Illinois Central R. R., 40 Iowa 341 (1875); *Maine*: Kennard v. Burton, 25 Maine 39, 42 (1845); Ward v. Maine Cent. R. R., 96 Maine 136, 51 Atl. 947 (1902); *Michigan*: Teipel v. Hilsendegen, 44 Mich. 461 (1880); *Missouri*: Callahan v. Warne, 40 Mo. 131 (1867); *North Carolina*: See Owens v. Richmond & Danville R. R., 488 N.C. 490, 502 (1883), as interpreted in Aycock v. Raleigh & Augusta Air-Line R. R., 89 N.C. 321 (1883); *Vermont*: Bovee v. Danville, 53 Vt. 183 (1880); *Wisconsin*: Chamberlain v. Milwaukee & M. R. R., 7 Wis. 425 (1858).

In Massachusetts and North Carolina the rule was later changed by statute: Mass. Acts (1914) c. 553 [Mass. Ann. Laws (1933) c. 231, §85]; N.C. Laws (1887) c. 33 [N.C. Gen. Stat. (1943) §1-139]. It is interesting to note that in Massachusetts the burden of proving freedom from contributory negligence is still cast upon the plaintiff in railway crossing cases. See Mass. Gen. Laws, c. 90, §15, as interpreted in Fortune v. New York, New Haven and Hartford R. R., 271 Mass. 101, 170 N.E. 923 (1929). In Wisconsin, Missouri and Indiana the New York rule has been abrogated in later decisions. See, for example, Hoyt v. Hudson, 41 Wis. 105 (1876).

Despite the North Carolina statute the courts of that state have managed to maintain some degree of control of the jury on the contributory negligence issue through nonsuit. See Neal v. Carolina Cent. R. R., 126 N.C. 634 (1900). Blair, Automobile Accidents at Railroad Crossings in North Carolina (1945) 23 N.C. L. Rev. 223.

[38] See, for example, Tolman v. Syracuse, Binghamton & New York R. R., 31 Hun. 397 (N.Y. 1884), with which compare Tolman v. Syracuse, Binghamton & New York R. R., 98 N.Y. 198 (1885) and Wiwirowski v. Lake Shore & Mich. So. Ry., 124 N.Y. 420, 26 N.E. 1023 (1891).

the plaintiff would not have avoided the accident and thus dispense with proof of freedom from contributory negligence.[39] An unusual insight into the processes behind these cases is afforded by the following statement from *Johnson v. Hudson River Railroad Company*:[40]

> "Upon this I have to remark that in the absence of a statement of the nature and extent of the defendant's negligence, it is impossible to say what it was incumbent upon the plaintiff to show. If slight and not such as necessarily or probably to endanger a person on foot, then the plaintiff was bound to show that she did not by her negligence bring the misfortune upon her."[41]

Once the court had made possible the use of the plaintiff's fault as a device for dispensing with the jury, it facilitated the process by treating the evidence in typical judge fashion. Items of plaintiff's conduct at crossings fall naturally into a limited number of fact patterns which are repeated in case after case. Since they are readily classified, they lend themselves to stereotyped treatment by the court. This makes for a tighter control of the jury's operations, both by affording an opportunity for detailed instructions which, in turn, give rise to reversible error, and by offering material which can be easily translated into conduct that is negligent "as a matter of law."[42] To fail to look when a view is available or to listen when sound can be heard, to approach a crossing with which one is familiar

[39] Smedis v. Brooklyn & Rockaway Beach R. R., 88 N.Y. 13 (1882); Tolman v. Syracuse, Binghamton & New York R. R., 31 Hun. 397 (N.Y. 1884); Cranston v. New York Cent. & Hudson River R. R., 39 Hun. 308 (N.Y. 1886); Pruey v. New York Cent. & Hudson River R. R., 58 N.Y.S. 797 (1899), *aff'd* without opinion 166 N.Y. 616, 59 N.E. 1129 (1901). With these cases compare Wieland v. Delaware & Hudson Canal Co., 167 N.Y. 19, 60 N.E. 234 (1901).

[40] 20 N.Y. 65 (1859).

[41] *Id.* at 72. Compare Chadbourne v. Delaware, Lackawanna & Western R. R., 6 Daly 215 (N.Y. 1875). Another statement that reveals the inextricable relationship between the conduct of both parties appears in Borst v. Lake Shore & Mich. So. Ry., 4 Hun. 346 (N.Y. 1875), a case in which the court was inclined toward recovery: "The conduct of the plaintiff in all this class of cases is generally so mixed with, and so dependent upon, the conduct and acts of the defendant and the surrounding circumstances of the case that this question [the question of contributory negligence], in most cases, fairly belongs to the jury, in the general consideration of the whole facts of the case." (4 Hun. at 349.)

[42] ". . . the cases arising from injuries suffered at railroad crossings have been so numerous, and upon certain points there has been such absolute accord, that what will constitute ordinary care in such a case will have been precisely defined, and, if any element is wanting, the courts will hold as a matter of law that the plaintiff has been guilty of negligence." Herbert v. Southern Pac. Co., 121 Cal. 227, 230, 53 Pac. 651 (1898). See also Nixon, Changing Rules of Liability in Automobile Accident Litigation (1936) 3 Law & Contemp. Prob. 476, 478, 481.

without first ascertaining that no train is approaching, to proceed to cross in the face of smoke[43] or noise[44] — all these fragments of behavior which recur frequently in the experience of crossing litigation can be handled by rule-of-thumb judgment which soon become regarded as rules of law and leave nothing to be considered by the jury.

The hand of the court was further strengthened by the nature of the evidence that can be employed to prove the fact of plaintiff's negligence. The so-called "physical facts approach" became a familiar means of establishing beyond doubt that a view *was* available to the plaintiff, or that the whistle *could* be heard. Arbitrary measurements began to take the place of human narrative. A train two hundred yards down the track could be seen at a distance of twenty feet from the crossing, because someone has gone down to the scene of the accident with a tape and has measured off the distance. This kind of evidence has a convincing ring and tends to deprive the jury of even its rudimentary function of fact finding. The physical facts approach ignores, of course, the human element. It takes no account of the urgency of the victim's situation or the physical handicaps under which he may have been laboring at the time. It leaves out of reckoning the fact that the purpose of a standard of reasonableness is to allow some tolerance for the frailties of human behavior. Yet the statement "not to look when one can see, is careless" makes mighty convincing stuff in opinions when courts are determined that recovery is not to be allowed.[45]

Here again, however, means of expression are available for the accommodation of both parties. The physical facts doctrine can be either accepted or discounted by the court, and both positions have been adopted.[46] The judge is free to say

---

[43] Heaney v. Long Island Ry., 9 N.Y. St. 707 (1887); Heaney v. Long Island R. R., 112 N.Y. 122, 19 N.E. 422 (1889); Swift v. Staten Island Rapid Transit R. R., 123 N.Y. 645, 25 N.E. 378 (1890); Whalen v. New York Cent. & Hudson River R. R., 15 N.Y.S. 941 (1891); McNamara v. New York Cent. & Hudson River R. R., 19 N.Y.S. 497 (1892); Foran v. New York Cent. & Hudson River R. R., 19 N.Y.S. 417 (1892).

[44] Morse v. Erie Ry., 65 Barb. 490 (N.Y. 1873).

[45] The following are representative instances where the physical facts type of argument was used effectively: Woodard v. New York, Lake Erie & Western R. R., 106 N.Y. 369, 13 N.E. 424 (1887); Tucker v. New York Cent. & Hudson River R. R., 124 N.Y. 308, 26 N.E. 916 (1891); Rodrian v. New York, New Haven & Hartford R. R., 125 N.Y. 526, 26 N.E. 741 (1891); Swart v. New York Cent. & Hudson River R. R., 80 N.Y.S. 906 (1903), *affirmed* without opinion 177 N.Y. 529, 69 N.E. 1131 (1903); Dolfini v. Erie R. R., 178 N.Y. 1, 70 N.E. 68 (1904).

[46] With the cases in note 45, *supra*, compare the following cases where the argument was discounted: Massoth v. Delaware & Hudson

that the mere perfunctory turning of the eyes in a certain direction does not meet the requirement of the law,[47] or that to look means to see,[48] that the plaintiff is not entitled to go heedlessly upon the track assuming that the defendant will give the required signal.[49] There are equally available stock expressions which color the decision in favor of the plaintiff. "There is no absolute rule requiring the traveller to use his eyes in a particular manner at a particular instance of time."[50] The remark has been made that the victim is not presumed to have intended suicide by going carelessly upon the tracks,[51] or that he was entitled to assume that the signal would be sounded if a train were approaching.[52] In this confusing welter of language, almost any decision can be made to sound plausible or even convincing.

### How the Doctrine was Employed

HERE, then, in the issue of contributory negligence, was an ingenious device which gave the court almost complete freedom to accept or reject jury participation at its pleasure. How was it to be used? No one who has read the cases can escape the conclusion that plaintiff fault, as such, had at best a very uneven bearing on the disposition of these controversies. In one case a avictim whose conduct seems impervious to reasonable reproach may suffer a nonsuit at the hands of a court, while in another the victim's obvious carelessness may be dismissed or dealt with only lightly as a matter for jury consideration. The outcome seems to be determined by the complexion of the controversy as a whole, rather than by the impact of the plaintiff's carelessness. Commentaries on contributory negligence that account for the doctrine in terms of the individualism of the common law,[53] or by the notion

---

Canal Co., 64 N.Y. 524 (1876); Casey v. New York Cent. & Hudson River R. R., 78 N.Y. 518 (1879); Byrne v. New York Cent. & Hudson River R. R., 83 N.Y. 620 (1881); Shaw v. Jewett, 86 N.Y. 616 (1881); Greany v. Long Island R. R., 101 N.Y. 419, 5 N.E. 425 (1886).

[47] McAuliffe v. New York Cent. & Hudson River R. R., 84 N.Y.S. 607 (1903), *affirmed* 181 N.Y. 537, 73 N.E. 1126 (1905).

[48] Swart v. New York Cent. & Hudson River R. R., 80 N.Y.S. 906 (1903), *affirmed* without opinion 177 N.Y. 529, 69 N.E. 1131 (1903).

[49] Rodrian v. New York, New Haven & Hartford R. R., 125 N.Y. 526, 26 N.E. 741 (1891).

[50] O'Bierne v. New York Cent. & Hudson River R. R., 56 N.Y.S. 236 (1899), *affirmed* without opinion 167 N.Y. 568, 60 N.E. 1117 (1901).

[51] Danforth, J., dissenting in Woodard v. New York, Lake Erie & Western R. R., 106 N.Y. 369, 376, 13 N.E. 424, 427 (1887).

[52] Sherry v. New York Cent. & Hudson River R. R., 104 N.Y. 652, 10 N.E. 128 (1887); Palmer v. New York Cent. & Hudson River R. R., 112 N.Y. 234, 19 N.E. 678 (1889).

[53] Bohlen, Contributory Negligence (1908) 21 Harv. L. Rev. 233.

that the plaintiff is disentitled to recovery by reason of his own guilt,[54] tell only a small part of the story. These accounts rest upon the easy premise that controversies are severable in administration as well as in theory into separate issues, each of which is susceptible of being resolved in isolation from the others. No such idea obtains in practice. The first impress of the case upon the court is a totality, and the resolution of the controversy into separate issues is a refinement imposed by the judicial intellect for the purpose of explaining the decision or apportioning parts of the dispute between the judge and jury. An item of plaintiff conduct may be treated as indisputably negligent when the defendant's fault was slight, or the causal connection was attenuated, or the testimony was incredible;[55] while the same item of conduct will be regarded as a matter only for the jury's consideration when the defendant ran its train at excessive speed in a congested area, or its engineer was not at his post, or a crossing gate was left unattended.

The Illinois courts attempted for a time to proceed openly upon the premise of balancing fault in the mine-run of negligence cases.[56] But when they found that the approach resulted in jury participation to an intolerable extent they reverted to the orthodox procedure.[57] The same idea of comparative negligence has achieved open doctrinal expression nearly everywhere when the situation becomes extreme, and we find such rules as the last clear chance and the dogma that contributory negligence is not a defense to gross or wanton wrong.[58] But the notion of balancing fault does not begin merely on the doctrinal level. It supplies a large part of the impulse that determines the choice between those cases that will be thrown out on nonsuit and those that will be retained for the jury's consideration.

We have previously observed that for a time the failure to give the crossing signal was the chief and indeed almost the only cause of complaint in the crossing cases. The New York court immediately adopted the practice of nonsuiting the plaintiff because of his negligence in nearly every instance when the accident occurred in a rural area and there was a clear

---

[54] See Harper, A Treatise on the Law of Torts (1933) §132.
[55] As in Swart v. New York Cent. & Hudson River R. R., 80 N.Y.S. 906, 910 (1903), *affirmed* without opinion 177 N.Y. 529, 69 N.E. 1131 (1903); Dolfini v. Erie R. R., 178 N.Y. 1, 70 N.E. 68 (1904).
[56] Galena & Chicago Union R. R. v. Jacobs, 20 Ill. 478 (1858).
[57] Green, Illinois Negligence Law (1944) 39 Ill. L. Rev. 36, 47-54.
[58] See James, Last Clear Chance: A Transitional Doctrine (1938) 47 Yale L.J. 704.

view of the train upon the approach.[59]  Doubtless it was felt
that further refinement was impossible from the viewpoint of
practical administration and that the defendant's wrong could
not be presumed to have figured with sufficient prominence
in the picture to warrant the inevitable jury verdict for plaintiff that would follow a more compromising view.  Furthermore this simple approach afforded the comforting refuge of
rule-of-thumb action which enabled the courts to shield themselves from the moral responsibility that would follow any
further individualization of the controversies.  Even the presence of intermittent obstacles to the victim's clear view of the
approaching train seldom altered the adamant position of the
court.[60]  The necessity of drawing tenuous distinctions in
terms of the physical surroundings was a prospect from which
the court retreated.[61]  It did leave sufficient latitude in its
formulae, however, to permit of compromise whenever com-

---

[59] Spencer v. Utica & Schnectady R. R., 5 Barb. 337 (N.Y. 1849);
Haring v. New-York & Erie R. R., 13 Barb. 9 (N.Y. 1852); Brooks v.
Buffalo & Niagara Falls R. R., 25 Barb. 600 (N.Y. 1854); Sheffield &
Herrender v. Rochester & Syracuse R. R., 21 Barb. 339 (N.Y. 1856);
Dascomb v. Buffalo & State Line R. R., 27 Barb. 221 (N.Y. 1858);
Steves v. Oswego & Syracuse R. R., 18 N.Y. 422 (1858); Wilcox v.
Rome, Watertown etc. R. R., 39 N.Y. 358 (1868); Reynolds v. New York
Cent. & Hudson River R. R., 58 N.Y. 248 (1874); Bronk v. New York
& New Haven R. R., 5 Daly 454 (N.Y. 1874); Salter v. Utica & Black
River R. R., 13 Hun. 187 (N.Y. 1878), *reversed* 75 N.Y. 273 (1878); Con-
nelly v. New York Cent. & Hudson River R. R., 88 N.Y. 346 (1882);
Winslow v. Boston & Albany R. R., 11 N.Y. St. 831 (1887); Cullen v.
Delaware & Hudson Canal Co., 113 N.Y. 667, 21 N.E. 716 (1889); Nash
v. New York Cent. & Hudson River R. R., 4 N.Y.S. 525 (1889), *reversed*
125 N.Y. 715, 26 N.E. 266 (1891); Fleissner v. New York Cent. & Hud-
son River R. R., 16 N.Y.S. 18 (1891); Nolan v. New York Cent. & Hud-
son River R. R., 16 N.Y.S. 826 (1891); Burke v. New York Cent. &
Hudson River R. R., 25 N.Y.S. 1009 (1893); Shires v. Fonda, J. & G.
R. R., 30 N.Y.S. 175 (1894); Miller v. New York Cent. & Hudson River
R. R., 30 N.Y.S. 751 (1894); Bates v. New York Cent. & Hudson River
R. R., 32 N.Y.S. 337 (1895); Morris v. Lake Shore and Mich. So. Ry.,
148 N.Y. 182, 42 N.E. 579 (1896).
[60] Gorton v. Erie Ry., 45 N.Y. 660 (1871); Haight v. New York
Cent. R. R., 7 Lansing 11 (N.Y. 1872); McCall v. New York Cent. R. R.,
54 N.Y. 642 (1873); Kellogg v. New York Cent. & Hudson River R. R.,
79 N.Y. 72 (1879); Young v. New York, Lake Erie & Western R. R.,
107 N.Y. 500, 14 N.E. 434 (1887); Rodrian v. New York, New Haven &
Hartford R. R., 125 N.Y. 526, 26 N.E. 741 (1891); Krauss v. Wallkill
Valley R. R., 23 N.Y.S. 432 (1893); Hood v. Lehigh Valley R. R., 96
N.Y.S. 431 (1905), *affirmed* without opinion 186 N.Y. 517, 78 N.E. 1105
(1906); Hagglund v. Erie R. R., 210 N.Y. 46, 103 N.E. 770 (1913).
[61] "Every tree or pole in a highway cannot be made the excuse for
a man's failure to observe a coming train, and it is not to be assumed
that he cast his eyes trainward just at the nick of time when the tree
or pole may possibly be in the focus of his vision."  Hood v. Lehigh
Valley R. R., 96 N.Y.S. 431 (1905).
"But these obstacles, if they existed and hid from view the railroad
and approaching trains to the extent claimed, did not relieve the plaintiff from the duty of looking for an eastbound train at the first opportunity, but rather rendered a cautious approach to the crossing the
more necessary."  Gorton v. Erie Ry., 45 N.Y. 660, 664 (1871).

promise seemed desirable.[62] Such was the wondrous plasticity of the device that it had created.

Unreasonable speed of the train was seldom urged as negligence in the early cases except when the accident took place in a congested urban area.[63] Accidents in such places, however, soon became numerous, and in most cases of this sort the jury's verdict for the plaintiff was sustained on appeal. Whatever may have been the advantages of speed on the open track, the need for fast and efficient transportation did not demand reckless haste in places where the crossings were congested with vehicles and pedestrians.[64] Despite the inefficient braking system of the time the courts were convinced that a sufficiently low speed in these areas would be productive of some measure of safety. In such places the tracks were numerous; several trains might be proceeding in different directions at the same time with a resulting din and uncertainty of view. The general scene was likely to be highly confusing to a public forced to navigate the elaborate network of crossings. Under these circumstances a high rate of speed tended substantially to disarm the crosser by making his estimate of distance and time uncertain. Such conduct then was highly blameworthy and the courts were of a mind to deal with it as such.[65] Of course

[62] Contributory negligence held for jury: Renwick v. New York Cent. R. R., 36 N.Y. 132 (1867); Davis v. New York Cent. R. R., 47 N.Y. 400 (1872); Leonard v. New York Cent. & Hudson River R. R., 42 N.Y. Super. 225 (1877); Kelsey v. Staten Island Rapid Transit R. R., 28 N.Y.S. 974 (1894).
Where the defendant was responsible for the erection or maintenance of the obstruction the court showed a manifest leniency toward the plaintiff's alleged negligence: Mackay v New York Cent. R. R., 35 N.Y. 75 (1866); McGuire v. Hudson River R. R., 2 Daly 76 (N.Y. 1866); Eaton v. Erie Ry., 51 N.Y. 544 (1873); Ingersoll v. New York Cent. & Hudson River R. R., 6 Thomp. & Cook 416 (N.Y. 1875).

[63] In a few of the later cases in which the accident arose at an open rural crossing excessive speed was charged against the defendant. The plaintiff was held guilty of contributory negligence as a matter of law in each instance. Bomboy v. New York Cent. & Hudson River R. R., 47 Hun. 425 (N.Y. 1888); Cullen v. Delaware & Hudson Canal Co., 113 N.Y. 667, 21 N.E. 716 (1889); Collins v. New York Chi. & St. Louis R. R., 36 N.Y.S. 942 (1895).

[64] "It would seem to me to be no more than reasonable to require railroad companies to run their trains through cities and villages at such moderate rate of speed as that by the use of brakes the train may be speedily stopped, so that neither person nor property should be exposed to injury from it; and this without regard to whether there was a municipal regulation as to the speed at which trains should be run. This imposes no great burden on the company, and it would relieve the people from the reckless disregard of life so frequently shown by persons employed in running trains." Mullin, P. J., in Costello v. Syracuse, Binghamton & N. Y. Ry., 65 Barb. 92, 103 (N.Y. 1873).

[65] In the following cases the unreasonable speed of the train seemed to have figured prominently and the courts refused to nonsuit the plaintiff on the contributory negligence issue: Keller v. New York Cent. R. R., 24 How. Prac. 172 (N.Y. 1861); Ernst v. Hudson River R. R., 35 N.Y.

unreasonable speed was often coupled with failure to give warning and other manifestations of general indifference.[66]

Early in the history of English railway development Parliament recognized the dangers attendant upon grade crossings.

9 (1866); Beisiegel v. New York Cent. R. R., 34 N.Y. 622 (1866); Cook v. New York Cent. R. R., 3 Keyes 476 (N.Y. 1867); Costello v. Syracuse, Binghamton & N.Y. Ry., 65 Barb. 92 (N.Y. 1873) Keese v. New York, New Haven & Hartford R. R., 67 Barb. 205 (N.Y. 1875); Fallon v. Central Park, N. & E. R. R. R., 64 N.Y. 13 (1876); Massoth v. Delaware & Hudson Canal Co., 64 N.Y. 524 (1876) McGovern v. New York Cent. & Hudson River R. R., 67 N.Y. 417 (1876); Leonard v. New York Cent. & Hudson River R. R., 42 N.Y. Super. 225 (1877); Casey v. New York Cent. & Hudson River R. R., 78 N.Y. 518 (1879); Powell v. New York Cent. & Hudson River R. R., 22 Hun. 56 (N.Y. 1880); Wasmer v. Delaware, Lackawanna & Western Ry., 80 N.Y. 212 (1880); Byrne v. New York Cent. & Hudson River R. R., 83 N.Y. 620 (1881); Northrup v. New York, Ontario & Western Ry., 37 Hun. 295 (N.Y. 1885); Greany v. Long Island R. R., 101 N.Y. 419, 5 N.E. 425 (1886); Scott v. Pennsylvania Ry., 9 N.Y.S. 189 (1890), 130 N.Y. 679, 29 N.E. 289 (1891); Richardson v. New York Cent. & Hudson River R. R., 15 N.Y.S. 868 (1891), *affirmed* 133 N.Y. 563, 30 N.E. 1148 (1892); Doyle v. Pennsylvania & N. Y. Canal & Ry., 139 N.Y. 637, 34 N.E. 1063 (1893); De Loge v. New York Cent. & Hudson River R. R., 36 N.Y.S. 697 (1895); Waldele v. New York Cent. & Hudson River R. R., 38 N.Y.S. 1009 (1896).

[66] In the following cases arising from accidents at congested crossings, the contributory negligence of the plaintiff was held properly for the consideration of the jury, with the resulting plaintiff verdict. In most, but not all, instances the defendant was also charged with unreasonable speed or failure to give the crossing signal: Brown v. New York Cent. R. R., 32 N.Y. 597 (1865) (flying switch); Green v. Erie Ry., 11 Hun. 333 (N.Y. 1877) (cars released on their own momentum); O'Bierne v. New York Cent. & Hudson River R. R., 56 N.Y.S. 236 (1899) (same); McGrath v. Hudson River R. R., 32 Barb. 144 (N.Y. 1860) (brakeman not at post; confusing arrangement of track); O'Mara v. Hudson River R. R., 38 N.Y. 445 (1868) (train in charge of fireman); Dickens v. New York Cent. R. R., 1 Keyes 23 (N.Y. 1864) (confusion due to failure to call station); Costello v. Syracuse, Binghamton & N.Y. Ry., 65 Barb. 92 (N.Y. 1873) (defective crossing caused child to fall in path of train); Oldenburg v. New York Cent. & Hudson River R. R., 9 N.Y.S. 419 (1890), *affirmed* 124 N.Y. 414, 26 N.E. 1021 (1891) (defective crossing caused plaintiff to look downward); Maginnis v. New York Cent. & Hudson River R. R., 52 N.Y. 215 (1873) (sudden acceleration of unlighted train); Berkery v. Erie R. R., 67 N.Y.S. 189 (1900), *affirmed* without opinion 172 N.Y. 636, 65 N.E. 1113 (1902) (sudden reversal of train); Chadbourne v. Delaware, Lackawanna & Western R. R., 6 Daly 215 (N.Y. 1875) (sudden starting of train); Casey v. New York Cent. & Hudson River R. R., 78 N.Y. 518 (1879) (no view for operator of train); Palmer v. New York Cent. & Hudson River R. R., 112 N.Y. 234, 19 N.E. 678 (1889) (unusual design of locomotive cab impaired vision of operator); Smedis v. Brooklyn & Rockaway Beach R. R., 88 N.Y. 13 (1882) (train traveling at night without headlights); Doyle v. Pennsylvania & N. Y. Canal & Ry., 139 N.Y. 637, 34 N.E. 1063 (1893) (deceptive layout of track); Woodworth v. New York Cent. & Hudson River R. R., 66 N.Y.S. 1072 (1900), *affirmed* 170 N.Y. 589, 63 N.E. 1123 (1902) (same); Judson v. Central & Vermont R. R., 158 N.Y. 597, 53 N.E. 514 (1899) (same); St. John v. New York Cent. & Hudson River R. R., 165 N.Y. 241, 59 N.E. 3 (1901) (lumber protruding from car struck plaintiff); Flanagan v. New York & Hudson River R. R., 75 N.Y.S. 225 (1902), *affirmed* 173 N.Y. 631, 66 N.E. 1108 (1903) (train operator knew that electric crossing signal upon which public depended had ceased to operate, yet failed to give crossing signal).

The Railway Clauses Consolidation Act of 1845[67] required the erection of overpasses or underpasses at all public crossings at the railroad's expense, except that on permission of local authorities crossings at grade were permissible if gates were erected and maintained. Doubtless this practice was acceptable and desirable in a settled insular community where distances were short and roads were both well established and heavily trafficked. In sprawling America, however, with its loose network of shifting trails and sparsely travelled roads, where the need for railway expansion was ever urgent, such a requirement was not likely to be favored. The first New York crossing act in 1853[68] made no mention of such protection. The first statutory requirement of this nature was imposed as late as 1884.[69] Even this act failed to supply indiscriminate coverage. It provided only for the establishment of watchmen at designated crossings upon the demand of local authorities.

The New York courts regarded the matter of such safeguards as being exclusively within the province of the legislature, and they refused to allow the jury to determine whether the dictates of reasonable care demanded the erection of gates or the establishment of a watchman.[70] Later, however, as the hazards increased and certain crossings became notoriously dangerous, they showed signs of retreating from this position.[71]

If the railroad, acting either on its own motion or in obedience to statute, erected a gate or established a watchman, its subsequent dereliction in maintaining the warning was dealt with sternly by the courts. In such instances the alleged carelessness of the victim was usually regarded lightly, and the case nearly always reached the jury.[72] The placing of the

---

[67] 8 & 9 Vict. c. 20.
[68] N.Y. Laws (1853) c. 62.
[69] N.Y. Laws (1884) c. 439, §3.
[70] Weber v. New York Cent. & Hudson River R. R., 58 N.Y. 451, 459 (1874), with which compare Grippen v. New York Cent. R. R., 40 N.Y. 34 (1869).
[71] "A railroad company is not bound and owes no duty so to station a flagman, and negligence cannot be predicated on the omission. The fact may be proven as one of the circumstances under which the train was moved, and by which the degree of care requisite in its handling and running may be affected; so that the question never is whether there should have been a flagman, or one ought to have been stationed at the crossing, but whether, in view of his presence or absence, the train was moved with prudence or negligence." Houghkirk v. Delaware & Hudson Canal Co., 92 N.Y. 219, 227 (1883).
[72] Ernst v. Hudson River R. R., 35 N.Y. 9 (1866); Kissenger v. New York & Harlem R. R., 56 N.Y. 538 (1874); McGovern v. New York Cent. & Hudson River R. R., 67 N.Y. 417 (1876); Dolan v. Delaware & Hudson Canal Co., 71 N.Y. 285 (1877); Leonard v. New York Cent. & Hudson River R. R., 42 N.Y. Super. 225 (1877); Casey v. New York Cent. & Hudson River R. R., 78 N.Y. 518 (1879); Glushing v.

watchman or the erecting of the gate amounted to a recognition of a special peril at a particular place.  Such precautions, unlike the sounding of the statutory signal, were likely to be immediately arresting and effective even with only a modicum of cooperation on the part of the public.  Added to this of course was the deceptive condition created when the warning upon which the victim had learned to depend was suddenly removed without his knowledge.

The street railways, particularly those of New York City, furnished their quota of personal injury cases; but the tide of litigation from this source was late in reaching full surge, and the chief developments came during the 1880's.  This was probably due to the fact that horses supplied the motive power in most instances.  Substantial congestion and the increasing demand for more speed did not create a highly hazardous situation until comparatively late in the century.

The street railway cases were more difficult to administer than the crossing situations.  Time reactions and emergency adjustments were typical of these accidents.  The dilemma of the operators was a difficult one.  They were acutely aware of the pressure of the public demand for faster and yet faster service.  Nevertheless they were obliged to proceed down crowded thoroughfares where pedestrians and other travellers had as much right as they.  Cooperation by all parties concerned was essential if accidents were to be avoided.  Obviously a substantial latitude for judgment was required by the courts and the contributory negligence of the victim figured prominently in the decisions in order to furnish the flexibility needed.

The situation usually turned upon the inquiry as to whether or not the victim had interjected himself upon the track so suddenly that it was impossible for the driver to bring his car to a halt from a permissible speed in time to avoid mishap.

Sharp, 96 N.Y. 676 (1884); Lindeman v. New York Cent. & Hudson River R. R., 42 Hun. 306 (N.Y. 1886); Fitzgerald v. Long Island R. R., 10 N.Y. St. 433 (1887); Palmer v. New York Cent. & Hudson River R. R., 112 N.Y. 234, 19 N.E. 678 (1889); Oldenburg v. New York Cent. & Hudson River R. R., 9 N.Y.S. 419 (1890); Kane v. New York, New Haven & Hartford R. R., 9 N.Y.S. 879 (1890); Richardson v. New York Cent. & Hudson River R. R., 15 N.Y.S. 868 (1891); Bond v. New York Cent. & Hudson River R. R., 23 N.Y.S. 450 (1893); Waldele v. New York Cent. & Hudson River R. R., 38 N.Y.S. 1009 (1896).
    Apparently *contra*:  Warner v. New York Cent. R. R., 44 N.Y. 465 (1871); Woodard v. New York, Lake Erie & Western R. R., 106 N.Y. 369, 13 N.E. 424 (1887); Tucker v. New York Cent. & Hudson River R. R., 124 N.Y. 308, 26 N.E. 916 (1891).

Hence the speed[73] of the vehicle and the attentiveness of the operator figured prominently in each case. Both factors found convenient expression through the rulings on the plaintiff's carelessness.

> ". . . but they have no right to drive immoderately, and it is in the highest degree dangerous for them to do so. Still, if they offend in that respect and the driver of a common carriage will negligently or wilfully place himself or remain in their path he has no right to claim damages. It is not, however, unreasonable for the private traveler to assume that the railroad car will be driven moderately and prudently. He can calculate distances and the time required to effect his own change of position, in order to prevent injury in such cases. But if he encounter a car driven furiously through a crowded street, and makes a mistake as to time attempting to get out of the way, culpable negligence is not necessarily to be imputed to him."[74]

Since the street railways merely enjoyed a franchise to share the public highway and could not demand a landowner's immunity, curt phrases that enjoined the public to watch out or stay off the tracks could not be used appropriately by the courts. Due to the fact that these cases did not lend themselves to stereotyped treatment plus the fact that the driver of the streetcar had a better control than the train operator and was more frequently called upon to exercise it, directed verdicts on the issues of contributory negligence were perhaps less frequent here than in the crossing cases. Where inattention,[75] excessive speed,[76] or defective brakes[77] contributed materially to the accident the jury's verdict was usually accepted by the court.

---

[73] Streetcar speeds in New York City as late as 1903, after the adoption of electric power, were very slow. The maximum did not exceed 11.75 miles per hour, and the average was around 7 miles per hour. Passenger Transportation Service in the City of New York, A Report to the Merchants' Association of New York by its Committee on Engineering and Sanitation (1903) 14.

[74] Hagan v. Eighth Ave. R. R., 15 N.Y. 380, 383 (1857).

[75] Mentz v. Second Ave. R. R., 3 Abb. App. Dec. 274 (N.Y. 1869); Fenton v. Second Ave. R. R., 9 N.Y.S. 162 (1890); Freidman v. Drydock, East Broadway and Battery R. R., 110 N.Y. 676, 18 N.Y. St. 1029 (1888); O'Toole v. Central Park, North River and East River R. R., 12 N.Y.S. 347 (1890); Kerr v. Atlantic Ave. R. R. of Brooklyn, 30 N.Y.S. 1070 (1894).

[76] Hagan v. Eighth Ave. R. R., 15 N.Y. 380 (1857); Aaron v. Second Ave. R. R., 2 Daly 127 (N.Y. 1867); Wells v. Brooklyn City R. R., 12 N.Y.S. 67 (1890); Huerzeler v. Central Cross Town R. R., 20 N.Y.S. 676 (1892); Young v. Atlantic Ave. R. R., 31 N.Y.S. 441 (1894); Arnesen v. Brooklyn City R. R., 29 N.Y.S. 748 (1894). R. R., 29 N.Y.S. 748 (1894).

[77] Aaron v. Second Ave. R. R., *supra* note 76. Hand brakes, which permitted of poor control or threatened injury to passengers by sudden

The pat phrases concerning the plaintiff's fault were often reshaped to favor the victim's situation and thus invite a fuller jury participation in the controversies. The arbitrary duty to look both ways before crossing, which had been used so effectively to bar recovery in the railroad cases, became merely an obligation to use reasonable care, which, in turn, was to be determined by the facts of the particular case.[78]  The absolute duty to get off the tracks in the face of the oncoming steam train was softened into an obligation to "fairly and in a reasonable manner respect the paramount right of a street railway."[79]

In most, but not all, of the cases in which the court held the plaintiff guilty of contributory negligence as a matter of law it will be found that the evidence of the defendant's carelessness was meager.  Usually the victim's conduct had produced a situation with which the defendant could not reasonably be expected to cope.[80]

### The Last Clear Chance

THE rule of the last clear chance was slow in achieving recognition by the New York courts.  The early decisions made no reference to it as a distinct reason for ignoring the plaintiff's negligence.[81]  There were a few intimations that some such notion might apply, but these are to be found chiefly in cases involving accidents at urban crossings or arising out of the operation of street railways.  In the early railroad cross-

---

uneven stopping, were still in use in New York City until after 1903. Passenger Transportation Service in the City of New York, *op. cit. supra* note 73, at 39.

[78] "It is true that a different rule prevails in regard to crossing steam railroads, where the danger is greater; but it has never been held that it is necessary to look both up and down before crossing an ordinary street where there was no steam railway."  Pyne v. Broadway and Seventh Ave R. R., 19 N.Y.S. 217, 219 (1892).

[79] Fleckenstein v. Drydock, East Broadway and Battery R. R., 105 N.Y. 655, 656, 11 N.E. 951, 952 (1892).

[80] Suydam v. Grand Street and New Town R. R., 41 Barb. 375 (N.Y. 1864) ; Brown v. Broadway and Seventh Ave. R. R., 50 N.Y. Super. 106 (1884) ; Motel v. Sixth Ave. R. R., 2 How. Prac. (N.S.) 30 (N.Y. 1885) ; Donnelly v. Brooklyn City R. R., 109 N.Y. 16, 15 N.E. 733 (1888) ; Cowan v. Third Ave. R. R., 1 N.Y.S. 612 (1888) ; Enk v. Brooklyn City R. R., 19 N.Y.S. 130 (1892) ; Winter v. Crosstown Street Ry. of Buffalo, 28 N.Y.S. 695 (1894) ; Roth v. Metropolitan Street Ry., 34 N.Y.S. 232 (1895) ; Jager v. Coney Island & Brooklyn Ry., 84 Hun. 307, 32 N.Y.S. 304 (1895).

But with these compare Scott v. Third Ave. R. R., 16 N.Y.S. 350 (1891) ; Winch v. Third Ave. R. R., 33 N.Y.S. 615 (1895).  In these last cases nonsuit was entered because of plaintiff's fault, although the defendant's conduct seemed clearly negligent.

[81] Unless Owen v. Hudson River R. R., 20 N.Y. Super. 329 (1860) could be regarded as such a decision.

ing cases there was in fact seldom a last chance situation for the simple reason that there were no adequate means whereby the defendant could seize any such chance when it was presented. The typical picture of the last clear chance involves a braking system which can be brought into effective play at the final moment, and this we know was impossible at that time.

Even in situations where the last clear chance doctrine might have been availed of there was little need for its use in assisting the plaintiff so long as the whole controversy could conveniently be passed along to the jury through other means. Thus, in cases which today would be moderated through last chance rules the New York courts of the last century found it easier to minimize the plaintiff's negligence and refuse to enter a nonsuit.[82]   The jury could be depended upon to do the rest. Despite the indirect nature of this kind of attack on the problem and irrespective of how unacceptable it may be according to modern legal theory, it nevertheless offers the marked advantage of permitting a freehanded determination of the merits of each individual case without exposing the mechanics of decision.   Through the use of this procedure, excessive speed or inadequate brakes, which preclude the defendant from availing itself of what would otherwise be a last chance, can be fairly considered without the embarrassment of running afoul of doctrinal limitations.[83]   Later developments of formal

---

[82] In the following cases the situation might be fairly regarded as lending itself to last clear chance treatment under present procedures. The courts regarded the plaintiff's negligence in each instance as a matter for jury determination: Bernhart v. Rensselaer & Saratoga R. R., 18 How. Prac. 427 (N.Y. 1859) ; Mentz v. Second Ave. R. R., 3 Abb. App. Dec. 274 (1869) ; Costello v. Syracuse, Binghamton & N.Y. Ry., 65 Barb. 92 (N.Y. 1873) ; Thurber v. Harlem Bridge, Morrisania & Fordham R. R., 60 N.Y. 326 (1875) ; Fallon v. Central Park, N. & E.R. R. R., 64 N.Y. 13 (1876) ; Friedman v. Drydock, East Broadway and Battery R. R., 3 N.Y. St. 557 (1886) ; McClain v. Brooklyn City R. R., 116 N.Y. 459, 22 N.E. 1062 (1889) ; Wells v. Brooklyn City R. R., 12 N.Y.S. 67 (1890) ; Fenton v. Second Ave. R. R., 9 N.Y.S. 162 (1890) ; Swift v. Staten Island Rapid Transit R. R., 123 N.Y. 645, 25 N.E. 378 (1890) ; Kerr v. Atlantic Ave. R. R., of Brooklyn, 30 N.Y.S. 1070 (1894) ; Young v. Atlantic Ave. R. R., 31 N.Y.S. 441 (1894).
The following cases fairly presented the issue, but it is clear that the court was not convinced that the chance was available to the defendant.   A nonsuit was granted in each instance on the ground off the plaintiff's contributory negligence: Owen v. Hudson River R. R., 20 N.Y. Super. 329 (1860) ; Chrystal v. Troy & Boston R. R., 105 N.Y. 164, 11 N.E. 380 (1887), 124 N.Y. 519, 26 N.E. 1103 (1891) ; Fenton v. Second Ave. R. R., 126 N.Y. 625, 26 N.E. 967 (1891).
[83] Young v. Atlantic Ave. R. R., 31 N.Y.S. 441 (1894) (excessive speed and inadequate brakes on electric street railway; the negligence of the plaintiff could hardly be open to serious dispute) ; Costello v. Syracuse, Binghamton & N. Y. Ry., 65 Barb. 92 (N.Y. 1873). It is interesting to contrast the academic disputes that result from an attempt by the court to consider similar factors under last clear chance rules.   See Bohlen, The Rule in British Columbia Railroad Company v. Loach

last chance rules can scarcely be said to have added any appreciable certainty in the determination of such matters. Even after a recognition of the last clear chance doctrine by the General Term of the Supreme Court in 1875[84] it was seldom used by any of the courts of record until after the close of the century.[85] They found it easier to continue the attack from ambush.

### Cross Currents

IT has been previously pointed out that much of our doctrinal treatment of contributory negligence is open to the objection of over-simplification.[86] Plaintiff fault as such is at best only a partial explanation as to why these contributory negligence cases turn out as they do. But the antithesis is equally extreme and unacceptable. The bare proposition that careless plaintiffs cannot recover for the sole reason that they are unworthy of legal protection has become too deeply impressed into the consciousness of judges and lawyers to be disregarded lightly. This notion is sincerely subscribed to by courts everywhere. It is only when a judge attempts to translate it into practice that it becomes seriously intervolved with other considerations, which in turn are likely to dominate the deliberations on the controversy.

The idea of plaintiff fault has little independent existence outside the facts of some concrete dispute. It acquires its meaning only from the full context of the picture to which it is applied. Nevertheless, like all legal doctrines, contributory negligence is discussed by judges and writers in bulk, and lump sum evaluations of it are always being made. These take the form of doctrinal statements such as we have referred to. When a proposition has been thus translated into a generality, it tends to develop an integrity all its own, and a judge will generally refuse any use of the proposition that runs directly contrary to its doctrinal characteristics as he has learned to understand them from cases and texts. There is a limit as to how far practical utility and theory can be reconciled in the mind of the trier. This conflict is well presented in those cases where the victim was a child of tender years.

(1917) 66 U. of Pa. L. Rev. 73 and Prosser, A Handbook of the Law of Torts (1941) 415.

[84] Kenyon v. New York Cent. & Hudson River R. R., 5 Hun. 479 (N.Y. 1875).

[85] Only occasional reference is found. See Chrystal v. Troy & Boston R. R., 105 N.Y. 164, 11 N.E. 380 (1887), 124 N.Y. 519, 26 N.E. 1103 (1891); Huerzeler v. Central Cross-town R. R., 20 N.Y.S. 676 (1892).

[86] P. 22 of ms., *supra.*

### The Contributory Negligence of Infants and Children

W E know that an adult who is struck at an open rural crossing by a train that failed to give the crossing signal has a poor chance of recovery. The reason is that the protection of the rule requiring signals does not extend to those whose conduct does not afford sufficient indicia that the scheme of cooperation would have worked if the railroad had done its part.[87] This idea can be expressed in several ways, and plaintiff fault has been chosen by the courts as the vehicle simply because it is more fluent, more expressive, and affords a much better means of jury control than any competing doctrine. But were it not for these advantages of contributory negligence, cause in fact or the duty issue might as well have been selected.

If duty or cause had met the court's favor for the purpose, there would be no difficulty in treating adults and children alike in the crossing cases; but the selection of plaintiff's fault as the vehicle of articulation interposes serious doctrinal barriers where the plaintiff is a child. Fault has become the touchstone, and fault is a thing that the child is incapable of. Thus doctrinal integrity and practical utility are likely to come at loggerheads.

Whenever possible, reconciliation will be effected in the trier's mind. This will nearly always happen if some halfway plausible means of mediation can be made available through fiction or otherwise. We know, for example, that the contributory negligence of a deceased person remains an issue in any action brought by his surviving dependents despite their complete freedom from personal fault.[88] This is accomplished by the fiction of treating the cause as a surviving claim merely. It is easy to conclude that the dependents receive only those rights the victim would have had if had survived; thus reconciliation is accomplished.

In cases involving injury to infants at railroad crossings the court had no difficulty early in its experience in retaining the practical benefits of the contributory negligence doctrine as a jury control device. In the case of *Hartfield v. Roper*[89] it adopted the amazingly simple trick of *imputing* the parents' negligence to the infant. This satisfied the court completely in preserving the integrity of the contributory negligence doctrine, particularly since it was known that the careless parents

---

[87] Pp. 17-19 ms., *supra*.
[88] Wettach, Wrongful Death and Contributory Negligence (1938) 16 N.C. L. Rev. 211.
[89] 21 Wend. 615 (1839).

would receive the benefits of any judgment secured. This rule persisted, despite the protests of critics, until 1935 when it was abrogated by statute[90] upon the recommendation of the New York Law Revision Commission.[91]

Of course negligence of the parents might exist even though the conduct of the infant had been such as to recommend recovery, or even though the negligence of the defendant was of a sufficiently severe character that recovery should be allowed. In such an instance the rule of *Hartfield v. Roper* would have defeated its own purpose. But again, the ingenuity of the court was equal to the occasion. In several instances it simply sent the issue of the parent's negligence to the jury.[92] But a more direct approach was made available. The court devised a corallary rule that the negligence of the parent would not be imputed where the conduct of the infant was such that it met the standard of care for an adult, nor where the child's conduct was not a substantial factor in bringing about the accident.[93] This was justified in the jargon of proximate cause. Thus an adult was placed in the shoes of the child, the judge was enabled to proceed just as in any other crossing case and still sleep with a clean doctrinal conscience that night.

For older children the court had means for reconciliation. Reasonable care was abandoned as the test and the care of average children of the same age and experience was substituted. This, it is believed, made very little difference in the outcome of the cases. Such shades of expression are important principally in the language to be used in the giving of instructions, which is not a matter of great moment unless an appellate court decides that it wants to make something of it. Virtually all the accidents in which children were the victims occurred in congested areas, and the verdict for the plaintiff was usually allowed to stand.[94]

---

[90] N.Y. Laws (1935) c. 796.

[91] Report of the New York Law Revision Commission (1935) 47.

[92] Fallon v. Central Park N. & E.R. R. R., 64 N.Y. 13 (1876) (Plaintiff was child of five. Defendant was charged with driving at high speed and giving no attention to danger. The contributory negligence of the parent was held proper for jury.); Aaron v. Second Ave. R. R., 2 Daly 127 (N.Y. 1867) (Plaintiff was an infant. Defendant was charged with excessive speed and inattention. The court held that the issue of the negligence of his sister who was attending him was properly a matter for the jury's consideration.)

[93] Aaron v. Second Ave. R. R., 2 Daly 127 (N.Y. 1867); Ihl v. Forty-Second Street & Grand Street Ferry R. R., 47 N.Y. 317 (1872); Huerzeler v. Central Cross Town R. R., 20 N.Y.S. 676 (1892).

[94] In the following cases the child-plaintiffs were allowed recovery. In each instance their alleged contributory negligence was held proper for the jury: Reynolds v. New York Cent. & Hudson River R. R.,

There is no moral from the foregoing pages to impress upon the reader.   Courts wanted to control juries during the last century, they want to control them today, and they will probably want to continue to control them in the future.   If we take away contributory negligence from the judges, they will find some other way.   It's hard to beat judicial ingenuity.

2 Thomp. & Cook 644 (N.Y. 1874) (boy of 12; crossing near schoolhouse.   Defendants failed to give statutory signals.); Thurber v. Harlem Bridge, Morrisania & Fordham R. R., 60 N.Y. 326 (1875) (boy of nine tried to run across in face of streetcar; defendant charged with high speed and inattention); Haycroft v. Lake Shore & Michigan So. Ry., 2 Hun. 489 (1874), 64 N.Y. 636 (1876) (girl of sixteen; congested crossing); Byrne v. New York Cent. & Hudson River R. R., 83 N.Y. 620 (1881) (girl of ten; locomotive backing at high speed in congested area); Mentz v. Second Ave. R. R., 3 Abb. App. Dec. 274 (1869) (boy of seven; defendant guilty of inattention); Young v. Atlantic Ave. R. R., 31 N.Y.S. 441 (1894) (boy of seven; defendant charged with driving at high speed in congested area).   See also Kupchinsky v. Vacuum Oil Co., 263 N.Y. 128, 188 N.E. 278 (1933).

In the following cases the defendant was charged with inattention, but in each instance the court found that there was no opportunity to avoid the accident.   In each case the child-plaintiff was held guilty of contributory negligence as a matter of law: Motel v. Sixth Ave. R. R., 2 How. Prac. (N.S.) 30 (N.Y. 1885) (boy of eight); Fenton v. Second Ave. R. R., 126 N.Y. 625, 26 N.E. 967 (1891) (boy of nine).

# 10

# SOCIAL CHANGE AND THE LAW OF INDUSTRIAL ACCIDENTS

## LAWRENCE M. FRIEDMAN & JACK LADINSKY

# SOCIAL CHANGE AND THE LAW OF INDUSTRIAL ACCIDENTS

## LAWRENCE M. FRIEDMAN* AND JACK LADINSKY**

Sociologists recognize, in a general way, the essential role of legal institutions in the social order.[1] They concede, as well, the responsiveness of law to social change and have made important explorations of the interrelations involved.[2] Nevertheless, the role law plays in initiating—or reflecting—social change has never been fully explicated, either in theory or through research. The evolution of American industrial accident law from tort principles to compensation systems is an appropriate subject for a case-study on this subject. It is a topic that has been carefully treated by legal scholars,[3] and it is also recognized by sociologists to be a significant instance of social change.[4] This essay, using concepts drawn from both legal and sociological disciplines, aims at clarifying the concept of social change and illustrating its relationship to change in the law.

## I. THE CONCEPT OF SOCIAL CHANGE

Social change has been defined as "any nonrepetitive alteration in the established modes of behavior in . . . society."[5] Social change is change in the way people relate to each other, not change in values or in technology. Major alterations in values or technology will, of course, almost invariably be followed by changes in social relations—but they are not in themselves social change. Thus, although the change from tort law to workmen's compensation presupposed a high level of technology and certain attitudes toward the life and health of factory workers, it was not in itself a change in values or technology but in the patterning of behavior.

Social change may be revolutionary, but it normally comes about in a more-or-less orderly manner, out of the conscious and unconscious attempts of

* Professor of Law, University of Wisconsin. A.B., 1948, J.D., 1951, M.LL., University of Chicago, 1953.
** Assistant Professor of Sociology, University of Wisconsin. B.A., 1954, M.A., University of Missouri, 1957; Ph. D., University of Michigan, 1962.
The authors wish to acknowledge the support of the Russell Sage Foundation's Law and Sociology Program at the University of Wisconsin. They also wish to express their gratitude to Professor J. Willard Hurst, who read the manuscript and made many valuable suggestions.
   1. *See, e.g.,* T. PARSONS, STRUCTURE AND PROCESS IN MODERN SOCIETY 190-92 (1960).
   2. *See, e.g.,* J. WILLARD HURST, LAW AND SOCIAL PROCESS IN UNITED STATES HISTORY (1960).
   3. *See generally* C. AUERBACH, L. GARRISON, W. HURST & S. MERMIN, THE LEGAL PROCESS (1961) [hereinafter cited as AUERBACH].
   4. *See, e.g.,* W. OGBURN, SOCIAL CHANGE WITH RESPECT TO CULTURE AND ORIGINAL NATURE 213-36 (Viking ed. 1950).
   5. R. FREEDMAN, A. HAWLEY, W. LANDECKER & H. MINER, PRINCIPLES OF SOCIOLOGY 312 (1st ed. 1952) [hereinafter cited as FREEDMAN].

## LAW AND SOCIAL CHANGE                    51

people to solve social problems through collective action. It is purposive and rational; although social actions have unanticipated consequences and often arise out of unconscious motivations, nonetheless social change at the conscious level involves definition of a state of affairs as a "problem" and an attempt to solve that problem by the rational use of effective means. The *problem* defined collectively in this instance was the number of injuries caused to workmen by trains, mine hazards, and factory machinery. It is clear that the number of accidents increased over the course of the century, but it is not self-evident that this objective fact necessarily gave rise to a correspondent subjective sense of a problem that had to be solved in a particular way. To understand the process of social change, one must know how and why that subjective sense evolved. This requires knowledge of how and why various segments of society perceived situations—whether they identified and defined a set of facts or a state of affairs as raising or not raising problems.[6] It also requires an understanding of what were considered appropriate and rational means for solving that problem. The perspective of a particular period, in turn, sets limits to the way a people collectively defines problems and the means available for their solution.[7]

This essay deals with behavior at the societal level. At that level, social change necessarily means changes in powers, duties, and rights; it will normally be reflected both in custom and law, in formal authority relations and informal ones. In mature societies, law will be an important indicator of social change; it is institutional cause and institutional effect at the same time, and a part of the broader pattern of collective perceptions and behavior in the resolution of social problems. The essay will therefore also deal with the way in which legal systems respond to their society—the social impact on law, modified and monitored by the institutional habits of the legal system.

In legal terms, this is the story of the rise and fall of a *rule*, the fellow-servant rule, as the legal system's operating mechanism for allocating (or refusing to allocate) compensation for industrial injuries. It is an exploration of how the rule originated, how it changed, how and when it was overthrown.

## II. DEVELOPMENT OF THE LAW OF INDUSTRIAL ACCIDENTS

### A. *Background of the Fellow-Servant Rule*

At the dawn of the industrial revolution, the common law of torts afforded a remedy, as it still does, for those who had suffered injuries at the hands of others. If a man injured another by direct action—by striking him, or slander-

---

6. A "collective problem solving" approach to the study of social change is set forth in detail by Guy E. Swanson, in FREEDMAN 554-621.

7. Thus, for example, the problem of sickness and feebleness of the aged can be "solved" by euthanasia, prayer, medicare, socialized medicine, or left alone—depending on the society.

ing him, or by trespassing on his property—the victim could sue for his
damages. Similarly, the victim of certain kinds of negligent behavior had a
remedy at law. But tort law was not highly developed. Negligence in particular
did not loom large in the reports and it was not prominently discussed in books
of theory or practice.[8] Indeed, no treatise on tort law appeared in America
until Francis Hilliard's in 1859;[9] the first English treatise came out in 1860.[10]
By this time, the field was rapidly developing. A third edition of Hilliard's
book was published in 1866, only seven years after the first edition. The
explosive growth of tort law was directly related to the rapidity of industrial
development. The staple source of tort litigation was and is the impact of
machines—railroad engines, then factory machines, then automobiles—on the
human body. During the industrial revolution, the size of the factory labor
force increased, the use of machinery in the production of goods became more
widespread, and such accidents were inevitably more frequent. In Hilliard's
pioneer treatise, railroads already played a major role in tort litigation—a role
which he ascribed to their "great multiplication and constant activity; their
necessary interference, in the act of construction, with the rights of property . . .
the large number and various offices of their agents and servants; and the
dangers, many of them of an entirely novel character, incident to their mode
of operation. . . ."[11]

In theory, at least, recovery for industrial accidents might have been
assimilated into the existing system of tort law. The fundamental principles
were broad and simple. If a factory worker was injured through the negligence
of another person—including his employer—an action for damages would lie.
Although as a practical matter, servants did not usually sue their master nor
workers their employers, in principle they had the right to do so.

In principle, too, a worker might have had an action against his employer
for any injury caused by the negligence of any other employee. The doctrine
of *respondeat superior* was familiar and fundamental law. A principal was liable
for the negligent acts of his agent. As Blackstone put it:

---

8. Blackstone's *Commentaries* has virtually no discussion of negligence. In early
19th century America, tort law (and particularly the law of negligence) remained
fairly obscure. Dane's *Abridgment*—an eight-volume compendium of British and American law—has a short, miscellaneous chapter on negligence: cases "which cannot be
brought conveniently under more particular heads." 3 N. DANE, A GENERAL ABRIDGMENT
AND DIGEST OF AMERICAN LAW 31 (1824). These include some commercial and maritime
instances ("If the owner of a ship, in the care of a pilot, through *negligence* and want
of skill, sinks the ship of another, this owner is liable," *id.* at 35); and some cases
of negligence in the practice of a trade or profession ("if a register of deeds neglects to
record a deed as he ought to do, this action lies against him for his negligence," *id.* at
32). Under this latter heading comes one of the very few examples of personal injury—
a doctor's negligent practice of his art. *Id.* at 32. (Another example had to do with
the negligent owner of a dog or other animal, *id.* at 33.) But, in general, personal injury
cases are rare in Dane; and the shadow of the industrial revolution has not yet fallen
on this corner of the law.
9. F. HILLIARD, THE LAW OF TORTS (1st ed. 1859); *see* C. WARREN, HISTORY OF THE
AMERICAN BAR 450 (1911).
10. C. ADDISON, WRONGS AND THEIR REMEDIES (1st ed. 1860).
11. 2 F. HILLIARD, THE LAW OF TORTS 339 (3d ed. 1866).

he who does a thing by the agency of another, does it himself . . . .
If an innkeeper's servants rob his guests, the master is bound to restitution. . . . So likewise if the drawer at a tavern sells a man bad wine,
whereby his health is injured, he may bring an action against the
master.[12]

Conceivably, then, one member of an industrial work force might sue his
employer for injuries caused by the negligence of a fellow worker. A definitive
body of doctrine was slow to develop, however. When it did, it rejected the
broad principle of *respondeat superior* and took instead the form of the so-called
fellow-servant rule. Under this rule, a servant (employee) could not sue his
master (employer) for injuries caused by the negligence of another employee.
The consequences of this doctrine were far reaching. An employee retained the
right to sue the employer for injuries, provided they were caused by the
employer's personal misconduct. But the factory system and corporate ownership of industry made this right virtually meaningless. The factory owner was
likely to be a "soulless" legal entity; even if the owner was an individual
entrepreneur, he was unlikely to concern himself physically with factory operations. In work accidents, then, legal fault would be ascribed to fellow employees, if anyone. But fellow employees were men without wealth or insurance. The fellow-servant rule was an instrument capable of relieving employers
from almost all the legal consequences of industrial injuries. Moreover, the
doctrine left an injured worker without any effective recourse but an empty
action against his co-worker.

When labor developed a collective voice, it was bound to decry the rule
as infamous,[13] as a deliberate instrument of oppression—a sign that law served
the interests of the rich and propertied, and denied the legitimate claims of the
poor and the weak. The rule charged the "blood of the workingman" not to
the state, the employer, or the consumer, but to the working man himself.[14]
Conventionally, then, the fellow-servant rule is explained as a deliberate or
half-deliberate rejection of a well-settled principle of law in order to encourage
enterprise by forcing workmen to bear the costs of industrial injury. And the
overthrow of the rule is taken as a sign of a conquest by progressive forces.

It is neither possible nor desirable to avoid passing judgment on human
behavior; but one's understanding of social processes can sometimes be hindered by premature moral assessments. The history of industrial accident law

---

12. 1 W. BLACKSTONE, COMMENTARIES *429-30.
13. And Labor was not alone. "Lord Abinger planted it, Baron Alderson watered
it, and the devil gave it increase," said the Secretary for Ireland in a famous remark
to the House of Commons in 1897. *Quoted in* W. DODD, ADMINISTRATION OF WORKMEN'S
COMPENSATION 5 n.7 (1936). Lord Abinger wrote the decision in Priestley v. Fowler,
150 Eng. R. 1030 (Ex. 1837); Baron Alderson in Hutchinson v. York, N. & B. Ry.,
155 Eng. R. 150 (Ex. 1850).
14. The slogan "The cost of the product should bear the blood of the working man"
has been attributed to Lloyd George; it expresses the theory that the price of the
commodity should include all costs, including that of industrial accidents. *See*
W. PROSSER, TORTS 554-55 & n.3 (3d ed. 1964).

is much too complicated to be viewed as merely a struggle of capital against labor, with law as a handmaid of the rich, or as a struggle of good against evil. From the standpoint of social change, good and evil are social labels based on *perceptions* of conditions, not terms referring to conditions in themselves. Social change comes about when people decide that a situation is evil and must be altered, even if they were satisfied or unaware of the problem before. In order, then, to understand the legal reaction to the problem of industrial accidents, one must understand how the problem was perceived within the legal system and by that portion of society whose views influenced the law.

## B. *Birth and Acceptance of the Rule*

The origin of the fellow-servant rule is usually ascribed to Lord Abinger's opinion in *Priestley v. Fowler*,[15] decided in 1837. Yet the case on its facts did not pose the question of the industrial accident, as later generations would understand it; rather, it concerned the employment relationships of tradesmen. The defendant, a butcher, instructed the plaintiff, his servant, to deliver goods which had been loaded on a van by another employee. The van, which had been overloaded, broke down, and plaintiff fractured his thigh in the accident. Lord Abinger, in his rather diffuse and unperceptive opinion, reached his holding that the servant had no cause of action by arguing from analogies drawn neither from industry nor from trade:

> If the master be liable to the servant in this action, the principle of that liability will . . . carry us to an alarming extent . . . . The footman . . . may have an action against his master for a defect in the carriage owing to the negligence of the coachmaker. . . . The master . . . would be liable to the servant for the negligence of the chambermaid, for putting him into a damp bed; . . . for the negligence of the cook in not properly cleaning the copper vessels used in the kitchen. . . .[16]

These and similar passages in the opinion suggest that Abinger was worried about the disruptive effects of a master's liability upon his household staff. These considerations were perhaps irrelevant to the case at hand, the facts of which did not deal with the household of a nobleman, great landowner, or rich merchant; *a fortiori* the decision itself did not concern relationships within an industrial establishment. Certainly the opinion made extension of the rule to the factory setting somewhat easier to enunciate and formulate technically. But it did not justify the existence of an industrial fellow-servant rule. The case might have been totally forgotten—or overruled—had not the onrush of the industrial revolution put the question again and again to courts, each time more forcefully. *Priestley v. Fowler* and the doctrine of *respondeat superior* each stood for a broad principle. Whether the one or the other (or neither) would find a place in the law relative to industrial accidents depended

---

15. 150 Eng. R. 1030 (Ex. 1837).
16. *Id.* at 1032.

upon needs felt and expressed by legal institutions in response to societal demands. Had there been no *Priestly v. Fowler*, it would have been necessary —and hardly difficult—to invent one.

In the United States, the leading case on the fellow-servant situation was *Farwell v. Boston & Worcester Railroad Corp.*,[17] decided by Massachusetts' highest court in 1842. The case arose out of a true industrial accident in a rapidly developing industrial state. Farwell was an engineer who lost a hand when his train ran off the track due to a switchman's negligence. As Chief Justice Shaw, writing for the court, saw it, the problem of *Farwell* was how best to apportion the risks of railroad accidents. In his view, it was superficial to analyze the problem according to the tort concepts of fault and negligence. His opinion spoke the language of contract, and employed the stern logic of nineteenth century economic thought. Some occupations are more dangerous than others. Other things being equal, a worker will choose the least dangerous occupation available. Hence, to get workers an employer will have to pay an additional wage for dangerous work. The market, therefore, has already made an adjustment in the wage rate to compensate for the possibility of accident, and a cost somewhat similar to an insurance cost has been allocated to the company. As Shaw put it, "he who engages in the employment of another for the performance of specified duties and services, for compensation, takes upon himself the natural and ordinary risks and perils incident to the performance of such services, and *in legal presumption, the compensation is adjusted accordingly.*"[18] The worker, therefore, has assumed the risk of injury— for a price. The "implied contract of employment" between the worker and employer did not require the employer to bear any additional costs of injury (except for those caused by the employer's personal negligence).

In *Priestley v. Fowler* too, counsel had argued in terms of implied contract.[19] But Lord Abinger had not framed his logic accordingly. Shaw did, and his opinion had great influence on subsequent judicial reasoning. The facts of the case were appropriate and timely, and Shaw saw the issue in clear economic terms. His decision helped convert the rules and concepts of the status-bound law of master and servant to the economic needs of the period, as he understood them.[20]

---

17. 45 Mass. (4 Met.) 49 (1842). Murray v. South Carolina R.R., 26 S.C.L. (1 McMul.) 385 (1841), was decided a year earlier and came to the same result. But *Farwell* is the better known case, the one usually cited and quoted. In England, Baron Alderson extended *Priestley* to a railroad accident situation in Hutchinson v. York, N. & B. Ry., 155 Eng. R. 150 (Ex. 1849). The House of Lords, in Barton's Hill Coal Co. v. Reid, 111 Rev. R. 896 (1858), held the rule applicable in Scotland as well as in England. Lord Cranworth cited *Farwell* with great praise as a "very able and elaborate judgment." *Id.* at 906.

18. Farwell v. Boston & W.R.R., 45 Mass. (4 Met.) 49, 57 (1842) (emphasis added).

19. 150 Eng. R. 1030, 1031 (Ex. 1837).

20. The same impulse motivated Timothy Walker, who introduced his discussion of master and servant in his text on American law with these words:

The title of *master and servant*, at the head of a lecture, does not sound very

Shaw's opinion makes extreme assumptions about behavior, justified only by a philosophy of economic individualism.[21] Partly because of this, it has a certain heartlessness of tone. A disabled worker without resources was likely to be pauperized if he had no realistic right to damages. Unless his family could help him, he would have to fall back upon poor relief, the costs of which were borne by the public through taxation. The railroads and other industrial employers paid a share as taxpayers and, in addition, a kind of insurance cost as part of their wage rate—but no more. Additional damages had to be borne by the worker; if he could not bear them, society generally would pay the welfare costs. Thus the opinion expresses a preference for charging the welfare cost of industrial accidents to the public generally, rather than to the particular enterprise involved.

It is not surprising that such a preference was expressed. Shaw's generation placed an extremely high value on economic growth. As Willard Hurst has noted, that generation was thoroughly convinced it was "socially desirable that there be broad opportunity for the release of creative human energy," particularly in the "realm of the economy."[22] The establishment of a functioning railroad net was an essential element in economic growth. Furthermore, Shaw's resolution of the *Farwell* case is cruel only insofar as society makes no other provision for the victims of accidents—that is, if social insurance and public assistance are inadequate, degrading, or unfair. In a society with a just and workable system of state medical insurance and disability pensions, the *Farwell* solution would be neither inhumane nor inappropriate, even today. Indeed, it could be argued that the broader social responsibility is preferable to one which taxes a particular industry for the claims of its workers. Whether the one side or the other is correct, in economic or political terms, is not here relevant.

Of course, from today's viewpoint, the word "inadequate" is too weak a judgment on what passed for public relief in the early nineteenth century.

---

harmoniously to republican ears. . . . But the legal relation of master and servant must exist, to a greater or less extent, wherever civilization furnishes work to be done, and the difference of condition makes some persons employers, and others laborers. In fact, we understand by the relation of master and servant, nothing more or less than that of *employer* and *employed*. It is, therefore, a relation created by contract, express or implied, and might properly be treated under the head of contracts; but custom has placed it among the personal relations, and I shall so treat it.
T. WALKER, INTRODUCTION TO AMERICAN LAW § 114, at 275 (6th ed. 1837).
    21. "[*Farwell* represents] the individualistic tendency of the common law, which took it for granted that an employee was free to contract and was not bound to risk life or limb in any particular employment . . . ." W. DODD, *supra* note 13, at 7. "[T]he leading employers' liability cases, from which the whole subsequent juristic development received its tone and direction, were decided at the very moment when the *laissez faire* movement in economic and political thought reached its culmination." E. DOWNEY, HISTORY OF WORK ACCIDENT INDEMNITY IN IOWA 13 (1912). *See also* F. BOHLEN, STUDIES IN THE LAW OF TORTS 461-65 (1926).
    22. J. WILLARD HURST, LAW AND THE CONDITIONS OF FREEDOM IN THE NINE-TEENTH-CENTURY UNITED STATES 5-6, *passim* (1956).

Social insurance was unknown. Local poor relief was cruel, sporadic, and pinchpenny. Institutions for the helpless were indescribably filthy and heartless. Villages sometimes shunted paupers from place to place, to avoid the burden of paying for them. Moreover, the whole system was shot through with what strikes us today as an inordinate fear of the spread of idleness and a perverse notion that pauperism generally arose out of the moral failings of the poor. The most that can be said is that the system usually made a minimum commitment to keeping the poor alive.[23]

But our condemnation of nineteenth century welfare administration is based on a certain amount of hindsight. Social welfare is looked upon today as a task of government, and government can lay claim to far greater resources to accomplish welfare goals. In Shaw's day, private charity was assigned a higher place in the relief of misery. Probably most people would have agreed then that the disabled and wretched poor ought not to starve. Where private philanthropy failed, local poor relief stepped in. It was the most miserable sort of minimum, but its deficiencies were not apparent to the average middle or upper class citizen who seldom gave the matter a second thought—just as today the inadequacies of mental hospitals and prisons are only vaguely known and rarely given a second thought by most Americans. Poor relief was not *perceived* as a major social problem in the most literal sense. Furthermore, in Shaw's day certain kinds of crises and risks had to be accepted as inevitable, far more than they would be accepted today. High mortality rates from disease threatened all classes of society. Business entrepreneurs ran heavy risks; business failure was common and could be avoided only by great skill and good fortune. The instability of the monetary system threatened an entrepreneur with sudden, unpredictable, and uninsurable ruin. At the onset of the great business panic of 1857, for example, banks failed by the score; currency turned to ashes, and chain reactions of default were set off by distant collapse or defalcation.[24] Hardly any businessman was safe or immune. Furthermore, imprisonment for debt was still a living memory when Shaw wrote; the present national bankruptcy system did not exist, and local insolvency laws were chaotic and unpredictable.[25] Men like Shaw, the bearers of power and influence, might have conceded that the misfortunes of factory workers were real, but insecurity of economic position cursed the lot of all but the very rich. The problem was one of *general* insecurity.

Shaw and his generation placed their hopes of salvation on rapid economic

---

23. *See, e.g.*, D. SCHNEIDER & A. DEUTSCH, THE HISTORY OF PUBLIC WELFARE IN NEW YORK STATE 1609-1866, at 211-30 (1938). For a vivid description of early nineteenth century poor relief administration, see M. Rosenheim, *Vagrancy Concepts in Welfare Law*, 54 CALIF. L. REV. 511, 528-30 (1966).

24. *See* B. HAMMOND, BANKS AND POLITICS IN AMERICA (1957).

25. For a discussion of legal and political aspects of the short-lived national bankruptcy acts before 1898, see C. WARREN, BANKRUPTCY IN UNITED STATES HISTORY (1935).

growth.[26] Perhaps they were anxious to see that the tort system of accident compensation did not add to the problems of new industry. Few people imagined that accidents would become so numerous as to create severe economic and social dislocations. On the contrary, rash extension of certain principles of tort law to industrial accidents might upset social progress by imposing extreme costs on business in its economic infancy. The 1840's and 1850's were a period of massive economic development in New England and the Midwest, a period of "take-off" (perhaps) into self-sustaining economic growth.[27] Textiles, and then iron, spearheaded the industrial revolution; westward expansion and the railroads created new markets. Communities and states made a social contribution to the construction of railroads through cash subsidies, stock subscriptions, and tax exemptions. The courts, using the fellow-servant doctrine and the concepts of assumption of risk and contributory negligence,[28] socialized the accident costs of building the roads. That these solutions represented the collective, if uneasy, consensus of those with authority and responsibility is supported by the fact that every court of the country, with but one transient exception,[29] reached the same conclusion in the years immediately following *Farwell*. Moreover, the fellow-servant rule was not abolished by any legislature in these early years. Although legislative inaction is not a necessary sign of acquiescence, it at least indicates lack of a major feeling of revulsion.

---

26. It is generally assumed that the "considerations of policy" invoked by Shaw in the Farwell case were those in favor of the promotion of railroad and industrial expansion. Charles Warren . . . observed that railroads began to operate only 8 years before the Farwell decision, and quoted an 1883 writer to the effect that the decision was "a species of protective tariff for the encouragement of infant railway industries." The United States Supreme Court has said that the "assumption of risk" doctrine was "a judicially created rule ⸱ . . developed in response to the general impulse of common law courts . . . to insulate the employer as much as possible from bearing the 'human overhead' which is an inevitable part of the cost—to someone—of the doing of industrialized business." "The general purpose behind this development in the common law," the Court continued, "seems to have been to give maximum freedom to expanding industry." Tiller v. Atlantic Coast Line Railroad, 318 U.S. 54, 58-59 (1943). AUERBACH 84-85; *see* W. DODD, *supra* note 13, at 7; E. DOWNEY, *supra* note 21, at 15; E. FREUND, STANDARDS OF AMERICAN LEGISLATION 21 (1917); A. Brodie, *The Adequacy of Workmen's Compensation as Social Insurance: A Review of Developments and Proposals,* 1963 WIS. L. REV. 57, 58.

27. The 1840's were marked by rail and manufacturing development in the East. The 1850's brought heavy foreign capital inflow and the railroad push into the Midwest. W. ROSTOW, THE STAGES OF ECONOMIC GROWTH 38 (1960).

28. For these doctrines see W. PROSSER, *supra* note 14, at 426-28, 450. Both are essentially 19th century doctrines—indeed, Prosser feels assumption of risk "received its greatest impetus" from *Priestley v. Fowler. Id.* at 450 & n.3. On the significance in American law of the doctrine of contributory negligence, see the important article by Wex Malone, *The Formative Era of Contributory Negligence,* 41 ILL. L. REV. 151 (1946).

29. Wisconsin, in Chamberlain v. Milwaukee & M.R.R., 11 Wis. 248 (1860), rejected the fellow-servant rule, but one year later, in Moseley v. Chamberlain, 18 Wis. 700 (1861), the court reversed itself and adopted the rule which was "sustained by the almost unanimous judgments of all the courts both of England and this country . . . [an] unbroken current of judicial opinion." *Id.* at 736.

## C. *Weakening the Rule*

A general pattern may be discerned which is common to the judicial history of many rules of law. The courts enunciate a rule, intending to "solve" a social problem—that it, they seek to lay down a stable and clear-cut principle by which men can govern their conduct or, alternatively, by which the legal system can govern men. If the rule comports with some kind of social consensus, it will in fact work a solution—that is, it will go unchallenged, or, if challenged, will prevail. Challenges will not usually continue, since the small chance of overturning the rule is not worth the cost of litigation. If, however, the rule is weakened—if courts engraft exceptions to it, for example—then fresh challenges probing new weaknesses will be encouraged. Even if the rule retains *some* support, it will no longer be efficient and clear-cut. Ultimately, the rule may no longer serve *anybody's* purposes. At this point, a fresh (perhaps wholly new) "solution" will be attempted.

The history of the fellow-servant rule rather neatly fits this scheme. Shaw wrote his *Farwell* opinion in 1842. During the latter part of the century, judges began to reject his reasoning. The "tendency in nearly all jurisdictions," said a Connecticut court in 1885, was to "limit rather than enlarge" the range of the fellow-servant rule.[30] A Missouri judge in 1891 candidly expressed the change in attitude:

> In the progress of society, and the general substitution of ideal and invisible masters and employers for the actual and visible ones of former times, in the forms of corporations engaged in varied, detached and widespread operations . . . it has been seen and felt that the universal application of the [fellow-servant] rule often resulted in hardship and injustice. Accordingly, the tendency of the more modern authorities appears to be in the direction of such a modification and limitation of the rule as shall eventually devolve upon the employer under these circumstances a due and just share of the responsibility for the lives and limbs of the persons in its employ.[31]

The rule was strong medicine, and it depended for its efficacy upon continued, relatively certain, and unswerving legal loyalty. Ideally, if the rule were strong and commanded nearly total respect from the various agencies of law, it would eliminate much of the mass of litigation that might otherwise arise. Undoubtedly, it did prevent countless thousands of law suits; but it did not succeed in choking off industrial accident litigation. For example, industrial accident litigation dominated the docket of the Wisconsin Supreme Court at the beginning of the age of workmen's compensation; far more cases arose under that heading than under any other single field of law.[32] Undoubt-

---

30. Ziegler v. Danbury & N.R.R., 52 Conn. 543, 556 (1885).
31. Parker v. Hannibal & St. J.R.R., 109 Mo. 362, 397 (1891) (Thomas, J., dissenting).
32. Unpublished survey and classification of all Wisconsin Supreme Court cases 1905-1915, by Robert Friebert and Lawrence M. Friedman.

edly, this appellate case-load was merely the visible portion of a vast iceberg of litigation. Thus, the rule did not command the respect required for efficient operation and hence, in the long run, survival.

One reason for the continued litigation may have been simply the great number of accidents that occurred. At the dawn of the industrial revolution, when Shaw wrote, the human consequences of that technological change were unforeseeable. In particular, the toll it would take of human life was unknown. But by the last quarter of the nineteenth century, the number of industrial accidents had grown enormously. After 1900, it is estimated, 35,000 deaths and 2,000,000 injuries occurred every year in the United States. One quarter of the injuries produced disabilities lasting more than one week.[33] The railway injury rate doubled in the seventeen years between 1889 and 1906.[34]

In addition to the sheer number of accidents, other reasons for the increasing number of challenges to the rule in the later nineteenth century are apparent. If the injury resulted in death or permanent disability, it broke off the employment relationship; the plaintiff or his family thereafter had nothing to lose except the costs of suit. The development of the contingent fee system provided the poor man with the means to hire a lawyer. This system came into being, in the words of an investigating committee of the New York State Bar:

> shortly after the beginning of that which we now call the age of machinery. With the advent of steam and the vast variety of machines for its application to the service of mankind, came a multitude of casualties. This resulted in . . . a class of litigants, whose litigation theretofore had only involved controversies in small transactions . . . calling for the services of inexpensive lawyers. In the new era . . . the poor man found himself pitted . . . against corporations entrenched in wealth and power. . . . Thus resulted a great crop of litigation by the poor against the powerful. . . .[35]

The contingent fee system was no more than a mechanism, however. A losing plaintiff's lawyer receives no fee; that is the essence of the system. The

---

33. E. DOWNEY, *supra* note 21, at 1-2, gives these estimates based on U.S. BUREAU OF LABOR BULL. No. 78, at 458.

34. Accidents were about 2.5 per 100 railway employees in 1889 and 5 per 100 in 1906. Calculated from ICC figures reported in [1909-1910] WIS. BUREAU OF LABOR AND INDUSTRIAL STATISTICS FOURTEENTH BIENNIAL REP. 99 (1911).

Railroads had been the earliest major source of industrial accidents, and most of the leading American and English fellow-servant cases arose out of railroad accidents. Railroads accounted for more serious industrial accidents than any other form of enterprise in the middle of the 19th century. But in the late 19th century, mining, manufacturing, and processing industries contributed their share to industrial injury and death. For example, close to 80% of the employer liability cases that reached the Wisconsin Supreme Court before 1890 related to railroad accidents; from 1890 to 1907 less than 30% were railroad cases. [1907-1908] WIS. BUREAU OF LABOR AND INDUSTRIAL STATISTICS THIRTEENTH BIENNIAL REP. 26 (1909). In 1907-1908, manufacturing injuries and deaths were more than double those of the railroads. [1909-1910] WIS. BUREAU OF LABOR AND INDUSTRIAL STATISTICS FOURTEENTH BIENNIAL REP. 79 (1911).

35. Report of Committee on Contingent Fees, 31 PROCEEDINGS OF THE N.Y. ST. B. ASS'N 99, 100-01 (1908). The elite of the bar always looked with suspicion upon the contingent fee. But the system was a source of livelihood to many members of the bar, and it suited the American proposition that justice was classless and open to all.

fact is that plaintiffs won many of their lawsuits; in so doing, they not only weakened the fellow-servant rule, but they encouraged still more plaintiffs to try their hand, still more attorneys to make a living from personal injury work. In trial courts, the pressure of particular cases—the "hard" cases in which the plight of the plaintiff was pitiful or dramatic—tempted judges and juries to find for the little man and against the corporate defendant. In Shaw's generation, many leading appellate judges shared his view of the role of the judge; they took it as their duty to lay down grand legal principles to govern whole segments of the economic order. Thus, individual hardship cases had to be ignored for the sake of higher duty. But this was not the exclusive judicial style, even in the appellate courts. And in personal injury cases, lower court judges and juries were especially prone to tailor justice to the case at hand. For example, in Wisconsin, of 307 personal injury cases involving workers that appeared before the state supreme court up to 1907, nearly two-thirds had been decided in favor of the worker in the lower courts. In the state supreme court, however, only two-fifths were decided for the worker.[36] Other states undoubtedly had similar experiences. Whether for reasons of sympathy with individual plaintiffs, or with the working class in general, courts and juries often circumvented the formal dictates of the doctrines of the common law.

Some weakening of the doctrine took place by means of the control exercised by trial court judge and jury over findings of fact. But sympathy for injured workers manifested itself also in changes in doctrine. On the appellate court level, a number of mitigations of the fellow-servant rule developed near the end of the nineteenth century. For example, it had always been conceded that the employer was liable if he was personally responsible (through his own negligence) for his worker's injury. Thus, in a Massachusetts case, a stable owner gave directions to his employee, who was driving a wagon, that caused an accident and injury to the driver (or so the jury found). The employer was held liable.[37] Out of this simple proposition grew the so-called vice-principal rule, which allowed an employee to sue his employer where the negligent employee occupied a supervisory position such that he could more properly be said to be an alter ego of the principal than a mere fellow-servant. This was a substantial weakening of the fellow-servant doctrine. Yet some states never accepted the vice-principal rule; in those that did, it too spawned a bewildering multiplicity of decisions, sub-rules, and sub-sub-rules. "The decisions on the subject, indeed, are conflicting to a degree which, it may safely be affirmed, is without a parallel in any department of jurisprudence."[38] This

---

36. [1907-1908] Wis. Bureau of Labor and Industrial Statistics Thirteenth Biennial Rep. 85-86 (1909).
37. Haley v. Case, 142 Mass. 316, 7 N.E. 877 (1886). In *Priestley v. Fowler* itself the same point was made.
38. 4 C. Labatt, Master and Servant 4143 (1913).

statement appeared in a treatise, written on the eve of workmen's compensation, which devoted no fewer than 524 pages to a discussion of the ramifications of the vice-principal rule.

There were scores of other "exceptions" to the fellow-servant rule, enunciated in one or more states. Some of them were of great importance. In general, an employer was said to have certain duties that were not "delegable"; these he must do or have done, and a failure to perform them laid him open to liability for personal injuries. Among these was the duty to furnish a safe place to work, safe tools, and safe appliances. Litigation on these points was enormous, and here too the cases cannot readily be summed up or even explained. In *Wedgwood v. Chicago & Northwestern Railway Co.*[39] the plaintiff, a brakeman, was injured by a "large and long bolt, out of place, and which unnecessarily, carelessly and unskillfully projected beyond the frame, beam or brakehead, in the way of the brakeman going to couple the cars."[40] The trial court threw the case out, but the Wisconsin Supreme Court reversed:

> It is true, the defendant . . . is a railroad corporation, and can only act through officers or agents. But this does not relieve it from responsibility for the negligence of its officers and agents whose duty it is to provide safe and suitable machinery for its road which its employees are to operate.[41]

So phrased, of course, the exception comes close to swallowing the rule. Had the courts been so inclined, they might have eliminated the fellow-servant rule without admitting it, simply by expanding the safe place and safe tool rules. They were never quite willing to go that far, and the safe tool doctrine was itself subject to numerous exceptions. In some jurisdictions, for example, the so-called "simple tool" rule applied:

> Tools of ordinary and everyday use, which are simple in structure and requiring no skill in handling—such as hammers and axes—not obviously defective, do not impose a liability upon employer[s] for injuries resulting from such defects.[42]

Doctrinal complexity and vacillation in the upper courts, coupled with jury freedom in the lower courts, meant that by the end of the century the fellow-servant rule had lost much of its reason for existence: it was no longer an efficient cost-allocating doctrine. Even though the exceptions did not go the length of obliterating the rule, and even though many (perhaps most) injured workers who had a possible cause of action did not or could not recover, the instability and unpredictability of operation of the common law rule was a significant fact.

---

39. 41 Wis. 478 (1877).
40. *Id.* at 479.
41. *Id.* at 483.
42. Dunn v. Southern Ry., 151 N.C. 313, 315, 66 S.E. 134-35 (1909); *see* 3 C. LABATT, *supra* note 38, at 2476-84.

The numerous judge-made exceptions reflected a good deal of uncertainty about underlying social policy. The same uncertainty was reflected in another sphere of legal activity—the legislature. Though the rule was not formally abrogated, it was weakened by statute in a number of jurisdictions. Liability statutes, as will be seen, were rudimentary and in many ways ineffective. This was partly because of genuine uncertainty about the proper attitude to take toward industrial accident costs—an uncertainty reflected in the cases as well. The early nineteenth century cannot be uncritically described as a period that accepted without question business values and practices. Rather, it accepted the ideal of economic growth, which certain kinds of enterprise seemed to hinder. Thus in the age of Jackson, as is well known, popular feeling ran high against financial institutions, chiefly the chartered banks. Banks were believed to have far too much economic power; they corrupted both the currency and the government. They were a "clog upon the industry of this country."[43] But many a good judge, who decried the soulless corporation (meaning chiefly the moneyed kind) in the best Jacksonian tradition, may at the same time have upheld the fellow-servant rule. One did not, in other words, necessarily identify the interests of the common man with industrial liability for personal injuries.

Later on, the railroads replaced the banks as popular bogeymen. By the 1850's some of the fear of excessive economic power was transferred to them. Disregard for safety was one more black mark against the railroads; farmers, small businessmen, and the emerging railroad unions might use the safety argument to enlist widespread support for general regulation of railroads, but the essential thrust of the movement was economic. The railroads were feared and hated because of their power over access to the market. They became "monopolistic" as the small local lines were gradually amalgamated into large groupings controlled by "robber barons." Interstate railroad nets were no longer subject to local political control—if anything, they controlled local politics, or so it plausibly appeared to much of the public. Farmers organized and fought back against what they identified as their economic enemy. It is not coincidental that the earliest derogations from the strictness of the fellow-servant rule applied *only* to railroads. For example, the first statutory modification, passed in Georgia in 1856, allowed railroad employees to recover for injuries caused by the acts of fellow-servants, provided they themselves were free from negligence.[44] A similar act was passed in Iowa in 1862.[45] Other statutes were passed in Wyoming (1869)[46] and Kansas (1874).[47] The chron-

---

43. T. Sedgwick, Jr., *What is a Monopoly?* (1865), *quoted in* SOCIAL THEORIES OF JACKSONIAN DEMOCRACY 220, 231 (Blau ed. 1954).
44. No. 103, [1855] Ga. Acts 155.
45. Ch. 169, § 7, [1862] Iowa Laws 198.
46. Ch. 65, [1869] Wyo. Terr. Laws 433.
47. Ch. 93, §1, [1874] Kan. Laws 143.

ology suggests—though direct evidence is lacking—that some of these statutes were connected with the general revolt of farmers against the power of the railroad companies, a revolt associated with the Granger movement, which achieved its maximum power in the 1870's.[48] Wisconsin in 1875 abolished the fellow-servant rule for railroads; in 1880, however, when more conservative forces regained control of the legislature, the act was repealed.[49]

The Granger revolt, and similar movements, were not without lessons for the railroad companies. Despite the fall of Granger legislatures, the legal and economic position of the railroads was permanently altered. Great masses of people had come to accept the notion that the power of the railroads was a threat to farmers and a threat to the independence and stability of democratic institutions. Out of the ashes of ineffective and impermanent state regulation of railroads arose what ultimately became a stronger and more systematic program of regulation, grounded in federal power over the national economy.

The Interstate Commerce Commission was created in 1887,[50] chiefly to outlaw discrimination in freight rates and other practices deemed harmful to railroad users. The original legislation had nothing to say about railroad accidents and safety. But this did not long remain the case. The railroads had become unpopular defendants relatively early in American legal history. By 1911, twenty-five states had laws modifying or abrogating the fellow-servant doctrine for railroads.[51] Railroad accident law reached a state of maturity earlier than the law of industrial accidents generally; safety controls were imposed on the roads, and the common law tort system was greatly modified by removal of the employer's most effective defense. The Interstate Commerce Commission called a conference of state regulatory authorities in 1889; the safety problem was discussed, and the Commission was urged to investigate the problem and recommend legislation.[52] In 1893, Congress required interstate railroads to equip themselves with safety appliances, and provided that any employee injured "by any locomotive, car, or train in use" without such appliances would not "be deemed . . . to have assumed the risk thereby occasioned."[53]

The Federal Employers' Liability Act of 1908[54] went much further; it abolished the fellow-servant rule for railroads and greatly reduced the strength

48. *See generally* R. HUNT, LAW AND LOCOMOTIVES (1958).
49. Ch. 173, [1875] Wis. Laws 293 (*repealed*, Ch. 232, [1880] Wis. Laws 270). A new act, somewhat narrower than that of 1875, was passed in 1889. Ch. 348, [1889] Wis. Laws 487.
50. Interstate Commerce Act § 11, 24 Stat. 379 (1887). As much as workmen's compensation, the development of utility regulation was a kind of compromise among interests. Under public regulation, companies gain freedom from local political harassment and uncontrolled competition; they are virtually guaranteed a "fair" but limited return on investment. In exchange, they agree to accept supervision and regulation by the general government.
51. 1 A. LARSON, WORKMEN'S COMPENSATION § 4.50, at 30 (1965).
52. 1 I. SHARFMAN, THE INTERSTATE COMMERCE COMMISSION 246 n.4 (1931).
53. Safety Appliance Act, 27 Stat. 531-32 (1893) (now 45 U.S.C. § 7 (1964)).
54. 35 Stat. 65 (1908).

of contributory negligence and assumption of risk as defenses. Once the employers had been stripped of these potent weapons, the relative probability of recovery by injured railroad employees was high enough so that workmen's compensation never seemed as essential for the railroads as for industry generally. The highly modified FELA tort system survives (in amended form) to this day for the railroads.[55] It is an anachronism, but one which apparently grants some modest satisfaction to both sides. Labor and management both express discontent with FELA, but neither side has been so firmly in favor of a change to workmen's compensation as to make it a major issue.[56]

FELA shows one of many possible outcomes of the decline in efficacy of the fellow-servant rule. Under it, the rule was eliminated, and the law turned to a "pure" tort system—pure in the sense that the proclivities of juries were not interfered with by doctrines designed to limit the chances of a worker's recovery. But the railroads were a special case. Aside from the special history of regulation, the interstate character of the major railroads made them subject to national safety standards and control by a single national authority. For other industrial employers, the FELA route was not taken; instead, workmen's compensation acts were passed. In either case, however, the fellow-servant rule was abolished, or virtually so. Either course reflects, we can assume, some kind of general agreement that the costs of the rule outweighed its benefits.

## D. *Rising Pressures for Change*

The common law doctrines were designed to preserve a certain economic balance in the community. When the courts and legislatures created numerous exceptions, the rules lost much of their efficiency as a limitation on the liability of businessmen. The rules prevented many plaintiffs from recovering, but not all; a few plaintiffs recovered large verdicts. There were costs of settlements, costs of liability insurance, costs of administration, legal fees and the salaries of staff lawyers. These costs rose steadily, at the very time when American business, especially big business, was striving to rationalize and bureaucratize its operations. It was desirable to be able to predict costs and insure against fluctuating, unpredictable risks. The costs of industrial accident liability were not easily predictable, partly because legal consequences of accidents were not predictable. Insurance, though available, was expensive.

In addition, industry faced a serious problem of labor unrest. Workers and their unions were dissatisfied with many aspects of factory life. The lack of compensation for industrial accidents was one obvious weakness. Relatively

---

55. The 1908 act was limited to railroad employees injured while engaged in interstate commerce. A 1906 act [Act of June 22, 1906, ch. 3073, 34 Stat. 232] had been declared invalid by the Supreme Court in the Employers Liability Cases, 207 U.S. 463 (1908), because it applied to employees not engaged in interstate commerce. The 1908 act was liberalized in 1910 and in 1939. *See* 45 U.S.C. §§ 51-60 (1964). *See generally* V. Miller, *FELA Revisited*, 6 Catholic U.L. Rev. 158 (1957).

56. Arguments by supporters and opponents of FELA are reviewed in H. Somers & A. Somers, Workmen's Compensation 320-25 (1954).

few injured workers received compensation. Under primitive state employers' liability statutes, the issue of liability and the amount awarded still depended upon court rulings and jury verdicts. Furthermore, the employer and the insurance carrier might contest a claim or otherwise delay settlement in hopes of bringing the employee to terms. The New York Employers' Liability Commission, in 1910, reported that delay ran from six months to six years.

> The injured workman is driven to accept whatever his employer or an insurance company chooses to give him or take his chance in a lawsuit. Half of the time his lawsuit is doomed to failure because he has been hurt by some trade risk or lacks proof for his case. At best he has a right to retain a lawyer, spend two months on the pleadings, watch his case from six months to two years on a calendar and then undergo the lottery of a jury trial, with a technical system of law and rules of evidence, and beyond that appeals and perhaps reversals on questions that do not go to the merits. . . . If he wins, he wins months after his most urgent need is over.[57]

When an employee did recover, the amount was usually small. The New York Commission found that of forty-eight fatal cases studied in Manhattan, eighteen families received no compensation; only four received over $2,000; most received less than $500. The deceased workers had averaged $15.22 a week in wages; only eight families recovered as much as three times their average yearly earnings.[58] The same inadequacies turned up in Wisconsin in 1907. Of fifty-one fatal injuries studied, thirty-four received settlements under $500; only eight received over $1,000.[59]

Litigation costs consumed much of whatever was recovered. It was estimated that, in 1907, "of every $100 paid out by [employers in New York] on account of work accidents but $56 reached the injured workmen and their dependents." And even this figure was unrepresentative because it included voluntary payments by employers. "A fairer test of employers' liability is afforded by the $192,538 paid by these same employers as a result of law suits or to avoid law suits, whereof only $80,888, or forty-two percent, reached the beneficiaries."[60] A large fraction of the disbursed payments, about one-third, went to attorneys who accepted the cases on a contingent basis.[61]

These figures on the inadequacy of recoveries are usually cited to show how little the workers received for their pains. But what did these figures mean to employers? Assuming that employers, as rational men, were anxious to pay as little compensation as was necessary to preserve industrial peace and maintain a healthy workforce, the better course might be to pay a higher *net* amount direct to employees. Employers had little or nothing to gain from

---

57. *Quoted in* W. DODD, *supra* note 13, at 23-24.
58. *Id.* at 19.
59. *Id.* at 20-21.
60. E. DOWNEY, *supra* note 21, at 83.
61. *See* W. DODD, *supra* note 13, at 22-23.

their big payments to insurance companies, lawyers, and court officials. Perhaps at some unmeasurable point of time, the existing tort system crossed an invisible line and thereafter, purely in economic terms, represented on balance a net loss to the industrial establishment. From that point on, the success of a movement for change in the system was certain, provided that businessmen could be convinced that indeed their self-interest lay in the direction of reform and that a change in compensation systems did not drag with it other unknowable and harmful consequences.

As on many issues of reform, the legal profession did not speak with one voice. Certainly, many lawyers and judges were dissatisfied with the status quo. Judges complained about the burdens imposed on the court system by masses of personal injury suits; many felt frustrated by the chaotic state of the law, and others were bothered by their felt inability to do justice to injured workmen. One writer noted in 1912:

> [A]mendatory legislation in scores of separate jurisdictions have made employers' liability one of the most involved and intricate branches of the law, have multiplied definitions more recondite and distinctions more elusive than those of the marginal utility theory, and have given rise to conflicts of decisions that are the despair of jurists.[62]

Some influential judges despaired of piecemeal improvements and played an active role in working for a compensation system. In a 1911 opinion, Chief Justice J. B. Winslow of Wisconsin wrote:

> No part of my labor on this bench has brought such heartweariness to me as that ever increasing part devoted to the consideration of personal injury actions brought by employees against their employers. The appeal to the emotions is so strong in these cases, the results to life and limb and human happiness so distressing, that the attempt to honestly administer cold, hard rules of law . . . make[s] drafts upon the heart and nerves which no man can appreciate who has not been obliged to meet the situation himself . . . . These rules are archaic and unfitted to modern industrial conditions . . . .
> When [the faithful laborer] . . . has yielded up life, or limb, or health in the service of that marvelous industrialism which is our boast, shall not the great public . . . be charged with the duty of securing from want the laborer himself, if he survive, as well as his helpless and dependent ones? Shall these latter alone pay the fearful price of the luxuries and comforts which modern machinery brings within the reach of all?
> These are burning and difficult questions with which the courts cannot deal, because their duty is to administer the law as it is, not to change it; but they are well within the province of the legislative arm of the government.[63]

---

62. E. Downey, *supra* note 21, at 17.
63. Driscoll v. Allis-Chalmers Co., 144 Wis. 451, 468-69, 129 N.W. 401, 408-09 (1911); *see* Monte v. Wausau Paper Mills Co., 132 Wis. 205, 209, 111 N.W. 1114, 1115 (1907) (Winslow, C.J.).

Justice Roujet D. Marshall propagandized for workmen's compensation in his judicial opinions.[64] He claimed in his autobiography "to have been largely the exciting cause of the establishment of the workmen's compensation law" in Wisconsin.[65] He also wrote part of the governor's message to the 1909 legislature appealing for a workmen's compensation statute, and he helped induce the Republican Party to back a workmen's compensation plan in its 1910 platform.[66] Legal writers and law teachers also spoke out against the common law and in favor of a compensation system. Roscoe Pound voiced a common opinion in 1907:

> [I]t is coming to be well understood by all who have studied the circumstances of modern industrial employment that the supposed contributory negligence of employees is in effect a result of the mechanical conditions imposed on them by the nature of their employment, and that by reason of these conditions the individual vigilance and responsibility contemplated by the common law are impossible in practice.[67]

In 1911, when the New York Court of Appeals unanimously declared the nation's first workmen's compensation statute unconstitutional,[68] Dean Pound and thirteen other "experts in political and Constitutional law" issued a lengthy statement in an influential New York City weekly newspaper, *The Outlook*, which the editors summarized as demonstrating that the "decision of the Court of Appeals of the State of New York is not in accordance with the best legal authorities in the United States."[69]

When considerations of politics were added to those of business economics and industrial peace, it was not surprising to find that businessmen gradually withdrew their veto against workmen's compensation statutes. They began to say that a reformed system was inevitable—and even desirable. A guaran-

---

64. *See, e.g.,* Houg v. Girard Lumber Co., 144 Wis. 337, 352, 129 N.W. 633, 639 (1911) (separate opinion); Monaghan v. Northwestern Fuel Co., 140 Wis. 457, 466, 122 N.W. 1066, 1070 (1909) (dissenting opinion).

65. 2 AUTOBIOGRAPHY OF ROUJET D. MARSHALL 53 (Glasier ed. 1931).

66. *Id.* at 239-46.

67. R. Pound, *The Need of a Sociological Jurisprudence,* 19 GREEN BAG 607, 614 (1907). The entire April 1906 issue of *The Green Bag* was devoted to employers' liability and workmen's compensation. See, particularly, R. Newcomb, *The Abuse of Personal Injury Litigation,* 18 GREEN BAG 196, 199-200 (1906). *See also* F. Walton, *Workmen's Compensation and the Theory of Professional Risk,* 11 COLUM. L. REV. 36 (1911); E. Wambaugh, *Workmen's Compensation Acts: Their Theory and Their Constitutionality,* 25 HARV. L. REV. 129 (1911).

68. Ives v. South Buffalo Ry., 201 N.Y. 271, 94 N.E. 431 (1911), *declaring unconstitutional* Ch. 674, [1910] N.Y. Laws 1945.

69. *The Workmen's Compensation Act: Its Constitutionality Affirmed,* 98 THE OUTLOOK 709-11 (1911). Lyman Abbott, editor of *The Outlook,* and his contributing editor, Theodore Roosevelt, wrote frequently about employers' liability and compensation statutes. See especially the issue of April 29, 1911, 97 THE OUTLOOK 955-60 (1911).

Roosevelt, as President, had stated as early as 1907 that "it is neither just, expedient, nor humane; it is revolting to judgment and sentiment alike that the financial burden of accidents occurring because of the necessary exigencies of their daily occupation should be thrust upon those sufferers who were least able to bear it. . . ." E. DOWNEY, *supra* note 21, at 277 n.540.

teed, insurable cost—one which could be computed in advance on the basis of accident experience—would, in the long run, cost business less than the existing system.[70] In 1910, the president of the National Association of Manufacturers (NAM) appointed a committee to study the possibility of compensating injured workmen without time-consuming and expensive litigation, and the convention that year heard a speaker tell them that no one was satisfied with the present state of the law—that the employers' liability system was "antagonistic to harmonious relations between employers and wage workers."[71] By 1911 the NAM appeared convinced that a compensation system was inevitable and that prudence dictated that business play a positive role in shaping the design of the law—otherwise the law would be "settled for us by the demagogue, and agitator and the socialist with a vengeance."[72] Business would benefit economically and politically from a compensation system, but only if certain conditions were present. Business, therefore, had an interest in pressing for a specific kind of program, and turned its attention to the details of the new system. For example, it was imperative that the new system be in fact as actuarially predictable as business demanded; it was important that the costs of the program be fair and equal in their impact upon particular industries, so that no competitive advantage or disadvantage flowed from the scheme. Consequently the old tort actions had to be eliminated, along with the old defenses of the company. In exchange for certainty of recovery by the worker, the companies were prepared to demand certainty and predictability of loss—that is, limitation of recovery. The jury's caprice had to be dispensed with. In short, when workmen's compensation became law, as a solution to the industrial accident problem, it did so on terms acceptable to industry. Other pressures were there to be sure, but when workmen's compensation was enacted, businessmen had come to look on it as a positive benefit rather than as a threat to their sector of the economy.

## E. *The Emergence of Workmen's Compensation Statutes*

The change of the businessman's, the judge's, and the general public's attitudes toward industrial injuries was accelerated by the availability of fresh information on the extent of accidents and their cost to both management and workers. By 1900, industrial accidents and the shortcomings of the fellow-servant rule were widely perceived as *problems* that had to be solved. After 1900, state legislatures began to look for a "solution" by setting up commissions to gather statistics, to investigate possible new systems, and to recommend

---

70. For a comparison of the cost efficiency of the two systems, see generally W. DODD, ADMINISTRATION OF WORKMEN'S COMPENSATION 737-83 (1936).

71. NATIONAL ASSOCIATION OF MANUFACTURERS, PROCEEDINGS OF THE FIFTEENTH ANNUAL CONVENTION 280 (1910).

72. NATIONAL ASSOCIATION OF MANUFACTURERS, PROCEEDINGS OF THE SIXTEENTH ANNUAL CONVENTION 106 (1911) (remarks of Mr. Schwedtman).

legislation.[73] The commissions held public hearings and called upon employers, labor, insurance companies, and lawyers to express their opinions and propose changes. A number of commissions collected statistics on industrial accidents, costs of insurance, and amounts disbursed to injured workmen. By 1916, many states and the federal government had received more-or-less extensive public reports from these investigating bodies.[74] The reports included studies of industrial accident cases in the major industries, traced the legal history of the cases, and looked into the plight of the injured workmen and their families.

From the information collected, the commissions were able to calculate the costs of workmen's compensation systems and compare them with costs under employers' liability. Most of the commissions concluded that a compensation system would be no more expensive than the existing method,[75] and most of them recommended adoption, in one form or another, of workmen's compensation. In spite of wide variations in the systems proposed, there was agreement on one point: workmen's compensation must fix liability upon the employer regardless of fault.

Between 1910 and 1920 the method of compensating employees injured on the job was fundamentally altered in the United States. In brief, workmen's compensation statutes eliminated (or tried to eliminate) the process of fixing civil liability for industrial accidents through litigation in common law courts. Under the statutes, compensation was based on statutory schedules, and the responsibility for initial determination of employee claims was taken from the courts and given to an administrative agency. Finally, the statutes abolished the fellow-servant rule and the defenses of assumption of risk and contributory negligence. Wisconsin's law, passed in 1911, was the first general compensation act to survive a court test.[76] Mississippi, the last state in the Union to adopt a compensation law, did so in 1948.[77]

Compensation systems varied from state to state, but they had many features in common. The original Wisconsin law was representative of the earlier group of statutes. It set up a voluntary system—a response to the fact that New York's courts had held a compulsory scheme unconsitutional on

---

73. For example, in 1907, Illinois required employers to report their employees' accidents to the State's Bureau of Labor Statistics. [1907] Ill. Laws 308.

74. *See* W. Dodd, *supra* note 70, at 18.

75. For example, the Wisconsin Bureau of Labor and Industrial Statistics argued, on the basis of cost estimates in 1908, that:

> Employers' liability insurance costs now in Wisconsin from 12 cents per $100 of wages in knitting mills to at least $9.00 in some building operations — an average of 50 or 60 cents. But it is very probable that this expense would be increased in the near future by weakening the defense of the employer in the courts. . . . The cost of the present system would be sufficient to inaugurate a general system of compensation if properly administered.

[1907-1908] Wis. Bureau of Labor and Industrial Statistics Thirteenth Biennial Rep. (1909), *quoted in* Auerbach 588.

76. Borgnis v. Falk Co., 147 Wis. 327, 133 N.W. 209 (1911).

77. Ch. 354, [1948] Miss. Laws 507.

due process grounds.[78] Wisconsin abolished the fellow-servant rule and the defense of assumption of risk for employers of four or more employees. In turn, the compensation scheme, for employers who elected to come under it, was made the "exclusive remedy" for an employee injured accidentally on the job. The element of "fault" or "negligence" was eliminated, and the mere fact of injury at work "proximately caused by accident," and not the result of "wilful misconduct," made the employer liable to pay compensation but exempt from ordinary tort liability.[79] The state aimed to make it expensive for employers to stay out of the system. Any employer who did so was liable to suit by injured employees and the employer was denied the common law defenses.

The compensation plans strictly limited the employee's amount of recovery. In Wisconsin, for example, if an accident caused "partial disability," the worker was to receive 65% of his weekly loss in wages during the period of disability, not to exceed four times his average annual earnings.[80] The statutes, therefore, were compensatory, not punitive, and the measure of compensation was, subject to strict limitations, the loss of earning power of the worker. In the original Wisconsin act, death benefits were also payable to dependents of the worker. If the worker who died left "no person dependent upon him for support," the death benefit was limited to "the reasonable expense of his burial, not exceeding $100."[81] Neither death nor injury as such gave rise to a right to compensation—only the fact of economic loss to someone, either the worker himself or his family. The Wisconsin act authorized employers to buy annuities from private insurance companies to cover projected losses. Most states later made insurance or self-insurance compulsory. Some states have socialized compensation insurance, but most allow the purchase of private policies.[82]

In essence, then, workmen's compensation was designed to replace a highly unsatisfactory system with a rational, actuarial one. It should not be viewed as the replacement of a fault-oriented compensation system with one unconcerned with fault. It should not be viewed as a victory of employees over employers. In its initial stages, the fellow-servant rule was not concerned with fault, either, but with establishing a clear-cut, workable, and predictable rule, one which substantively placed much of the risk (if not all) on the worker. Industrial accidents were not seen as a social problem—at most as an economic problem. As value perceptions changed, the rule weakened; it developed exceptions and lost its efficiency. The exceptions and counter-exceptions can be looked at as a

78. Ives v. South Buffalo Ry., 201 N.Y. 271, 94 N.E. 431 (1911).
79. Ch. 50, § 1, [1911] Wis. Laws 43, 44.
80. Ch. 50, § 1, [1911] Wis. Laws 46.
81. Ch. 50, § 1, [1911] Wis. Laws 48.
82. *See* A. REEDE, ADEQUACY OF WORKMEN'S COMPENSATION 231-38 (1947); H. SOMERS & A. SOMERS, *supra* note 56, at 93-142.

series of brief, ad hoc, and unstable compromises between the clashing interests of labor and management. When both sides became convinced that the game was mutually unprofitable, a compensation system became possible. But this system was itself a compromise: an attempt at a new, workable, and predictable mode of handling accident liability which neatly balanced the interests of labor and management.

### III. THE LAW OF INDUSTRIAL ACCIDENTS AND SOCIAL THEORY: THREE ASPECTS OF SOCIAL CHANGE

This case study, devoted to the rise and fall of the fellow-servant rule, utilizes and supports a view of social change as a complex chain of group bargains—economic in the sense of a continuous exchange of perceived equivalents, though not economic in the sense of crude money bargains. It also provides a useful setting for evaluating three additional popular explanations of the origin or rate of social change. First, the apparently slow development of workmen's compensation is the classic example of what Ogburn called "cultural lag." Second, since German and English statutes were enacted prior to the American laws, the establishment of compensation schemes in America can be viewed as a case of cross-cultural influence. Third, the active role of particular participants (in Wisconsin, for example, Judge Marshall and John R. Commons) may substantiate the theory which advances the causal influence of "great men" in the process of social change. A thorough examination of these theories is not contemplated here. Students both of law and of sociology, however, may profit from a brief discussion of these theories in the context of the social change embodied in workmen's compensation statutes.

### A. *The Concept of Cultural Lag*

The problem of "fair and efficient incidence of industrial accident costs," in the words of Willard Hurst, "followed a fumbling course in courts and legislature for fifty years before the first broad-scale direction [leading to workmen's compensation] was applied."[83] In a famous book written in 1922, the sociologist William Fielding Ogburn used the example of workmen's compensation and the fifty-year period of fumbling to verify his "hypothesis of cultural lag."[84] "Where one part of culture changes first," said Ogburn, "through some discovery or invention, and occasions changes in some part of culture dependent upon it, there frequently is a delay . . . . The extent of this lag will vary . . . but may exist for . . . years, during which time there

---

83. J. WILLARD HURST, LAW AND SOCIAL PROCESS IN UNITED STATES HISTORY 69 (1960).
84. W. OGBURN, SOCIAL CHANGE WITH RESPECT TO CULTURE AND ORIGINAL NATURE 200 (Viking ed. 1950). *See generally id.* at 199-280. In the book cultural lag was offered as a hypothesis; in later writing Ogburn referred to it as a theory.

may be said to be a maladjustment."[85] In the case of workmen's compensation, the lag period was from the time when industrial accidents became numerous until the time when workmen's compensation laws were passed, "about a half-century, from 1850-70 to 1915." During this period, "the old adaptive culture, the common law of employers' liability, hung over after the material conditions had changed."[86]

The concept of cultural lag is still widely used, in social science and out— particularly since its popularization by Stuart Chase in *The Proper Study of Mankind*.[87] And the notion that law fails to adjust promptly to the call for change is commonly voiced. In popular parlance, this or that aspect of the law is often said to "lag behind the times." This idea is so pervasive that it deserves comment quite apart from its present status in sociological thought.

The lesson of industrial accident law, as here described, may be quite the opposite of the lesson that Ogburn drew. In a purely objective (nonteleological) sense, social processes—and the legal system—cannot aptly be described through use of the idea of lag. When, in the face of changed technology and new problems, a social arrangement stubbornly persists, there are *social* reasons why this is so; there are explanations why no change or slow change occurs. The legal system is a part of the total culture; it is not a self-operating machine. The rate of response to a call for change is slow or fast in the law depending upon who issues the call and who (if anybody) resists it. "Progress" or "catching up" is not inevitable or predictable. Legal change, like social change, is a change in behavior of individuals and groups in interaction. The rate of change depends upon the kind of interaction. To say that institutions lag is usually to say no more than that they are slow to make changes of a particular type. But why are they slow? Often the answer rests on the fact that these institutions are controlled by or respond to groups or individuals who are opposed to the specific change. This is lag only if we feel we can confidently state that these groups or individuals are wrong as to their own self-interest as well as that of society. Of course, people *are* often wrong about their own self-interest; they can be and are short-sighted, ignorant, maladroit. But ignorance of this kind exists among progressives as well as among conservatives—among those who want change as well as among those who oppose it. Resistance to change is "lag" only if there is only one "true" definition of a problem—and one "true" solution.

There were important reasons why fifty years elapsed before workmen's compensation became part of the law. Under the impact of industrial conditions

---

85. *Id.* at 201.
86. *Id.* at 236.
87. See S. Chase, The Proper Study of Mankind 115-17 (1st ed. 1948). For other applications of cultural lag, see H. Hart, *Social Theory and Social Change*, in Symposium on Sociological Theory 196, 219-25 (Gross ed. 1959). *See generally* H. Hart, *The Hypothesis of Cultural Lag: A Present Day View*, in Technology and Social Change 417-34 (Allen ed. 1957).

Americans were changing their views about individual security and social welfare. Dean Pound has remarked that the twentieth century accepts the idea of insuring those unable to bear economic loss, at the expense of the nearest person at hand who can bear the loss. This conception was relatively unknown and unacceptable to judges of the nineteenth century.[88] The fellow-servant rule could not be replaced until economic affluence, business conditions, and the state of safety technology made feasible a more social solution. Labor unions of the mid-nineteenth century did not call for a compensation plan; they were concerned with more basic (and practical) issues such as wages and hours. Note the form that the argument for workmen's compensation took, after 1900, in the following quotation; few Americans reasoned this way fifty years earlier.

> [S]uppose you carry an accident policy and are negligent in stepping from a street car. Do you not expect the insurance company to pay? If you negligently overturn a lamp and your house burns, do you not expect the fire insurance company to pay? That is what insurance is for—to guard against the slips and mistakes that are characteristics of human nature. . . .
> Before granting a pension do we ask whether a man used due care in dodging the bullets, or do we plead that he voluntarily assumed the risk? Then why, when a man courageously volunteers to do the dangerous work in transportation, mining, building, etc., should it seem wrong to grant him or his dependents compensation in case of accidents?[89]

Social insurance, as much as private insurance, requires standardization and rationalization of business, predictability of risk, and reliability and financial responsibility of economic institutions. These were present in 1909, but not in 1850.

Prior to workmen's compensation, the legal system reflected existing conflicts of value quite clearly; the manifold exceptions to the fellow-servant rule and the primitive liability statutes bear witness to this fact. These were no symptoms of "lag"; rather, they were a measure of the constant adjustments that inevitably take place within a legal system that is not insulated from the larger society but an integral part of it. To be sure, the courts frequently reflected values of the business community and so did the legislatures, but populist expressions can easily be found in the work of judges, legislatures, and juries. In the absence of a sophisticated measuring-rod of past public opinion—and sophisticated concepts of the role of public opinion in nineteenth century society—who is to say that the legal system "lagged" behind some hypothetical general will of the public or some hypothetically correct solution?

The concept of lag may also be employed in the criticism of the courts' use of judicial review to retard the efficacy of social welfare legislation. In

---

88. R. Pound, *The Economic Interpretation and the Law of Torts*, 53 HARV. L. REV. 365, 376 (1940).
89. [1907-1908] WIS. BUREAU OF INDUSTRIAL AND LABOR STATISTICS THIRTEENTH BIENNIAL REP. (1909), *quoted in* AUERBACH 586.

1911, the New York Court of Appeals declared the state's compulsory work-men's compensation act unconstitutional. As a result of this holding, the state constitution had to be amended—two years later—before workmen's compensation was legally possible in New York.[90] Because of the New York experience, six states also amended their constitutions and others enacted voluntary plans. The issue was not finally settled until 1917, when the United States Supreme Court held both compulsory and elective plans to be constitutional.[91] But it adds little to an understanding of social process to describe this delay in terms of the concept of cultural lag. Courts do not act on their own initiative. Each case of judicial review was instigated by a litigant who represented a group in society which was fighting for its interests as it perceived them; these were current, real interests, not interests of sentiment or inertia. This is completely apart from consideration of what social interests the courts thought they were serving in deciding these cases—interests which hindsight condemns as futile or wrong, but which were living issues and interests of the day.

Conflicts of value also arose in the legislatures when they began to consider compensation laws. The Massachusetts investigating commission of 1903 reported a workmen's compensation bill to the legislature, but the bill was killed in committee on the ground that Massachusetts could not afford to increase the production costs of commodities manufactured in the state.[92] Once more, the emergence of compensation depended upon a perception of inevitability—which could cancel the business detriment to particular states which enacted compensation laws—and of general economic gain from the new system. It is not enough to sense that a social problem exists. Rational collective action demands relatively precise and detailed information about the problem, and clear placement of responsibility for proposing and implementing a solution. For many years legislatures simply did not consider it their responsibility to do anything about industrial injuries. Since they did not view accidents as a major social problem, and since state legislatures were weak political structures, they were content at first to leave accidents to tort law and the courts.[93] Moreover, state agencies were not delegated the task of collecting information on the nature and extent of industrial accidents until relatively late. The Wisconsin legislature created a Bureau of Labor and Indus-

---

90. N.Y. Const. art. 1, § 19, was added in 1913; the new compensation law it authorized was enacted that same year. *See* Ch. 816, [1913] N.Y. Laws 2277.

91. New York Cent. R.R. v. White, 243 U.S. 188 (1917); Hawkins v. Bleakly, 243 U.S. 210 (1917). In Mountain Timber Co. v. Washington, 243 U.S. 219 (1917), the Court also held an exclusive state insurance fund to be constitutional.

92. R. Warner, *Employers' Liability as an Industrial Problem*, 18 Green Bag 185, 192 (1906).

93. "Laying the personal injury burdens of production upon the things produced . . . should have been efficiently recognized long ago, and would have been had the lawmaking power appreciated that it is its province, not that of the courts, to cure infirmity in the law." Borgnis v. Falk Co., 147 Wis. 327, 370, 133 N.W. 209, 223 (1911) (Marshall, J., concurring).

trial Statistics in 1883, but did not provide for the collection of data on industrial accidents until 1905.[94] When a need for accident legislation was perceived, individual legislators, under pressure of constituencies, began to introduce work accident indemnity bills. Some were inadequately drafted; most were poorly understood. In order to appraise potential legislation, investigating commissions were created to collect information, weigh the costs and report back alternative solutions.

What appears to some as an era of "lag" was actually a period in which issues were collectively defined and alternative solutions posed, and during which interest groups bargained for favorable formulations of law. It was a period of "false starts"—unstable compromise formulations by decision makers armed with few facts, lacking organizational machinery, and facing great, often contradictory, demands from many publics. There was no easy and suitable solution, in the light of the problem and the alignment of powers. Indeed, workmen's compensation—which today appears to be a stable solution —was only a compromise, an answer acceptable to enough people and interest groups to endure over a reasonably long period of time.

Part of what is later called "lag," then, is this period of false starts—the inadequate compromises by decision makers faced with contradictory interest groups pressing inconsistent solutions. There may not *be* a "solution" in light of the alignment of interests and powers with respect to the problem at any given point in time. Perhaps only a compromise "solution" is possible. What later appears to be the final answer is in fact itself a compromise—one which is stable over some significant period of time. Sociologically, that is what a "solution" to a problem is: nothing more than a stable compromise acceptable to enough people and interest groups to maintain itself over a significant period of time. Theoretically, of course, total victory by one competing interest and total defeat of another is possible. But in a functioning democratic society, total victories and defeats are uncommon. Total defeat would mean that a losing group was so utterly powerless that it could exert no bargaining pressure whatsoever; total victory similarly would imply unlimited power. In the struggle over industrial accident legislation, none of the interests could be so described. Different perceptions of the problem, based at least in part on different economic and social stakes, led to different views of existing and potential law. When these views collided, compromises were hammered out. Workmen's compensation took form not because it was (or is) perfect, but because it represented a solution acceptable enough to enough interests to outweigh the costs of additional struggle and bargaining. If there was "lag" in the process, it consisted of acquiescence in presently acceptable solutions which

---

94. Ch. 416, §§ 1, 4, [1905] Wis. Laws 680, 682.

turned out not to be adequate or stable in the long run. "Lag" therefore at most means present-minded pragmatism rather than long-term rational planning.[95]

### B. *Cross-Cultural Borrowing*

The adoption of workmen's compensation in America does represent an instance of what can be called conscious cross-cultural borrowing. Workmen's compensation was not an American innovation; there were numerous European antecedents. Switzerland passed a workmen's compensation act in 1881; Germany followed in 1884 with a more inclusive scheme. By 1900 compensation laws had spread to most European countries. In 1891 the United States Bureau of Labor commissioned John Graham Brooks to study and appraise the German system. His report, published in 1893, was widely distributed and successfully exposed some American opinion-leaders to the existence of the European programs.[96] Most of the state investigating commissions also inquired into the European experience, and a number of early bills were modeled after the German and British systems.

Though workmen's compensation can therefore be viewed as an example of cross-cultural borrowing, care must be exercised in employing the concept. Successful legal solutions to social problems are often borrowed across state and national lines but this borrowing must not be confused with the actual "influence" of one legal system over another. "Influence" carries with it an implication of power or, at the least, of cultural dominance. The forces that led to a demand for workmen's compensation were entirely domestic, as this study has argued. The fact that European solutions to similar problems were studied and, to an extent, adopted here shows not dominance but an attempt to economize time, skill, and effort by borrowing an appropriate model. It would be quite wrong to detect European legal "influence" in this process. The existence of the European compensation plans was not a cause of similar

---

95. Other instances of supposed cultural lag can be analyzed in similar terms. For example, Ogburn used exploitation of the forests and the tardy rise of conservation laws as another illustration of the lag. *See* W. OGBURN, *supra* note 84, at 203-10. Professor Hurst's elaborate study of law and the Wisconsin lumber industry demonstrates that the legal system supported the exploitation of the forests of Wisconsin in the 19th century; the public did not and would not consider the ultimate social costs of destroying the forests. "Common opinion through the lumber era considered that the public interest *had no greater concern* than the increase of the productive capacity of the general economy." J. WILLARD HURST, LAW AND ECONOMIC GROWTH 261 (1964) (emphasis added). "[T]he dominant attention of nineteenth-century policy was upon promotional rather than regulative use of law." *Id.* The crucial problem was how to develop and settle the continent, not how to conserve or reforest. Certainly no one was concerned with playgrounds for unborn urban masses. People backed demands arising out of immediate interests: the development of stable, economically prosperous communities. Courts reflected these attitudes. Blindness to future needs for natural resources did not result from evil intentions or from a yielding to the "pine barons"; the law reflected "prevailing community values," seeking concrete solutions to problems concretely and currently perceived. *Id.*

96. *See* 1 A. LARSON, WORKMEN'S COMPENSATION § 5.20 (1964).

American statutes. Rather, the interest shown in the foreign experiences was a response to American dissatisfaction with existing industrial accident law.[97] Similarly, the current drive for an American *ombudsman* is not an example of the "influence" of Scandinavian law. A foreign model here sharpens discussion and provides a ready-made plan. Yet the felt need for such an officer has domestic origins.

## C. *Great Men and Social Change*

Sociologists are fond of pointing out the inaccuracy of the "great-man theory of history," which holds that particular persons play irreplaceably decisive roles in determining the path of social change. The influence of single individuals, they say, is hardly as critical as historians would have us believe.[98] The role of outstanding persons in bringing about workmen's compensation acts seems on one level quite clear. In Wisconsin, Roujet Marshall excoriated the existing system from the bench; off the bench he was a vigorous champion of the new law and, indeed, helped draft it. John R. Commons worked tirelessly for passage of the act, and served on the first Industrial Commission whose obligation it was to administer the law.[99] His writings and teachings helped mobilize informed public opinion and virtually created a lobby of academicians for workmen's compensation. Political figures, businessmen, union leaders, and others played active roles in the passage of the law. It is quite tempting to say that the Wisconsin law would be unthinkable but for the work of Marshall, or Commons, or LaFollette and the Progressive tradition in the state, or the craftsmanship of Wisconsin's pioneering legislative reference service under the skilled leadership of Charles McCarthy.[100] Reformers and academicians served as important middlemen in mediating between interest groups and working out compromises. Their arguments legitimated the act; their zeal enlisted support of middle-class neutrals. They were willing to do the spadework of research, drafting, and propagandizing necessary for a viable law. In the passage of many other welfare and reform laws, outstanding personalities can be found who played dominant roles in creating and leading public opinion—for example, Lawrence Veiller for the New York tenement housing law of 1901,[101] Harvey Wiley for the Federal Food and Drug Act.[102]

The great-man hypothesis is not susceptible of proof or disproof. But the course of events underlying workmen's compensation at least suggests that

97. Of course, cross-cultural borrowing of legal institutions presupposes a certain level of world interchange of culture. At the time workmen's compensation was adopted, American intellectuals were in close communication with Europe, and academics were in particular infatuated with things German. African or Asiatic models—had they existed—most likely would have been ignored. America was disposed to learn from Englishmen and Germans, not from Chinese or Bantus.
98. *See, e.g.,* FREEDMAN 83 (rev. ed. 1956).
99. *See* 2 J. COMMONS, INSTITUTIONAL ECONOMICS 854 (1934).
100. On McCarthy, see J. COMMONS, MYSELF 107-11 (1934).
101. *See generally* R. LUBOVE, THE PROGRESSIVES AND THE SLUMS (1962).
102. *See* O. ANDERSON, JR., THE HEALTH OF A NATION (1958).

social scientists are properly suspicious of placing too much reliance on a great-man view. If the view here expressed is correct, then economic, social, political and legal forces made workmen's compensation (or some alternative, such as FELA) virtually inevitable by the end of the nineteenth century. Outstanding men may be necessary in general for the implementation of social change; someone must take the lead in creating the intellectual basis for a change in perception. Nonetheless, when a certain pattern of demand exists in society, more than one person may be capable of filling that role. Particular individuals are normally not indispensable. The need is for talent—men with extraordinary ability, perseverance, and personal influence, men who can surmount barriers and accomplish significant results. Obviously, the absence of outstanding persons interested in a particular cause can delay problem solving or lead to inept, shoddy administration. The appearance of truly exceptional persons at the proper moment in history is undoubtedly not automatic. But talent, if not genius, may well be a constant in society; and the social order determines whether and in what direction existing talent will be exerted.

Thus, it would be foolish to deny that specific individuals exert great influence upon the development of social events, and equally foolish to conclude that other persons could not have done the job as well (or better) if given the opportunity. "Great men," however, must be in the right place, which means that society must have properly provided for the training and initiative of outstanding persons and for their recruitment into critical offices when needed. In difficult times, great businessmen, political leaders, musicians, or physicists will emerge. "Great men" appear "when the time is ripe"—but only insofar as society has created the conditions for a pool of creative manpower dedicated to the particular line of endeavor in which their greatness lies.

### POSTSCRIPT: WORKMEN'S COMPENSATION AND AFTER

We have called workmen's compensation a solution to the problem that called it forth, defining a solution as a stable compromise. In what sense can the present system be called stable? A literature of attack on it is certainly at hand.[103] It has been criticized as not "adaptable enough to keep abreast of a changing environment";[104] some say it has not "removed litigiousness";[105] at mid-century, others report that "despite the progress from the modest beginnings of 50 years ago, employers and labor are both dissatisfied with workmen's compensation."[106] In what sense, then, has workmen's compensation been a solution at all?

---

103. *See generally* H. Somers & A. Somers, *supra* note 56, at 268-89; A. Brodie, *The Adequacy of Workmen's Compensation as Social Insurance: A Review of Developments and Proposals,* 1963 Wis. L. Rev. 56, 63-91.
104. H. Somers & A. Somers, *supra* note 56, at 269.
105. *See id.* at 178; A. Brodie, *supra* note 103, at 63.
106. A. Brodie, *supra* note 103, at 74.

It has certainly not been stable in the sense of unchanging. Few, if any statutory programs have been so frequently tampered with. Not a session of the Wisconsin legislature, for example, goes by without amendments—some major, some minor—proposed and frequently passed.[107] Many changes have also come about through judge-made law, or through judicial ratification of changes initiated by the various state commissions. The original concept of the industrial accident almost seems buried under layers of statutory and judicial accretion. In some states compensation may be paid for heart attacks suffered on the job.[108] Not *all* heart attacks, to be sure, are compensable; the hairline distinctions and causistry involved in deciding which ones bring recovery rival the ramifications of the fellow-servant rule at its height.[109] Thousands of accidents are compensable that have nothing to do with the impact of machine upon man in an industrial setting. A bartender hit by a stray bullet fired by a customer's wife,[110] a teacher struck by a student's missile,[111] and a traveling salesman burnt in his sleep by a hotel fire[112] have recovered for their losses. Moreover, the law seems to have wandered from the notion that compensation covers only economic loss. Thus, losses of arms and legs are compensable without showing a connection with the injured man's power to earn,[113] and awards have been occasionally made for disfigurement seemingly unrelated to earning capacity.[114] The full significance of these and other changes would require extensive treatment in itself. But the stupendous number of reported cases, the huge bulk of the technical literature on the law of compensation, and the constant statutory tinkering with the program indicate that workmen's compensation has embarked on a voyage comparable to that of the fellow-servant rule, except that the direction is toward expanding rather than contracting a principle. Compensation is stable, then, only in the sense that it is the base onto which accretions are added. The many changes are in it and to it, not from it. In this respect it is similar to the federal income tax law—constantly amended and tinkered with, but in the predictable future accepted in essential structure as a fact of legal and social life.

If all the tendencies of the case law were followed to their logical limit, then workmen's compensation would end up covering workers for all illnesses, injuries, and disabilities which might be linked somehow to the job—either

---

107. Thus, in 1963 the Wisconsin statute was amended so that (among other things) a worker who suffers injury on the job and whose hearing aid is damaged, can recover also for the damage to his hearing aid. WIS. STAT. ANN. § 102.01 (Supp. 1966).

108. *E.g.*, Rebsamen West, Inc. v. Bailey, 396 S.W.2d 822 (Ark. Sup. Ct. 1965).

109. *See generally* 1 A. LARSON, *supra* note 96, at § 38.64 (1965); J. Wigginton, *The Heart of the Working Man—A Post Mortem*, 17 U. FLA. L. REV. 543 (1965).

110. Industrial Indem. Co. v. Industrial Accident Comm'n, 95 Cal. App. 2d 804, 214 P.2d 41 (Dist. Ct. App. 1950).

111. Whitney v. Rural Independent School Dist. No. 4, 232 Iowa 61, 4 N.W.2d 394 (1942).

112. Wiseman v. Industrial Accident Comm'n, 46 Cal. 2d 570, 297 P.2d 649 (1956).

113. Alaska Indus. Bd. v. Chugach Elec. Ass'n, 356 U.S. 320, 323 (1958).

114. See 2 A. LARSON, *supra* note 96, at § 58.32.

causally, or because they happened during working hours. Present law is far from reaching this point, and most likely it cannot reach it, within the limits of a compensation system. Vastly increased coverage would levy an unacceptable tax on industry, and if compensation reached the point where it became a kind of total social insurance for workers, industry would demand further spreading of the risk. Institutionally, it is difficult for courts and legislatures to go fast or far *within* a compensation system, since the traditional limits of the system help define its legitimacy, and its legitimacy in turn suggests definite limits. The words of the statute prevent judges from going past a certain invisible point in stretching language. Legislatures make only marginal changes because of the absence, so far, of a strong sustained call for a great broadening of scope.

One possible change in direction would be an abandonment of compensation in favor of a more comprehensive plan secured by state insurance. Such a change would give up the theory that compensation costs are allocated in accordance with industrial responsibility for the injuries of employees and replace it with a more general social theory of welfare and risk. The British have reached this stage.[115] Whether the United States will in the near future is doubtful. Old-age assistance, medicare and other welfare programs may blunt the demand—or, conversely, they may prepare the way for it. Perhaps workmen's compensation will fall if the irrationalities of the present system become so gross that all parties in interest agree to abandon it, just as the fellow-servant rule was abandoned.

In short, workmen's compensation is in the second of the three stages which the fellow-servant rule itself went through—the stage of technical complexity and unstable compromise. Nothing here is intended to suggest that the third stage must come within some definite time-period or that it must come at all. To make definite predictions would be foolish. Even sensible guessing is not possible without careful comparative study of the life-cycle of legal rules and doctrines. It is clear, however, that the general three-stage pattern followed by the fellow-servant rule is quite common.[116] This is because such a pattern is the natural result of the impact of social change, moving more or less in one

---

115. National Insurance (Industrial Injuries) Act of 1946, 9 & 10 Geo. 6, ch. 62, *as amended*, 11 & 12 Geo. 6, ch. 42 (1948).

116. Another example is provided by the national quotas system in immigration law, which was unpopular with some groups and under attack throughout its history. Immigration Act of 1924, ch. 190, 43 Stat. 153. It went through a period of high complexity and unstable compromises before being abolished in 1965. Act of Oct. 3, 1965, Pub. L. No. 89-236, § 1, 79 Stat. 911. In the middle stage, the basic restrictive features of immigration law were complicated by private immigration and naturalization bills, as well as special statutory provisions for relatives of citizens, refugees, and others. Between 1952 and 1965 probably "two out of every three immigrants entered the United States outside the quota restrictions." It was finally replaced by a more "liberal" bill, which carefully protected the vital interests of those groups which opposed free, open immigration, while removing the complexity and iniquity of the system of national quotas. *See* T. Scully, *Is the Door Open Again?—A Survey of our New Immigration Law*, 13 U.C.L.A.L. Rev. 227, 236 (1966). *See generally id.* at 242-44.

definite direction, upon a given area of law. If the proper societal demands are made, wide-reaching changes in law inevitably come about; and the process of change in the law, despite enormous diversities, produces noticeable regularities of behavior.

# 11

# THE HISTORICAL BACKGROUND OF THE AMERICAN LAW OF ADOPTION

*STEPHEN B. PRESSER*

# THE HISTORICAL BACKGROUND OF THE AMERICAN LAW OF ADOPTION

Stephen B. Presser*

## I. INTRODUCTION

Over 150,000 children are now legally adopted in the United States each year.[1] The American law of adoption, however, is of quite recent vintage, and there remain in our law vestiges of an older attitude that would sacrifice the interests of families created by adoption in favor of natural relationships.[2] The legally-sanctioned custom of adopting children as heirs was unknown to the common law, although it was well-known in Roman practice, and passed nearly unchanged in the civil law.[3] No general adoption statutes were passed in America before about 1850, however, and no British statute was enacted before 1926.[4] Once American legislatures had begun to act on the problem of adoption, however, it was not long before a host of states enacted some form of adoption law. Within twenty-five years of the passage of the first statutes, twenty-four states had adoption legislation.[5] This chronology raises a series of intriguing questions for the legal historian: Why was the Roman practice of adoption not incorporated into the common law? Why did the English and American legislatures wait so long before passing adoption laws? Since there had been virtually no law on adoption

---

* A.B., Harvard College 1968; J.D., Harvard Law School 1971; member, Massachusetts State Bar; clerk, United States Court of Appeals, D.C. Circuit.

For constant inspiration and encouragement in connection with the writing of this article, the author wishes to thank Professor Morton Horwitz of the Harvard Law School.

[1] UNITED STATES CHILDREN'S BUREAU, STATISTICAL SERIES NO. 92, SUPPLEMENT TO CHILD WELFARE STATISTICS—1967: ADOPTIONS IN 1967, at 1 (1968).

[2] *See, e.g.*, Oelsner, *Adoption: Toward a Limit on Natural Mother's Claim,* N.Y. Times, April 25, 1971, § 4, at 8, col. 5.

[3] *See generally* Huard, *The Law of Adoption: Ancient and Modern,* 9 VAND. L. REV. 743 (1956) (hereinafter cited as Huard).

[4] Great Britain Statutes, 1926, 16 & 17 Geo. 5, c. 29. *See generally* ABBOT, THE CHILD AND THE STATE 204-228 (1938).

[5] *See* notes 111 & 112 *infra.*

for over a thousand years in what had become the Anglo-American system of jurisprudence, why were so many adoption statutes passed in America in such a comparatively short time?[6] Definitive answers to these questions may not be possible, in part because few documentary sources exist which explain the motivations of the adoption lawmakers,[7] and in part because the phenomenon of adoption is inseparable from many social and legal problems having to do with child-care and inheritance. Nevertheless, this article is an attempt to grapple with the perplexing history of the law of adoption, and in particular with the passage of the adoption legislation in the third quarter of the nineteenth century in America. In the discussion which follows, some suggestions are made as to solutions of the historical problems of adoption.

In the first sections of this article, the different views that the law has taken of the practice of adoption are presented, beginning with a brief examination of the law of Rome and some earlier civilizations. Next, the medieval English law relating to adoption and inheritance and the child-rearing methods of the time are examined for purposes of contrasting them with those of the Roman empire and of illustrating how children were brought up in a system that did not permit legal adoption. The discussion then shifts to the treatment of children in early America, particular attention being paid to the practice of caring for orphans in the seventeenth and eighteenth centuries, to see how *this* system operated before children could be legally adopted. Next, the first legislation on adoption in America, the "private" adoption laws, will be discussed, along with some contemporary judicial comment. The general statutes then will be considered, laws which provided a mechanism for adopting children. Next, a contemporary analysis and criticism of the general adoption legislation will be presented, and the historical background of the American adoption legislation will be discussed. The roots in the nineteenth century movement for child welfare will be emphasized to shed some light on some of the difficulties of the adop-

---

[6] To a very limited extent, the question "Why was the first British law passed so long after the first American law?" will also be considered.

[7] *See* text accompanying notes 125-127 *infra.*

tion laws. These difficulties, in the form of the opinions of courts which interpreted the adoption law during the second half of the nineteenth century, will be considered last.

As some of the material to be considered will show, and as common sense would indicate, it *was* possible for children to be "adopted" into a family before there was any legislation about adoption. In such a situation, of course, the child was entirely dependent on his adopting parents for his maintenance and support, and could usually expect no assistance from the law in enforcing any obligations which his adopting parents might have toward him. It may be helpful in the course of the discussion which follows for the reader to bear in mind the distinctions between this kind of informal adoption and what is here referred to as "legal" adoption.[8] One who has adopted a child will usually be referred to as the "adopted parent."

## II.   ADOPTION AMONG THE ROMANS AND EARLIER CIVILIZATIONS

Sir Henry Maine, in his *Ancient Law*, takes the position that the early patriarchal civilizations would not have been able to grow out of their "swaddling clothes" without the custom of adoption.[9] It is Maine's contention that without the fiction of adoption, primitive tribes could not have absorbed each other, or could not have combined except on terms of "absolute superiority on one side and absolute subjection on the other."[10] Primitive peoples also found a strong motive for the artificial extension of the family in their desire for male issue to perpetuate the family rites of ancestor worship.[11]

---

[8] Following *Black's Law Dictionary*, the latter type of adoption may be defined as "The act of one who has taken another's child into his own family, treating him as his own, and giving him all the rights and duties of his own child in a manner provided by and with consequences specified in statute." BLACK'S LAW DICTIONARY 70 (4th ed. 1968).

[9] MAINE, ANCIENT LAW 125ff., 26 (1861). Sir Henry Maine's theory is quoted and analyzed in 1 HOWARD, A HISTORY OF MATRIMONIAL INSTITUTIONS (1904).

[10] MAINE, *supra* note 9, at 125ff.

[11] HOWARD, *supra* note 9, at 13. The same motive of ancestor worship apparently resulted in the old Chinese custom whereby a childless male was entitled (as recently as ninety years ago) to claim the first-born male child of any of his younger brothers. This

We can document the practice of adoption among the ancient Babylonians,[12] Egyptians,[13] and Hebrews,[14] as well as the Greeks,[15] but the most advanced early law on adoption which we have is from the Romans.[16] In contrast with current adoption law, which has as its purpose the "best interests" of the child,[17] it appears that ancient adoption law, and particularly the Roman example, was clearly designed to benefit the *adoptor*, and any benefits to the adoptee were secondary.[18] There were two broad purposes that Roman adoption law served: (1) to avoid extinction of the family, and (2) to perpetuate rites of family religious worship.[19] The exact provisions of the Roman law varied over time, from the beginning of the empire when the basic unit of Roman society was the family, to the later days when, under the Code of Justinian, "the individual had, to a great extent, become the unit of society, and the law had adapted itself to the change."[20] In the beginning, the law was that the adopted child had all his relations with his former family severed, but according to Justinian, the adopted child usually retained his right to the succession of his natural father.[21] This change in policy is an early example of what we will see to have occurred

---

was because "[o]ne of the gravest calamities to be apprehended by a Chinaman is to die without leaving a male posterity to care for his ashes and decorate his grave, thereby pacifying his wandering spirit in purgatory." Note, *Laws of Adoption in China*, 15 CHIC. L.N. 362 (1883).

[12] *See* Huard 744.

[13] *Exodus* 2:10 (The Egyptian princess adopts Moses).

[14] *Id.; see also Esther* 2:5-8 (Mordecai adopts his niece, Esther).

[15] *See* Huard 743.

[16] *Id.* at 744.

[17] *See generally* WITMER, HERZOG, et al., INDEPENDENT ADOPTIONS 24ff. (1963) (hereinafter cited as WITMER).

[18] Huard 745. *See also* Brosnan, *The Law of Adoption*, 22 COL. L. REV. 332 (1922); Quarles, *The Law of Adoption—A Legal Anamoly*, 32 MARQ. L. REV. 237 (1949). Rather than having a great concern for the unwanted child, ancient tribes appear to have often resorted to the handy expedient of infanticide. *See, e.g.,* 1 HOWARD, *supra* note 9, at 78, 79, 87. Both the Roman's and Greeks also indulged in that practice. *See, e.g.,* SLINGERLAND, CHILD PLACING IN FAMILIES 28 (1919). The practice of infanticide was particularly offensive to the nineteenth century child-welfare reformers, who were bent on eradicating the practice. *See* N.Y. Times, Dec. 12, 1857, at 8, col. 1.

[19] Brosnan, *supra* note 18.

[20] Note, *The Effect of the Law of Adoption Upon Rights of Inheritance*, 1 SO. L. REV. 70, 76 (1875).

[21] *Id., quoting* JUSTINIAN'S INSTITUTES (Sandars) 369, lib. III, tit. I, 10.

in American adoption law, where adoption law also reflects changes in the social structure which it serves.[22] However, it is to the early character of the Roman laws, and in particular the singularly Roman notions involved in the idea that one can have a connection with one family only, that we now turn. This notion from the early Roman law is bound up in the Roman concept of the *patria potestas*, which bears explaining in some detail.

Under either of the two types of adoption permitted by Roman law,[23] the adopted child subjected himself to the *patria potestas*, the "parental power," of his new father. In its original form (later emperors made it somewhat less encompassing), the *patria potestas* was a complete power over the offspring and descendants, including even the power of life and death.[24] This aspect of the Roman law of adoption had a strong effect on some American judges, who were repelled by the Roman parental power since "with us, every man who has reached his majority is free from [anyone else's] power."[25] The Connecticut Supreme Court thought that the *patria potestas* was illustrative of a deep organic difference between Roman society and our own, and in 1908, in *Woodward's Appeal*,[26] that court offered the explanation that it was the inherent notion of the free individual of the Anglo-American common law which prevented adoption, with its concept of the *patria potestas*, from being included in it.[27] This "individualistic" character of the common law, and its abhorrence of the *patrias potestas*, is a neat explanation for the non-incorporation of adoption, but it falls short of providing the

---

[22] *See, e.g.,* text accompanying note 143 *infra.*

[23] The two types were 1) "arrogation," or "adrogation," where a child who was not a member of another family (presumably because his parents had died), entered into a new one on his own, and 2) "adoption" in the strict sense, which applied to children already under a *patria potestas.* Huard 745.

[24] BLACK'S LAW DICTIONARY 1283 (4th ed. 1968).

[25] Woodward's Appeal, 81 Conn. 152, 163 (1908).

[26] *Id.*

[27] The Connecticut court was also disturbed by the fact that the *patria potestas* cut both ways. Not only did the father gain power over the child, but the children (even the adopted ones) had a "quasi interest or ownership in [their father's] property during his life," and were thus entitled to take in cases of intestacy. The court could not accept this, since "[w]ith us a child has no interest in his father's property, which in case of intestacy is taken possession of by the law and distributed among those related to the intestate by blood according to prescribed rules." 81 Conn. at 163.

answers to the questions which are sought here, particularly in light of the fact already noted, that the *patria potestas* had lost most of its awesome significance by the time of the later emperors. Indeed, it finally dwindled to "little more than a right in the *paterfamilias* to hold as his own any property or acquisitions of one under his power."[28] It would seem, then, that the early framers of the common law, if they were familiar with Roman law at all,[29] would have realized, how the *patria potestas* had diminished, and it alone would not have deterred them from accepting the idea of adoption had they thought such acceptance necessary.

III.   EARLY ENGLISH LAW RELATING TO ADOPTION AND IN-
HERITANCE

The usual explanation for the absence of a legal recognition of adoption in the English common law is the inordinately high regard for blood lineage of the English.[30] As one commentator observed fifteen years ago:

> The primitive understanding of adoption required the adoptee to become a member of the adopter's family, to acquire a quasi-interest in the adopter's property while the latter lived and to succeed to such property upon the adopter's death. But to the English, heirs meant legitimate children who were heirs of the blood.[31]

This feeling was epitomized in the oft-quoted statement of Glanvill, "Only God can make a *heres*, not man."[32] Maitland in his great work with Sir Frederick Pollock tells us, however, that Glanvill's maxim may be of relatively recent vintage:

> [F]ar back in remote centuries Englishmen had seen no difficulty in giving the name *heres* to a person chosen by a land-holder to succeed him in his holding at his death. And so with the English word for which *heres* has been an equivalent. It was not inconceivable that a man should name an *yrfeweard* to succeed him. We are far from

---

[28] BLACK'S LAW DICTIONARY 1283 (4th ed. 1968), *citing* MACKELD, ROMAN LAW, § 589.

[29] Evidence indicates that at least in the period of English history with which we are concerned, English lawyers *were* quite familiar with Roman law and practice. 1 F. POLLOCK AND F. MAITLAND, THE HISTORY OF ENGLISH LAW 111ff. (2d ed. 1898) (hereinafter cited as P&M).

[30] *See, e.g.,* Huard 745; WITMER 21-23.

[31] *See* Huard 745-46.

[32] Glanvill, vii., 1., *quoted in* 2 P&M 254.

believing that this could be done of common right, or that this nomi-
nated *yrfeweard* was a *heres* in the Roman sense of that term; but
while in Glanvill's day it would have been a contradiction in terms
to speak of an heir who was not of the blood of the dead man, this
had not been so in the past.[33]

Glanvill's rule also may have had much more to do with expressing a sentiment against testamentary bequests and inter vivos
gifts to non-related persons than it did with adoption.[34]

By the time of Shakespeare, it seemed evident that an heir
to the crown could not be created by adoption. In *Henry VI* the
Bard has a scene in which Henry attempts to establish his title
in an argument with York on the grounds that King Richard had
resigned the crown to his grandfather, Henry IV.[35] But it is
pointed out to Henry that Richard was forced to abdicate, and
even if Richard's abdication were "unconstrain'd," "he could
not so resign his crown but that the next heir should succeed and
reign."[36] In the Middle Ages, the feeling that an outsider could
not be brought into the family to inherit to the prejudice of the
expected heirs undoubtedly extended throughout all the classes
which owned property in the English realm, since in Maitland's
words, "[i]n the thirteenth century no wide gulf could be fixed
between the inheritance of a kingdom and other impartible inheritances."[37]

At the time of Bracton the law may have been leaning toward some kind of recognition of adoption,[38] and in some cases
courts would go far to legitimize an heir. Maitland refers to one
case during the reign of Edward I which involved a decedent who
had been beyond the seas for three years immediately after
marrying his wife.[39] About a month before the husband's return,

---

[33] 2 P & M 254.

[34] *Id.* at 293, 308ff. The rule pertains to a system of land ownership before the
Statute of Wills in 1540, and at a time when the consent of a man's heirs was necessary
before he could alienate land, if he would be permitted to alienate it at all. *See also*
WITMER 23.

[35] 3 *Henry VI* at I, i.

[36] For a discussion of Shakespeare's understanding of adoption, *see* WITMER 22.

[37] 2 P & M 300.

[38] *Id.* at 398-99, *citing Bracton* f.63b.

[39] 2 P&M 398. The case is Y.B., 32-33 Edw. I, p. 63.

the wife gave birth to a female child who had brought an assize of *mort d'ancestor* on the death of the husband. The assize concluded, sensibly it would seem, that the plaintiff should lose, but the justices sitting on appeal reversed, and treated the girl as his lawful child. Their *ratio decidendi:* "[F]or the privities of husband and wife are not to be known, and he might have come by night and engendered the plaintiff."[40] Maitland concludes, ever, that the law's seeming tendency toward permitting variations in the strict inheritance scheme was really "no more than the result of a very strong presumption—a presumption which absolves the court from difficult inquiries—and from the time when it rejects the claims of the 'mantle-children' onwards to our own day, we have no adoption in England."[41]

The dispute over the "mantle-children" to which Maitland refers illustrates another possible reason for the reluctance of English courts to incorporate adoption into the English law in the thirteenth century. In Germany, France, and Normandy there was an ancient custom whereby children, who were born out of wedlock but whose parents afterwards intermarried, could be legitimated. "The children, together with the father and mother, stood under a cloth extended while the marriage was solemnized. It was in the nature of adoption. . . . They were called 'mantle children.' "[42] Even in England, this custom apparently legitimated children in the eye of the canon law.[43] A great controversy over whether to accept the canon law rule into the common law preceded the *Statute of Merton*, 20 Henry III,

---

[40] 2 P&M 398.

[41] *Id.* at 398-99.

[42] BLACK'S LAW DICTIONARY 1264 (*Pallio Cooperire*) (4th ed. 1968). *See also* 2 P&M 397. The ceremonial legitimation of the "mantle children" is reminiscent of another ceremonial adoption reported by Margaret Kirnitzer:

> The real beginnings of adoption take us back into mythology, and *The Golden Bough* relates a story of Diodours to the effect that when Hera adopted Hercules, 'the goddess got into bed, and clasping the burly hero to her bosom, pushed him through her robes and let him fall to the ground in imitation of a real birth;' and the historian adds that in his own day the same mode of adopting children was practised by the barbarians. M. KIRNITZER, CHILD ADOPTION IN THE MODERN WORLD 346 (1952).

[43] 2 P&M 397-98.

A.D. 1236. But by the statute this rule was firmly rejected in the course of "a famous scene":[44]

> And all the Bishops instanted the Lords, that they would consent, that all such as were born before matrimony should be legitimate, as well as they that be born within matrimony, as to the succession of inheritance, forsomuch as the Church accepteth such for legitimate. And all the Earls and Barons with one voice answered, that they would not change the laws of the realm, which hitherto have been used and approved.[45]

There may have been various reasons for the refusal of the *Statute of Merton* to recognize the "mantle-children," but one in particular appears to have struck commentators:

> The remarkable opposition to the introducing this part of the civil law probably arose from its being proposed by one of the Poictevine favorites of Henry the Third. The sturdy Barons not approving of the proposer rejected the proposal *una voce*. You are a foreigner and shall not introduce foreign laws, be they good or bad.[46]

While the legitimation of children is not strictly the same as adoption, it does appear that the problem of the "mantle-children" was thought of in terms of adoption,[47] and thus the common law's failure to incorporate adoption may be attributable to some extent to English xenophobia.

Recent scholarship suggests one more, albeit somewhat problematical, reason for the unwillingness to accept adopted heirs. According to Maitland, there was a right of inheritance of fiefs held by military service in legitimate children which dated from the days of the Conquest.[48] Professor Samuel Thorne has questioned this assumption of Maitland's and has suggested that

---

[44] *Id.*

[45] Et rogaverunt omnes Episcopi magnates ut consentirent quod nate anti matrimonium essent legitimi sicut illi qui nate sunt post matrimonium quantum ad successionem hereditariam quia ecclesiatales habet pro legitimis. Et omnes comites et barones una voce responderunt quod nolunt leges angliae mutare que hucusque usitate sunt et approbate.
(Translation from I Statutes at Large 9 (Queen Anne) (1704).)

[46] BARRINGTON, OBSERVATIONS ON ANCIENT STATUTES 44, 45 (1796), *discussed in* Joachimsen, *The Statute to Legalize the Adoption of Minor Children*, 8 ALB. L.J. 353, 355 (1873).

[47] 2 P&M 397-98.

[48] 2 P&M 314-16.

452          *JOURNAL OF FAMILY LAW*          [Vol. 11

from the Conquest until about the year 1200, the military fief, a chief mode of land tenure at that time, was *not* heritable. Thorne argues that the Lord over the land, to whom the military service was owed, was free to award the land to whom he pleased upon the death of his tenant for service.[49] According to Thorne, the choice of a new tenant was originally made on the basis of who could best provide the military service that was desired. Over the years, however, it came to be accepted, through convenience and expectancy, that the land would pass to the children of the former tenant.[50] If it were true that immediately after the Conquest the Lord could choose whomever he wanted to succeed his tenant, then at that time there really were no heirs except heirs by "adoption" (although it was the Lord who was doing the "adopting," not the tenant who was succeeded). If there were many capricious choices made by Lords which caused resentment in enough of the offspring of former tenants who were left landless, perhaps this resentment eventually resulted in a reluctance on the part of the common law judges to recognize "adopted" heirs of the tenant himself.

Whatever the ostensible reasons for the English common law's refusal to incorporate adoption, in light of the generally utilitarian character of the law,[51] it seems probable that at that time there was no strongly felt need for a practice of adoption as there was for the Romans of antiquity or the Americans of the nineteenth century. It will be remembered that the Roman practice served two purposes: the perpetuation of religious rites and the avoidance of the extinction of the family. The first purpose was clearly inappropriate to a land that had turned away from the pagan dieties of Rome to the Roman Catholic Church. While there may have been some sympathy with the second purpose,[52] it does not appear to have been overwhelming or widespread enough to have necessitated accommodation by the law.

---

[49] Thorne, *English Feudalism and Estates in Land*, 1959 CAMB. L.J. 193.

[50] *Id.* at 196-99.

[51] *See, e.g.*, HOLMES, THE COMMON LAW 5 (Howe ed. 1963). "The substance of the law at any given time pretty nearly corresponds so far as it goes, with what is then understood to be convenient. . . ." *Id.*

[52] The most accessible record of the manifestation of this desire is the case of the unfortunate Grace of Saleby, as told by Maitland. 2 P&M 391-92. Very briefly, in Old

The purpose of the American adoption statutes passed in the middle of the nineteenth century was to provide for the welfare of dependent children, a purpose quite different from that of the old Roman laws. If there was a perceived need for a similar mechanism to provide for the welfare of children in England in the late Middle Ages, adoption might have been introduced into the law. It appears, however, that at that time, and for many years to come, there were mechanisms for the care of children, dependent and otherwise, that made adoption for social welfare purposes unnecessary. These mechanisms, which were instituted early[53] and which were very well developed by the seventeenth century,[54] were the institutions of "putting out" and "apprenticeship." In a very real sense these institutions were a form of "adoption," although the purpose was neither inheritance nor the perpetuation of the adoptor's family, but the temporary training of the child:

> Apprentices . . . were workers who were also children, extra sons or extra daughters (for girls could be apprenticed too), clothed and educated as well as fed, obliged to obedience and forbidden to marry, unpaid and absolutely dependent until the age of 21.[55]

Apparently very nearly all young people during the 16th century in England were shifted out of their homes for some extended period of time. "Most young people in service, except, of course, the apprentices, seem to have looked upon a change

---

Lincolnshire there lived an ancient childless Knight, Thomas of Saleby. Thomas' wife did not want the patrimony to pass out of the immediate family, so she took to her bed and claimed that she had born a daughter. This child, Grace, was actually the child of a villager's wife. Bishop Hugh, upon hearing of the fraud, threatened to excommunicate Thomas if he kept the child as his own. As Maitland puts it, however, Thomas "feared his wife more than he feared God," and he would not give up the child. Thomas died soon afterwards, apparently because of his defying of the deity's representative, and the rest of Grace's short life was spent in controversies between her husbands (there were three in succession) and the Bishop as to whether or not she was really an heir. In the end Grace died childless, and Thomas' property "at length fell to the rightful heir," where it would have gone had there been no Grace.

[53] The beginnings go back to the feudal system and the patriarchial society in the dimness before. *See* ARIES, CENTURIES OF CHILDHOOD 192 (Baldick transl. 1962) (hereinafter cited as ARIES) and LASLETT, THE WORLD WE HAVE LOST 150 (1965) (hereinafter cited as LASLETT).

[54] *See generally* LASLETT 1-3, 53-80.

[55] *Id*. at 3.

of job bringing them into a new family as the normal thing every few years."[56] The "putting out" system extended to the houses of rich and poor alike, although there was a tendency for the poor to pass their children on to the rich, where, perhaps, they could be better trained and cared for.[57] Although there may have been formal schooling in institutions of learning for some, in particular for the wealthy, by far the more common method of education was through "putting out," "a period in which the child left his home and was sent to another house, where he had to learn the manners (or the trade) of the head of the family"[58]:

> It was by means of domestic service that the master transmitted to a child, and not his child, but another man's, knowledge, practical experience, and human worth which he was supposed to possess.[59]

The psychological framework in which these child-rearing practices operated was not the same as that of the reformers of the nineteenth century in America. It has been suggested that until very recently a sharp distinction between the world of the child and the world of the adult was not perceived at all, and it was thought that the best way to bring up the child was not through the extended nurturing by parents, but by thrusting him out into the adult world at what we would consider a tender age (six to nine years or younger) to learn a service or a trade:

> [T]he family at that time was unable to nourish a profound existential attitude between parents and children. This did not mean that the parents did not love their children, but they cared about them less for themselves, for the affection they felt for them, than for the contribution those children could make to the common task.[60]

Assuming that this was the attitude toward children in the thirteenth through the seventeenth centuries, it is difficult to believe that the English at that time would have seen the necessity for laws on adoption like those that came later, laws designed to insure that adoption fulfilled the necessary task of giving the adopted child loving, nurturing surrogate parents. Thus, a few

---

[56] *Id.* at 7.
[57] *Id.* at 69-70.
[58] ARIES 290-91.
[59] *Id.* at 366.
[60] *Id.* at 268.

hundred years ago the "adoption" practice was probably limited to the application of "service" or "apprenticeship." While in a sense "adoption" went on as an every day occurrence, there may have been no need for laws to regulate it, since the indenture or apprenticeship contract might have been sufficient.[61] In any case, the model of "apprenticeship," of "putting out" children, soon came to serve as a convenient means for solving the problem of dependent children, a problem which the adoption statutes later would be designed to deal with.[62]

Many of the most detailed descriptions of the "putting out" and "apprenticeship" systems to be found in the literature are of those that existed in the seventeenth century and before,[63] but it is nonetheless true that "the great families of the nobility and the artisan class remained faithful to the old system of apprenticeship" through the 17th Century, and "in the working class, the apprenticeship system would continue down to our own times."[64] Indeed, for Europe at least, "[i]n the early nineteenth century, a large part of the population, the biggest and poorest section, was still living like the medieval families, with the children separated from their parents."[65]

Having examined the Roman adoption laws, and the climate in which they operated, and having compared these with a social structure a few centuries ago in England which had no real need for such laws, and indeed would not admit them, the next step is to move across the Atlantic to America and discuss the care of children and the practices of adoption there.

---

[61] The later apprenticeship arrangements and contracts are very detailed in the provisions that they make for the child's welfare. *See, e.g.,* REMINISCENCES OF THE BOSTON FEMALE ASYLUM 60ff. (1844). For examples of some early nineteenth century apprenticeship indentures, see the reports of the Boston child welfare societies discussed at note 137 *et seq., infra.*

[62] *See* text accompanying notes 125-170 *infra.*

[63] *See generally* LASLETT 1-3, 53-80.

[64] ARIES 371.

[65] *Id.* at 404.

## IV.  EARLY AMERICAN METHODS FOR THE CARE OF DEPENDENT CHILDREN

As they had existed in sixteenth century England, the customs of "apprenticeship" and "service" were brought to America by the New England Puritans.[66] Historians studying the Puritans are unable to furnish a conclusive, documented explanation for the phenomenon of "putting out" the children from one "well-off" household to another, but the most plausible suggestion seems to be that "Puritan parents did not trust themselves with their own children, . . . they were afraid of spoiling them by too great affection," so they placed them in the homes of others who would bring them up more objectively.[67]

The practice of "putting out," although often done voluntarily by the parent, also was done at the prompting of the state; the Laws of the Massachusetts Colony of 1648 provided that when children were allowed to become "rude, stubborn, and unruly," the state might take them from their parents and place them in another's home.[68] The early laws of Connecticut provided similarly, and indeed, the laws of both colonies provided the death penalty "for a rebellious son and for any child who should smite or curse his parents,"[69] although the courts preferred to put the child out rather than to exterminate him. A study of the Massachusetts town of Dedham has revealed that the town selectmen also possessed the power to place children out of their parents' homes, in furtherance of the "Christian Utopian Closed Corporate Community" that was taking form there.[70] Thus, the governments of these New England colonies and towns were providing services which the public and private adoption acts would provide two hundred years later. In short, the practice of placing a child with foster parents was hardly a new invention of nineteenth century American reformers.[71]

---

[66] *See, e.g.*, DEMOS, FAMILY LIFE IN PLYMOUTH COLONY 70-72 (1970) (hereinafter cited as DEMOS).

[67] MORGAN, THE PURITAN FAMILY 77 (2d ed. 1966).

[68] *Id.* at 78.

[69] *Id.*

[70] LOCKRIDGE, A NEW ENGLAND TOWN: THE FIRST HUNDRED YEARS 15-16 (1970).

[71] There were even occasions when English and American courts would approve of a child being placed in the custody of those not his parents when it would be for the

Through early records concerning the treatment of orphans, it can be seen that "putting out" and "apprenticeship" formed the models for some very early American "adoptions":

> Still another factor behind many of these arrangements for putting children out was the death of one or both of the natural parents. In short, this was the way that seventeenth-century communities took care of orphans.[72]

The usual practice was to provide for the disposition of the child in the will of the parent, and to have him "adopted" by a relative:

> Widow Mary Ring who died in 1631 left her young son Andrew to grow up in the family of her son-in-law Stephen Deane—requiring Deane "to help him forward in the knowledge and feare of God, not to oppresse him by any burdens but to tender him as he will answere to God."[73]

As the example of young Andrew Ring indicates, there was a great dependence on religion as the force that would insure the success of the adoption and the quality of the upbringing of the child. Indeed, it would appear that when there was this great a role for religious belief to play in the process of adoption, and when religion permeated the lives of all,[74] there may have been no need for state laws to oversee the adoption process.[75]

Even where there was no will which gave explicit directions, there was apparently a similar pattern of placing orphans in the homes of relatives. John Demos relates a history of four orphans in Barnstable which merits examining in some detail.[76] The orphans' father died in about 1648; their mother remarried one John Finney, but the mother then died five years later. Finney soon was ready to marry another, but he felt a need to make sure that the four orphans (who were still with him) were properly

---

welfare of the child. These cases are really the earliest "adoption" cases in Anglo-American law. *See generally* Huard 746-47, WITMER 24ff.

[72] DEMOS 73.

[73] *Id.*

[74] *See, e.g.,* MORGAN, *supra* note 67, at 69.

[75] Even when there was a need for adoption law, it may have been the force of religion which motivated reformers who succeeded in getting the laws passed. *See* text accompanying notes 150-155 *infra.*

[76] DEMOS 122.

provided for. Finney wrote to the children's grandfather (his former wife's father) and asked what he should do with the orphans. The grandfather wrote back saying that the only girl of the four was "speedy to come home to me for I purpose to take her as a Daughter." As to the three boys, the grandfather instructed Finney that the first was to be committed "to youer care and trust that you doe provide for him and keep him as youer owne child taking his meanes to help to his maintenance."[77] The second son was to be bound over as an apprentice to be taught a trade, and the third was to remain with Finney "as youer owne sonne to Schoole and to write and read till hee bee fitt for a Master." This episode demonstrates two striking characteristics of the period. One is the great importance that was attached to having the decision as to the disposition of the children made by a blood relative. Although Finney had been the children's stepfather for five years, it was their grandfather who was to decide what was to be done with them.[78] Second, it is inescapable that the seventeenth century Americans *did* have an advanced notion of the child welfare and nurturing purposes of adoption, as the phrases in the grandfather's letter ("I purpose to take her as a Daughter . . . keep him as your owne child . . . as youer owne sonne to Schoole") indicate.[79]

It would appear that orphans who had no relatives were put into homes or "bound out," as it was called in the seventeenth century.[80] This custom affected very large numbers of children,

---

[77] This particular provision is probably more reflective of early law on guardianship, an arrangement whereby a child's guardian maintained him out of his (the child's) estate. *See generally* REEVE, THE LAW OF BARON & FEMME 311ff. (1816). This is to be contrasted with adoption, where the child is maintained usually at the expense of his adopted parents, and where the child may have no estate at all.

[78] This deference to blood relations in matters of dependent children was also a powerful factor in court decisions which interpreted the adoption laws more than two hundred years later. *See* text accompanying notes 171-267 *infra*.

[79] It should be noted that the practice of "putting out" does not appear to be universal in the colonies. Grevn, *Family Structures in Seventeenth Century Andover*, 23 WM. & MARY Q. 234 (3d ser. 1966). In Andover, at least, the aim was to keep the sons tied to the family farm rather than to put them in the care of someone else. It is not clear, however, whether the failure to practice the custom of "putting out" had any influence on the treatment of orphans.

[80] *See generally* 1 CALHOUN, A SOCIAL HISTORY OF THE AMERICAN FAMILY 57ff. (1917) (hereinafter cited as CALHOUN).

and unhappily there are indications that the custom often may
have been utilized more for the economic uses of child labor than
for the good of the children.[81] The colonization of the new world
seemed, indeed, to furnish an ideal place to make use of the
orphans of England:

> In England under Elizabeth poor children were to be trained for some
> trade and the idle were to be punished. In the reign of James I the
> statutes of Elizabeth for binding children were utilized for sending
> them to America. The apprenticing of poor children to the Virginia
> Co. began as early as 1620. . . . A record of 1627 reads: "There are
> many ships going to Virginia, and with them 1400 or 1500 children
> which they have gathered up in divers places."[82]

Fortunately, laws were soon passed which provided that apprentices and indentured servants who were orphans must be well
cared for and trained, or the state would remove them from their
masters.[83]

Particularly in the South, it was customary in the eighteenth
century for those of great wealth to incorporate large groups of
orphans and others into their "families." In Georgia, for instance, in 1740 there lived a Mr. Whitefields, who was said to
have "by far the largest family of any in this colony." Whitefield's "family" consisted of almost one hundred and fifty individuals and was made up of "[s]ixty persons, including bond
servants, 61 orphans and other poor children, 25 working tradesmen, and others. . . ."[84] By the middle of the nineteenth century, this method of caring for dependent children by placing
them into new families, and in particular by placing the child in
a family to whom he was related by blood, was widely practiced.
By this time the custom had come to be referred to as "adoption," and its effects made a great impression upon the observor:

> "One blessed custom they have in America," wrote an English visitor
> in 1848, "resulting from the abundance which they enjoy; a man dies,
> his widow and children are objects of peculiar care to the surviving
> branches of his family; the mother dies—her orphans find a home
> among her friends and relatives."[85]

---

[81] 1 CALHOUN 171-72.

[82] 1 CALHOUN 306-07.

[83] *Id.* at 308.

[84] *Id.* at 232.

[85] 2 CALHOUN 23. *See also id.* at 144: "The different members of the family," wrote
an observer of 1833-1834, "are firmly united together." When a brother or sister dies

Another impressed visitor wrote in 1852 that he was struck by "how easily and frankly children are adopted in the United States, how pleasantly the scheme goes on, and how little of the wormwood of domestic jealousies, or the fretting prickle of neighbors' criticisms" interfered with it. The custom's spectacular success in America led the visitor to speculate why "the benevolent practice" was so common in this country. He concluded that there were a number of reasons why adoption existed and was so successful in America. One was the vast abundance of the country, which made it easy to feed more hungry mouths; another was the need on the part of "the sons of labor" for more hands to help with their work, which made them "quite as ready to adopt a child as the wealthy." A third reason given by this visitor was the absence of primogeniture in America. His final assessment of the American practice of adoption was that "if one in a hundred [adopted parents] tired or failed to do by the adopted as they would have done by their own, it was *but* one in the hundred."[86]

The adoption picture at the middle of the nineteenth century was not completely genial, however. Parents were often quite careless about letting their children be placed in the far-off homes of strangers. Children's societies were placing thousands of "uninvestigated children in uninvestigated homes all over the prairies."[87] Later in the century, "there was a widespread habit of advertising children for adoption, and parents sold or gave them away."[88] Indeed, one British adoption authority has suggested that it was this seamier side of American child-placing practice that kept Britain from passing an adoption statute until after the first World War. "It may well be that our legislators saw it as something merely wide, brash and 'Yankee.' "[89]

Having made this brief historical review of adoption practice in the United States and illustrated that the need for some

---

leaving orphan children, wrote another person, "[t]hey are readily adopted into the families of their uncles and other kindred, who treat them entirely as their own."

[86] 2 CALHOUN 23.

[87] KIRNITZER, *supra* note 42, at 347.

[88] *Id.* at 347.

[89] *Id.* at 348.

kind of regulation had manifested itself by the middle of the
century, it is now pertinent to examine the first legal steps concerned with adoption.

## V.   THE "PRIVATE" ACTS WHICH AUTHORIZED ADOPTION

The first American adoption statutes were private acts,
passed in the fourth and fifth decades of the nineteenth century.[90]
The form and text of these acts vary considerably, and the genesis and purposes of the private acts could themselves be the
subject of a scholarly article, but because the necessary research
still remains to be done, they will be treated here only summarily, as an introduction to the more general statutes which will
be considered next.

The leading decision on the interpretation of the private
statutes is the Louisiana case of *Vidal v. Commagere* (1858).[91]
*Vidal*'s use here as a general precedent may be somewhat proble-
matic, since it was decided in a state which had historically
followed civil law adoption practice, and in particular a Spanish
statute which was repealed in 1808,[92] but since later courts in
common-law jurisdictions also turned to the civil law for help in
interpreting the word "adoption,"[93] perhaps *Vidal* may be taken
as authoritative. The 1837 statute which was interpreted in *Vidal*
authorized Pierre Jean Baptiste Vidal and his wife "to adopt a
young orphan child named Adele, aged about seven years, who
has been brought up by them," provided that the adoption was
evidenced by an act which was to be executed before a notary
within six months after the passage of the statute.[94] The act was
subsequently executed by the Vidals, and the text of the notarized
act provided in part that they adopted "irrevocably now and

---

[90] *See, e.g.,* Ill. Laws, 1853, at 485; Ky. Acts, 1841, at 163; Wis. Gen. Acts, 1855,
at 14; Ga. Laws, 1852, at 499; N.Y. Sess. Laws, 1844, at 11; (list compiled in WITMER
19-20). *See also* La. Acts 26, 65 of 1837; La. Acts 69, 139, 217 and 235 of 1852; La.
Act 100 of 1859. On old Louisiana adoption law, *see generally* Comment, *Adoption,* 1
LA. L. REV. 196 (1938).

[91] 13 La. Ann. 516.

[92] *Id.* at 517.

[93] *See, e.g.,* Markover v. Krauss, 132 Ind. 294, 31 N.E. 1047 (1892), Morrison v.
Session's Estate, 70 Mich. 297, 38 N.W. 249 (1888); *contra,* Comm. v. Nancrede, 32
Pa. 389 (1859).

[94] Act of March 15, 1837, § 2; *quoted by* the court, 13 La. Ann. at 517.

forever the said orphan . . . and they desire and intend thence-
foreward she shall enjoy the same right, and advantages and
prerogatives, as if she had been the issue of the marriage of the
parties to the act."[95] Soon afterward, Pierre Jean died, and this
action was brought by some nephews and nieces of the Vidals to
determine who was entitled to the property of the succession of
the wife. Apparently the nephews and nieces argued that they
should inherit as collateral heirs, and that the adopted child
gained no rights by the act of adoption, which was limited in
effect to conferring a right in the Vidals to "take the orphan into
the family to reside."[96]

The court rejected this argument, holding that the statute
could not be construed so narrowly. Because "it cannot be presumed that a formal exertion of the sovereign power was made
for a trivial purpose," the court concluded that "the legislature
intended to confer some substantial right by its action" in passing the private act. To accept the nephews' and nieces' argument,
the court reasoned, would be to impute to the act "a slight
significance," since the right to take in the orphan "was a right
with which no one would likely interfere, even in the absence of
any action of the sovereign power."[97] The court then saw as its
task the determination of the meaning of the term "adoption,"
and noted that Webster defined the act as "to take a stranger
into one's family, as son and heir; to take one who is not a child
and treat him as one, giving him a title to the privileges and
rights of a child."[98] Turning to history and to the Louisiana
adoption practice under the Spanish law, the court concluded
that the legislature must have meant for the word "adoption"
to have the meaning it had in Webster's dictionary and under the
Spanish statute, and that meaning was identical with that expressed in the Vidals' notorial act.[99]

The court dealt with the contention by the nephews and
nieces that since adoption was in derogation of the positive laws

---

[95] *Id.* at 519.
[96] *Id.* at 517.
[97] *Id.*
[98] *Id.*, quoting definition of *adopt* from Webster's Dictionary.
[99] 13 La. Ann. at 517-19.

of inheritance, any adoption acts should be strictly construed. The court rejected this contention, in a rather clever argument,[100] but the notion that adoption acts should be strictly construed was to carry over to the general acts with much more success than it had in *Vidal*.[101] The happy ending to the *Vidal* case, however, was that the nephews and nieces lost, and the adopted girl was awarded the succession.

Although *Vidal v. Commagere* was instructive in the sophistication of its analysis, this sophistication was not universal with the private adoption statutes. The variation in the private acts may be demonstrated by an analysis of three Pennsylvania acts which were passed over an eleven year period, from 1844 to 1855.[102]

These private acts reveal an increasing awareness of what

---

[100] The argument that the statute must be strictly construed, because it is in derogation of the law in regard to inheritances, which law has been created and molded by positive legislation, can have, we think, no great weight; for the argument assumes, that the state authorizing plaintiff's adoption only intended to grant *Vidal* and wife the control over the person of the plaintiff. Now, it might be assumed with equal propriety, that tutorship [guardianship] is regulated by general laws operating upon all persons of the same class, and that therefore, the Legislature could not have intended, by the indefinite expression used, to give *Vidal* and wife control over the person of the plaintiff, and thus derogate from the laws on the subject of tutorship. Put these two arguments together, and they prove; 1st, that the Act of the legislature did not intend to give the plaintiff any right as heir, because that would be in derogation of the law of inheritance; and 2d, that it did not create the reciprocal relations of protector and protected, and consequent control over the person of the minor, because that would be in derogation of the general laws as to tutorship; and thus the statute is deprived of all meaning. 13 La. Ann. at 518-19.

[101] *See generally* text accompanying notes 171-267 *infra*.

[102] The first of these acts, Pub. L. No. 212, 1844, was "An Act to change the names of certain persons therein named," and provided, *inter alia*:

> *Be it enacted . . .* that Eliza Jane Jarvis, of Allegheny county, the daughter of Oliver J. Jarvis, and now the adopted child of James and Hannah Miles, shall henceforth be called and known by the name of Eliza Jane Miles, and by this name to be capable of suing and being sued, and of granting or taking any estate in the same manner she could have done if no change had been made therein.

A law passed four years later, Pub. L. No. 167, 1848, was somewhat more explicit. It was called "An act to change the name of David Richardson Bair," and provided:

> *Be it enacted . . .* that henceforth the name of David Richardson Bair, an adopted son of Thompson Richardson, of Westmoreland county, shall be

is accomplished in the legal act of adopting a child. Thus, the first of the three acts is simply an act "to change the name of certain persons," but the last act is to enable the petitioners "to adopt a child as their lawful heir." Similarly, the first act seems concerned with merely assuring the adopted child the right to sue and be sued and to grant or take an estate in his new name, but by the last of the three acts the intent is that the adopted child "have capacity to take and inherit from said petitioners . . . in manner as if she were their lawful child." Indeed, although the first private act is sketchy in its purpose and provisions, the text of the last of the acts bears a strong resemblance to Pennsylvania's first general adoption act, which was passed in the same year, 1855.[103] Although generalizations are risky over such a short period of time, the three Pennsylvania statutes might be said to show a change of attitude from a time when all that was wanted out of adoption was to take a child into a new family and give him a new name, to a time when the child was to be assured not only a new name, but also the security of having the right to succeed to his new parents' property should they die intestate.[104] Whatever the genesis and development of the private acts, by the middle of the nineteenth century legislatures grew weary of the routine action on private bills for adoption[105] and began to provide an easier way to take new children into the family legally. It is to these general acts that we now turn.

---

David Richardson; in which name he shall be competent to sue and be sued, and to transact business, and he is hereby invested with all the legal rights of a legitimate son of said Thompson Richardson.

Finally, Pub. L. No. 100, passed in 1855 is the most comprehensive of all. This time the law was called an act "To enable John H. and Rebecca Bugher to adopt a Child as their lawful heir, by the name of Emily Bugher," and the legislature said:

*Be it enacted* . . . that it shall be lawful for John H. Bugher and Rebecca Bugher to adopt, in pursuance of their petition to the legislature, as and for their child and heir at law, Rachel Clark, now living with them at Fayette city, by the name of Emily Bugher, and the said child shall hereafter be known by the latter name, and have capacity to take and inherit from said petitioners real and personal estate in manner as if she were their lawful child; *Provided*, that said petitioners shall further present their petition to the court of common pleas of Fayette county, consenting to such adoption and capacity to inherit by said child, and said court shall by its decree approve of the same.

[103] Pub. L. No. 430, Act of 4 May, 1855.

[104] The latter was apparently the purpose of the general acts. *See* text accompanying note 109 *infra*.

[105] *See* WITMER 28. *See also* Bancroft v. Heirs of Bancroft, 53 Vt. 9 (1880). "The object the legislature intended to accomplish by the passage of the [adoption] act of

## VI. THE GENERAL ADOPTION ACTS

The first comprehensive adoption statute was passed in 1851 in Massachusetts.[106] Among its key provisions were requirements 1) that written consent be given by the natural parents of the child to be adopted, or by a legal guardian; 2) that the child himself must consent if he is fourteen years of age or older; 3) that the adoptor's wife or husband (if he or she were married) must join in the petition for adoption; 4) that the probate judge to whom the petition for adoption was presented must be satisfied that the petitioner(s) were "of sufficient ability to bring up the child . . . and that it is fit and proper that such adoption should take effect," before he could decree and confirm the adoption; 5) that once the adoption was approved by the probate court, the adopted child would become "to all intents and purposes" the legal child of the petitioner(s); 6) that the natural parents would be deprived by the decree of adoption of all legal rights and obligations respecting the adopted child; and 7) that any petitioner or child who is the subject of such a petition might appeal to the Supreme Judicial Court from the decree of the probate judge.[107]

The "avowed object" of the Massachusetts act, and presumably of the other acts that were passed over the next quarter of the century,[108] according to one closely contemporary source, was that of "securing to adopted children a proper share in the estate of adopting parents who should die intestate."[109] The twenty-four different statutes accomplished this object in differ-

---

November 22d, 1870, was to provide a certain, simple, and inexpensive method, by which names might be changed, and persons be adopted, and constituted heirs at law of other persons; and to effectuate that intent, forms were prescribed to be used and allowed, and were made a part of that act." 53 Vt. at 12.

[106] Earlier statutes which provided simplified methods for recording adoptions, but which did *not* well provide for the welfare of adopted children were passed in Mississippi (1846), Texas (1850), and Vermont (1850). On the Mississippi statute, *see generally,* McFarlane, *The Mississippi Law on Adoptions,* 10 MISS. L.J. 239, 240 (1938).

[107] Acts of 1851, ch. 324.

[108] Many, if not most, of the adoption statutes were directly copied from the Massachusetts law. Kuhlman, *Intestate Succession By and From the Adopted Child,* 28 WASH. U.L.Q. 220, 225 (1943).

[109] WHITMORE, THE LAW OF ADOPTION iii-iv (1876) (hereinafter cited as WHITMORE).

466        *JOURNAL OF FAMILY LAW*        [Vol. 11

ent ways, however, although they have been conveniently classified into two broad types "based on their provision or lack of
provision for public inquiry into and control over proposed
adoptions."[110] One type of act included those "that may be regarded as being predominantly statutes to authenticate and
make public record of private agreements of adoption."[111] In the
second class were those acts which "provided, in greater or less
degree, for judicial supervision over adoptions, although the lines
along which the courts' inquiries were required to proceed varied
considerably."[112]

There is only one contemporary treatise which reviews the
various laws, and although this is inaccurate in some parts, it is
a valuable source for determining the perspective of one kind of
legal mind which viewed many of the features of the adoption
statutes with alarm. The treatise, *The Law of Adoption* (1876),
by William H. Whitmore, A.M., was originally a report prepared "for the purpose of assisting a committee of the Massachusetts Legislature in considering the question of a proposed
change in the [adoption] laws of that state."[113]

Whitmore noted that the adoption law of Massachusetts
(and by implication the laws in the other states which had followed the Massachusetts lead) was "unnecessarily and unwisely
broad in its terms." Not only did adopted children receive an
intestate share, but the laws could also be interpreted to give the
adopted children "entails and other dispositions of property, in
cases where the testator could have had no prevision of such a

---

[110] WITMER 30.

[111] *Id.* These are the acts which come closest to being merely measures designed to
ease the burden on the legislature caused by the many private acts. Witmer places in this
class the acts of Texas (1850), Vermont (1850), Tennessee (1851-52), Missouri (1857),
and Iowa (1858). Added to this list should be Mississippi (1846), and Louisiana (1870).
"None of these make express provision for public supervision of the adoption agreement,
or for inquiry into its propriety or its effect on the welfare of the child." WHITMER 30.

[112] *Id.* at 30-31. Witmer placed in this second class the acts of Massachusetts (1851),
Pennsylvania (1855), Indiana (1855), Georgia (1855-56), Wisconsin (1858), Ohio (1859),
Michigan (1861), New Hampshire (1862), Oregon (1864), Connecticut (1864), Kansas
(1868), California (1870), Maine (1871), Rhode Island (1872), North Carolina (1872-
73), and New York (1873). Added to this list should be Illinois (1873-74). The texts of
most of these, including the acts in note 111 *supra*, are collected in WHITMORE 1-66.

[113] WHITMORE iii.

result."[114] According to Whitmore, many of the difficulties with the adoption statutes were probably attributable to the novel nature of the topic of adoption itself, since "the whole subject is one which has received little discussion from writers upon legal topics, except so far as it was part of the civil law, and very few decisions have been made under any of our state laws." An even more ominous feature, as Whitmore saw it, was the fact that all adoption legislation had been made "from the philanthropic standpoint," and adoption had become a topic which, unhappily, "one may discuss from a nonprofessional point of view, without incurring the imputation of presumption."[115]

Whitmore reviewed in some detail the similarities and differences as well as the lacunae of the various state statutes,[116] and some of his comments furnish valuable insights into the bewilderment with which the pragmatic late nineteenth-century legal mind contemplated the adoption laws. For example, Whitmore seemed puzzled by the fact that most of the statutes made no provision regarding the duration of the relation that was to be created between adopted parents and children:

> In this country, in most of the states, when the relationship of an adopted child has been established, it is irrevocable. . . . Considering the fact that the subjects of adoption are so largely taken from the waifs of society, foundlings or children whose parents are depraved and worthless; considering also the growing belief that many traits of mind are hereditary and almost irradicable; it may be questioned whether the great laxity of the American rule is for the public benefit.[117]

Whitmore saw the purpose of the law as protecting adopted children during their minority should their adopted parents die intestate or somehow neglect to provide for them in their wills. Because of his nervousness about the possibly "irradicable" unpleasant traits of character that adopted children might carry, Whitmore suggested that adoption be only a temporary relationship, extending perhaps throughout the period of the child's mi-

---

[114] *Id.* at iv. Whitmore is here referring to the case of Sewell v. Roberts, 115 Mass. 262 (1874), discussed *infra*.

[115] *Id.* at vii.

[116] *Id.* at 73-86.

[117] *Id.* at 73-74.

nority, with an option to ratify at the end of that period, depending on how the child actually turned out. Even if the adoption were not ratified, however, Whitmore felt a need to provide the adopted child some "reasonable provision" upon setting him out in the world at his majority, presumably so that he would not sink completely back into the milieu from which he was raised by adoption.[118]

Although some aspects of Whitmore's view of the nature of adopted children are unappealing, it is particularly interesting to note how far the adoption law had come from the time of the Romans to the era when Whitmore wrote. Whatever Whitmore thought of adopted children, he conceived of the law on adoption as affording them, at the very least, temporary protection of their welfare, a view quite different from the Roman laws, which were almost exclusively for the perpetuation of the family of the adopted parents.

Whitmore saw problems with the new laws other than the difficulties owing to the nature of the adopted children themselves. Perhaps chief among these was the prospect that many of the statutes appeared to allow the adoption of one's illegitimate offspring. If this were to be allowed, reasoned Whitmore, a "great barrier to illegal connections" would be removed. Before the passage of the adoption laws, he argued, men could be restrained from having sexual relations with women whom they never intended to marry, out of concern for what might happen to any children from such an illicit union. But if men could adopt such children without marrying the mother, as the laws in many states permitted, such restraint would be lost.[119]

---

[118] *Id.*

[119] *Id.* at 75. In a higher vein Whitmore observes another problem that could come about through an unorthodox adding to the family by means of adoption: "In Vermont, it seems that a married woman cannot be the subject of adoption. In view of the confidential relation presumed to exist between parent and child, this provision may be deemed reasonable. Should matrimony entail an innumerable succession of mothers-in-law?" *Id.* at 76.

While many of Whitmore's misgivings about the adoption statutes have to do with problems unrelated to the welfare of the adopted child himself, he does observe that the fact that many of the statutes could be read to permit subsequent adoptions might be deleterious for the adopted:

It may be inferred that as the general rule is to place an adopted child in the position of one lawfully born to the adopter, the new parent may dispose of

Most of Whitmore's comments, however, are not so obviously moral but have to do with the problem of some unwary testator's intent being frustrated by an act of adoption. Whitmore points to the situation, existing under the adoption laws of many states, where single persons could adopt as many children as they might desire:

> Formerly a devise for life to an old maid with remainder over in the expected contingency of her death without children, might well keep the testator's property in the channels by him intended. Now the spinster of eighty may rear a thriving family, to inherit at her death.[120]

The central problem which seems to disturb Whitmore is the lack of clarity as to the extent the adopted child was to sever his relationship with his blood relations and become like a natural son to his adopted parents. The capricious nature of economic conditions at the time made the question of whether the adopted child could still inherit from his natural parents particularly important. "In this country, with the rapid mutations of fortunes, this question is not merely speculative."[121] Unfortunately, the nineteenth century adoption laws often were opaque as to whether the natural or the adopted family would inherit from the adopted child if he died intestate, and they were similarly uncertain as to which relatives would be gained by adoption.[122]

---

this child to a second adopting parent, and so indefinitely. Wherever the law prescribes that the lawful parent, by consenting to the act of adoption, severs all his previous natural relations with it, a second adoption would be an easy method of terminating his responsibilities. Obviously this may be greatly to the disadvantage of a minor and therefore may well be the subject of [remedial] legislation. *Id.* at 76.

[120] *Id.* at 77. As well as this problem of the artificially-fertile octogenarian, Whitmore is concerned with the reverse. "In the United States, the wise rule that there should be a reasonable diversity of ages between parent and child, equivalent to that existing in nature, seems unduly realized. A youth might adopt a centenarian." *Id.* at 78.

[121] *Id.* at 80.

[122] *Id.* at 81-82. The problem of the adopted child's taking by a devise to children of his adopted parent is still with us. *See* note 282 *infra.*

Somewhat tangentially related to the problem of who was to be in the adopted family, for Whitmore, at least, was the problem of sexual crimes. Whitmore appears to have taken the position that if adopted families were really going to be like natural families, laws would have to be passed which made them equally subject to severer penalties for certain sexual offenses.

> In none of the states is any attempt made to follow out the chain of ideas, and to settle the point whether sexual crimes are created or are aggravated in law by the artificial relationship of adoption. Yet as marriage is prohibited between near blood relatives, so are sexual crimes immensely augmented by such affinity. Such important results flow from the decision of this point, that it should also be the subject of definite enactments. *Id.* at 84.

470        *JOURNAL OF FAMILY LAW*        [Vol. 11

Whitmore finished his evaluation of the different statutes with the observation that rules of comity were sorely needed to insure that a child adopted in one state would be treated equitably in all.[123] Whitmore's conclusion aptly sums up his views on the state of the adoption laws at the time he wrote: "Evidently as the matter stands, the attempts of philanthropists to cure a small evil may have resulted in a serious injury to the rights of many other persons."[124]

In a later section of this article, we will return to the problem of interpreting the adoption statutes and examine the treatment they received in the first court decisions to pass upon the new laws. But at this point, we turn to the motives that led the men Whitmore called the "philanthropists" to press for the adoption statutes. We now return to some of the questions posed at the beginning of this article: What were the conditions that brought about the need for adoption statutes at the middle of the century? What was it about the kind of adoption being practiced at that time that required the incorporation of adoption into a legal system that had existed for so long without it?

## VII. THE SOCIAL BACKGROUND OF THE ADOPTION LAWS

The available official legislative history of the adoption laws gives no indication of the motivation or the intention of the legislators who passed the first adoption statutes. Legislative journals record the men who introduced the bills, the committees that considered them, and the dates they became effective, but little else.[125] This lack of material has been attributed to the fact that although these statutes appear highly significant to the twentieth century observor, "the passage . . . of the first general adoption laws . . . was not one of the great issues of the day."[126] As one commentator put it, the passage of the general adoption laws "created little stir because they were then looked upon as little more than a normal and desirable next step in a develop-

---

[123] *Id.* at 84-85.

[124] *Id.* at 85.

[125] *See, e.g.,* The Pennsylvania Journals of the House and Senate, with reference to the Act of 4 May, 1855, Pub. L. No. 430.

[126] WITMER 19.

ment that was already taking place."[127] This "normal and desirable next step" that was taking place in the development of adoption law was the move from the private statutes to the more generalized methods for the legal adoption of children.

It must be pointed out, however, that at least one of the statutes, the Massachusetts act of 1851, did not pass completely without notice. The *Boston Advertiser* of May 26, 1851, included the following observation in an editorial about the significant bills that had been passed in the recently-prorogued legislative session:

> As usual, the names of a large number of persons have been changed by acts of the legislature, but a law has been passed by which persons may hereafter have their names changed by authority of the judges of probate without the necessity of application to the legislature. *A general law authorizing and regulating the adoption of children, has been passed.* [Emphasis added.][128]

Although the passage of the act was not unattended, the fact that it is only mentioned in passing seems to indicate that just as was demonstrated in some of Pennsylvania's early private laws,[129] the men in Massachusetts might not have thought of adoption as much more than a change of name for the adopted child. Thus, it may not be surprising that there does not seem to be any discussion in the press of the implications of the passage of the adoption statute.

While the Boston press does not furnish much assistance in determining why the legislation was enacted at this time, a law review comment published some twenty years later does hint at an answer:

> [The Massachusetts statute] was, as we are informed, originally passed as a remedy for the distressing cases arising under the custom of adopting children, which was then increasing rapidly in that state, through the efforts of foundling societies.[130]

The cases were "distressing," the article observed, because the

---

[127] *Id.*

[128] Boston Daily Advertiser, Vol. LXXVII, No. 124, at 2, col. 4.

[129] *See* text accompanying notes 102-105 *supra*.

[130] Comment, *The Law of Adoption*, 9 AM. L. REV. 74 (1874).

adopted child might be worse off if his adopting parents died intestate than if he had not been adopted at all.

It is naive to attribute the passage of adoption statutes in so many states solely to the activities of "foundling societies." The activity of these societies *is* demonstrative of a larger movement for child welfare of which the passage of the adoption statutes also represents a part. This movement came about as a resultof the economic changes which made the stop-gap institutions of apprenticeship, service, and indenture quite unable to cope with the great numbers of children who had been neglected by their families and also were neglected, until about the middle of the nineteenth century in most cases, by the society and the state.[131] In order to understand better the motives that lay behind the passage of the adoption statutes, it is important to understand some of these other developments in child welfare work. In particular, it is instructive to examine the extent, scope, and purposes of the private agencies which began to aid children during the first half of the nineteenth century. It was to these agencies which the author of the passage quoted above probably referred when he used the term "foundling societies."

Before considering in detail the private agencies, however, it is important to understand the conditions that gave rise to the private agencies, that is, the provisions that had been made for the care of dependent children by public means from about the beginning of the nineteenth century until the period with which we are concerned. The chief public institution from the colonial days until the middle of the nineteenth century for the care of children, and indeed all dependent persons, was the almshouse. In some places there were systems of "outdoor relief," by which pecuniary support was given to indigents who were not cared for in public institutions, but this system apparently fell out of use by the middle of the nineteenth century. In general, the children would be taken from the almshouses between seven and fourteen years of age and given in indenture or apprenticeship by the overseers of the poor. There were laws regulating this indenturing as early as the beginning of the eighteenth century, but they were

---

[131] *See generally* Kuhlman, *Intestate Succession By and From the Adopted Child,* 28 WASH. L.Q. 221, 223 (1943).

not always strictly observed. The children who remained in the almshouses usually were poorly cared for by women consigned to prison terms; many were taken ill with opthalmia or other contagious diseases, and very many died. To sum up the situation, as noted by one historian of the plight of dependent children in America, "[F]ew persons, if any, will dissent from the statement that the direct care of destitute children by American municipalities prior to 1875 was, as a rule, a pitiful failure."[132]

Thus, from philanthropic motives most probably inspired by the continuing plight of dependent children in the hands of public authorities, private agencies for the care of such children were founded.[133] Even before the beginning of the nineteenth century, private agencies for the care of dependent children existed in New Orelans, Savannah, New York, Philadelphia, Baltimore, and Boston. In the first half of the nineteenth century, at least seventy-seven such agencies were founded, with fifty-six of them being founded between the years 1830 and 1850. After 1850 the increase in the number of such agencies was even more rapid, with approximately forty-seven new institutions founded in the fifties, and seventy-nine in the sixties (the public agencies notwithstanding).[134] The form of child care given by the private agencies varied somewhat with the type of the institution and the religious orientation of its founders and administration, but there was a general pattern of care which did not differ drasti-

---

[132] FOLKS, THE CARE OF DESTITUTE, NEGLECTED AND DELINQUENT CHILDREN 33 (1902) (hereinafter cited as FOLKS). On public provision for the care of destitute children before 1875, *see* FOLKS v-42. The experience of Ohio seems typical of many states at this time:

> As early as 1824 laws were passed permitting the incorporation of private orphan asylums and permitting the trustees of townships to "bind out" an orphan child to serve as a clerk, apprentice or servant to the person to whom bound. The child was supposed to have redress in court in case of cruelty or abuse, but justice was seldom secured due to prejudice against "pauper brats." MCCLAIN, CHILD PLACING IN OHIO 10 (1928).

[133] The definition of public and private agencies used here is that given by Folks: "[P]ublic . . . indicates such agencies or institutions for the care of children which are under the direct control of governmental bodies and are supported from public funds. The term 'private' indicates all other agencies, whether managed by individuals or by societies, churches, or corporations." FOLKS 12.

[134] These figures are somewhat low, as they do not include associations founded in some of the central and western states at that time, since data on them is not as readily available. FOLKS 55.

cally from that employed by the public agencies which have already been discussed. Before 1850, the private agencies sought to teach their charges to read and write and then to indenture them for service or apprenticeship. While "[m]ost of the . . . agencies made more or less use of indenture, adoption, or placing out of children," and while this activity of the agencies is the most probable force behind the passing of the adoption statutes, the "placing out" activity initially was regarded by many of the administrators of the private agencies "rather as a convenient means of disposing of their older wards than as an essential part of the plan by which they were to benefit homeless children."[135] Prior to the establishment of the public school systems and compulsory attendence, the agencies felt their primary service should be to give to their children the rudiments of an education before they were placed out in indenture or service.

Around 1850, however, private agencies began to be founded with the avowed purpose of placing younger children in a suitable family atmosphere. The work of some of the "infant's hospitals," "foundling asylums," and "maternity hospitals" in New York and Boston stands out in this regard, as does the work of the Children's Aid Societies started in those cities in 1853 and 1865, respectively. Similar societies existed in Baltimore (1860), Brooklyn (1866), Buffalo (1872), and Philadelphia (1882). The Children's Aid Societies made efforts to place children in suitable homes, usually homes far from the city, in the expanding states and territories of the West. The best known of these societies, the Children's Aid Society of New York, placed over twenty thousand children in homes out of New York City in the twenty years after it was founded.[136] Although the childplacing efforts on the grandest scale came after the first Massachusetts statute was passed in 1851, the records of some of the nine Boston

---

[135] *Id.* at 64. Folks goes on to add: "[T]here is little evidence of any adequate inquiry [before 1850] into the circumstances of the persons receiving children, or of any system of subsequent oversight. The children after leaving the doors of the institutions, were in too large measure lost sight of." *Id.* at 64-65.

[136] A review of the years in which the twenty-three states, following the example of Massachusetts, passed general adoption statutes shows that the statutes were passed during a period which coincided with this peak child-placing activity. One is hard-pressed not to draw the inference that the passage of the statutes and this monumental child-placing effort are related.

private associations founded before 1850[137] indicate the beginnings of the problems to which the 1851 statute must have been
a response.[138]

The most general problem with which the private agencies
dealt, of course, was the great poverty that existed in many of
the urban centers during the nineteenth century. The 1933 annual
report of the Boston Children's Friend Society eloquently sum-
marizes the conditions that existed at the time of the founding
of the Society, one hundred years earlier:

> While the city could boast of her culture and intellectual achievements
> as well as the gracious gentility of living associated with the Boston
> of those days, there was also unfortunately squalor and misery. Hand
> in hand with the concentration of wealth in urban districts goes pov-
> erty in its direst forms, and all this opulence in early Victorian Boston
> had its counterpart in the rapidly rising slums. At this time there was
> no public provision for dependent children except in almshouse or
> jail. There was no school for the feeble-minded child, nor the child
> requiring special disciplinary training. There was no free public hospi-
> tal to care for the destitute sick. Boston was not alone in these re-
> spects for no other city in the country was better provided with insti-
> tutions for the poor.[139]

In order to gain more perspective on these child-placing
activities, it is appropriate to consider the problems of the mid-
nineteenth century city from a more strictly sociological point of
view. Historically, there seem to be two main reasons why
groups of people have come together to form large settlements.
The first of these reasons is that the settlers wish to live near each

---

[137] These nine societies were the Boston Female Orphan Asylum (1800), The Boston
Asylum for Indigent Boys (1813), St. Vincent's Orphan Asylum (R.C.) (1831), The
Farm School Society (1832), The Children's Friend Society (1833), The Infant School
and Children's Home Association (later the Hunt Asylum for Destitute Children) (1833),
The Nickerson Home for Children (1835), The Temporary Home for the Destitute (later
the Gwynne Temporary Home for Children) (1847), and the Children's Mission to the
Children of the Destitute (1849).

[138] For the topics discussed in the preceding two paragraphs, see generally FOLKS
43-71 and sources cited therein.

[139] BOSTON CHILDREN'S FRIEND SOCIETY, ANNUAL REPORT 5 (1933). At this time
it was not unusual to place dependent children, especially in cases where they were
suspected of criminal activity or had actually committed crimes, in jailhouses, for lack
of anywhere else to keep them. It was by no means unusual to find children as young as
eight or ten years of age in such questionable quarters. See, e.g., FIRST REPORT OF THE
EXECUTIVE COMMITTEE OF THE BOSTON CHILDREN'S AID SOCIETY 14 (1865).

476          *JOURNAL OF FAMILY LAW*          [Vol. 11

other "in order to realize a way of life made possible by production activities carried on elsewhere." This type of settlement is called, in sociological terms, "consumption-oriented," and is typified by such settlements as the modern residential suburb, the traditional rural village, the ceremonial capital or "court" city, and the modern "resort" city. The other of these reasons is that the settlers wish to live within the immediate vicinity of the production facilities where they are employed, or where they seek to find employment. This second type of settlement is called "production-oriented," and some examples of this type are the manufacturing city, the market town, and the governmental administrative center. Before the industrial revolution most settlements would have been classed as consumption-oriented, but in modern times the production-oriented center has become the more common. The problems of Boston and other nineteenth century urban centers which lie behind many of the topics discussed in this article are those of the production-oriented city. In particular, the production-oriented settlement does not appear to have the stable, well-integrated, coherent social organization that seems to typify the consumption-oriented center. Instead, production-oriented cities may contain many highly diverse and possibly antagonistic groups who have come together not through any basic compatibility, but only for the purpose of contributing to production. The creation of a satisfactory mode of living among such disparate groups has been said to be one of the major  problems facing the cities today, and the child-placing efforts of the nineteenth century, insofar as they sought to integrate many children from the indigent masses into more stable environments, are an early means of coping with this problem.[140]

Nonetheless, many of the agencies which placed children tended to be somewhat careless about the choice of homes, although many of the Boston agencies did take special pains to make sure that the placement was proper, and perhaps this care was instrumental in securing the passage of the Massachusetts adoption statute at such an early date. The procedure outlined

---

[140] This sociological discussion has been drawn from Anderson, *City: Comparative Urban Structure*, 2 INT. ENCY. SOC. SCI. 466 (1968).

in a report from the Boston Asylum for Indigent Boys seems typical for Boston agencies. The boys were admitted to the asylum at the age of four and were tutored by the asylum's matron and instructress until they were old enough to enter Boston's public schools. Then, at the age of 12, the boys would be apprenticed to local farmers. The most impressive feature of the asylum's plan was the care with which the boys' masters were chosen:

> The character and situation of those to whom the boys are apprenticed, are made the subjects of particular inquiry; and the testimonies of clergymen and selectmen, of the town where they live are required, respecting their fitness to take charge of the young. They are also required to give obligation, that they will furnish the objects of their care with instruction in reading, writing, arithmetic, and the principles of the Christian religion.[141]

The fact that the Boston Asylum for Indigent Boys (and doubtless other children's agencies as well) made use of the Boston public school system as an integral part of their child-rearing plans suggests another reason why the Massachusetts adoption statute may have been passed in advance of so many others. The public schools of Massachusetts were among the very first in the United States.[142] Once the public school system was established, there was less need to tutor children in asylums and orphanages, since the necessary rudiments of education could now be provided at public expense. Thus, it was no longer as necessary to keep the children in institutions for extended periods of time, and they could be placed into foster homes at an earlier age. Since many of the children who were placed in foster homes were "adopted" by their foster parents, there must have been acute pressure on the Massachusetts legislature to pass a generalized statute and allow these foster parents to complete the legal adoption of their children without the bother of private legislative action.

Another factor which contributed to the decline of the pattern of extended institutional care followed by apprenticeship was the changing economic conditions which came about as a

---

[141] An Account of the Boston Asylum for Indigent Boys (3d ed. 1832).
[142] *See generally* 7 Ency. Britt. 980-81 (1961 ed.).

result of industrialization. By the 1840's it had become apparent to those who ran the Boston agencies that the old methods of child welfare, and in particular the institution of "putting out" for service, were becoming obsolete. Although in the "olden time," mistresses of families had been very willing to clothe and instruct poor children in return for their services, the changing times had rendered this relationship much less profitable from the point of view of the children:

> The increase in wealth and variations in the forms of society, have at the same time increased the demand for service, and removed the mistress of a family farther from that direct supervision of those who perform it, which is so especially important to the young. Now a girl, long before she is eighteen, can obtain wages, which enables her to indulge that love of dress, which is a prevailing folly, and give her a feeling of independence, the desire for which, is often most strong in those who least know how to use it.[143]

In short, not only were mistresses and masters no longer instructing and supervising as extensively as they had in the past, but apprentices and servants were beginning to realize that their contemporaries who were working as wage-earners possibly had a more pleasant position, at least as far as the immediate tangible benefits of material remuneration were being conferred on them. Thus the lure of "the precarious and often elusive good of having an earlier command of wages" began to turn many apprentices away from the master-servant relationship. Furthermore, putting the child out into service was failing as a method of child welfare because the nature of the market had altered so that it was often too profitable for masters or mistresses to use their charges simply as cheap labor, and put aside the old duties of combining instruction and tutorship with service:

> It is true that some who apply [for female apprentices] may have little other purpose than that of obtaining a selfish convenience; the most service at the least price at which it can be procured; that in the idea of *servant* some may lose sight of the *child*, of one needing all the instruction, forbearance, encouragement and restraint that youth always requires. That disappointed in their expectation of finding at once an obedient and useful domestic, some become impatient and unmindful of their obligations.[144]

---

[143] REMINISCES OF THE BOSTON FEMALE ASYLUM 58 (1844).

[144] *Id.* at 60. *See also* 3 CALHOUN 190. ("The binding of apprentices by hard and fast indenture fell into disuse before the middle of the century. . . .")

It appears that as the managers of the agencies became aware of the obsolescence of the old "service" relationship in placing out children, they began to strive to place children in families where they would be treated more like natural children. That is, the agencies began to move further away from the old notions of apprenticeship and service for child placing and closer to what we now know as "adoption." This change in emphasis is evident in the period immediately before the passage of Massachusetts' first adoption act, as a touching passage in the Annual Report of the Boston Female Asylum for 1850 indicates:

> [Y]ou should see the neglected and exposed, for whom vice and infamy seemed waiting as for their certain prey, when some messenger of mercy has led them away, and brought them here in safety from the contagion and ruin. And, following these children farther into life, you should see some adopted into families, where they are loved and cherished as if natural members of the household; . . . finding in those among who they were placed friends, who care kindly for them, and toward whom their affections are called warmly forth, although there is none to claim kindred of blood with them. You should see a happy wife, the mother of a promising family, . . . and to hear such a one say, "What would have become of me, had it not been for the asylum, and the family in which its managers placed me?"[145]

Another factor which was related to the economic changes which were taking place, and which also made it difficult for the agencies to maintain their old policies of keeping children for extended periods in the institutions and then placing them out for service, was the tremendous increase in immigration that occurred in the middle of the nineteenth century. This tide of immigration hit Boston particularly hard:

> By 1854 the great number of immigrants that poured into our city from Europe, chiefly the British Isles, well nigh crippled the resources of private charities here, for Boston, rather than New York, was then the favorite port of entry to America.[146]

The large numbers of indigent immigrant dependent children with which the agencies were confronted in the forties and fifties forced them to give up the notion of early education and rearing for all the children in the institutions, and made it inevitable that

---

[145] ANNUAL REPORT OF THE BOSTON FEMALE ASYLUM 32 (1850).
[146] BOSTON CHILDREN'S FRIEND SOCIETY, ANNUAL REPORT (1933).

children be placed out in foster homes at an earlier age. Many of these children were adopted by their foster parents, and some of them apparently were taken in when they were mere infants. One can find in the contemporary press accounts of "foundlings" who had been adopted, or placed in institutions for dependent children,[147] and it is most likely that it was this kind of activity that led later commentators to conclude that it was the "efforts of foundling societies" that led to the passage of the Massachusetts statute.[148]

Still another force which helped change the methods of caring for dependent children was the intense religious devotion which seems to have motivated many of the men and women who were active in the reforms made for the care of dependent children. There are signs of this zeal in some of the literature of the Boston agencies,[149] but to get the full flavor of the religious fervor, one must examine the records left by the Children's Aid Society of New York.

The founder of the New York Children's Aid Society, Reverend Charles Loring Brace, in his writing about the work of the society, gives a lucid description of the faith that motivated its workers and tells how this faith was characteristic of a great revival occurring in the middle of the nineteenth century. Thus, in 1866 Brace wrote that during the past twelve or fifteen years,

---

[147] *See, e.g.*, Boston Daily Advertiser, Jan. 30, 1851, Vol. LXXVII No. 26, col. 3: During last week, a male infant, six or eight months old, was left on the door steps of the residence of Mr. Cutler, on Summer street, Cambridge, and has since been adopted by a driver of one of the omnibuses. Later in the week, a female infant, but a few days old, was left at the door of another omnibus driver. Mr. Howe, who resides in North Avenue, Cambridge, but as he had no desire to harbor the unknown stranger, she was provided with a home at the almshouse.

[148] *See* note 130 *supra* and accompanying text.

[149] As well as having the recognized requirement that foster homes should provide religious care (*see* text accompanying note 142 *supra*), the Boston agencies depended upon the religious faith of the foster parents to insure generally that the foster care provided would be beneficial:

You take a *child*; you must not expect to make her, without care, and instruction and patience a useful domestic. Encourage what you may find good in her, and in punishing her faults, consider how you should endeavor to correct those of your own children; for is not One the father of us all? REMINISCES OF THE BOSTON FEMALE ASYLUM 62 (1844).

there had been a new religious "wave of feeling and opinion" passing over the country. This rebirth directed the minds of religious people away from the "New England teachings" with its "morbid reflection" and preoccupation with one's own spiritual state and moved instead in the direction of bringing religion to others:

> The saving of one's own soul, which had often been a kind of elevated selfishness, was almost disregarded in the eagerness to save the souls of others. . . . How to preach the gospel to the poor become the great question for all conscientious and religious persons. . . . Our great effort was to put these poor creatures—the vagrants, the houseless, the needy and criminal, and the uncared-for children of the great cities, where they could be most easily reached by Christian influences. . . . The hopeful field was evidently among the young. There, crime might possibly be checked in its very beginnings, and the seed of future good character and order and virtue be widely sown. . . .[150]

As a result of these feelings, the Children's Aid Society of New York was founded in 1853. While Brace and his fellow reformers were ultimately interested in saving the souls of the poor, they realized that the only way to achieve their goal was by first ministering to the more mundane needs of the indigents. In the course of feeding and caring for the poor, Brace and others hoped to inculcate "consciously or unconsciously, refinement, purity, self-sacrifice and Christian obligation."[151]

Perhaps it is difficult for us to realize the power of the purely religious commitment that these men had, but it is still possible for us to be impressed by the eloquence with which Brace motivated his fellow reformers and sought contributions to his cause by offering a glimpse of divine reward for present efforts, however small. Brace told his workers that though they might see little progress as they attempted to help the children of "crime and penury," still "in distant lonely convict cells, in far-away prison-courts, in gloomy halls of justice, your deeds of

---

[150] BRACE, SHORT SERMONS TO NEW BOYS 5ff. (1866).

[151] BRACE, ADDRESS UPON THE INDUSTRIAL SCHOOL MOVEMENT 9 (1857). The industrial schools were institutions where many of the youthful poor of New York were taught a trade. Many of these pupils were subsequently placed in homes in the West, as seemed to be the case with almost every enterprise with which the good Reverend Brace was associated.

goodness and Christian love have penetrated and bear pleasant fruit." But the most reassuring thought, it seemed, was the effect of the reformers' efforts to be enjoyed in a later life:

> Will not, in the far-away dim Eternity, a day come in which a voice, sweeter than all earthly music, shall sound to the depth of your soul, bringing rich peace and joy, and saying, "Inasmuch as ye did it unto one of the least of these, ye did it unto me!" Ye did it unknowing, unseen, for me of the poorest and basest of your fellows, and ye find in that day, it was done for humanity, for Christ, for God.[152]

Thus, if the words and deeds of the Reverend Brace are any indication, religious dedication was a powerful force indeed in the movement for child welfare of which adoption was a part.

The purpose of dealing at length with the religious inspiration that lay behind the view that Brace and his followers had of the children of the poor makes it easier to understand how that view differed so radically from that articulated by such men as Whitmore.[153] A comparison of these disparate conceptions of the nature of the poor, and in particular of poor dependent children, suggests what may be the underlying basis of the legal disputes about the nature of adoption which occurred shortly after the passage of the statutes.[154] In contrast to the view of Whitmore, Brace saw the children of the poor as being essentially the same as the children of the rich:

> [T]he same principles which influence the good or evil development of every child in comfortable circumstances, will effect, in greater or less degree, the child of poverty. Sympathy and hope are as inspiring to the ignorant girl, as to the educated; steady occupation is as necessary for the street boy, as the boy of a wealthy house; indifference is as chilling to the one class, as to the other; the prospect of success is as stimulating to the young vagrant, as to the student in the college.[155]

---

[152] *Id.* at 19.

[153] *See* text accompanying note 117 *supra.*

[154] *See* text accompanying notes 269-70 *infra.*

[155] BRACE, THE BEST METHOD OF DISPOSING OF PAUPER AND VAGRANT CHILDREN 4 (1859) (hereinafter cited as BEST METHOD). That Brace's view of the pauper children was dictated by his religious views is evident in the following extract from another of his pamphlets, discussing what type of men should engage in child welfare work:

> Let only those who are in earnest. Such work is not for a few Sabbaths—for a passing religious enthusiasm. It must be patient, steady, hearty; to be urged on through discouragements, difficulties, even apparent want of success. You want *live men* in it. Men who really believe that the poor outcast boy has a

Brace realized, however, that not all men had his paternalistic attitude toward the children of the poor, for many opposed the main effort of the Children's Aid Society, that of placing children in families, because they looked upon the poor differently. "It is feared," conceded Brace, "that these children would corrupt the morals of the families to which they are sent, and that thus the enterprise would become an imposition and a nuisance. . . ."[156] But he countered this argument with the observation that since the districts to which he had been sending children kept asking for more, and since the demand at times even exceeded the supply, the children must be doing good, and not evil, in the new homes to which they were sent. As might be expected, Brace attributed this phenomenon to the innately noble nature of the children:

> We must remind such persons [who would doubt the wisdom of the child-placing plan of the society] of the wonderful capacity for improvement in children's natures under new circumstances; and we assert boldly, that a poor child taken in thus by the hand of Christian charity, and placed in a new world of love and of religion, is *more likely to be tempted to good*, then to tempt others to evil.[157]

Although it was by a slightly different logical route than that used by the Boston societies (who apparently were under sore pressure from immigration and the changing economy), Brace also concluded that the old methods of caring for dependent children, were no longer the best methods. In particular, Brace was struck by what he perceived as the psychological dan-

---

soul immortal, within him; and that ONE has died for him, even as for the child of the rich. Men who feel for the poor, the helpless, the forsaken as their brethren; and who do not forget that in working for the least of these they are working for Christ. BRACE, A TRACT FOR THE TIMES! 1-2 (1858).

[156] BEST METHOD 13.

[157] *Id*. at 13-14 (original emphasis). Brace goes on:

The fact is, such children of misfortune are, very often, by no means as bad as they seem. A considerable experience has alone confirmed this in our minds. The vice which in a child of better circumstances would be proof of an utter depravation of character, in these unfortunate creatures, victims of circumstances, is often only an external habit and soon eradicated by pure and kindly influence. *Id*.

ger of placing dependent children in large groups, as was customary for the institutions of his time:

> Nature seems especially to indicate small groups of parents and children, or old and young, as the best forming-institution for young minds. Children in large numbers together, in constant intercourse, appear never to exert a healthful influence on each other; in the higher classes, habits of deceit, and unnatural vices are spread among them; and in the lower, all the seeds of vice which might otherwise lie dormant, spring up and grow noxiously.[158]

Brace realized that many would object to his method of placing dependent children in families simply because of the accumulated prestige of the method of institutional care, a prestige which probably was due to its long use in England.[159] To mollify these doubts, Brace made an economic argument, which is reminiscent of that used by more recent historians to explain the widespread custom of adoption:[160]

> America has the accidental, but the immense advantage, of an unlimited demand for labor, especially for juvenile labor. In England, on the contrary—though in this respect a favorable change is commencing—the market is over-supplied, and the great difficulty in regard to each youthful criminal, or vagrant, or pauper, is to know what to do with him, even if he be reformed. The consequence is, that the English institutions are obliged to keep large numbers of children together, and their great attention is turned to what is a necessity to them—the management of young persons in masses.[161]

Thus, according to Brace, the demand for labor in America made it possible to place children in families, rather than in institutions. This situation, then, made the plan of the Children's Aid Society practically an inescapable one since, "[t]he Emigration plan of the . . . Society, is simply to connect the supply of juvenile labor of the city with the demand from the country, and

---

[158] *Id*. at 13.

[159] *Id*.

[160] *See* text accompanying notes 84-86 *supra*.

[161] BEST METHOD 6. If what Brace says about the English system is true, that it was forced to remain with institutional care for longer than America, this might be another reason why the British adoption statute was passed later. There may have been fewer children placed in homes, and thus less pressure for adoption legislation since there might have been fewer people wanting to adopt.

to place unfortunate, destitute, vagrant and abandoned children at once in good families in the country."[162]

Even though the plan of the Children's Aid Society for placing children in families did have economic benefits, for Brace, at least, it seems clear that these were secondary to the great psychological and religious virtues of his plan:

> The family is God's Reformatory; and every child of bad habits who can secure a place in a Christian home, is in the best possible place for his improvement. All the individual impulses which help to make our children what they are, are applied to him—sympathy, kind care, personal interest, association with the virtuous, the approbation of the good, and direct religious influence.[163]

Perhaps the most striking feature of the Children's Aid Society's plan for sending children to families in the West, however, was that the children were not indentured to the families to which they were sent. This system of child-placing represented a rather radical departure from that employed by other institutions, such as many of the Boston agencies which have been discussed. This aspect of the plan, according to the literature of the Society, seemed to work:

> [I]n most cases it will be found, I apprehend, that boys sent [to country homes who have not been indentured] will do better, and stay more contentedly, than they would if bound to service. The master, too, if a good man, will do as well, and even better, for the boy, than if he should be bound to him for a term of years. There are so many hardminded men who would abuse the confidence reposed in them by having a defenseless and unfortunate boy bound to them, that the subject, at least, of indenturing boys to masters, . . . is of doubtful propriety.[164]

---

[162] *Id.* at 12.

[163] *Id.* at 12-13. Brace goes on to note the happy effects of bringing the child up among the country working class:

> [The child who is placed in a family] feels, too, the great impelling powers which help everywhere to elevate the laboring class in America; the instinct of property (for we find that farmers wisely give these boys or girls some animal, or tool, or garden bed which they may have as their own); the consciousness of equality; the chance of great success; and, at an early period, a liberal payment for labor. No artificial system could ever supply these influences; they are continuous, unconscious, and necessary in the family life of this country. *Id.*

[164] *Id.* at 14, *quoting* CHILDREN'S AID SOCIETY, ANNUAL REPORT (1859).

Since the children were not indentured, they were more or less at liberty to move out of one home in which they were placed into another, and indeed "the older boys and girls change[d] their places frequently, with the hope of bettering themselves."[165] It was, however, quite possible for the children placed in families to run away and return to New York or engage in other misadventures, and the scheme's ultimate success was really dependent on the family atmosphere which the child found. Thus, Brace's child-placing would be judged successful or unsuccessful on the same grounds as would the process of adoption itself in the years to come, and there are many indications that the children themselves were thought of in the same way that we now think of adopted children:

> I . . . know a large number of the boys who are doing well, and have by their good conduct taken such a strong hold upon the affection of their foster parents, that they would not part with them under any circumstances, and the mutual attachment could not be easily severed. I might mention the names of many foster parents, whose affections have centered in these little hitherto homeless ones, who are now made comfortable, joyous, and happy around the firesides of the homes of their adoption.[166]

Just as the activities of the Boston children's associations were instrumental in pressing for the passage of the first Massachusetts general adoption legislation, it appears that the efforts of Brace and men like him made apparent the need for legislation in New York. Thus, in 1865, the Commissioners of the proposed Civil Code for New York (David Dudley Field and his colleagues) wrote:

> The total absence of any provision for the adoption of children is one of the most remarkable defects of our law. Thousands of children are actually, though not legally, adopted every year; yet there is no method by which the adopting parents can secure the children to themselves except by a fictitious apprenticeship, a form which, when

---

[165] *Id.* at 14.

[166] Letter to the Children's Aid Society from a correspondent in Battle Creek, Michigan, dated Dec. 5, 1859; quoted by Brace in BEST METHOD 27. The words "adoption" and "adopted parents" were frequently used to describe the relation between the children and their homes in the West, as these letters to Brace demonstrate. *See also* BEST METHOD 29, 30, 32.

applied to children in the cradle, becomes absurd and repulsive. It is, indeed, so inappropriate a form in every case that it is rarely resorted to.[167]

The first New York statute was passed a few years later in 1873,[168] although arguments have been made that adoption was legal in the state as early as twenty years before.[169] In any case, it seems undeniable that the movement of which Brace's activities were a part led to the passage of the 1873 statute. Moreover, these efforts did not cease to be effective with the passage of that statute, and two years later we find that Brace's theories on child-rearing had caught on to the extent that the Congress of the State Boards of Charities resolved that legislation should be passed to remove all dependent children from county poorhouses, city almshouses and common jails, and "from all association with adult paupers and criminals," and place them "in families, asylums, reformatories or other appropriate institutions." Thus, in New York state alone in the year following that resolution, over one thousand children were taken from poorhouses and were placed in families or in orphan asylums.[170]

---

[167] NEW YORK COMMISSIONERS OF THE CODE, CIVIL CODE OF THE STATE OF NEW YORK 36, *quoted in* WITMER 24. Witmer observes that though the civil code failed to pass in New York, its adoption provisions were picked up in California.

[168] An Act to Legalize the Adoption of Minor Children, 1873, N.Y. Sess. Laws, ch. 830, at 1243.

[169] The thirteenth section of the New York act provided that "nothing herein contained shall prevent proof of the adoption of any child heretofore made, according to ANY method practiced in this State, from being received into evidence, nor such adoption from taking the effect of an adoption hereunder." One contemporary commentator interpreted this to mean that adoption had been completely legal even before the statute.

> I assert that there is no such definition in any previous statute, or in the published opinions of our courts, and that no one can maintain that the matter intended to be legalized was ever an illegal transaction. Joachimsen, *The Statute to Legalize the Adoption of Minor Children*, 8 ALB. L.J. 353 (1873).

More likely is the interpretation by the New York Court of Appeals in Matter of Thorne, 155 N.Y. 140, 144, 49 N.E. 661 (1898):

> We think the only construction [of the section] permissible is that it refers to those forms of adoption theretofore existing by virtue of special statutory enactments contained in the charters of charitable societies that received destitute and homeless children, and whose officers were permitted to execute agreements of adoption on their behalf with suitable persons willing to assume the obligations of parents. This is illustrated by the act to incorporate the American Female Guardian Society, a well-known charitable institution in the city of New York (Ch. 244, Laws of 1849). . . ."

[170] *See generally* THURSTON, THE DEPENDENT CHILD (1930).

Before passing on to the next section of the paper, it will be helpful to summarize briefly the social background of the adoption legislation. In the first half of the nineteenth century, it became apparent that public means for the care of dependent children were grossly inadequate for the welfare of the children. At first the system of private care was like the old methods of public care, with an initial period where the children were kept in an asylum or institution to receive rudimentary education, followed by indenture or apprenticeship. It soon became apparent that the old systems of apprenticeship and indenture were failing to educate and provide for the needs of children because of changing economic conditions, and through the efforts of philanthropists, private agencies were formed for the care of dependent children. As it became impossible to provide early institutional care for all, private agencies began to channel their energies toward placing children, often at very early ages, in foster homes where they would be treated more like members of the family than like servants. Motivating many, if not all, of these child-welfare reformers was a strong religious spirit which was an offshoot of a religious revival then taking place. The reformers believed that the children of the poor were not basically different from the children of the rich. These religious and egalitarian views of many of the child welfare workers led them to abandon the system of indentures and to conclude that the best way of caring for dependent children was to have them accepted into "God's Reformatory," a family. Since a child who was not indentured could not be bound to a family in which he was not properly cared for, the effort to provide a proper family atmosphere became paramount. Many of the children placed by such agencies as the New York Children's Aid Society found themselves in situations which not only resembled "adoption" as we know it today, but which was called by the same name. As the phenomenon of children in adopted homes became more common, there was increased pressure not only to pass laws regulating and insuring the legal relations between adopted children and their natural and adoptive parents, but to guarantee that some benefits of heirship were conferred on the adopted child. This pressure, which originated with the activities of the

charitable associations working in child welfare, led to the passage of the general adoption statutes in the third quarter of the
nineteenth century.

In the final section of the paper, how these adoption statutes
fared in the legal forum of the courts will be examined.

## VIII.   The Adoption Law In The Courts

This discussion of the adoption law in the courts is concerned only with those cases that shed some light on the thinking
of judges in connection with adoption law during the period
which is roughly contemporaneous with the passage of the adoption legislation. The main concern of this article is with the
second half of the nineteenth century, and in particular the
1870's and 1880's.[171] The most salient issues which the courts
confronted at that time were: a) the acceptance to be accorded
to adoption law and customs which existed prior to the wave of
adoption legislation, b) the construction that would be placed
upon the new legislation and whether or not methods for adoption other than those prescribed by the statutes should be permitted to take effect, c) the extent to which adopted children should
be treated the same as natural children of the adopted parent,
and d) the extent to which the rights of the adopted child should
be given protection against attack. As will become quite evident,
the treatment of most of these matters in the courts was anything
but uniform.

### a)   Acceptance of Laws and Customs

The custom of adoption was practiced extensively by the
American Indians[172] and by native Hawaiians.[173] The Oregon
Supreme Court, in what appears to be the typical response to the
request to recognize Indian adoption, in *Non-She-Po v. Wa-
Win-Ta* (1900)[174] said that such adoption could not be recognized

---

[171] There are a veritable host of articles which discuss the law of adoption and
consider more modern court decisions. In particular the reader is referred to Huard;
Brosnan, *The Law of Adoption*, 22 Col. L. Rev. 332 (1922); and Quarles, *The Law of
Adoption—Legal Anomaly*, 32 Marq. L. Rev. 237 (1949).

[172] Non-She-Po v. Wa-Win-Ta, 37 Ore. 213, 62 Pac. 15 (1900); *see also* Henry v.
Taylor, 16 S. D. 424, 93 N.W. 641 (1903).

[173] Kiaiaina v. Kahanu, 3 Haw. 368 (1871). *See also* Melish v. Bal, 3 Haw. 123
(1869), and Estate of Nakupa, 3 Haw. 410 (1873).

[174] 37 Ore. 213, 62 Pac. 15.

unless the procedure specified by the Oregon adoption law was followed. This formality was necessary, said the court, because "[i]t never was in the power of an individual, either by the common law of England or the Roman law, to adopt the child of another at his own volition, or by the consent of its parents." Rather, some special authority of law was always required.[175] The courts of Hawaii, on the other hand, did recognize and enforce the heirship of a *Keiki Hanai*, or foster child, provided that the adoption occurred at a time before the Hawaiian law was passed requiring that adoptions be made in writing. It also was required that the adoption made by the ancient oral mode was "clear, definite, and reasonably notorious."[176]

Courts have differed as to the extent of recognition to be accorded adoptions made pursuant to the Spanish law formerly in force in some states. In *Fuselier v. Masse* (1832),[177] for instance, the Louisiana court refused to recognize an adoption because the Spanish law had not been strictly adhered to, although the court still managed to interpret the arrangement to the benefit of the individual child concerned.[178] The Texas court, in *Ortiz v. De Benavides* (1884),[179] however, decided that they could give the benefit of the doubt to the adopted child under Spanish law, and although the record of the adoption (made in about 1813) was rather sketchy, the court nevertheless presumed:

> . . . that such a state of facts existed as would have authorized him to adopt and thus make [the child] his sole heir. . . . She had been reared in his house, was a niece of his wife, who is not shown to have been alive at the time, towards whom, in his childless condition, his affections would extend as do those of a father to his child. . . . The act [of adoption] was one which ordinary affection under the circumstances would prompt.[180]

---

[175] 37 Ore. at 216.

[176] Estate of Nakupa, 3 Haw. 410 (1873). Interestingly enough, the Hawaiian act that provided for written adoptions was passed in 1843, which would make it the earliest general act which has been mentioned here. 3 Haw. at 402.

[177] 4 La. Rep. 423.

[178] The court construed the written act by which the parties intended to adopt the child as a quasi-testamentary document to designate him as the universal heir of the adopted parents' estate. 4 La. Rep. at 428-30.

[179] 61 Tex. 60.

[180] 61 Tex. 60, 68.

It would appear, however, that the Texas court was not as lenient in cases where the adopting parent also had natural children. In the case of *Teal v. Sevier* (1863)[181] the court held that "[a]ccording to the [Spanish] laws of Texas in 1832, a person who had a legitimate child could not adopt a stranger as his co-heir with such a child" and decided that the adopted child would only be entitled to the amount of property that a father was entitled to give in his will to one not his heir.[182]

The reaction of courts to the use of Roman law precedents in interpreting the adoption statutes of the mid-nineteenth century also was inconsistent. While an adoption was upheld in *Woodward's Appeal* (1908),[183] the Connecticut court remarked that in interpreting the Connecticut statute, it refused to be controlled by analogies to Roman law, "[S]ince adoption is foreign to the common law, the statute [itself] is the measure" of the rights which it confers.[184] In sharp contrast to this view, the Michigan court twenty years earlier in *Morrison v. Session's Estate* (1888)[185] observed that since "the real object [of the Roman adoption] proceedings [was] to change the succession of property of persons dying intestate, and to create relations of paternity and affiliation not before recognized as legally existing," and since "[o]ur statute has the same object," Roman practices could be incorporated into the court's decision. Following the Roman custom, the Michigan court then decided that the child could be presumed to assent to the adoption.[186] Similarly, the Indiana court in *Markover v. Krauss* (1892),[187] when confronted with the question of whether "adopted children" should be included in a proviso regarding "children by a former wife," turned to Roman law. Citing an earlier Indiana case,[188] the *Markover* court remarked:

> [S]ince the rule [about adoption] is adopted from the civil law, it is there that we must look for its interpretation. . . . It is established

---

[181]  26 Tex. 516.
[182]  This amount, under the Spanish law, was one-fifth of the estate.
[183]  81 Conn. 152, 70 A. 453 (1908).
[184]  81 Conn. 163.
[185]  70 Mich. 297, 38 N.W. 249.
[186]  70 Mich. at 306.
[187]  132 Ind. 294, 31 N.E. 1047.
[188]  100 Ind. 274 (1884).

> law that where a rule is borrowed from another body of laws, courts will look to the source from which it emanated to ascertain its effect and force.[189]

The court went on to note from the *Institutes* of Gaius[190] that "[h]e who is either adopted or arrogated is assimilated in many points to a son born in lawful matrimony," and the court concluded that the adopted child was enough like a natural child that he should be considered the child "of the adoptive father by the adoptive mother."[191]

### b)   Construction of the Adoption Laws

Another striking contrast in the treatment of the adoption laws is that of the clear social welfare purpose of the adoption laws themselves[192] with the strict construction that those laws often received in the courts. In *Long v. Hewitt* (1876),[193] for instance, an instrument intended to effect the adoption of a child was signed and acknowledged by the child's surviving parent, but the adoption failed in execution because the justice who had possession of the instrument (and who was to approve it) was taken ill and died. Eighteen months later the adopted father also became sick and passed away. Throughout these events, the adopted child remained with his adopted parents. Shortly after the death of the adopted father, this action was brought as a bill in equity to declare that the adoption be given effect pursuant to the equity doctrine of accident. The *Long* court refused, however, to give a remedy:

> If courts of equity should hold that an inquiry may be made as to what were the causes which prevented a compliance with the statute by the proper execution of an agreement for adoption, it would be a most dangerous doctrine, and would be in effect permitting that which the statute requires shall be in writing to be shown by parol; thus allowing estates to be distributed upon what might be shown by

---

[189] 132 Ind. at 300.

[190] 1 Sandar's JUSTINIAN 45, § 105.

[191] 132 Ind. at 302.

[192] *See, e.g.*, Wolf's Appeal, 22 W.N.C. 93 (1888), where the Pennsylvania court noted: "The purpose of our adoption act is to promote the welfare of the child to be adopted, and any one desirous of adopting a child may invoke the power of the court of the county in which he or she may reside."

[193] 44 Iowa 363 (1876).

> parol to have been the intention of the intestate. . . . This is contrary
> to the whole policy of the law of descents and distribution. As well
> might we hold that the non-execution of a will is a fraud upon some
> devisee named therein, because the deceased was stricken with death
> before he signed it.[194]

Thus the *Long* court's conservatism in the area of the distribution of property forced it to turn away from what was best for the welfare of the child.

The courts were not consistently strict in this matter, for in *Barnard v. Barnard* (1886),[195] an Illinois equity case, the court permitted the adopted child to be declared heir at law, although the original adoption petition may have been deficient in that certain facts necessary for jurisdiction were not alleged.[196] The view of the *Barnard* court seems rather unique. For instance, in *Ferguson v. Jones* (1888),[197] the court observed that "[c]onsent lies at the foundation of statutes of adoption and when it is required to be given and submitted, the court cannot take jurisdiction of the subject-matter without it," and that a child's father who had not had his day in court would not be presumed to consent to the child's adoption.[198] This conclusion was held even in a case such as this one, where the father had been divorced from the mother and the mother had been given custody of the child and had consented to the child's adoption. The *Ferguson* court, in its strict construction, took what became a classic position:

> The permanent transfer of the natural rights of a parent was against
> the policy of the common law. The right of adoption, as conferred
> by this statute, was unknown to it, and repugnant to its principles.
> Such right was of civil law origin, and derived its sanction from its

---

[194] 44 Iowa at 367.

[195] 119 Ill. 92, 8 N.E. 320.

[196] The petition omitted the name of the father of the child, whether he consented, whether he was dead, or whether he had abandoned the child. The *Barnard* court held that it was sufficient to state the mother's name, and that she consented to the adoption. It will be presumed, said the court, that the father was either dead or had abandoned the child. The court was thus willing to presume facts necessary for the jurisdiction to accept the adoption petition. 119 Ill. at 99.

[197] 17 Ore. 204, 20 Pac. 842, 3 L.R.A. 620.

[198] "It is a rule as old as the law, and never more to be respected than now, that no one shall be personally bound until he has had his day in court. . . . Galpin v. Page, 18 Wall. 350." 17 Ore. at 211.

code. The right of adoption, then, being in derogation of common law, is a special power conferred by statute, and the rule is that such statutes must be strictly construed.[199]

*Tyler v. Reynolds* (1880) previously used strict interpretation of adoption statutes.[200] In *Tyler* the court dealt with the Iowa statute which required that an instrument of adoption be executed, signed, acknowledged and filed for record by the adopting parties before an adoption be final. All of these procedures were gone through in the case except for the last, since the adopting father had died before he could file. The adoption instrument *was* subsequently filed for record, but by someone who was *not* a party to the adoption. The court decided that this failure to record by a party to the adoption was fatal, since the provisions of the statute must prevail, even though in a case like this one such a holding might be "inconsistent with our views as to what constitutes natural rights, or justice and equity."[201]

Another issue over which the courts differed was the extent to which adoptions in the form of contractual arrangements would be enforced. In *Van Dyne v. Vreeland* (1857),[202] a New Jersey case pertaining to an adoption which occurred in 1832, several years before the first New Jersey general adoption statute was passed,[203] the court upheld such an arrangement. The father of the adopted child concerned had made an agreement with the child's uncle, at the uncle's request, that the uncle would take the child, adopt him as his own son, and transfer his property to the adopted son at the death of the uncle and his wife. The uncle took the child to live in his home; the child was baptised, assumed his uncle's surname, and lived with the uncle for twenty-five years. In the meantime, however, the uncle's wife had died and he had married a second wife. Apparently through the uncle's relations with his new wife, a rupture occurred in the relationship between

---

[199] 17 Ore. at 217.

[200] 53 Iowa 146, 4 N.W. 902.

[201] 53 Iowa at 148. *See also* Shearer v. Weaver, 65 Iowa 578, 9 N.W. 907 (1881). Somewhat later in the century the courts began to take a more liberal view in construing the adoption statutes for the benefit of the adopted children. *See, e.g.*, Gilliam v. Guaranty Trust Co., 186 N.Y. 127, 78 N.E. 697 (1906).

[202] 3 Stock. 370, 12 N.J. Eq. 142.

[203] The first New Jersey adoption law was enacted March 9, 1877.

the uncle and his adopted son. The uncle and his second wife proceeded to engage in several schemes to place the uncle's property in other hands, thereby insuring that it would not go to the adopted son upon the death of the uncle. The adopted son brought this action to have the arrangements resulting from these schemes set aside for fraud, as the arrangement amounted to a breach of the original adoption contract. The court held for the adopted son as the third-party beneficiary of the adoption contract between his natural father and his uncle. The court's remarks on its decision are quite different from those of the strict-construction courts that have just been examined:

> Why should not the complainant have redress? It is said the character of the agreement is such that the court ought not to entertain a bill upon it. There is no consideration of public policy which should forbid the court's countenancing such an agreement. Considering the situation of the parties, and their circumstances in life, it was beneficial to all the parties, and cannot be considered as injudicious or unreasonable. The father made a beneficial arrangement for his offspring, and [the uncle's] affections were satisfied by the adoption of a son. The agreement is alleged to have been unreasonable, because it deprived [the uncle] of the free disposal of his property. But this is not so. It provided him with a son, and only obligated him, in the disposal of his property, to make such provision for the child of his adoption as might reasonably be expected from parental obligation and affection.[204]

To be compared with the *Van Dyne* case is a Pennsylvania case of more recent vintage, *Evan's Estate* (1911),[205] where the court refused to hold that a written agreement by a husband and wife to adopt, support, maintain and educate a child until she arrived

---

[204] 3 Stock, at 380-81. The New Jersey courts, however, did not always countenance these contractual arrangements. For a New Jersey case where an adoption which was initially an oral agreement failed, *see* Luppie v. Winans, 37 N.J. Eq. 245 (1883). In the *Luppie* case, the court was much less sympathetic to the welfare considerations than was the *Van Dyne* court:

> It seems entirely manifest that in this case the welfare of the child would be very greatly promoted by the adoption, especially in view of the very handsome pecuniary provision which it was said on the hearing Mr. Winans [the adopted father] had made for it in his will, if the decree of adoption stands. That consideration, however, while it makes decision painful, cannot affect my judgment as to the legal validity of the decree."37 N.J. Eq. at 249.

[205] 47 Pa. Super. 196.

at the age of eighteen operated as an immediate and complete adoption which would make the child an heir.[206]

The most striking cases where the courts have denied adoptions are those in which a blood relative of the adopted child seeks to have the adoption nullified. A case representative of this genre is *Vandermis v. Gilbert* (1899).[207] In *Vandermis* the Pennsylvania court was confronted with an adopted child's grandmother who was trying to set aside a lower court's decree of adoption, on the ground of lack of consent on the part of the adopted child's parents. The facts of the case were that the child's mother had died long before the adoption petition was brought to the court and had not consented to the adoption. The child's father, however, *had* consented to the petition, but he died the day before the petition was presented to the court. The lower court had granted the adoption petition because the adopting father was "a man of good moral character, and of sufficient ability to properly maintain" the child. Furthermore, said the lower court, it was clear that "the welfare of the said Henry Bastin [the adopted child] will be promoted by the adoption." It appeared that the adopted child had been living for some time with the adopted parent, and until the petition was filed the grandmother took no interest in his welfare. Nevertheless, the court held for the grandmother and voided the adoption:

> This child had neither parent living at the time the petition was presented and the decree [of adoption] made. The fact that its father, who was the surviving parent, had died only one day prior to the presentation of the petition, and the making of the decree leaves the child as much without parents as if he had died a year before. . . . In this case, the father, by his death, lost his power to consent.[208]

---

[206] The *Evans* case illustrates some of the intriguing problems that have arisen in Pennsylvania as a result of the Act of April 2, 1872, Pub. L. No. 31. Among other provisions it demonstrated a legislative intent to give to the "common-law method of adoption by deed" the same force and effect as the record of an adoption in the mode provided in the Act of May 4, 1855, Pub. L. No. 430 (the earlier act provided the method for adoption with judicial approval). The problems are intriguing because, as has been demonstrated in an earlier section of this paper, *there was no common law method of adoption by deed. See also* 47 Pa. Super. at 199.

A topic closely related to adoption is that of legitimation of illegitimate children so that they might inherit as if they had been born within wedlock. As in the *Evans* case in the realm of adoption, courts have been strict with the kind of arrangements that will serve to legitimate children for heirship purposes. *See, e.g.,* Estate of Samuel Sandford, 4 Cal. 12 (1854); Pina v. Peck, 31 Cal. 12 (1866).

[207] 10 Pa. Super. 570.

[208] 10 Pa. Super at 575.

Another, and perhaps a more dramatic case where the court's high regard for blood bonds blinded them to the welfare of the adopted child, was *Johnson v. Terry* (1867).[209] In 1860 the mother of the adopted child (and two other children) left the children's father. That same year he divorced her. Having furnished no support for the three children, the father did not seek custody of them. In 1865 a man named Terry asked the mother whether her eldest son might come and live with him. The wife consented, and for some time the boy lived with Terry as his adopted son. Some months later the father (who was the plaintiff in the case) employed two men to take the child from Terry's home and bring the boy to him. The two men drove to Terry's house, found the child in the street, and invited him for a ride. He got into the carriage with the men, and as they drove along they passed Terry. The child called out repeatedly for Terry to save him. Hearing the child's cry, Terry immediately took a horse and wagon and followed the carriage to the father's house where the boy was delivered. Terry attempted to take the boy from his father by force, and the father subsequently brought this action for assault and battery.[210] The court held for the father, deciding that there was legally no adoption, and thus Terry had no right to recover custody of the child, and *a fortiori* no right to use force to obtain custody. The court decided that it was not in the father's power to divest himself by contract, even with the child's mother, of the custody of his children.[211] Thus, the father

---

[209] 34 Conn. 259.

[210] 34 Conn. at 260.

[211] In support of this point the court cited Torrington v. Norwich, 21 Conn. 543 (1852), in which it was said in plaintiff's argument:

Residence out of the family is no emancipation; nor working for others . . . nor the removal of the parent to a distance, leaving the child in the care of another until eighteen, *to be treated as an adopted child*, nor if the minor lived about, in several places, and the father refused to take care of him. . . ." (Emphasis added.) 21 Conn. at 545-46.

In its opinion, the *Torrington* court said:

The duties and legal relations of minor children and their parents toward each other, are imposed by the law, not merely in accordance with the natural obligation, but from considerations of high public policy and the general welfare of the community; and cannot be divested or varied by any private agreement between them. 21 Conn. at 548.

could not have been said to consent to the adoption, and it was void.[212]

The courts' predilection to award inheritances to consanguineous heirs over adopted children led them into some exceedingly technical and bizarre interpretations of the statutes, and in particular, of the Pennsylvania statute of 1872 which made legal the "common-law form of adoption by deed."[213] The two Pennsylvania cases which best illustrate this point are *Ballard v. Ward* (1879)[214] and *McCully's Appeal* (1881).[215]

The *Ballard* case concerned a child who had been adopted by a deed in 1863. The lower court recognized the deed as setting up an arrangement by which the adopting father bound himself to care for the adopted child, but the court was incapable of

---

[212] For still another interesting case, where the court's emphasis on consanguinity led them to overturn an adoption, *see* Booth v. Van Allen, 7 Phila. 401 (1870). In that case, A, a married man, had a child by B, an unmarried woman. A told B he would acknowledge and adopt the child, but instead A had his sister adopt the child, representing to the court that the child had been abandoned. B brought the action to void the decree whereby the sister adopted the child. In giving the decision to B, the mother, the court said:

> That the court may, in a proper case, permit a stranger to a minor to act as next friend will not be denied, but the right of those related by consanguinity or affinity, or whose claim is based upon an equitable ground, will not be set aside to permit a mere stranger to act in that capacity. It is plain that this is meant to be a right to the office, based on a legal or equitable ground, the act affects the interest of the child in the most important respects; it is to become in many instances subject as a child and heir, to one who is a stranger to its blood, and who must shape to a great extent its future. A Guardian of the Poor, or a charitable institution, can only be allowed to consent to a decree of adoption after they shall have supported the child one year; how can one who does not establish that right, who stands as an intruder before the court, be permitted to give a binding consent to a decree of this kind, to affect the custody and interests of the infant, and the claim of a father and mother, without notice to them, or an opportunity having been afforded to be heard by way of protest or objection? 7 Phila. at 404.

For a case with a strong civil law flavor which emphasizes the importance of blood ties in cases of adoption, *see In re* Upton, 16 La. Ann. 175 (1861), which preserves to the natural parent the right to appoint a tutor (a guardian in civil law jurisdictions) to the exclusion of the exercise of the power by the adopted father.

[213] *See* note 206 *supra*.

[214] 89 Pa. 358.

[215] 10 W.N.C. 80.

conceiving of the deed as making the child an heir:

> I am unable to see how Mr. Ward could impart to his niece inherita-
> ble blood by deed, so as to make her capable in law of inheriting his
> property as a natural child . . . The alleged deed is but a proposition
> to adopt, followed by an agreement for maintenance . . .[216]

On appeal, the Pennsylvania Supreme Court was barely able to conceive of the creation of heirs by adoption.[217] They decided that though the 1872 act *was* intended to validate adoption by deed, and though the act *was* intended to be retroactive, "it is too plain for argument that a proceeding under it could not divest the estate of the defendants in error, which had vested by the death of their father."[218] Thus, by virtue of the fact that the adopted father had died in 1870, two years before the statute in question was passed, the court decided that the rights of the other heirs had vested, and the court neatly defeated the inheritance of the adopted child. Thus the court's notion of vested property rights was used to frustrate the intent of the 1872 statute.

In *McCully's Appeal*[219] an instrument executed in 1848 was in issue. The instrument was an indenture of apprenticeship for fourteen years in the usual form, but a clause was added at the end which provided that "The full intent and meaning of this indenture is that the said apprentice is to be the adopted child of the said [adopting father] and his wife, and to be brought up and educated as their own child." Both the adopted mother and father signed and sealed the deed, and it was acknowledged before an alderman by all the parties, although there was no separate acknowledgement by the wife. The adopted child served the full term of apprenticeship, and continued to live with her adopted parents for the rest of their lives, the adopted father being survived a few years by his spouse. Upon the death of the

---

[216] 89 Pa. at 360.

[217] The court expressed its uneasiness about the notion of permitting adoption by deed by a reference to ancient adoption practices. They observed that even under Roman law,

> [s]ome special authority of law was necessary to constitute an adoption . . . .
> Before the times of the empire, arrogation was authorized only by a vote of
> the people, and ordinary adoption by an edict of the praetor . . . and under
> the Code Napoleon the judge must intervene. . . . 89 Pa. at 361.

[218] 89 Pa. at 361.

[219] 10 W.N.C. 80.

adopted mother, the child brought this action to claim her rights
to administer the estate, as her adopted parents' heir. The court,
however, decided that she had no such rights. The decision of the
court appears to have rested on two grounds. The first was that
"[a] married woman is incapable of binding herself by deed so
as to confer a future right of inheritance in favor of an adopted
child. Even if she were so capable, the absence of a proper separate acknowledgement would be fatal to the validity of such an
instrument." The court went on to add, "Nor does the Act of
1872 (P.L. 31) give any validity of such a deed. No deed invalid
at common law is within its operation."[220] The court's argument
here seems irrelevant, both because the intent of the adopted
mother was completely clear, as indicated by her signing and
sealing of the indenture, and because, since there was no such
thing as a common law deed of adoption, it is hairsplitting to
speak of fine distinctions among such deeds. It would seem more
consistent with the spirit of the Act of 1872 simply to affirm the
adoption.

The second ground of the court's decision was bottomed on
the terms of the deed itself:

> The deed of 1848 must be construed upon its own terms, and with
> reference to the law as it then existed; and conceding, what is far from
> being clear, that the period of adoption was not limited to the term
> of apprenticeship, it certainly cannot, by anything in the language
> used, or by any legal operation then known, be extended beyond the
> lifetime of the master and mistress, in whose estates it does not pro-
> fess to give any present or future right whatever.[221]

Yet a "legal operation" recognized in 1848 was the technique
of passing a private act to authorize adoption, and indeed some
of the acts passed did provide that the adopted child be "invested
with all the legal rights of a legitimate son."[222] Among those
rights would presumably be the right to inherit and administer.
Thus the court's conclusion that no legal operation existed which
would serve as an analogy by which to attribute a meaning to
the words "adopted child" and thereby give the adopted child a
present or future right in the estates of the adopted parents appears incorrect.

---

[220] *Id.*

[221] 8 W.N.C. at 16.

[222] *See, e.g.*, Pub. L. No. 167 of 1848, cited in note 102 *supra*.

## c) Adopted Children As "Natural" Children

The confusion over the incidents of the status of adopted children was by no means limited to the question of whether the adopted child could inherit from his adopted parents. A sampling of the decisions that interpreted the adoption acts in the years following their passage shows that courts felt that the rights of adopted children differed significantly from those that might have been accorded to natural children of the adopting parents. For example, it was held that the natural parents, not the adopted parents, inherited from the adopted child when he died intestate;[223] that adopted children are children of their adopted father, but are not children of his wife, thus being excluded from the category of "children by a previous wife," if the adopted father remarried;[224] that adopted children are not brothers and sisters of any natural children of the adopted parents;[225] that adopted children must pay the "collateral inheritance" tax which natural children did not have to pay;[226] and that the adoption of a child would not operate to allow a court to correct a last will and testament, as the court could following the birth of a natural child.[227]

The status of adopted children has also been the subject of early court decisions concerned with comity, that is, the extent to which a child adopted in one state will be accorded the same status in the courts of another state. The leading case in this area is *Ross v. Ross* (1878).[228] In the course of a discussion which touched upon most common law precedents from the time of the *Statute of Merton*, the *Ross* court set the standard which was to guide in questions of status for adopted children:

> It is a general principle, that the status or condition of a person . . .
> by which he is qualified or made capable to take certain rights in . . .
> property, is fixed by the law of the domicil; and that this status and
> capacity are to be recognized and upheld in every other State, so far
> as they are not inconsistent with its own laws and policy. . . . But

---

[223] Hole v. Robbins, 53 Wis. 514, 10 N.W. 617 (1881).

[224] Barnes v. Allen, 25 Ind. 222 (1865).

[225] Barnhizel v. Ferrell, 47 Ind. 335 (1874).

[226] Comm. v. Nancrede, 32 Pa. 389 (1859).

[227] Bowdlear v. Bowdlear, 112 Mass. 184 (1873).

[228] 129 Mass. 243.

> the status or condition of any person, with the inherent capacity of
> succession or inheritance, is to be ascertained by the law of the domi-
> cil which creates the status, at least when the status is one which may
> exist under the laws of the State in which it is called into question,
> and when there is nothing in these laws to prohibit giving full effect
> to the status and capacity acquired in the State of the domicil.[229]

Applying this standard, the *Ross* court decided that a child adopted in Pennsylvania, where the consent of the adopting father's wife was not required, would be recognized in Massachusetts, even though under Massachusetts adoption law the consent of the wife was required.

In *Keegan v. Geraghty* (1881[230] the Illinois court applied the *Ross* standard, but this time to rule against the adopted child. *Keegan* involved an inheritance from a natural child of an adopted father. The adopted child sought to receive the inheritance as the closest relative of the deceased natural child. This position was contested by the intestate's grandmother. The adoption had occurred in Wisconsin and the family had subsequently moved to Illinois. In the course of a comparison between the Wisconsin and the Illinois statutes the court noted that although an adopted child might be able to inherit from his brothers and sisters by adoption in Wisconsin, this was not true in Illinois. Comparing the texts of the two statutes, however,[231] it would

---

[229] 129 Mass. at 246-47.

[230] 101 Ill. 26.

[231] The relevant Wisconsin statutory provision was section six of Chapter 49 of the Revised Statutes of 1871:

> A child so adopted as aforesaid, shall be deemed, for the purpose of inherit-
> ance and succession by such child, custody of the person and right of obedi-
> ence by such parent or parents by adoption, and all other legal consequences
> and incidents of the natural relation of parents and children, the same to all
> intents and purposes as if such child had been born in lawful wedlock of such
> parent or parents by adoption, saving only that such child shall not be deemed
> capable of taking property expressly limited to the heirs of the body or bodies
> of such petitioner or petitioners.

The comparable Illinois statutory provision was the Illinois Adoption Statute of 1874, section five:

> A child so adopted shall be deemed, for the purpose of inheritance by such
> child, and his descendents and husband or wife, and other legal consequences
> and incidents of the natural relations of parents and children, the child of the
> parents by adoption, the same as if he had been born to them in lawful
> wedlock, except that he shall not be capable of taking property expressly
> limited to the [heirs of the] body or bodies, of the parents by adoption, nor

appear that the court's decision against the adopted child, and in favor of the grandmother was based on other considerations which the court elaborated:

> When such an adoptive parent dies intestate, having had no children born to him in wedlock, it is reasonable and just that the property he leaves should go to a stranger to his blood, his adopted child. It would be a consequence of his own desire and request in the taking of the adoption proceeding. But another person [here referring to the natural child of the adopting father], who has never been a party to any adoption proceeding, who has never desired or requested to have such artificial relation established as to himself, why should his property be subjected to such an unnatural course of descent? To have it turned away upon his death from blood relations, where it would be the natural desire to have property go, and pass into the hands of an alien in blood,—to produce such effect, it seems to us, the language of the statute should be most clear and unmistakable, leaving no room for any question whatever.[232]

Thus it would seem that the court's decision was dictated more by its notions of what was "reasonable and just" and "the natural desire to have property go [to blood relations]" than by the requirements of the Illinois statute and the doctrine of the *Ross* case.[233]

The same court that decided *Ross* found limits to the extent to which it would recognize the principles of comity. In *Foster*

---

property from the lineal or collateral kindred of such parents by right of representation.

In comparing the texts of these two statutes, it appears clear that under both states' laws the adopted child should be permitted the "legal consequence of . . . the natural relation of parents and children," that is, the right to take in cases of intestacy from brothers and sisters by adoption. The court attempts to get around this by looking at another section of the Illinois statute which prohibits the adopted parents from taking any property which intestate adopted child had acquired from his natural kindred (Act of 1874, section six). The court's argument here seems to emphasize consanguinity rather than strict logical analysis.

> We cannot admit this anomalous right [that of taking from the natural child by the adopted child], here claimed in a stranger in blood to take by descent in exclusion of kindred, to be given by any doubtful implication or vague generality of language. As against the adopted child, the statute should be strictly construed, because it is in derogation of the general law of inheritance, which is founded on natural relationship, and is a rule of succession according to nature, which has prevailed from time immemorial. 101 Ill. at 39.

[232] 101 Ill. at 35-36.
[233] *See also* note 231 *supra*.

*v. Waterman* (1878)[234] the court was passing upon the validity of an act of adoption in New Hampshire. A New Hampshire probate judge had approved the petition of Massachusetts domiciliaries who sought to adopt a child residing in New Hampshire. In a puzzling reading of the New Hampshire statute,[235] the court refused to recognize the adoption.

> Such a statute is not to be presumed to extend to a case in which the domicil of those petitioning for leave to adopt a child is in another state; the provision, in the statute of New Hampshire, that the decree may be made in the county where the petitioner or the child resides, implies that the statute is intended to be limited to cases in which all parties have their domicil in that state; and there is no presumption in favor of the jurisdiction of a probate court, exercising a special authority conferred by state, and not according to the usual course of proceedings at common law or in chancery.[236]

Again, it seems that the court's decision was not dictated by the meaning of the statute (which is ambiguous at best). Rather, the nature of adoption, which was, after all, an operation "not according to the usual course of proceedings at common law or in chancery" was controlling. Fortunately for adopted children, not all courts took the same view as the *Foster* court, and a few years later, an Illinois court recognized the validity of the temporary-resident adoption. *Van Matre v. Sankey* (1893).[237]

The last issue to be examined concerning the status of adopted children is the extent to which they were allowed to take under testamentary bequests. The earliest case to be considered is *Shafer v. Eneu* (1867).[238] A Pennsylvania woman had adopted a child pursuant to the 1855 Act.[239] The adopted child joined the woman's family which already included several children. The woman's father had died in 1851, bequeathing his property to trustees "for the sole and separate use of [his daughter] for life, and on her death to be conveyed to her children and the heirs of her children for ever." Upon the woman's death, the adopted child brought this action to recover under the devise, as one of

---

[234] 124 Mass. 592.
[235] N.H. Gen. Stats. ch. 169 (1867).
[236] 124 Mass. at 594-95.
[237] 148 Ill. 536, 36 N.E. 628.
[238] 54 Pa. 304.
[239] Pub. L. No. 430, Act of 4 May, 1855.

the woman's children. Interpreting the language of the devise, the court decided against the adopted child:

> [H]is gift of the remainder was to the children of his daughter Theresa Clark, and heirs of her children. Adopted children are not children of the person by whom they have been adopted, and the Act of Assembly [the 1855 act] does not attempt the impossibility of making them such.[240]

The 1855 statute had provided however, with reference to the natural and adopted children of an adopted parent, "[t]hat if such adopting parent shall have other children, the adopted shall share the inheritance only as one of them, in case of intestacy, and he, she, or they shall respectively inherit from, and through each other, as if all had been the lawful children of the same parent."[241] From the text of the statute it could be argued that the adopted child should be treated exactly as if he were a natural child born after the death of the husband, and thus that he should be allowed to take under the devise. The court rejected this argument, however, and decided that the natural children alive at the father's death "had a vested interest in the devise when the Act of 1855 took effect which the legislature could not take away and give to persons adopted by the [daughter] for life."[242] Thus, the courts' notion of vested property rights in consanguineous relatives once again served to frustrate the interests of the adopted child.[243]

Providing sharp contrast to the view of the *Shafer* court that adopted children are not the children of their adoptors for the purposes of taking in a testamentary bequest is the Massachusetts case of *Sewell v. Roberts* (1874).[244] The *Sewell* case involved an irrevocable trust with the income to the adopted father for life and a gift over to his "children or issue." The adopted child brought the action to be declared within the terms "children or issue." The relevant provision of the Massachusetts

---

[240] 54 Pa. at 306.

[241] Pub. L. No. 430, Act of 4 May, 1855.

[242] 54 Pa. at 304.

[243] *See also* Ballard v. Ward, 89 Pa. 358 (1879), discussed at text accompanying notes 216-218 *supra*.

[244] 115 Mass. 262.

adoption statute of 1851 was section six:

> A child so adopted . . . shall be deemed, for the purposes of inheritance and succession by such child, custody of the person and right of obedience by such parent or parents by adoption, and all the other legal consequences and incidents of the natural relation of parents and children, the same to all intents and purposes as if such child had been born in lawful wedlock of such parents or parent by adoption, saving only that such child shall not be deemed capable of taking property expressly limited to the heirs of the body or bodies of such petitioner or petitioners.[245]

Observing that "[t]his language is very broad and comprehensive, and it was manifestly the intention of the legislature to provide with the exception named, that the adopted child should . . . 'to all legal intents and purposes be the child of the petitioner,'" the court decided that the terms "child or children," "issue," and "lawful issue" included adopted children.[246]

Fourteen years after *Sewell*, however, an Alabama court in *Russell v. Russell* (1888)[247] decided that the Alabama adoption act,[248] which provided that the adopted child would be made capable of inheriting the estate of his adoptor, does not authorize one adopted under its provisions by a testator to take under the term "my children" in his will:[249]

---

[245] Acts of 1851, ch. 324.

[246] 115 Mass. at 277. Another Massachusetts case, which expressly followed *Sewell*, Burrage v. Briggs, 120 Mass. 103 (1876), shows the courts' acceptance of the notion that adopted children would really be treated like natural offspring. In *Burrage*, the testatrix had made a special provision for her adopted daughter, and had bequeathed the rest of her estate to her (the testatrix's) brother as residuary legatee. The brother died, and the testatrix failed to change her will. The heirs of the brother then argued:

> The delay or omission of the testatrix to change her will after the death of [her brother] does not show that she intended her adopted child to take as her sole heir the residue, but rather, that, having amply provided for her, she intended the residue to go to the heirs of [the brother], who were also her heirs and next of kin by blood. *Id.*

The court refused to accept this argument, and gave the residuary bequest to the adopted child, apparently accepting her as the nearest of kin to the testatrix.

[247] 84 Ala. 43, 3 So. 900.

[248] ALA. CODE § 2367 (1886).

[249] 84 Ala. at 51-53.

> The statute enables [the adopted child] to inherit from him by whom
> he was adopted because the statute says so; not because he is the child
> of the decedent. . . . All the rights he has are given him by the
> statute, and that confers nothing but a mere right of inheritance,—to
> share the estate of [the adopted father] left undisposed by will. . . .
> Even a known wish or intention of the testator can avail nothing, if
> he failed to take the legal steps necessary to carry it into effect.[250]

The court decided that it was in no way bound by the decision
in such Massachusetts cases as *Sewell v. Roberts*:[251]

> The Massachusetts statute is much more comprehensive than ours.
> It confers on the adopted child, not only the right of inheritance, but
> 'all other legal consequences and incidents of the natural relation of
> parents and children. . . .' Their decisions shed no light on the inter-
> pretation of our statutes.[252]

Taken together, then, the *Shafer, Sewell*, and *Russell* cases show
that in the area of interpretation of testamentary bequests the
views of the courts were no more uniform than they were in the
other areas that have been reviewed here.

### d)   Protection of the Adopted Child

There appears to be a uniformity of decision in this area
which favors the rights of the adopted child. This area concerns
attacks on the adoption by parties other than the adopting parents and general protection of the rights of the adopted child. The

---

[250] 84 Ala. at 51-52.

[251] Note 244 *supra*, and accompanying text.

[252] 84 Ala. at 52-53. For another case in which a court arrived at the same holding
as the *Russell* case, although as a result of reasoning based more on the nature of deeds
of adoption than the adoption statute, *see* Reinders v. Keppelman, 94 Mo. 344, 7 S.W.
290 (1888). In the testament concerned in that case, the adopted father made specific
provision for his adopted daughter, so the court decided that the term, "nearest the
lawful heirs," used in another bequest in the same will did not include the adopted child.
Had this not been the case, however, the court indicated it would still have come out the
same way:

> If, however, the testator had not hung out this light, by which his meaning
> may be easily read, it would seem that the very terms, "nearest and lawful
> heirs," would be sufficient to exclude the idea of an adopted heir. . . . The
> *status* or relation of an adopted heir is a lawful one, since the law sanctions
> and provides a method for its creation; but the relation is not the creature of
> the law, but the deed of adoption; a child by adoption is, in a limited sense,
> made an heir, not by the law, but by contract evidenced by deed. "Adopted
> heir," or "heir by adoption," [not "nearest and lawful heir"] would be
> appropriately descriptive of such relation. *Id.*

cases to be reviewed here occurred near the end of the nineteenth century and show a trend to give the adopted child more benefits than earlier cases had allowed.

In the first of these cases, *Wolf's Appeal* (1888),[253] a California resident had adopted a Pennsylvania child in 1878. The California adopted father died in 1886. In 1887, natural relatives of the decedent brought this action to set aside the adoption (and to defeat the adopted child's inheritance) on the ground that the adopted father did not have necessary consent. Remarking that "the purpose of our adoption act is to promote the welfare of the child to be adopted,"[254] the court decided that since the attackers were bringing the action as the "heirs and next of kin" of the adopted father, that is, since they derived their status by virtue of their relationship to him, just as the adopted father would be estopped from trying to set aside the adoption decree which he had obtained, they would similarly be estopped. This, said the court, would be the best way to insure the welfare of the child, as the statute intended:[255]

> On the argument many cases were cited where decrees of adoption have been set aside at the instance or in the interests of the adopted child, but none were cited, nor will any likely ever be found where such decrees were revoked at the instance of the party who invoked the power of the court and sought and obtained its decree, when such revocation would be to the prejudice of the innocent child.[256]

The same concern for the welfare of the adopted child, here resulting in a restraining of the activities of the adopted parent, showed up in the case of *Succession of Uforsake* (1896).[257] The *Uforsake* court engaged in a brief historical survey of ancient adoptions and of adoptions by assorted kings and noblemen, in the course of which the court noted the hostility that the custom

---

[253] 22 W.N.C. at 93.

[254] 22 W.N.C. at 95.

[255] Compare this result with the non-allowance of the adoption by the temporary resident in Foster v. Waterman, 124 Mass. 592 (1878), discussed at text accompanying notes 234-237 *supra*.

[256] 22 W.N.C. at 96. For a later case where the disappointed relatives from *Wolf's Appeal* sought to disinherit the adopted child in another forum, and were similarly unsuccessful, *see* Van Matre v. Sankey, 148 Ill. 536, 36 N.E. 628 (1893), notes at text accompanying note 237 *supra*.

[257] 48 La. Ann. 546, 19 So. 602.

of adoption has encountered at different times. But the court
concluded:

> The extent of the right and meaning of the word [adoption] can not
> be determined with precision by reference to history. It is ever vary-
> ing, . . . with the times, customs and ideas. In modern times when
> antagonism to the laws and customs [of adoption] has been de-
> feated—justly defeated, as we may say—the purpose seems to have
> been assistance to the one adopted. . . .[258]

In line with this view, the *Uforsake* court decided that though a
tutor[259] may adopt his ward with the consent of the child's parent, this does not remove the adopted father from his obligation
to account for his tutorship, nor does it give him all the rights
of a natural parent, such as the right of usufruct to the property
of the adopted child.[260]

The culmination of the growth of the attitude that the
*Wolf's Appeal* and *Uforsake* cases illustrate appears to have
occurred at the turn of the century, in the Pennsylvania case of
*Brown's Adoption* (1903).[261] The attitude of the court had come
a long way from some of the more conservative stands that have
been examined:

> While the statutes authorizing adoption are in derogation of the com-
> mon law, and for this reason are in some respects to be strictly
> construed, yet their construction should not be narrowed so closely
> as to defeat the legislative intent which may be made obvious by their
> terms, and by the mischief to be remedied by their enactment.[262]

Following this principle, the court sustained the adoption in
question from an attack by the widow who had married the
adopted father subsequent to the adoption. She sought to overturn it twenty-one years after the decree, on the grounds that the
adoption proceedings described the decedent as of "Brooklyn,
New York," without indicating that at the time he was a tempo-

---

[258] 48 La. Ann. at 550.
[259] A "tutor" under Louisiana laws was roughly equivalent to a "guardian," under
the common law. *See In re* Upton, 16 La. Ann. 175 (1861).
[260] 48 La. Ann. at 550.
[261] 25 Pa. Super. 259.
[262] *Id.* at 262.

rary resident of Pennsylvania, as required under statute. In the court's words:

> It has been well said, that it requires more than mere irregularities to annul the relationship [of adoption] when [it] was entered into with honesty of purpose, especially when lived up to for many years and severed only by the hand of death.[263]

The court concluded that even if there were irregularities, since the adopted father benefited from his relationship with the children for so many years, no court would have allowed him to question the regularity of the original proceeding. Thus, his widow, who claimed under him, could not question its validity.

Reviewing the early case law on adoption, we have seen that courts differed in the extent to which they gave force to laws and customs of adoption from the period before the legislation passed at the middle of the nineteenth century, and that there was a tendency to look more favorably upon these laws and customs when there were no natural children of the adopted parent.[264] In general, courts construed the adoption laws strictly, since they were "in derogation of the common law." This was sometimes done to an extent "inconsistent with our views as to what constitutes natural right, or justice and equity."[265] The courts' acceptances of methods of adoption outside those provided by the early statutes varied, but there appears to have been a tendency to be more favorably inclined to the adoption when the child adopted was a blood relative, and to be much less favorably inclined when the child adopted was *not* a blood relative of the adopted parents and a natural relation of the child objected to the adoption.[266] Unhappily for the adopted child, courts occasionally allowed notions of vested property rights or strained interpretations to defeat the intent of adoption statutes.[267]

---

[263] *Id.* at 264.

[264] *Compare* Ortiz v. De Benavides, 61 Tex. 60 (1884) (text accompanying notes 179-180 *supra*) *with* Teal v. Sevier, 26 Tex. 516 (1863) (text accompanying notes 180-81 *supra*).

[265] Tyler v. Reynolds, 53 Iowa 146, 148 (1880). *See* text accompanying note 201 *supra*.

[266] *Compare* Van Dyne v. Vreeland, 3 Stock. 370, 12 N.J. Eq. 142 (1857) (text accompanying notes 202-204 *supra*) *with* Johnson v. Terry, 34 Conn. 259 (1867) (text accompanying notes 209-212 *supra*).

[267] *See, e.g.*, McCully's Appeal, 10 W.N.C. 80 (1881), and text accompanying notes 219-222 *supra*.

Adopted children were accorded significantly fewer rights than natural children, and the court opinions which dealt with the recognition of the status of the adopted child in questions of comity and testamentary bequests went both ways. Often the determining factor in these decisions may have been the notion that *blood* relations should prevail "where it would be the natural desire to have property go."[268] Fortunately for adopted children, courts at the beginning of the twentieth century seemed to be moving in a direction which would insure the safety of the adopted child against collateral attacks on his status, and even against poor management of his own assets by an adopted parent.

What was the cause of the divergences in the courts opinions on questions of adoption? In particular, why did courts so often tend to favor natural relations over relationships artificially created by the adoption laws? It is pertinent to recall at this point that in the late nineteenth century there were two differing views on the nature of many of the children who were adopted. One view stressed the similarity of all children, with particular emphasis on the parallels between children in wealthy families and children from deprived backgrounds.[269] The other, much less sympathetic view, held that many of the subjects of adoption were taken "from the waifs of society, foundlings or children whose parents are depraved and worthless." This view considered "the growing belief that many traits of mind are hereditary and almost irradicable," and was thus pessimistic about the prospects for adopted children.[270] It is tempting to attribute the different trends in the adoption decisions to adherence to one or the other of these two views by individual judges, with those that adhered to the latter view feeling more acutely the need to favor natural relations over artificial ones.

Another reason for the tendency of courts to favor consanguineous relationships over those created by adoption is suggested by a consideration of changes that were occurring in the form, function, and conception of the family in late nineteenth

---

[268] Keegan v. Geraghty, 101 Ill. 26 (1881). *See* text accompanying note 232 *supra*.

[269] *See* text accompanying note 155 *supra*.

[270] WHITMORE 73-74. *See* text accompanying notes 117-118 *supra*.

512          *JOURNAL OF FAMILY LAW*          [Vol. 11

century America. In early America, and in Europe before the industrial revolution, it was usual for children to inherit "home, source of economic support, and special occupational status (especially a farm or family enterprise) from their fathers."[271] In that kind of a family structure there was great pressure on the children to conform to the wishes and life style of their parents. The modern American family, however, according to many sociologists and anthropologists, is quite different from the older more traditional model. There is no longer "a strong emphasis on a line of descent which would insure conformity of status of the kinship unit from generation to generation."[272] Rather, the American family is now characterized by a nonauthoritarian, democratic attitude where children are usually able to make choices on their own.[273]

During periods of great social change, it is not uncommon for those who live through such change to make the family a kind of "whipping boy" for the dislocations that have come about, and for it to be believed that if only the family were to be as it was in past halcyon days, all would be well.[274] Similarly, some theorists believe that in order to adapt to the demands of industrialism, cultures often must preserve a "stem family" system in which the main family or "stem" must be maintained through the use of "a regular mode of inheritance designed to prevent fragmentation" and ensure both the continuity and the integrity of the familial estate.[275]

It is possible, then, that the nineteenth century court decisions which favored the blood line over the interests of the adopted child may have been a reaction against what, at that time, was becoming the modern American family, where free choice and individuality were growing in importance. The favoritism of some of the courts may have demonstrated a desire to

---

[271] Parsons, *The Social Structure of the Family*, in THE FAMILY: ITS FUNCTION AND DESTINY 173, 178-79 (Anshen ed. 1949).

[272] *Id.*

[273] Benedict, *The Family: Genus Americanum*, in THE FAMILY: ITS FUNCTION AND DESTINY 159-69 (Anshen ed. 1949).

[274] *Id.* at 159-61.

[275] *See generally* Smith, *Family: Comparative Structure*, 5 INT. ENCY. SOC. SCI. 301, 310 (1968).

return to the more stable sureness of an imagined past where kinship ties were paramount. In short, individual judges, feeling that it would be better if the American family were the way it once was, may have reacted to modern development such as the new law of adoption by clinging to a last vestige of what they remembered from the old family structure; thus, they tried to preserve the continuity of the patrimony in the blood line.[276]

Whatever may have been the orientation of the individual judges, however, it does seem likely that had it not been for the imprecise language of many of the adoption statutes, and their susceptibility to varying interpretations under different circumstances, the courts would not have had the freedom to diverge as widely as they did. One possible reason advanced for this imprecision and loose draftsmanship is that these statutes were the work of men who were attempting to remedy one small defect in the provisions for child welfare, and were unmindful of the profound complications they would cause in the law of inheritance.[277] Those who passed the first laws apparently believed that they would be clearly understood when they said that "a child . . . adopted shall be deemed, for the purposes of inheritance . . . and all other legal consequences and incidents of the natural relation of parents and children . . . the same as if he had been born . . . in lawful wedlock."[278] But, and this may itself be an independent reason for the courts' vacillation on adoption, it appears that in the second half of the nineteenth century it was by no means clear what the legal meaning of the term "family" was, or what indeed *were* the "legal incidents of the natural relation of parents and children."[279] Thus, the varying treatment

---

[276] Another way of looking at these opinions is to say that the judges were reacting against the growing trend to think of the family in what might be called "contractual" terms, and to think of the family's interactions as being regulated by contract rather than ascriptive status. *See generally* Smith, *supra* note 275, at 305. This feeling on the part of these judges is particularly ironic coming at a time when there was a great surge in the law to think of almost everything in contractual terms. *See, e.g.*, HURST, LAW AND THE CONDITIONS OF FREEDOM IN THE NINETEENTH-CENTURY UNITED STATES 911 (1967), and when the courts themselves were speaking of family relations in terms that seemed to be in the language of contract. *See, e.g.*, text accompanying note 232 *supra*.

[277] WHITMORE 84.

[278] Mass. Gen. L. ch. 110 (1860).

[279] Joachimsen, *The Statute to Legalize the Adoption of Minor Children*, 8 ALB. L.J. 353, 354 (1873).

in the courts of the adoption statutes may be indicative of a larger problem: the courts and legislatures which had made such brilliant strides forward in formulating an American law of property, torts, contracts, and corporations,[280] had not yet grappled with some of the elementary aspects of domestic relations.

## IX.   CONCLUSION

We can now advance answers to the questions posed at the beginning of the paper.

*Why was the Roman practice of adoption not incorporated into the common law?* The Roman adoption practice was tailored to a social system which was quite different from that which came to exist in the common law countries. Roman adoption served the adoptor, not the adoptee, with its chief aims of continuity of the family and the perpetuation of family religious rites. The English medieval social system had no place for religious rites like those of the Romans. Although many Englishmen were sensitive to the need for perpetuating the family line through adopted heirs, this sensitivity was not strong enough to overcome the English notion that heirs should be of the blood, made by God, not by man. It is not completely clear how this notion came about, but it is possible that it was related to the type of land tenure which grew up immediately after the Norman Conquest, when there may have been *only* adopted heirs. This early situation may have bred a strong reaction to adoption which lasted hundreds of years. Over the years there were attempts to introduce practices like adoption into the law, but these attempts were rejected for a variety of reasons, not the least of which may have been English xenophobia. In the final analysis, however, it may be that adoption was not introduced into the common law because the child-rearing practices that existed a few hundred years ago served many of the needs that adoption now does. The customs of "putting-out" for service and apprenticeship appear to have been adequate to provide for the basic needs of child welfare.

---

[280] *See generally* R. POUND, THE FORMATIVE ERA OF AMERICAN LAW (1938).

*Why did the English and American legislatures wait so long before passing adoption legislation?* The putting-out system grew over the centuries into the system of indentures for apprenticeship and service which persisted in England until the late nineteenth century, was brought over to America with the first settlers, and continued here nerly as long as it did in England. For two hundred years, this system, and the custom of placing orphaned children with relatives, was as adequate for the child welfare needs of America as putting-out had been for the child welfare needs of early England. With the advent of industrialization, and the influx of immigrants, however, the appealing educational and beneficial qualities of the master-apprentice and mistress-servant relationship began to diminish as it became economically unfeasible. Similarly, the system of placing orphaned children with relatives may not have been appropriate for the new masses of urban, usually immigrant, poor, since there may have been neither the blood affinity nor the economic means to support a new addition to the family. New means were needed for child welfare in the middle of the nineteenth century, and in the movement for reform in child welfare practices which began to grow, adoption was accepted as one of these new means. Eventually the American, and later the British legislatures came to realize that there were problems in this custom of adoption requiring corrective legal action, and general legislation dealing with adoption began to be enacted.[281]

*Why were so many adoption statutes passed in America in such a comparatively short time?* The answer to this question lies in the pervasiveness of the economic and social conditions that gave rise to the movement for child welfare reform in the nine-

---

[281] The principal problem that has been dealt with here, because it is the one that most persistently crops up in the legal literature, is that of the adopted child whose parent dies intestate, that is, the problem of inheritance from the adopted parents. Two other problems were also important, and should be mentioned in passing. (1) The adopted parents, having no legal rights in their adopted child, could never be sure that the natural parents, who still had the legal rights before the legislation, might not come back and take the child from them. *See* WITMER 24, where he discusses this problem as it was observed by David Dudley Field and his associates in New York. (2) The adopted child would normally have no redress if his adopted parents grew tired of him and decided to cut off their support, since no laws bound them to their assumed obligations. This fact appears to be one that had a good deal to do with the eventual passage of the British legislation. *See* ABBOT, THE CHILD AND THE STATE 204ff. (3d ed. 1947).

teenth century, and in the vastness of the efforts undertaken by the reformers. In particular, the Children's Aid Society of New York was placing thousands of children in homes in many different states each year. The widespread failure of public child-care institutions to provide adequately for child welfare gave birth to private philanthropic efforts to remedy the situation through child-placing which ended in the adoption of children in many different states. Thus, many state legislatures found it necessary to respond with laws to facilitate legal adoption.

The materials presented in this article, and in particular the decisions of the late nineteenth century courts demonstrate the difficulties that can arise when an idea that has been out of a legal system for over a thousand years returns to it. One of the lessons to be learned from the history of the adoption law in America is that a legal reform prompted by lofty social and religious ideals can be accompanied by frustrating machinations in the courts. When the lofty ideals are not accompanied by careful draftsmanship that takes account of potential repercussions, and when judges are either uncomfortable about the sentiments of the reformers, or feel an equally strong obligation to uphold the property rights with which they have worked for many years, there are bound to be problems. In the case of the law of adoption, these difficulties, which began with the passage of the laws a century ago, are still with us.[282]

---

[282] *Compare* Riggs v. Summmerlin, No. 23,437 (D.C. Cir. 1971) (word "issue" in specific document does not include within its meaning adopted children), *with* Johns v. Cobb, 402 F.2d 638 (1968), *cert. denied*, 393 U.S. 1087 (1969) (word "issue" includes adopted children).

# 12

# FROM JUDICIAL GRANT TO LEGISLATIVE POWER: THE ADMIRALTY CLAUSE IN THE NINETEENTH CENTURY

*NOTE*

FROM JUDICIAL GRANT TO LEGISLATIVE POWER: THE ADMIRALTY
CLAUSE IN THE NINETEENTH CENTURY. — "The most bigoted idolizers
of state authority, have not thus far shown a disposition to deny the
national judiciary the cognizance of maritime causes. These so generally
depend on the laws of nations, and so commonly affect the rights of
foreigners, that they fall within the considerations relative to the public
peace."[1] With these two sentences in the *Federalist Papers,* Hamilton
disposed of the admiralty grant. Born as an element of foreign policy,
virtually uncontested at Philadelphia and in the state ratifying conventions,[2] the constitutional grant of federal judicial power over all cases
of admiralty and maritime jurisdiction[3] within a century had come to
rank with the Commerce Clause[4] as a far-reaching source of congressional legislative power over the vast system of navigable lakes, rivers,
and canals in the interior of the United States. It became the constitutional basis for the twentieth century outpouring of congressional enactments touching the law of the sea.[5]

The admiralty grant has had a tortuous history.[6] For the first half-
century, its very existence as a significant judicial power was in doubt.
Opponents of federal judicial power sought to confine maritime jurisdiction to those few cases cognizable in the debilitated English admiralty
courts of 1789. Virtually because of a single man, the scholarly, determined New Englander, Justice Joseph Story, the federal courts, in contrast to their English counterparts, gradually came to assert jurisdiction
over a broad field of maritime cases. But English precedent determined
one point of key importance: admiralty's scope was limited to the high
seas and tidal waters. The few federal statutes governing navigation on
the Great Lakes and the 15,000-mile Mississippi-Ohio-Missouri river
system of the Middle West seemingly were based on the Commerce
Clause. Not until 1851, in a decision written by Chief Justice Roger B.
Taney, was it held that all navigable waters, tidal or nontidal, fresh or
salt, fell within the admiralty power.[7] And it was not the Court, but
Congress — acting under the Commerce Clause — that gave the impetus to this reversal.

---

[1] THE FEDERALIST, No. 80 at 590–91 (J. C. Hamilton ed. 1864).
[2] See Putnam, *How the Federal Courts Were Given Admiralty Jurisdiction,* 10
CORNELL L.Q. 460 (1925); *cf.* Stevens v. The Sandwich, 23 Fed. Cas. No. 13,409, at
30 (D. Md. 1801).
[3] U.S. CONST. Art. III, § 2: "The judicial Power shall extend . . . to all Cases
of admiralty and maritime Jurisdiction . . . ."
[4] U.S. CONST. Art. I, § 8.
[5] See, *e.g.,* Detroit Trust Co. v. The Thomas Barlum, 293 U.S. 21, 39 n.5 (1934).
[6] A brief summary is in 4 BENEDICT, AMERICAN ADMIRALTY §§ 726–34 (6th ed.
1940). See Sprague, *The Extension of Admiralty Jurisdiction and the Growth of
Substantive Maritime Law in the United States since 1835* in 3 LAW: A CENTURY
OF PROGRESS 294 (1937); COLBY, DEVELOPMENT OF THE ADMIRALTY LAW OF THE
UNITED STATES (unpublished thesis in Harvard Law School Library, 1933); Goulder,
*Evolution of the Admiralty Law in America,* 5 AM. LAWYER 314 (1897); *History
of Admiralty Jurisdiction in the Supreme Court of the United States,* 5 AM. L. REV.
581 (1871). For the historic difficulties of the English admiralty courts, see p. 1216
*infra.*
[7] The Genesee Chief v. Fitzhugh, 12 How. 443 (U.S.). The sweep of this
holding is somewhat limited by the defining of "navigable waters" in terms of interstate commerce. See p. 1237 *infra.*

Only with difficulty in the second half-century did the Court develop the full import of the enlarged scope of the admiralty jurisdiction. Hesitantly, it rejected a definition of admiralty jurisdiction based on the limitations of the federal commerce power. And only as the century closed did the Court explicitly hold that under the judicial grant of admiralty jurisdiction Congress had the power to legislate in the field of maritime law. It is this nineteenth century history of the development of the admiralty grant as a broad source of federal judicial and legislative power that forms the subject matter of this Note.

*Admiralty Comes to Nontidal Waters: Territorial Expansion of Judicial Power* — (a) The Thomas Jefferson. — In the summer and fall of the year 1819, the 250-ton steamboat *The Thomas Jefferson* made a pioneer voyage from Shippingport, Kentucky, up the Missouri River and back, carrying foodstuffs and matériel on private contract to supply the Army's Yellowstone exploratory expedition.[8] Steamboat traffic was already well established on the Mississippi and Ohio rivers, but this voyage marked the first such ascent of the Missouri. It proved a financial disaster, and on return to Shippingport the crewmen were not paid. They sought relief in the federal district court for Kentucky, sitting in admiralty. On appeal to the circuit court, the libel was dismissed for lack of jurisdiction. The case was again appealed, to the Supreme Court of the United States in the February Term, 1825.

Justice Joseph Story, the high tribunal's ardent supporter and great student of the admiralty, wrote a four-paragraph opinion for the unanimous court, summarily affirming the dismissal.[9] He cited not a single case. Nevertheless, he rooted his decision in the precedent of history: [10] never in all its centuries in England had the admiralty claimed for itself jurisdiction further upriver than the ebb and flow of the tide.[11] In later

---

[8] Some accounts report that *The Thomas Jefferson* sank on this voyage. P. E. CHAPPELL, HISTORY OF THE MISSOURI RIVER 70 (1905). This is inaccurate; it was a keelboat carrying the cargo of the ship further upstream that met with this misfortune. H.R. Doc. No. 110, 16th Cong., 2d Sess. 169 (1821). See J. HALL, THE WEST: ITS COMMERCE AND NAVIGATION 162 (1848).

[9] The Thomas Jefferson, 10 Wheat. 428 (U.S. 1825). In December 1821 the district court entered judgment for the libelants, see note 38 *infra*, but apparently later reversed itself and dismissed for want of jurisdiction. The record of the case on file with the Supreme Court indicates that the circuit court affirmed a dismissal for want of jurisdiction entered in December Term, 1822.

[10] Story brushed aside the argument that the First Congress, in including within the admiralty jurisdiction all seizures made on waters navigable from the sea by vessels of ten or more tons burthen, 1 STAT. 77 (1789), had recognized the inapplicability in America of the tidewater doctrine: "[T]his is a statuteable [sic] provision, and limited to the cases there stated." 10 Wheat. at 430. Taney, in The Genesee Chief v. Fitzhugh, 12 How. 443, 457 (U.S. 1851), used the same statute to buttress his overruling of Story's decision.

The seizure jurisdiction was a departure from the English practice of handling such cases in the Court of Exchequer. Nevertheless, the provision was upheld in two early decisions, United States v. La Vengeance, 3 Dall. 297 (U.S. 1796), and United States v. The Betsey and Charlotte, 4 Cranch 443 (U.S. 1808), marking the first departure in American admiralty history from the English standards. The latter case explained the purpose of Congress as avoiding "the great danger to the revenue if such causes should be left to the caprice of juries." *Id.* at 446 n.(a) (Chase, J.).

[11] The most common applications of the tidewater doctrine occurred in actions of tort and contract. In tort, the cause of action must have arisen on the high seas or within the ebb and flow of the tide. Contracts, to be cognizable in admiralty,

years, this was explained as a patent fact of English geography. Since there was in that country no navigable stream beyond the tide's limit, tide water and navigable water were synonymous terms.[12] At best, this was only a partial explanation. In the early fourteenth century at the time of the establishment of the admiralty court, internal navigation was virtually non-existent. Not until that dynamic period of growth after the reign of the first Elizabeth did river transport become a factor in English life.[13] Beginning about 1600, "river navigation was 'in the air.' Members of parliament and country gentlemen discussed in the lobby of the house or the parlour of a country inn the merits and demerits of water transport."[14] Numerous schemes were undertaken to improve the navigability of English rivers, and at least occasionally nontidal waters were involved.[15] In the years after 1750, canal building began in earnest, markedly increasing the amount of navigable but nontidal waters. But throughout this period of the growth of internal navigation, admiralty jurisdiction was undergoing a steady decline.[16] The common law courts at Westminster, interpreting early statutes with great bias, issued writ after writ of prohibition against suits in admiralty.[17] Far from concerned with expanding its jurisdiction to nontidal waters, the admiralty was fighting a losing battle to retain what river jurisdiction it already had. By the time of the American revolution, admiralty power and prestige was at its nadir; virtually all that remained within its jurisdiction were events occurring exclusively on the high seas.

A germinal source of Story's decision perhaps lay with the definition of "navigable waters" developed by the common law courts. That term was a factor in determining three important common law property rights: fishing, navigation, and river-bed ownership.[18] Relying on dubious interpretations of English authorities, the early American courts

---

had to be "maritime," which was interpreted to mean that their subject matter dealt with events on the high seas or on tide waters.

[12] See The Genesee Chief v. Fitzhugh, 12 How. 443, 454–55 (U.S. 1851). "And, indeed, until the discovery of steamboats, there could be nothing like foreign commerce upon waters with an unchanging current resisting the upward passage." *Id.* at 455.

[13] The extent of this transport has generally gone unnoticed in English histories. For a sound modern study, from which the material for this paragraph is taken, see WILLAN, RIVER NAVIGATION IN ENGLAND: 1600–1750 (1936).

[14] *Id.* at 6.

[15] As early as 1650, supporters of a bill to make navigable the upper Wye were blocked by the common law rule holding nontidal streams the private property of the riparian owner. *Id.* at 21–22, app. III.

[16] The classic exposition of the struggle between admiralty and the common law remains Story's opinion in De Lovio v. Boit, 7 Fed. Cas. 418, No. 3,776 (C.C.D. Mass. 1815). For more modern treatment, see 4 BENEDICT, AMERICAN ADMIRALTY §§ 672–704 (6th ed. 1940); ROSCOE, ADMIRALTY JURISDICTION AND PRACTICE 1–36 (5th ed., Hutchinson, 1931).

[17] These actions, led by Lord Coke, have generally been ascribed to an inherent jealousy and even enmity toward the admiralty. A perhaps more intriguing explanation, advanced by a mid-nineteenth century writer, is that in former times the judges of common law courts depended for their means of support upon the fees paid by suitors. Hence, every cause of admiralty was so much subtracted from their salaries; and, of course, every writ of prohibition brought a pound or two more to their own pockets. See 2 PARSONS, MARITIME LAW 497 n.1 (1859).

[18] See ANGELL, WATERCOURSES (1st ed. 1824) *passim*. The development of the definition of "navigable waters" in this country is exhaustively discussed in 1

held that at law only tidal rivers were navigable rivers.[19]  Only Pennsylvania, in a case involving fishing rights in the Susquehanna River, perceived the utter inapplicability of the English rule to the vast river system of this country, and rejected it.[20]  The inaccuracy of the standard American interpretation of the ancient English definition of "navigable waters" appears beyond dispute.  It was at best only a rule of evidence, creating prima facie proof of navigability.[21]

Nevertheless, in the year that Story decided *The Thomas Jefferson*, navigable waters in American jurisprudence were at law tidal waters, and admiralty jurisdiction was generally limited thereto.  Story paid homage to stare decisis.[22]  Admiralty was declared to halt at the tide's upper limit.[23]  The case stands virtually alone, a curious landmark of admiralty abnegation in a judicial career marked otherwise by determined support of a broadened scope for the American maritime courts.[24]  The anomaly of such a decision from Story's pen puzzled Chief Justice Taney twenty-six years later.  He sought a plausible explanation:

[T]he great importance of the question . . . could not be foreseen; and the subject did not therefore receive that deliberate consideration which at this time would have been given to it . . . . For the decision was made in 1825, when the commerce on the rivers of the west and on the lakes was in its infancy, and of little importance, and but little regarded compared with that of the present day.[25]

However, experiments in steamboat navigation dated back before the Constitution.[26]  After the triumphal run of the 371-ton *New Orleans* from Pittsburgh to New Orleans in 1811 — the first steamboat voyage

---

FARNHAM, WATERS AND WATER RIGHTS §§ 22–23g (1904). See McManus v. Carmichael, 3 Iowa 1 (1856).

[19] *E.g.*, Palmer v. Mulligan, 3 Caines 307, 318–19 (N.Y. 1805). The harshness of the rule deeming nontidal rivers the private property of the riparian owner was mitigated by the view that the public held an easement to travel on all rivers navigable in fact.

[20] Carson v. Blazer, 2 Binn. 475 (Pa. 1810).

[21] 1 FARNHAM, *op. cit. supra* note 18, § 23g. See BENEDICT, AMERICAN ADMIRALTY § 253 (2d ed. 1870).

[22] The continental codes had no such tidewater limitation. ANGELL, TIDE WATERS 79 (2d ed. 1847). In other contexts, Story had a tendency to make much use of the civil law. See Pound, *The Place of Judge Story in the Making of American Law*, 7 CAMB. HIST. SOC. PUBS. 33, 41 (1912).

[23] The mechanics of tidal rivers are explored in WHEELER, TIDAL RIVERS (1893). The Amazon is the longest tidal river in the world, with a rise and fall perceptible over 900 miles from the sea. *Id.* at 108. Tidal effect on the Mississippi ceases shortly above New Orleans. Locks built on rivers also block off the tidal effect, such as the Teddington Lock on the Thames, 64 miles upstream. Whether admiralty jurisdiction could thus be diminished from former limits apparently was never litigated.

[24] "It was said of the late Justice Story, that if a bucket of water were brought into his court with a corn cob floating in it, he would at once extend the admiralty jurisdiction of the United States over it." Note, 37 AM. L. REV. 911, 916 (1903). The only other example of a Story Supreme Court opinion restricting admiralty jurisdiction is The General Smith, 4 Wheat. 438 (U.S. 1819) (absent state law, no lien exists in admiralty on a ship in its home port).

[25] The Genesee Chief v. Fitzhugh, 12 How. 443, 456 (U.S. 1851). This explanation was repeated in The Hine v. Trevor, 4 Wall. 555, 563 (U.S. 1867).

[26] Two excellent studies of the steamboat era are J. T. FLEXNER, STEAMBOATS COME TRUE (1944), and HUNTER, STEAMBOATS ON THE WESTERN RIVERS (1949).

on the Western rivers — steamboat traffic grew rapidly; in 1816 a committee of Congress reported that the success of steam navigation on the Ohio and Mississippi was no longer in doubt.[27] Lower federal courts, responding to this development, rejected the argument that admiralty jurisdiction was limited to tidal rivers.[28] Such interior maritime courts, argued one judge, were essential to proper control of commerce by Congress.[29] He, unlike Story, found no tidewater precedent in English history. Thus, when *The Thomas Jefferson* was appealed in 1825, neither the steamboat nor nontidal jurisdiction was a curiosity.[30] It is difficult to believe that Story, the author seventeen years later of the opinion in *Swift v. Tyson*,[31] could have failed to appreciate the significance of a broad admiralty power in achieving uniformity of law over Western water commerce.

The explanation of the decision may lie in the powerful extra-legal forces playing upon Story and the Court in the 1825 Term. For several years past, the criticism of federal judicial power had been increasing in intensity.[32] Resentment centered particularly in Kentucky,[33] whose laws on land settlement[34] had already been struck down as unconstitutional, and whose restrictive enforcement of judgments statute went unheeded in diversity cases in the federal circuit court.[35] Moreover, the Supreme Court decisions barring state taxation of the Bank of the United States[36] had added to the monetary crisis. In this background, the displacement of state power by the federal admiralty was an added irritation. It was not surprising then that a leader of the congressional advocates of judicial reform was Senator Richard Johnson.[37] Not only

---

[27] American Telegraph, May 11, 1816, quoting the report of the committee on the National Turnpike.

[28] Federal courts in Kentucky, Pennsylvania, and perhaps Virginia sat in admiralty over nontidal maritime cases. See 17 NILES WEEKLY REGISTER 31 (1819); THOMAS SERGEANT, CONSTITUTIONAL LAW 195 n.(*l*) (2d ed. 1830). The Kentucky case is Savage v. The Buffaloe, 21 Fed. Cas. 547, No. 12,382 (D. Ky. 1819) (opinion, not now accessible, summarized in THOMAS SERGEANT, *op. cit. supra*, at 195). The federal judge was Robert Trimble, a follower of the Marshall school. At a time when state feeling was strongly against the federal judiciary, he did not hesitate to uphold the national government. John Quincy Adams appointed Trimble to the Supreme Court in 1827.

[29] Sheckler v. The Geneva Boxer, 21 Fed. Cas. 1218, No. 12,735 (W.D. Pa. 1819) (opinion, not now accessible, summarized in THOMAS SERGEANT, *op. cit. supra* note 28, at 195, which lists date incorrectly as 1829).

[30] In addition to the lower court cases, the Supreme Court itself had dealt the previous term with a problem arising out of the new invention. Gibbons v. Ogden, 9 Wheat. 1 (U.S. 1824).

[31] 16 Pet. 1 (U.S. 1842).

[32] HAINES, THE ROLE OF THE SUPREME COURT IN AMERICAN GOVERNMENT AND POLITICS: *1789–1835* 463–97 (1944); 1 WARREN, THE SUPREME COURT IN UNITED STATES HISTORY 652–85 (1937 ed.).

[33] Kentucky's peculiar role in the battle against the Court is given in 1 *id.* at 633–51.

[34] Green v. Biddle, 8 Wheat. 1 (U.S. 1823).

[35] Wayman v. Southard, 10 Wheat. 1 (U.S. 1825); Bank of the United States v. Halstead, 10 Wheat. 51 (U.S. 1825).

[36] Osborn v. Bank of the United States, 9 Wheat. 738 (U.S. 1824), following McCulloch v. Maryland, 4 Wheat. 316 (U.S. 1819).

[37] Vice-President of the United States under Van Buren, 1837–41. The story of his financial difficulties is set out in MEYER, THE LIFE AND TIMES OF COLONEL

did he represent Kentucky, but he himself was an early investor in Western steamboats, and three of his brothers were the owners of *The Thomas Jefferson*. The failure of the Yellowstone venture, heightened by the collapse of a bank in which they were involved, created a perilous financial situation for the Johnson family. In late 1821, barely two weeks after the adverse decision of the Kentucky district court in *The Thomas Jefferson*,[38] Johnson bitterly attacked in the Senate the federal admiralty jurisdiction over Western rivers.[39] He claimed that those who engaged in steam navigation would be ruined if subjected to the processes of the federal admiralty courts.[40] His words had effect; his bill to limit the admiralty jurisdiction specifically to tidal waters passed the Senate in 1822 and went to the House.[41]

But perhaps the sentiments of the Senator were more familial than statewide. In 1823, with Johnson's statute awaiting action, a fellow Kentuckian, Representative John Breckenridge, asked that the House act upon his measure to facilitate admiralty suits by authorizing the United States district court to sit at Louisville, Kentucky's center of river navigation, as well as at Frankfort, the state capital.[42] He said that he was under the impression it would not excite debate. But Representative John T. Johnson, the Senator's brother and a co-owner of *The Thomas Jefferson*, responded with violent opposition. "The bills of the tavernkeeper . . . the account of the merchant . . . the charges of the carpenters and mechanics . . . all crowded into the district court of the United States, as a Court of Admiralty, subject to all the rigor of its processes before, and a different execution of law after judgment . . . ."[43] Breckenridge broke in to withdraw his proposal, since to his surprise it had resulted in controversy.[44] But Senator Johnson's bill did not pass the House either.

The 1825 Term of the Court has been characterized by one writer as the turning point in which decisions began to reflect more closely public

---

RICHARD M. JOHNSON OF KENTUCKY 189–206 (1932). See also H.R. DOC. NO. 110, 16th Cong., 2d Sess. (1821).

[38] The original libel was filed May 22, 1820, and a month later the district court sustained a demurrer to the shipowners' plea of lack of jurisdiction. Judgment for the libelants was decreed on Dec. 13, 1821. United States District Court, E.D. Ky., Order Book H, 158, 159, 206–09. See note 9 *supra*.

[39] 38 ANNALS OF CONG. 44–47 (1821).

[40] Johnson mentioned the requirement of the federal courts that judgments be paid in gold. 38 *id.* at 45–46. State courts allowed payment in paper and judgments were subject to the stay-laws. 1 WARREN, *op. cit. supra* note 32, at 634. Other prevalent objections were: (1) loss of trial by jury, (2) inconvenient location of the federal courts, (3) depriving the state courts of cases, (4) tying up of vessels for a few hundred dollars of debt, (5) unfamiliarity of the state bar with the admiralty procedure. See The Orleans v. Phoebus, 11 Pet. 175, 178 (U.S. 1837) (argument of counsel); Waring v. Clarke (The De Soto), 5 How. 441, 470 (U.S. 1847) (dissenting opinion).

[41] For the course of the bill in the Congress, see 38 ANNALS OF CONG. 48, 197–98, 200, 289, 292 (1821–22); 39 *id.* at 1307, 1309–10, 1453–54, 1464 (1822).

[42] The debate which followed is reported in 40 *id.* at 1024–29 (1823).

[43] 40 *id.* at 1028.

[44] The prior year, Representative Hardin of Kentucky also had supported the federal admiralty jurisdiction on nontidal rivers in the course of a debate with John T. Johnson. 39 *id.* at 1458–59 (1822).

opinion.[45] In *The Thomas Jefferson*, as had not been true in the earlier Kentucky cases, the Court had a precedent, the English tidewater doctrine, on which it could stand with honor while satisfying the public opinion of the day.[46] But perhaps because of misgivings about the effect of the decision,[47] Story carefully stated the corrective, by which, twenty years later, he himself was able to initiate reform:

> Whether, under the power to regulate commerce between the states, Congress may not extend the remedy, by the summary process of the admiralty, to the case of voyages on the western waters, it is unnecessary for us to consider. If the public inconvenience, from the want of a process of an analogous nature, shall be extensively felt, the attention of the legislature will doubtless be drawn to the subject.[48]

(b) *Tidewater Years and the Statute of Reform.* — The West boomed on in an extraordinary growth. Migrants pouring over the Appalachians to the vast fertile lands of the Middle West formed the population of seven new states. The Erie Canal was completed; commerce on the Great Lakes, as on the rivers, soared.[49] By 1845, half the total steamboat tonnage of the nation was in western traffic.[50] The steamboat formed the lifeline of this new empire, bringing "to the remotest villages of our streams, and the very doors of the cabins, a little Paris, a section of Broadway, or a slice of Philadelphia."[51] But for creditors, all was not

---

[45] "[T]he Chief Justice and his Associates began to temper their decisions to accord more nearly to the prevailing public sentiment of the country. The change in judicial decisions which is particularly noticeable in the decade from 1825 to 1835 came in time to ward off attempts to reform or to reorganize the Court . . . . This change in attitude by the federal Justices probably resulted from the public agitation for the reform of the federal Judiciary." HAINES, *op. cit. supra* note 32, at 497, 526. See HOLMES, THE COMMON LAW 1 (1881): "The felt necessities of the time, the prevalent moral and political theories . . . even the prejudices which judges share with their fellow-men, have had a good deal more to do than the syllogism in determining the rules by which men should be governed."

[46] *Cf.* Justice Washington in Green v. Biddle, 8 Wheat. 1, 93–94 (U.S. 1823): "We hold ourselves answerable to God, our consciences and our country, to decide this question according to the dictates of our best judgment. . . . If we have ventured to entertain a wish as to the result of the investigation which we have laboriously given to the case, it was that it might be favorable to the validity of the laws; our feelings being always on that side of the question, unless the objections to them are fairly and clearly made out." And see letter of Story to Todd in 1 LIFE AND LETTERS OF JOSEPH STORY 422, 423 (W. W. Story ed. 1851).

A final element that may have been not unimportant was the fact that also in the 1825 Term, the Court decided the case of De Wolf v. Johnson, 10 Wheat. 367 (U.S. 1825). The defendants were Senator Richard Johnson and James Johnson, among others. The Court held against the defendants, reversing a circuit court decision and ordering a mortgage on their lands foreclosed.

[47] The Chief Justice thought the case wrongly decided: "He [Marshall] said (and he spoke of it as one of the most deliberate opinions of his life) . . . that he had always been of opinion that we in America, had misapplied the principle upon which the admiralty jurisdiction depended . . . ." New York Rev., Oct. 1838, quoted in Horace Gray, "Chief Justice Marshall," published in 1 J. F. DILLON, JOHN MARSHALL 74 (1903).

[48] The Thomas Jefferson, 10 Wheat. 428, 430 (U.S. 1825).

[49] See generally BARTON, COMMERCE OF THE LAKES (1847); Monette, *The Progress of Navigation and Commerce on the Waters of the Mississippi River and the Great Lakes, A.D. 1700–1846*, 7 MISS. HIST. SOC. PUBS. 479 (1904).

[50] See table of official figures in HUNTER, *op. cit. supra* note 26, at 33.

[51] Western Monthly Rev., May 1827, p. 25, quoted in F. J. TURNER, RISE OF THE NEW WEST 104 (1906).

so lyrical. Vessel owners were difficult to determine; often they were located at distant points; steamboat officers had a reputation of general irresponsibility. Under maritime law the vessel itself would have been liable for its operations; but admiralty's benefits had been denied the nontidal states by Story's decision. Some of the states responded to the situation and provided for in rem proceedings against steamboats.[52] But certain debtor-minded legislatures remained inactive, such remedies as were passed tended to be incomplete, and the lack of legal uniformity was disconcerting. However, Story, given a second chance on an appeal to the Supreme Court in 1837, continued to adhere to his views expressed in *The Thomas Jefferson*.[53]

Only one exception to the rule of tidewater limits was made. The Judiciary Act of 1789 had provided for enforcement in admiralty of revenue seizures made on "waters which are navigable from the sea by vessels of ten or more tons burthen."[54] On the nontidal areas of the upper St. Lawrence and Lake Ontario,[55] such seizures were frequent, and the federal court for the Northern District of New York took jurisdiction without hesitation. Not until the 1840's was this practice challenged as an unconstitutional extension by Congress of judicial power.[56] The argument, "altogether novel," was rejected by the court with the comment that "a jurisdiction which has been constantly exercised and acquiesced in without complaint for half a century" should be renounced only at the order of a higher tribunal.[57]

On the Eastern seaboard, unhampered by tidewater difficulties, complainants became increasingly aware of the judicial advantages of the admiralty. Not only great clipper ships, but even canal boats[58] and river sloops[59] were subjected to libel in admiralty. The Great Lakes states, the scene of an ever-growing water commerce, began to complain of discrimination "because God, in His wisdom, did not cause salt water instead of fresh to fill these Great Lakes, and create a tide that would ebb and flow upon them."[60] They pressed for equal treatment with the

[52] See statutes cited in *The Limits of the Exclusive Jurisdiction of Admiralty in the United States*, 3 AM. L. REV. 597, 604 n.1 (1869). The state courts had upheld such statutes on the ground that the admiralty jurisdiction of the federal courts in in rem actions was not exclusive. This view was reversed by the Supreme Court in The Moses Taylor, 4 Wall. 411 (U.S. 1867); The Hine v. Trevor, 4 Wall. 555 (U.S. 1867). Of course, less satisfactory attachment remedies existed at common law. See note 68 *infra*.

[53] The Orleans v. Phoebus, 11 Pet. 175 (U.S. 1837). Story held that even though one terminus was in tidal waters, the voyage was "substantially" nontidal, and hence without the admiralty jurisdiction.

[54] 1 STAT. 77.

[55] While it is true that no strictly tidal effect is felt on the Great Lakes, an analogous phenomenon known as seiches occasionally causes a perceptible rise and fall in the lake level. For a reported instance, see Eastern Journal, Aug. 1, 1851, quoted in BENEDICT, AMERICAN ADMIRALTY 128 n.3 (1870 ed.).

[56] The Black Hawk (N.D.N.Y.), reported in CONKLING, UNITED STATES COURTS 350 n.(a) (2d ed. 1842).

[57] *Ibid.*

[58] Van Santwood v. The John B. Cole, 28 Fed. Cas. 1075, No. 16,875 (N.D.N.Y. 1846).

[59] Smith v. The Pekin, 22 Fed. Cas. 620, No. 13,090 (E.D. Pa. 1831).

[60] BARTON, *op. cit. supra* note 49, at 56. See SEN. DOC. NO. 234, 27th Cong., 3d

seaboard areas, both in federal expenditures for navigation improvements and in maritime law and admiralty courts.[61] But blocking the latter was *The Thomas Jefferson.* For a statute to solve the dilemma, Congress turned to the man who had created it.[62] Story carefully followed the line of his query in *The Thomas Jefferson* nearly twenty years before,[63] and based his statute [64] on the congressional commerce power. Jurisdiction was limited to federally licensed vessels employed in interstate commerce on the Great Lakes and their connecting waters. Doubt as to Congress' authority to extend a constitutional grant of judicial power was met by providing that the applicable law and modes of procedure should be "the same as" in admiralty. To meet the standard complaints of admiralty opponents, Story inserted a provision for jury trial at the request of either party,[65] and specifically reserved any concurrent remedy which might be given under state law. Even the title was innocuous: "An Act extending the jurisdiction of the district courts in certain cases, upon the lakes and navigable waters connecting the same." As a final safeguard, Story took the extraordinary step of submitting the draft to all the justices of the Supreme Court then in Washington; the Act received their approval.[66]

With this supreme stamp of authority, albeit unofficial and probably little-known, the bill was submitted to the Senate. It came to the floor at the height of the great debate over the annexation of Texas; but in the space of six days both houses of Congress, apparently without a dissent-

---

Sess. (1843), for a complete report on the navigation situation in the West, especially with respect to harbor improvements.

[61] The specific impetus for the upsurge of interest in admiralty jurisdiction in at least one state may be ascribed to the decision that maritime law did not apply on the Lakes, even in a state court. The court said that absent *The Thomas Jefferson*, it would have applied the law, but it felt "bound to yield to that policy which teaches us, that in respect to the commerce and navigation of the United States . . . uniformity of rules and decisions, is of the highest importance . . . ." Rossiter v. Chester, 1 Doug. 154 (Mich. 1843).

[62] Story was no novice at statute-writing for Congress. He had been instrumental in preparing several judiciary acts and a crimes bill. See 1 LIFE AND LETTERS OF JOSEPH STORY 293–303, 315, 437 (W. W. Story ed. 1851).

[63] See p. 1220 *supra.*

[64] 5 STAT. 726 (1845), codified as amended in 28 U.S.C. § 1873 (Supp. 1952).

[65] That the jury trial objection was more for popular appeal than for litigant protection is shown by the subsequent use of that provision. Twenty-five years after the statute's enactment, there was no reported case using the provision. *The Limits of the Exclusive Jurisdiction of Admiralty in the United States*, 3 AM. L. REV. 597, 607 (1869). The problem, however, has occasionally arisen. See note 117 *infra.*

[66] *Cf.* Correspondence of the Justices (1793), published in 3 CORRESPONDENCE AND PUBLIC PAPERS OF JOHN JAY 486–89 (Johnston ed. 1891). However, instances of extra-judicial opinions by Supreme Court justices, while unusual, are by no means unprecedented. See HART AND WECHSLER, THE FEDERAL COURTS AND THE FEDERAL SYSTEM 79–80 (1953). Story's part in this statute was apparently not widely publicized, probably in recognition of his status as a remnant of the old national-minded court in a time of strong states' rights feeling. The part of Story and the Court in its enactment is reported in 2 WEST. L.J. 563 (1845), and in later years by Justices Daniel and Campbell in Jackson v. The Magnolia, 20 How. 296, 315, 342 (U.S. 1858). The article states that Story drew up the bill at the request of the judiciary committee; Daniel indicates that it was on the application of a portion of the Court.

ing voice, approved the measure.[67] On February 26, 1845, with the signature of outgoing President John Tyler, the bill became law. But its author never lived to see the fruition of his work. Less than seven months later, Joseph Story was dead.

(c) The Genesee Chief *Ends an Era*. — On the 15,000 miles of the great river system of the Middle West, with steamboat traffic approaching its golden age of the decade before the Civil War, state courts remained a complainant's only source of relief. But the statutory extension of admiralty to the nontidal Great Lakes turned Western minds to its advantages.[68] The new Supreme Court rules of admiralty procedure [69] and the publication of two complete treatises [70] put within the reach of every lawyer a relatively easy means of mastering the new system. Shortly after the passage of Story's Act, a Cincinnati law journal complained that it should have encompassed all the Western waters.[71] Steamboat operators too, plagued by labor unrest and the tendency of crews to jump ship in mid-voyage, may well have seen a powerful weapon in the maritime law making strikes mutiny and jumping ship desertion.[72]

A new spirit toward admiralty jurisdiction became apparent in the Supreme Court as well. In 1847, a case came to the Court which highlighted the inherent anomaly of the tidewater rule as applied in this country.[73] A collision occurred between two steamboats some ninety-five miles above New Orleans. Conflicting evidence of the tide at that point was introduced, which showed that, at best, only a slowing in the steady current occurred. The Court held this sufficient for admiralty jurisdiction. Taney, four years later, made clear that the justices had recognized the "purely artificial and arbitrary" distinction that subjected

---

[67] The course of the bill through Congress may be traced in CONG. GLOBE, 28th Cong., 2d. Sess. 43, 320, 328, 337, 345 (1844–45). No opposition to the Act is reported. However, on memorial of a number of citizens of Michigan, the Senate debated a bill to extend federal jurisdiction over certain crimes committed on board vessels engaged in interstate commerce. Senator Tappan of Ohio opposed the measure, stating that the other Lake states had not applied for such a bill. He did not feel that those states wanted to give up a portion of their judicial power. Both Michigan senators indicated their support of the bill. CONG. GLOBE, *id.* at 350. And see p. 1224 *infra.*

[68] "[W]hy does an actor, with an option of remedies, almost invariably resort to a court of admiralty? The reason is . . . that the party aggrieved has a speedy, certain and efficacious remedy in his lien upon the offending thing, and his right to arrest it and subject it to the payment of his claim. . . . It is true that at common law he may attach the ship as the property of the defendant, but subject to all existing liens and mortgages, a security very different from a maritime lien. As the admiralty court is always supposed to be open for business, and witnesses may be examined *de bene esse* as soon as the libel is filed, the case may be tried, freed of all technicalities, before the vessel leaves port." Brown, *Jurisdiction of the Admiralty in Cases of Tort*, 9 COL. L. REV. 1, 11 (1909).

[69] 3 How. iii (1845). The rules were authorized in 1842. 5 STAT. 518.

[70] BENEDICT, AMERICAN ADMIRALTY (1st ed. 1850); CONKLING, ADMIRALTY (1st ed. 1848).

[71] 2 WEST L.J. 563 (1845). See introductory note to *Admiralty Practice*, 6 *id.* 414 (1849), reprinting article in 12 MONTHLY L. REP. 1 (1849).

[72] 1 STAT. 131 (1790); 1 CONKLING, ADMIRALTY 92–101 (1st ed. 1848). See HUNTER, *op. cit. supra* note 26, at 473–78.

[73] Waring v. Clarke (The De Soto), 5 How. 441 (U.S. 1847). The opinion was by Wayne, an unswerving advocate of an expanded admiralty jurisdiction. Woodbury, Daniel, and Grier dissented. Woodbury had died by the time of *The Genesee Chief*, four years later. Grier apparently changed his mind.

"one part of a public river to the jurisdiction of a court of the United States, and den[ied] it to another part equally public and but a few yards distant."[74] But an equally far-reaching effect of the decision was its announcement that the English authorities did not control the general American admiralty law and that they "[a]t most . . . furnish only analogies to aid us in our constitutional expositions."[75] The following Term, the Court reiterated this view,[76] and two years after did not even bother to answer a dissent based on English limitations.[77] Yet even as the Court was refusing to follow other English precedents, the tidewater doctrine was still faithfully acknowledged.[78] Likewise, the Congress, petitioned by Ohio Valley citizens to duplicate with respect to the river system its 1845 action, declined to do so. The House Judiciary Committee reported that "to extend this jurisdiction . . . to the *internal* commerce of the country, would seem not to be commended by any necessity perceptible to the committee."[79]

But in 1847 an event had happened which was to reshape American law. The schooner *Cuba*, en route from Ohio to New York on Lake Erie, was rammed and sunk by the steamboat, *The Genesee Chief*. A plea of lack of jurisdiction in answer to the libel in the federal admiralty court was rejected. The case by successive appeals came up for decision by the Supreme Court in the December 1851 Term.[80] Chief Justice Taney delivered the opinion. He held that any extension of quasi-admiralty jurisdiction under the Commerce Clause would be unconstitutional,[81] and that the validity of Story's 1845 Act must depend upon

[74] The Genesee Chief v. Fitzhugh, 12 How. 443, 457 (U.S. 1851).
[75] Waring v. Clarke (The De Soto), 5 How. 441, 459 (U.S. 1847).
[76] New Jersey Steam Nav. Co. v. Merchants' Bank of Boston, 6 How. 344, 391 (U.S. 1847). Daniel Webster, in argument, gave an interesting insight into contemporary thinking on the 1845 Act: "The only objection to this necessary law seems to be, that Congress, in passing it, was shivering and trembling under the apprehension of what might be the ultimate consequence of the decision of this court in the case of The Thomas Jefferson. It pitched the power upon a wrong location.
"Its proper home was in the admiralty and maritime grant, as in all reason, and in the common sense of all mankind out of England, admiralty and maritime jurisdiction ought to extend, and does extend, to all navigable waters, fresh or salt." *Id.* at 378.
[77] Newton v. Stebbins, 10 How. 586 (U.S. 1850). The decision followed as settled law Waring v. Clarke (The De Soto), 5 How. 441 (U.S. 1847). Daniel again dissented for the reasons he stated in the earlier case.
[78] See, *e.g.*, New Jersey Steam Nav. Co. v. Merchants' Bank of Boston, 6 How. 344, 392 (U.S. 1848). However, in 1850 Erastus Benedict devoted a whole chapter of his new work to a scholarly examination of the tidewater doctrine and showed how it was completely unsuited to the needs of this country. BENEDICT, AMERICAN ADMIRALTY 125–45 (1st ed. 1850).
[79] H.R. REP. No. 72, 31st Cong., 1st Sess. 2 (1850). The committee also alluded to "the great force" of "the great constitutional question as to the power of Congress to extend maritime jurisdiction beyond the ground occupied by it at the adoption of the Constitution . . . ." *Ibid.*
[80] The Genesee Chief v. Fitzhugh, 12 How. 443 (U.S. 1851).
[81] Reporting without name a case in the Northern District of New York upholding the Act, Conkling had followed Story's analysis: ". . . Congress may doubtless define the force and effect of commercial contracts, and, independently of state laws, devise and prescribe remedies for their violation, and for torts and injuries committed in the prosecution of commerce . . . . And this, in effect, is what Congress may be supposed to have designed to do . . . ." 1 CONKLING, ADMIRALTY 5

the fact that the Lakes fell within the constitutional grant of admiralty jurisdiction. While every prior decision of the Court was to the contrary,[82] he proceeded in a masterly argument to reject all precedents. While he thought both sensible and sound the early American adoption of the English tidal rule, it had lost meaning with the acquisition of the Western territory and the invention of the steamboat. Now such a distinction was purely arbitrary without any foundation in reason. The Lakes particularly were in truth inland seas, in times of war floating hostile fleets and bordered on the north by a foreign country.[83]

Taney strengthened his argument by speaking of the admiralty not as an onus but a privilege, due to all states in a Union founded on a basis of equal rights among its members. That equality would not exist, he asserted, if the commerce on the Lakes and on the navigable waters of the West were denied the benefits of the same courts and the same jurisdiction for its protection which the Constitution secured to the eastern seaboard states. Finally, by its specific preservation of both concurrent state remedies and the right to jury trial, the Act "effectually removes the great and leading objection, always heretofore made to the admiralty jurisdiction."[84] His arguments were of great power. Only Justice Daniel,

(1st ed. 1848). In the second edition of his treatise, he virtually admitted that it had been sheer rationalization. 1 *id.* at 9–12 (2d ed. 1857).

[82] Taney might possibly have dodged the issue by treating the Lakes as "high seas" for admiralty purposes. *Cf.* United States v. Rodgers, 150 U.S. 249 (1893) (Lakes "high seas" within meaning of federal statute); Moore v. American Transp. Co., 24 How. 1 (U.S. 1861) (Lakes not within statutory exception of "inland navigation").

[83] The Canadian experience with the tidewater doctrine on the Lakes offers an interesting comparison. In early cases, the common law courts issued writs of prohibition against the admiralty as freely as in England. See, *e.g.*, Hamilton v. Fraser, Stuart L.C.K.B. 21 (Quebec 1811). This practice was halted by 3 & 4 VICT., c. 65, § 6 (1840) (Great Britain). The courts at first appeared to accept the tidewater rule in deciding Lake-shore trespass cases, Parker v. Elliott, 1 U.C.C.P. 470 (1852), but later held that in Canada, navigable in law meant navigable in fact. Gage v. Bates, 7 U.C.C.P. 116 (1857). In 1869, a conviction for a crime committed on the Lakes, under a statute giving authority to punish all offenses committed where the admiralty had jurisdiction, was upheld. The Queen v. Sharp, 5 Pr. Rep. 135 (Ontario 1869).

The first Canadian admiralty court on the Lakes was established in 1877. Maritime Jurisdiction Act, 40 VICT., c. 21 (Canada). The history of the passage of this Act and the prior difficulties of the tidewater limitation were outlined in a speech given by the first judge of the new court at its opening. "This all-important Act . . . abrogates for ever the narrow and old fashioned ideas which confined the authority of maritime rules and laws within the ebb and flow of the tide . . . ." *The Maritime Court of Ontario*, 14 CAN. L.J. (N.S.) 287, 290 (1877). But as late as 1893, a seaman on a boat on Lake Winnipeg experienced the frustration that must have been frequent in our Middle West until 1851, when the court denied him a lien on the boat as there was no admiralty court established for that province at the time his wage claim arose. Bergman v. Aurora, 3 Ex. C.R. 228 (1893). At present, the exchequer court in Canada sits as a court of admiralty, with jurisdiction over "all navigable waters, tidal and non-tidal, whether naturally navigable or artificially made so." Admiralty Act, 1934, 24 & 25 GEO. 5, c. 31, § 18 (Canada).

[84] 12 How. at 459. This argument did not apply, of course, to the extension of admiralty over the Western rivers. It might be argued that although the validity of the 1845 Act depended upon constitutional admiralty jurisdiction over the Lakes, such jurisdiction would not be assumed in the absence of an empowering statute. Later the same Term, however, the Court took jurisdiction over the Western river system as well. Fretz v. Bull, 12 How. 466 (U.S. 1851). That this was completely independent of the 1845 statute was made definitely clear by The Eagle, 2 Wall. 15 (U.S. 1869). See pp. 1229–30 *infra*.

an extreme states' righter, dissented.[85] The decision marked one of the great expansions of federal judicial power.[86]

The new jurisdiction was apparently well-received. As soon as the decision became generally known, admiralty cases involving Western rivers increased rapidly.[87] Only occasional statements of discontent came from steamboat owners that the seamen's status as "wards of the admiralty" gave their crews a means to harass them unreasonably.[88] One attempt was made in Ohio to urge Congress to restore the tidewater limits.[89] But in most respects, it seems that there was "a ready acquiescence on the part of the profession and of the public interested in the navigation of the interior waters of the country."[90]

*Commerce and Admiralty as Coordinate Grants of Maritime Power.* — The extension of admiralty jurisdiction to all navigable waters was accompanied by another development which was to temper for almost two decades the full impact of *The Genesee Chief.* The feeling for states' rights which was to plunge the nation into civil war affected the justices as it did the general populace. In the field of commerce, the concept that there were limits upon the scope of congressional power under the Commerce Clause, suggested by Chief Justice Marshall in *Gibbons v. Ogden,*[91] was given specific application with respect to water-borne commerce in *Veazie v. Moor,*[92] decided the year after *The Genesee Chief.*[93] The state of Maine had given an exclusive license to a ship

---

[85] Daniel remained a bitter foe of the admiralty to his death, however hopeless the cause. "[E]ven the conviction of an inability to accomplish this result [of returning to the English standards], is with me no dispensation from the duty of resistance." Ward v. Peck (The Mopang), 18 How. 267, 271 (U.S. 1856) (dissenting opinion). A later writer termed him in this respect "the Coke of the Supreme Bench." Brown, *Jurisdiction of the Admiralty in Cases of Tort,* 9 COL. L. REV. 1, 5 (1909).

[86] The import of this decision in its extension of federal judicial power has been commented on in strong terms. See BUTLER, A CENTURY AT THE BAR OF THE SUPREME COURT OF THE UNITED STATES 212 (1942); 2 WARREN, *op. cit. supra* note 32, at 239; The Plymouth (Hough v. Western Transp. Co.), 3 Wall. 20, 22 (U.S. 1866) (argument of counsel). The influence of the decision in areas of the law other than admiralty is remarked on in Smith, *The Genesee Chief,* 9 A.B.A.J. 527 (1923). Remarkably enough, the most recent biography of Taney relegates the case to a footnote. SWISHER, ROGER B. TANEY 409 n.20 (1935).

[87] See The Hine v. Trevor, 4 Wall. 555, 566 (U.S. 1867). *Cf.* 9 WEST. L.J. 287 (1852).

[88] See, *e.g.,* Foster v. The Pilot No. 2, 9 Fed. Cas. 569, No. 4,980 (W.D. Pa. 1853). Three principal facts served as cause of the complaints: (1) wages had priority over all other liens; (2) in all disputes, summary action was given; (3) in bringing suit, the seaman was not required to post bond for costs in the event he lost. This last was the loudest source of complaint. See HUNTER, *op. cit. supra* note 26, at 476.

[89] Cincinnati Gazette, Feb. 13, 1869, cited in HUNTER, *op. cit. supra* note 26, at 477.

[90] The Hine v. Trevor, 4 Wall. 555, 562 (U.S. 1867). See Jackson v. The Magnolia, 20 How. 296, 299 (U.S. 1858). Occasionally, of course, exuberance with the new remedy led to excesses. Thus, in Illinois, an unsuccessful attempt was made to assert a maritime lien against a bridge. Rock Island Bridge, 6 Wall. 213 (U.S. 1867).

[91] 9 Wheat. 1, 194–95 (U.S. 1824). "The completely internal commerce of a state, then, may be considered as reserved for the state itself." *Id.* at 195. *Cf.* North River Steam Boat Co. v. Livingston, 3 Cow. 711 (N.Y. 1825).

[92] 14 How. 568 (U.S. 1852).

[93] For a highly readable discussion of the Commerce Clause under Marshall and

to ply the wholly intrastate Penobscot River on a portion not navigable from the sea. A writ of prohibition issued by the state court against a federally licensed competitor vessel was affirmed by the Supreme Court. The nature of the commerce was wholly "internal"; therefore, unlike *Gibbons v. Ogden*, the federal license could bestow no rights.

This restriction of federal power over intrastate commerce, first thought of in terms of congressional action under the Commerce Clause, began to expand into a restriction on the federal admiralty jurisdiction as well. With the extension of admiralty jurisdiction from the seaboard states into the interior of the nation, where state courts of necessity had been until 1851 the sole arbiters of maritime disputes, possibilities of conflict with state courts were sharply increased. Justice Samuel Nelson [94] was the leader of the Court in developing, largely through dicta, a theory dividing the respective federal and state jurisdictions. Two distinct bodies of law were envisioned; as the federal admiralty courts could generally ignore state statutes,[95] so, it was indicated, state courts could enforce their own statutes touching even interstate vessels.[96] In in rem proceedings state and federal courts were equal in stature; the first to attach the vessel held jurisdiction to the exclusion of the other.[97] Finally, to minimize conflict, an attempt was made to limit the constitutional admiralty jurisdiction to interstate vessels.

The wellhead of this latter view was a dictum by Justice Nelson in 1848: "The exclusive jurisdiction of admiralty cases was conferred on the national government, as closely connected with the grant of the commercial power . . . . There seems to be ground, therefore, for restraining its jurisdiction, in some measure, within the limit of the grant of the commercial power . . . ."[98] In three cases in the December 1857 and 1858 Terms, the thought was further elaborated. The first involved the sinking on the Alabama river of a steamboat running from New Orleans to Montgomery.[99] The ramming vessel operated exclusively within one state. The majority opinion upheld jurisdiction without adverting to this fact, but it troubled Justice McLean. In a concurring opinion he said that the Commerce Clause "limits the power of Congress in the regulation of commerce to two or more states . . . . The admiralty and maritime jurisdiction is essentially a commercial power, and it is necessarily limited to the exercise of that power by Congress."[100] However, he argued, the interstate vessel which was sunk

---

Taney, see FRANKFURTER, THE COMMERCE CLAUSE 1–73 (1937). This concept was until 1870 more a matter of dicta than of firm holdings. *E.g.*, The License Cases, 5 How. 504, 588 (McLean, J.), 620 (Woodbury, J.) (U.S. 1847); The Passenger Cases, 7 How. 283, 400 (U.S. 1849) (McLean, J.). See note 129 *infra*.

[94] Appointed in 1845 after 23 years on New York state courts, Nelson remained on the Supreme Court until 1872. Thus, his term spanned the second era of admiralty grant history, as Story's did the first and Bradley's the third.

[95] The New York v. Rea, 18 How. 223, 225–26 (U.S. 1856).

[96] The Globe, 10 Fed. Cas. 477, No. 5,483 (C.C.N.D.N.Y. 1852) (state sale of vessel under local statute upheld).

[97] Taylor v. Carryl, 20 How. 583 (U.S. 1858) (5–4 decision).

[98] New Jersey Steam Nav. Co. v. Merchants' Bank of Boston, 6 How. 344, 392 (U.S. 1848).

[99] Jackson v. The Magnolia, 20 How. 296 (U.S. 1858).

[100] *Id.* at 304.

was within federal power and protection; therefore, the intrastate vessel, while normally solely within state jurisdiction, was on these facts subject to libel in the federal courts.

The next Term, two cases involving contracts for intrastate carriage of goods were appealed on jurisdictional grounds. The first libel was on a Great Lakes steamboat running from Wisconsin to Illinois.[101] Justice Nelson, writing for the Court, interpreted the controlling Act of 1845 in light of his dictum ten years before. He admitted that there was "some ground" for holding that intrastate contracts on ships operating between two states were within the jurisdiction conferred by the Act but held that the better interpretation was that the contract, as well as the ship, must be for interstate transport. Three justices dissented without opinion. In the second case, Nelson extended this view to the general admiralty law.[102] The claim was for coal furnished *The Goliah*, a ship operating on the Sacramento river in California. The Court ordered the district court to dismiss the libel, noting that "the admiralty would be exercising this jurisdiction simply in the enforcement of the municipal laws of the State, as these laws, under the conceded limitation of the commercial power, regulate the subject as completely as Congress does commerce with 'foreign nations and among the several States' . . . . So in respect to the completely internal commerce of the States . . . contracts growing out of it should be left to be dealt with by its own tribunals." [103] It was this philosophy, he said, that had prompted the Court to amend its rules of admiralty procedure to remove from federal jurisdiction proceedings against vessels in their home port for supplies and repairs.[104]

With the coming of the Civil War and the withdrawal from the Union of the most fervent states' rights elements, a new spirit of ardent nationalism swept the country. The personnel of the Court underwent a sharp change.[105] Lower courts, restive under the attempted commerce limitation on their jurisdiction, distinguished Nelson's holdings.[106] The

---

[101] Allen v. Newberry (The Fashion), 21 How. 244 (U.S. 1859).

[102] Maguire v. Card (The Goliah), 21 How. 248 (U.S. 1859).

[103] *Id.* at 250–51. See Nelson v. Leland, 22 How. 48, 56 (U.S. 1860). *But cf.* Bondies v. Sherwood, 22 How. 214, 217 (U.S. 1859).

[104] *Id.* at 251. The rule change is at 21 How. iv (1858). However, in The St. Lawrence, 1 Black 522 (U.S. 1862), Taney enforced a lien arising under the old rule, holding that the change was made not by constitutional compulsion but for reasons of convenience in admiralty administration. Taney apparently had little sympathy for Nelson's attempts to link admiralty to the Commerce Clause: "Nor can the jurisdiction of the courts of the United States be made to depend on regulations of commerce. They are entirely distinct things, having no necessary connection with one another, and are conferred in the Constitution by separate and distinct grants." The Genesee Chief v. Fitzhugh, 12 How. 443, 452 (U.S. 1851).

[105] Between 1858 and 1864 six new justices were appointed to the Court: Clifford (1858), Swayne (1862), Miller (1862), Davis (1862), Field (1863), Chase (1864). WORLD ALMANAC 177 (1954 ed.). Only one of the vacancies came about as a result of the Civil War; Justice John Campbell of Alabama resigned to follow his state into the Confederacy.

[106] See, *e.g.*, Carpenter v. The Emma Johnson, 5 Fed. Cas. 109, No. 2,430 (C.C.D. Mass. 1861); The Sarah Jane, 21 Fed. Cas. 456, No. 12,349 (D. Mass. 1868). *But cf.* Poag v. The McDonald, 19 Fed. Cas. 903, No. 11,239 (C.C.S.D.N.Y. 1860). Earlier cases had accepted jurisdiction over intrastate vessels without question. See, *e.g.*, The Flash, 9 Fed. Cas. 252, No. 4,857 (S.D.N.Y. 1847).

Court responded to these developments. In 1862, just four years after Nelson and McLean's strong language with respect to intrastate contracts, a tort case arose in which the steamboat *Commerce* had rammed a canal boat on the Hudson river. A unanimous court deemed irrelevant the argument made that both vessels were exclusively intrastate.[107] It held that admiralty jurisdiction over torts depends upon location alone, and if committed on navigable waters, such torts are cognizable in admiralty. But not until 1869 did the Court hold that Nelson's 1858 decisions "must be regarded as incorrect" and declare that the admiralty jurisdiction extended over all maritime contracts as well as torts, unfettered by Commerce Clause limitations.[108] Justice Nelson, still on the Court, did not dissent.[109] To reinforce its new view, the Court restored the rule giving district courts cognizance of domestic liens.[110]

Throughout this period, the limitations of the statute of 1845, inserted under the belief that the Commerce Clause was its constitutional base, seemed to have served as both a source of and a reinforcement for the belief that general admiralty jurisdiction was similarly limited. In 1859, the Court declared that the provision restricting jurisdiction to interstate vessels was merely "declaratory of the law." [111] After the overruling of this view, the Act's continued validity with respect to the Great Lakes was recognized by the district courts, despite occasional dissents; [112] and surprisingly enough, even though the statute clearly did not cover the Western river system, the opinion seemed common throughout the Middle West that all nontidal admiralty jurisdiction depended upon its force.[113] Thus, with admiralty jurisdiction held in *The Genesee Chief* to extend over nontidal as well as tidal waters, the statute, enacted to expand judicial power, by its terms limited it. In 1869, Justice Nelson, for a unanimous Court, recognized this absurdity.[114] On an appeal from a Great Lakes district court, the objection was made that the jurisdictional requirements of the 1845 Act had not been fulfilled. The Court found that in fact they had been adequately met but in an extended dictum judicially discarded the entire Act, save the optional jury clause. "We must . . . regard it as obsolete and of

---

[107] The Commerce (Commercial Transp. Co. v. Fitzhugh), 1 Black 574 (U.S. 1862). The libel alleged that one of the vessels was bound for Philadelphia. This fact was contested for the first time before the Supreme Court.

[108] The Belfast, 7 Wall. 624, 641–42 (U.S.). The decision was presaged by Chief Justice Chase on circuit in The Mary Washington, 16 Fed. Cas. 1006, No. 9,229 (C.C.D. Md. 1865).

[109] In 1868 a district judge had accepted jurisdiction over an intrastate vessel, despite the precedent of Maguire v. Card (The Goliah), 21 How. 248 (U.S. 1859). He said that he knew that "Mr. Justice Nelson does not adhere to the views expressed by him" in an opinion based on that precedent. The Brooklyn, 4 Fed. Cas. No. 1,938, at 240 (S.D.N.Y. 1868).

[110] 13 Wall. xiv (1871). The post-Civil War period also saw the Court declare that in rem actions in admiralty were exclusively cognizable in the federal judiciary. This finally ended the state court practice which had grown up during the years when federal admiralty jurisdiction was limited to tidewater. The Moses Taylor, 4 Wall. 411 (U.S. 1867); The Hine v. Trevor, 4 Wall. 555 (U.S. 1867).

[111] Maguire v. Card (The Goliah), 21 How. 248 (U.S.).

[112] See the contemporary discussion of the problem in 1 WEST. JUR. 241 (1867).

[113] See The Hine v. Trevor, 4 Wall. 555, 566 (U.S. 1867).

[114] The Eagle, 8 Wall. 15 (U.S.).

no effect."[115] Following this opinion, the compilers of the Revised Statutes in 1875 retained the jury provision.[116] Despite calls for its abolishment, this right continues occasionally to be sought in cases arising on the Lakes.[117] It remains on the books only as an anachronistic vestige of a constitutional struggle over a century past.

With this decision, admiralty jurisdiction was cut from its direct links with the Commerce Clause as a measurement of judicial power.[118] The way was now open for its development as a source of untrammeled legislative power as well. This was to be the history of the next twenty years.[119]

*The Admiralty Grant as Legislative Power.* — Congressional statutes touching maritime matters date from the First Congress,[120] but the reports show little recognition of the admiralty grants as a possible constitutional basis for such legislation.[121] The validity of these statutes, though virtually unchallenged, seems to have been assumed as resting on the taxation or commerce power; this was to be expected in an era when commerce was primarily water-borne. Moreover, the maritime law was viewed less as a municipal code than as an international law of the sea, a set of rules accepted by all seafaring nations.[122] Chief Justice Marshall in 1828 denied that maritime cases arose under "the Constitution or laws of the United States"; rather they were ruled by "the law, admiralty and maritime, as it has existed for ages."[123] In addition, many in the

---

[115] *Id.* at 25. At the same time, Nelson declared inoperative the clause in the Judiciary Act of 1789 limiting seizures under the revenue laws to waters navigable from the seas by vessels of ten or more tons burthen. See p. 1221 *supra.* Since *The Genesee Chief,* the effect of the clause would be restrictive, instead of extensive, as, he said, was originally intended.

[116] REV. STAT. § 566, codified as amended in 28 U.S.C. § 1873 (Supp. 1952).

[117] The most recent case involving the statute is Miller v. Standard Oil Co., 199 F.2d 457 (7th Cir. 1952), *cert. denied,* 345 U.S. 945 (1953), 52 MICH. L. REV. 139. See also 50 HARV. L. REV. 350 (1936) and cases cited.

[118] A possible exception is in the definition of "navigable waters of the United States." See p. 1237 *infra.* The reaffirmation of admiralty jurisdiction over intrastate vessels came as river traffic, unable to compete with the railroad, diminished chiefly to short, often intrastate hauls. HUNTER, *op. cit. supra* note 26, at 606.

[119] For a discussion of this period in admiralty history, see GOODNOW, SOCIAL REFORM AND THE CONSTITUTION 39–54, 153–57 (1911); COOKE, THE COMMERCE CLAUSE §§ 43–46 (1908). And see Miller, *The Foreclosure of Vessel Mortgages in Admiralty,* 70 U. OF PA. L. REV. 22–23 (1921).

[120] See, *e.g.,* Tonnage Duty, 1 STAT. 27 (1789); Ship Registry, 1 STAT. 55 (1789); Government and Regulation of Seamen, 1 STAT. 131 (1790). One early statute indicated that Congress had a broad view of the scope of its navigation laws, as including river as well as ocean commerce. "All persons employed in navigating any . . . boat, raft, or float" down the Mississippi river to New Orleans were to be considered as "seamen of the United States, and entitled to the relief established by law to sick and disabled seamen." 2 STAT. 192–93 (1802).

[121] See United States v. Bevans, 3 Wheat. 336, 386, 388–89 (U.S. 1818) (criminal); Janney v. Columbian Ins. Co., 10 Wheat. 411, 418 (U.S. 1825) (insurance); United States v. Jackson, 26 Fed. Cas. No. 15,458, at 561 (S.D.N.Y. 1841) (license).

[122] See the compilation of quotations by Daniel in Jackson v. The Magnolia, 20 How. 296, 332–35 (U.S. 1858); see also Martin v. Hunter's Lessee, 1 Wheat. 304, 335 (U.S. 1816); Marshall to Peters, Peters Papers MSS, Sept. 5, 1807, quoted in 1 WARREN, *op. cit. supra* note 32, at 568. For a somewhat similar sentiment expressed in comparatively recent times, see the dissent in The Robert W. Parsons, 191 U.S. 17, 48 (1903).

[123] American Ins. Co. v. Canter, 1 Pet. 511, 545, 546 (U.S. 1828).

first half-century thought admiralty constitutionally bound by the un-alterable limits of its 1789 English counterpart.[124]

But in 1848, the Court definitively rejected this view, adverting to congressional power: "It would be a denial to Congress of all legislation upon the subject. It would make, for all time to come, without an amendment of the constitution, that unalterable by any legislation of ours, which can at any time be changed by the Parliament of England, — a limitation which never could have been meant . . . ."[125] This opinion in modern cases has been cited apparently as an early assertion of congressional power through the admiralty grant.[126] But such a view seems unwarranted in light not only of the tenor of the decision but of the Court's indications in the following terms that the legislative as well as judicial admiralty power was limited by the scope of the Commerce Clause.[127] The persistence of this attitude until its final rejection in 1869 may explain in part the absence of any discussion of the admiralty grant as a source of congressional power.

Moreover, such statutes as did exist were directed more toward regulating conditions under which interstate waters should be navigated and protecting and increasing their navigability, than toward a substantive change in the law governing water-borne transactions;[128] and the courts naturally considered them in light of the doctrine of Commerce Clause limits.[129] The most marked example of such treatment occurred with respect to the federal law requiring licenses for all vessels on navigable waters.[130] Early district court cases had split on congressional authority to require such licenses for intrastate vessels, and the Supreme Court in 1849 indicated a lack of such legislative power.[131] In

---

[124] See, *e.g.*, Johnson, J., concurring in Ramsay v. Allegre, 12 Wheat. 611, 614 (U.S. 1827). "I think it high time to check this silent and stealing progress of the admiralty in acquiring jurisdiction to which it has no pretentions."

[125] Waring v. Clarke, 5 How. 441, 457 (U.S. 1847) (Wayne, J.).

[126] See, *e.g.*, O'Donnell v. Great Lakes Dredge & Dock Co., 318 U.S. 36, 41 (1943).

[127] *See* New Jersey Steam Nav. Co. v. Merchants' Bank of Boston, 6 How. 344, 392 (U.S. 1848) (dictum by Nelson; opinion concurred in by Wayne); The Passenger Cases, 7 How. 283, 400 (U.S. 1849) (McLean, J.).

[128] The suggestion has been made that the source of congressional power over navigable waters may be divided between the Commerce Clause and the admiralty grant on this standard. 2 WILLOUGHBY, THE CONSTITUTION 950 (2d ed. 1929).

[129] The great bulk of congressional legislation in this field went unchallenged. Not until the closing decades of the nineteenth century, it should be remembered, did the extension of federal power under the Commerce Clause become a key factor in the Court's work. Prior to that time, the great constitutional Commerce Clause litigation was over state legislation. Gibbons v. Ogden, 9 Wheat. 1 (U.S. 1824); Cooley v. Board of Port Wardens, 12 How. 299 (U.S. 1851); Gilman v. Philadelphia, 3 Wall. 713 (U.S. 1866). The first case holding unconstitutional an act of Congress under the Commerce Clause appears to be United States v. Dewitt, 9 Wall. 41 (U.S. 1870).

[130] 5 STAT. 304 (1838), as amended, 10 STAT. 61 (1852). Statutes for licensing of vessels had been in effect since the founding of the nation. The statutes are listed in United States v. Jackson, 26 Fed. Cas. No. 15,458, at 561 (S.D.N.Y. 1841). However, the 1838 Act was the first which was interpreted positively to require such licenses.

[131] The Passenger Cases, 7 How. 283, 400 (U.S. 1849) (McLean, J.). *Compare* United States v. Jackson, 26 Fed. Cas. 559, No. 15,458 (S.D.N.Y.

1868 a Supreme Court justice on circuit declared in dictum that Congress had no such power:

> It has been strongly urged that the admiralty jurisdiction in the federal courts extends to all the navigable waters of the United States, though the voyage may be limited to the ports of the same state; and that a corresponding rule should be applied to the power of congress over the commerce so carried on. But if we concede that the proposition is true as to admiralty jurisdiction, a concession [which must be] made in the face of many decided cases, the inference claimed by no means follows. By the Federal Constitution, admiralty jurisdiction is granted to the courts of the United States; the power to regulate commerce is granted to congress.[132]

The Supreme Court in 1871 utilized the Commerce Clause in upholding the application of the licensing statute to intrastate vessels. *The Daniel Ball*, a steamship operated wholly within the state of Michigan, had not obtained a federal license. The district judge stated that in his view the vessel was subject to congressional power under the Commerce Clause. He distinguished prior cases to the contrary on the ground that there it was not positively shown that the vessels transported goods received from or destined for a second state. However, since the practice of other district judges was to dismiss such suits, he did likewise in the interests of conformity.[133] The Supreme Court affirmed the Circuit Court's reversal of this decree.[134] It found, first, that the vessel was operating on navigable waters of the United States within the meaning of the license statute, and second, that since the ship carried goods from or to other states, it was an "instrument of interstate commerce," and hence within congressional power under the Commerce Clause. No mention was made of legislative power under the admiralty grant.

But subsequent cases in the district courts suggested a possible weakness in the Commerce Clause basis of *The Daniel Ball*. The next year, 1872, Judge Samuel Blatchford[135] dismissed a libel for a violation during an intrastate excursion of the passenger load limit set by federal statute.[136] He argued that unlike *The Daniel Ball*, this ship was not

---

1841), *with* United States v. The James Morrison, 26 Fed. Cas. 579, No. 15,465 (D. Mo. 1846). See United States v. The William Pope, 28 Fed. Cas. 629, No. 16,703 (D. Mo. 1852); United States v. The Seneca, 27 Fed. Cas. 1021, No. 16,251 (D. Wis. 1861).

[132] The Bright Star, 4 Fed. Cas. No. 1,880, at 142 (C.C.D. Mo. 1868) (Miller, J.).

[133] The Daniel Ball, 6 Fed. Cas. No. 3,564, at 1165 (W.D. Mich. 1868).

[134] The Daniel Ball, 10 Wall. 557 (U.S. 1871). *Cf.* The Passenger Cases, 7 How. 283, 400 (U.S. 1849).

[135] Later Mr. Justice Blatchford. He was elevated to the Supreme Court in 1882 by President Arthur.

[136] The Thomas Swan, 23 Fed. Cas. 1011, No. 13,931 (S.D.N.Y. 1872). The court apparently overlooked an alternative ground for the holding in *The Daniel Ball*: "[The commercial] power authorizes all appropriate legislation for the protection or advancement of either interstate or foreign commerce, and for that purpose such legislation as will ensure the convenient and safe navigation of all the navigable waters of the United States, whether that legislation consists . . . in prescribing the form and size of the vessels employed upon them, or in subjecting the vessels to inspection and license, in order to assure their proper construction and equipment." The Daniel Ball, 10 Wall. 557, 564 (U.S. 1871). *But cf.* The City of Salem, 37 Fed. 846, 849 (D. Ore. 1889).

engaged in interstate commerce at the time of the violation and hence was outside the scope of congressional power. Seventeen years later, an Oregon judge, faced with a similar argument, posited as the test, "whether a regulation limiting the number of passengers which a steamboat may carry over a navigable water of the United States, between ports of the same state, is necessary to maintain this highway of foreign and interstate commerce in a safe and desirable condition for the use of vessels and passengers engaged in the same." [137] He considered the application highly doubtful. On similar reasoning an Ohio court held an intrastate barge not bound to obey a navigation law requiring life preservers.[138] Cases that affirmed congressional power over intrastate vessels rested on a broad interpretation of *The Daniel Ball* to hold that "[i]t is not their use, but the fact that they navigate the highways of commerce, which brings them within the constitutional grant of power." [139] A single court suggested a solution through the admiralty grant. Ruling on an intrastate vessel that had failed to obtain an excursion permit, the court put forward the proposition that "the power of Congress over navigation may be derived from the double sources of the commercial power and the admiralty power; in some cases from one power, and in other cases from both." [140] But in its view, the court stood alone.

In 1851, Congress for the first time substantially modified a rule of admiralty as laid down by the Supreme Court. In 1848, the Court had held that shipowners were fully liable for all torts committed by their vessels.[141] The Limited Liability Act of 1851 overturned this rule.[142] The first Supreme Court decision touching the statute declared in a dictum that "[t]he act can apply to vessels only which are engaged in foreign commerce, and commerce between the States." [143] And a

---

[137] *Ibid.* The court rejected the assertion that the federal passenger load limit statute might be upheld under the admiralty grant. "The admiralty jurisdiction of the United States is a part of its judicial power, and not its legislative." *Id.* at 849.

[138] The Gretna Green, 20 Fed. 901 (S.D. Ohio 1883).

[139] The Oyster Police Steamers of Maryland, 31 Fed. 763, 766 (D. Md. 1887). See The Hazel Kirke, 25 Fed. 601 (E.D.N.Y. 1885). This view with respect to the Commerce Clause power rests on the alternative holding of *The Daniel Ball*. See note 136 *supra. Cf.* Southern R.R. v. United States, 222 U.S. 20 (1911) (Safety Appliance Acts). Under the admiralty grant, the statement would appear unquestionable. *Cf.* People *ex rel.* Pennsylvania R.R. v. Knight, 171 N.Y. 354, 364, 64 N.E. 152, 155 (1902), *aff'd*, 192 U.S. 21 (1904).

[140] United States v. Burlington & Henderson County Ferry Co. 21 Fed. 331, 339 (S.D. Iowa 1884). A more tentative statement to the same effect, written with respect to the Limited Liability Act of 1851, was made in *In re* Long Island North Shore Passenger & Freight Transp. Co., 5 Fed. 599, 616 (S.D.N.Y. 1881).

[141] New Jersey Steam Nav. Co. v. Merchants' Bank of Boston, 6 How. 344 (U.S. 1848).

[142] 9 STAT. 635 (1851), as amended, 46 U.S.C. § 188 (1946). At the behest of "those who represent the interior waters of the country," all vessels used on "rivers or inland navigation" were exempted. CONG. GLOBE, 31st Cong., 2d Sess. 717–18 (1851). This exemption was later removed. See Sprague, *Limitation of Shipowners' Liability*, 12 N.Y.U.L.Q. REV. 568 (1935).

[143] Moore v. American Transp. Co., 24 How. 1, 39 (U.S. 1861) (Nelson, J.). In 1850, Congress passed a statute providing for recording of mortgages on federally licensed vessels. 9 STAT. 440 (1850). The statute was upheld as constitutional on the theory that Congress, "having conferred upon it [the mortgagee's

lower court suggested that "undoubtedly" the power of Congress so to legislate was found only in the Commerce Clause.[144] But when in 1868 admiralty jurisdiction was held to extend over intrastate as well as interstate vessels, the way was opened for a direct clash between the Commerce Clause limits on legislation over intrastate vessels and the admiralty power extending over all vessels in navigation.

As Story in the tide water struggle and Nelson in the period of the Commerce Clause limitation had been the key figures, so Justice Joseph P. Bradley of New Jersey was to represent the gradual evolution of the admiralty grant as a legislative power. Appointed at the age of 57 by President Grant in 1870, over the bitter protests of Southern senators who wanted one of their own,[145] Bradley almost immediately became the Court's chief architect of admiralty decisions. Five years after taking his seat on the bench, he gave the first complete analysis of the sources of the admiralty law since the days it was viewed as a branch of the law of nations.[146] He expounded the theory of a nationwide maritime law composed not only of decisions of the Supreme Court, based on judicious selection of the best from the codes of other lands, but also of statutes enacted from time to time by Congress. "It cannot be supposed that the framers of the Constitution contemplated that the law should forever remain unalterable. Congress undoubtedly has authority under the commercial power, if no other, to introduce such changes as are likely to be needed."[147] Acting on this view of a general maritime law subject to the will of Congress, Bradley at first upheld the Limited Liability Act in terms of the Commerce Clause.[148] But in 1889, a significant shift in emphasis occurred.[149] Striking down a Massachusetts law which had restored the unlimited liability of shipowners, Bradley held that Congress by its 1851 enactment had forbidden all such state modifications. "We cannot doubt its power to do this. As the Constitution extends the judicial power of the United States to 'all cases of admiralty and maritime jurisdiction,' and as this jurisdiction is held to be exclusive, the power of legislation on the same subject must necessarily be in the national legislature and not in the state legislatures."[150] The consequences of this embryonic thought were fully brought out in In

interest] its chief value under the power . . . to regulate commerce," may regulate the protection of title. White's Bank v. Smith, 7 Wall. 646, 656 (U.S. 1869).

[144] *In re* Vessel Owners' Towing Co., 26 Fed. 169, 170 (N.D. Ill. 1886).

[145] For a further explanation of the Senate's opposition, see Fairman, *Mr. Justice Bradley's Appointment to the Supreme Court and the Legal Tender Cases,* 54 HARV. L. REV. 977, 1028 (1941).

[146] The Lottawanna, 21 Wall. 558 (U.S. 1875).

[147] *Id.* at 577.

[148] Providence & N.Y.S.S. Co. v. Hill Manufacturing Co., 109 U.S. 578 (1883). See Norwich Co. v. Wright, 13 Wall. 104 (U.S. 1872). Lower courts applied a similar analysis. The War Eagle, 29 Fed. Cas. 225, No. 17,173 (C.C.W.D. Wis. 1875); *In re* Vessel Owners' Towing Co., 26 Fed. 169 (N.D. Ill. 1886); The Mamie, 5 Fed. 813 (E.D. Mich. 1881).

[149] Occasional district courts from 1881 had been exploring the potentialities in the admiralty grant as a source of legislative power. *In re* Long Island North Shore Passenger & Freight Transp. Co., 5 Fed. 599 (S.D.N.Y. 1881); United States v. Burlington & Henderson County Ferry Co., 21 Fed. 331 (S.D. Iowa 1884); The Garden City, 26 Fed. 766 (S.D.N.Y. 1886).

[150] Butler v. Boston & S.S.S. Co., 130 U.S. 527, 557 (1889).

re *Garnett* [151] two years later. In 1886, the Limited Liability Act had been amended to include within its scope all vessels on navigable waters of the United States.[152] The amendment was powerfully attacked in the Supreme Court as an unconstitutional attempt to control intrastate commerce. Reversing the practice of all prior decisions, Bradley considered congressional power not under the Commerce Clause but the admiralty grant.

It is unnecessary to invoke the power given to Congress to regulate commerce with foreign nations, and among the several states, in order to find authority to pass the law in question. The act of Congress which limits the liability of ship owners was passed in amendment of the maritime law of the country, and the power to make such amendments is coextensive with that law. It is not confined to the boundaries or class of subjects which limit and characterize the power to regulate commerce; but, in maritime matters, it extends to all matters and places to which the maritime law extends. . . .
. . . [T]he act in question . . . is a constitutional and valid law.[153]

Bradley was not troubled by the fact that this implication of federal legislative power in the judicial clause of the Constitution was unique. Judicial lawmaking in admiralty had the analogy of *Swift v. Tyson*[154] with respect to a federal common law; but the Court had never interpreted the grant of power over diversity cases to authorize congressional legislation on the controlling law.[155] However, a distinction may well rest in the respective purposes of the grants. Admiralty jurisdiction was created for other purposes than to assure an impartial forum, since any possible bias could be avoided through the federal diversity jurisdiction. The framers of the Constitution were probably thinking in terms of a uniform maritime law of nations.[156] And if that law was not to remain forever static and yet maintain some semblance of uniformity, legislative power must necessarily vest in Congress.

This new basis of congressional power was immediately utilized in lower court opinions in a number of contexts.[157] But in two respects especially, its full statement by Bradley in 1891 was of paramount im-

---

[151] 141 U.S. 1 (1891).
[152] 24 STAT. 80 (1886), 46 U.S.C. § 188 (1946).
[153] *In re* Garnett, 141 U.S. 1, 12, 18 (1891).
[154] 16 Pet. 1 (U.S. 1842).
[155] Goodnow, writing when *Swift v. Tyson* was good law, suggested that other congressional legislative powers might be derived from the judicial article, by analogy to the implied power in the admiralty grant. GOODNOW, SOCIAL REFORM AND THE CONSTITUTION 150–202 (1911).
[156] *Cf.* Frankfurter, J., dissenting in Madruga v. Superior Court, 346 U.S. 556, 566 (1954): "[T]he need for a body of maritime law, applicable throughout the Nation and not left to the diversity of the several States, was the one basis for the creation of a system of inferior federal courts, authorized by the Constitution, which was recognized by every shade of opinion at the Philadelphia Convention."
[157] *E.g.*, The City of Norwalk, 55 Fed. 98 (S.D.N.Y. 1893), *rev'd in part on other grounds sub nom.* The Transfer No. 4, 61 Fed. 364 (2d Cir. 1894), *appeal dismissed*, 163 U.S. 693 (1895) (validity of state law); United States v. Banister Realty Co., 155 Fed. 583 (C.C.E.D.N.Y. 1907) (damming inlet); The Scow No. 1, 169 Fed. 717 (E.D.N.Y. 1909) (life preservers). In the first Federal Employers' Liability Act cases, in which the Act was successfully attacked as unconstitutional, the defendants' brief distinguished congressional limitation of vessel liability on the ground that that

portance. First, by placing the constitutionality of congressional statutes on an admiralty rather than a commerce basis, it cautioned against the direct application to land commerce of doctrines developed for water commerce.[158] On this ground, Chief Justice Fuller denied the binding force of an earlier water commerce decision, *Lord v. Goodall, N. & P.S.S. Co.*,[159] in determining whether a railroad operating between two points in Pennsylvania but passing through a second state on the trip was engaged in interstate commerce. He rejected the analogy to the *Lord* case on the ground that that decision involved the maritime power of Congress under the admiralty grant.[160]

Second, and perhaps more significantly, the separation of both legislative and judicial power in admiralty from the Commerce Clause enabled maritime development to take an independent course. From Bradley's doctrine came the series of cases that rejected the Commerce Clause rule that state legislation was valid absent an overriding need for national uniformity in the law, and held that in Congress lay the exclusive, nondelegable power to legislate on the maritime law with respect to all but highly local activities.[161] Thus, by the end of the nineteenth century, the concept of a maritime law extending to all vessels on navigable waters of the United States and subject to amendment by Congress under the admiralty grant had fully matured. In this context have operated the admiralty statutes and decisions of modern times.

The linking of commerce and admiralty is still with us, however, in

---

measure was based on the admiralty grant, not the Commerce Clause. Employers' Liability Cases, 207 U.S. 463, 483, 488 (1907).

Bradley's broad language in In re *Garnett* was presumably not necessary, since the vessel libeled was clearly engaged in interstate commerce. However, the Limited Liability Act has subsequently been sweepingly applied to virtually all vessels within the admiralty jurisdiction, without question as to the Act's constitutional validity. See, *e.g.*, Petition of Liebler (The Francesca), 19 F. Supp. 829 (W.D.N.Y. 1937) (limited liability granted to owner of 19-foot pleasure motorboat), and cases cited. *Cf. In re* Eastern Dredging Co., 138 Fed. 942 (D. Mass. 1905).

[158] *Cf.* Baltimore & Ohio R.R. v. Maryland, 21 Wall. 456, 470 (U.S. 1874): "Commerce on land between the different States is so strikingly dissimilar, in many respects, from commerce on water, that it is often difficult to regard them in the same aspect with reference to the respective constitutional powers and duties of the State and Federal governments" (Bradley, J.). For a reverse application of land doctrines to water commerce, see Hutton v. Webb, 124 N.C. 749, 33 S.E. 169 (1899).

[159] 102 U.S. 541 (1881) (opinion by Waite, C.J.). In that case, the Limited Liability Act was held applicable to a ship traveling from San Francisco to Los Angeles. The Court reasoned that since the ship went out onto the high seas, it was to that extent engaged in interstate or foreign commerce, and hence fell within the Commerce Clause power.

[160] Lehigh Valley R.R. v. Pennsylvania, 145 U.S. 192, 203 (1892). *But cf.* Central Greyhound Lines, Inc. v. Mealey, 334 U.S. 653 (1948).

In the *Lord* case, the Court had specifically stated: "Having found ample authority for the act as it now stands in the commerce clause of the Constitution, it is unnecessary to consider whether it is within the judicial power of the United States over cases of admiralty and maritime jurisdiction." Lord v. Goodall, N. & P.S.S. Co., 102 U.S. 541, 545 (1881). Counsel had argued: "No case can be found in which this court has based the validity of any Act of Congress upon the provision defining the jurisdiction of the judiciary." 26 L. Ed. at 224.

[161] See Conlen, *Ten Years of the Jensen Case*, 76 U. OF PA. L. REV. 926 (1928), and cases cited; Knickerbocker Ice Co. v. Stewart, 253 U.S. 149, 166 (1920); London Guarantee & Accident Co. v. Industrial Accident Commission, 279 U.S. 109 (1929). The Court in recent years has retreated from the extreme position to some extent. *E.g.*, Just v. Chambers, 312 U.S. 383 (1941).

one respect. Admiralty jurisdiction continues to depend upon the fact that the vessel involved operated on "navigable waters of the United States."[162] The definition as laid down in *The Daniel Ball*, though perhaps somewhat modified in recent years,[163] basically remains valid: "Those rivers must be regarded as public navigable rivers in law which are navigable in fact. . . . And they constitute navigable waters of the United States . . . when they form . . . by themselves, or by uniting with other waters, a continued highway . . . [for interstate and foreign commerce]."[164] Thus, the interstate commerce character of the waters affected appears to be a prerequisite to admiralty jurisdiction; and waters wholly within one state seem excluded.[165] Examples of such waters are rare; but should such a case arise, this final remnant of admiralty's links with the early nineteenth century limitations on the commerce power might be discarded. The Court might assume admiralty jurisdiction simply because vessels were involved. But if the internal waters were at all navigated by vessels in the chain of interstate commerce, it might be reasoned that these waters, as highways of commerce clearly within the commercial power of Congress, fell within the admiralty jurisdiction as "navigable waters of the United States." Thus, in the last analysis, a total separation of admiralty and commerce may be unrealistic; since they both so largely touch the same subject matter, the future may well see continued the cross-fertilization that marked their development in the nineteenth century.

---

[162] See ROBINSON, ADMIRALTY 34–41 (1939), and cases cited. *But cf.* United States v. Banister Realty Co., 155 Fed. 583 (C.C.E.D.N.Y. 1907).

[163] United States v. Appalachian Elec. Power Co., 311 U.S. 377 (1940), indicates that waters potentially navigable, through improvement works, are "navigable waters of the United States," for Commerce Clause purposes at least. The case illustrates the possibility for confusion which arises from the fact that one definition of that phrase is carried over and applied to a totally different context. It should be noted that in *The Daniel Ball* the exact issue was the definition of the phrase as used in a congressional statute, not as an interpretation of the constitutional limits of admiralty jurisdiction.

[164] The Daniel Ball, 10 Wall. 557, 563 (U.S. 1871). See The Montello, 11 Wall. 411 (U.S. 1871), 20 Wall. 430 (U.S. 1874).

[165] Thus, in Stapp v. The Clyde, 43 Minn. 192, 45 N.W. 430 (1890), the court upheld a state statute affecting a ship navigating Lake Minnetonka, lying wholly within Minnesota. See also Commonwealth v. King, 150 Mass. 221, 22 N.E. 905 (1889) (Connecticut river above dam at Holyoke is exclusively within state jurisdiction and a state license may be required for vessels navigating thereon). See Waite, *Admiralty Jurisdiction and State Waters*, 11 MICH. L. REV. 580 (1903).

[1] 48 STAT. 74, as amended, 15 U.S.C. §§ 77a *et seq.* (1946).

[2] See §§ 5, 12, 17, 38 STAT. 77, 84 (1933), as amended, 15 U.S.C. §§ 77e, *l*, q (1946); LOSS, SECURITIES REGULATION 120 (1951).

# 13
## LAW AND ECONOMIC DISTRESS: SANGAMON COUNTY, ILLINOIS, 1837-1844

*GEORGE L. PRIEST*

Reprinted for private circulation from
THE JOURNAL OF LEGAL STUDIES
THE UNIVERSITY OF CHICAGO LAW SCHOOL
Volume II(2) June 1973
PRINTED IN U.S.A.

# LAW AND ECONOMIC DISTRESS: SANGAMON COUNTY, ILLINOIS, 1837-1844

*GEORGE L. PRIEST\**

T HIS essay attempts to analyze the impact in one county of Illinois of the depression which began in 1837 and continued into the mid-1840s, and to examine the effects of some of the laws enacted by the Illinois legislature as relief measures. The study employs simple statistical techniques to analyze records of judgments and executions issued in Sangamon County, Illinois during that period. Historians have not ignored the depression and the relief laws, but their accounts are impressionistic and incomplete. Part I considers these historical accounts and presents a brief description of the relief laws. Part II discusses the plausibility of inferences about economic conditions from court records and Part III presents and analyzes the data. Part IV discusses the general problem of retrospective legislation aimed at redistributing wealth.

## I. THE HISTORICAL ACCOUNTS

In the 1830s and 1840s the United States experienced extraordinary monetary fluctuation. A moderate inflation developed in the early 1830s and was interrupted by a mild contraction in 1834; then from 1835 to 1837 prices raced upwards. In 1837 the boom ended: hundreds of banks suspended operations; severe deflation occurred. Although there was partial recovery in 1838, prices fell again in 1839 and did not recover until the middle 1840s. During this period the country suffered one of the more serious depressions in its history.[1]

Illinois at this time was a state on the western frontier. It is reasonable to suppose that the monetary fluctuations experienced in the eastern states would have been felt less severely in a state primarily agricultural. Historical accounts, however, although incomplete and inadequately supported, indicate that the state did not escape the inflation and subsequent depression.

There are no reliable price indices for Illinois for the period, but there is

\* University of Chicago Law School. I wish to express my gratitude to Stanley N. Katz for helpful suggestions and comments. John P. Brown, James L. Huffman, and John L. Peterman gave valuable advice.

[1] Hugh Rockoff, Money, Prices, and Banks in the Jacksonian Era, in The Reinterpretation of American Economic History 448, 449 (Fogel and Engerman eds. 1971).

evidence that intense speculation drove up land prices and that this flourishing land business affected markets in other products. A contemporary, Thomas Ford, who had been Governor of Illinois, explains that speculation on town lots and unimproved land began in the spring and summer of 1836, primarily in Chicago. Expectation of rising prices became feverish, according to Ford, and spread to all towns and villages in the state. "The story of sudden fortunes made there [Chicago], excited at first wonder and amazement, next a gambling spirit of adventure, and lastly, an all-absorbing desire for sudden and splendid wealth."[2] Ford's account is corroborated by Henry Brown, who writing in 1844 remembered that the speculative spirit of 1836 had ". . . filled every bosom, possessed every class in the community, controlled every avenue to business, monopolized every species of influence."[3] It is plausible that widespread increases in land values would influence the demand for other products. According to Ford, "During the inflation of the bank currency . . . every one had got into debt. The merchants had purchased on a credit, and they had again sold on a credit. This system brought a great many goods into the State; more than the people, according to their means, ought to have consumed. But the merchants were anxious to sell, and freely credited the people up to about the value of their property."[4]

There is other evidence indicating unusual expectation of growth. Until the depression struck, the state legislature attempted to encourage commercial development through extravagant, perhaps profligate, charters and appropriations. In the special session of 1835-1936 the legislature chartered eleven railroads. In the next regular session, 1836-1837, it enacted a system of internal improvements committing eight million dollars to finance nine railroads and the improvement of the Great Western Mail Route.[5] Ford explains, "It was argued that Illinois had all the natural advantages which constitute a great State; a rich soil, variety of climate, and great extent of territory. It only wanted inhabitants and enterprise. These would be invited by a system of improvements; timber would be carried by railroad to fence the prairies; and the products of the prairies, by the same means, would be brought to market."[6] The state did not possess the eight million dollars it had pledged—there was no system of state taxation—but the legislature hoped that values of state land along the Illinois-Michigan canal would rise, allowing the improvement system to be financed from land sales.[7] Ford, who acceded to office after the system

[2] Thomas Ford, A History of Illinois 181 (1854) (hereinafter cited as Ford).

[3] Henry Brown, The History of Illinois 418 (1844).

[4] Ford, 310.

[5] Theodore C. Pease, The Frontier State 1818-1848, 194-215 (1922).

[6] Ford, 182.

[7] Theodore C. Pease, *supra* note 5, at 212; cf. Ford, 188.

had failed, described these hopes as another example of the "general phrenzy" of the times.[8]

The nationwide inflation ended in 1837. A panic struck the eastern states in the spring of that year. In New York there were large numbers of business failures in April[9] and by May banks had suspended specie payments.[10] It is not clear when the crisis reached Illinois. Bessie Pierce maintains that by July 1937 trade in Chicago was dwindling, and that by December "all money payments at Chicago had ceased; hard times had set in; business was demoralized and confidence destroyed; almost every business man was ruined or heavily involved."[11] Her statements have support in other accounts.[12] On the other hand, Ford, a contemporary, argues that at the end of 1837, "Money was as plenty as dirt." He dates the onset of depression nearer to 1841 or to February 1842 when the Bank of Illinois "exploded."[13] As late as January 1839 the legislature appropriated an additional $800,000 for the internal improvement system, and imposed the first state property tax, to raise revenue to pay interest on the improvement loan.[14] Such legislation would be extraordinary had depression been widespread. One month after increasing the improvement appropriation, however, the legislature relaxed the residency requirement for qualification as a pauper, presumably as a measure of relief. The actions of the legislature, as we will see, become less ambiguous in the session which convened in December 1839 and thereafter. Apparently by this time the effects of the depression were sufficiently extensive to influence a majority of representatives.

Descriptions of the effects of the depression on the people of the state and on the state's commerce are, unfortunately, contradictory and unsystematic. As mentioned, it is plausible that an agricultural community would be less dependent on the exchange of goods and thus less susceptible to injury from general economic reverse. Turner's safety-valve theory implies that: cheap western lands would have provided little release, were the inhabitants of the frontier as sensitive to hard times as inhabitants of eastern cities. Still, barter cannot have been totally adequate; money must have been necessary in

---

[8] Ford, 182-88.

[9] John B. McMaster, 6 A History of the People of the United States 395 (1906).

[10] Reginald G. McGrane, The Panic of 1837, 93 (1924).

[11] Bessie L. Pierce, 1 A History of Chicago 67-68 (1937).

[12] Professor McLear finds that the panic reached Chicago in November. Patrick E. McLear, Speculation, Promotion, and the Panic of 1837 in Chicago, 62 J. Ill. St. Hist. Socy's 135, 142 (1969); John Denis Haeger, Eastern Money and the Urban Frontier, 64 J. Ill. St. Hist. Soc'y 267, 282 (1971); Robert M. Sutton, Illinois' Year of Decision, 1837, 58 J. Ill. St. Hist. Soc'y 34, 48 (1965).

[13] Ford, 196, 223.

[14] Theodore C. Pease, *supra* note 5, at 221; Ford, 192-93.

Illinois in the 1830s and 1840s and, therefore, the depression must have been felt. First, immigrants needed substantial cash reserves to establish themselves. Professor Danhof's essay on farm-making costs indicates that $550 in cash was required to settle a forty-acre farm in Illinois in 1852 and $785 was required for an eighty-acre farm in Illinois in 1857.[15] Governor Ford asserts that the depression stopped immigration,[16] but census figures do not confirm him. A comparison of state censuses of 1835 and 1845 with the federal census of 1840 shows an increase in population between 1835 and 1840 from about 270,000 to 476,000, and between 1840 and 1845 from 476,000 to 662,000. (One should note, however, that the population of Sangamon County, according to the same reports, declined between 1835 and 1840 from about 18,000 to 15,000, but increased to about 19,000 by 1845.)[17] Clearly there was immigration and some immigrants needed loans.

Second, established residents, though perhaps relying on their own farm products for food, needed cash to pay taxes, to meet mortgage payments, to purchase other goods, and to pay off debts incurred during the preceding boom. Ford maintains that purchase on credit was prevalent before the depression and that commerce was dominated by credit competition. Merchants "were forced to sell on a credit or not at all. The people were encouraged to buy on credit, and when their debts became due, for want of money to pay them, they gave their notes to the merchants with twelve per cent interest. . . ."[18] It is thus a reasonable conclusion that a capital market existed in Illinois, that it was affected by the depression, and that inability to pay debts was one consequence of it.

Agreement with this proposition is not entirely unanimous, however. Professor McLear suggests that trade in Chicago continued to flourish during the the depression's hardest days, and Professor Pease declares that the state's "rank and file" (presumably the nonmerchant classes) did not suffer greatly.[19] Conversely, Ford was convinced that ruin was widespread and payment of debts infrequent. As Governor he had first-hand knowledge that the depression created a general inability and unwillingness to pay taxes.[20] Bessie Pierce has concluded from a study of Chicago newspapers that "Practically all of the leading business men of 1836 were either bankrupt

[15] Clarence H. Danhof, Farm-making Costs and the "Safety Valve": 1850-60, 49 J. Pol. Econ. 317, Table 1 at 327 (1941).

[16] Ford, 445.

[17] Illinois census of 1835 in J. M. Peck, A New Guide for Emigrants to the West 295 (2d ed. 1837); 1845 returns in John Moses, 1 Illinois, Historical and Statistical 549 (1889); 1840 returns in Sixth Census of the United States 376-96 (1841). Ford admits that population increased greatly from 1843-1846 while he was Governor. Ford, 446.

[18] Ford, 232.

[19] Patrick E. McLear, *supra* note 12, at 144; Theodore C. Pease, *supra* note 5, at 263.

[20] Ford, 223, 310, 278.

or greatly impoverished by 1842."[21] J.B. McMaster reports that a southern Illinois tax collector was implored by men in his district to allow them to work out their taxes at twelve and a half cents a day; such cases, he says, were common.[22] There is evidence of extensive failure to pay debts and a general resort to law for a remedy. Joseph N. Balestier in 1840 recalled the previous three years as "the era of protested notes; it was the harvest to the Notary and the Lawyer—the year of wrath to the mercantile, producing, and laboring interests. . . . The land resounded with the groans of ruined men. . . ."[23]

Historians have been less clear in indicating when the depression abated. Ford claims that recovery began around the time of his inauguration· as Governor in 1842 and was complete by the end of his term in 1846.[24] Professor Haeger states that in Chicago the worst of the depression had passed by 1842.[25] Professor Pierce draws attention to a boom market in wheat in September 1841, but concludes, safely, that there was revival by autumn 1844.[26] A price index for the Ohio River valley shows that prices were lowest in 1842 and that there was recovery, although slight, in 1844-1845; prices in 1845, however, were still far below the 1834 level.[27]

Whatever the merits of the historical accounts, the existence of the depression is evident in the acts of the Illinois legislature. From 1839 through 1843 the legislature enacted a multitude of measures extending relief. It has generally been thought that laws passed in response to the depression granted relief to the "class" of debtors as opposed to the "class" of creditors.[28] This descrip-

---

[21] Bessie L. Pierce, *supra* note 11, at 69.

[22] 7 John B. McMaster, *supra* note 9, at 44-45.

[23] Patrick E. McLear, *supra* note 12, at 143; accord, Theodore C. Pease, *supra* note 5, at 231-32.

[24] Ford, 445-46.

[25] John Denis Haeger, *supra* note 12, at 284.

[26] Bessie L. Pierce, *supra* note 11, at 128, 195.

[27] The price index, below, was taken from George Macesich, Sources of Monetary Disturbances in the United States, 1834-45, 20 J. Econ. Hist. 407, 412 (1960), who took it from A. H. Cole, Wholesale Commodity Prices in the U.S. 1700-1861 (1938).

| 1834 | 84  | 1840 | 92 |
|------|-----|------|----|
| 1835 | 103 | 1841 | 79 |
| 1836 | 128 | 1842 | 64 |
| 1837 | 116 | 1843 | 64 |
| 1838 | 114 | 1844 | 68 |
| 1839 | 122 | 1845 | 77 |

Base: Average 1834-42.

[28] James Willard Hurst, Law and the Conditions of Freedom in the Nineteenth-Century United States 13-14, 66 (1956); Samuel Rezneck, The Social History of an American Depression, 1837-1843, in Business Depressions and Financial Panics 73-101 (1968); Henry W. Farnam, Chapters in the History of Social Legislation in the United States to 1860, 148-52 (1938, repr. 1970).

tion is misleading because it is unlikely that these classes were mutually exclusive, that those who had loaned money were not debtors themselves. In addition, several acts of this period strengthened the rights of creditors specifically. In 1839 the legislature withdrew from judgment debtors the right of replevin on execution or attachment;[29] in 1840 it allowed sheriffs to pursue absconding debtors into any county of the state[30] and extended the right of attachment to goods in the hands of joint debtors;[31] in 1841 it extended retrospectively a right of redemption of property sold at a foreclosure sale to both mortgagors and their judgment creditors.[32] Other relief laws did not concern debtor-creditor relations at all. Acts passed in 1839 and 1841 lowered the residency requirement for qualification as a pauper and increased pauper benefits.[33] The legislature also granted relief to those having dealings with the Bank of Illinois.[34]

The Illinois legislature did enact measures aimed at relieving debtors in this period, and it is this legislation that is examined in more detail below. Laws passed in 1841[35] and 1843[36] sought to make the forced sale of a debtor's property more difficult by requiring that no property be sold unless two-thirds of its value, as appraised by three disinterested householders, was bid at the sale. This limitation was applied, in each act, only to contracts or causes of action originating prior to the date of passage. In addition, the legislature extended the coverage of the exemption to property from sale on execution in 1840, 1841, and 1843.

## II. What Court Records Can Show

This study examines a period of depression and the effects of relief laws, using court records. The study is based on the statistics of judgments and executions issued by the circuit court of Sangamon County, Illinois between 1835 and 1844. Courts do not record every debt incurred in the community, but only those that become the subject of judicial proceedings. Our sample is

---

[29] An Act supplemental to an act entitled "An act to regulate the action of replevin," approved January 29, 1827 (1839), Ill. Laws, 11 G.A., 77.

[30] An Act concerning attachments (1840), Ill. Laws, 11 G.A. Spec. Sess., 30.

[31] An Act to amend "An act concerning attachments," approved February 12, 1833 (1840), Ill. Laws, 11 G. A. Spec. Sess., 31.

[32] An Act to amend "An act concerning judgments and executions, approved January 17th, 1825" (February 19, 1841), Ill. Laws, 12 G.A., 168.

[33] An Act to amend an act entitled "An act for relief of the poor," approved March 1, 1833 (1839), Ill. Laws, 11 G.A., 138; An Act in relation to Paupers (1841), Ill. Laws, 12 G.A., 190.

[34] Theodore C. Pease, *supra* note 5, at 310, 311, 314.

[35] An Act regulating the Sale of Property (February 27, 1841), Ill. Laws, 12 G.A., 172.

[36] An Act entitled "an act regulating the sale of property on judgments and executions" (1843), Ill. Laws, 13 G.A., 186.

further limited to cases that proceeded through a full trial to judgment.[37] How representative a sample is this?

Recent scholarship has advanced our understanding of the conditions that determine when disputes are settled out of court and when they are tried to judgment.[38] Generally parties to a dispute will litigate when litigation appears cheaper to each than settlement. This requires that the expected value of the litigation to the plaintiff exceed the expected cost of the litigation to the defendant. More precisely, litigation will occur if the expected value of a judgment to the plaintiff (the probability of his winning, as he sees it, times the stakes— the amount of judgment) minus the expected cost of a judgment to the defendant (the probability of the plaintiff's winning, as the defendant sees it, times the stakes) is greater than the total of the parties' litigation and court costs minus their settlement costs. Since it usually requires fewer resources to settle a dispute than to go through a trial (litigation and court costs minus settlement costs are greater than zero), litigation will occur only when the plaintiff thinks he has a better chance of winning than the defendant thinks the plaintiff has. Factors unrelated to the costs of litigation (or settlement) or to the stakes will not affect the settlement rate unless they differentially affect the parties' optimism. If, for example, judges or juries had become more disposed to decide in favor of defendants than plaintiffs during the depression, the settlement rate would be unaffected so long as the change of disposition was recognized equally by plaintiffs and defendants, although the sum settled for would be lower.[39]

---

[37] Data were collected only on money judgments and thus show only those disputes where the plaintiff won, or the defendant won on a counterclaim. Where the plaintiff lost the amount in issue was not recorded. The percentage per year of judgments entered without a debt or damages figure is presented below. These can include judgments where defendants won and judgments in chancery, including divorces.

|      |        |      |        |
|------|--------|------|--------|
| 1835 | 32.1%  | 1840 | 22.5%  |
| 1836 | 52.9   | 1841 | 28.1   |
| 1837 | 39.0   | 1842 | 15.9   |
| 1838 | 30.2   | 1843 | 26.9   |
| 1839 | 20.5   | 1844 | 35.2   |

It has not been possible to distinguish judgments for failure to repay a note from judgments for personal injuries. We assume, not unreasonably, that the proportion of personal injury or chancery actions remains constant throughout the depression. Statistics of the satisfaction of judgments or executions are unaffected by the character of the cause of action.

[38] Richard A. Posner, An Economic Approach to Legal Procedure and Judicial Administration, 2 J. Leg. Studies 399 (1973); John P. Gould, The Economics of Legal Conflicts, 2 J. Leg. Studies 279 (1973); William M. Landes, An Economic Analysis of the Courts, 14 J. Law & Econ. 61 (1971).

[39] The likelihood of litigation would be increased if the potential defendant had learned that defendants received sympathy and the potential plaintiff had not because

It is possible to estimate, roughly, court costs and lawyers' fees in this period, allowing a guess to be made of the "litigation threshold."[40] Court costs, which were set by statute, consisted of fees paid to the officials superintending the trial for performing their various duties.[41] Yearly averages of these fees, taken from judgments in the sample, range slightly less than $10 in 1838 to slightly more than $13 in 1836. The weighted average, 1835-1843, is $11.10.[42] Court costs were paid by the losing party. If the case was settled before the verdict, costs were shared. It is interesting to note that fees were paid not in advance (except possibly witness fees to each witness), but after judgment was given. Clerks and sheriffs thus had to collect court costs from losing parties.[43]

Evidence has survived of lawyers' fees in this period in the account books of the law firms in which Abraham Lincoln was a partner. Lincoln lived in Springfield and practiced in Sangamon County. One might expect Lincoln's fees to be higher than average; he was a member of the Illinois legislature

---

the difference between the expected value to the plaintiff and the expected cost to the defendant would be larger than it was before the change of disposition. Sympathy may also reduce the size of judgments.

[40] "Litigation threshold" will be defined as total litigation costs minus settlement costs. We assume that the expected judgment is the same for both plaintiff and defendant. Expected judgment is related to ability to predict outcomes and to discount rates. See Richard A. Posner, *supra* note 38. The assumption of parity in the ability to predict outcomes is not unreasonable since, as we show below, lawyers—professional outcome predictors—were accessible at relatively low prices. This study has not considered differences in discount rates. Institutional lenders, who might have lower discount rates, were not active in this period in Champaign County, Illinois, admittedly a county with less commerce. Severson, Niss, Winkelman, Mortgage Borrowing as a Frontier Developed: A Study of Mortgages in Champaign County, Illinois, 1836-1895, 26 J. Econ. Hist. 147, Table 4 at 160 (1966).

[41] An Act regulating the Salaries, Fees, and Compensation of the several officers and persons therein mentioned (1827), Ill. Revised Laws 281 (1833).

[42]

AVERAGE COURT FEES, 1835-1844
(current dollars)

| 1835 | $12.1 | 1840 | $13.1 |
|------|-------|------|-------|
| 1836 | 13.4 | 1841 | 11.0 |
| 1837 | 11.4 | 1842 | No record |
| 1838 | 9.6 | 1843 | 8.0 |
| 1839 | 11.0 | 1844 | No record |

Weighted average $11.10

*Source:* Sangamon County Judgment Docket, Books A, B, C.

The range of court costs in this period was large: $3-$142, but most appeared to be within a range of two dollars of the average. The parties could affect the level of court costs only in the choice between trial by judge or jury and in the number of witnesses called. In 1843 the legislature reduced docket fees ($2.50-$5 paid to the victorious lawyer) by half. An Act relating to docket fees (1843), Ill. Laws, 13 G.A., 142.

[43] Fees Act, *supra* note 41, § 6, 296.

at the time and a rising politician. His fees, however, seem low: generally between $5 and $10.[44]

The costs to the parties of their participation in a trial and the costs of settlement are impossible to determine. Trials appear to have taken very little time in court. In 1836 nine judgments were entered each day for the first two days the court met in the spring term.[45] The day labor wage in the period was $1.25.[46] This amount is so small that one cannot err greatly by assuming that the costs of preparation and trial (excluding legal fees and court costs) equaled the costs of settlement.

The total costs of litigation of a dispute can thus be estimated as $11 in court costs plus $15 in lawyers' fees ($7.50 per party). For litigation to occur, the difference between the subjective probabilities to the parties of the plaintiff's winning, times the stakes in the dispute, would have to exceed $26. This "litigation threshold" remained constant over the period of study. Records of court cost show small variation; the statutory fees were not changed. Lincoln's ledgers do not indicate a rise or fall in prices in current dollars. The threshold —$26—is very low, implying that quite small differences between the parties' estimates would have sufficed to induce litigation.[47]

The foregoing analysis suggests that changes in the statistics of judgments are probably fairly good proxies for changes in the generation of claims in the community. Since it is unlikely that factors existed which had systematic differential effects on the optimism of the parties, and since the costs of litigation and settlement were stable, the settlement rate for a given claim size was probably constant throughout the period. Further, the low "litigation threshold" implies that a large fraction of claims, especially larger claims, were tried to judgment.

Once a judgment was entered, the plaintiff had a strong incentive to cause

[44] H.E. Pratt, Personal Finances of Abraham Lincoln 25-37 (1943). In one case Lincoln received a $20 fee, but he had appeared in court ten times. *Id.* at 37. Note that $7.50 is only 2.8 per cent of the average judgment in 1840.

[45] Sangamon County, Judgment Docket, Book A.

[46] Diary of William Sewall 1797-1846, 194, 204 (J. Goodell ed. 1930).

[47] Values below indicate the minimum difference in probability estimates (of plaintiff's winning) sufficient to induce litigation for various expected judgments:

| Expected Judgment | | Expected Judgment | |
|---|---|---|---|
| $ 50 | 52.0% | $ 500 | 5.2% |
| 100 | 26.0 | 1000 | 2.6 |
| 200 | 13.0 | 2600 | 1.0 |

These differences will induce litigation only where the plaintiff's estimate exceeds the defendant's. If we assume a standard distribution of probability differences, defendant's estimates will exceed plaintiff's for half the disputes.

an execution to issue, unless he had been paid. An execution must issue within one year of the judgment date for the judgment. More important, all costs of the execution were charged to the judgment debtor, so the plaintiff lost only the time required to make a request. One would therefore expect that all (or at least most) judgment creditors who did not cause an execution to issue had been paid by their judgment debtors. Executions are a good proxy for unsatisfied debts.

## III.  THE EMPIRICAL EVIDENCE

### A.  *The Depression*

The information gleaned from historical accounts about Illinois in the period 1836-1844 shows that there was serious inflation in the years preceding 1837. Historians have been less clear in sketching the course of the depression that followed. The crisis and sudden deflation that occurred in eastern states in early 1837 reached Illinois, according to one account (Pierce) in December 1837, according to another (Ford) in 1841. We do know that the Illinois legislature enacted relief laws as early as December 1839. Balestier claims that there were great numbers of protested notes between 1837 and 1840; Ford claims there was widespread ruin after 1841; Pierce has found prevalent bankruptcy in 1842; others (Pease, McLear) argue that the depression was not serious. Commerce began recovering from what depression there was in 1842 according to Ford and Haeger, in 1844 according to Pierce. A price index of wholesale commodity prices in Cincinnati and the Ohio River valley shows inflation through 1836, a decline in prices in 1837 and 1838 and a resurgence in 1839, followed by a precipitous drop through 1842 and a slight rise in 1844 and 1845.

Tables 1-4 record the number and value of judgments rendered in Sangamon County each year during this period.[48] Table 5 records the percentage of judgments satisfied before a sale of the judgment debtor's property.[49] The

[48] Sangamon, at this time, was the second most populous county of the state; thus the statistics may not be representative of counties of the state more exclusively agricultural. Sangamon may be peculiar because it lost population between 1835 and 1840, while the state's population increased by 75 per cent. The capital of Illinois was located in Springfield in 1839, the middle of the period studied. It is not known what this circumstance meant to the commerce of the county. After 1839 disputes involving the state were litigated in the Sangamon County court; a large number of judgments in 1842 and executions in 1842 and 1843 represent disputes over the bonds of the Bank of Illinois, which had defaulted. A significant limitation of this study is the failure to consider actions in the federal courts between out-of-state citizens and Illinois residents.

[49] To determine the number of judgments satisfied before execution, I multiplied the percentage of executions which were issued within 0-3 months of the date of judgment by the total number of executions issued for the year and subtracted this product from the total number of judgments. A debtor also could pay the judgment after execution. Allowing execution added between $2.50 and $4 in costs. Fees Act, *supra* note 41; Bryan v. Smith,

TABLE 1A
VALUE OF JUDGMENTS

| Period[1] | Average Judgment (current $) | Total Judgment (current $) | Average Judgment (constant $) | Total Judgment (constant $) |
|---|---|---|---|---|
| 1835 | 158.6 | 4441 | 154.0 | 4312 |
| 1836 | 155.9 | 2651 | 121.8 | 2071 |
| 1837 | 183.8 | 7539 | 158.4 | 6499 |
| 1838 | 266.4 | 16784 | 233.7 | 14723 |
| 1839 | 271.7 | 19833 | 222.7 | 16257 |
| 1840 | 270.6 | 19213 | 294.1 | 20884 |
| 1841[2] | 319.3 | 20119 | 404.2 | 25467 |
| 1842 | 367.0 | 25323 | 573.4 | 39567 |
| 1843 | 310.3 | 16134 | 484.8 | 25209 |
| 1844 | 213.1 | 11505 | 313.4 | 16919 |

*Sources:* Judgment Docket, Books A, B, C, Sangamon County Circuit Court, Illinois.
[1] Year beginning spring term.
[2] One judgment equal to $15,505 was excluded from the tally.

TABLE 1B
VALUE OF JUDGMENTS BY TERM

| Period[1] | Current $ | Period | Current $ |
|---|---|---|---|
| 1835 | | 1840 | |
| 3 | 2889 | 3 | 8654 |
| 7 | 493 | 7 | 4807 |
| 10 | 1059 | 11 | 5752 |
| 1836 | | 1841 | |
| 3 | 805 | 3 | 6074 |
| 7 | 1696 | 7[2] | 6276 |
| 10 | 150 | 11 | 7769 |
| 1837 | | 1842 | |
| 3 | 3172 | 3 | 8768 |
| 7 | 1075 | 7 | 5619 |
| 10 | 3292 | 11 | 10936 |
| 1838 | | 1843 | |
| 3 | 2112 | 3 | 4844 |
| 7 | 6733 | 7 | 10 |
| 10 | 7939 | 11 | 11280 |
| 1839 | | 1844 | |
| 3 | 6768 | 3 | 3635 |
| 7 | 7658 | 7 | 7059 |
| 11 | 5407 | 11 | 811 |

*Sources:* Judgment Docket, Books A, B, C, Sangamon County Circuit Court, Illinois.
[1] Month term begins.
[2] One judgment equal to $15,505 was excluded from the tally.

---

3 Ill. (2 Scammon) 47 (1839); if the debtor did not pay the sheriff at the levy, any property he had sufficient to satisfy the judgment would be sold. It is unlikely that a debtor would allow a sale if he could pay since forced sales usually bring lower prices and increase court costs.

TABLE 2
AVERAGE JUDGMENT

| Period[1] | Current $ | | Constant $ | |
|---|---|---|---|---|
| | 0-200 | 200+ | 0-200 | 200+ |
| 1835 | 82.0 | 649.0 | 79.6 | 630.0 |
| 36 | 43.8 | 810.6 | 34.2 | 633.3 |
| 37 | 98.4 | 1114.2 | 84.8 | 960.5 |
| 38 | 74.7 | 785.1 | 65.5 | 688.7 |
| 39 | 100.8 | 704.2 | 82.6 | 577.2 |
| 40 | 98.1 | 609.9 | 106.6 | 662.9 |
| 41[2] | 92.6 | 651.8 | 117.2 | 825.0 |
| 42 | 80.3 | 845.7 | 125.5 | 1321.4 |
| 43 | 72.9 | 854.7 | 113.9 | 1335.4 |
| 44 | 85.3 | 693.9 | 125.4 | 1020.4 |

*Sources:* Judgment Docket, Books A, B, C, Sangamon County Circuit Court, Illinois.
[1] Year beginning spring term.
[2] One judgment equal to $15,505 was excluded from the tally.

historians are unanimous in the view that in the years 1836 and 1837 commerce was expanding rapidly and the currency was inflating. Court statistics reveal an unusual decline in both the number and total value of judgments in 1836. The number and value of judgments increased generally in 1837; averages above and below $200 rose substantially; but the number of judgments below $200 rose relatively much more. Perhaps this indicates the existence of the credit competition in goods described by Ford.

If the historians are correct that deflation did not strike Illinois until late in 1837, we cannot ascribe the increase in the value of judgments in that year to the depression. This conclusion is supported by the results in Table 5, which show in 1837 the highest level of payment of judgments of the period. The

TABLE 3A
RELATIVE NUMBER OF JUDGMENTS

| Period[1] | $0-200 | $200+ |
|---|---|---|
| | % | % |
| 1835 | 73.7 | 26.3 |
| 1836 | 62.5 | 37.5 |
| 1837 | 80.0 | 20.0 |
| 1838 | 56.8 | 43.2 |
| 1839 | 60.3 | 39.7 |
| 1840 | 50.8 | 49.2 |
| 1841 | 43.4 | 56.6 |
| 1842 | 53.5 | 46.5 |
| 1843 | 56.4 | 45.6 |
| 1844 | 60.0 | 40.0 |

*Sources:* Judgment Docket, Books A, B, C, Sangamon County Circuit Court, Illinois,
[1] Year beginning spring term.

TABLE 3B
YEARLY CHANGE IN NUMBER OF JUDGMENTS

| Period[1] | $0-200 % (loss) | $200+ % (loss) |
|---|---|---|
| 1835 | | |
| 1836 | (56.7) | (29.2) |
| 1837 | 196.6 | 23.5 |
| 1838 | 47.7 | 357.1 |
| 1839 | 34.6 | 16.7 |
| 1840 | (18.7) | 19.6 |
| 1841 | (26.6) | (1.5) |
| 1842 | 53.9 | (20.5) |
| 1843 | (32.5) | (21.9) |
| 1844 | 1.9 | (12.2) |

*Sources:* Judgment Docket, Books A, B, C, Sangamon County Circuit Court, Illinois.
[1] Year beginning spring term.

TABLE 4
PROPORTION OF JUDGMENTS BY VALUE

| Period[1] | 0-200 % total judgment | 201+ % total judgment |
|---|---|---|
| 1835 | 25.9 | 73.1 |
| 1836 | 8.3 | 91.7 |
| 1837 | 26.2 | 73.9 |
| 1838 | 11.1 | 88.9 |
| 1839 | 17.8 | 81.6 |
| 1840 | 14.3 | 85.7 |
| 1841[2] | 9.2 | 90.7 |
| 1842 | 5.9 | 93.9 |
| 1843 | 10.0 | 90.1 |
| 1844 | 15.6 | 84.5 |

*Sources:* Judgment Docket, Books A, B, C, Sangamon County Circuit Court, Illinois.
[1] Year beginning spring term.
[2] One judgment equal to $15,505 was excluded from the tally.

more detailed information in Table 1B shows an exceptionally large increase in the dollar value of judgments in the summer term of 1838. The lag is reasonable and confirms the historical accounts of when the depression began.

Tables 3 and 4 disclose that the increase in number and dollar value in 1838, which we have associated with the beginning of the depression, is attributable primarily to an increase in the number of judgments over $200. It is interesting that the averages of judgments both above and below $200 declined. The larger number of defaults included debts of lower amounts.

The dollar value of judgments increased gradually from 1838 through 1842. Historians have implied that the deflation was sudden, that the low point

482      THE JOURNAL OF LEGAL STUDIES

TABLE 5
JUDGMENTS SATISFIED BEFORE SALE

| Period[1] | (1)<br>Before<br>Execution[2]<br>% | (2)<br>After<br>Execution<br>% | (3)<br>Total<br>(1) + (2)<br>% |
|---|---|---|---|
| 1836 | 44.3 | 6.4 | 50.7 |
| 1837 | 51.4 | 5.6 | 57.0 |
| 1838 | 13.5 | 26.6 | 40.1 |
| 1839 | 0.3 | 25.9 | 26.2 |
| 1840 | 1.1 | 31.0 | 32.1 |
| 1841 | 27.7 | 17.3 | 42.0 |
| 1842 | 45.4 | 11.8 | 57.2 |
| 1843 | 31.2 | 16.0 | 47.2 |
| 1844 | 36.7 | 12.5 | 49.2 |

*Sources:* Judgment Docket, Books A, B, C; Execution Docket, Book D, Sangamon County Circuit Court, Illinois,

[1] Year beginning spring term.

[2] See note 49.

of the depression was reached early (within six months of the crisis), and that this level persisted until a recovery in 1842 or 1844. If this thesis were correct, the level of unpaid debts should rise sharply (after some lag), and then decline as lenders adjusted to hard times by making fewer loans that might fail. There is no evidence of decline in dollar values until 1843, although the number of large judgments declines in 1842. The price index for Cincinnati also refutes the "sudden deflation" thesis, indicating slight deflation in 1837 and 1838 and violent deflation in 1840 and 1841.

A better measure of the effect of depression on the ability to repay debts is the percentage of judgments paid before sale on execution (Table 5). This index shows a gradual but substantial drop in the percentage satisfied in 1838 and 1839, a slight increase in 1840, a recovery in 1841 to the 1838 level and a full return to the pre-crisis level by 1842. There is thus no evidence after 1937 of the cataclysmic failure to pay that the historical accounts assert. Furthermore, the steep deflation of 1840-1842 shown by the Ohio River valley price index does not correspond to the rates of satisfaction before sale in Sangamon County, implying either the inapplicability of the Ohio price index or an adjustment by the credit market to the second wave of the depression that is not evident in the dollar value of judgments.

Table 5 measures also the time taken to pay by debtors after judgment. The astonishing decline in 1838 and especially 1839 and 1840 in the percentage of judgments that debtors paid before execution might indicate either a decline in the liquidity of property generally (it took the judgment debtor longer to raise the money), or the increasing discount rates of judgment debtors (postponing paying is equivalent to borrowing the amount for the period between judgment and levy).[50]

It is peculiar that the highest percentage of judgments satisfied before sale occurred in 1842, the year the federal bankruptcy act was in effect. One would expect a law providing federal release of debts to inspire creditors to seek judgments in order to authenticate claims for shares of the debtor's surviving assets. These judgments would not be recorded as having been satisfied. Other evidence indicates the presence of judgments sought for this reason: the total dollar value of judgments rose (Table 1A), the proportion (by value) of larger judgments rose (Table 4), and the average larger judgment rose (Table 2), although (a contradiction) the 1843 average was about the same. That the level of satisfaction rose, despite the additional bankruptcy judgments, suggests recovery by 1842.

Additional evidence supports the conclusion of recovery. In 1843 and 1844 the total dollar value of judgments declined. The percentage of judgments satisfied dropped from the unusually high 1842 amount, but to a level near that before the depression. Table 6A shows that the proportion (by value) of executions uncollected also dropped to the pre-depression level.

In sum, if the percentage of judgments satisfied before sale and the dollar

TABLE 6A
VALUE OF EXECUTIONS COLLECTED

| Period[1] | (1) Collected % total execution $ | (2) Uncollected % total execution $ | (3) Misc. % total execution $ |
|---|---|---|---|
| 1836 | 61.5 | 37.3 | 1.1 |
| 1837 | 23.1 | 76.7 | .01 |
| 1838 | 63.0 | 21.5 | 15.5 |
| 1839 | 48.9 | 40.8 | 10.2 |
| 1840 | 49.1 | 38.2 | 12.6 |
| 1841 | 31.1 | 62.5 | 6.2 |
| 1842 | 51.8 | 46.2 | 1.9 |
| 1843 | 55.6 | 38.8 | 5.5 |
| 1844 | 54.8 | 36.8 | 8.5 |

*Sources:* Table 6B, *infra;* Collected = categories (1), (2), (3), and part of (4) collected. Uncollected = part of (4) uncollected, (5) (6), and (7).
[1] Year beginning spring term.

[50] Judgment debtors paid six per cent per year from the date of judgment. It is not clear how much time debtors gained by allowing execution. A statute required the sheriff to return the execution within 90 days or be liable personally for the amount of the judgment. I have attempted to determine whether the time between issue and return is related to the size of the judgment. Crude results indicate no relation.

value of judgments are reasonably good proxies for the general economic condition, the statistical evidence from the court records implies a different history of the crisis in Illinois from that of the traditional historical accounts. There was a large increase in the dollar value of judgments in the summer of 1838 and a gradual increase through 1842, implying not sudden deflation, but slowly worsening economic conditions. The percentage of judgments satisfied dropped sharply in 1838, and reached low points in 1839 and 1840. These were the difficult years of the depression. The very high level of judgments satisfied indicates that there was recovery by 1842. This conclusion is substantiated by the stability of the percentage of judgments satisfied in 1843 and 1844 and by the decline in the dollar value of judgments and in the proportion of unsatisfied executions.

## B.  *The Relief Laws*

Earlier we described the laws passed by the Illinois legislature to relieve the burdens of the depression. Here we attempt to assess the importance of two types of relief laws in operation in this period: laws requiring appraisal and a minimum bid before sale, and laws exempting property from sale on execution.

1. *Appraisal Laws*. The Illinois legislature in 1841 and 1843 approved laws forbidding sales on execution or foreclosure unless two-thirds of the property's value, as appraised by three disinterested householders, was bid at the sale.[51] Both laws operated primarily retrospectively. The 1841 law (approved February 27) applied to all sales of mortgaged property, and to sales based on any cause of action or contract prior to May 1, 1841.[52] The 1843 law applied only to sales based on contracts, bonds, and notes made before January 1, 1843.

It may seem peculiar that any property would not sell for two-thirds of its value; indeed, if the appraisers had defined value as what the property would bring at a sale at the time of the appraisal, the requirement would have meant nothing. But the 1841 law leaves the definition to the householders chosen as appraisers, and the 1843 law explicitly defines value at appraisal as "its fair and reasonable value in ordinary times." The Illinois legislature must therefore

[51] See Act, *supra* notes 35 and 36. The Illinois legislature originated this form of relief in 1823, in response to a depression then. An Act concerning Judgments and Executions (1823), Ill. Laws, 1 G.A., 169; see Ford, 311. The two-thirds requirement was repealed in 1825. An act concerning Judgments and Executions (1825), Ill. Revised Laws 370 (1833).

[52] This means that the law applied retrospectively to all contracts or causes prior to the date of passage, and to all judgments which had not been satisfied by the date of passage. Curiously (poor drafting?) the law operated prospectively on all contracts or causes entered into or arising between February 27 and May 1.

have anticipated that householders would attach a value to the property sufficiently high to prevent the sale, or at least to make it difficult.[53]

Table 6B presents the precentage of total execution dollars by each type of return over the period. Column (5) shows the percentage of execution dollars (also the number of executions and the dollar amounts) which the sheriff returned unsatisfied because the property would not bring two-thirds of the appraised value.[54] It is obvious that neither the 1841 nor the 1843 law had much significance in terms of preventing sales, once the execution had been levied.

Although the appraisal law had little apparent effect in preventing sales, it might have had a deterrent effect, convincing creditors not to proceed to the sale stage by reducing the probability of collection. The decision to litigate could be affected for causes of action that had not been settled or litigated prior to the date of passage. But there could be no deterrence to the execution of judgments rendered prior to the date of passage since there was no cost to the judgment creditor of causing an execution to issue. Column (5) shows that in 1841 and 1842, when judgments rendered prior to passage would have been executed,[55] the law prevented sales on fewer than two per cent of the executions (by value). This is good evidence of the ineffectiveness of the law.[56]

2. *Exemption from Execution.* Debtors were allowed to retain certain items of personal property upon execution throughout the period of study. An 1825

---

[53] Householders cooperated to retain property from speculators in claims' associations. James Willard Hurst, *supra* note 28, at 3-5; Theodore C. Pease, *supra* note 5, at 182-83; Allan G. Bogue, From Prairie to Corn Belt 31-39 (1963). The assumption of high valuation to prevent sale requires some reservation. The 1841 and 1843 laws provided that one appraiser was to be appointed each by the creditor, the debtor, and the sheriff. Possibly the legislature was responding to the common presumption that the price of property is lower at a forced sale, rather than expecting illegitimate valuations. What the definition of value was can be determined empirically.

[54] The 1841 and 1843 acts provided that if the three appraisers could not agree on the value of the property the sheriff would return the execution as not levied. Evans v. Landon, 6 Ill. (1 Gilman) 307 (1844). Column (7), returns not levied, shows a large increase in 1841 and 1842. These executions may represent appraiser disagreement and thus sales prevented. Also this study has not considered actions in the federal court which applied the two-thirds requirement on sales on federal executions in Illinois until Bronson v. Kinzie, 42 U.S. (1 How.) 311 (1843).

[55] The 1843 law, although applied retrospectively, may not have had the hypothesized effect since parties to contracts had had notice after February 27, 1841, that the legislature considered this type of limitation appropriate. Cf. Bronson v. Kinzie, *supra* note 54 (McLean, J., dissenting).

[56] McMaster reports that a mob threatened to use force against any court officer yielding to the Supreme Court's decision in *Bronson* that the 1841 appraisal law was unconstitutional. This suggests that some thought the appraisal law was effective. 7 John B. McMaster, *supra* note 9, at 47.

TABLE 6B
VALUE OF EXECUTIONS BY RETURN

| Period[1] | Plaintiff Withdrew % (1) | Satisfied % (2) | Satisfied by Sale % (3) | Partially Satisfied by Sale % (4) | Sale Impossible % (5) | No Property[2] Found % (6) | Not Levied[3] % (7) | Misc. % (8) |
|---|---|---|---|---|---|---|---|---|
| 1836 | 0 | 6.5 | 54.5 | 0.9 | 0 | 36.9 | 0 | 1.1 |
| 1837 | 0 | 7.2 | 0.4 | 57.7 | 0 | 34.5 | 0 | 0 |
| 1838 | 20.6 | 25.4 | 12.8 | 16.8 | 0 | 8.0 | 0.9 | 15.5 |
| 1839 | 11.5 | 14.9 | 10.8 | 29.0 | 0 | 18.5 | 5.0 | 10.2 |
| 1840 | 20.2 | 12.9 | 12.3 | 15.8 | 0 | 16.3 | 9.8 | 12.6 |
| 1841[4] | 13.2 | 13.7 | 4.2 | 0 | 1.3<br>1 = $235 | 36.2 | 25.0 | 6.2 |
| 1842[5] | 9.6 | 3.6 | 18.2 | 25.7 | 0.9<br>2 = $234 | 16.9 | 23.1 | 1.9 |
| 1843 | 24.5 | 7.7 | 22.8 | 2.1 | 0 | 32.7 | 4.6 | 5.5 |
| 1844 | 19.1 | 10.9 | 22.5 | 9.9 | 6.5<br>2 = $796 | 19.7 | 3.0 | 8.5 |

*Source:* Execution Docket, Book D, Sangamon County Circuit Court, Illinois.
[1] Year beginning spring term.
[2] See note 64.
[3] See note 54.
[4] Two executions equal to $47,396 were excluded from the tally.
[5] One execution equal to $31,882 was excluded from the tally.

act exempted one milch cow and calf, wearing apparel, beds, cooking utensils and household furniture, one spinning wheel and a pair of wool-cards, and provisions for a family for three months.[57] (The exemption only applied to the property of persons who were heads of families, living with their families.) The depression in the 1830s and 1840s revised legislative interest in this form of relief. In February 1840 the legislature extended the exemption to include one horse or a yoke of oxen worth no more then $60 for a farmer or $60 in tools for a mechanic.[58] In February 1841, the legislature changed the exemption to include just farmers and mechanics, $60 worth of property suited to any person's occupation, not just a farmer's or a mechanic's.[59] In March 1843, the legislature added one spinning wheel, one weaving loom, one stove, two sheep or their fleeces for each member of the family, and fuel for three months.[60]

It is possible to attach approximate dollar values to these successive exemptions. The exemptions allowed by the 1825 law, in effect throughout the period of study, were worth $87.[61] The 1840 law specifically added $60 in horse, oxen, or tools. The 1841 law applied the exemption more widely. The 1843 law added about $57 to the amount exempted.[62]

A law exempting property from execution reduces the amount that can be

[57] An Act concerning Judgments and Executions, § 19 (1825), Ill. Revised Laws (1833) 376.

[58] An Act exempting certain articles from execution, in addition to those already exempt by the laws of this State (1840), Ill. Laws, 11 G.A. Spec. Sess., 89.

[59] An Act to exempt certain articles from execution (1841), Ill. Laws, 12 G.A., 171.

[60] An Act to exempt certain articles from execution (1843), Ill. Laws, 13 G.A., 141.

[61] Peck in 1837 wrote that a cow was worth $7-15. J. M. Peck, *supra* note 17, at 286; Sewall paid $26 for two year-old heifers in 1840. William Sewall, *supra* note 46, at 211. A milch cow and calf were thus worth about $20. Constable Wickersham told the Probate Court in March 1841 that three months' provisions were worth $32. Scott v. Butler, Sangamon County Probate Court Book I and J 66-68 (1841); Sewall paid $35 for a bed, a stove, and a dining table in 1840. Sewall at 220. Beds, one spinning wheel and wool cards, and cooking utensils were therefore worth about $20. $15 of household furniture, in addition, was exempted explicitly.

[62] Based on Sewall's purchase of household furniture in 1840, *supra* note 61, one spinning wheel, one loom, and one stove was worth about $30. The issue is complicated regarding the exemption for two sheep or fleeces for each member of the family. Mitchell claimed that wool was selling for 50 cents a pound in Illinois. S. Augustus Mitchell, Illinois in 1837, A Sketch 42 (1837); in 1964 the world-wide average for wool per sheep was five pounds. 2 Encyc. Brittanica 728 (1964); the average family size in Sangamon County according to the 1840 Census was six (the number of children less than 15 years divided by the number of females 15-40 years, plus two). Sixth Census, *supra* note 17. Two sheep times 5 pounds times 50 cents times 6 members equals $30. This seems high. Professor Bogue declares that in the early 1840s sheep could be imported from the East to Illinois for about $1 per head. Bogue, *supra* note 53, at 116. At this price the sheep exemption was worth $15. We will use the average of the two calculations: $22. Fuel for three months was probably not worth more than $5.

Professor Hurst interprets the exemption laws of the 19th century as critical because collected from any debtor. As discussed more fully in the final section, the parties to a contract or a loan will take such a law into account in assessing the value of the security for the agreement. But when an exemption is (1) extended, and (2) given retrospective effect (*i.e.*, exempting the property of debtors from sale on agreements made prior to the extension), the law lessens the value of the security of an existing agreement. If the property owned by the debtor, besides that exempted, is worth less than the value of the loan, the probability of collecting the full amount of the loan will be reduced. And if there are many debtors in this position, the reduced probability of collection should be reflected in the court statistics, both in the number of judgments collected and in the decision to go to court. Fewer judgments issued before the passage of the extension and executed after passage will be collected; and where the decision to settle or litigate has yet to be made, the settlement rate will be higher.[63] We suggest, as a hypothesis, that there will be a larger percentage of debtors with limited additional property when the value of the judgment is less than $200 than when the value of the judgment is greater.

Table 7 extracts from Table 6B those executions returned "no property found."[64] If the exemption from execution laws had the hypothesized effect, Table 7 should show increases in the percentage of small no-property-found executions in the years immediately following the passage of exemption extensions: 1840, 1841 (less), and 1843. It does not. The largest percentages of smaller no-property-found executions appear in 1839, 1840, and 1841, years that we know from other data were the worst of the depression.

It is peculiar to note that the proportion (by value) of judgment dollars involving small (below $200) judgments declined in 1840, 1841, and 1842

---

they preserved a nucleus of working capital necessary to permit continued freedom of maneuver. James Willard Hurst, *supra* note 28, at 66. We have seen that by the mid-1840s, laws in Illinois exempted about $200 from execution. Professor Danhof, in his study of farm-making costs in the decade 1850-1860, shows that the lowest estimates of the capital settlers in Illinois needed to establish themselves were $550 for a 40 acre farm, $785 for an 80 acre farm, and $896 for a 34 acre farm. Clarence H. Danhof, *supra* note 15, Table 1 at 327. Subtracting the cost of land (for squatters) and items exempt the estimates are $450, $685, and $726. If Danhof's figures resemble the level of costs in the 1840s, the exemption laws in Illinois preserved a nucleus of capital quite inadequate to allow resettlement. Furthermore, the exemption laws applied only to heads of families; single persons were permitted to retain only wearing apparel.

[63] If the "litigation threshold" and the difference in probability estimates are the same, a lower probability of collection will reduce the expected judgment and increase the likelihood of settlement.

[64] "No property found" can mean no property found that is not exempt. It also can mean that the debtor has skipped the county. The executions listed in Table 7 are those where the execution was issued within three months of the judgment; that is, alias executions (included in Tables 6A and B) have been omitted, in order to eliminate executions harassing the debtor or simply requiring the sheriff to look around again.

LAW AND ECONOMIC DISTRESS                      489

TABLE 7
PROPORTION (BY VALUE) OF EXECUTIONS RETURNED "NO PROPERTY FOUND"[1]

| Period[2] | $0-200 % | $200+ % |
|---|---|---|
| 1836 | 14.3 | 85.7 |
| 1837 | 6.0 | 94.0 |
| 1838 | 1.3 | 98.7 |
| 1839 | 35.8 | 64.2 |
| 1840 | 25.1 | 74.9 |
| 1841[3] | 28.4 | 71.6 |
| 1842 | 14.1 | 85.9 |
| 1843 | 11.0 | 89.0 |
| 1844 | 100.0 | 0 |

*Source:* Execution Docket, Book D, Sangamon County Circuit Court, Illinois.
[1] See note 64.
[2] Year beginning spring term.
[3] One execution equal to $15,505 was excluded from the tally.


(Table 4). One would expect loans and judgments of smaller amounts, not larger, to become relatively more frequent as the market adjusted to lower rates of collection and resulting higher interest rates. We will discuss three possible explanations of this eccentric evidence: sympathy, stamina, and exemption.

One hypothesis is that as economic conditions deteriorated, the feelings that had motivated legislators to enact relief laws motivated judges and juries to favor debtors over creditors. Judgments against debtors would become smaller and less frequent. Further, as potential litigants recognized the change of disposition, disputes involving smaller amounts would be settled more often (since sympathy also reduces the size of the judgment), so the judgment rate would decline precipitously.

Although it is clear that the number of small judgments decreased in 1840 (Table 3), this comes too late to support the sympathy theory. There is no indication of a decline in the average smaller judgment prior to 1840 except in 1838, and in the following year there were more small judgments, not fewer. Moreover, it is difficult to imagine that sympathy for debtors would be limited to debtors for less than $200. One should find some indication of sympathy in larger judgments as well. Instead the average larger judgment rose after 1840, parallel to the small judgments' decline.

An alternative explanation is that larger judgments predominated as the depression progressed because those who borrowed larger amounts of money characteristically possessed larger resources, and thus were able to withstand the depression longer before failing. However, the decline after 1840 both in the number of larger judgments (Table 3B) and in the number of larger judgments relative to smaller (Table 4) contradicts this hypothesis. There is good evidence that the stamina of large borrowers lasted no longer than 1838, when the number of large judgments increased fourfold.

The third hypothesis is that the decline in the relative value of smaller judgments reflects the influence of the laws exempting property from execution. Evidence of the number of small judgments rendered (Table 3) supports this hypothesis: there were substantial decreases in 1840, 1841, and 1843, the years in which the property exemption was extended. But other evidence contradicts it. In particular, the decline in the average small judgment after 1840 (Table 2) is inconsistent with *all* three of the hypotheses. Each hypothesis presupposes that the decline in the relative proportion of small-judgment dollars reflects the fact that fewer small judgments were being rendered. Yet the hypotheses simultaneously imply that the *average* small judgment should increase, as a larger proportion of the lower-valued judgments in the small-judgment category drop out; in fact it declines.[65] (There is an indication of an increase in the average small judgment in constant dollars but it is unlikely that this is the correct measure, since court costs were fixed, and there is no evidence of lawyers' deflating their fees.)

The execution statistics show conclusively that the appraisal laws were ineffective. The evidence is less clear for the property exemptions, but there is no indication of a decrease in the rate of collection of smaller executions or of a substantial change in judgments that can be traced to these laws. The analysis has shown the improbability of significant judicial sympathy in the period and that the stamina of large borrowers was exhausted early in the depression.

---

Empirical studies of the legal system can provide useful information to historians and to those interested in the effectiveness of laws. The statistics of judgments and executions in Sangamon County give definite and unimpeachable evidence of economic conditions and the operation of the relief laws. Historians of the period have based their accounts on contemporary sources, but the evidence is impressionistic (with some exceptions) and lacks comprehensiveness. Our conclusions from court records confirm the historical judgment of the beginning of the depression, but substantially revise and give greater depth to the description of the depression and recovery. The appraisal and exemption laws have been praised widely as important examples of relief.[66] Our statistics show the effects of the laws to be minimal. As this essay attests, the empirical study of the legal system is in infancy. Such studies are prom-

[65] The exemption laws may appear ineffective because the proportion of debtors with limited additional resources, the beneficiaries of such laws, is no greater for smaller judgments than for larger.

[66] Henry W. Farnam, *supra* note 28, at 150-52; Ford, 311; James Willard Hurst, *supra* note 28, at 13-14, 66. See note 62, *supra*, and note 68, *infra*; 7 John B. McMaster, *supra* note 9, at 43-48; Samuel Rezneck, *supra* note 28, at 95.

ising tools of historical research and indispensable methods of determining the effectiveness of laws.

## IV. A NOTE ON RETROSPECTIVE LEGISLATION

Many of the relief laws enacted by the Illinois legislature extended relief primarily to individuals who had incurred debts prior to the date the law was approved. The appraisal laws, for example, only restricted sales based on agreements or causes of action that had accrued before enactment. Though one might think that the legislators were half-hearted or miserly in their reluctance to grant relief generally, a principle of common sense underlies the limitation of the law's application. The appraisal laws were to provide relief (as were the laws creating redemption rights for mortgagors and extending property exemptions) by altering the mechanism through which individuals enforced private agreements. These laws attempted to make the enforcement of an obligation more difficult for the creditor in order to provide relief for the debtor.

A private agreement by definition is an exchange of resources that is mutually beneficial. No agreement will be made unless each party considers that what he is receiving is worth more than what he is giving up. This simple relationship indicates the futility of laws which attempt to provide relief by applying restrictions to the enforcement of agreements that have not yet been made. If the change in the mechanism of enforcement reduces the value of the agreement to one of the parties, he will not agree.[67] If a party to a contract knows while he is negotiating terms that the property of the other party, his assurance of collection, cannot be sold at an execution or a foreclosure sale because of the two-thirds requirement, he will ask for better terms—higher interest, larger payments, more security—to compensate him for the greater risk he is taking. An appraisal law, if applied prospectively, cannot possibly increase the value of the rights of debtors relative to creditors.

But where the terms of the contract were negotiated in the expectation that a sale would take place if the first party defaulted, and later the sale is made impossible by a change of law, creditors as a class find their rights under existing contracts worth less and debtors find their rights worth more. Those debtors whose land will not bring the two-thirds price will be better off because, although the judgment against them will not be extinguished, it is unenforceable, at least until someone is willing to pay the two-thirds. This analysis, evidently, was well understood by members of the Illinois legislature in the 1840s.[68]

---

[67] Cf. Richard A. Posner, Economic Analysis of Law ch. 3 (forthcoming).

[68] Recent commentators have shown less comprehension of the effects of prospective and retrospective laws relating to contracts. Professor Hurst in his provocative essay describes

The U.S. Supreme Court in 1843 considered the effects of the Illinois appraisal and and mortgage redemption laws and held that they violated the Constitution as impairments of the obligation of contracts.[69] In the famous case of *Sturges v. Crowninshield*, in 1819, Chief Justice Marshall had laid down the standards by which such laws would be considered: if the state law modified retrospectively the obligation of a contract, it was void; but if the law modified only the remedy by which the contract was to be enforced, it was within the state's powers.[70] In *Sturges* Marshall found that a New York insolvency act that retrospectively discharged the applicant's debts was unconstitutional. The difficulty in *Bronson* was that the laws appeared to reduce the value of the contract to the creditor yet seemed to be remedies. Justice Taney, for the Court, found that when entering the agreement, the parties mutually expected that the obligations would be enforced, but the redemption and appraisal laws so changed the enforcement mechanism as to make the remedy "hardly worth pursuing." The Court admitted that sometimes a change in remedy could impair an obligation.

The distinction between obligation and remedy is, indeed, untenable. The form of the change made by the state is less important than the extent to which the change raises or lowers the value of the contract right to the various parties. This is an empirical question—and the evidence we have presented above suggests that the appraisal law had negligible effect on the rights and welfare of the parties to agreements.

---

laws elaborating lien and debtor's exemptions as the "main area of legislative contribution running through the century." Exemption laws, according to Hurst, correspond to the contemporaneous judicial development of contract law, which created "a framework of reasonable expectations," thereby increasing "the scope of individual discretion in the management of resources." Both the legislative and judicial developments are examples of the predominant 19th century principle of promoting the release of creative human energy. James Willard Hurst, *supra*, note 28, at 13-14; Professor Hurst's argument is curious because, according to our analysis, debtors' exemptions applied retrospectively represent the converse of creating reasonable expectations; applied prospectively, the exemptions will be taken into account in the agreement and thus have no redistributive effect, but will decrease the scope of individual discretion for those debtors wanting to stake personal property now exempt as security for a loan.

[69] Bronson v. Kinzie, 42 U.S. (1 Howard) 311 (1843).

[70] 17 U.S. (4 Wheaton) 122 (1819).

Errata: "Law and Economic Distress:  Sangamon County,
          Illinois, 1837-1844", 2 J. Leg. Studies 469 (1973)

Page 473, first full paragraph, last line should read
          "1835 level.".

Page 478, line 2:  After "for the judgment", add "to act
          as a lien on the debtor's property."

Page 487, line 5 should read "revived".  The words "just
          farmers and mechanics," should be deleted from
          line 9.

NOTE:  The figures in Tables 1A and 1B (at 479) represent
        sample totals only.  The sample included the same
        proportion (one-fifth) of total judgments for each
        term.

The author neglected to express appreciation to Hans Zeisel
for advice, and to Kathy Kiefer for help with the statistica
work.  He apologizes.

# D. CONSTITUTIONAL ISSUES

# 14
## THE CHEROKEE CASES: A STUDY IN LAW, POLITICS, AND MORALITY

*JOSEPH C. BURKE*

# The Cherokee Cases: A Study in Law, Politics, and Morality[*]

## Joseph C. Burke[†]

An air of doom settled over the Supreme Court when the Justices gathered for the 1832 Term. The Court approached the case of *Worcester v. Georgia*[1] as though caught in the clutches of fate and irresistible events. Georgia had imprisoned two white missionaries for living in Cherokee Territory without a license from the State, and the missionaries had appealed the case to the Supreme Court by challenging the authority of State law within the Cherokee territories. The Governor, legislators, and judges of Georgia had publicly dared the Supreme Court to interfere; and the President of the United States, who had encouraged—or at least winked at—this outrage, now seemed prepared to stand by and watch the State defy the Constitution, laws, and treaties of the United States. With a sense of duty and a premonition of defeat, the Justices issued the fateful decree that reversed the conviction of the missionaries and exposed the Court to the wrath of Georgia and of Jackson. Surely the *Worcester* case had all the elements of high tragedy.

Yet, somehow this tragic act seems out of character for the Marshall Court. Only the year before, in *Cherokee Nation v. Georgia*,[2] the Court had averted a similar clash. At least two of the Justices had been prepared for a confrontation then; and one of them, Joseph Story, had written: "At this moment, it would have been desirable to have escaped it; but you know it is not for Judges to choose times and occasions. We must do our duty as we may."[3] Even if Story knew better, and he probably did, John Marshall did not find the confrontation inevitable in 1831. Yet, a year later in the *Worcester* case he might have been paraphrasing Story when he wrote that the Judiciary Act of 1789 "imposed on [the Court] the duty, of exercising jurisdiction in this case. This duty, however unpleasant, cannot be avoided.

---

* This Article represents a considerable revision of a paper delivered at the Organization of American Historians meeting on April 19, 1968. This Article, Donald Roper's, and Kent Newmyer's were delivered at the session entitled "Law, Morality, and the Marshall Court." The revisions are the result of further research and further thought about the subject. I have drawn heavily on the excellent comments of Kent Newmyer, who served as commentator for the panel at Dallas, and on the penetrating criticism by Professor Gerald Gunther of the Stanford Law School, who chaired the panel, and the students who participated in his seminar on the Supreme Court.

† B.A. 1954, Bellarmine College; M.A. 1958, Ph.D. 1965, Indiana University. Associate Professor of History, Duquesne University.

1. 31 U.S. (6 Pet.) 515 (1832).
2. 30 U.S. (5 Pet.) 1 (1831).
3. Letter from Joseph Story to George Ticknor, Jan. 22, 1831, in 2 THE LIFE AND LETTERS OF JOSEPH STORY 49 (W. Story ed. 1851).

Those who fill the judicial department have no discretion in selecting the subjects to be brought before them."[4]

The two Indian cases raise interesting questions. Why did the Supreme Court take the fateful plunge in 1832 rather than in 1831? Why did it take the plunge at all? And, finally, was that plunge in 1832 as fateful as it seemed? Unfortunately, neither the words nor the actions of the Justices speak loud enough for conclusive answers to these questions. Still, tentative answers may be arrived at by examining those words and actions in connection with the history of the federal government's relations—both in theory and in practice—with the Indians, the chain of events that brought the two cases before the Court, and the alternatives available to the Court in disposing of them. The Cherokee cases offer a fascinating study in judicial motivation, for they mingled complex considerations of law, politics, and morality.

The nation long avoided facing Indian relations as a legal, political, or moral problem. The ambivalent Indian policy of the federal government, the irresistible push of white settlers, and the official "willingness" of the tribes to sell their lands long hid the conflict between the theory and practice of our Indian relations. In theory, the Government treated with the tribes as sovereign nations, purchasing only the lands they chose to sell and guaranteeing forever their title to the lands they chose to keep. In practice, the constant encroachment of white settlers, which the state governments would not and the federal government could not prevent, made a mockery of Indian sovereignty by forcing tribes to sell lands they wanted but could not peacefully keep. Written treaties that spoke of Indian nations, Indian boundaries, and Indian political rights remained on file, while time and the lack of records concealed the bribery, threats, and force that so often preceded their signing. Because the Indians, under pressure, usually sold the lands that the settlers demanded, the President, the Congress, and the Supreme Court could maintain the formal position that cession had been voluntary.[5]

The cases that first came before the Supreme Court complicated the difficult task of forging legal principles to reconcile theory and reality in dealings with the Indians. The early cases arose between white men with

---

4. 31 U.S. (6 Pet.) at 541.
5. For a discussion of the United States Indian relations see the excellent study by F. Prucha, American Indian Policy in the Formative Years: The Indian Trade and Intercourse Acts, 1790–1834 (1962). For the legal side of these relations see U.S. Dep't of the Interior, Federal Indian Law (1958) and Digest of Decisions Relating to Indian Affairs (K. Murchison comp. 1901). For the treaties and correspondence relating to Indian affairs see 2 American State Papers: Indian Affairs (1834). The treaties can be found in 2 Indian Affairs: Laws and Treaties: Indians of North America—Treaties (C. Kappler ed. 1904) and in 7 Stat. (1846). The presidential messages appear in 1 & 2 A Compilation of the Messages and Papers of the Presidents 1789–1897 (J. Richardson comp. 1902) [hereinafter cited as Messages].

conflicting claims to land that once belonged to Indians[6] rather than between states and Indian nations with rival claims to soil and sovereignty.
Since these cases did not directly confront the Court with questions of the
political and property rights of the tribes, its decisions only suggested
answers to these problems. The questions were novel, and the technical
terms originating in the relationship between lord and tenant in feudal
times were ill-suited to describe the peculiar relationship between the red
men and the white men in colonial America.

The Supreme Court first touched the question of Indian rights in 1810
when it decided the famous Yazoo land case, *Fletcher v. Peck*.[7] Chief Justice Marshall ruled that Georgia had a right in 1795 to grant this territory to
land companies, since it lay within the boundaries of the State, even though
the Indians retained possession of the soil. While conceding the difficulty
in regarding a state as holding a fee simple in land still occupied by tribes,
he declared that the "nature of the Indian title, which is certainly to be respected by all courts, until it be legitimately extinguished, is not such as to
be absolutely repugnant to seisin in fee on the part of the State."[8] In a concurring opinion William Johnson called the Indians of the Yazoo Territory
an "independent people" with the "absolute proprietorship of the soil."[9]

The Supreme Court returned to this question 13 years later in *Johnson
v. McIntosh*.[9] Later both sides in the Cherokee controversy would quote
from the *McIntosh* decision,[10] but in reality Marshall's opinion supported
neither those who considered the tribes independent nations and proprietors of the soil nor those who regarded them as subject people and
tenants at will. He spoke of the peculiar situation of the Indian—"in some
respects . . . a dependent, and in some respects . . . a distinct people, occupying a country claimed" first by Britain and then by the United States.[11]
In *McIntosh* the doctrine of Indian property rights was explained in greater
historical detail than in the *Yazoo* case, though hardly with less ambiguity.
The United States held the ultimate right to the soil; the tribes retained the
right of possession with the limitation that they could sell only to the United
States. Marshall suggested that the right of the United States might be compared to a "seisin in fee" and the Indian right to a "lease for years."[12] In so

---

6. *See* Danforth v. Wear, 22 U.S. (9 Wheat.) 673 (1824); Johnson v. McIntosh, 21 U.S. (8
Wheat.) 543 (1823); Danforth's Lessee v. Thomas, 14 U.S. (1 Wheat.) 155 (1816); Preston v.
Browder, 14 U.S. (1 Wheat.) 115 (1816); Fletcher v. Peck, 10 U.S. (6 Cranch) 87 (1810).
7. 10 U.S. (6 Cranch) 87, 142–43 (1810).
8. *Id.* at 142–43.
9. 21 U.S. (8 Wheat.) 543 (1823).
10. *See, e.g.*, letter from Jeremiah Evarts to Sidney Morse, Nov. 16, 1829, Miscellaneous Collection, New-York Historical Society; [J. Evarts] ESSAYS ON THE PRESENT CRISIS IN THE CONDITION OF
THE AMERICAN INDIANS; FIRST PUBLISHED IN THE NATIONAL INTELLIGENCER, UNDER THE SIGNATURE
OF WILLIAM PENN 84, 105–08 (1829) [hereinafter cited as ESSAYS OF WILLIAM PENN]; Richmond
Enquirer, Dec. 9, 1830, at 4, col. 1.
11. 21 U.S. (8 Wheat.) at 596.
12. *Id.* at 592.

stating Indian rights Marshall claimed not to be building a doctrine, but to be conforming his decision to the "actual condition of the two people." Yet even as he wrote, conditions were changing.

Both the legal doctrines of the Supreme Court and the Indian policy of the federal government had been developed with the assumption that the tribes would continue to sell their lands at roughly the same rate the settlers demanded them; so did the famous agreement between the United States and Georgia in 1802. Georgia ceded her western land claims in return for the promise of the United States Government to extinguish the Indian title to lands within the state boundary as soon as it could be done "peaceably" and on "reasonable terms."[13] But by the early 1820's the Cherokees and other southern tribes had refused to cede another foot of soil. These Indian nations, persuaded by federal officials and aided by federal funds, had abandoned hunting for farming. The change attached them to their lands, created in them a sense of property, and made the wild lands west of the Mississippi seem uninviting.[14] This economic change had its political counterpart. In 1827 the Cherokees adopted a constitution modeled after that of the United States, and declared themselves an independent nation with an absolute right to soil and sovereignty within their boundaries.[15] By these two acts, the Cherokees reasserted their autonomy with respect to Georgia and their independence from the United States.

The reaction from Georgia and Georgians was immediate and extreme. Inspired by the rhetoric of states' rights and encouraged by the clamor for Indian lands on which gold had recently been discovered, Georgia in 1828 and 1829 enacted a series of laws that distributed the Cherokee territory to several counties and declared that after June 1, 1830, Georgia law would be enforced within this territory and all Indian customs and laws would be null and void. These laws also denied Indians the right to testify in cases involving whites and punished any person or groups who tried to prevent Indians from emigrating from the State.[16] The time lag was to give the federal government the chance to persuade the Cherokees and Creeks to move west of the Mississippi. The lag also represented an expression of faith in the new President and old Indian fighter, Andrew Jackson. The faith was not misplaced.

---

13. Georgia Cession, Apr. 26, 1802, in 1 AMERICAN STATE PAPERS: PUBLIC LANDS 126 (1832).
14. *See* letter from Cherokee Council to United States Commissioners, Oct. 20, 1823, in 2 AMERICAN STATE PAPERS: INDIAN AFFAIRS 468 (1834); extract of letter from Commissioner Campbell to Secretary of War, Nov. 28, 1823, in *id.* at 464; letter from United States Commissioners to Cherokee Council, Oct. 25, 1823, in *id.* at 471; letter from Secretary of War to Cherokee Delegation, Jan. 30, 1824, in *id.* at 473; letter from Georgia Delegation in Congress to the President, Mar. 10, 1824, in *id.* at 476–77; memorial of the Senate and House of Representatives of Georgia to the President, Dec. 20, 1823, in *id.* at 490–91; views of the Cherokees in relation to the further cession of their lands, communicated to the U.S. Senate, Apr. 16, 1824, in *id.* at 502.
15. For the constitution see H.R. Doc. No. 91, 23d Cong., 2d Sess. 10 (1827).
16. Act No. 545 of Dec. 20, 1828, and Act No. 546 of Dec. 19, 1829, in A COMPILATION OF THE LAWS OF THE STATE OF GEORGIA 198 (W. Dawson comp. 1831).

Like Jackson, James Monroe and John Quincy Adams had concluded that the Indians could not permanently remain within the limits of the states, and that their removal west of the Mississippi offered the only practical solution to the Indian problem.[17] Still, a vital difference remained between their policy and that of Jackson. While Monroe and Adams had urged removal by every kind of inducement, officially they continued to treat the tribes as more or less sovereign nations and to respect their right to remain on the treaty lands.[18] Whereas circumstances had permitted them to postpone decision on the Indian question, the intransigence of Georgia and the Cherokees did not allow Jackson such a luxury.

The Cherokee delegation in Washington could hardly have been comforted by Jackson's inaugural address, which promised as much "humane and considerate attention to their rights" as was "consistent with the habits of our Government and the feelings of our people."[19] All remaining doubt about Jackson's position vanished when in April 1829 the new Secretary of War John Eaton sent the delegation a letter outlining the President's views on the Indian problem.[20] The Cherokees had no right to set up an independent nation within the limits of Georgia, and the President had no authority to interfere with the internal legislation of one of the states of the Union. The choice seemed simple to Eaton and Jackson. The Indians must move or submit to Georgia law. The President thought removal offered the only practical solution. In his annual message on December 8, 1829,[21] Jackson recommended a bill setting aside territory west of the Mississippi and outside the boundaries of any existing state or territory for the Indians. The choice of removing or staying remained with the Indians; but those who

---

17. Monroe, First Annual Message, Dec. 2, 1817, in 2 MESSAGES, *supra* note 5, at 16; Monroe, Second Inaugural Address, Mar. 5, 1821, in *id.* at 92; Monroe, Message to the Senate and House of Representatives of the United States, Jan. 27, 1825, in *id.* at 283; Adams, Fourth Annual Message, Dec. 2, 1828, in *id.* at 416; report from the Secretary of War to the House of Representatives on the Condition of the Several Tribes, Feb. 8, 1822, in 2 AMERICAN STATE PAPERS: INDIAN AFFAIRS 275 (1834); Report of the Secretary of War on Extinguishment of Indian Title to Lands in Georgia, Mar. 29, 1824, in *id.* at 461.

18. For the background of the Treaty of Indian Springs and its aftermath see Phillips, *Georgia and States Rights,* in 2 ANNUAL REP. OF THE AM. HIST. ASS'N 56–59 (1902); S. BEMIS, JOHN QUINCY ADAMS AND THE UNION 79–87 (1956).

19. Jackson, First Inaugural Address, Mar. 4, 1829, in 2 MESSAGES, *supra* note 5, at 438. As early as 1817 Jackson had written to Monroe, and in 1820 and 1821 he wrote to the Secretary of War, John C. Calhoun, advising an end to the practice of treating the tribes as sovereign nations. Jackson considered them subjects of the United States whose only right to the land was that of occupancy for hunting purposes. Letter from Jackson to Monroe, Mar. 4, 1817, in 2 CORRESPONDENCE OF ANDREW JACKSON 279, 281 (J. Bassett ed. 1927); letter from Jackson to Calhoun, Sept. 2, 1820, in 3 CORRESPONDENCE OF ANDREW JACKSON 32 (J. Bassett ed. 1928); letter from Jackson to Calhoun, Jan. 18, 1821, in *id.* at 36, 38.

20. Eaton's letter, Apr. 18, 1829, is printed in Niles' Weekly Register, May 30, 1829, at 258, col. 1. For the best legal statement of the Jacksonian point of view see the opinion of Attorney General and former Georgia Senator John Macpherson Berrien, 2 OP. ATT'Y GEN. 305 (1829).

21. Jackson, First Annual Message, Dec. 8, 1829, in 2 MESSAGES, *supra* note 5, at 442. Jackson postponed the question of rechartering the Bank with the terse comment that many Americans question its "constitutionality" and "expediency." *Id.,* at 462.

stayed had to submit to state law and could retain only such property as they had "improved by their industry."[22]

Even before the presidential message, the Indian question had become a political issue. The Washington *National Intelligencer* fired the opening shot when it announced in August of 1829 the forthcoming appearance of a series of articles on this question over the signature of William Penn.[23] These articles, published in book form late in 1829 and in 1830, soon became the holy writ, the reference work, and the legal brief of the many preachers, congressmen, and lawyers interested in defending the Cherokees, attacking Georgia, and condemning Jackson. In over 100 pages of fine print, these essays ransacked treaties, statutes, and federal and state court decisions for every shred of evidence supporting the Cherokee claims. Jacksonians and Georgians saw a dark political purpose behind these essays; and Wilson Lumpkin, later Governor of Georgia, charged that their author had "much more of the character of the politician and lawyer than of an humble missionary."[24]

The Cherokees' first appeal was not to the Court but to Congress. Jeremiah Evarts, the chief official of the American Board of Commissioners for Foreign Missions, began the *Essays*, in August of 1829, with the declaration that the Indian question "will be among the most important, and probably the most contested, business of the 21st Congress."[25] In December the Cherokee Nation petitioned Congress to protect their political and property rights against the recent Georgia laws.[26] Evarts and others organized meeting after meeting throughout the Northeast at which memorials to Congress were drafted begging it to defend the national honor by protecting the Cherokees.[27] The presses and pulpits of the Northeast echoed these pleas and castigated Jackson for abandoning the benign policy of his predecessors toward the Indians.[28] Jacksonians charged that a conspiracy of church, party, and section had been formed to overthrow the administration.[29] Most of the leaders of this movement were opposed to Jackson, did come from the Northeast, and did make their appeal to religious groups, especially in the politically crucial states of New York and Pennsylvania. The be-

22. *Id.* at 459.
23. ESSAYS OF WILLIAM PENN, *supra* note 10, at 2.
24. Speech of Governor Lumpkin to the Georgia Legislature, May 1830, in 1 W. LUMPKIN, THE REMOVAL OF THE CHEROKEE INDIANS FROM GEORGIA 73 (1907).
25. ESSAYS OF WILLIAM PENN, *supra* note 10, at 2.
26. The memorial is printed in Niles' Weekly Register, Mar. 13, 1830, at 53, col. 1.
27. *See* letter from Ambrose Spencer and Henry Storrs to John Trumbull, Jan. 25, 1830, Simon Gratz Collection, Pennsylvania Historical Society; Niles' Weekly Register, Feb. 27, 1830, at 5, col. 1; Wash. Daily Nat'l Intelligencer, Jan. 5, 1830, at 2, col. 1; Jan. 26, 1830, at 2, col. 1; Richmond Enquirer, Jan. 5, 1830, at 2, col. 3; Jan. 23, 1830, at 4, col. 2; Feb. 18, 1830, at 3, col. 2; Feb. 26, 1830, at 2, col. 5; Mar. 2, 1830, at 3, col. 2; Mar. 9, 1830, at 2, col. 3; Apr. 6, 1830, at 2, col. 2.
28. *See* article from New Eng. Weekly Rev. reprinted in Richmond Enquirer, Feb. 4, 1830, at 4, col. 1; *cf.* Richmond Enquirer, Feb. 18, 1830, at 3, col. 2.
29. *See* Richmond Enquirer, Feb. 18, 1830, at 3, col. 2; Feb. 26, 1830, at 3, col. 2; Mar. 12, 1830, at 3, col. 5; Apr. 30, 1830, at 3, col. 3.

lated conversion of a number of these leaders to the Indian cause also seemed to confirm the charge that their inspiration was political. Henry Clay, for example, while in Adams' cabinet, had thought the red men "a race not worth preserving," since the hunter had to give way to the farmer.[30] As chief justice of the New York supreme court in 1822, Ambrose Spencer, an outspoken friend of Indian sovereignty in 1830, had upheld the extension of state law to the New York tribes.[31] Of course, Indian removal had been accepted as the only practical answer to the Indian question by most of the supporters of Monroe and Adams, although both administrations insisted that the removal be voluntary.[32]

The memorials, however, were ignored, and the committees on Indian affairs of both houses of Congress reported bills that set aside territory west of the Mississippi to be exchanged for tribal lands within the states. These bills provided funds to assist Indian removal.[33] The reports merely elaborated on Jackson's advice to the Cherokees, insisting that the states retained full control over all persons and lands within their chartered limits and that the President lacked the authority to interfere.

The long congressional debate on the Removal Bill, which lasted from late February to late May 1830, explored the moral and legal implications of the Indian question and exposed it as a partisan and sectional issue. The Bill's opponents charged that President Jackson had discarded the policy of every President since George Washington and had ignored the many treaties and laws that recognized the tribes as foreign nations and guaranteed forever the Indian right to their lands. The Bill before Congress promised to protect the rights of the Indians in the new lands; but in time, the westward push of settlers would make a farce of these new guarantees, just as it had the old ones.[34]

Jacksonians accused the Bill's opponents of attempting to build an opposition party on false morality and sectional politics. They insisted that every President since Jefferson had approved of Indian removal. Now Northerners, whose states had gotten rid of their Indian problem by removing or legislating over them, cursed Georgia, Alabama, and Mississippi for doing what they had once considered both natural and necessary. Ex-

---

30. *See* 7 MEMOIRS OF JOHN QUINCY ADAMS 90 (C. Adams ed. 1875).

31. Jackson v. Goodell, 20 Johns. 188, 189–94 (N.Y. Sup. Ct. 1822). As late as January 17, 1833, Spencer had renewed doubts. *See* letter from Spencer to John Armstrong, Rokeby Collection, New-York Historical Society. James Kent overturned Spencer's opinion in Jackson v. Goodell, 20 Johns. 693, 713–17 (N.Y. 1822). The Indians of New York were independent of New York control until the state asserted control and the Indians acquiesced. As a nation of aliens governing themselves within their own territory, the Indians of New York had to be considered a foreign state.

32. *See* notes 17 & 18 *supra* and accompanying text.

33. S. Doc. No. 61, 21st Cong., 1st Sess. (1830).

34. For the best speeches in opposition to the Bill see those of Senators Theodore Frelinghuysen of New Jersey and Peleg Sprague of Maine and Congressman Henry Storrs of New York, in SPEECHES ON THE PASSAGE OF THE BILL FOR THE REMOVAL OF THE INDIANS DELIVERED IN THE CONGRESS OF THE UNITED STATES, APRIL AND MAY, 1830, at 1, 31, 79 ([J. Evarts? comp.] 1830) [hereinafter cited as SPEECHES ON THE REMOVAL BILL].

pediency and humanity, not a lack of authority, explained why some Southern states had only recently brought the Indian nations under their laws. The proposed Bill left to the Indians the choice of whether to remove or to submit to state law. Humanity and reason dictated removal, for west of the Mississippi they could govern themselves on their own land without the demoralizing influence of intruding whites.[35]

The element of choice in the Bill was seriously impaired when the Senate rejected, 27 to 20, an amendment providing that until the tribes decided whether or not to remove, the federal government should respect their political and property rights.[36] The sectional character of this crucial vote was obvious.[37] The final vote on the Removal Bill[38] in the House on May 26 also revealed, though less sharply, a sectional split.[39]

Passage of the Removal Bill did not end the controversy. On May 29, the day after Jackson signed the Bill, Webster wrote Clay concerning the results of informal consultations between National Republican leaders in Washington.[40] "The passage of the Indian bill, and the rejection of the Maysville Turnpike bill, have occasioned unusual excitement."[41] After speculating that Clay would lose the election unless Virginia, Pennsylvania, or New York were detached from Jackson, Webster stated that the Indian Bill and the Maysville Road veto would weaken Jackson in both Pennsylvania and New York and should be used for this purpose. Clay gave complete approval to the plan for keeping these two issues before the public.[42] The National Republican press responded by labeling the Removal Bill a stain on national honor and attacking Jackson for signing it.[43] And Jeremiah Evarts, encouraged by Webster and Ambrose Spencer,[44] hurried

---

35. For the best speech in support of the Bill see that of Senator John Forsyth of Georgia. 6 Cong. Deb. 324 (1830). For the extreme Georgia position see the speech of Congressman Wilson Lumpkin, 1 W. Lumpkin, *supra* note 24, at 57.

36. S. Jour., 21st Cong., 1st Sess. 266 (1829); 6 Cong. Deb. 383 (1830).

37. Senators from states north of the Potomac and from Ohio cast only eight votes against it, and four of these votes came from Indiana and Illinois, which still had Indian problems. All 18 southern senators voted against the amendment, while the New England senators supported it 11 to 1.

38. Act of May 28, 1830, ch. 148, §§ 1–8, 4 Stat. 411.

39. Southern congressmen approved the Bill 60 to 15; those from the North rejected it 79 to 42. Most of the 42 favorable votes from the North came from Jacksonian strongholds. The Senate vote seemed to run along party lines, but the House was different. Although there were 139 Democrats and 74 National Republicans in the House, the Bill passed 102 to 99, a majority of only five votes. Martin Van Buren later remarked on how the Indian question had cut away at the Jacksonian majority in the House. He noted that while 25 of the 26 representatives from Pennsylvania were Jacksonians, only six voted for the Removal Bill. Fear of the Quaker vote outweighed party loyalty. *The Autobiography of Martin Van Buren*, in 2 Annual Report of the American Historical Association for the Year 1918, at 289 (1920).

40. Letter from Webster to Clay, May 29, 1830, in The Private Correspondence of Henry Clay 274–76 (C. Colton ed. 1856).

41. *Id*. at 274.

42. *See* letter from Clay to Josiah Johnston, June 14, 1830, in *id*. at 278.

43. *See* the efforts of the Richmond Enquirer to counteract that charge. Richmond Enquirer, May 25, 1830, at 3, col. 3; May 28, 1830, at 3, col. 4; June 1, 1830, at 3, col. 6; June 4, 1830, at 3, col. 3, and at 4, col. 1; June 11, 1830, at 1, col. 5; June 15, 1830, at 2, col. 3, and at 4, col. 1; June 18, 1830, at 2, col. 1; June 25, 1830, at 2, col. 3, and at 4, col. 1; July 30, 1830, at 2, col. 3.

44. *See* letter from Webster to Evarts, June 28, 1830, and letter from Spencer to Evarts, June 21, 1830, Evarts Collection, Library of Congress.

into print the best speeches against the Removal Bill[45] and arranged for a reprinting of the *Essays of William Penn*.[46]

At about the time of these informal consultations in Washington, several prominent National Republicans in Congress, including Daniel Webster, Ambrose Spencer, and Peter Frelinghuysen, advised the Cherokee delegation, then in the capital, that they should hire eminent counsel to get the Supreme Court to protect their rights. They recommended William Wirt for the job.[47] The Cherokee case seemed tailor-made for Wirt. Wirt was not as open a partisan against Jackson as other leaders of the Washington bar. Despite his 12 years as Attorney General under Monroe and Adams, he gave the impression of being above politics. His loyalty to the federal courts in general and to the Supreme Court in particular was beyond question. His brand of legal oratory, which had both emotional and intellectual appeal, seemed admirably suited to a case that would be tried not only in the courts but in the press and at the polls.[48]

The efforts to get a case before the Supreme Court seemed only a part of the general plan to appeal the Cherokee cause to the people in the election of 1832. As his first act in the case, Wirt recommended that the Cherokees issue a public plea to the American people.[49] His second act was to write the Governor of Georgia, George Gilmer, suggesting that the State cooperate in settling the Cherokee controversy in the quiet and impartial atmosphere of the Supreme Court. He even speculated that the Supreme Court might uphold Georgia, since Georgia belonged to the Union while the Cherokee Nation was a foreign state.[50] This letter may well have been written by Wirt in order to make a public record of his willingness to settle. When published, the letter would absolve him of the charge of stirring up the controversy and would make Georgia appear in the wrong should she refuse to recognize the Court's jurisdiction. The sarcastic reply from the Governor[51] and the attacks on Wirt and the Supreme Court in the Jacksonian press[52] suggested that many Americans felt that the Supreme Court was far from an impartial tribunal and that the Cherokee issue could not be settled by judicial intervention.[53]

---

45. This volume ran over 300 pages. *See* SPEECHES ON THE REMOVAL BILL, *supra* note 34.

46. For the original printing see note 10 *supra*. The reprinting was in Philadelphia in 1830.

47. *See* letter from Wirt to Dabney Carr, June 21, 1830, in 2 J. KENNEDY, MEMOIRS OF THE LIFE OF WILLIAM WIRT, ATTORNEY-GENERAL OF THE UNITED STATES 290–92 (1849).

48. Apparently, Wirt would have been willing to continue as Attorney General under Jackson and only changed his mind about the General when it became clear that Jackson would not retain him. *Compare* his letter to his wife, Oct. 28, 1828, *with* one to Carr, Feb. 28, 1829, Wirt Papers, Maryland Historical Society. By 1830 Wirt was violently opposed to Jackson. *See* letter from Wirt to his wife, Jan. 28, 1830, *id.*

49. *See* letter from Spencer to Evarts, June 21, 1830, Evarts Collection, Library of Congress.

50. The letter was printed in Niles' Weekly Register, Sept. 18, 1830, at 69, col. 2.

51. *See* letter from Gilmer to Wirt, June 19, 1830, in Niles' Weekly Register, Sept. 18, 1830, at 70, col. 2.

52. *See* Richmond Enquirer, July 30, 1830, at 2, col. 5; Aug. 27, 1830, at 3, col. 2; Sept. 3, 1830, at 3, col. 4; Sept. 10, 1830, at 3, col. 1; Sept. 21, 1830, at 1, col. 6; Sept. 24, 1830, at 4, col. 3.

53. Jackson called "the course of Wirt . . . truly wicked." Letter to William B. Lewis, Aug. 25,

The letter to Gilmer and the decision to make a legal case out of the Indian question marked the beginning of a second change in the parties and the nature of the dispute. The controversy, first between the Cherokees and Georgia, and then between the Jacksonians and their opponents, was to become a contest matching the Supreme Court against Georgia and the President. The new issue was nothing less than the nature of the Union and the authority of the Supreme Court as the final arbiter of the constitutional system.

Wirt followed up his letter to the Governor with a long legal opinion supporting the Cherokee claims to soil and sovereignty.[54] The opinion first appeared in newspapers and later was widely circulated in pamphlet form.[55] Wirt drew heavily on the *Essays of William Penn*, the speeches in Congress on the Removal Bill, the New York decision of former Chancellor James Kent—*Jackson v. Goodell*[56]—and *Johnson v. McIntosh*.[57] The opinion argued that the Cherokee tribe was a foreign nation with full political and property rights within its boundaries, owing no duty of allegiance to either the State or the federal government. The condition that the Cherokees could sell their lands only to the United States was the sole limit on their property rights; the prohibition of relations with nations other than the United States was the sole limit on their political rights and sovereignty. Neither condition deprived them of their status as a foreign nation. The Cherokees, unlike many tribes in the Northeast, had grown in numbers and had never extinguished their national existence. The Georgia laws were unconstitutional because they violated federal treaties and laws, regulated a subject belonging exclusively to the federal government, and impaired the obligation of many contracts made by both the federal and state governments with the Indians. While this opinion fully supported the Cherokees' claim, not a single hint appeared as to how their rights might be tested in court.

Wirt never seemed to doubt the legality of the basic Cherokee claims: that Georgia could not legally enforce its laws in Indian territory and that Jackson did not have authority to remove the Indians forcibly. His doubts came on the method of getting a proper case before the Supreme Court.

1830, Jackson-Lewis Papers, New York Public Library. *See also* letters from Wirt to Thomas Swann, Sept. 13 & Oct. 4, 1830, Wirt Papers, Maryland Historical Society.

54. W. WIRT, OPINION ON THE RIGHT OF THE STATE OF GEORGIA TO EXTEND HER LAWS OVER THE CHEROKEE NATION (1830), reprinted in Niles' Weekly Register, Sept. 25, 1830, at 81, col. 1. As Attorney General, Wirt had been inconsistent on the question of Indian sovereignty and property rights. He had written an opinion in 1821 suggesting that the tribes were independent nations with a permanent right to the soil. 1 OP. ATT'Y GEN. 465 (1821). In 1824 he declared that the Cherokee tribe could not be considered a sovereign nation. 1 OP. ATT'Y GEN. 645 (1824). In 1828, in still a third opinion, he pronounced the Creeks a free and independent nation and found no reason to treat their contracts differently because "they resided within the local limits of the sovereignty of Georgia." 2 OP. ATT'Y GEN. 110, 135 (1828).

55. Copies were sent to all the governors, ex-presidents, "and other distinguished personages." Letter from John Ross to Wirt, Oct. 30, 1830, Wirt Papers, Maryland Historical Society.

56. 20 Johns. 693 (N.Y. 1823). *See* note 31 *supra*.

57. 21 U.S. (8 Wheat.) 543 (1823). *See* notes 9–12 *supra* and accompanying text.

In a long letter to his best friend, Dabney Carr of the Virginia Court of Appeals, Wirt explored the many difficulties in making a test case.[58] He thought that the Georgia courts would never enter a plea on their records that would permit an appeal to the Supreme Court by writ of error. This left only two courses: a suit by Chief John Ross against an officer of Georgia in a lower federal court, or a direct appeal to the original jurisdiction of the Supreme Court in the name of the Cherokee Nation. Success depended on whether the Justices of the Supreme Court considered the individual Cherokees to be aliens—as had Kent in *Jackson v. Goodell*—and their tribe to be a foreign state.

The letter also contained an unusual request. Would Carr ask Chief Justice Marshall for his unofficial opinion on these questions especially his interpretation of *Johnson v. McIntosh*? The possibility of conflict between the Supreme Court on one side and Georgia and the President on the other prompted this request, for Wirt believed that the State would resist and the President would refuse to enforce a decision favorable to the Indians. Answers from the Chief Justice might prevent mischief, for if the Cherokees had "no hope from the Supreme Court," they would move west rather than submit to Georgia law.[59] Carr should tell Marshall that while no case was pending one might be started if the past opinions of the Supreme Court did not prevent it.

After dismissing any thought of impropriety in Wirt's request, the Chief Justice declined to give an opinion on these "very interesting questions," which might soon come before him as a judge. Still, he had a confession to make:

> I have followed the debate in both houses of Congress with profound attention, and with deep interest, and have wished, most sincerely, that both the Executive and Legislative departments had thought differently on the subject. Humanity must bewail the course which is pursued, whatever may be the decision of policy.[60]

If Wirt failed to get Marshall's legal opinion, he got the next best thing: Marshall's personal sympathies. If the Chief Justice had wished to avoid the case, surely he would have replied differently. Apparently Wirt was not discouraged, for he afterwards planned to apply to the Chief Justice alone for an injunction to prevent the Georgia officials from enforcing the State's Indian laws. Delay in collecting the necessary documents led him to abandon this effort, however, in favor of an appeal to the entire Court during its regular session.[61]

---

58. Letter of June 21, 1830, in 2 J. KENNEDY, *supra* note 47, at 253–58.
59. *Id.* at 255.
60. Letter from Marshall to Carr, June 26, 1830, in 2 J. KENNEDY, *supra* note 47, at 296–97.
61. *See* letter from Wirt to John Ross, Nov. 15, 1830, in G. WOODWARD, THE CHEROKEES 165–66 (1963).

The Jacksonian press attacked Wirt for taking the case and accused the friends of the Cherokees of consulting with the Chief Justice and several of his associates.[62] John Ross, the principal chief of the Cherokees, was said to have consulted with William Johnson about the possibility of getting a case before his Circuit Court.[63] One anonymous correspondent, calling himself "Amicus Curiae," accused Story of prejudging the case because he had spoken at a party feast in Boston on the Fourth of July at which toasts were offered upholding the Cherokee rights and denouncing the actions of Jackson and Georgia.[64] The newspapers also insisted that the southern Indians would have moved after the passage of the Removal Bill if Wirt had not assured them more favorable treatment from appointed judges than they had received from the elected representatives of the people.[65] The deft hand of Henry Clay was seen in this assurance. The Kentuckian was attacked for sacrificing the sovereignty of Georgia in the interest of political ambition and personal hostility to Andrew Jackson.[66] Whether or not Clay intervened, Jeremiah Evarts certainly encouraged the suit. He had assured the Cherokee chiefs in July that if their case came "fairly before the Supreme Court your rights will be defended. It is so clear a case that the Court cannot mistake it. All the great lawyers in the country are on your side."[67]

Most of the "great lawyers" did support the Cherokee claims. Wirt's doubts on whether the Supreme Court would accept original jurisdiction in a suit brought by the Cherokee Nation led him to demand that Ross obtain legal opinions from a number of prominent lawyers.[68] John Sergeant —who served as counsel with Wirt—Ambrose Spencer, Daniel Webster, Horace Binney, and James Kent agreed that the Court could take jurisdiction.[69] Apparently only Binney and Kent wrote formal opinions.[70] Wirt especially prized the one submitted by Kent. The questions submitted to Kent revealed the doubts of Wirt and Evarts on the question of jurisdiction. These questions can be reduced to two important ones: Did the Cherokee

---

62. Both the Richmond Enquirer, Sept. 10, 1830, at 2, col. 5, and Niles' Weekly Register, Sept. 18, 1830, at 69, col. 1, reprinted such charges from the Georgia Journal, Aug. 28, 1830. *See also* Savannah Republican, Aug. 19, 1830; letter from Jackson to William B. Lewis, Aug. 25, 1830, Jackson-Lewis Papers, New York Public Library.

63. *See* articles from the Augusta Chronicle and the Georgia Journal, reprinted in Richmond Enquirer, Sept. 10, 1830, at 2, col. 5; *cf.* Niles' Weekly Register, Sept. 18, 1830, at 69, col. 1.

64. Richmond Enquirer, Nov. 5, 1830, at 3, col. 3.

65. *See* Richmond Enquirer, Oct. 29, 1830, at 2, col. 5; July 30, 1830, at 2, col. 2.

66. *See* Richmond Enquirer, Sept. 24, 1830, at 4, col. 3.

67. Letter of [July 30, 1830?], in G. WOODWARD, *supra* note 61, at 163.

68. *See* letter from Wirt to Carr, undated 1830, in 2 J. KENNEDY, *supra* note 47, at 303.

69. A letter from Wirt to his wife, Feb. 10, 1831, stated that "Kent, Binney, Sergeant, and Webster (I understand) concurred with me in thinking, that the Court had jurisdiction . . . ." Wirt Papers, Maryland Historical Society.

70. *See* letter from Wirt to Ross, Nov. 15, 1830, in G. WOODWARD, *supra* note 61, at 166.

Nation constitute a foreign state? Did their claims raise legal rather than political questions?[71]

Kent's opinion answered both questions favorably to the Indians and encouraged Wirt to appeal directly to the Supreme Court. But Wirt's doubts about the Court's willingness to accept original jurisdiction remained.[72] His decision to make the direct appeal came not so much by choice as by the elimination of other alternatives. Wirt had toyed with the idea of having a Cherokee gold-digger sue as an alien in a federal circuit court on a charge of false imprisonment,[73] and with having Ross seek an injunction against the Georgia officials who were executing the State's Indian laws, especially those expropriating the tribal gold mines.[74] Ross probably had one of these cases in mind when he consulted with Justice Johnson, in whose circuit such a case would have been brought.[75] Given Johnson's unfavorable opinion in *Cherokee Nation v. Georgia*,[76] it seems unlikely that he encouraged a suit. Both Wirt and Evarts had also seriously considered bringing a case before the Supreme Court by writ of error.[77] Wirt had foreseen difficulties in such a course from the beginning,[78] and the case of *Georgia v. Tassel* seemed to document these difficulties.[79]

The execution of George Tassel, a Cherokee convicted by a Georgia court for murder committed in Indian territory, revealed the State's determination to resist a writ of error from the Supreme Court of the United States.[80] The state court decision, allegedly written by William H. Crawford completely vindicated Georgia's sovereign right to govern the Indians and denounced Northern fanatics for making the Cherokee question a party issue.[81] The Governor and state legislature publicly vowed never to let the *Tassel* case, or any other case, be carried to the Supreme Court.[82] The execution of George Tassel in the face of a writ of error issued by Chief Justice John Marshall showed that Georgia meant business. The Jacksonian press warned the Supreme Court not to interfere,[83] and Congress echoed the

---

71. Kent's opinion, which is dated October 23, 1830, is printed in R. PETERS, THE CASE OF THE CHEROKEE NATION AGAINST THE STATE OF GEORGIA: ARGUED AND DETERMINED AT THE SUPREME COURT OF THE UNITED STATES, JANUARY TERM, 1831, App. No. I, at 225 (1831). The questions submitted to him appear at 225–26.

72. *See* letter from Wirt to his wife, Feb. 10, 1831, Wirt Papers, Maryland Historical Society.

73. *See* letter from Evarts to Ross, in G. WOODWARD, *supra* note 61, at 163.

74. *See* letter from Wirt to Carr, in 2 J. KENNEDY, *supra* note 47, at 295.

75. For references to this meeting and Ross' comments see the materials cited in note 63 *supra*.

76. 30 U.S. (5 Pet.) at 20.

77. *See* letter from Wirt to Carr, June 21, 1830, in 2 J. KENNEDY, *supra* note 47, at 294; letter from Evarts to Ross, in G. WOODWARD, *supra* note 61, at 163.

78. *See* letter from Wirt to Carr, June 21, 1830, in 2 J. KENNEDY, *supra* note 47, at 294.

79. See the facts and the decision printed in the Richmond Enquirer, Dec. 9, 1830, at 4, col. 1.

80. For the circumstances of the execution and the attempt to deliver the citation see *id.*, Jan. 8, 1831, at 3, col. 6. The writ appears in *id.*, Jan. 4, 1831, at 2, col. 5.

81. Richmond Enquirer, Dec. 9, 1830, at 4, col. 1.

82. For the message of the Governor and the resolutions of the legislature see Niles' Weekly Register, Jan. 8, 1831, at 338, col. 1.

83. Richmond Enquirer, Jan. 4, 1831, at 2, col. 5; Jan. 8, 1831, at 3, col. 6; Jan. 13, 1831, at 3, col. 2; article from the Georgia Journal in the Richmond Enquirer, Feb. 5, 1831, at 4, col. 1.

warning by debating late in January 1831 a resolution calling for the repeal of section 25 of the Judiciary Act of 1789, which permitted the review of state court decisions by writ of error.[84] The *Tassel* case and the debate in Congress revealed on the eve of the *Cherokee Nation* case that the controversy had become a battle between those who would defy and those who would defend the authority of the Supreme Court.

The Court itself seemed on trial when on March 5 Wirt and Sergeant moved for an injunction to stop Georgia from executing her Indian laws. No counsel appeared for Georgia. The State refused to submit to the indignity of being hauled before the Supreme Court by a band of Indians. Wirt and Sergeant tried to prove that the Cherokees had the right to sue directly in the Supreme Court as a foreign nation and that the Court had the power to grant the injunction against Georgia. They insisted that the Cherokees owed allegiance neither to Georgia nor to the United States. The Cherokees, a nation of aliens whose rights to govern themselves within their own territory had been repeatedly recognized by treaties, had to constitute a foreign nation. No one had questioned the foreign status of the small nations of Europe who had long been surrounded by and under the protection of a stronger power. The law of nations and the treaties and laws of the United States had all recognized the Cherokee Nation as a foreign state. While admitting that not all of the treaty rights of the Cherokees could be judicially protected, Wirt and Sergeant insisted that the Supreme Court could defend their rights to both soil and self-government.[85]

In his eloquent peroration Wirt came to the question that must have been on the mind of all who heard him. How could the Court enforce its decree? Instead of an answer, he gave a ringing defense of the Supreme Court as the final arbiter of the Constitution. Wirt compared the Union without this Court to a solar system without a sun.[86]

> [I]*f we have a government at all*, [said Wirt,] there is no difficulty . . . . In pronouncing your decree you will have *declared the law*; and it is a part of the sworn duty of the President of the United States, to "take care that the laws be faithfully executed." It is not for him, nor for the party defendant, to sit in appeal on your decision. The constitution confers no such power. He is authorized to call out the military power of the country to enforce the execution of the laws. It is your

---

84. *See* 7 CONG. DEB. 532, 534–35, 542, 620, 659, 665, 731, 739, app. lxxvii, lxxxi (1831). The debates certainly worried the judges. *See* letter from Story to George Ticknor, Jan. 22, 1831, in 2 LIFE AND LETTERS OF JOSEPH STORY, *supra* note 3, at 48–49; letter from Story to his wife, Jan. 28, 1831, in *id.* at 43–44; 8 MEMOIRS OF JOHN QUINCY ADAMS 302 (C. Adams ed. 1876). Charles Warren says that "[i]n 1831 there occurred the most determined and the most dangerous attack on the Supreme Court and its jurisdiction under the 25th Section." Warren, *Legislative and Judicial Attacks on the Supreme Court of the United States—A History of the Twenty-Fifth Section of the Judiciary Act*, 47 AM. L. REV. 161 (1913).

85. The arguments were printed in R. PETERS, *supra* note 71, at 38 (Sergeant) and 65 (Wirt). They can also be followed in the detailed notes taken by Thompson, now in the Huntington Library. They were favorably reported in the Am. Spectator & Wash. City Chronicle, Mar. 19, 1831; Niles' Weekly Register, Mar. 26, 1831, at 61, col. 2.

86. R. PETERS, *supra* note 71, at 156.

function to say what the law is. It is his to cause it to be executed. If he refuses to perform his duty, the constitution has provided a remedy.[87]

Wirt dared the Court to challenge President Jackson by issuing the injunction. In effect he was asking the Justices to turn the case of *Cherokee Nation v. Georgia* into *Supreme Court v. Andrew Jackson.* He told them that while they were the judges the people would be the jury. "At all events let us do our duty, and the people of the United States will take care that others do theirs."[88]

Only 4 days after the argument closed, and on the last day of the session, the Supreme Court declined Wirt's challenge. The *National Intelligencer* reported that Marshall read the decision of the Court denying jurisdiction and that Henry Baldwin and William Johnson delivered concurring opinions, which agreed in dismissing the case but differed with the reasoning of the Chief Justice.[89] Nine days later the *Intelligencer* commented with surprise that it had only recently learned that Smith Thompson and Joseph Story had dissented.[90] A correspondent for the *Richmond Enquirer,* writing on the day the decision was given, stated that while Thompson and Story were not present "it is said they dissented on every point."[91] Those present in the courtroom on March 18 heard only three opinions read: the majority opinion of Marshall and the concurring opinions of Baldwin and Johnson.

Considering the pressures under which he wrote, Marshall delivered an ingenious opinion. His approach to the *Cherokee* case is reminiscent of *Marbury v. Madison.*[92] Then too, when faced by the resistance of a popular President and unencumbered by the arguments of defense counsel, the Chief Justice had commented favorably on the plaintiff's claims, had criticized the President, and had avoided the threatened disobedience of the Court's decree by dismissing the case for want of jurisdiction. Opinions on the political status of the tribes had polarized since *Johnson v. McIntosh,*[93] and both sides in the Cherokee controversy now tended to agree that the tribes must be considered either foreign or subject nations.[94] Marshall accepted neither alternative: to declare them subject nations and leave them at the mercy of the states, or to pronounce them foreign nations and free them from federal control. Instead he chose a third alternative, which was suited to the peculiar relations between the United States and the Indian tribes, and which he had suggested earlier in *McIntosh.*[95] In the

---

87. *Id.* at 155.
88. *Id.*
89. Mar. 19, 1831, at 3, col. 5. *See also* Niles' Weekly Register, Mar. 26, 1831, at 67, col. 2.
90. Daily Nat'l Intelligencer, Mar. 28, 1831, at 3, col. 2.
91. Richmond Enquirer, Mar. 24, 1831, at 3, col. 3.
92. 5 U.S. (1 Cranch) 137 (1803).
93. *See* text accompanying notes 9–12 *supra.*
94. *See, e.g.,* Andrew Jackson's Message to the Senate, Feb. 22, 1831, in 2 MESSAGES, *supra* note 5, at 539; W. WIRT, *supra* note 54, at 3.
95. *See* note 11 *supra* and accompanying text.

*Cherokee* case he described the tribes as "domestic dependent nations," whose relation to the United States resembled that of a "ward to his guardian."[96]

Still, Marshall did not stop with a nod to past precedents and judicial practices; he left a hint as to future actions. While rejecting the Cherokee claim to sue as a foreign nation, Marshall let it be known that a majority of the Justices did regard this tribe "as a distinct political society separated from others, capable of managing its own affairs and governing itself" and retaining an "unquestionable" right to its lands.[97] Some of the complaints in the bill of injunction, such as those concerning the tribes' powers of self-government, raised political questions beyond the authority of the Court; but others, touching its property rights, might be decided in the "proper case with the proper parties."[98] While Marshall decided against the Cherokees on the question of jurisdiction, he hinted that he sided with them on the merits and even suggested a method of getting a case properly before the Court in the future.

Justice Baldwin justly complained that "the reasons for the judgment . . . seem to be more important than the judgment itself."[99] He joined Marshall in denying jurisdiction, but his concurring opinion reads like a dissent; he even refers to himself as a dissenting judge.[100] Baldwin denied that the Indian tribes could be considered states or distinct political communities. Marshall, himself, in *Johnson v. McIntosh* had not called them "nations or states" or declared them to possess "any national capacity or attributes of sovereignty in their relations to the general or State governments." A lengthy examination of Indian relations from the Revolution to his own day convinced Baldwin that within its borders Georgia possessed full political jurisdiction over the Indians and absolute title to the Indian lands, subject only to a temporary right of occupancy. Justice Johnson also doubted that the Cherokees could be considered a sovereign state. The treaties signed with the Cherokees secured for them merely the property rights needed by a nation of hunters, and had ceded to the states and the United States the ultimate title to the soil. The federal government had never intended and lacked power to create permanent Indian communities within the limits of the states.

Johnson conceded that the privilege of personal self-government had never been taken from the Cherokees, but argued that the tribe could retain that privilege only by moving west.[101] Johnson emphasized that the entire

96. 30 U.S. (5 Pet.) at 17.
97. *Id.* at 16, 17.
98. *Id.* at 20.
99. *Id.* at 32.
100. *Id.* at 42, 48.
101. *Id.* at 20–27.

case presented a political question for the President rather than a legal question for the Court. The Court lacked both the authority to decide such questions of policy and the power to enforce its decisions.

When the Supreme Court ended its session, the public knew about only these three opinions. While Marshall had spoken of the Cherokees' political and property rights and even hinted that the Court might protect their property rights in some future case, his denial of jurisdiction meant that he could not fully discuss the merits in *Cherokee Nation*. The weight of argument marshalled in the lengthy opinions of Baldwin and Johnson against the Cherokees' claims seemed overwhelming. Baldwin's use of *Johnson v. McIntosh* in rejecting the Cherokees' argument for sovereignty must have disturbed Marshall; the shouts of glee from the Jacksonian press that the *Cherokee* decision vindicated the President's Indian policy surely angered him; the rumors that the decision had so discouraged the Cherokees that they were preparing to treat with Jackson must have saddened the Chief Justice.[102] If Marshall had second thoughts about his decision, especially about its effect on the public,[103] it seemed too late: The opinions had been read, and the Court had risen.

The Chief Justice chose an unusual solution to his problem. This judge, who had made almost a fetish of the unity of the Supreme Court, now encouraged the dissenters, Thompson and Story, to write an opinion. Story later wrote that "neither Judge T. nor myself contemplated delivering a dissenting opinion, until the Chief Justice suggested to us the propriety of it, and his own desire that we should do it."[104] Thompson wrote a dissent that appeared after the Court had risen. It clearly replies to the arguments of Johnson and Baldwin on the merits of the case—points that Marshall had necessarily left largely untouched. Baldwin even accused Thompson of drafting the dissent to answer his own opinion.[105]

Thompson relied heavily on the arguments of Wirt and Sergeant. He quickly pointed out that he and Story differed from Marshall only in regarding the Cherokees as a foreign nation; all three agreed they were a nation. The Cherokees had always held the land and governed themselves; and after treating with the United States they continued to do so, save only that they accepted the protection of the United States and agreed to sell their land only to their protector. Neither these restrictions nor the location of their territory within the chartered limits of Georgia deprived them of their foreign status, stated Thompson. In spite of these restrictions, said

---

102. *See, e.g.*, Richmond Enquirer, Mar. 24, 1831, at 3, col. 3; Mar. 29, at 3, col. 1; Apr. 29, 1831, at 2, col. 2; June 14, 1831, at 3, col. 3; Nat'l Intelligencer, Mar. 29, 1831, at 1, col. 1; Apr. 5, 1831, at 3 col. 1; Niles' Weekly Register, Apr. 2, 1831, at 82, col. 1.
103. *See* letter from Marshall to Richard Peters, May 19, 1831, Peters Papers, Pennsylvania Historical Society.
104. Letter from Story to Peters, May 17, 1831, *id.*
105. *Id.*

Thompson, Justice Johnson in *Fletcher v. Peck* had declared the Indian tribes of Georgia independent states with the absolute title to their soil. A nation of aliens governing themselves within their own territory had to be considered a foreign state,[106] and the treaties with the United States clearly recognized the Cherokee Nation as a foreign state.

After concluding that the Supreme Court had original jurisdiction, Thompson took up the question of whether the Court could provide a remedy for the wrongs that the Cherokees suffered at the hands of Georgia. Like Marshall, he conceded that the Court could not grant relief against state laws that were inconsistent with recognition of the national character and political independence of the Cherokees; and like Marshall, he thought the Court could protect the property rights of the tribe. The Chief Justice had only hinted at the nature of such a future case. Thompson explained it in detail. He singled out an act of Georgia passed in December of 1830 that authorized state officials to seize the gold mines and survey the land within the Cherokee territory. He thought the Supreme Court could enjoin the state officials from executing such an act because it infringed property rights secured by treaties.[107] Ironically, the property-minded Justice ignored another act passed in 1830 that prohibited white men from living in the Cherokee territory without a license from the Governor. Several ministers, including Samuel A. Worcester, had already been arrested under this law.[108]

While Thompson's dissent could not change the legal effect of the decision, it changed its political effect. On March 18 the Court had rejected the Cherokees' plea for protection. Two of the three opinions read that day had belittled the political and property rights of the Cherokees; only one had hinted that the tribe had rights that the Court might protect in some future case. Publication of Thompson's opinion reinforced those hints. Actually, the six man court (Duvall was absent) had split into three pairs. Marshall, ostensibly speaking for the majority but actually only for himself and John McLean, ruled that the Court lacked jurisdiction because the Cherokees were not a foreign nation—though they were a distinct political community with an unquestionable right to their lands. Baldwin and Johnson, while concurring in rejecting jurisdiction, thought very little of the political and property rights of the Cherokees. Thompson and Story pronounced the Cherokees a foreign state entitled to at least part of the remedy they requested. Thus on the question of jurisdiction, the Court split four to

---

106. 30 U.S. (5 Pet.) at 50–74. Thompson drew on Johnson's opinion in *Fletcher v. Peck* and Chancellor Kent's in *Jackson v. Goodell. See* notes 6–8, 31 *supra* and accompanying text. Thompson took lengthy notes on the arguments of Wirt and Sergeant, which are now in the Huntington Library.

107. 30 U.S. (5 Pet.) at 75–80. Story was "entirely satisfied with . . . Thompson's opinion." Letter from Story to Peters, Sept. 2, 1831, Peters Papers, Pennsylvania Historical Society.

108. *See* note 115 *infra* and accompanying text.

two against the Cherokees; but on the merits, which should not have been discussed by the majority, the Court divided four to two in favor of the Cherokees. At the heart of it all was John Marshall: He wrote the decision and was at least a silent partner in the dissent.

The court reporter, Richard Peters, gave another unusual twist to the case by announcing that he would publish a separate report to be sold to the public.[109] The items that Peters printed certainly bolstered the Cherokee side of the question. The volume included the arguments of Wirt and Sergeant (which ran to 128 pages), the legal opinion of James Kent on the Cherokee claims, the treaties with the Cherokees, the Federal Intercourse Act of 1802, the Georgia Indian laws, and naturally the opinions of the Justices. Though it did publish the opinions of Baldwin and Johnson, they took up only 30 pages of the 286 page book. A reader of this volume would put it down with a much different view of the Court's attitude on Cherokee rights than he would have carried from the Courtroom on March 18th after hearing the opinions of Marshall, Baldwin, and Johnson.

Marshall, Story, and Thompson were among the strongest supporters of this volume, while Baldwin was its staunchest opponent. The comments of Marshall and Story are worth quoting at length.

> I should be glad to see the whole case [wrote Marshall]. It is one in which a very narrow view has been taken in the opinion which is pronounced by the Court. The judge who pronounced that opinion had not time to consider the case in its various bearings; and had his time been so abundant, did not think it truly proper to pass the narrow limits that circumscribed the matter on which the decision of the court turned. The dissenting opinion, it is true, go [sic] more at large into the subject, but those which were delivered in Court look to one side of the question only, and the public must wish to see both sides.[110]

Story hoped for great things from the volume.

> The publication will do a great deal of good—the subject unites the *moral* sense of all New England—It comes home to the religious feelings of our people. It touches their sensibilities, and sinks to the very bottom of their sense of Justice— Depend on it there is a depth of degradation in our national conduct, which will irresistibly lead to better things.[111]

On May 10, John Ross, the Cherokee Chief, had written to Wirt begging for a clear explanation of the Court's decision. He indicated then that the tribe would remain until their claims were adjudicated "by the proper tribunal."[112] Eleven days later the Cherokee Nation issued still another

---

109. R. PETERS, *supra* note 71. For a contemporary announcement of the publication see Niles' Weekly Register, Mar. 26, 1831, at 68, col. 2. Martin Van Buren later labeled this volume a cheap electioneering trick. *The Autobiography of Martin Van Buren, supra* note 39, at 292.

110. Letter from Marshall to Peters, May 19, 1831, Peters Papers, Pennsylvania Historical Society. *See also* letter from Thompson to Peters, May 27, 1831, *id.*

111. Letter from Story to Peters, June 24, 1831, *id.* Kent "hoped it would be a useful publication." Letter from Kent to Peters, June 30, 1831, *id.*

112. Letter from John Ross to Wirt, May 10, 1831, Wirt Papers, Maryland Historical Society.

appeal to the American people.[113] While admitting that the Supreme Court had refused for the present to redress the wrongs done to the Cherokees of Georgia, the appeal stressed the Court's acceptance of their nation as a sovereign state immune from the laws of Georgia. It concluded with the declaration that the *Cherokee Nation* decision clearly bound President Jackson to protect the political and property rights of their tribe against Georgia. Thus the friends of the Cherokees continued to follow the two-fold plan of appealing to both the public and the courts.

Marshall's dicta, later supported by Thompson's dissent, had encouraged a second Cherokee case at the 1832 Term of the Court. *Worcester v. Georgia* may not have been the type of case Marshall had in mind, for it involved personal rather than property rights; but it could hardly have been better from a political point of view. The trials and tribulations of Samuel A. Worcester seem straight out of a heroic epic—a genre always irresistible to the American public. Worcester was a white missionary, the nephew of the founder of the powerful American Board of Commissioners for the Foreign Missions, and the eighth generation in an unbroken line of Congregational ministers. He had abandoned the pleasant life of a Vermont minister to teach the gospel and civilization to the Cherokees. Letters from him had been used in the *Essays of William Penn* and in the debate on the Removal Bill; and for years he had served as an unofficial adviser to the editor of the *Cherokee Phoenix*, an influential Indian newspaper.[114] Worcester was prepared to risk even his freedom by defying a Georgia law that prohibited white men from residing in the Cherokee Territory after December 1830, without a license from the state.

On a quiet Sunday in March 1831, just following church services, the Georgia Guard arrested Worcester and several others for violating the 1830 law.[115] Only the day before in Washington John Sergeant had asked the Supreme Court to protect Cherokee rights in *Cherokee Nation v. Georgia*. On March 26, a Georgia court, obviously trying to avoid an appealable case, upheld the Georgia law but released Worcester and another missionary on the grounds that the support they received from the United States government made them federal employees, who were specifically exempted from the law. The missionaries, who had deliberately courted prosecution in order to bring the question of Cherokee sovereignty before the Supreme Court, had tried to avoid this result by refusing to plead that they were federal officials.[116] When Worcester and the other missionary

    113. Niles' Weekly Register, June 25, 1831, at 298, col. 1, printed the appeal.
    114. D. Van Every, Disinherited: The Lost Birthright of the American Indian 62–63 (1966).
    115. The account of the arrest in the Cherokee Phoenix was reprinted in Niles' Weekly Register, Apr. 9, 1831, at 95, col. 2.
    116. State v. Worcester (Gwinnett County Super. Ct., Mar. 26, 1831), in Niles' Weekly Register, June 4, 1831, at 244, col. 2.

still refused to leave the Indian country, the Governor persuaded President Jackson to deny that they were federal employees and to remove Worcester as Postmaster of New Echota.[117] With these obstacles removed Georgia again arrested them and a state court in September convicted all the missionaries of violating the licensing law and sentenced them to 4 years of hard labor.[118] Nine of them accepted pardons, but Worcester and Elizur Butler rejected offers of freedom in order to get the Cherokees their second day in Court.[119]

When that day arrived, the pressures on the Court seemed almost an exaggerated replay of those in 1831. Again the Governor, legislature, and courts of Georgia publicly vowed to disregard any unfavorable ruling from the Supreme Court.[120] Indeed, it seems astonishing that the clerk of the Georgia court returned the record in reply to the writ of error. Again rumors, which few questioned, declared that President Jackson would never enforce a decree ordering the release of Worcester and Butler.[121] If anything the political complexion of the case was even more obvious than in 1831. The lawyers for Worcester and Butler were deeply involved in the presidential contest of 1832: Wirt as Anti-Masonic candidate for the presidency, and Sergeant as the vice-presidential nominee of the National Republicans.

The National Republican Convention on December 24, 1831, had already seized the Indian question and the missionaries' plight as party issues. James Barbour's address to the Convention emphasized their importance.[122] After attacking Jackson's policies on removals from office, on the tariff, on internal improvements, and on the Bank of the United States, Barbour turned to the Indian question, which he called "perhaps the most important of all." Instead of resisting Georgia's violations of Indian rights by military force, Jackson had left the Indians at the mercy of Georgia by withdrawing federal troops. But Barbour saved his most biting comments for Georgia's jailing of the missionaries.

> The recent inhuman and unconstitutional outrages committed under the authority of Georgia upon the persons of several unoffending citizens heretofore residing as missionaries within the territory of the Cherokees, constitutes, perhaps, the most unjustifiable portion of these proceedings. They have received, like the rest, the countenance and approbation of the general executive. Few examples can be

---

117. Phillips, *supra* note 18, at 79.
118. State v. Missionaries (Gwinnett County Super. Ct., Sept. 15, 1831), in Niles' Weekly Register, Oct. 29, 1831, at 174, col. 1.
119. *See* Phillips, *supra* note 18, at 80; Niles' Weekly Register, Oct. 29, 1831, at 176, col. 2; Oct. 8, 1831, at 102, col. 1.
120. *See, e.g.,* Message of Governor Lumpkin to Georgia Legislature, Nov. 25, 1831, in Niles' Weekly Register, Dec. 24, 1831, at 212, col. 1; Richmond Enquirer, Dec. 13, 1831, at 3, col. 3.
121. The Richmond Enquirer suggested in an editorial that if the Court ruled in favor of Worcester and Butler, Jackson would probably not enforce the decree. Dec. 10, 1831, at 1, col. 6.
122. The address appears in Niles' Weekly Register, Dec. 24, 1831, at 307, col. 1.

found, even in the history of barbarous communities, in which the sacred character of a minister of religion has furnished so slight a protection against disrespect and violence to the persons invested with it. We rejoice to learn that this subject will shortly be presented to congress and to the people, in full detail, and in a form fitted to excite the attention which it so well deserves.[123]

While Barbour failed to mention that the *Worcester* case was pending before the Supreme Court, his concluding remarks censured Jackson for openly encouraging attacks on the Supreme Court such as the efforts to repeal section 25 of the Judiciary Act of 1789. He praised the presidential nominee of the National Republicans, Henry Clay, as a man who would "assert the supremacy of the laws."

The National Republican press and the Cherokee delegation carried Barbour's message to the people. Party newspapers gave the public bulletins on the deplorable conditions in the Georgia penitentiary where Worcester and Butler were held. The Cherokee delegation toured northern cities making new converts, speaking to meetings, and encouraging new memorials to Congress.[124] Joseph Story had felt their spell when he met them in Philadelphia on his way to the Court session in Washington. Story was so busy telling his wife how the Cherokee chiefs "conversed with singular force and propriety of language upon their own case, the law of which they perfectly understood," that he forgot to explain the propriety of discussing a pending case with interested parties.[125]

Both Story and the Cherokee chiefs were present on February 20 when Wirt and Sergeant began their argument in *Worcester v. Georgia*.[126] Georgia again refused to appear. Wirt and Sergeant first argued that *Cohens v. Virginia* established the Supreme Court's authority to issue writs of error in criminal cases. To the charge that the Georgia court would never execute a decree from the Supreme Court ordering the release of the missionaries, they replied that the decisions of the highest court bound the state judges and were "final and conclusive." They not only attacked the constitutionality of the Act of 1830, but claimed that all Georgia's Indian laws violated the Constitution by regulating a subject that belonged exclusively to the federal government and by conflicting with the laws and treaties of the United States. Wirt and Sergeant could have argued the case on the narrow ground that the Georgia Act of 1830 conflicted with the Federal Act of 1802. They chose instead to argue their case on the broadest grounds in

---

123. *Id.* at 311, col. 2.
124. Niles' Weekly Register, Nov. 19, 1831, at 227, col. 2; letter from Cherokee Chief John to Robert Vaux, Jan. 18, 1832, Vaux Papers, Pennsylvania Historical Society.
125. Letter from Story to his wife, Jan. 13, 1832, in 2 THE LIFE AND LETTERS OF JOSEPH STORY, *supra* note 3, at 79.
126. The arguments have been taken from the manuscript brief of John Sergeant, Sergeant Papers, Pennsylvania Historical Society, and from the short outline in Peters' report, 31 U.S. (5 Pet.) at 534–36.

order to get the general question of Cherokee rights before the Supreme Court.

This time Marshall took 2 weeks to write his opinion. And this time, speaking for Thompson, Story, and Duvall, he braved the wrath of Georgia and Jackson and risked the prestige of the Court by declaring all of the recent Georgia Indian laws unconstitutional and ordering the missionaries released. He borrowed freely from Thompson's dissenting opinion in *Cherokee Nation* and the legal arguments of Wirt and Sergeant. The tone, reasoning, and direction of his decision suggests that he tried to write a reply to the opinions of Baldwin and Johnson in *Cherokee Nation*. In other words, he wrote in 1832 the opinion that he could not write in 1831.[127]

Parts of his argument rest on questionable interpretations of the history of Indian relations, and some conflict with statements he made in *Johnson v. McIntosh*. The *Worcester* opinion declared that the tribes had never been conquered and that the British Crown claimed only the exclusive right to purchase whatever land the Indians were willing to sell.[128] The *Worcester* decision also claimed that the British had never interfered with the internal affairs of the Indians or coerced a surrender of Indian lands.[129] The *Johnson* decision had stated that the British had maintained by the sword their claims to ultimate soil and sovereignty as far west as the Mississippi. The *Johnson* opinion had also asserted that the act of discovery had conferred upon the colonies, and thus the states, the right to seize land by conquest.[130]

Marshall examined the Indian treaties at length in *Worcester*, especially those of Hopewell and Holston, which had received so much attention from Johnson and Baldwin in the *Cherokee Nation* case. In none of these treaties had the Indians yielded their sovereignty. The Chief Justice saw only one limitation on Indian sovereignty—the treaties excluded them from intercourse with any foreign powers; but he reasoned that placing themselves under the protection of a larger state did not rob the Cherokee Nation of sovereignty any more than it did some of the smaller nations of Europe. The United States called the tribes nations and it used the term in the same sense as it did when treating with all the other nations of the world.[131] The arguments Marshall used in *Worcester* to show that the Cherokees were sovereign and therefore free from the control of Georgia were the same ones Wirt, Sergeant, and Thompson had used in *Cherokee Nation* to prove the quite separate proposition that the tribe was a foreign nation for the purposes of establishing original jurisdiction under article III.

---

127. The presence of Duvall and the absence of Johnson meant that the Court was more favorable toward Cherokee rights in 1832 than it had been in 1831.
128. 31 U.S. (6 Pet.) at 545–46.
129. *Id.* at 547.
130. 21 U.S. (8 Wheat.) at 574.
131. 31 U.S. (6 Pet.) at 551, 560–61.

But merely freeing them from Georgia did not satisfy Marshall, for this would leave them at the mercy of the federal government in the person of Andrew Jackson. He insisted that the Act for the promotion of civilization passed in 1819 revealed the intention of the federal government to preserve the national character of the tribes and showed its "settled purpose to fix the Indians in their country by giving them security at home."[132]

Most of Marshall's opinion was an elaborate argument for Cherokee independence and most of it was unnecessary to a decision resting on the conflict between federal and Georgia law. His 28 page decision did not reach Worcester and his predicament until the next-to-last page. That Marshall would have preferred a property-right case was obvious. But he insisted that Worcester could not be less entitled to protection because his liberty was affected rather than his property rights.[133] The Chief Justice ruled that Georgia had arrested Worcester while he was "under guardianship of treaties guaranteeing the country in which he resided," and "performing, under the sanction of the chief magistrate of the Union, those duties which the humane policy adopted by Congress had recommended." He was convicted under a law "repugnant to the Constitution, laws, and treaties of the United States."[134] But Marshall did not confine himself to these narrow grounds. He chose instead to declare the whole "system of legislation lately adopted by the Legislature of Georgia in relation to the Cherokee Nation . . . repugnant to the Constitution, laws, and treaties of the United States," because it interfered forcibly with the relations established according to the Constitution between the United States and the Cherokee Nation.[135]

Justice McLean refused to accept Marshall's broad vindication of Cherokee rights. He rested his concurring opinion on the treaties of the United States and on the Intercourse Act of 1802. But while admitting the right of the Indian tribes to remain in Georgia under these laws and treaties, McLean thought that

> the exercise of the power of self-government by the Indians, within a State, is undoubtedly contemplated to be temporary. . . . [A] sound national policy does require that the Indian tribes within our States should exchange their territories . . . or, eventually, consent to become amalgamated in our political communities.[136]

---

132. *Id.* at 557.

133. *Id.* at 562. In the *Cherokee Nation* case Marshall had hinted that the proper case would be one involving property. *See* text accompanying note 98 *supra*. Wirt in preparing for the *Worcester* case had been especially interested in the property of the Missionary Board in Cherokee territory. *See* letter from David Green, Secretary of the Board, to Wirt, Sept. 24, 1831, Wirt Papers, Maryland Historical Society.

134. 31 U.S. (6 Pet.) at 562.

135. *Id.* at 561.

136. *Id.* at 593. *See also* his circuit decisions in United States v. Bailey, 24 F. Cas. 937 No. 14,495 (C.C. Tenn. 1834), and United States v. Cisna, 25 F. Cas. 422 No. 14,795 (C.C. Ohio 1835).

However, if the policy of the government is to withdraw its protection from Indians who have uniformly exercised the power of self-government,

> the laws and treaties which impose duties and obligations on the general government should be abrogated by the powers competent to do so. So long as those laws and treaties exist, having been formed within the sphere of the federal powers, they must be respected and enforced by the appropriate organs of the federal government.[137]

Worcester had "entered Cherokee country . . . under the protection of the treaties of the United States, and the law of 1802," and was deprived of his liberty by the administration of Georgia laws that were repugnant to them.[138]

McLean also differed from Marshall in declaring that the plaintiff could complain of the Georgia laws only insofar as they affected him and not of their general effect on the political and property rights of the Cherokee Nation. McLean, always the political candidate, even suggested that these Georgia laws might flow from the sense of wrong that the State felt because 30 years had passed "since the Federal government had engaged to extinguish the Indian title within the limits of Georgia."[139]

Baldwin dissented on the technical ground that the record had been signed by the clerk instead of by the judge of the state court. On the merits of the case, the official report merely stated that his opinion remained the same as in the *Cherokee Nation* decision. The reporter, Richard Peters, simply noted that Baldwin's opinion had not been delivered to him; a newspaper later reported that Baldwin had written a long opinion.[140] Johnson, who would probably have dissented, had been kept away from the entire session of the Court by illness.

The Court had delivered its opinion on March 3, 1832. Two days later it issued a special mandate to the Georgia court ordering it to reverse its decision and to release Worcester and Butler.[141] The Court's decision had hardly been delivered when the anti-Jackson press began to berate President Jackson for not enforcing the decree of the Supreme Court. Article after article depicted the poor missionaries languishing in the Georgia penitentiary while the President allowed Georgia to defy federal laws, treaties, and the decision of the Supreme Court.[142] Most historians, with the exception of Charles Warren, have echoed these cries. Invariably, they conclude their

---

137. 31 U.S. (6 Pet.) at 594.
138. *Id.* at 595–96.
139. *Id.* at 595.
140. Richmond Enquirer, Mar. 30, 1832, at 3, col. 1.
141. OPINION OF THE SUPREME COURT OF THE UNITED STATES, AT JANUARY TERM DELIVERED BY MR. CHIEF JUSTICE MARSHALL, IN THE CASE OF SAMUEL A. WORCESTER, PLAINTIFF IN ERROR, VERSUS THE STATE OF GEORGIA 20. The official report does not give the date the mandate was issued.
142. For a summary of the press comments see 2 C. WARREN, THE SUPREME COURT IN UNITED STATES HISTORY 217–22 (1924).

discussion of the *Worcester* case with the quote: "John Marshall has made his decision, now let him enforce it." While most admit that they cannot prove what Jackson said, none seems to doubt that he thought it and acted on it. The impression left by these discussions is that Jackson ignored his constitutional duty to enforce the Court decree.[143]

Such an interpretation ignores the deficiencies in federal laws that probably would have made it impossible to execute the *Worcester* decree, even if Jackson had wished to enforce it. It ignores the fact that the Court ensured that its decree could not be enforced until its 1833 Term. Finally, it accepts as competent criticism the partisan use of this decision by the National Republicans in the election of 1832.

The decree issued on March 5 merely told the Georgia court to reverse its decision and to release the missionaries. Only after the state court refused could the Supreme Court order the federal marshal to free Worcester and Butler.[144] A special messenger had gone to Georgia to obtain the necessary official document showing that the state court had refused to enter the *Worcester* mandate. Though this messenger rushed back to Washington in order to get the second decree from the Supreme Court before the end of its session, the Court rose before he arrived.[145] A letter from Ambrose Spencer to Daniel Webster on March 14 revealed the necessity of the second decree and the political importance of tagging Jackson with the charge of refusing to enforce the *Worcester* decision:

> Will a final mandate issue from the Supreme Court to deliver the missionaries during the present Term? If not, is it not all important to collect and embody proof, if such exists, that General Jackson declares he will not aid in enforcing the judgment and mandate of the Court? It seems to me very important, if he has made the declarations imputed to him; but the proof of them should be spread before the public, in an authentic shape. The effect of fastening upon him such declarations would be incalculably great.[146]

William Wirt, Worcester's own attorney, doubted that the Court decree could be enforced even in 1833, or that the Court could do anything for the missionaries.[147] Shortly after the *Worcester* decision, he and Sergeant, anticipating the resistance of the Georgia court, had met to discuss this problem before Sergeant rushed off to Philadelphia on business. Sergeant's

---

143. Warren takes the position that Jackson had no obligation to enforce the Court's decree. *Id.* at 216–29. For the opposite view see 2 J. BASSETT, THE LIFE OF ANDREW JACKSON 688–92 (1911); M. JAMES, ANDREW JACKSON: PORTRAIT OF A PRESIDENT 304–05 (1937); G. VAN DEUSEN, THE JACKSONIAN ERA 1824–48, at 49 (1959); C. WILTSE, JOHN C. CALHOUN: NULLIFIER, 1829–1839, at 146–47 (1949).

144. The *Niles' Weekly Register*, Mar. 31, 1832, at 78, col. 1, and the *National Intelligencer*, Apr. 5, 1832, at 3, col. 4, clearly explained what would have to be done before Jackson could be called on to execute its decree. And even a layman's glance at the Judiciary Act of 1789 would have made this clear. Law of Sept. 24, 1789, ch. 20, § 25, 1 Stat. 85.

145. Richmond Enquirer, Apr. 3, 1832, at 2, col. 4.

146. Webster Papers, Library of Congress, printed in 2 C. WARREN, *supra* note 142, at 218.

147. Letter from Wirt to Lewis Williams, Apr. 28, 1832, Wirt Papers, Library of Congress. This and the next four paragraphs are based on that letter.

"*prima facie* impression" was that when the state court refused to execute the decree any judge of the Supreme Court could issue a writ of habeas corpus. Wirt replied that a writ of habeas corpus could not be issued by a single judge, the Circuit Court for Georgia, or the Supreme Court, since the Judiciary Act of 1789 clearly allowed federal judges and courts to issue such writs only when prisoners were held under federal authority.[148] Wirt also thought that the Supreme Court would not be able to award execution by the means provided for in section 25 of the Judiciary Act of 1789, even in its 1833 Term. Though the Judiciary Act permitted the Court, when a case had once been remanded without effect, to proceed to a final decision and award execution, this action required a written record of the state court's refusal to carry out the first decree. Since the Georgia court never put its refusal in writing, the Supreme Court could not have awarded execution in its next Term.

Given these defects in the laws, Wirt admitted that nothing could be done for the missionaries by the Supreme Court. He recommended that the missionaries follow four steps after the Supreme Court issued its mandate in the *Worcester* case. First, the mandate from the Supreme Court had to be presented to the Georgia court. Second, when the state court refused to obey it, the missionaries by petition had to demand that the Governor of Georgia order their release. Third, when the Governor ignored their plea, they had to call on the President to execute the laws that clearly required that they be freed. Fourth, when the President refused, the prisoners had to appeal to Congress. Wirt believed that if Jackson refused to use force if necessary to release the missionaries that the House of Representatives, which had the power to impeach, should pass a resolution that he do so.

After thoroughly discussing these problems, Wirt recommended a new law and a series of amendments to cure the defects that this case had revealed in the judicial processes. The new law would have authorized all federal judges to issue writs of habeas corpus to free persons held under state authority for violating a law that had been declared unconstitutional by the Supreme Court. Section 25 of the Judiciary Act of 1789 would have been amended to permit the Supreme Court to execute immediately its own sentence in a case where the state court seemed likely to resist. Finally, Wirt wished to change the Militia Act of 1795,[149] which merely authorized the President to call out the militia to execute the laws of the Union. Though Wirt thought Jackson could act in the *Worcester* case under the 1795 law, he wanted Congress to amend it to "require" him to act.

---

148. Section 14 of the Judiciary Act authorized federal courts and judges to issue writs of habeas corpus, "*provided*, that writs of *habeas corpus* shall in no case extend to prisoners in gaol, unless where they are in custody, under or by colour of the authority of the United States . . . ." Law of Sept. 24, 1789, ch. 20, § 14, 1 Stat. 81.

149. The Act speaks of "whenever it may be necessary, in the judgment of the President, to use the military" to execute the laws. Act of Feb. 28, 1795, ch. 26, § 3, 1 Stat. 424.

Wirt suggested that the *Worcester* controversy provided the "golden opportunity" for getting the needed changes in these acts "while this resistance on the part of Georgia is creating a strong interest for the authority of the Supreme Court. If this occasion is lost, will it ever return?" He stated that the authority of the Court and the continuance of the Union demanded that Congress act to remedy these deficiencies in the laws of the United States. Wirt's letter clearly indicates that he felt the Supreme Court could do no more in the *Worcester* case. The next move was up to Congress and the people of the United States. In the conclusion of his argument in *Cherokee Nation* in 1831 he had told the Court that it was the President's duty to execute the laws.[150] Apparently Story agreed when he exclaimed after the Court delivered the *Worcester* decision: "The Court has done its duty. Let the nation now do theirs."[151]

A long speech on October 18, 1832, by Benjamin Butler, later Jackson's Attorney General, indicates that he too was aware of the procedural problems attending the *Worcester* case and the importance of the Indian question in the campaign of 1832.[152] Butler attempted to answer the charge that Jackson had violated the Constitution by refusing to enforce the *Worcester* decree. He first noted that whatever general statements the Court had made about the rights of the Cherokees, the judgment of that case extended no farther than to declaring the Georgia law of 1830 unconstitutional. Jackson's oath to the Constitution did not bind him to surrender his own deliberate judgment in this case, since the Supreme Court had ended its session without issuing the necessary mandate. Butler pointed out that the required second decree would go to the federal marshal, who was authorized by the Militia Act of 1795 to enforce the orders of the Court. If combinations too powerful to be suppressed by ordinary judicial proceedings obstructed the marshal, "then, and then only, is the President authorized by the same act of 1795, if he thinks it proper to do so, to interfere by calling out the 'militia of the State' . . . to cause the Laws to be duly executed."[153] Thus the President had not unlawfully refused to enforce the mandate, because at the present stage of the case he lacked the authority to interfere. Still the "great proportion of the Opposition papers" continued to give currency to this false charge to win the clergy and the religious to the anti-Jackson movement. Butler pleaded with the "respectable portion of our opponents" to disavow such tactics.

Despite Butler's plea and the wide circulation given to his speech, the opposition press continued to accuse Jackson of tearing up the Constitution

---

150. R. PETERS, *supra* note 71, at 155.
151. Letter from Story to George Ticknor, Mar. 8, 1832, in 2 THE LIFE AND LETTERS OF JOSEPH STORY, *supra* note 2, at 83.
152. Printed in Richmond Enquirer, Nov. 2, 1832, at 1, col. 5; Nov. 6, 1832, at 1, col. 5; Nov. 9, 1832, at 1, col. 5.
153. *Id.*, Nov. 9, at 1, col. 6.

by failing to execute the *Worcester* decree. The *Boston Daily Advertiser*, for example, stated late in October:

> The Judiciary has nobly taken its stand in defense of the right, but, without the cooperation of the executive, its interposition will probably be ineffectual. It is only by a change in the character of the administration that we can expect to redress this wrong. . . . If there were no other objection to our present rulers, this alone ought to be considered decisive, and it is therefore of the highest importance that the facts in this case should be constantly kept before the public mind. Will the Christian people of the United States give their sanction, by placing him again in office, to the conduct of a President who treats the ministers of the Christian religion with open outrage, loads them with chains, drags them from their peaceful homes to prison, commits them in defiance of law like common criminals to the penitentiary, and violently keeps them there against the decision of the highest law authority affirming their innocence? [They] are violently detained in prison by the authorities of Georgia in defiance of a decree of the Supreme Court declaring [their] . . . innocence.[154]

Though the Bank issue received more attention during the 1832 election campaign than the Cherokee controversy, it was often linked with the *Worcester* case in the party presses. The debates on the Bank and on the missionaries' imprisonment frequently ran side by side; and the partisans of the missionaries were in most instances supporters and even employees of the Bank of the United States. Wirt, Binney, Webster, and Clay, to name only a few, were either permanently retained by the Bank or had many times argued its cases in court.[155] The link made in the press between the Bank and the *Worcester* controversies was that in both Jackson refused to recognize the supremacy of the Constitution as interpreted by the Supreme Court.

Historians have long emphasized the paragraph in Jackson's veto of the Bank Bill declaring that the decisions of the Court ought not to control "the coordinate authorities" of the federal government—that "the Congress, the Executive, and the Court must each for itself be guided by its own opinion of the Constitution."[156] But historians have usually neglected to mention that this paragraph was written at a time when the opposition press was denouncing Jackson for refusing to enforce the *Worcester* decision. At least 4 months before the President sent his veto message to Congress, the *Utica Observer* sought to answer the charge that Jackson defied the Constitution by refusing to force Georgia to release the missionaries.

> Will the president, to carry into effect a decision he believes unconstitutional and wrong, wage war against Georgia, and attempt to force submission with a bayonet? . . . [W]e do not believe he will. He is a *co-ordinate* and INDEPENDENT

---

154. Printed in the Pittsburgh Gazette, Oct. 26, 1832, at 2, cols. 1 & 2.
155. *See* M. BAXTER, DANIEL WEBSTER AND THE SUPREME COURT, ch. 7 (1966).
156. Veto messages of Andrew Jackson to Senate, July 10, 1832, in 2 MESSAGES, *supra* note 5, at 582.

branch of the government, bound by his oath to support the constitution *as it is*, and not as it shall be *interpreted* by the federal judges. He is no more responsible to them than they are to him. The constitution has clearly defined their separate powers; and to deny the president the right of acting *independently* ON ALL CONSTITUTIONAL QUESTIONS, is to convert our republican form of government into an odious monarchy—not with *one* but with *five sovereigns*. We claim for him in this matter the RIGHT to act as HE may think proper. . . . It is with him a question of Constitutional duty; and HE MAY EITHER ACT OR REFUSE TO ACT IN SUPPORT OF THE DECISION OF A CO-ORDINATE BRANCH OF THE GOVERNMENT.[157]

This paragraph from the *Observer* contained the doctrine and even some of the phrases that Jackson used in his veto message.

Whether or not Jackson and his advisers had the *Worcester* case in mind when they included that paragraph in his veto message, the National Republicans often linked the two. The *National Gazette* printed a parody of Jackson's veto message, connecting it with the imprisoned missionaries:

There is a constitution of the United States. But every man has a right to judge of its provisions and no one is bound to obey or enforce it if he believes it to be unconstitutional. Ministers of the Gospel are under the protections of the laws. But when falsely imprisoned the President is not bound to enforce a decision declaring them so—if it will in his opinion injure his re-election to office.[158]

*Niles' Weekly Register* and the *Pittsburgh Gazette* both copied an article from the *Cherokee Phoenix* that warned that the doctrine in the veto message

bears directly upon the interest of the Cherokees—it is, that *the executive is not bound by the decisions of the supreme court*. That such was the opinion of President Jackson it was frequently intimated after the decision of the court in the case of the missionaries, but it has not been before publicly and officially avowed. . . . According to the doctrine in the veto message, he will disregard it even when he is called upon by a regular process from the supreme court.

What sort of hope have we then from a president, who feels himself under no kind of *obligation to execute*, but has abundance of *inclination to disregard* the laws and treaties as interpreted by a proper branch of the Government? We have nothing to expect from such an executive—and if general Jackson is disposed to act as he pleases, the remedy is not with us, but with the people of the United States.—We shall see whether that remedy will be promptly applied.[159]

What effect charges such as these had in the election is difficult to assess. Though Jackson won an overwhelming victory at the polls, Martin Van Buren, who should have known, thought that in his own New York these charges meant a loss of from eight to ten thousand votes for Jackson.[160]

---

157. As reprinted in Niles' Weekly Register, Apr. 14, 1832, at 112, col. 1.
158. Pittsburgh Gazette, Aug. 28, 1832, at 3, col. 1.
159. Niles' Weekly Register, Sept. 15, 1832, at 47, col. 2.
160. AUTOBIOGRAPHY OF MARTIN VAN BUREN, *supra* note 39, at 293.

When the Court met in January 1833 the reelection of Jackson and the need for a united front against nullification had dramatically changed attitudes toward the *Worcester* case. The Cherokees and the missionaries had become an embarrassment. The President's message to Congress in December 1832 had been conciliatory regarding the Indians and his nationalistic proclamation against nullification had been read with wonder and approval by the Justices and the friends of the Supreme Court.[161] Prominent Jacksonians had pleaded with Governor Lumpkin of Georgia to pardon Worcester and Butler on the grounds that it would remove the pretext for bringing together Georgia and South Carolina on nullification.[162] And the missionaries' own attorneys had begged them to drop the case for the same reasons.[163] Wirt and Webster advised the Cherokees not to renew the contest in the Supreme Court since a suit might destroy the united front against the nullifiers.[164] Both sides must have breathed a sigh of relief when Worcester and Butler gave up the struggle in return for a pardon from Governor Lumpkin.[165] By late January, Justice Story could write that Jackson had asked him to the White House for dinner and could add that "what is more remarkable, since his last proclamation and message, the Chief Justice and myself have become his warmest supporters . . . ."[166] Surely the missionaries and the Cherokees must have wondered how a cause so connected with politics, law, and morality in 1832 could be of so little interest to politicians and lawyers in 1833. Perhaps the Cherokees merely concluded that politicians, judges, and lawyers spoke with forked tongues.

Still, the Cherokees would have been wrong. It was not that the Justices and lawyers such as Wirt loved the Indians less, it was only that they loved the Court more. The key to understanding the Cherokee cases is to realize that the Court and the Constitution, as the Justices interpreted it, always came first. In *Cherokee Nation v. Georgia* Chief Justice Marshall resisted the political and moral pleas of the Cherokees because he believed that the

---

161. Andrew Jackson, Fourth Annual Message to Congress, Dec. 4, 1832, in 2 MESSAGES, *supra* note 5, at 602; Proclamation of Andrew Jackson, Dec. 10, 1832, in *id.* at 640; letter from Story to Peters, Dec. 22, 1832, Peters Papers, Pennsylvania Historical Society; letter from Story to Judge Fay, Feb. 10, 1833, in 2 LIFE AND LETTERS OF JOSEPH STORY, *supra* note 3, at 121; letter from Story to Reverend John Brazer, Feb. 11, 1833, in *id.* at 122; letter from Ambrose Spencer to John W. Taylor, Feb. 8, 1833, Taylor Papers, New-York Historical Society.

162. *See, e.g.,* letter from Martin Van Buren to John Forsyth, Dec. 18, 1832, Van Buren Papers, Library of Congress; letter from Wilson Lumpkin to Lewis Cass, Jan. 2, 1833, to Silas Wright, Jr., *et al.*, Jan. 5, 1833, to Lewis Cass, Jan. 19, 1833, and to John Forsyth, Jan. 19, 1833, in 1 W. LUMPKIN, *supra* note 24, at 195–208.

163. A letter from Worcester to Sergeant on January 22, 1833, explains the various moves that led to the request and the granting of the pardon. Sergeant Papers, Pennsylvania Historical Society. The Niles' Weekly Register on February 16, 1833, printed his letters to the Governor—perhaps as a sort of official notice that the Indian cause had been compromised in order to maintain the united front against nullification. Niles' Weekly Register, Feb. 16, 1833, at 419, col. 1.

164. Letter from Wirt to Colonel John Williams, Feb. 26, 1833, Wirt Papers, Maryland Historical Society.

165. Niles' Weekly Register, Feb. 16, 1833, at 419, col. 1.

166. Letter from Story to his wife, Jan. 27, 1833, in 2 THE LIFE AND LETTERS OF JOSEPH STORY, *supra* note 3, at 119.

Constitution would not allow the Court to accept jurisdiction. The best he would do for the Cherokee Nation and the National Republicans was to suggest through his opinion and Thompson's dissent that the Cherokee claims had merit and that the Court might rule differently in a future case. If considerations of politics and morality clashed with those of law in the *Cherokee Nation* case, *Worcester v. Georgia* represented a remarkable blending of these three considerations. The Court clearly had jurisdiction; the majority of the Justices believed that the Georgia law of 1830 was unconstitutional; and a decree ordering the release of the missionaries would play a part in the election of 1832. For most of the Justices the election of 1832 was not simply a contest of parties but a battle for the Court and the Constitution.

Nullification and Jackson's stand against it changed all this. Law again clashed with politics and morality. The need to defend the Constitution and the Union meant that the Cherokee cause had to be dropped and the Jackson Administration supported. Perhaps the real winner in the Cherokee cause was the Supreme Court. For years every effort to extend the jurisdiction of the federal courts had been defeated. The *Worcester* case revealed glaring deficiencies in the Judiciary Act of 1789. Wirt felt that the public outrage over the continued imprisonment of the missionaries afforded a "golden opportunity" to make the necessary amendments.[167] Still, it was not the missionary cause but the nullification controversy that turned Wirt's hopes into reality. The Force Act of 1833 reads more like the revisions recommended by Wirt in April of 1832 than those suggested by Jackson in his message to Congress in January of 1833.[168] In fact Daniel Webster felt obligated to deny that "there was the slightest reference to the Georgia case in my own mind, or ever, as far as I know, in that of any other gentleman, in preparing and passing the bill for the better collection of revenue. It is true that some of the provisions of the bill ought, in my judgment, to be permanent."[169]

Legal considerations kept the Court from taking the plunge in 1831, even though both politics and morality called for it. The Court did take the plunge in 1832, when law, politics, and morality all pushed for the same decision. And finally, the plunge in 1832 was not as fateful as it seemed, for no direct confrontation with the President could have occurred in the *Worcester* case without a second writ of error. The Marshall Court was moved by politics and morality in the Cherokee cases but it moved no farther than the law allowed.

---

167. Letter from Wirt to Colonel John Williams, Apr. 28, 1832, Wirt Papers, Library of Congress.
168. Act of Mar. 2, 1833, ch. 57, 4 Stat. 632. The Force Act permitted any Justice of the Supreme Court or any district judge to issue writs of habeas corpus to state courts—a recommendation that Wirt had made and Jackson had not. *See* Jackson's Message to Congress, Jan. 16, 1833, in 2 MESSAGES, *supra* note 5, at 630.
169. Letter from Webster to Mr. Perry, Apr. 10, 1833, in 1 THE PRIVATE CORRESPONDENCE OF DANIEL WEBSTER 534 (F. Webster ed. 1875).

# 15

# FAIRNESS AND FORMALISM IN THE TRIALS OF BLACKS IN THE STATE SUPREME COURTS OF THE OLD SOUTH

*A. E. KEIR NASH*

# FAIRNESS AND FORMALISM IN THE TRIALS OF BLACKS IN THE STATE SUPREME COURTS OF THE OLD SOUTH

*A. E. Keir Nash**

*The Editors of the* Virginia Law Review *have selected for publication Professor Nash's scholarly historical discussion of judicial attitudes toward blacks in the antebellum South because of the contribution it makes to the limited legal literature on slave conditions in the pre-Civil War South. The Article should prompt controversy in Black Studies classes and, for that reason alone, is timely. In addition, however, antebellum history is a part of the heritage of all Americans, and in a period when improved race relations is a high national priority, Professor Nash offers an analysis of the past which may promote the understanding essential to full racial reconciliation.*

> An officer of the town having a *notice to serve on the defendant,* without any authority whatever, *arrests him and attempts to tie him!!* Is not this gross oppression? . . . What degree of cruelty might not the defendant reasonably apprehend after he should be entirely in the power of one who had set upon him in so high-handed and lawless a manner? Was he to submit tamely?—Or, was he not excusable in resorting to the natural right of self defense?[1]

THE time was December, 1859—less than a year before Lincoln's election; the place, the Supreme Court of North Carolina. So saying, Chief Judge Richmond Munford Pearson[2] reversed the conviction of a free black who had resorted to "self-help" against "police brutality." [3] The tenor of Judge Pearson's opinion is striking when viewed in the perspective of twentieth century judicial decisions affecting black defendants in the South. In the 1920's, for example, the Arkansas Su-

---

* Assistant Professor of Political Science, University of California, Santa Barbara, California. A.B., Harvard College, 1958; M.A., University of North Carolina, 1961; Ph.D., Harvard University, 1967.

1 State v. Davis, 52 N.C. 52, 54-55 (1859).

2 Judge Pearson was on the court as Associate Judge, 1848-58, and Chief Judge, 1859-1878. He was a Unionist Whig, who viewed the Constitution of 1789 as "an obligatory covenant of perpetual union." Dick, *Richmond Munford Pearson* in 5 BIOGRAPHICAL HISTORY OF NORTH CAROLINA 295, 301 (S. Ashe ed. 1906).

3 A New Bern constable had been required to serve a tax delinquency notice upon the free black. To prevent the attempted arrest, the black had beaten the constable. 52 N.C. at 52-53.

*Fairness and Formalism*                    65

preme Court found nothing fundamentally unfair about passing a death sentence upon a black whose trial for murder had been conducted with an angry mob assembled outside the courtroom.[4] In the 1930's a majority of the judges on the Mississippi Supreme Court discerned nothing shocking to the conscience in a capital conviction based on a confession procured by whipping the black defendant over a three-day period.[5] These more recent cases tend to support the thesis advanced by the late Ulrich B. Phillips that the central theme of southern history has been the maintenance of white supremacy.[6]

By contrast, Judge Pearson's words and a similar opinion by his Tennessee contemporary, Judge Nathan Green[7]—if they are at all representative of the behavior of southern state supreme courts before the Civil War—suggest an overlooked antebellum tradition of solicitude for the black defendant. Certainly these decisions are not easily explained in terms of the standard historical interpretations of the racial climate in the pre-Civil War South.[8]

---

[4] Moore v. Dempsey, 261 U.S. 86 (1923).

[5] Brown v. Mississippi, 297 U.S. 278 (1936).

[6] *See* U. PHILLIPS, THE COURSE OF THE SOUTH TO SECESSION 151-65 (1939).

[7] Rejecting the argument that as a mere chattel a slave could not sue, Judge Green declared:

> [A slave] is made after the image of the Creator. He has mental capacities . . . that constitute him equal to his owner but for the accidental position in which fortune has placed him . . . but the law under which he is held as a slave have not and cannot extinguish his high-born nature . . . .

Ford v. Ford, 26 Tenn. 92, 95-96 (1846). Judge Green was on the Tennessee appellate court from 1831 to 1852. He was a Jacksonian who became a Whig and was a strong Unionist and a Presbyterian.

[8] This difficulty seems to obtain with respect both to the dominant post-bellum northern view that the South was always morally retarded in its enthusiasm for slavery, and to the Southern Revisionist interpretation which has prevailed in most twentieth-century historiography. The latter has tended to find a crucial turning-point from "Jeffersonian liberalism" to "hegemonic pro-slavery conservatism" in four events occurring at the end of the 1820's: the incendiary Walker pamphlet of 1829; the first publication of William Lloyd Garrison's *The Liberator* in 1831; the Nat Turner revolt in 1831; and Virginia's ensuing legislative debates on the institution of slavery narrowly resulting in the defeat of its opponents. Within a few years, after these four events, virulent northern abolition and the spectre of insurrection had united the South in a concert of defense: "Jeffersonian liberalism was dead. The South was on the road to nationhood—and to Appomattox." W. OSTERWEIS, ROMANTICISM AND NATIONALISM IN THE OLD SOUTH 22 (1949).

As regards the processes of justice, "[a]ll over the South mob action began to replace orderly judicial procedure." J. FRANKLIN, THE MILITANT SOUTH ix (1956). Nothing in the course of southern events from 1830 to 1860 diminished the vast gap between the existence of laws protecting blacks from cruel treatment and their application. "[W]herever protection was on the one hand theoretically extended, it was practically cancelled on the other by the universal prohibition in southern law

This Article will examine the extent to which this apparent libertarianism was characteristic of the treatment accorded the black in the era of slavery by southern state appellate judges.[9] The pattern of judicial behavior is a complex one, encompassing manumission cases[10] as well as criminal prosecutions both against blacks and against whites who abused blacks. Many appellate judges preferred to emancipate slaves than to uphold the contentions of their would-be inheritors.[11] Few judges appear to have been eager to find loopholes to excuse white attacks upon blacks. When appeals of convicted black felons reached them, virtually all judges applied at least the benefits of strict procedural formalism so that indictments were quashed under the same or stricter rules of construction than were applied to whites.[12] Thus, even the least activist judge observed a neutral deference to statutes and precedents. Many of the more activist jurists, on the other hand, vigorously expanded the trial rights of black defendants.

This inquiry into judicial behavior will begin with an examination of the most basic issue affecting the adjudication of black rights: application of the common law. If the judiciary had determined that the slave was purely a creature of statute, unprotected by the common law, activists would have been severely hindered in their efforts to extend fair trial procedures to blacks. By 1834 two of the most influential benches—those of North and South Carolina—had split on the applica-

---

against permitting slaves to testify in court, except against each other . . . . Even the murder of a slave found the law straining all its resources to avoid jurisdiction." S. ELKINS, SLAVERY 56-58 (2d ed. 1968). For an extended discussion of changing interpretations, see T. PRESSLY, AMERICANS INTERPRET THEIR CIVIL WAR (1954).

Nineteenth century northern views are referred to as "Rhodesian"—after James Ford Rhodes—and their contemporary manifestations as "Neo-Rhodesian." *See, e.g.,* K. STAMPP, THE PECULIAR INSTITUTION (1956); S. ELKINS, *supra.* Southern views are referred to as Revisionist, after the school of historians trained as graduate students at Columbia under Dunning in the 1890's, of which the most influential was Ulrich Bonnell Phillips of Georgia. *See* U. PHILLIPS, AMERICAN NEGRO SLAVERY (1928).

[9] It is important to stress that we are here concerned with the behavior of only a sector of the antebellum southern elite—the judges of the Supreme Courts of nine states which seceded in 1861. See note 13 *infra* regarding the exclusion of Virginia and Louisiana. *We are not concerned with lower-court, vigilante, or "plantation justice" unless it reached the appellate level. Throughout this Article the terms "liberal," "libertarian," and "conservative" are used with reference to prevalent nineteenth-century cultural standards, not with reference to contemporary views.*

[10] See notes 125-36 *infra* and accompanying text.

[11] *See* A. Nash, Negro Rights and Judicial Behavior in the Old South, Ph.D. Dissertation, Harvard University, June 1, 1968 [hereinafter referred to as Nash HUD].

[12] See notes 52-124 *infra* and accompanying text.

tion of the common law.[13] Thus, judges in other states, faced with the issue at a later date, had an option to decide either for or against the extention of the common law to the black defendant.

## THE QUESTION OF COMMON LAW PROTECTION
### 1800-1830

Not until the end of the 18th century did much litigation concerning personal rights of slaves reach the appellate level, and not until the early 19th century were the Carolina courts involved with the first and most fundamental question of black criminal jurisprudence: Did the slave fall under the protection of the common law—or did he have to rely on the more flimsy armor of statutory law? Was his life wholly at the mercy of his owner, or was he within the general peace of the State? The answer that the South Carolina court gave to this issue was unequivocal: "There can be . . . no offense against the State for a mere beating of a slave. . . . The peace of the State is not thereby broken; for a slave is not *generally* regarded as legally capable of being within the peace of the State." [14]

---

[13] Of the 11 states which seceded in 1861, only five had sufficient population to engender substantial litigation during the 1790-1830 period—the two Carolinas, Virginia, Georgia, and Louisiana. Virginia is excluded from the discussion in the succeeding section because her Court of Appeals was restricted to civil jurisdiction until 1851; Georgia, because her legislature ignored constitutional requirements and failed to create a supreme court until 1845; and Louisiana, because of the difficulty of comparing her code-law with the Anglo-Saxon common law of other states.

[14] State v. Maner, 22 S.C.L. 453, 454-55 (1834); *cf.* Helton v. Caston, 2 S.C.L. 95 (1831). South Carolina judges never considered the issue as a group prior to 1830, though the archly-conservative Chancellor DeSaussure indicated the eventual answer in an opinion which he delivered while on circuit. Bynum v. Bostick, 4 S.C.E. 266 (1812). For a discussion of the Chancellor's views, see Nash HUD, *supra* note 11, at 47-51.

The acceptance or rejection of the common law view of slavery did not require a different sensitivity to the procedural incidents created by statute. When the South Carolina bench was asked to affirm procedurally dubious trials of slaves, it refused. For example, Judge Colcock, the leading pro-slavery jurist on the court before 1830, agreed that the 1788 Debtors' Act should be construed to include free blacks since it did not expressly exclude them and it would not "be just, after forcing them into Court, to withhold a privilege so important, and which is granted to all others." Rodgers ads. Norton, Harper 5, 6 (S.C. 1823) (Huger, J.). Similarly, the court reversed a conviction of shooting with intent to kill because one freeholder at trial did not comply with residency requirements even though the court could have relied on waiver to uphold the lower court. *Ex parte* Richardson, Harper 308 (S.C. 1824).

In South Carolina v. Hudnal, 2 Nott & McCord 419 (S.C. 1820), the court voided the kangaroo trial of a slave charged with trying to poison a white. Two private citizens, falsely claiming to be justices of the peace and several others, falsely acting as freeholders, had sentenced the slave to death. Judge Colcock, hearing the case on

By contrast, the North Carolina bench waged a full-scale debate among the three most prominent members of that court before 1830. Curiously, the two who chose the common law protection—Chief Judge John Louis Taylor[15] and his successor Leonard Henderson[16]—were Federalists inclined to judicial restraint in the face of legislative hostility to manumission.[17] Their opponent, John Hall,[18] was an activist Democrat who criticized them for being too passive on that issue.[19]

Taylor and Hall had been on the bench barely a year when the

---

circuit, had refused to issue a prohibition: The grounds for issuance did not, he said, appear on the face of the proceedings. He did not sit on the appeal which was argued successfully before the constitutional court. That court asked:

> Would it not be in direct violation of the principles of natural justice, as well as the order of civil government, for unauthorized individuals to usurp jurisdiction . . . and carry into execution the solemn and awful sentence of death?

*Id.* at 423. Judge Gantt was thoroughly appalled:

> Every feeling of humanity and justice revolts at the idea, that any other mode of trial, less formal and substantial than what the Act [of 1740] has prescribed, should be sanctioned . . . . the defendants are prohibited from all further proceedings . . . against negro [*sic*] Manuel.      :

*Id.* at 424. *Hudnal* shows that five of the six judges would not permit improper procedures in trying suspected slaves. *Ex parte* Richardson, *supra,* decided four years later, suggests that the sixth judge, Charles Colcock, had simply not considered the question raised in *Hudnal* adequately on circuit. It seems fair to conclude that in South Carolina before 1830, Unionists and States' Righters voiced equal demands for fair trials under the law.

15 Judge Taylor was on the court from 1800 to 1829. Born in London, he emigrated at the age of 12 to Virginia; after working his way through William and Mary, he moved to North Carolina where, as a member of the State Legislature in 1794 and 1795, he sponsored several unsuccessful bills promoting manumission of slaves.

16 Judge Henderson was a popular Federalist lawyer appointed to the court in 1808 by a Republican legislature. A native North Carolinian, he was Chief Judge from 1829 to 1833.

17 See note 19 *infra.*

18 Judge Hall was an associate judge from 1800 to 1832. Born in Virginia, he was an agnostic until just before he died, when he became an Episcopalian.

19 See Hall's dissent in Trustees of the Contentnea Soc'y of Quakers v. Dickenson, 12 N.C. 189, 206 (1827) (per curiam), where Taylor and Henderson viewed a bequest of blacks to a religious organization hostile to slavery as an attempt to skirt the 1741 law limiting manumission to blacks who had performed "extraordinary services." Taylor thought that the Quakers' "benevolence," though "virtuous and just in the abstract," would result in the blacks covertly being allowed to work for themselves, in "quasi-emancipation" as the phrase went. *Id.* at 202. For a discussion of a series of eight such manumission cases from 1816 to 1827 in which the North Carolina judges seemingly ignored personal preferences for freeing slaves in deference to legislative intent, see Nash HUD, *supra* note 11, at 52-65. For a discussion of what could be done by an activist judge to undermine anti-manumission statutes, see Nash, *Negro Rights, Unionism, and Greatness on the South Carolina Court of Appeals: The Extraordinary Chief Justice John Belton O'Neall,* 21 S.C.L. Rev. 141 (1969).

dispute opened with *State v. Boon.*[20] Despite an assertion that the defendant's murder of a slave was "a crime of the most atrocious and barbarous nature; much more so than killing a person . . . on an equal footing," [21] the conviction was reversed because of the relevant statute's vagueness. Two of the four judges penned lengthy dicta which delineated their respective positions on the question of common law treatment for slaves. Despite his personal distaste for North Carolina's "unfortunate connection with slavery," [22] Judge Hall took a logical path which would become the trademark of pro-slavery judges. Rejecting the analogy between American slaves and English villeins who were within the protection of the common law, he asserted that English law had never contained the notion of slavery, and therefore that the American slave had to be the creation of colonial statute.[23] Absent legislative mandate to the contrary, the captor's right to kill followed the bill of sale.

John Louis Taylor objected to the thrust of Hall's logic. With anguished words he urged a logically-strained mixture of Anglo-Saxon common law and natural law in opposition to Hall's "continental doctrine." [24]

---

[20] 1 N.C. 103 (1801).

[21] *Id.* at 110 (Johnston, J.).

[22] *See, e.g.,* Trustees of the Contentnea Soc'y of Quakers v. Dickenson, 12 N.C. 189, 207 (1827) (dissenting opinion).

[23] As the king's subjects, villeins had the right of suit against all but their lords. By contrast, the condition of American slaves was "more abject; they are not parties to our constitution." 1 N.C. at 108. They had no such right to sue. Utilizing the authority of Montesquieu and Blackstone, Hall argued that English law cast no light on slavery. Rather, it negated the institution on English soil: The moment the slave "lands in England he undergoes a change, . . . in . . . law . . . he is . . . a free man." *Id.* at 107. But conversely, were his condition "not altered, the laws would not extend their protection . . . ." In Hall's judgment, Montesquieu and Blackstone had rightly defined "slavery to be, that whereby an absolute power is given to the master, over the life . . . of the slave." Any rights to protection

> were the consequence of positive laws: they did not exist before these laws imposed them; they were unknown in a pure state of slavery . . . . he that was taken in battle, remained bound to his taker forever, and he could do with him as with his beast; he could kill him with impunity.

*Id.*

[24] The Natural Law components appear to be: (1) Hobbes' minimal restraint to killing only from unavoidable necessity; (2) Locke's ethics of abstention from injury; (3) Hooker's positive duty to "do all the good we can." Blackstone, in the passages to which Hall referred, was clearly drawing from Continental philosophers—besides Montesquieu, primarily Grotius and Pufendorf. F. Meinecke, Die Idee der Staatsraeson in der Neueren Geschichte (2d ed. 1925). For an exegesis of the different effects of such "Anglo-Saxon" and "Continental" philosophic starting points in another area, see Wolfers, *Statesmanship and Moral Choice,* 1 World Politics 175 (1949).

> Upon what foundation can the claim of a master to an absolute do-
> minion over the life of his slave, be rested? The authority for it is
> not to be found in the law of nature, for that will authorize a man
> to take away the life of another, only from the unavoidable neces-
> sity of saving his own; and of this code, the cardinal duty is to ab-
> stain from injury, and do all the good we can. It is not the necessary
> consequence of the state of slavery, for that may exist without it;
> and its natural inconveniences ought not to be aggravated by an evil,
> at which reason, religion, humanity and policy equally revolt. . . .
> [Despite legislative alterations] the crime is unchanged in its es-
> sence, undiminished in its enormity. The scale of its guilt exists in
> those relations of things which are prior to human institutions, and
> whose sanctions must forever remain unimpaired.[25]

*Boon* thus placed into competition two possible evolutionary themes
in American slave jurisprudence.

The decisive battle on the North Carolina Court came twenty-two
years later. In 1823 in *State v. Reed*[26] a white appealed to the court
from a conviction for the murder of a black under an indictment which
had charged a common law crime. Judge Hall, dissenting, relied upon
his own opinion in *Boone;* if the murder of a slave were an offense at
common law, any other injury, assault for example, would also be in-
dictable. Judge Taylor retorted: "[A] law of paramount obligation
to the statute was violated . . . , the Common Law, founded upon the
law of nature, and confirmed by revelation." [27]

Judge Leonard Henderson, who held the balance of power, agreed
with Taylor's result, but was far more ingenious. His deciding opinion
demonstrated a considerable capacity for covering a sinuous logical path
with a veneer of reasoned inevitability. He restated Reed's argument that
as a chattel, the slave's fate was of no more interest to the state "independently of the acts of the Legislature . . . than . . . the death of a
horse." [28] Then he wrote two amazing sentences:

> This is argument, the force of which I cannot feel, and leads
> to consequences abhorrent to my nature:—yet if it be the law of
> the land, it must be so pronounced. I disclaim all rules or laws in
> investigating this question, but the Common Law of England, as
> brought to this country by our forefathers when they emigrated

---

[25] 1 N.C. at 112.
[26] 9 N.C. 454 (1823).
[27] *Id.* at 455.
[28] *Id.*

hither, and as adopted by them, and as modified by various declarations of the Legislature since. . . ."[29]

The judicial self-restraint proclaimed in the first sentence is sharply undercut by the second, which transforms the central question into a premise. After several pages of dubious argumentation,[30] Judge Henderson wound up with an analogy subject to the same flaw as his initial thesis—the answer came by fiat rather than by convincing logic:

> [A]nd I would ask, what law is it that punishes at this day the most wanton and cruel dismemberment of a slave, by severing a limb from his body, if [his] life should be spared? There is no statute on the subject, it is the Common Law, cut down, it is true, by statute or custom, so as to tolerate slavery, yielding to the owner the services of the slave, . . . but protecting the life and limbs of the human being; and in these particulars, it does not admit that he is without the protection of the law. I think, therefore, that [the] judgment of death should be pronounced against the prisoner.[31]

The "therefore" is hard to believe. Judge Henderson's opinion is perhaps best described as advancing by a strategy of dubious statement. Strangest of all, its weaknesses were not necessary to obtain a conviction. The court could have arrested the judgment, allowing the prosecutor to bring a new indictment *"in formam statuti."*

Six months later Judge Taylor began his opinion in *State v. Hale,*[32] which broadened application of the common law to include assault and

---

[29] *Id.*

[30] *E.g.,* Henderson's observation:

> [W]ith me it has no weight to shew, that by the laws of ancient Rome or modern Turkey, an absolute power is given to the master over the life of his slave:—I answer, these are not the laws of our country, nor the model from which they were taken; it is abhorrent to the hearts of all those who have felt the influence of the mild precepts of christianity . . . .

*Id.* at 456. But note the three pecularities of this passage. First, equating the laws of Rome with those of Turkey was seemingly intended to minimize their relevance. Of course, the laws of Turkey in 1823 were not the laws of "our country" nor their model. But the laws of American slavery were hardly founded without regard to the laws of ancient Rome. As Hall had noted in *Boon,* the common law abrogated the status of slave in England. And, English decisions recognizing slavery in the colonies reasoned from something other than the common law—from continental theorists who drew ultimately from Rome. Second, Henderson joined the laws of slavery and the laws of free persons in the phrase, "the laws of our country." Third, as if to distract attention from this elision, he remarked that "it" was abhorrent to Christianity.

[31] *Id.* at 454.

[32] 9 N.C. 582 (1823).

battery against slaves, by declaring that the absence of a statute necessitated deduction from "general principles, from reasonings founded on the common law. . . ."[33] Such was the great tactical advantage created by Judge Henderson's opinion in *Reed*. Judge Taylor could simply announce that the common law was the basis for the decision and then observe:

> The public peace is thus broken, as much as if a free man had been beaten, for the party of the aggressor is always the strongest, and such contests usually terminated by overpowering the slave and inflicting on him a severe chastisement, without regard to the original cause of the conflict. There is consequently, as much reason for making such offenses indictable, as if a white man had been the victim.[34]

Almost simultaneously with *Boon*, the Supreme Court of North Carolina in *State v. Sue*,[35] had made another advance by settling an important jurisdictional question in favor of the black: the power of a county court to impose the death sentence upon a slave guilty of attempted murder. Although the statutory punishment of a free person was imprisonment, no specific enactment governed the punishment of slaves. The State argued that the 1741 Slave Code had given discretionary power of punishment to the court of freeholders and magistrates, and that the Act of 1793, granting jury trials to slaves accused of felonies, had simply transferred that power to the county court. The majority disagreed:

> The discretion given . . . is a legal discretion, not the power of altering punishment, or affixing to any offence, a punishment unknown to the law. This would be for the Court to legislate not to adjudicate. . . .[36]

Judge Taylor dissented. One clause of the 1741 Code had provided capital punishment for slaves convicted of conspiracy to rebel, and the next clause had empowered the freeholders' court after convicting a slave of "*any other crime or misdemeanour*, [to pass] such judgment . . . according to the[ir] discretion . . . as the nature of the crime or offense shall require."[37] Thus, in Taylor's view there was little reason

---

[33] *Id.*

[34] *Id.* at 584.

[35] 1 N.C. 54 (1800).

[36] *Id.* at 62.

[37] *Id.* at 59. There were two reasons to believe that the legislature had intended

to doubt that the 1793 law, granting a county court trial by jury to slaves accused of capital offenses, transferred plenary discretion in sentencing to the county court. Judge Taylor disliked the result, but felt bound by the legislature: "[A] sense of duty compels me to pronounce it, however repugnant it may be to my private notions of humanity." [38]

Twelve years later, Judge Taylor was more successful in squaring his private notions of humanity with judicial neutrality. *State v. Washington*[39] presented a basic question overlooked in an earlier case: Could a slave appeal at all from a county court decision? Washington, a slave sentenced to death for raping a white woman, had assumed so, but the State resisted on the ground that appeals had not been allowed from freeholders' courts under the 1741 Code.[40]

All of the judges except John Hall agreed with Washington. Hall saw ground for dissent in the 1793 Act itself, which provided for a county court trial *only* when the slave was arrested not more than two weeks before, or during a regular court term. If arrested at another time the slave still received a jury trial, but the bench consisted of three justices of the peace. Consequently, Washington's argument led to a situation of complete chance. Arrested "out of judicial season," a slave could not appeal because special courts did not come under the 1777 appeals law. Arrested "in season," he could appeal. Such an anomaly should not, Hall argued, be attributed to the legislature. Certainly, Judge Hall's logic was more neutral than that of his colleagues,[41] but *Washing-*

---

this clause to be a plenary grant. First, if the legislature intended the 1741 Code to forbid the freeholders to impose capital punishment in crimes which were non-capital offenses for whites, it could have said so explicitly. Second, a 1786 law had taken away the master's right to compensation for an executed slave if the State could show that the master had treated him cruelly. The law was designed to discourage a particular form of maltreatment—not providing sufficient food and clothing—which led the slave to steal in desperation. But the very fact of passing the law demonstrated that between 1741 and 1786 slaves could be punished capitally for larceny, whereas a white would merely have been imprisoned or burned on the hand.

[38] 1 N.C. 61.

[39] 6 N.C. 100 (1812).

[40] Washington argued that the 1793 transfer of slaves' trials brought the slave under a 1777 Act which allowed appeal by any person dissatisfied with a county court's verdict. Certainly, the 1793 Act said nothing explicit about appeals, but the right to appeal could, he argued, be inferred from its provisions for trial-by-jury and right-to-counsel. Act of 1793, Ch. 381, §§ 1, 3, at 1 N.C. Code 706 (1821).

[41] Hall's neutralism was not without its advantages. Thus, in State v. Ben, 8 N.C. 434 (1821), his insistence that only positive statute affected the slave opened up a benefit to a black defendant which the common law theory of Taylor and Henderson foreclosed. Ben had been indicted for burglary, but the only evidence connecting

*ton,* like *Sue,*[42] was a decision wherein "justice of the heart" prevailed. The difference was that in *Washington,* Judge Taylor joined the sentimentalists.

Five black felony cases reached the court between 1820 and 1830. In each the judges made strict demands upon the State, producing unanimous reversals.[43] In *State v. Poll,*[44] the court granted a new trial to two blacks accused of conspiring with a white man to poison the latter's father. Both the son and the slaves' master consented to a change in venue. Judge Taylor insisted that the consent did not bind the blacks, successfully overturning North Carolina's adherence to the doctrine that a slave on trial was a "non-willing chattel." When in the

---

him with the crime was given by a slave. Under the 1741 Code such evidence would have been insufficient to convict, for a slave's testimony had to be supported by "pregnant circumstances." Ben's counsel argued that the sentence of death should accordingly be arrested.

Taylor and Henderson found that argument doomed by the very Act of 1793 which had so improved the general condition of accused slaves. In their view, the 1793 statute operated to repeal anything in the 1741 Code which differed "from the Common Law rule of evidence." *Id.* at 436. Thus, "pregnant circumstances" were no longer required to corroborate a slave's testimony. Furthermore, an Act of 1816, which gave exclusive original jurisdiction to superior courts in capital cases, provided:

> the trial shall be conducted in the same manner, and under the same rules, regulations and restrictions, as trials of freemen for a like offence are now conducted.

Ch. 912, § 1, at 2 N.C. Code 1354 (1812).

Justice Hall disagreed. As far as he could see, the Act of 1816 was

> altogether silent, both as to the competency and credibility of witnesses: that, as I apprehend, was left to the law as it then stood, I mean the law of 1741 . . . . [T]he policy of the law of 1741 was founded on a sense of the degraded state in which those unhappy beings existed . . . .
>
> [A] humane policy forbade that the life of a human being (one of themselves) should be taken away upon testimony coming from them, unless some circumstance appeared in aid. . . .

Hall would not admit the effect of the 1793 and 1816 Acts to be a general bringing of the slave within the sphere of the common law. Unless the statute specifically mentioned a common law protection, the slave's position remained determined by the 1741 Code. *State v. Ben* was truly an ironic case. Hall's strict continental absolutism would have spared Ben's life; Taylor's and Henderson's "humaneness" required its taking.

[42] See note 35 *supra* and accompanying text.

[43] In addition, see two slightly earlier cases, State v. Dick, 6 N.C. 388 (1818) (arresting a judgment for rape since an indictment had failed to conclude "*contra formam statuti*"); State v. Jim 7 N.C. 3 (1819) (because the indictment referred to "statute" rather than to "statutes"). In *State v. Jim* Judge Taylor invoked the following justification for his strict attention to detail: "To observe . . . this particular, is in effect to comply with the . . . Bill of Rights, by apprising every man . . . of the specific charges against him." *Id.* at 6.

[44] 8 N.C. 442 (1821).

dock a black could exert his own will even though it might be con-
tary to his master's.

*State v. Isham*[45] and *State v. Allen*[46] both involved convictions for
grand larceny, an offense punishable under the Slave Code by whipping
for the first conviction and by death without benefit of clergy for a
second offense. In *Isham* the State's attempt to secure capital punishment failed, not because of any real doubt about guilt, but because the
seal on the record of the first conviction was defective. In *Allen* the
indictment failed to charge a second offense. Because the court would
not permit the State to adduce proof of a prior conviction dehors the
indictment, the defendant was held entitled to benefit of clergy.[47]

In 1826 a black was tried for carnal assault, a crime which had been
elevated to a capital felony under an 1823 act.[48] After one verdict for
the State had been reversed,[49] the defense counsel sought to exclude the
testimony of the principal prosecution witness, a white female, on the
basis of minor inconsistencies in her testimony. While the trial judge
refused counsel's request for complete rejection of the testimony, he did
instruct the jury to accept only the credible part of her testimony
and to "act on such part as they did believe." When the case reached the
Supreme Court of North Carolina for the second time in 1828, Judge
Taylor ruled that the whole testimony should have been discarded,
adducing as a principle of the English Common Law the phrase *"falsum
in uno, falsum in omnibus."* [50]

This decision, handed down three years after the anti-slavery Ohio
Resolutions had first infuriated southern state legislators and scarcely a

---

[45] 10 N.C. 185 (1824).

[46] 10 N.C. 614 (1825).

[47] The State had to be ultra-careful about procedural niceties. Thus, the solicitor
saw his indictment quashed when he brought a grand larceny case before the superior
court. State v. Daniel, 10 N.C. 617 (1825). Since the first offense—which it was in
*Daniel*—was not punishable "in life or limb," the State should have tried to convict in
the county court.

[48] State v. Jim, 12 N.C. 142 (1826), and 12 N.C. 508 (1828).

[49] Defendant appealed on two grounds. One, not all the jurors had been slaveowners
as required by law; and two, the indictment had failed to allege that the assault had
been committed "violently . . . against the will" of the white female. Taylor agreed
with Jim's lawyer. Community outrage at the supposed rapist constituted no excuse
for failing to secure a proper jury. Furthermore, the charge amounted to "no more
than a misdemeanor at common law, . . . as it still continues in relation to all but the
colored population." 12 N.C. at 143. Finally—and most notably—the very fact of a
racially discriminatory punishment gave "an additional reason for . . . adhering to the
established forms." *Id*. at 144.

[50] *Id*. at 510.

year before the discovery of the incendiary Walker pamphlet among slaves on North Carolina coastal plantations, was quite generous. As another North Carolina Chief Judge, Richmond Pearson, was to observe thirty years later:

> Any one, upon the first blush, after reading *Jim's case*, would suppose that he could hardly open an English law book without meeting with the general rule *"falsum in uno, falsum in omnibus,"* yet, strange as it may seem, he will not be able to find the rule laid down in any English book of reports or by any writer upon evidence. This is not merely full negative proof against the existence of any such rule, but there is full positive proof that there is no such rule.[51]

But such was the behavior of the Supreme Court of North Carolina; the longer Chief Judge Taylor sat on the bench, the more liberal the court seemed to become. With the exception of his construction of manumission legislation, he carved out lines of jurisprudence which increasingly improved the black's condition.

### COMMON LAW DEVELOPMENT AND FAIR TRIALS, 1830-1860

Although sectional animosities increasingly marked national politics from the end of the 1820's to the Civil War, Judge Taylor's doctrine of common law protection for slaves became a dominant characteristic of southern appellate jurisprudence. In 1829, the Tennessee Supreme Court adopted it with little concern for logical niceties. In *Fields v. State*[52] the Tennessee judges simply stated that villeinage and slavery resembled each other and that the defendant's argument from continental theory was too "monstrous" [53] to accept. In 1843 the Alabama Supreme Court sustained a conviction for manslaughter in which the indictment had been "framed as at common law" but had concluded "against the form of the statute." [54] The Alabama judges reasoned in much the same manner as had the North Carolina court a quarter of a century earlier in *Reed*.[55] The Alabama statute was held merely to have increased the penalty for a pre-existing common law offense. Finally, in 1847, the Supreme Court of Texas held that the absence of a specific statute pertaining to manslaughter of slaves in no way hindered a common law conviction for that offense.[56] Judge Royall T.

---

[51] State v. Williams, 47 N.C. 257, 263 (1855).
[52] 9 Tenn. 141 (1829).
[53] *Id.* at 148.
[54] State v. Flanigin, 5 Ala. 477, 480 (1843).
[55] See notes 26-31 *supra* and accompanying text.
[56] Chandler v. State, 2 Tex. 305 (1847).

Wheeler thought that the "learned court" of Tennessee had reached a conclusion "so consonant to reason and principle as scarcely to require the support of argument or authority," and that "the only matter of surprise is that it should ever have been doubted." [57] Eight years later Judge Wheeler was to express himself with yet more vigor on the subject: Knifing a slave was "a crime against the law of nature and the laws of society, and equally within the spirit and intention of the statute, as if . . . committed upon a free person." [58] Only South Carolina and Georgia—the most conservative antebellum court—rejected Judge Taylor's doctrines.[59]

Between 1830 and 1860 the appellate courts of eight southern states considered the appeals of fifty-five whites convicted of inflicting injuries upon blacks. Seventeen of these defendants secured new trials, an incidence of success substantially below that achieved by black appellants during the same period. Examination of the records in these prosecutions of whites reveals no bias in favor of slaveowners or against defendants lacking a property connection with the victims of their crimes.[60] Indeed, forty-one percent of the slave murder prosecutions

---

[57] *Id.* at 309.

[58] Nix v. State, 13 Tex. 575, 579 (1855).

[59] See Whig Judge Eugenius A. Nisbet's compelling opinion in Neal v. Farmer, 9 Ga. 555 (1851), which does a rather thorough logical dissection of common law doctrines. The Georgia court—under the Chief Judgeship of Joseph Lumpkin, brother of the redoubtable State Rights Governor, Wilson Lumpkin, who defied Andrew Jackson over the Cherokee Indians' fate—was the only consistently pro-slavery court. *See* Nash HUD, *supra* note 11, at 182-202. Nisbet characterized *Fields v. State* as resulting from a "fervid zeal in behalf of humanity to the slave." 9 Ga. at 583. In 1859, by a two-to-one majority, the Mississippi Supreme Court broke from an earlier libertarian tradition which it had hewn out during the 1840's. In George v. State, 37 Miss. 316 (1859), Judge William Harris—a rabid fire-eater—asserted that the North Carolina and Tennessee decisions were founded upon the "unmeaning twaddle . . . of 'natural law'." *Id.* at 320. *See also* Mitchell v. Wells, 37 Miss. 235 (1859), discussed at note 126 *infra*.

[60] APPEALS FROM CONVICTIONS FOR HOMICIDE
AND ATTEMPTED HOMICIDE IN SEVEN SOUTHERN STATES, 1830-1860

| State | *Master** | | *Overseer** | | *"Unconnected"* | *White** |
|---|---|---|---|---|---|---|
| Alabama | 4 | 3 | 1 | 0 | 6 | 3 |
| Georgia | 2 | 1 | 1 | 0 | 1 | 0 |
| Mississippi | 2 | 1 | | | 4 | 3 |
| North Carolina | 2 | 0 | | | | |
| South Carolina | 3 | 0 | | | 8 | 1 |
| Tennessee | | | | | 1 | 0 |
| Texas | | | | | 2 | 0 |
| Totals: | 13 | 5 | 2 | 0 | 22 | 7 |

* First column indicates appeal taken; second column indicates reversals.

were brought against masters or overseers, and an analysis of the reversals in such slave homicide cases[61] suggests a predominant concern for fair procedures.[62]

It might be reasonable to suspect that in an era of mounting sectional hostility such a concern would not have extended to the trials of black defendants, especially in cases where guilt had been substantially es-

---

APPEALS FROM CONVICTIONS FOR INJURIES TO SLAVES AND FREE BLACKS

| State | Abuse of Slaves by: Master* | | Overseer* | | Other Whites* | | Murders of Free Blacks* | | Lesser Assaults on Free Blacks* | |
|---|---|---|---|---|---|---|---|---|---|---|
| Alabama | 1 | 1 | | | | | | | | |
| Mississippi | | | 1 | 0 | | | | | | |
| N. Carolina | | | | | 1 | 0 | 2 | 1 | 4 | 2 |
| S. Carolina | 1 | 0 | | | 3 | 0 | | | 1 | 0 |
| Tennessee | 2 | 0 | | | | | | | | |
| Texas | | | | | 1 | 0 | | | | |
| Totals: | 4 | 1 | 1 | 0 | 5 | 0 | 2 | 1 | 5 | 2 |

Total "slave" appeals: 10/1          Total "free black" appeals: 8/3

* First column indicates appeals taken; second column indicates reversals.

[61] For an extended discussion of this and other types of cases—lesser injuries to slaves, and attacks upon free blacks, see Nash HUD, *supra* note 11, at 377-413.

[62] None of the reversals could have been readily withheld. Thus, three Mississippi cases illustrated the clear need for new trials or acquittals because of prosecutors' carelessness. In Dowling v. State, 13 Miss. (5 S. & M.) 664 (1846), the prosecution had not proved that the victim had died from the cause charged in the indictment. Bradley v. State, 18 Miss. (10 S.&M.) 353 (1848), found the State without any proof directly connecting the defendant with the black's death. All that was offered was one witness' testimony that some hours prior to the homicide, the defendant had been pursuing the victim with a knife and had threatened to kill him. In Jenkins v. State, 30 Miss. 408 (1855), there was no evidence in the official record that, prior to trial, a valid indictment had ever been found by a grand jury. The grounds for the four reversals granted by the Alabama Court between the Mexican War and Lincoln's election exemplify the neutrality of that court throughout the antebellum decades: an unclear verdict, Cobia v. State, 16 Ala. 781 (1849); error in the indictment as to ownership of the deceased black, Eskridge v. State, 25 Ala. 30 (1854); prosecution under the wrong statute, *Ex parte* Howard, 30 Ala. 43 (1857); and the admission of incompetent testimony, Dupree v. State, 33 Ala. 380 (1859). In one South Carolina case, State v. Winningham, 10 Rich. Law 257 (S.C. 1857), the defendant had never been provided with an accurate copy of the indictment. The Georgia reversal, Martin v. State, 25 Ga. 494 (1858), was granted because of one juror's manifest prejudice against the defendant. Shortly before the trial had begun, the juror had declared that the defendant ought to be hanged. Afterwards, he had observed "in justification of the verdict of guilty which he and his fellow jurors had rendered, that the Martins were bad men *anyhow*, for that he had heard they had beat a man pretty nigh to death the spring before." *Id.* at 513. Green Martin was probably a "bad man," but a fair-minded court could hardly rule that he had received an unbiased trial. In the eighteen cases reaching the appellate benches, reversals of white convictions for lesser injuries to slaves and for attacks on free blacks were similarly granted only where clearly "proper."

tablished. Surprisingly, however, procedural fairness was almost always demanded by appellate judges in the trials of blacks. While prosecutions of blacks were numerous—there were 238 appeals taken during this period—defendants secured reversals in 136 instances.[63] Thus, blacks won reversals in more than half the cases that reached the appellate level. The qualities of appellate behavior in these cases are illustrated by decisions concerning four major grounds for appeal: flaws in the indictment process, biased judges and jurors, lack of counsel and involuntary self-incrimination.

## The Indictment Process

Even before an accused black reached the prisoner's dock, the state could impair the fairness of his trial by using unqualified persons to draft the indictment, by overreaching jurisdictional restrictions or by permitting flaws in the form of the indictment itself. On the few occasions when objections concerning the qualifications of judges and jurors were raised, even the pro-slavery Georgia Supreme Court weighed them without regard to the nature of the crime or the color of the defendant.[64] The judges of the South Carolina appellate court once insisted on a new trial, not because of genuine doubts about a slave's guilt, but rather because he had been tried in the parish where he had

---

[63]      APPEALS FROM CONVICTIONS BY WHITES AND BLACKS
                   IN NINE STATES, 1830-1860

| State | All Injuries* to Blacks | | All Trials* of Slaves | | All Trials of* Free Blacks | |
|-------|----|----|----|----|----|----|
| Alabama | 12 | 7 | 40 | 25 | 0 | 0 |
| Arkansas | 0 | 0 | 9 | 8 | 2 | 0 |
| Florida | 0 | 0 | 0 | 2 | 1 | 1 |
| Georgia | 4 | 1 | 14 | 2 | 1 | 1 |
| Mississippi | 7 | 4 | 34 | 21 | 3 | 1 |
| N. Carolina | 9 | 3 | 43 | 22 | 28 | 14 |
| S. Carolina | 16 | 2 | 9 | 6 | 3 | 1 |
| Tennessee | 3 | 0 | 33 | 23 | 10 | 7 |
| Texas | 4 | 0 | 3 | 2 | 1 | 0 |
| Totals | 55 | 17 | 185 | 111 | 49 | 25 |

* First column indicates appeals taken; second column indicates reversals.

[64] Stephen v. State, 11 Ga. 225 (1852). *See* Green v. State, 23 Miss. 509 (1852) (error in the indictment as to the county where the attempt to rape occurred); Abram v. State, 25 Miss. 589 (1853) (record failed to show that the grand jury had ever been duly sworn).

inflicted the injury instead of the parish where the victim had actually died.[65]

More substantial objections arose from defective indictments which lacked an adequate description of the offense, misjoined offenses or sought convictions for nonexistent crimes. Six of the seven courts which heard objections based on these flaws awarded new trials.[66] Reversals were always granted for failure to give the defendants fair warning as, for example, when the indictment specified a plurality of statutes rather than just the single relevant one,[67] or when it failed to charge an assault in conjunction with a rape.[68]

Some judges appear to have gone further than necessary to insure that defendants were adequately apprised of the nature of the accusation. While the North Carolina Supreme Court refused to reverse where the indictment used the word "intention" rather than "intent," [69] it did not allow much more variation, reversing two rape convictions—one where the word "feloniously" had been omitted,[70] and the other where the black had been indicted for "attempt" rather than "intent" to rape.[71] In Tennessee a conviction for robbery failed because the indictment omitted to aver that the slave had taken the property contrary to the will of its owner.[72] A capital conviction for assault with intent to kill failed in Mississippi because the court insisted that malice be averred in the indictment,[73] while the conviction of an Alabama slave for attempt-

---

[65] State *ex rel.* Matthews v. Toomer, 1 Cheves 106 (S.C. 1840). Judge Bayliss Earle agreed with the State that a 1793 law under which he ordered a *venire de novo* was "perhaps . . . not intended, at the time, to embrace the homicide of one slave by another. At least, considering the policy of the country, then, in regard to slaves, it may well be doubted . . . ." *Id.* at 107. Nonetheless, he argued, since "the tendency of our modern legislation has been . . . to promote a more favorable regard for the life of the slave . . . [t]he . . . Act, on a fair and liberal construction, applies as well to the trial of slaves as of white persons. . . ." *Id.* at 108.

[66] The refusal of the seventh court, Georgia's, to reverse was neutral. Anthony v. State, 9 Ga. 264 (1851).

[67] State v. Sandy, 25 N.C. 570 (1843).

[68] Sullivan v. State, 8 Ark. 400 (1848). Both the Alabama and Tennessee courts reversed for failure of an indictment to specify that the victim was white—even though the prosecution offered ample proof at trial. Nelson v. State, 6 Ala. 394 (1844); Grandison v. State, 21 Tenn. 451 (1841). These appellate demands for proper procedure are the more noteworthy since they seem to have been voiced even when the accusation was for rape.

[69] State v. Tom, 47 N.C. 414 (1855).

[70] State v. Jesse, 19 N.C. 297 (1837).

[71] State v. Martin, 14 N.C. 329 (1832).

[72] Kit v. State, 30 Tenn. 167 (1850).

[73] Anthony v. State, 21 Miss. (13 S. & M.) 263 (1850).

ing to poison a white was reversed because the indictment had omitted to allege that the administered substance was poisonous.[74] One of the cases upholding the conviction of a black further illustrates the impartiality of antebellum judges. In *Ben v. State*[75] "administering and causing to be administered" was determined not to be fatally duplicitous because a prior conviction of a white had been sustained under an indictment charging "receiving and concealing stolen goods."

## Biased Judges and Jurors

From time to time antebellum judges heard appeals seeking the disqualification of juries or lower court judges. The Supreme Court of Texas, for example, awarded a new trial for murder where the record failed to show that the jury had been sworn,[76] and the Supreme Court of Alabama threw out a unanimous verdict of guilty for the murder of a white man, on the ground that one juror's share in an undistributed estate of slaves did not qualify him as a slave-holder and thus as a juror.[77] Similarly, Tennessee jurors were held to be acting *ultra vires* since the indictment under which they were proceeding did not specify that the black defendant was free; had he been a slave there would have been no jurisdiction.[78] In *Jim v. State*,[79] however, the Georgia Supreme Court denied a new trial for the murder of an overseer even though one of the jurors "had formed and expressed an opinion, (before being sworn as a Juror,) that prisoner ought to be hung [*sic*]."[80] The Tennessee judges, by contrast, were willing to reverse when the jurors had separated from each other during their impanelling and were permitted to go home for the weekend.[81] Although the defendant had consented to the separation, Judge Nathan Green insisted that

the consent of the prisoner, in such case, [ought not] to be taken. And in a case like this, where the prisoner is a slave, and ignorant of

---

[74] State v. Clarissa, 11 Ala. 57 (1847). There was little doubt that the defendant in this case had been properly apprised of the nature of the crime since the indictment had charged him with administration of "Jimson weed," the deadly properties of which were common knowledge in the neighborhood.

[75] 22 Ala. 9 (1853), *citing* State v. Murphy, 6 Ala. 846 (1844).

[76] Nels v. State, 2 Tex. 280 (1847). *But see* Peter v. State, 11 Tex. 762 (1854) (complaint that the deputy county clerk was an impostor failed because it did not appear on the lower court record).

[77] Spence v. State, 17 Ala. 192 (1850).

[78] Bennett v. State, 31 Tenn. 411 (1852).

[79] 15 Ga. 535 (1854).

[80] *Id.* at 537.

[81] Wesley v. State, 30 Tenn. 502 (1851).

his rights, and the case one calculated to excite the community against him, the rules of law for securing an impartial trial of the case, ought to be the more firmly enforced.[82]

Apparently the Tennessee court was moved by a genuine and substantial concern for fair play and for humane treatment of the accused black. Moreover, at least in this case, the court was free of any baser motive to protect the master's interest by keeping costly property alive, because the defendant was on trial for the murder of his master.[83]

In four cases the Mississippi judges proceeded considerably beyond a neutral position. In *Lewis v. State*,[84] the court took to task a juror who conversed and exchanged notes with a bystander during trial:

> This conduct was highly reprehensible, and should have subjected the juror to punishment. . . . Confidence in the administration of justice can only be preserved by removing even the shadow of suspicion from those in whose hands it is entrusted.[85]

In the second case, *Sam v. State*,[86] the court disqualified two jurors. The first juror had listened the day before Sam's trial to the proceedings against an accused accomplice, and the appellate court felt the opinions so formed were too strong to be tolerated. The second man, however, had merely formed an opinion on the basis of rumor. Judge Clayton recognized the difficulty of laying "down a rule of universal application, upon a subject so hard to place within precise limits," [87] and his rejection of the second juryman seems to have been based on the feeling that the lower court could have done better by the slave. Judge Clayton observed that, in rare cases, such as Aaron Burr's trial, notoriety might

---

[82] *Id.* at 505.

[83] The Tennessee judges would not disqualify jurors who had formed opinions prior to the trial solely on rumor and who convinced the judge that they were capable of changing their minds according to the evidence presented at the trial. *Cf.* Alfred and Anthony v. State, 32 Tenn. 581 (1853); Moses v. State, 30 Tenn. 232 (1850). The doctrine comes from two earlier cases involving whites: Payne v. State, 22 Tenn. 375 (1842); McGowan v. State, 17 Tenn. 184 (1836).

[84] 17 Miss. (9 S. & M.) 115 (1847).

[85] *Id.* at 121. But note that the court did not actually rule on the prisoner's objection that the juror should not be allowed to serve despite the fact that the notes were on another subject. A new trial was awarded on other grounds. Note also that the trial judge had disqualified one juror because he had "told the court that he had conscientious scruples about finding any man guilty of murder, and could not conscientiously take the oath in a capital case." *Id.* at 116.

[86] 21 Miss. (13 S. & M.) 189 (1849).

[87] *Id.* at 195.

be so great that finding jurymen totally free of prior opinions would be almost impossible.

> In such cases, some modification of . . . doctrine may be impera-
> tively required. The rule must yield to the necessity, but only so
> far as the necessity demands. Yet the more nearly we approach the
> point of entire freedom from preconceived opinion, and of complete
> equality between the parties, the more nearly we approach the per-
> fection of the system of trial by jury.[88]

Seven years later, the Mississippi court heard a case in which the judge had refused a new trial when the black had discovered after his conviction that one juror might have been biased against him. Two witnesses swore they had heard the juror declare prior to the trial "that if the evidence . . . should be the same as that given on a previous trial [of the same case] . . . the defendant was guilty of murder, and ought to be hung [*sic*]." [89] The juror submitted an affidavit denying he had made such a statement, and the judge, despite holding that the affidavit was incompetent evidence, refused a new trial. On appeal, the Mississippi Supreme Court, with the secessionist Judge Alexander Handy dissenting, reversed. Finally, in 1859, the Mississippi court overturned a conviction because a juror had been impanelled after stating on exami-nation "that it would require testimony to remove or destroy" the opinion which he had already formed on the basis of rumor.[90]

## The Right to Counsel

Given the numerous complaints during the past thirty years that indigent defendants have not been provided with adequate legal assis-tance in conducting their defense,[91] the record of antebellum southern courts is striking, especially since the right to counsel under English Common Law of the eighteenth century meant only that if a de-fendant had the money to hire a lawyer, the attorney could not be barred from the courtroom.[92] In very few antebellum cases does it

---

[88] *Id.*

[89] Sam v. State, 31 Miss. 480, 483 (1856).

[90] Alfred v. State, 37 Miss. 296 (1859).

[91] *E.g.,* Gideon v. Wainwright, 372 U.S. 335 (1963); Hudson v. North Carolina, 363 U.S. 697 (1960); Tomkins v. Missouri, 323 U.S. 485 (1945); Betts v. Brady, 316 U.S. 455 (1942); Avery v. Alabama, 308 U.S. 444 (1940); Powell v. Alabama, 287 U.S. 45 (1932).

[92] *See* C. PRITCHETT, AMERICAN CONSTITUTIONAL ISSUES 400-05 (1962). *See also* Betts v. Brady, 316 U.S. 455 (1942).

appear that blacks lacked counsel either at their original trial or on appeal. Perhaps the abundance of distinguished lawyers lined up on the blacks' side was the result of the master's desire to keep a valuable piece of property, but that does not explain the instances in which future governors and judges appeared to argue for free blacks.[93]

Two sample cases suggest that courts were active in insisting on counsel regardless of the master's property interests. The first case discloses that the court appointed two of the more distinguished members of the Tennessee Bar.[94] In the second case, even the pro-slavery Georgia judiciary showed concern. In *Jim v. State*,[95] the slave had been accused of murdering his overseer, and so heavy was the evidence against him that his master had declined to hire a lawyer. The lower court provided assistance for the trial, and hearing of the master's refusal on appeal, Judge Ebenezer Starnes became angry:

> [I]n our State, no man, white or black, bond or free, can be tried without the assistance of counsel, as the humane provisions of our law require the appointment of counsel by the Court, for every one . . . who is unable to procure counsel for himself . . . . [T]he master's duty . . . is, that he should . . . see to it, that his slave has the benefit of counsel . . . at the earliest convenient moment of his need . . . .[96]

In all probability the other more liberal courts had similar attitudes. Thus, it appears that the right to counsel may have been better secured to indigent blacks during the antebellum era than in any later period prior to *Gideon v. Wainwright*.[97]

### Coerced Confessions

Perhaps no protection is more vital to a fair trial than the exclusion of coerced confessions; no other inequity increases the likelihood of an unfair conviction so greatly as the admission of an involuntary confession. Since this aspect of criminal jurisprudence is currently contested in the Supreme Court of the United States, the surprisingly modern record compiled by five of the six slave state supreme courts which adjudicated appeals from convictions based on coerced confessions is

---

93 *See, e.g.*, State v. Manual, 20 N.C. 20 (1838).

94 John Marshall and R. C. Foster, in Henry v. State, 30 Tenn. 224 (1850). Normally, antebellum reports do not make clear whether the lawyer was court-appointed.

95 15 Ga. 535 (1854).

96 *Id.* at 539-540.

97 372 U.S. 335 (1963).

worthy of detailed examination. Working without the compulsions of the fourteenth amendment, the courts of North Carolina, Tennessee, Florida, Georgia, Alabama and Mississippi granted new trials in fourteen of the twenty-four cases heard between 1830 and 1861. With the possible exception of the Georgia bench, these courts evolved standards of at least minimal fairness. Safeguards ranged from a position such as that of the late Mr. Justice Robert Jackson, who sought a relatively close nexus between threats, or application, of force and the making of the confession, to a position similar to that of Mr. Justice Douglas, which goes beyond concern for the reliability of the confession to insistence on civilized police behavior by barring any confession which appears to have been the result of official overreaching.[98] Between these two stances, courts adopted mesne positions as they faced three problems: whether to recognize non-physical coercion; whether the magistrates had a duty to warn the suspect of his rights prior to interrogation; and whether evidence procured by virtue of a coerced confession was admissible.

Not surprisingly, the Tennessee court reacted rather liberally to the problems of non-physical coercion and of "tainted fruit." In *Ann v. State*,[99] there was no doubt that force had been used; the only question was whether the force was sufficiently proximate to the confession to make it inadmissible. Ann, a fifteen-year-old slave, was accused of administering an overdose of laudanum to her master's five-week-old baby, contrary to a general command not to give the baby any medicine. Following the baby's death, the master became very excited, inflicted blows with his hand and threatened to shoot Ann. He was induced to desist by his wife, but the next evening Ann broke her silence and confessed. Since she was no longer in imminent danger of violence, the court could have held that the nexus between force and confession was insufficient. Yet, Judge Robert McKinney observed that

> in the case of a timid girl, of tender age, ignorant and illiterate, a slave and in chains, whose life had been threatened by her master, and against whom the hand of everyone, even those of her own color and condition, seems to have been raised, . . . the law . . . conclusively presumes that an influence was exerted upon . . . the prisoner.[100]

---

[98] *Compare* Ashcraft v. Tennessee, 322 U.S. 143, 156 (1944) (dissenting opinion) (Jackson, J.), *with* Malinski v. New York, 324 U.S. 401 (1945) (Douglas, J.).
[99] 30 Tenn. 159 (1850).
[100] *Id.* at 163.

The North Carolina court, which considered coerced confession issues in three slave cases and in one case involving a free black, attempted to judge admissibility by the reliability theory. Before reversing a conviction, the court demanded proof that the confession had been induced either by threats of violence or by promises of reward or leniency.[101] The court applied this test to uphold a conviction based on a confession to a white man who had said somewhat angrily to the prisoner: "If you belonged to me, I would make you tell." [102] The condition "carried with it the assurance that the witness would inflict no suffering upon him." [103] In the free black case, *State v. Fisher*,[104] there were two confessions. The first, made one day after the homicide was committed, was an indirect product of a whipping. The black had been "struck . . . five or six licks with a whip on his bare back, when he agreed to show the gun." [105] Though the witnesses promised "that they were not going to whip him to make him confess the murder," [106] but only to make him reveal the whereabouts of the gun used in the killing, the nexus between coercion and confession was sufficiently close for the court to exclude it on the grounds that the officer had "treated him in . . . a cruel and unlawful manner." [107] However, the second confession, made the next day to another white, was valid because "it is conceded that the second . . . did not proceed from the same influence which induced, or rather, cruelly extorted the first." [108] The court would not exclude the later confession, procured while the prisoner was in jail and safe from further violence,

> upon the ground of public policy, for the purposes of discountenancing, and thus putting an end to such gross violation of the law as the officer and his party . . . were guilty of . . . . We think the purposes of justice will be best accomplished by having the officer indicted and punished for his unlawful and tyrannical abuse of his official power.[109]

The court, in brief, would not accept the libertarian argument for

---

101 State v. Jefferson, 28 N.C. 304 (1846) (alternative holding).
102 State v. Patrick, 48 N.C. 443, 445 (1856).
103 *Id*. at 449.
104 51 N.C. 478 (1859).
105 *Id*. at 479.
106 *Id*.
107 *Id*. at 480.
108 *Id*. at 482.
109 *Id*. at 484.

"civilizing the police" which supports the modern exclusionary rule. In the fourth case, *State v. George*,[110] the lower court judge had admitted confessions which the Supreme Court thought

> were extracted by means calculated to excite *the fear of present death in the firmest mind*. The prisoners were in irons; a large crowd . . . became very much excited; one strikes Gauzey in the face, and threatens to kill him . . .; another says to George: "Tell about it, '*they*' will hang you if you don't," and there they stood—an infuriated crowd! This was as direct an appeal to his fear as could have been made . . . .[111]

The appellate judges rejected the State's argument that an hour's lapse between this "confrontation" and the slave's confession legitimated it:

> [*T*]*he circumstances of terror remained the same*. There was the same infuriated crowd. . . . Some of them said "the Negroes who did it deserve to be burnt." True, the prisoner did not hear this, but the demonstrations of a crowd where such sentiments are uttered, can be . . . felt by an unfortunate being, who knows that he is within its power, without hearing what is said.[112]

Alabama and Mississippi both developed very liberal views on the subject of confessions. In 1847 the wealthy Whig Judge, John J. Ormond, speaking for the Alabama court, rejected a confession obtained by questioning the defendant three days after a whipping.[113] In 1850, testimony that the master customarily whipped his slaves whenever he suspected them of wrongdoing until they confessed discredited a

---

[110] 50 N.C. 233 (1858).

[111] *Id*. at 235.

[112] *Id*. at 235-36. The most conservative Florida court—that of 1851 to 1853—heard a similar case, and reached the same result. The city mayor, while trying to stop a crowd from hanging the suspected slave, suggested to him that he should turn state's evidence and that his accomplices would be put on trial instead. The majority excluded both a confession made then and another made the next day to his master. Chief Judge Wright, dissenting, delivered the rather astounding declaration that
> in this case no undue means were used. I cannot regard the crowd outside, and their excited declarations, as constituting such undue means. The natural and probable effect of these excited declarations was . . . to induce him to persist in his denial . . . .
Simon v. State, 5 Fla. 285, 301 (1853).

[113] State v. Clarissa, 11 Ala. 57 (1847) (slave's confession is almost *per se* coerced).

confession given to a third party who had used no force, but whom the master had left in charge of the prisoners.[114]

During the 1850's the Alabama court became increasingly liberal with respect to "the duty to warn." In 1852, in *Seaborn v. State*,[115] the judges rejected the doctrine that the slaves' ignorance of the consequences of confessions made them altogether inadmissible. The failure to warn only affected the credibility which the jury should attach to the confession. While the magistrate "undoubtedly ought to have" cautioned them, still "we find no case excluding confessions for want of such caution. The question is . . . were the confessions voluntary, and uninfluenced by fear of personal injury or the hope of some benefit." [116] Two years later, however, the court qualified *Seaborn*, holding inadmissible both a first confession made to the master and a second made to a magistrate who failed to caution the slave.[117]

Perhaps the most striking Alabama decision was *Bob v. State*[118] in 1858. The court rejected a string of confessions by a black convicted of murdering his master. The first few confessions had clearly been induced by beating. The last, however, occurred after he was in jail. Judge A. J. Walker stated that while the circumstances might have been

> sufficient to have removed the impression from the mind of a white man, accustomed to, and understanding the proceedings of a criminal trial. . . . we cannot affirm the same thing of a slave. An ignorant slave, knowing nothing of judicial proceedings, perhaps not even understanding the nature of the duties discharged by the different persons engaged in his trial, and confused . . . by the scenes transpiring around him, might witness an offer of testimony against him, and hear an argument upon its admissibility [without realizing that the object was to procure his conviction].[119]

Furthermore, the court stated, the slave should have been treated specially because he might well have feared that changing his story in mid-stream would result in further punishment.[120]

Between 1839 and 1852 the Mississippi court became no less de-

---

114 Spence v. State, 17 Ala. 192 (1850).
115 20 Ala. 15 (1852).
116 *Id.* at 18.
117 Wyatt v. State, 25 Ala. 9 (1854).
118 32 Ala. 560 (1858).
119 *Id.* at 567-68.
120 *Id.* at 568.

termined than the Alabama court to exclude dubious confessions. In 1839, although reversing the conviction on other grounds, it admitted a confession which, though procured without threats or promises, had been made while a crowd had milled around outside the jail where the suspected slave was incarcerated.[121] The black went through a second trial, secured another reversal on different grounds, and finally in 1844 came before the court once more on the subject of a coerced confession. The defense counsel successfully argued that the court should presume that the defendant's fear of imminent coercion had continued after the crowd had dispersed and while a magistrate had questioned him about his actions, failing to warn him of his right to remain silent. Judge Joseph Thacher took much the same line as Judge Walker of Alabama.[122] Eight years later in *Van Buren v. State*[123] the Mississippi court took an even firmer approach. Not only did the magistrate have to warn the prisoner, but according to the Unionist Whig Judge William Yerger, he had to make sure that "the prisoner understood such warning."[124]

---

[121] Peter v. State, 3 Howard 433 (Miss. 1839).

[122] It is true that by adopting this rule the truth may sometimes be rejected; but it effects a greater object, in guarding against the possibility of an innocent person being convicted who by weakness has been seduced to accuse himself in hopes of obtaining thereby more favor.
Peter v. State, 12 Miss. (4 S. & M.) 31, 38-39 (1844).

[123] 24 Miss. 512 (1852).

[124] *Id.* at 516. Although in 1856 the Mississippi court—by then changed to a more States' Rights make-up—limited this libertarian position by holding that a private citizen did not have to caution a black prisoner in his charge, and although it also held valid a confession volunteered without hope of gain, *cf.* Dick v. State, 30 Miss. 593 (1856), it certainly did not effect a shift towards reaction in regard to self-incrimination parallel to that which it abruptly executed two years before Secession in respect to suits pertaining to emancipation. The few cases lost by blacks appealing from felony convictions did not amount to egregious miscarriages of justice. *See, e.g.,* Simon v. State, 36 Miss. 636 (1859); Simon v. State, 37 Miss. 288 (1858); Sam v. State, 33 Miss. 347 (1857). For the 1859 shift regarding manumission, see notes 125-26 *infra*.
One misdemeanor case is noteworthy because it suggests that judicial demands for fair trials were not limited to slaves in felony trials. In State v. Jacobs, 5 Jones 259 (N.C. 1858), the free black defendant—convicted for illegally carrying a gun under a statute applicable only to blacks—complained that his privilege against self-incrimination had been denied because his presence in court before the jury had allowed the jurors to determine his color. The Attorney General pointed out that the defendant had to be present at his trial and that the jury would be bound to see him. Yet, Judge William Battle replied: "[W]e are decidedly of the opinion that he *can not*" be compelled "to stand or sit within view of the jury." *Id.* at 259-60. Battle could see no reason for "an exception to that great conservative rule which the generous spirit of the common law has established for the protection of accused persons." *Id.* at 260. This was an

THE MANUMISSION CASES

Strict nineteenth century formalism might have been the sole cause of appellate insistence on procedural safeguards in antebellum criminal trials of slaves and free blacks. Formalism alone, however, cannot adequately explain a parallel fairness in many civil suits for freedom from slavery. Such cases raised substantive questions of law involving an underlying philosophy toward slavery as an institution and toward the black as an individual.

Manumission suits involved a basic policy judgment whether a grant of freedom was a laudable act of benevolence which judges should underwrite, or a "subversive" attempt to undermine an institution which the judges had a duty to preserve. This issue was manifested in a variety of subsidiary questions but was particularly apparent in those involving the right to a hearing, damages for wrongfully holding a person as a slave, the capacity of blacks to exercise a legal choice, and the deference to be given to northern or foreign laws conflicting with domestic slave law.

The initial problem was insuring the black a day in court. Virtually all judges in the states which were later to join the Confederacy were willing to do that much, and some went so far as to hold whites who attempted to thwart manumission hearings in contempt of court.[125] Only the Supreme Court of Mississippi after 1858 could be faulted for denying access to the judicial process.[126] Once the black had his

---

unusual sort of conservatism—one which allowed the defendant the right to a partition—as well as a privilege—against self-incrimination.

[125] *See* Spear v. Rice, 1 Harper 20 (S.C. 1823); Campbell v. Campbell, 13 Ark. 513 (1853); Sylvia v. Covey, 12 Tenn. 297 (1833) (removing slaves from the owner's custody pending trial).

[126] *See* Mitchell v. Wells, 37 Miss. 235 (1859), where Judge William Harris attained an extraordinary pitch of "mad rationality" in urging that no civil suits brought by blacks be heard at all in Mississippi courts on the grounds that blacks should be regarded as enemies of the State. Judge Harris reached this striking conclusion in a rage at Ohio's affliction "with a negromania, which inclines her to descend . . . to embrace, as citizens, the neglected race . . . occupying, in the order of nature, an intermediate state between the irrational animal and the white man." *Id.* at 262-63. Yet, Harris displayed an unusual pathology and his dissenting colleague, Judge Alexander Handy, objected that Harris' viewpoint would amount to resurrecting "the barbarian rules which prevailed in the dark ages." *Id.* at 282. More representative of southern judicial behavior was the answer of Judge Nathan Green of Tennessee to the contention that blacks as property could not sue. Green declared that the black was the equal of the white and opened the courts to freedom-seeking slaves. See note 7 *supra* and accompanying text. Most judges did not overtly display such egalitarian

day in court and prevailed, however, his ability to collect damages was uncertain. In general, the courts allowed juries to award damages in individual cases. Only the Virginia Supreme Court of Appeals expressly denied damages on the ground that such practice might ruin a white who had wrongfully held a freed slave in good faith.[127] On this count the Texas and Tennessee courts were the most favorable to free blacks, allowing them to bring a second suit for damages after receiving freedom.[128]

Closely related to the argument that chattels could not sue was one concerning wills authorizing a slave to choose between freedom and bondage or permitting him to select a home in the event that domestic laws prohibited freed blacks from remaining within the state as freedmen. Drawing from Continental theories, opponents of such bequests argued that a grant of freedom was "the exercise of a power conferred on the owner by the law, with which the slave has nothing to do."[129] Libertarians thought such a contention absurd, particularly since criminal statutes ascribed capacity and responsibility for criminal choices to the slave.[130] This issue, more than any other, separated pro-slavery judges from pro-manumission activists. Texas, Tennessee and North Carolina judges consistently rejected restrictive interpretation,[131] as did the Mississippi judges of the early 1840's whose libertarianism sufficiently annoyed the state legislature that it overruled them.[132] During

---

general *attitudes* as did Green, but their holdings as to the right to a hearing (their specific judicial *behaviors*) were closer to Green's attitude than to Harris's.

[127] *See* Paup v. Mingo, 31 Va. (4 Leigh) 163 (1833).

[128] *See* Moore's Adm'r v. Minerva, 17 Tex. 20 (1856); Woodfolk v. Sweeper, 21 Tenn. 88 (1840) (holding in favor of a Maryland black previously convicted for helping slaves to escape on the underground railroad); Matilda v. Crenshaw, 12 Tenn. 299 (1833).

[129] Williamson v. Coalter, 55 Va. (14 Gratt.) 394, 398-99 (1858) (Allen, P.) (3-2 decision).

[130] Moderately pro-slavery judges less inclined than others to impose their distaste for manumission upon the law were similarly dubious. Thus, Thomas Ruffin of North Carolina, despite his shift from regarding slavery as an evil in the late 1820's to viewing it as a positive good for both races in the middle 1850's, repudiated the Virginia position in 1858: "It is not true in point of fact or law that slaves have not a mental or a moral capacity to make the election." Redding v. Findley, 4 Jones Eq. 216, 218-19 (N.C. 1858). *Compare* his statement in State v. Mann, 2 Devereux 263 (N.C. 1829), *with* his Address Before the State Agricultural Society of North Carolina, 1 CAROLINA CULTIVATOR 309 (December, 1855).

[131] *See* Reeves v. Long, 5 Jones Eq. 355 (N.C. 1860); Harrison v. Everett, 5 Jones Eq. 163 (N.C. 1859); Redding v. Findley, 4 Jones Eq. 216 (N.C. 1858); Purvis v. Sherrod, 12 Tex. 140 (1854).

[132] *See* Leech v. Cooley, 14 Miss. (6 S. & M.) 93 (1846); and the argument be-

the decade before the creation of Georgia's Supreme Court in 1845, the circuit judges in that State also rejected the oppressive rule.[133] Finally, Virginia jurists of the 1830's recognized the slave's capacity for choice. Passivists, whose personal liberal tendencies were seemingly overcome by judicial self-restraint, they sought diligently to distinguish rather than overrule earlier Virginia decisions against liberty.[134] In the Deep South, only one state court, Alabama, consistently denied the slave's capacity for choice;[135] in the Upper South only Virginia after 1858 did so.

Another indicator of judicial attitudes emerged in the conflict between foreign law favorable to freedom and local slave statutes which resticted manumission. Libertarian judges strained to apply northern and foreign laws, while the most pro-slavery judges rejected outside authority altogether.[136]

---

tween Judges Harris and Handy in Mitchell v. Wells, 37 Miss. 235 (1859), as to the libertarian thrust of earlier decisions.

[133] *See* Jordan v. Bradley, 1 Ga. 443 (1930).

[134] *Compare* Maria v. Surbaugh, 23 Va. (2 Rand.) 228 (1824), *with* Elder v. Elder's Ex'r, 31 Va. (4 Leigh) 252 (1833), Emory v. Erskine, 34 Va. (7 Leigh) 267 (1836), Emory v. Henry, 36 Va. (9 Leigh) 188 (1838), *and* Parks v. Hewlett, 36 Va. (9 Leigh) 511 (1838).

[135] *See* Carroll v. Brumby, 13 Ala. 102 (1848); Creswell's Ex'r v. Walker, 37 Ala. 229 (1861).

[136] Three such types of conflict illustrate the point. First, courts struggled with the effect of northern statutes when the southern master had taken his slave north to free him and brought him back again simply to skirt his own state's requirement that freed slaves leave the jurisdiction for good. Tennessee and the pre-1858 Virginia judges upheld this procedure. Foster's Adm'r v. Foster, 51 Va. (10 Gratt.) 485 (1853); Blackmore v. Phill. 7 Yerger 452 (Tenn. 1835); Betty v. Horton, 32 Va. (5 Leigh) 667 (1833). The Mississippi Court took the opposite position. Hinds v. Brazealle, 2 Howard 837 (Miss. 1838).

Second, courts divided on the question whether a slave with a grant to future freedom—a *statu liberi*, as he was called—could enforce that grant when it fell due, if in the meantime he had been taken into another jurisdiction whose statutes prohibited such grants to its own slaves. The courts of South Carolina, Texas and Alabama permitted enforcement. Guillemette v. Harper, 4 Richardson 186 (S.C. 1850); Jones v. Laney, 2 Tex. 342 (1847); Moore's Adm'r v. Minerva, 17 Tex. 20 (1856); Sidney v. White, 12 Ala. 728 (1848); Union Bank v. Benham, 23 Ala. 143 (1853); Fields v. Walker, 23 Ala. 155 (1853). The Georgia court held a different view. Its Chief Judge considered the relevant laws of Maryland and other "quasi-slave States" prejudicial to Georgia's rights and interests, argued that the South Carolina and Alabama courts had not considered the matter with adequate thoroughness, and—apparently genuinely—asserted: "[A]s a man, I do not regret the failure of this bequest. . . . [W]hat friend of the African . . . would desire to see these children of the sun . . . perish with cold in higher altitudes?" Knight v. Hardeman, 17 Ga. 253, 262 (1855); *see* Adams v. Bass, 18 Ga. 130, 138-39 (1855).

Third, courts questioned the right of a slave, who had been taken North and freed by his master, to inherit the master's property left to him in the South. Before 1859 the Mississippi judges all thought that comity—no matter how inconveniently—took

Manumission cases and attitudes add a substantive dimension to the climate of procedural fairness which prevailed in criminal trials. They support the thesis that more than mere formalism motivated the reasonable, if not equal, treatment accorded to slaves and free blacks. Rejecting formalism as the sole motive for judicial behavior, it thus becomes necessary to search for an answer.

## An Explanation for Judicial Behavior

The foregoing sketch of antebellum judicial behavior suggests two issues for analysis. First, to what extent did a climate of relative fairness prevail throughout the framework of southern justice? It seems safe to assume that "plantation justice" was rarely replete with insistence upon "fairness," but what of the lower levels of formal adjudication? How many lower trial court judges were motivated either by a formalist insistence upon proper procedures or by a concern for substantive fairness? Second, what factors account for the quality of appellate decision-making?

The range of questions inherent in the first issue must be left for subsequent research. Any satisfactory answers would require substantial samplings of county court records and a statistical analysis of "plantation justice"—records which, in all probability, are inadequate for the task. Such an effort lies beyond the scope of this Article. An attempt may be made, however, to answer the second inquiry through the use of a common social science technique—development of a link between behavior on the bench and a number of social and political characteristics of the judges.

A classification of judges according to their behavior on the bench is the first requisite of such a study, but classification necessarily requires a reduction of each judge's behavior into generalized patterns. Judicial decisions in suits for freedom offer—because of the frequency with which manumission issues produced different judicial solutions—the most promising basis for grouping judges. Arguably, the data suggests three major groups: a "libertarian" group whose members decided to free slaves in cases where an opposite choice would have been logically

precedent; in 1859, by a majority of one, they reversed themselves. Leiper v. Hoffman, 26 Miss. 615 (1853), *overruled*, Mitchell v. Wells, 37 Miss. 235 (1859). In 1860 the conservative South Carolina equity appeals court sought to bar such a bequest. On appeal to the newly-formed combined Supreme Court in Law and Equity, a pro-Union majority of one reversed, and thus aligned itself with the North Carolina court which had recently upheld a bequest of $9000. Willis v. Jolliffe, 11 S.C. Eq. 447 (1860); Alvany v. Powell, 1 Jones Eq. 25 (N.C. 1853).

feasible; a "pro-slavery" group whose members generally made the opposite choice; and a "neutralist" group whose members followed precedent and legislative intent to reach results without regard to personal preferences about slavery.[137] Of the 106 judges who sat between 1830 and 1860 about whom at least some social and political data is available, 36 seem to have been libertarian, 23 pro-slavery, and 47 neutralist.

Birth, date of appointment and socio-economic status are all attributes which might be linked with judicial behavior. It might be reasonable to expect greater tendencies toward libertarianism among those born in the eighteenth century, among those appointed before the rise of virulent northern abolitionism in the 1830's, and—if a distinction is made between "Jeffersonian patricians" and "Jacksonian plebians"—among those who came from high socio-economic backgrounds. Yet, examination shows that the correlations of judicial behavior with birth and appointment are weak,[138] and that the relationship of behavior to socio-

---

[137] For a discussion of the methodological assumptions and cautions which this division entails, see Nash HUD, *supra* note 11, at 473-77. For a more elaborate analysis of the results of two similar techniques—of which the following is a much-abbreviated distillate—see *id.* at 477-91. Note also that the number of judges precludes a multi-factor analysis. Thus, it is feasible to separate, say, Episcopalians from other Protestants, or Democrats from Whigs, while it is not feasible to compare the behavior of Episcopalian Democrats and Episcopalian Whigs. For a "ranking" of each judge, see the charts showing the tenures of members of each court, *id*, at 525-35. For biographical summaries of the judges, see *id.* at 536-57.

[138]                          BEHAVIOR AND DATES OF BIRTH AND APPOINTMENT

| Date | Birth | | | Appointment | | |
|------|------|------|------|------|------|------|
| | *Lib.* | *Neut.* | *Cons.* | *Lib.* | *Neut.* | *Cons.* |
| 1760-79 | 3 | 4 | — | — | — | — |
| 1780-89 | 6 | 3 | — | — | — | — |
| 1790-99 | 7 | 7 | 5 | — | — | — |
| 1800-09 | 6 | 13 | 7 | — | 2 | — |
| 1810-19 | 5 | 7 | 5 | 1 | — | — |
| 1820-29 | 1 | — | 2 | 3 | 3 | — |
| 1830-39 | — | — | — | 12 | 13 | 2 |
| 1840-49 | — | — | — | 9 | 11 | 7 |
| 1850-59 | — | — | — | 11 | 15 | 13 |
| 1860-61 | — | — | — | — | 3 | 1 |
| Rejects*: | 8 | 13 | 4 | | | |

* Number of judges on whom data was not obtainable.

economic background is, if anything, more negative than positive.[139]

None of the conservatives was born before 1790, and their median date of birth fell in the first decade of the nineteenth century, while the median birth date of the libertarians was not much earlier—the last decade of the eighteenth century. No conservatives who sat between 1830 and 1860 were appointed before 1830, and their median date of appointment lay in the 1850's. By contrast, the median appointment date of both libertarians and neutralists lay in the 1840's. Yet, it would be incautious to make too much of this difference, since many conservatives were born and reached their maturity well before the rise of ardent Yankee abolition at the end of the 1820's. In addition, many libertarians and neutralists were born contemporaneously with conservatives, yet did not join in a "judicial concert of defense" against abolition. Libertarians and neutralists continued to be appointed to the courts in substantial numbers up to the beginning of the Civil War. The statistics indicate a rise of conservative strength in the last decade before the War, but not a general overpowering of liberals and neutralists.

In generalizing about the influence of background, the number of judges about whom relevant data is not obtainable requires caution. It is noteworthy, however, that what data is available indicates that conservatives and neutralists came in greater numbers from "Upper" and "Upper Middle" family environments than did the libertarians. None of the conservatives started out at the bottom of society; only two neutralists did; while almost one-quarter of the libertarians were "born poor." The data thus suggests precisely the reverse of what might have been anticipated; the most "upward mobile" judges were the most likely to support manumission.

Place of birth and place and extent of education relate to judicial

---

[139]                    SOCIO-ECONOMIC BACKGROUND AND BEHAVIOR

| Class Born Into (Fathers were:) | Lib. | Neut. | Cons. |
|---|---|---|---|
| Upper (wealthy planters, successful capital-city lawyers, businessmen, leading politicians) | 7 | 13 | 6 |
| Upper Middle (prosperous farmers, justices of the peace, small-town business, law) | 5 | 6 | 2 |
| Petty Bourgeoisie (apothecaries, tanners, innkeepers, etc.) | 5 | 7 | 4 |
| "Poor White" | 5 | 2 | — |
| Rejects* | 14 | 19 | 11 |

* Number of judges on whom data was not obtainable.

behavior more clearly than age, appointment or class. Among the conservative group, judges born in border and northern states, or in foreign countries are conspicuously absent, while three-quarters of the conservatives were born in the Lower South. By comparison, one-third of the neutralists and one-quarter of the libertarians came from that region. Unexpectedly, the Upper South was the strongest source of libertarians, whereas the border states, the North and England were most strongly represented by neutralists. Thus, from outside the seceding states came 8 libertarians and 14 neutralists; from the Upper South, 17 libertarians, 16 neutralists, and 5 conservatives; and from the Lower South, 7 libertarians, 12 neutralists, and 15 conservatives. Place of education suggests a similar spread: None of the conservatives went to college outside the South, but a quarter of both libertarians and neutralists did. Yet the Revisionist[140] thrust of these statistics stops at the clearest correlation of all, the relationship of behavior with extent of education. Only one of the conservatives about whom we have data did not go to college, while one-quarter of the neutralists and over a third of the libertarians never advanced beyond secondary school. This finding is consistent with that concerning socio-economic background: Both tend to rebut any hypothesis linking the growth of pro-slavery sentiment with the rise of "red-neck authoritarianism" as a consequence of Jacksonian democracy.

The data hints that politically inactive judges tended more towards neutrality than did their colleagues who also led active political careers off the bench. Twenty-three of the 47 neutralists were men whose party activities are unknown, whereas the party affiliations of two-thirds of both the libertarians and conservatives are available. Political activity, therefore, did not automatically produce greater conservatism; if anything, it made polarization of behavior more likely.

Contrasting party affiliations produces little insight into judicial behavior toward slavery. The proportion of conservatives to all judges among known Whigs and Democrats varies between a ratio of 1 to 3 and 1 to 4, respectively. Only among the neutralists does the number of Whigs much exceed the overall proportion of one Whig to every two Democrats. If, however, we proceed a step further and examine political attitudes of judges belonging to the Democratic party, a significant difference emerges. Among libertarians and neutralists, only one-third of the Democrats were States' Rights Democrats, and two-thirds were Cooperationist or Unionist. Among conservatives, the ratio was almost

---

140 See note 8 *supra*.

exactly reversed. With respect to all judges of both parties on the bench in 1850 and in 1860, Unionists dominated libertarian and neutralist ranks, whereas Secessionists were heavily in the majority in conservative ranks. All thirteen Unionists in 1850 who were libertarians remained opposed to secession in 1860. Of the 25 libertarians of 1850 whose political views at that time are not known, only 3 apparently became Secessionists by 1860. This analysis suggests a close link between pro-slavery attitudes and secessionism. Those judges whose behavior favored the slave and the free black were also the judges who, when it came to a crisis between the Union and the institution of slavery, chose the Union.

It is striking that so many Unionists on the bench in 1850 remained pro-Union a decade later. Many legislators, governors and newspaper editors who supported the Union in 1850 had changed sides by the time of Lincoln's election. Almost without exception, however, the judicial Unionists of 1850 did not alter their political beliefs. These judges represent a significant—but insufficiently examined—sector of elite southern opinion whose constancy to the values of 1787 prevailed over the ideology and economy of slavery.

Moreover, the existence of this influential body of opinion suggests an insufficiency in the principal sources used by analysts of the southern antebellum climate—the published and unpublished papers of prominent southern politicians, journalists and apologists for slavery. The importance of such documents in attempting to ascertain the contours of that era's opinion, of course, cannot be denied. The question is, rather, one of balance. It may be that these documents offer a biased representation of the actual distribution of attitudes among the southern elite. Perhaps inquiry should be refocused on the possible effect of particular political jobs, or roles, upon perceptions of slavery. For instance, if ever a political role was "gladiatorial," [141] surely it was the job of the southern Congressman or Senator in Washington. Called upon to defend slavery from northern attacks in the halls of Congress, these representatives of a beleagered culture might well have adopted a more "offensively defensive" stance than they would have had they been engaged in other political jobs. At the very least, these representatives were hardly the most likely men to mirror any minority doubts about slavery which may have obtained after 1830. A similar examination might be directed at apologists and southern journalists writing for a national audience. Journalists concerned with domestic

[141] *See* L. MILBRATH, POLITICAL PARTICIPATION 8 (1965).

southern circulation might have been inclined to reflect majority pro-slavery views rather than minority feelings of doubt. The documents of domestic southern politicians who occupied less visible gladiatorial positions than their colleagues in Congress—the journals of state legislative debates—frequently suggest that minority views of slavery persisted throughout the antebellum years.[142] In brief, historians may need to penetrate further behind the "Great Wall" of southern defense represented by the "Washington salient" and by the repressive laws passed to "bolster" the institution at home.

To return to the problem of explaining the judicial behavior, it is clear that the job of the state appellate judge was measurably less gladiatorial in nature than that of the Congressman, or indeed, than that of the state legislator.[143] Unlike the apologist or the politician, the

---

[142] For example, in 1805, a Virginia statute barring emancipated slaves from remaining in the State was first adopted as an amendment to another bill in the Senate by a vote of only 8 to 6. VIRGINIA S. JOUR. of 1805, at 67. Two days later, a motion to postpone the whole bill indefinitely lost on a 9 to 8 vote in which the Speaker cast the deciding vote. Twenty-five years later a move to repeal this provision was defeated by a vote of 22 to 9. *Id.* of 1830-31, at 129.

In Mississippi, well before the Missouri Compromise, a bill was passed with a provision preventing slaves from raising cotton for their own use. MISSISSIPPI S. JOUR. of 1818, at 119-20. In the same session the Mississippi House of Representatives passed a bill preventing further purchase or importation of slaves as merchandise, but the Senate postponed it indefinitely. Later, the Senate took a different approach by proposing a bill which allowed private manumission conditioned upon departure of the ex-slave within one year. The House, however, was adamantly opposed and the proposal was finally dropped. *Id.* of 1842, at 511, 513, 522, 659.

The Alabama Senate defeated legislation which would have barred all blacks from serving as steamboat pilots by a vote of 11 to 6. ALABAMA S. JOUR. of 1832, at 126. In 1858 the legislators defeated perhaps the most extraordinary of all designs for perpetuating slavery, a scheme for redistributing property. One Senator moved to require all owners of more than 100 slaves to put their "excess" slaves in a "kitty" in the county where they lived. Any white man, who did not own slaves but would like to, would have been permitted to take one slave from this kitty without payment. The purpose of this measure must have been to give all whites a vested interest in perpetuating the institution. What is surprising is not its defeat, but rather that it managed to pick up 9 votes, more than a third of the votes cast that day in the Senate. *Id.* of 1858, at 280.

The Tennessee journals offer perhaps the clearest indications of diversity of opinion. In 1831 the Senate, by 14 to 6, voted not to repeal an Act allowing slaves to sue to enforce bequests of freedom, and it also defeated by 15 to 5 an attempt to take away the judicial power to emancipate slaves. In the same session a bill was defeated which would have required the immediate departure of all free blacks from the State, TENNESSEE S. JOUR. of 1831, at 222, 303, while 11 years later the Senate rejected by 17 to 4 a bill to make gambling with slaves a felony. *Id.* of 1841-43, at 599.

[143] The role of state judges has always been in some sense "political," but it was in that era far less "gladiatorial" than that of the southern Congressman. While antebellum

judge was primarily called upon to decide specific cases, not to debate general issues. While the judge may not have been wholly unaware of the general import of his decision-making, it seems likely that he was far more occupied with the particularity of a dispute involving individual blacks than with the general problem of defending slavery in a hostile national environment. Furthermore, in contrast to the senatorial speech and the state legislative bill, the "form" of his behavior—the written opinion—was admirably suited to the expression of minority views. Moreover, despite the growth of Jacksonian demands for making judges more "democratic," southern appellate judges remained far more insulated than their legislative and executive colleagues from the voting population.[144] Judges had, therefore, far less need to cater to popular sensibilities. Finally, the judicial role may have impressed upon the judge a different view of slavery. Certainly, the jurist could carry his own attitudes into his professional decision-making, whatever those attitudes may have been. Thus, the characteristics of the judicial—as opposed to the political—vocation may best account for the relative fairness of appellate court behavior during the antebellum era.

## Epilogue

One aspect of the black's quest for equal protection in the South—and more generally in the whole United States—stands out: the frailty of statutory "enactments of equality" unaccompanied by willingness to enforce them at the highest state judicial levels. Appellate insistence on the rule of law after the passage of the Civil War amendments would not by itself have guaranteed complete security from violence at private and public hands anymore than antebellum judicial behavior abolished inequity. Yet, it is not quixotic to ask whether the black's existence was better aided by the judicial fairness and integrity of judges such as Pearson and Green minus the mandate of the fourteenth amendment

---

judges did at times react to northern taunts, such response was more the exception than the rule.

[144] "Constituency fence-mending" was not a required endeavor for the political success of a judge. Even when necessary allowances are made for different systems of selecting judges, the amount of electioneering typically required of a state supreme court judge was less than that of a member of Congress whose election was an open question every two or six years. The career of Chief Judge William Sharkey of Mississippi is a case in point: his strongly Democratic constituency favored repudiation of State Bonds, yet he was re-elected as an anti-repudiationist Whig in 1847 over a Democratic opponent who advocated repudiation. Henry S. Foote's observation that party affiliation was not a strong factor in appointing judges suggests another difference in political roles. H. Foote, Bench and Bar of the South and Southwest 59 (1876).

than by that mandate unaided by judicial compassion. It is surely not too soon to ask for a return to enforcing in full measure the law of the land as it stands, whether or not it is distasteful to the personal sensibilities of those responsible for its application. Possibly—in view of the political polarizations of the late 1960's—the hour is too late. One can only hope that the apparent similarities of the 1960's and the 1850's do not develop further, producing a contemporary replication of that earlier decade's successor. Certainly, it would be helpful if contemporary judges and lawmakers found unnecessary the trauma experienced a century ago by a gubernatorial candidate of the first "American Party." In 1856, Judge David S. Walker, standing as the nominee of the Know-Nothings, lost the Florida gubernatorial election by 400 votes.[145] Ten years later, he became that State's Chief Executive, and in the bitter aftermath of war declared: "The colored man and the white man are now in the same boat; if she goes down, they both go down. . . ." [146] Judge Walker's ethnic terminology may now be dated, but the same cannot be said of the substance of his sentiments.

---

[145] R. RERICK, MEMOIRS OF FLORIDA 230 (1902).
[146] The Semi-Weekly Floridian, April 22, 1867, at 1, col. 3.

# 16
## JOHN MARSHALL HARLAN I: THE PRECURSOR

*G. EDWARD WHITE*

# John Marshall Harlan I: The Precursor

*by* G. EDWARD WHITE*

I

For nearly forty years after his death in 1911 he was virtually ignored by scholars; in 1947 Justice Frankfurter called him an "eccentric exception" to the distinguished majority of judges, Frankfurter included, who had resisted making the Bill of Rights freedoms available against the states through the due process clause of the Fourteenth Amendment.[1] Two years later, however, a law review article predicted his "coming vindication;"[2] in 1954 he was hailed by the New York *Times* as the progenitor of *Brown v. Board of Education;*[3] by the 1960's he was listed among twelve Supreme Court justices singled out as deserving of special biographical treatment;[4] and in a 1972 survey he was ranked as one of the twelve "great" justices in the history of the Court.[5]

Thus has John Marshall Harlan I's reputation climbed from obscurity to prominence. The same factors that alienated him from most of his peers and the scholarly public during his lifetime and long after his death have, ironically, formed the basis of his reincarnation. More of an ideologue than a jurist, his views were once distinctly out of phase; recently they have come into fashion. None of these slights or exaltations of history would have concerned Harlan, according to contemporaries: he allegedly went to sleep with one hand upon the Constitution and the other on the Bible, and thus secured the untroubled sleep of the just and the righteous.[6]

---

* Associate Professor of Law, University of Virginia Law School. This article is adapted from a chapter in the author's forthcoming book, *The American Judicial Tradition.*

1. In *Adamson v. California,* 332 U.S. 46, 62 (1947).

2. Watt and Orlikoff, "The Coming Vindication of Mr. Justice Harlan," 44 *Ill. L. Rev.* 13 (1949).

3. *N. Y. Times,* May 23, 1954, §4, p. 10E, cols. 1, 2.

4. See A. Dunham and P. Kurland, *Mr. Justice* (1964).

5. See Blaustein and Mersky, "Rating Supreme Court Justices," 58 *A.B.A.J.* 1183 (1972).

6. That characterization of Harlan has been attributed to Justice David P. Brewer. See, *e.g.,* Waite, "How Eccentric was Mr. Justice Harlan," 37 *Minn. L. Rev.* 173, 181 (1953).

2          THE AMERICAN JOURNAL OF LEGAL HISTORY          Vol. XIX

The years of Harlan's judicial career, 1877 to 1911, formed a meeting ground for three distinct ideologies, each with its separate mandate for the federal judiciary. The period was dominated by two issues of immense legal significance, and the ideologies represented diverse responses to those issues. First was the impact of the Reconstruction Amendments, which augured two substantial changes in American law, a new orientation of the relationship between the federal government and the states and an expanded meaning of the rights of American citizenship. Second was the growth and consolidation of large-scale industrial enterprise, lending a new dimension to conflicts between individual property rights and the state. The great cases of Harlan's tenure—the Civil Rights cases of 1883,[7] the rate regulation cases of the 1890's,[8] the income tax decision of 1895,[9] the segregation cases[10] at the turn of the century, the trust-busting cases of 1895, 1901, and 1911[11] were manifestations of these two issues.

The recurrent governmental problems engendered by the ambiguous mandate of the Reconstruction Amendments and the growing presence of giant industry raised diverse expectations concerning the performance of the federal judiciary. The first set of these manifested itself in a reaffirmation of the role envisaged by social theorists of Jacksonian Democracy and practiced to some extent by the Taney Court. That role rested on a concurrent theory of state sovereignty in a federal system and a belief that the states, under the guise of their police powers, could infringe upon individual rights for the sake of community welfare. The implications of this model for the new conditions of the late nineteenth century were threefold: first, the states, which could previously have circumscribed the civil rights of Negroes at will, could now, in the face of the Reconstruction Amendments, only infringe upon them to the extent they could upon the civil rights of whites; second, the states could continue to regulate economic enterprise, not in order to promote the ventures of "special" interests, but to insure equality of economic opportunity; third, the federal judiciary was generally to defer to the wisdom of state legislatures in cases involving economic regulation, and was to maintain equilibrium be-

7. 109 U.S. 3 (1883).

8. *E.g., Chicago, Milwaukee & St. Paul Ry. Co. v. Minnesota*, 134 U.S. 418 (1890); *Smyth v. Ames*, 169 U.S. 466 (1898).

9. *Pollock v. Farmers' Loan & Trust Co.*, 157 U.S. 429 (1895).

10. *E.g., Plessy v. Ferguson*, 163 U.S. 537 (1896); *C. & O. Ry. Co. v. Kentucky*, 179 U.S. 388 (1900).

11. *U.S. v. E.C. Knight Co.*, 156 U.S. 1 (1895); *Northern Securities Co. v. U.S.*, 193 U.S. 197 (1904); *Standard Oil Co. v. U.S.*, 221 U.S. 1 (1911); *U.S. v. American Tobacco Co.*, 221 U.S. 106 (1911).

tween the federal and state systems. This model was adopted by the Court in such decisions as the *Slaughter House Cases,* whose rationale was a balanced federalism, and *Munn v. Illinois,* where the Court deferred to the Illinois legislature's policy of regulating grain storage rates in the public interest.

Continued use of the Jacksonian theory of the judicial function was opposed by an increasing number of Supreme Court justices in the 1880's and nineties, some of whom, such as Field, articulated a competing theory. That theory combined a sense that state regulation of industrial enterprise was economically inefficient with a philosophical conviction that private rights against the state were sacred and inalienable. State attempts to influence the conduct of private enterprise were deemed presumptively suspect; the federal judiciary was charged with the responsibility of protecting private property from state interference; the contracts clause, commerce clause, and due process clauses of the Constitution became barriers against state legislation and weapons in the arsenal of activist judges. Under this interpretation the scope of the Reconstruction Amendments was widened and the powers of the states reduced, but with respect to economic rights rather than social rights. Moreover, federal regulatory activity, personified by institutions such as the Interstate Commerce Commission, was deplored, so that although corporations increasingly went immune from both federal and state regulation, the rights of freed Negroes were continually circumscribed.

Laissez-faire was the contemporary term for the economic theory which this second model complemented; the negative activism of the model, its blanket suspicion of governmental regulation of private conduct, and its indifference toward the autonomy of the states were in sharp contrast to the tenets of the Jacksonian model. Opposed to laissez-faire in the minds of most late-nineteenth-century Americans, however, was not Jacksonian Democracy but paternalism. From Justice David Brewer, who announced in one opinion that "the paternalistic theory of government is to me odious"[12] to jurist Christopher Tiedeman, who felt that "the demand for a paternal government"[13] threatened to undermine traditional constitutional guaranties, advocates of free enterprise identified paternalism as the ideology most potentially subversive of time-honored American values.

Paternalism was a late nineteenth-century catchall phrase

---

12. *Budd v. New York,* 143 U.S. 517, 551 (1892).
13. Tiedeman, "The Doctrine of Natural Rights in its Bearing upon American Constitutional Law," in *Report of the Seventh Annual Meeting of the Missouri Bar Association* 117 (1887).

that lumped together such movements as populism, socialism, the single-tax movement and communism. In the minds of its opponents, each of these movements represented an approach to the relationship between the individual and the state which assumed that certain disadvantaged persons could not improve their condition without positive support by the government. Paternalistic philosophies denied the validity of the maxim that individual initiative was all that was necessary for success, and in addition refused to acquiesce in the belief that the state had no obligation to help those who had proven themselves unfit in the struggle for existence. As such they departed from previous philosophies based on egalitarian and democratic premises, such as Jeffersonian Republicanism or Jacksonian Democracy, since those movements had merely demanded government intervention to restore conditions of equal opportunity. The paternalistic theories of the late nineteenth century assumed that a free enterprise system in a mature industrial economy inevitably fostered conditions of inequality, and the casualties of the system needed affirmative support from a beneficent government.

Paternalism identified itself in several concrete proposals advanced in the 1880's and nineties, such as a national commission to regulate railroad rates, a graduated income tax, nationalization of the railroads, government support for labor unions, and workman's compensation legislation. These proposals shared two common assumptions: first, that the federal government should be the principal agent of change, because it could achieve a uniformity of standards and a detachment from parochial interests that the states could not; second, that large-scale industrialization required large-scale government intervention to assuage its costs and aid its victims. Implicit in these assumptions was a greater conferral of power on the federal government in a regulatory capacity and a consequent reduction of the power of the states. The various philosophies of the late nineteenth century differed on the purpose of federal regulation, some seeing it only as a means of cutting down on the costs of industrial enterprise, thereby allowing more groups to prosper under industrialization, others seeing it as a device to achieve radical economic equality through a government-imposed redistribution of wealth.

Renewed attention to the powers of the federal government and the rights of disadvantaged persons required, for paternalists, a role for the federal judiciary as enforcer of the guaranties of the Reconstruction Amendments and supporter of federal plenary power in the regulation of industrial enterprise. The federal judiciary was to be deferential toward federal regulatory legislation but suspicious of similar state legislation, especially if it appeared to usurp federal powers, and to be zealous in its protection of the rights of minority groups, whether economic or racial in composition. If the Jacksonian blueprint for the federal judiciary envisaged it as essentially passive, except where legislation served to promote special privilege, and that conceived by advocates of laissez-faire as essentially active, although in a preventive sense, the theory of the judicial function compatible with paternalism was one of selective activism, with the judiciary intervening to enforce private rights against legislative usurpation in some circumstances and not in others, depending on the legislative forum involved and the class of persons whose rights were being affected.

The constitutional history of the late nineteenth century can be characterized at one level as the gradual replacement of the Jacksonian model of judicial performance with the model advanced by proponents of laissez-faire. The tolerance for state regulation of industrial enterprise evidenced in *Munn* receded; the Court came to see itself as exercising supervisory powers over the Interstate Commerce Commission;[14] efforts on the part of Congress to regulate income or prevent the consolidation of industrial enterprise were invalidated;[15] federal enforcement of civil rights was circumscribed, but state discriminations against minorities were tolerated. The triumph at the Court of the laissez-faire model has been characterized as representing a "conservative" phase in the history of that institution;[16] in actuality the development was politically conservative only in a limited sense, since it favored the interests of enterprises who had only recently reached a position of economic dominance, and was radical in its conception of the role of the federal judiciary.

Many of the leading justices of the late nineteenth century can be identified with the first two models: Waite, the prime supporter of the first model; Field, the chief exponent of the second; Miller and Bradley imperceptibly and irregularly sliding from the first to the second. Harlan cannot be described in the same terms. He combined a passionate desire to vindicate the civil rights of blacks with a reverence for private property. He often opposed economic regulation by the states, but generally tolerated it when undertaken by the federal government. He had no affinity for the reform ideologies of the late nineteenth century, populism, syndicalism and socialism. Yet he joined supporters of those movements in railing against and attempting to regulate the giant industrial

---

14. See cases cited at note 8.

15. *Pollack v. Farmers' Loan & Trust Co., supra* note 8; *U.S. v. E.C. Knight Co., supra* note 10.

16. *E.g.*, A. Paul, *Conservative Crises and the Rule of Law*, (1960).

enterprises of the period. Harlan's model of judging was primarily designed to implement his individual convictions. It placed a premium on arriving at desirable results, not on theoretical consistency. It bound a judge only to his own intuitive sense of what was right. But Harlan's intuition that a paternalistic federal government could serve as a protector of the socially and economically disadvantaged has struck fire with social reformers in the early and middle years of the twentieth century. Once a maverick, Harlan has become a visionary prophet.

II

Harlan retained throughout his judicial life two convictions produced by his early experiences as a Kentucky politician. He was reared as a Whig, his father being a Whig Congressman from Kentucky and a confidant of Henry Clay, and he adopted and maintained the Whigs' belief in a strong national government. Harlan never lost his sense of the importance of the Union. Before the Civil War he attempted to reconcile support for slavery with opposition to secession. During the War he chose nationalism over states rights, repudiating his original position on slavery. In 1890 he declared the Union could not exist "without a government of the whole" and that the "general government" was "supreme" with respect to its "objects," which he defined as those purposes to which "America has chosen to be . . . a nation."[17]

If Harlan was a Whig, he was also a Southern slaveowner, and the two affiliations proved increasingly difficult to reconcile. In the 1850's the Whig party in Kentucky found itself bankrupt as a result of the death of Clay and the ominous aspects of nationalism at a time when slaveholding seemed compatible only with states rights. As the Kentucky Whigs disintegrated, Harlan sought other political bases from which he could simultaneously espouse slavery and support the Union: first the American party, whose chief issues were opposition to immigration and anti-Catholicism, then the Conservative Union party of the 1860's, which favored preservation of the Union but opposed emancipation and abolitionism. At various points from the 1850's to the 1870's Harlan spoke out against popular sovereignty,, threatened secession if the war were made a mandate for emancipation, charged that the Emancipation Proclamation of 1862 was unconstitutional, opposed any grant of political privileges to blacks, called the proposed Reconstruction Amendments symbols of "a complete revolution in our Republican govern-

---

17. Harlan, "Address," 134 U.S. 751, 755 (1890).

ment," and maintained that blacks were the social inferiors of whites and that segregation of the races was right and proper.[18]

Despite these efforts to defend the caste system of his youth, Harlan increasingly found himself prepared to support the Union even at the price of the eradication of slavery. In 1868 he joined the Republican party and in 1871 ran for Governor of Kentucky on the Republican ticket. In the course of that campaign he publicly repudiated his earlier views. He stated that he had "acquiesced in the irreversible results of the war," expressed regret at his earlier championing of slavery, and claimed that "there is no man on this continent . . . who rejoices more than I do at the extinction of slavery."[19] He supported Reconstruction legislation such as the Ku Klux Klan Act of 1870 and the Civil Rights Act of 1871, and renounced his earlier views on immigration. Defeated, he ran again 1875, reaffirming his support for Reconstruction and civil rights, and once again lost.

Harlan's conversion on the issue of Negro rights and his persistent faith in the federal government as a uniform and efficient distributor of economic benefits were to form the intellectual cornerstones of his approach to judging. In his 1871 gubernatorial campaign both traits were in evidence. In addition to supporting the civil rights legislation of Reconstruction, Harlan proposed an extension of "the powers of industry and national wealth" through the abolition of interstate railroad monopolies, a graduated income tax to avoid imposing burdens on the poor, and an equalization of school taxes, based on the principle that "the rich owed it to the poor to contribute to the education of the latter."[20] Six years after that campaign, Harlan had become a power in Republican party politics. When he successfully maneuvered to swing the Kentucky delegation to Rutherford Hayes in 1876, he was rewarded with an appointment to the Supreme Court the next year.

Personality traits that strongly influenced Harlan's interpretation of his judicial office had also been exhibited in his political campaigns. He had entered politics early in his life, making speeches for the American party in 1856 when he was 23, and rapidly acquired a self-confidence and a sureness of his convictions. After his first public speech he became conscious, he later wrote, "of a capacity to say what I desired to say, and to make myself understood."[21] His large size and striking appearance perhaps

18. For newspaper accounts of these speeches, see Hartz, "John M. Harlan in Kentucky," 14 *Filson Club History Quarterly* 17, 22-35 (1940). Harlan's reference to the Reconstruction Amendments is quoted at 31.

19. Quoted in *ibid*, at 34.        20. Quoted in *ibid*, at 34.

21. Harlan, "The Know-Nothing Organization," reprinted in 46 *Ky. L.J.* 321, 332 (1958).

contributed to this sense of self-esteem: Harlan's wife remembered that when she first saw him, when he was 21, he walked "as if the whole world belonged to him."[22] A religious fundamentalism augmented his self-righteousness: he believed that nothing which the Bible commanded could "be safely or properly disregarded" and nothing that "it condemn[ed] [could] be justified."[23] Enduring the taunts of opponents who reminded him of his conversion on Negro rights only strengthened his beliefs. "I would rather be right," he said in 1871, "than consistent."[24]

Strength of convictions combined in Harlan with an approach to judicial decisionmanking that emphasized the achievement of results. His troublesome choice between the Union and slavery, once resolved in favor of the former, produced a messianic commitment to Negro rights. Harlan almost never failed to uphold the civil rights of Negro plaintiffs, never invalidated civil rights legislation when it pertained to freed Negroes, and invariably dissented from cases which left Negro petitioners without a remedy against either discrimination by states or attacks by private citizens. To achieve those results, Harlan was prepared to read the Thirteenth and Fourteenth Amendments exceptionally broadly[25] or ignore procedural irregularities.[26]

In cases involving government regulation of economic affairs, Harlan was equally result-oriented. He believed in broad federal regulatory powers, and would complain that Court decisions emasculating or invalidating federal statutes constituted "judicial legislation."[27] On the other hand, he opposed state attempts at rate regulation, was suspicious of the powers of federal executive officers, and believed that federal regulatory powers, though broad in scope, were limited in nature. In espousing these positions he described the judiciary as a guardian of private property,[28] trumpeted the rights of individuals against the government,[29] and made use of orthodox laisscz-faire precepts, such as the liberty of contract doctrine.[30] At the same time that Harlan tolerated state regulation

---

22. Malvina Shanklin Harlan, "Some Memories of a Long Life," reprinted in *ibid*, at 329.

23. Quoted in Westin, "John Marshall Harlan and the Constitutional Rights of Negroes," 66 *Yale L.J.* 637, 639 (1957).

24. Quoted in Hartz, *supra* note 18, at 34.

25. See, *e.g.* Civil Rights Cases, *supra* note 7 at 33-59.

26. See *Clyatt v. United States*, 197 U.S. 207, 222 (1905) (dissent).

27. *E.g., United States v. Clark*, 96 U.S. 37, 44, 47 (1877) (dissent); *Standard Oil Co., v. U.S.*, 221 U.S. 1, 82 (1911) (dissent).

28. *Smyth v. Ames*, 169 U.S. 466, 527-28 (1898).

29. *E.g., Geer v. Connecticut*, 161 U.S. 519, 542 (1896) (dissent).

30. *E.g., Adair v. U.S.*, 208 U.S. 161 (1908).

of working hours, maintaining that the judiciary had no right to "enter the domain of legislation and . . . annul statutes that had received the sanction of the people's representatives,"[31] he invalidated a federal statute purporting to extend the commerce power to include private labor relations, claiming that it arbitrarily sanctioned and illegal invasion of personal liberty and property rights.[32]

Harlan's result-orientation testified to his sense that the law could be shaped to conform to a judge's personal convictions. He once stated to a group of students at George Washington University, where he taught Constitutional Law from 1889 until his death, that if the justices did not "like an act of Congress, we don't have much trouble to find grounds to declare it unconstitutional."[33] In his own case, a basis for animosity or preference was often deep-seated, and he was rarely at a loss to justify it and rarely influenced by the views of his fellow justices. Chief Justice White, speaking gingerly at a ceremony honoring Harlan, stated that Harlan's "methods of thought . . . led him to the broadest lines of conviction, and as those lines were by him discerned, . . . differences between himself and others became impossible of reconciliation."[34]

On at least two occasions, disagreements between Harlan and his brethren provoked open confrontations. During the reading of his dissent in the case of *Pollock v. Farmers' Loan & Trust Co.*, which declared the income tax unconstitutional, Harlan was reported to have "pounded the desk, [shaken] his finger under the noses of Chief Justice [Fuller] and Mr. Justice Field" and to have "several times . . . turned his chair" to glare at Field, Fuller, and Justice Gray.[35] Harlan claimed that Field had whispered and shuffled papers during the reading of Harlan's dissent and had "acted like a mad man" throughout the Court's consideration of the income tax cases.[36] At the end of his career, Harlan became equally perturbed at the *Standard Oil*[37] and *American Tobacco* decisions,[38] which gave the judiciary power to construe the Sherman Act in light of a "reasonableness" standard. The decision represented a

---

31. *Atkins v. Kansas*, 191 U.S. 207, 223 (1903).

32. *Adair v. U.S., supra* note 30 at 180.

33. Quoted in Abraham, "John Marshall Harlan," 41 *Va. L. Rev.* 871, 876 (1955).

34. White, "Proceedings on the Death of Mr. Justice Harlan," 222 U.S. xxvii (1912).

35. See *N.Y. Sun*, May 21, 1895, p. 1, col. 7; *N.Y. Tribune* May 21, 1895, p. 1, col. 5.

36. See Farrelly, "Harlan's Dissent in the Pollock Case," 24 *So. Calif. L. Rev.* 174, 179 (1951).

37. *Supra* note 27.

38. *U.S. v. American Tobacco Co.*, 221 U.S. 106 (1911).

personal blow to Harlan, since it modified his holding in the 1903 *Northern Securities* case,[39] where a judicial "rule of reason" had specifically been repudiated. In his dissent in *Standard Oil*, Harlan stated that "many things are intimated and said in the Court's opinion which will not be regarded otherwise than as sanctioning an invasion by the judiciary of the constitutional domain of Congress—an attempt by interpretation to soften or modify what some regard as a harsh public policy." He described this tendency toward "judicial construction" as "most harmful."[40] For Harlan federal anti-trust legislation was intended to insure that the weak were not mastered by the strong, which for him was an essential part of doing justice. In such circumstances he was intolerant of "mere metaphysical conceptions or distinctions of casuistry"[41] and ill-disposed toward those who would employ them to reach unjust results.

III

Harlan's orientation toward results and individualized views on economic issues have made his opinions on government regulation difficult to characterize. He has been alternatively called a "liberal nationalist,"[42] a "complete reactionary,"[43] a "premature New Dealer"[44] a "Whig-Progressive,[45] and "both an economic liberal and conservative."[46] Central to an understanding of Harlan's decisions involving government regulation of the economy is a sense of their timing. He came to the Court with well-developed ideas about the role of government in promoting and regulating industrial enterprise, but those ideas originally had no apparent applicability to contemporary circumstances, and later suggested solutions that were not entirely consistent with other aspects of Harlan's thought.

In summary, Harlan began his service on the Court holding economic views that were already outmoded, persisted in those views despite their obsolescence, then saw them take on different implications in the late 1880's and 90's with the advent of collectivist ideologies. The interaction of Harlan's attitudes with the

---

39. *Northern Securities Co. v. U.S.*, 193 U.S. 197 (1904).

40. *Supra* note 27, at 104, 105.

41. White, *supra* note 34, at xxvi.

42. A. Kelly and W. Harbison, *The American Constitution* 585 (1963).

43. G. Myers, *History of the Supreme Court* 678 n (1912).

44. Westin in Dunham & Kurland, *supra* note 4, at 118, attributing characterization to "most commentators."

45. Westin, *supra* note 23, at 697.

46. M. Porter, "John Marshall Harlan and the Laissez-Faire Court," 1 (unpublished doctoral dissertation, University of Chicago, 1971).

changing intellectual climate of his years of service made him appear first as an economic reactionary, then as something of a radical, but he disdained either characterization. If he and those favoring nationalization of the American economy were united in their hatred of giant corporate interests, this did not, Harlan felt, make him a socialist;[47] if he was anxious to secure entrepreneurs adequate returns on their investments, this did not affiliate him with captains of industry.

In 1877, when he joined the Court, Harlan had revealed himself as an Orthodox Whig. He favored a "strong national economy," by which was meant support for the free flow if interstate commerce against particularistic local interests. He supported active government promotion of entrepreneurial ventures and held to a Marshallian interpretation of the commerce clause, which emphasized plenary federal control of commerce in the interest of economic expansion. To these tenets Harlan added a personal sympathy for economically disadvantaged persons, manifested in his 1871 and 1875 economic reform proposals for Kentucky, which advocated the use of tax policies as a means of alleviating the burdens on the poor. There was, in the 1870's, virtually no intellectual home for these positions. The states, rather than the federal government, had emerged as the chief promoters and regulators of industrial enterprise. The focus of controversy in questions involving governmental regulation was not whether the states or the nation should do the regulating but whether governmental institutions had any right to regulate the use of private property. Pressure for federal regulation as a means of combatting excessive market power, as exemplified in the legislation creating the Interstate Commerce Commission in 1887, had not yet emerged. Poverty had not yet been "discovered";[48] the costs of industrialism were not yet so apparent that policies intended to aid the victims of an industrial society had much widespread appeal.

Consequently Harlan's earliest decisions on government regulation, which involved the responsibility of defaulting states and municipalities to their bondholders, indicated an appreciation of the risks taken by investors and employed a rigorous application of the impairment-of-contracts clause reminiscent of Marshall.[49] Recognition of the importance of capital investment in transportation ventures and a belief in the sanctity of contracts were ante-

47. Harlan to Augustus Willson, June 1, 1895, quoted in Westin, *supra* note 4, at 121.
48. *Cf.* R. Bremner, *From the Depths* ⅛1956).
49. *E.g., Taylor v. Ypsilanti*, 105 U.S. 60 (1882); *Thompson v. Perrine*, 106 U.S. 589 (1883); *Brenham v. German-American Bank*, 144 U.S. 173, 189 (1892) (dissent).

bellum Whig doctrines: Harlan persisted longer in use of the impairment-of-contracts clause than any other post-Civil War justice with the possible exception of Field.[50]

A chief bugaboo of Harlan's, as manifested in the municipal bond cases, was the restrictive effects of local legislatures on the development of enterprises financed by out-of-state investment. Harlan resorted to a number of devices to try to protect investors. In addition to invoking the contracts and commerce clauses to invalidate state legislation adversely affecting their interests, he attempted to avoid the Eleventh Amendment's barrier to suits against a state by citizens of another state,[51] supported efforts to expand the diversity jurisdiction of the federal courts and facilitate removal of cases from state courts,[52] and invoked the due process clause to invalidate state regulation of foreign corporations.[53] These were essentially negative decisions, linking him with an approach to judging represented by Field. But they did not imply opposition to all forms of government regulation; they were merely the obstructive half of a two-fold policy designed to insure a uniform national flow of capital and commerce. The other half of the policy was positive federal action.

Other factors complicating an assessment of Harlan's attitudes toward governmental regulation include his distinction between state efforts to interfere with capitalization and state efforts to regulate the use of other goods and services, and his embracement of Marshall's distinction, in commerce clause cases, between "local" and "national" objects. He was zealous to protect out-of-state insurance companies[54] and investors in railroads,[55] but he tolerated state regulation of liquor, oleomargarine, and grain futures.[56] He denied the states the authority to set railroad rates, but allowed them to preclude railroad traffic on Sunday or control the points of stoppage on railroad lines.[57] He invalidated a federal

---

50. *E.g., Stone v. Farmers' Loan & Trust Co.*, 116 U.S. 307, 337 (1886) (dissent).

51. *Plaquemines Tropical Fruit Co. v. Henderson*, 170 U.S. 511 (1898).

52. *Macon v. Atlantic Coast Line*, 215 U.S. 501, 511 (1910) (dissent); *Tennessee v. Union Planters' Bank*, 152 U.S. 454, 464 (1894) (dissent).

53. *Smyth v. Ames, supra* note 28.

54. *E.g., Hooper v. California*, 155 U.S. 648, 659 (1895) (dissent).

55. *County of Tipton v. Locomotive Works*, 103 U.S. 523 (1880); *Concord v. Robinson*, 121 U.S. 165 (1886).

56. *Mugler v. Kansas*, 123 U.S. 623 (1887); *Powell v. Pennsylvania*, 127 U.S. 678 (1888).

57. *Hennington v. Georgia*, 163 U.S. 299 (1896); *Lake Shore & Michigan South Ry. v. Ohio*, 173 U.S. 285 (1899); *Northern Pacific v. Dustin*, 142 U.S. 492, 500 (1897) (dissent).

statute attempting to regularize hours for union employees,[58] but sustained New York and Kansas statutes fixing hours for bakers and state employees against a similar challenge.[59] His result-orientation was doubtless partially responsible for the uneven pattern of these decisions. Religious and moral convictions affected his attitude toward Sunday closing laws, temperance legislation, and questionable business practices, while his strong desire to provide entrepreneurs a return on their investments made him suspicious of legislation that jeopardized the security of investors.

Harlan's philosophy of government regulation developed an added dimension after 1887, when federal regulatory statutes creating the Interstate Commerce Commission and prohibiting monopolies and conspiracies in restraint of trade provided an outlet for his dormant Whig attitudes. In the regulatory policies of a newly assertive federal government he saw the personification of the older American system, with its emphasis on the even-handed nationwide promotion of economic growth. "Aggregations of capital," he felt, threatened to impose "another kind of slavery" on the American people.[60] A vigorous federal regulatory commission and rigidly enforced anti-trust laws would prevent large enterprises from unfairly controlling the nation's business.

Thus the antebellum Whig became the late-century paternalist: the federal government was seen as an ally of those discriminated against by the captains of industry. The powers delegated to the Interstate Commerce Commission to set railroad rates were to be strictly upheld by the courts; Supreme Court decisions emasculating the Commission constituted blatant judicial legislation.[61] The Sherman Anti-Trust law meant what it said: any industrial combination formed for the purpose of restraining trade was illegal. Whether the restraint was "reasonable" or not was not a question for the courts.[62] Sophistical judicial distinctions between "manufacture" and "commerce" intended to defeat the purpose of the anti-trust laws were equally illegitimate.[63] A federal income tax whose effect was to place the costs of national economic growth on those who could most easily bear them was compatible with views

---

58. *Adair v. U.S., supra* note 30.

59. *Lochner v. New York,* 198 U.S. 45, 65 (1905) (dissent); *Atkin v. Kansas, supra* note 31.

60. *Standard Oil Co. v. U.S., supra* note 27, at 83.

61. *Texas & Pacific Ry. Co. v. ICC,* 162 U.S. 197, 239 (1896) (dissent); *ICC v. Alabama Midland Ry. Co.,* 168 U.S. 144, 176 (1897) (dissent); *Harriman v. ICC,* 211 U.S. 407, 423 (1908) (dissent).

62. *Standard Oil Co. v. U.S., supra* note 27, at 82.

63. *U.S. v. E. C. Knight Co., supra* note 11, at 18.

14             THE AMERICAN JOURNAL OF LEGAL HISTORY      Vol. XIX

long held by Harlan. Invalidation of that tax by the Court he considered disasterous.[64]

While enthusiastically accepting paternalistic regulatory legislation, Harlan retained his older beliefs in the sanctity of individual
rights. He decried "the effort of accumulated capital to escape the
burden of just taxation"[65] and maintained that "the greatest injury
to the integrity of our social organization comes from the enormous
power of corporations,"[66] but he protested against arbitrary governmental interference with the property rights of citizens.[67] When
these two beliefs came into conflict, such as when regulatory
statutes infringed upon economic "liberties," Harlan resolved the
tension by following his intuitions. He seemed to think that labor
unions did not need special protection;[68] he accepted state regulation of wages and hours[69] more easily than state interference with
creditor rights;[70] he did not usually maintain his general suspicion
of state attempts to interfere with property rights in the area of
taxation.[71] If this approach made Harlan unpredictable and inconsistent, it also prevented him from succumbing to the fear that in-
vaded many American judges when collectivist doctrines first began to be discussed in the late nineteenth century,[72] which often
manifested itself in attempts to define the emerging problems of
industrialization out of existence.

IV

In civil rights cases, the experiences of Harlan's years in
Kentucky immeasurably affected his stance. He had come to see the
barbarity of a system in which whites treated blacks as chattels,
and he could never look at cases involving the civil rights of
Negroes without invoking that vision. An incident from Harlan's
domestic life is revealing of the symbolic meaning of the antebellum
South for him. Shortly after his appointment to the Supreme Court,
he had discovered in the Marshal's office at the Court an inkstand

---

64. *Pollock v. Farmers' Loan & Trust Co., supra* note 9, at 608.

65. Harlan to Augustus Willson, June 1, 1895, quoted in Westin, *supra*
note 23, at 121.

66. Harlan to Willson, Dec. 1, 1905, quoted in *ibid*, at 120.

67. *International Postal Supply Co. v. Bruce*, 194 U.S. 601, 606 (1904)
(dissent).

68. *Adair v. U.S., supra* note 30.

69. *Lochner v. New York, supra* note 59.

70. See cases cited at note 49 supra.

71. *E.g. Texas Gross Receipts Tax Case*, 210 U.S. 217, 228 (1908)
(dissent).

72. Cf. O. W. Holmes, "The Path of the Law," in *Collected Legal
Papers* 184 (1920).

used by Taney in writing his decisions. On learning that Taney had used the inkstand to write *Dred Scott,* Harlan demonstrated such interest in it that he was given it as a present. After the inkstand had remained with Harlan for a time, he promised to give it to the wife of Senator George Pendleton of Ohio, who had expressed a desire to have it because Taney had been a relative of hers.

Mrs. Harlan, believing that her husband would regret giving up the inkstand, secretly retrieved it from his study and hid it. Harlan told Mrs. Pendleton that the inkstand had inexplicably disappeared and subsequently forgot about it. In 1883 the *Civil Rights Cases* came before the Court, and Harlan resolved to dissent, but was having difficulty writing a dissenting opinion. One Sunday morning, in the midst of his difficulties, Mrs. Harlan again decided to intervene. Knowing that Harlan would not fail to attend church, she declined to go, and while he was absent retrieved Taney's inkstand, polished it and filled it with ink, put it in a conspicuous place in his study and removed the other ink-wells. When Harlan returned she called it to his attention and confessed her part in keeping it in the Harlan household. With the inkstand serving as a catalyst, Harlan began his dissent, the Reconstruction Amendments and the abolition of slavery linked in his mind. Out of those associations came sentences such as "I insist that the national legislature may, without transcending the limits of the Constitution, do for human liberty and the fundamental rights of American citizenship, what it did, with the sanction of this court, for the protection of slaves and the rights of the masters of fugitive slaves."[73]

Harlan's civil rights opinions were his most representative performances. They brought together his emotional attachment to the plight of freed Negroes, his broad reading of national power to protect citizenship rights under the Reconstruction Amendments, his willingness to shape legal doctrines to justify preferred results, the strength and stubbornness of his moral convictions, and his independence from the views of his colleagues. The cases, which were largely but not exclusively concerned with the rights of Negro plaintiffs, underscored for Harlan the responsibility of the federal government to take affirmative action to protect the rights of disadvantaged minorities. In this area Harlan viewed the federal government's proper function as that of a benign despot, continually intervening on the side of the underprivileged, and would use whatever juristic tools were available to maintain the primacy of federal powers. The only extent to which he would tolerate alleged racial discrimination was in matters of proof: if an affirmative case for

---

73. *Supra* note 7, at 53.

discriminatory practices had not been made, Harlan would vote to deny a petitioner relief.[74] He was by all odds the leading judicial civil libertarian of his time, and the only nineteenth-century justice whose approach to civil rights cases even faintly resembled that taken by the Warren Court.

The bulk of the civil rights cases considered by the Court in the early years of Harlan's tenure concerned federal civil rights legislation preventing blacks from being tried by juries selected by racial discrimination or preventing jurors from being excluded on account of race. Of all the Negro rights cases, the Court was most sympathetic to black petitioners in this area. Three 1880 decisions sustained federal legislation conferring a right to be tried by a jury selected without racial discrimination,[75] providing indictments against state judges who excluded blacks from juries,[76] and allowing black petitioners the right to remove their cases to a federal court if a state did not allow them a right to an unsegregated jury.[77] Harlan joined all those decisions. In 1881 he wrote the opinion for the Court in a case where the state of Delaware had systematically excluded blacks from juries and a Negro petitioner had sued to have his conviction by an all-white jury reversed. Harlan read the 1880 jury cases as holding that the equal protection clause of the Fourteenth Amendment prevented blacks from being tried by juries on which black jurors had been forbidden to serve on the basis of race. He maintained, however, that a prima facie case of racial discrimination had to be made out; it could not merely be inferred from statistical evidence.[78]

For the rest of his tenure on the Court, Harlan followed the approach to jury cases he had taken in the 1880s, with the continual support of a majority of the justices. He invalidated state statutes excluding blacks from juries on the basis of race,[79] but only where real evidence of discrimination had been presented or where the states had not seriously entertained claims of proof.[80] In other instances, where a prima facie case of discrimination had not been made out, or where a state trial court had ruled the evi-

---

74. *E.g., Murray v. Louisiana,* 163 U.S. 101 (1896); *Thomas v. Texas,* 212 U.S. 278 (1909).

75. *Strauder v. West Virginia,* 100 U.S. 303 (1880).

76. *Virginia v. Rives,* 100 U.S. 313 (1880).

77. *Ex parte Virginia,* 100 U.S. 339 (1880).

78. *Neal v. Delaware,* 103 U.S. 370 (1881).

79. *Bush v. Kentucky,* 107 U.S. 110 (1883); *Williams v. Mississippi,* 170 U.S. 213 (1898).

80. *Carter v. Texas,* 177 U.S. 442 (1900); *Rogers v. Alabama,* 192 U.S. 226 (1904).

dence insufficient,[81] Harlan denied relief. He also gave a relatively
narrow scope to the right of removal from state courts in jury
discrimination cases.[82] His jury decisions were unique in that his
position harmonized with that of most of his fellow justices, and
also in that they evidenced a relatively cautious attitude to civil
rights claims.

In Fifteenth Amendment cases, Harlan's views gradually
deviated from that of the Court. In 1884, in the case of *Ex parte
Yarborough*,[83] the Court upheld federal legislation preventing private citizens from conspiring to deprive Negroes of their right to
vote in a federal election; Harlan joined the majority. Nineteen
years later, however, at a high-point in the Court's tolerance of
racial discrimination, *Yarborough* was distinguished away by the
majority in *James v. Bowman*.[84] That case involved the constitutionality of a federal statute preventing private citizens from interfering with Fifteenth Amendment rights through bribery or intimi-
dation. Two citizens of Kentucky were convicted under the statute
for harassing a black voter in Kentucky. The Court struck down the
application of the statute to them as overbroad, since the statute
did not limit its reach to federal elections, and the Fifteenth
Amendment did not prohibit private citizens, as opposed to states,
from interfering with voting rights. Harlan dissented; he rejected
that reading of the Amendment.

In *Giles v. Harris*,[85] another 1903 case, the Court showed its
then current tendency to avoid disturbing state schemes aimed at
disenfranchising blacks. Alabama had established certain voting
requirements which tended to preclude blacks from registering; a
Negro petitioned for equitable relief in federal court, claiming that
he and other blacks had been illegally prevented from registering.
The Court denied relief, claiming that if Alabama's registration
provisions were unconstitutional, it could not tolerate their
presence by adding blacks to the registration rolls, and that since
the Court could not enforce an equitable decree, it should not
impose its views on state legislatures. Harlan, in dissent, maintained that the petitioner had made out a case for equitable relief
and the federal courts had the power to grant it.[86]

---

81. *Smith v. Mississippi*, 162 U.S. 592 (1896); *Brownfield v. South
Carolina*, 189 U.S. 426 (1903); *Thomas v. Texas, supra* note 74.
82. *In re Wood*, 140 U.S. 278 (1891); *Gibson v. Mississippi*, 162 U.S.
565 (1896).
83. 110 U.S. 651 (1884).
84. 190 U.S. 127 (1903).
85. 189 U.S. 475 (1903).
86. *Ibid.* at 493, 503-04.

18          THE AMERICAN JOURNAL OF LEGAL HISTORY      Vol. XIX

Harlan's reading of the Thirteenth Amendment also diverged from that of his peers. He believed, as he stated in the *Civil Rights Cases*, that the Amendment prevented not only "incidents" of slavery, such as compulsory labor or disqualification from holding property or making contracts, but "badges" of slavery, such as exclusion of blacks from public accommodations. Harlan was willing to find evidence of "slavery" in acts of private creditors forcing Negro debtors to return to a state[87] or preventing blacks from working in a lumber mill,[88] in a state statute that made refusal to work prima facie evidence of an intent to defraud an employer,[89] and in state statutes compelling seamen on private vessels to honor their contracts.[90] In the last case, Harlan maintained that "the condition of one who contracts to render personal services in connection with the private business of another becomes a condition of involuntary servitude from the moment he is compelled against his will to continue in such service."[91] A prior practice in America of permitting the forcible return of seamen to their vessels was unjustifiable for Harlan after the passage of the Thirteenth Amendment. In only one of these cases was Harlan's position eventually upheld by the Court.[92]

It was in cases involving the Fourteenth Amendment, however, that Harlan demonstrated his most radical isolation from the Court. He had begun this estrangement in the *Civil Rights Cases,* where he had maintained that public accommodations and transportation franchises were instrumentalities of the states for the purposes of the "state action" clause of the Amendment, and that the Amendment's enforcement clause, taken together with its broad grant of citizenship rights, meant that Congress could determine what legislation was necessary to protect rights that were "fundamental in republican citizenship."[93] This meant, despite the apparent confinement of the Fourteenth Amendment's reach to discriminations by states, that the federal government had broad potential powers to prevent private discriminatory acts. From these positions stemmed Harlan's dissents in subsequent Fourteenth Amendment cases.

In the area of transportation Harlan steadfastly maintained that state-enforced segregation of blacks from whites was impermissible. The first major transportation case in his tenure was

87. *Clyatt v. U.S.*, 197 U.S. 207 (1905).

88. *Hodges v. U.S.*, 203 U.S. 1, 20 (1906) (dissent).

89. *Bailey v. Alabama*, 211 U.S. 452, 455 (1908) (dissent).

90. *Robertson v. Baldwin*, 165 U.S. 275, 288 (1897) (dissent).

91. *Ibid.* at 301. Italics in original.

92. *Bailey v. Alabama*, 219 U.S. 219 (1911).

93. *Supra* note 7, at 47.

*Louisville, New Orleans, and Texas Ry. v. Mississippi*,[94] in which the Fuller Court showed its inclination to uphold Southern states in their efforts to prevent racial intermingling. In 1877 the Court, in a case in which Harlan did not participate, had invalidated a Louisiana law forbidding racial discrimination on interstate steamboats passing through the state as an undue usurpation of federal commerce powers.[95] The *Louisville* case presented an analagous situation, since it tested the constitutionality of a Mississippi statute requiring racial segregation during the Mississippi portion of interstate railroad trips. The Court distinguished the earlier case, claiming that compelling white passengers to share their steamboat cabins with blacks was a far greater burden on interstate commerce than compelling whites and blacks to have separate accommodations in pullman cars. Harlan's dissent denounced the spuriousness of this reasoning and held the statute an interference with interstate commerce, technically not reaching the equal protection issue. He intimated, however, that the statute violated the Fourteenth Amendment as well.[96]

*Louisville* set the stage for *Plessy v. Ferguson*,[97] the notorious 1896 decision sustaining the constitutionality of a Louisiana statute requiring racially segregated railway cars against a Fourteenth Amendment challenge. The striking thing about Harlan's dissent in *Plessy v. Ferguson*, for modern Americans, has been the attitudes of racial toleration and the fears of racial antagonism that it expressed, as well as its conviction that "the destiny of the two races, in this country, are indissolubly linked."[98] But in a historical context, those aspects of the opinion were overshadowed by Harlan's overriding assumption that the Fourteenth Amendment had radically equalized the status of all Americans. Inequality of citizenship rights, after the Reconstruction Amendments, was simply impermissible for Harlan. He admitted no distinctions between state and private action, between slavery and its vestiges, between reasonable and unreasonable governmental discrimination. He read the Reconstruction Amendments as creating a domain of protection for American citizens against inequitable treatment before the law and making the federal government the supervisor of that domain. In his support for the civil rights conferred by the Amendments, his older beliefs in individual liberties against the government merged with his more recent sympathy for freed blacks, creating an phalanx of ideological and moral conviction.

---

94. 133 U.S. 587 (1890).
95. *Hall v. DeCuir*, 95 U.S. 485 (1878).
96. *Supra* note 94, at 594-95.
97. 163 U.S. 537 (1896).
98. *Ibid.* at 560 (dissent).

Thus Harlan went to extraordinary lengths to find support for his positions in the traditional authoritative sources of a judge. He read the Thirteenth Amendment as forbidding private actions that tended to foster incidents or badges of slavery despite strong evidence in the legislative history that its scope was confined to state activities.[99] He extended the scope of that Amendment to reach areas; such as public accommodations, that it was very likely never intended to cover.[100] He interpreted the Fourteenth Amendment to apply to unnaturalized Indians who chose not to live on Indian reservations.[101] He believed that federal civil rights legislation could be made to apply not only to protect citizens against attempted infringement of their rights by private persons, but to protect aliens as well.[102] Neither of these last two positions had the support of the Waite or Fuller Courts.

Most remarkable of all, perhaps, was Harlan's belief that the Fourteenth Amendment had assured that "not one of the fundamental rights of life, liberty or property, recognized by the Constitution of the United States, can be denied or abridged by a State in respect to any person within its jurisdiction."[103] Harlan meant by that statement that all of the first eight amendments to the Bill of Rights were incorporated in the Fourteenth Amendment's due process and equal protection clauses, and thereby applied against the states. He appears, in fact, to have meant even more than that, for he stated that fundamental United States citizenship rights were "principally" enumerated in the Bill of Rights, implying that others might be found and likewise applied as limitations on state conduct. In six cases between 1884 and 1908 involving the application of various Bill of Rights provisions to the states, Harlan affirmed this position.[104] No other member of the Court accepted it. Today, despite the long efforts of Justices Black and Douglas, "selective incorporation" of Bill-of-Rights provisions in the Fourteenth Amendment remains the majority doctrine. Yet for Harlan total incorporation was obvious: the Reconstruction Amendments had redefined the meaning of American citizenship and in the process had altered fundamentally the relation of the federal govern-

---

99. See Westin, *supra* note 23, at 702.

100. *Ibid.* at 704-05.

101. *Elk v. Wilkins*, 112 U.S. 94, 110 (1884) (dissent).

102. *Baldwin v. Franks*, 120 U.S. 678, 694 (1887) (dissent).

103. *O'Neil v. Vermont*, 144 U.S. 323, 366, 370 (1892) (dissent).

104. *Hurtado v. California*, 110 U.S. 516, 538 (1884); *Baldwin v. Kansas*, 129 U.S. 52, 57 (1889) (dissent); O'Neill, *supra* note 103; *Maxwell v. Dow*, 176 U.S. 581, 605 (1900) (dissent); *Twining v. New Jersey*, 211 U.S. 78, 114 (1908) (dissent).

ment to the states. United States citizens, after 1870, were wards of the nation.

## V

The dramatic turnabout in attitudes toward racial equality that occurred in the 1950's and 60's seems to have been the chief catalyst in augmenting Harlan's reputation. The spectacle of a Southerner laying bare the prejudices and sophistries of his peers, appealing in his rhetoric to the same humanitarian feelings that lay at the base of the twentieth-century civil rights movement, demonstrating in his own person the zealousness that can be produced by a combination of insight and guilt—this was an overwhelmingly attractive image to twentieth-century integrationists. Harlan's more general interest in the responsibilities of the federal government to its citizens also contributed to his enhanced stature in a century where national social welfare legislation came into existence. But although he was the only late nineteenth-century justice to find paternalism at all congenial, he was a precursor of rather than a spokesman for judicial attitudes that later came into vogue. He had no integrated theory of judging, only his own convictions; he read the imperatives of his office only as a mandate to dispense his individualized kind of justice. Ultimately, his jurisprudence resists categorization, except as result-orientation, and his reputation becomes peculiarly vulnerable to changes in social attitudes. One generation's eccentric has become another's visionary, but his stature remains indeterminate. His currently high status may be as transitory as his formerly low esteem.

# 17

# LAW AND THE FAILURE OF RECONSTRUCTION: THE CASE OF THOMAS COOLEY

*PHILLIP S. PALUDAN*

# LAW AND THE FAILURE OF RECONSTRUCTION: THE CASE OF THOMAS COOLEY

## By Phillip S. Paludan

In the literature discussing the failure of Reconstruction to provide equal liberty for the freedmen the role of law and legal preconceptions occupies a minor place. That this should be the case in a time obsessed with law and order is notable, but the fact remains. Writers who have given the subject attention have concentrated on the congressional concern for constitutional limitations. They have properly suggested that respect for the separation of powers and a commitment to federalism produced conflict in Washington and ultimately crippled the ability of the national government to protect the freedmen, both before and after the so-called "redemption" of the South.[1]

In so far as the focus of this writing is the particular problems of the post-Appomattox era such an emphasis is proper. But a better understanding of the disunion crisis and the stuggle for equality demands a broader view. The legal compunctions of Reconstruction congressmen were not generated on the spot. They arose from prewar and wartime beliefs shared throughout northern society. When attention is extended beyond Congress to the legal and constitutional thought of the mid-nineteenth century new possibilities arise for understanding the Civil War era.

For example, why did the North fight for four years to sustain a legal abstraction called the Union? What accounts for the tenacious devotion to the Constitution displayed by both the President and Congress during the war? Although the fact that secession had occurred and war followed revealed the incapacity of the Constitution to resolve serious antagonisms, respect for the document remained firm almost everywhere. Lincoln threatened to veto a confiscation bill because it seemed to violate Article III, section 3. He refused to expand emancipation beyond war zones without a constitutional amendment. He

---

[1]W. R. Brock, *An American Crisis, Congress and Reconstruction, 1865–1867* (New York, 1963), 1–14, 250–73; Eric McKitrick, *Andrew Johnson and Reconstruction* (Chicago, 1960), 93–119; Harold M. Hyman, "Reconstruction and Political-Constitutional Institutions" and Alfred Kelly, "Comment," *New Frontiers of the American Reconstruction* (Urbana, 1966), 1–39, 40–58. Hyman's article does mention constitutional discussion outside Congress but focuses on wartime ideas, despite its title. I have discussed the thought of one legal author and its relation to Reconstruction in "John Norton Pomeroy, State Rights Nationalist," *American Journal of Legal History*, **12** (Oct. 1968), 275–93.

598                        PHILLIP S. PALUDAN

spent almost a third of his first inaugural address discussing constitutional questions.[2]

Congress and the nation mirrored this interest. Legislators debated
extensively the constitutionality of every wartime measure, and outside
Washington the debate continued. Over forty pamphlets appeared to
argue the single question of whether the legislature or the executive
might suspend the writ of habeas corpus. This constant legal wrangling
provoked the influential *Nation* to remark, "Nothing has been more
remarkable during the war than the rapidity with which 'legal fictions'
sprang up as the strife progressed. Generally the sword tears all the
lawyer's fine spun webs to pieces . . . but our war has furnished an exception."[3]

The full question of the relationship between law and the disunion
crisis cannot be given here the attention it deserves. But a brief look at
the thought of one of the nineteenth century's most important jurisprudents may suggest the possibilities that arise from studying the legal
mind of the Civil War era. In 1868, as the Fourteenth Amendment
was being ratified, Thomas McIntyre Cooley published *Constitutional
Limitations*. It was a propitious conjunction of circumstances. The
amendment was an attempt to limit the ability of states to infringe
upon the liberties of their citizens. Cooley's book was lucid and
learned discussion of the restrictions imposed by the Constitution on
the legislative powers of the states. Men who sought to determine how
the amendment affected the exercise of state power in the post-Civil
War world soon came to regard *Constitutional Limitations* as authoritative and indispensable. As the importance of the amendment
expanded, so did Cooley's reputation. It became America's second
constitution. Cooley became the most influential legal author of the
late nineteenth and early twentieth centuries.[4]

Pervading the hundreds of cases, principles, and illustrations of

---

[2]*Collected Works of Abraham Lincoln*, ed. Roy P. Basler (New Brunswick, 1953),
IV, 262–71; VI, 428–29; James G. Randall, *Constitutional Problems under Lincoln*
(Urbana, 1951), 278–80.

[3]"Legal Fictions," *Nation*, 1 (Oct. 1865), 455–56; Sydney G. Fisher, "The Sus-
pension of Habeas Corpus during the War of the Rebellion," *Political Science
Quarterly*, 3 (Sept. 1888), 454–88.

[4]Sidney Fine, *Laissez Faire and the General Welfare State* (Ann Arbor, 1956), 128–
29; Charles Edward Larsen, "Commentaries on the Constitution, 1865–1900" (Unpublished Ph.D. dissert., Columbia Univ., 1952), 146; Alan Jones, "Thomas M. Cooley
and 'Laissez Faire Constitutionalism': A Reconsideration," *Journal of American History*, 53 (Mar. 1967), 759; Edward S. Corwin, *Liberty Against Government* (Baton
Rouge, 1948), 116–18. A former student of Cooley, George Sutherland, sat as a justice
of the United States Supreme Court from 1922–38 and promulgated his mentor's ideas
while there. See Joel Francis Paschal, *Mr. Justice Sutherland* (Princeton, 1951), 16–
20, 170–72.

*Constitutional Limitations* was fundamental Jacksonian faith in equality. "Equality of rights, privileges, and capacities," Cooley wrote, "unquestionably should be the aim of the law." Further, he emphasized that the word liberty had broad meaning; it was not confined to acting as a codeword to defend intrusions upon property rights. The word "embraces all our liberties, personal, civil, and political." Freedom of worship, of speech, "the right of self defense against unlawful violence," the right to attend the public schools, the equal right to buy and sell, all were included. Looking back in 1873 at the Civil War amendments Cooley saw a culmination of Jacksonian ambitions. "Freedom is no longer sectional or partial," he exulted. "There are no privileged classes." Apparently persons who needed protection for their liberties would now receive it.[5]

Corporate persons did. Black persons did not. With amazing swiftness lawyers and judges made the Fourteenth Amendment, intended to protect Negro freedmen, into corporate property. And they used Cooley's writings as their instrument. Again and again counsel turned to *Constitutional Limitations* to argue that their clients might not be deprived of liberty or property without due process of law. With equal frequency the bench cited the same book to agree with them and to strike down state regulative laws. The power of corporations increased as the century passed and national constitutional guarantees secured the environment of their growth.[6]

Meanwhile the position of the freedmen declined. The nationwide announcement of their access to equal liberty ceased to resound. Soon they became the prisoners of state laws, local custom, and private violence. Penned in by federalism they could only watch the progress of the corporate giants who had stolen their amendment from them. Although he intended neither industrial growth nor the Negroes' decline, Cooley's writings were an important vehicle in the accomplishment of both. His role in the first has been described. His importance in the second requires attention.[7]

Basic to the understanding of the legal and constitutional problems of Cooley and his era is a recognition that the men who struggled with them were products of Andrew Jackson's America. They had de-

---

[5]Thomas M. Cooley, *Constitutional Limitations* (Boston, 1890[6]), 393; Joseph Story, *Commentaries on the Constitution*, ed. Thomas Cooley (Boston, 1873), II, 689.

[6]Jones, "Cooley," *JAH*, **53** (1966), 751n; Fine, *Laissez Faire*, 128–29.

[7]Jones, "Cooley," 751–71; Clyde E. Jacobs, *Law Writers and the Courts* (Berkeley, 1954); Benjamin Twiss, *Lawyers and the Constitution* (Princeton, 1942). The most complete and thoughtful study of Cooley is Alan Jones, "The Constitutional Conservatism of Thomas McIntyre Cooley" (Unpublished Ph.D. dissert., Univ. of Michigan, 1960). I am very much indebted to this study and to Jones' other work on Cooley, although he slights the relationship between Cooley's thought and equal rights.

600                          PHILLIP S. PALUDAN

veloped their ideas about the uses of law and the limitations imposed
by the Constitution in the years when Jackson sat in the White House
and later when his spirit pervaded the nation. This is not to say that the
legal thinkers of the pre-Civil War period were predominantly Jacksonians. In fact the majority of the legal profession probably opposed
Jackson, recalling his attack on the Bank of the United States, and
feared the egalitarian visions that his name provoked. They probably
agreed with one of their number who in 1864 recalled Jackson as "a
concentrated mob."[8]

Whatever the feelings of the legal establishment the Jacksonian
view dominated the prewar era. The "monster bank" was destroyed.
Whigs and Democrats vied with each other to wear the mantle of
"party of the people" with Jackson's party dominating the nation's
elections. So strong a hold did the Jacksonian spirit have on the popular mind that even Lincoln, Whig-Republican that he was, described
the Civil War in Jacksonian terms:

This is essentially a People's contest [he said]. On the side of the Union, it is
a struggle for maintaining in the world, that form, and substance of government, whose leading object is, to elevate the condition of men—to lift artificial weights from all shoulders—to clear the paths of laudable pursuit
for all—to afford all an unfettered start, and a fair chance in the race of life.[9]

Thomas Cooley spoke for the majority side. He supported the Jef-
fersonian-Jacksonian ideology. He read and listened eagerly to the
apotheosis of this ideology, William Leggett. This was Leggett's theme:

We hope to see the day . . . when the maxim of "Let us Alone" will be acknowledged to be better, infinitely better than all this political quackery of
ignorant legislators, instigated by the grasping, monopolizing spirit of
rapacious capitalists. The country, we trust, is destined to prove to mankind
the truth of the saying that "The world is governed too much," and to prove it
by her own successful experiment in throwing off the clogs and fetters with
which craft and cunning have ever combined to bind the mass of men.[10]

It was an argument in support of greater freedom of foreign and
domestic trade, favorable to equality in rights, liberties, and opportunities. Resting on an image of a strong, independent yeoman, it was
an assertion of belief in the sort of government that Jefferson *talked*
about—one whose duty was simply to keep men from injuring one an-

---

[8]Sidney George Fisher, "A National Currency," *North American Review*, **99**
(July 1964), 217.

[9]*Collected Works of Abraham Lincoln*, ed. R. P. Basler, XIV, 438.

[10]*The Political Writings of William Leggett*, selected by Theodore Sedgwick
(New York, 1940), I, 104. Richard Hofstadter calls Leggett "The Spokesman of Jacksonian Democracy," *Political Science Quarterly*, **58** (Dec. 1943), 581–94.

other and otherwise, in Jefferson's words, to "leave them free to regulate their own pursuits of industry and improvements."[11]

These ideals were the bedrock of Cooley's thought. When antislavery sentiment led him to abandon his Democratic allegiance and
to join in founding the Michigan Free Soil party he did not reject them.
The party platform was of course antislavery but it was more basically
Jacksonian. It opposed what one of its leaders called "anti-democratic
social conditions." The movement reflected the general sentiment that
freedom from all unrestrained power was the goal of true democrats.[12]

That such ideals sought support outside Jackson's party revealed
an important phenomenon: a growing feeling that existing institutions
had failed and that men would have to discover other paths to the
realization of their dreams. Cooley's move from party regularity thus
suggested more than a personal feeling that slavery was incompatable
with his ideals. It revealed also a general feeling that society itself was
sick, that his youthful optimism was unfounded, that there was more to
liberty than unexamined egalitarian oratory. He showed a growing
awareness of the possibilities for evil and failure in man and society.
By the 1850's his favorite authors were no longer Emerson and Leggett,
but Hawthorne and Dickens.[13]

As the prewar crisis intensified and sectional quarreling threatened
to tear the nation apart his apprehension grew. Events in Kansas and
the Dred Scott decision troubled him, and when the national administration endorsed proslavery actions in Kansas, Cooley joined the ranks
of anti-Nebraska Democrats who would soon supply the new Republican party with such men as Salmon Chase, Lyman Trumbull, Benjamin Butler, Gideon Welles, Hannibal Hamlin, and Walt Whitman.
In 1856 he officially joined the Republicans. This party seemed to him
to be least equivocal in its devotion to equal liberty.

More important than his political affiliations, however, was the
effect of the prewar societal crisis on his legal thought. Although his
papers are scanty for this period, there is evidence of a growing interest
in Blackstone and the common law. Cooley came to revere James
MacKintosh, a noted apostle of conservative Edmund Burke. He became more and more interested in history and studied the relationship
between common law and American liberty. The Michigan jurisprudent focused on the history of England which told him that principles
of liberty were given by God to Anglo-Saxon nations who embodied

---

[11]Quoted in Marvin Meyers, *The Jacksonian Persuasion* (New York, 1957), 29.

[12]Jones, "Laissez Faire Constitutionalism," 753–54; Salmon P. Chase to Samuel
Beaman quoted in Jones, "Constitutional Conservatism of Cooley," 54; William O.
Lynch, "Anti-Slavery Tendencies of the Democratic Party in the Northwest, 1848–
1850," *Mississippi Valley Historical Review*, 11 (Dec. 1924), 319–31.

[13]Jones, "Constitutional Conservatism," 109.

them in their customs and traditions. Common law was the structure of tradition and custom which preserved and promoted individual liberty; it was the perfection of natural reason and artificial reason. He accepted Matthew Hale's reverence for the common law "not as the product of some one man or society of men in any one age; but of the wisdom, council, experience, and observation of many ages of wise and knowing men." Even as the nation apparently fell apart Cooley came more and more to believe that an institutional framework, such as that provided by the common law, was imperative for liberty. With the nation secured in 1868 he would extol the common law, in spite of its faults, as "on the whole the . . . best foundation on which to erect an enduring structure of civil liberty which the world has ever known.[14]

Cooley modified his Jacksonianism, but he did not repudiate it. While he was sensitive to the need for law and a respect for history in a democratic society, he was equally sensitive to the need for liberty. He was concerned with maintaining an open society; one which, though restrained by respect for law and history, left open to every man an equal chance to exercise his talents and abilities. In contrast to more conservative legalists 'Cooley disliked the Dartmouth College decision. He deplored the support given by the Supreme Court to an ancient contract over the popular desire to permit the legislature to change established institutions for the people's benefit. "It is under the protection of [that] decision," he said, "that the most enormous and threatening powers in our country have been created."[15]

The common law which Cooley admired protected liberty first, then order, though it protected both most tenaciously. It was a common law that was suspicious of legislation, insistent about the equality of law, and always opposed to arbitrary power. Cooley's common law respected Jacksonian goals when it emphasized the idea that constitutional government was limited government, and that under just law all men's rights were equal. The law which Cooley admired was one which opened opportunity and formed a structure which protected liberty and property already won, but which also guaranteed the continued search and reward for enterprise. It was a law for liberal capitalism which opposed privilege. Its spirit: no one shall receive from the law special privileges; all shall have equal opportunities, no one shall be allowed to concentrate power to such an extent that liberty is impossible.[16]

This fusion of liberty and institutional structure was a common feature of the American political environment. Foreigners such as Thomas Carlyle might describe America as "the most favored of all

[14]*Ibid.*, 102–08; Cooley, *Constitutional Limitations* (Boston, 1872), iii, 23.

[15]Cooley, *Constitutional Limitations* (Boston, 1890), 335; Jones, "Laissez Faire Constitutionalism," 755.

[16]"Laissez Faire Constitutionalism," 757–58.

COOLEY ON LAW AND THE RECONSTRUCTION          603

nations that have no government," but the phrase was a triumph of rhetoric over reality. Edmund Burke had warned British imperialists that Americans were extraordinarily sensitive where points of law and liberty were concerned. "[I]n no country in the world perhaps," he said, "is the law so general a study." Alexis de Tocqueville noted the same phenomenon with his observation that "scarcely any political question arises in the United States that is not resolved, sooner or later, into a judicial question." Americans equated the Union with the Constitution; thus precipitating protracted constitutional arguments throughout the disunion crisis over whether the North or South respected the document more. In their local experience Americans were constantly concerned with the lineaments of liberty. They created governing institutions daily as they expanded their settlements across the continent.[17]

The protean Jacksonian world increased institutional concern, especially among the nation's lawyers. The result was twofold. On the one hand it generated advocacy of the restraining power of the law (certainly a tenable position). But on the other hand it encouraged the tendency to equate the preservation of existing institutions with the survival of liberty (a considerably more suspect claim which had its uses in creating strong Union sentiment, but which was ominous, as I hope to demonstrate, for the Negro).[18]

Cooley engaged in this more dubious process by insisting that the Jacksonian goal of equal liberty under law might only be achieved safely if men recognized liberty's deep historical and institutional foundations. Supporting his contention he hit upon the common law roots of American liberty. Doing this he joined a widespread effort of the legal profession in the prewar years, and he revealed the basic weakness in the era's legal thought: its fear of the exercise of governmental power in innovative ways.

Although American law was heavily dependent on the English common law, reliance on its restraining influence was unnecessarily conservative here. In England the restraining power of common law is

[17]Thomas Carlyle, "Horoscope," *Collected Works*, Sterling Edition (Boston, n.d.), XII, 356–57; Burke quoted in Clinton Rossiter, *The First American Revolution* (New York, 1956), 135; Alexis de Tocqueville, *Democracy in America* (New York, 1954), ed. Phillips Brooks, I, 290; Paul Nagel, *One Nation Indivisible, The Union in American Thought* (New York, 1964), 53–58; Daniel Boorstin, *The Americans, The National Experience* (New York, 1967), 50, 65–69, 72–79.

[18]On growth of concern for legal institutions: Perry Miller, *The Life of the Mind in America* (New York, 1965), 99ff. The most thoughtful criticism of Miller's work by Lawrence Friedman does not affect the generalization about the concern for these institutions. See "Head Against Heart: Perry Miller and the Legal Mind," *Yale Law Review*, **57** (1947–48), 1244–59.

kept from being too effective by the unitary form of parliamentary government. Parliament not only makes the laws, it is responsible for their execution, and is the ultimate arbiter of their constitutionality. Although the principles of common law can restrain, they cannot inhibit Parliament from exercising the nation's power to any extent necessary to respond to challenge. "Parliament," Blackstone insisted, "may do anything but make a man into a woman, or a woman into a man."

In the United States, born of a rebellion against that assertion, the national government is restrained considerably short of parliamentary power. Our constitutional troika already restrains the exercise of national power, and federalism further diminishes the power that remains. The addition of the restraining power of the common law was in fact redundant. It revealed starkly just how fearful of unrestrained power many jurisprudents were. It mirrored a devotion to institutional restraints which made most of them equate liberty with the negation of power.[19]

Such an attitude was an effective antislavery instrument. Slavery involved the ultimate assertion of both state and national power against individuals. It also seemed to threaten the institutional sinews of the nation by the way that it turned representative bodies into armed encampments, courts into political forums for dubious constitutional rhetoric, and presidents into advocates of territorial tyranny. It was easy for Jacksonians like Cooley to believe that the death of slavery would mean an end to arbitrary power and to envision a future in which free men boldly and successfully exercised their now unshackled talents.[20]

But of course the fallacy of such a view was its failure to recognize that the age of the free omnicompetent individual was in the past, not in the future. Even when applied to the white man it was an illusion. Society grew more complex every day, concentrations of economic power grew, fostered by freedom from the exercise of adequate governmental regulative power. Freedom there was and would be, but not freedom equally enjoyed. The myth of a society of equality ran bluntly into the fact of a society of unequal individuals. Equal freedom would ultimately require not the negation but the exercise of governmental power. That power would not be provided in ample portion to protect even white men until the first half of the twentieth century. Blacks

[19]On idea in law of liberty against government: Edward S. Corwin, *Liberty Against Government, The Rise, Flowering and Decline of a Famous Judicial Concept* (Baton Rouge, 1948).

[20]On slavery as a threat to northern liberties: Russell Nye, *Fettered Freedom: Civil Liberties and the Slavery Controversy, 1830–1860* (East Lansing, 1963).

would wait an additional half century before they could claim its benefits. When such power was available and combined with a willingness
to use force to secure freedom, men not free might hope; without such
willingness the hope was chimerical.

Cooley would never clearly understand the contradiction between
equality and individualism. Neither would he recognize the extent to
which an exercise of power might help resolve the conflict. He was too
occupied with securing existing institutional arrangements to consider
the possibility that they might be inadequate to the nation's future
needs. In any event the Civil War effectively ended any possibility that
he might seek new options. As an attack on the old order it made the
salvation of that order the measure of victory. Coming as the culmination of a decade of doubt and disorder, it committed him all the more
to the maintenance of the institutions he had come to equate with the
survival of ordered liberty.

He was most anxious about the potential turmoil of wartime. He
did not agree with abolitionists who insisted that the conflict offered
an opportunity for revolution against all the institutions that protected
slavery. He did not agree with these reformers that the great benefit of
this conflict was that it opened minds for new ideas. Although certainly a great believer in democracy, Cooley's democratic faith was
woven with doubt. He did not share the practically unalloyed joy of
abolitionists and some reforming jurisprudents at the outpouring of
popular support for any new measure which might save the country.[21]

Given a chance to talk at length about the meaning of the war, the
Michigan lawyer spoke of the need for order in the midst of potential
revolution. Addressing a crowd assembled to dedicate the new law
building in Ann Arbor in the fall of 1863, he focused on the stable elements, the old institutions, for which the nation was fighting. He reminded his listeners of the Anglo-Saxon roots of American law. He
emphasized the long national experience with local self-government.
At a time when many were concerned with increasing nationalism,
Cooley insisted on the traditional benefits of local self-government in
the way that it "fitted men to larger responsibilities [and] made them
conscious of the public purposes which government was to serve." No
law that he ever taught, he insisted, would ever have "any tendency to
strengthen the State at the expense of the nation, or to exalt the nation
on the ruin of the state."

Recognizing that in wartime men might resort to what he termed

---

[21]Sidney G. Fisher, *The Trial of the Constitution* (Philadelphia, 1862), v-vi;
Francis Lieber, *Miscellaneous Writings* (Philadelphia, 1880), II, 147; James M.
McPherson, *The Struggle for Equality: Abolitionists and the Negro in the Civil War
and Reconstruction* (Princeton, 1964), 65–66.

606                          PHILLIP S. PALUDAN

"desperate remedies" Cooley still sought to limit the occasions and
justifications for their use. Echoing a widespread northern commitment to institutional stability, he insisted that in times of disorder it
was "the part of wisdom to keep an eye to the old landmarks, and so to
shape action that when the commotion is quelled there shall be apparent, not mere heaps of materials from which to build something
new, but the same good old ship of state, with some progress toward
justice and freedom." Great danger to those landmarks could result
from yielding to "those temporary excitements which sometimes
sweep over the people and from which no body of men can at all times
be free." Only respect for established legal tradition would protect
Americans from the dangers of such momentary passions.[22]

Further to secure the stability of the nation and society Cooley emphasized the crucial role that the legal profession was to play in guiding the nation through the war and in securing the results of the fighting. Echoing the urgings of lawyers and congressmen throughout the
nation he insisted that the legal profession was uniquely qualified for
such an important task. Untrained persons, he wrote, "would cut and
hew blindly in their ignorance until the beautiful fabric which has required ages to build may be utterly defaced by vandal hands." But
jurisprudents could promote change without loosing anarchy. "The
lawyer is and should be conservative," he insisted. "However radical
the change he may desire to make the lessons of our judicial history
admonish him that they can only be safely brought about in the slow
processes of time."[23]

A Jeffersonian who read Hawthorne, a Jacksonian who respected
Blackstone and the common law, a devotee of individual freedom who
feared the masses, Thomas Cooley encountered Reconstruction with
ideas and assumptions which would severely limit uncompromising
devotion to its legislation. Obstacles stood in the way of an uncondi-
tional commitment to human freedom. Innovations, he believed, required historical basis, and American history was singularly lacking in
precedents for national power used in behalf of individual freedom.
Distrusting power and revering liberty as he did, the Michigan lawyer
was sure to feel discomfort where force was exercised to protect
liberty. To Cooley, constitutional government was, by definition, government restrained. He was sure to suspect government action to
guarantee liberty. When the Civil War ended, he was inclined to feel
that the question of liberty and freedom for all men had been settled.
He was not prepared to understand that it had only begun to be argued.
He looked back at what had been preserved, too relieved to envision
what had possibly been won.

[22]Quoted in Jones, "Constitutional Conservatism," 112–19.          [23]*Ibid.*, 117.

COOLEY ON LAW AND THE RECONSTRUCTION          607

Writing additional chapters on the Civil War amendments for his
1873 edition of Joseph Story's *Commentaries on the Constitution*,
Cooley reviewed the impact of the war. He rejoiced that the "dangerous excrescence of slavery" had been removed from the nation.
Human bondage had not only been a moral wrong, it had threatened
the permanence of the nation by a controversy made all the more
bitter by the fact that each side had insisted that it alone defended the
sacred Constitution. This violent and fearful antipathy had been the
cause of war.

The war had killed slavery by releasing the force of pro-union sentiment against the institution. Prior to Sumter, concern for the integrity of the Union had restricted anti-slavery sentiment to a small
group of radicals. But when the South dissolved the bonds of union,
fears for union no longer restrained criticism or action. Emancipation ceased to be solely the dream of the revolutionary and became
the necessity of the patriot. The Thirteenth Amendment, born of necessity, had removed slavery as "a disturbance and danger to the body
politic."[24]

Cooley recognized the post-Appomattox fear of Congress that the
conflict might somehow resume should leaders of the rebellion regain
control of their states. He saw that Andrew Johnson's Reconstruction
measures "did not sufficiently protect the government against the danger of States passing under disloyal control." Neither did executive
action provide sufficient protection for freedmen or loyal southerners.
Southern states had passed the so called "Black codes" which practically reduced the freedmen to peonage. He understood the fears behind these codes but deplored them. They would only "perpetuate the
degredation of this [recently enslaved] people." He was, therefore,
pleased that Congress had responded to these measures with the Civil
Rights Act of 1866 which made the freedmen citizens. He was even
more pleased when Congress ended doubt about the constitutionality
of this act by initiating the Fourteenth Amendment. The subsequent
ratification of this measure settled for all time, he thought, the vexing
question of the status of the Negro in the United States.[25]

This was Cooley's history of the meaning of the war era. It con-
formed to his Jacksonian hopes and fears. As Huck Finn said of Mark
Twain, "He told the truth, mostly." But what Cooley left out was in
fact the crucial part, the spawning in the war era of new constitutional
possibilities which would make Jacksonian goals realities for the
freedmen. Hiding in the Michigan jurisprudent's apparent support for

[24]Story, *Commentaries*, Cooley's additions, II, 633–46.
[25]*Ibid.*, 649–54, 661–62.

egalitarian legislation were attitudes poorly designed to bring these measures to life.

To have impact the measures would have to be seen as the beginning of a new constitutional era—a promise by the national government that it would do what it had never done before—act in behalf of a citizen's personal liberty. Abolitionists and radicals, and even more advanced moderates, argued plausably that the power of the national government to free the slave implied a promise that such power would exist to secure that freedom should it be endangered. But to Cooley, the Fourteenth Amendment, the legitimizer of future federal action, was a promise kept, not a promise made. It was the end of a crusade, not its beginning.[26]

Cooley supported the amendment as a means to end doubts about the legal condition of the black man in America. The whole war crisis had been generated over this fundamental question. The time had come, he insisted, to cool this passion. The people wished to forget the war and to resolve its bloodstained uncertainties. They were turning their thoughts to new directions, but before they finally did so, they wished to tie together the loose ends of civil war. "The number was few indeed," he said, "who would have been disposed to deny citizenship to this portion of the people, or to object to a settlement of the question by express declaration of the Constitution."[27]

He spoke here for millions of war-weary Americans, but the ideas he expressed did not suggest to him an abandonment of equality as he understood it. He did not seek to achieve "normalcy" by knowingly sacrificing equal justice under law. He believed that the war, by purging the constitutional system of slavery, had secured that justice. With the Fourteenth Amendment securing to Negroes their citizenship rights, and the Fifteenth Amendment proscribing race or previous slavery as a condition of voting he insisted that no "particular or invidious distinction" could infringe upon the legal equality of Americans.[28]

Cooley did more than just write about equality, he showed his belief in it as a member of the Michigan Supreme Court. As example, an 1869 case raised the issue of educational discrimination against a Negro boy. In 1867 Michigan had amended her general school law to say that any resident of a school district might attend any school in the district so long as such attendance did not interfere with the system of grading schools according to the intellectual level of the students. The

---

[26]W. R. Brock, *An American Crisis: Congress and Reconstruction, 1865–1867* (New York, 1963), 250–54; Eric McKitrick, *Andrew Johnson and Reconstruction* (Chicago, 1960), 93–120.

[27]Story, 654.                                                    [28]*Ibid.*, 656.

COOLEY ON LAW AND THE RECONSTRUCTION        609

Detroit schools had, however, special legislation which allowed students to be segregated by race. When the youngster attempted to enroll in an all white school he was denied entrance. His parents insisted on his right to enroll and the case reached Cooley's bench. The judge ordered the school board of Detroit to admit the student, ruling that the state law overturned the city's special legislation, and meant that Negroes might not be excluded from white schools because of their race. In addition, Cooley observed that the young man had been deprived of advanced education, since the Negro schools in Detroit were only elementary schools. Although the judge was only enforcing a law, he intimated that even without the law the court would have taken the same position under the due process clause of the state constitution.[29]

This action and others like it on the bench showed that he meant it when he insisted in 1873 that the Fourteenth Amendment made it a "settled rule of constitutional law that color or race is no badge of inferiority and no test of capacity to participate in government." In addition he doubted "if any distinction whatever, either in right or privilege, which has color or race for its sole basis, can either be established in the law or enforced where it had previously been established." That question had been settled.[30]

But the only settlement that had in fact been made was a legal settlement, one to be defined in terms of existing legal limitations and structures. The amendment declared that "No State shall make or enforce any law which shall abridge the privileges or immunities of citizens of the United States; nor shall any State deprive any person of life, liberty, or property, without due process of law; nor deny to any person within its jurisdiction the equal protection of the laws." These were principles with which Cooley agreed. But the vital question was how these principles would secure *de facto* the equal justice promised *de jure*. How would they operate in relation to the federal system; would they change or preserve it?

As he described the actual working of the amendment it became clear that, despite sincere words of acceptance of its principles, Cooley would not allow them to be experienced as facts in the lives of the freedmen. Defying the intentions of Congress, ignoring expressed statements of law, rejecting the possibility that the war had altered the federal system, he offered an explanation which made the amendment simply rhetorical. Most importantly, his description was not *sui generis*; it rested securely on widely recognized and respected constitutional principles. Although Cooley falsified the intentions of the

---

[29]*People vs. Board of Education of Detroit, 18 Michigan* 400 (1869). *People vs. Dean,* 14 *Michigan* 406 (1866); Jones, "Cooley and the Michigan Supreme Court," 119; Cooley, *Constitutional Limitations* (Boston, 1878), 494.

[30]Story, 676.

610                                PHILLIP S. PALUDAN

framers of post-war changes, his argument was sufficiently plausible
to gain the acceptance of war-weary people who sought an explanation
that demanded little of them. There were many such.

The amendment, he said, had been passed to make more secure the
guarantee of citizenship provided under the 1866 Civil Rights Act. It
was passed to overturn the Dred Scott decision that blacks were not
citizens. According to the bill and the amendment he noted, "The
freedmen were to have the same right in every State and territory of
the United States to make and enforce contracts; to sue, be parties
and give evidence; to inherit, purchase, lease, sell, hold, and convey
real and personal property; and to full and equal benefit of all laws and
proceedings for the security of persons and property as is enjoyed by
white citizens, and to be subject to the like punishments, pains and
penalties and to none other, any statute, ordinance, regulation, or
custom to the contrary notwithstanding." (This was a direct quotation from the bill.) Then came an immensely crucial qualifier. These
rights, which the national legislature was establishing for the freedmen
became, in his words "the privileges and immunities of citizens of the
State."[31]

These last words are so important because Cooley believed that the
phrase "No state shall make or enforce any law which shall abridge
the privileges or immunities of citizens of the United States" did not
refer to the rights of state citizens but only to those of national citizenship. "The difference," he stated, "is in high degree important . . . the
privileges which pertain to citizenship under the general government
are as different in their nature from those which belong to citizenship
in a State as the functions of the one government are different from
those of the other." The vital question then became what were the
privileges and immunities which each government protected. On this
definition would hang the extent of protection that could be claimed
by the freedmen, in short, their access to equal justice rested on it.

Cooley's catalogue of federally protected rights was miniscule. He
suggested that the 1823 definition of those rights provided by the
Supreme Court in *Corfeld vs Coryell* was the only proper one. The
following were exclusively federal rights: protection against wrongful
action by foreign governments, use of passports, use of all navigable
waters of the nation, use of post office facilities. "Such rights and
privileges," Cooley magnanimously asserted, "the general government must allow and insure, and the several States must not abridge or
obstruct; but the duty of protection to a citizen of a State in his privileges and immunities as such is not by this clause [of the Fourteenth

[31]*Ibid.*, 653–56.

Amendment] devolved upon the general government, but remains with the State itself, where it naturally and properly belongs."[32]

Had this view been isolated it would deserve only passing mention. But it was not isolated. It was the opinion adopted by the United States Supreme Court in April of 1873, the same year that Cooley offered his views. In the Slaughterhouse cases Justice Samuel Miller, for a 5—4 court, accepted that 1823 definition as the interpretation of the Fourteenth Amendment. It would be 1935 before the court would expand upon this list of federally protected privileges and immunities. Neither Cooley nor Miller provided reasons why the amendment should be so emasculated. Both were so firmly gripped by a commitment to the old federal Union that they seemed not to think that their assumptions required argument. Both simply made a fact out of a personal belief. Miller declared that it was not possible to believe that the framers had intended to change the nature of the Union. And Cooley simply asserted that the duty of protecting a citizen in the exercise of his fundamental rights remained with the state. Why? Because that was "where it naturally and properly belongs."[33]

An amendment that was intended by its authors to provide national protection for rights to life, liberty, and property had been transformed into an innocuous declaration of the permanence of the old federal Union. Although Cooley had insisted that the amendment constitutionalized the Civil Rights Act, when it came to describing the constitutional changes wrought by the amendment, he simply ignored what the act said. Its purpose was to end interference with citizenship rights of all kinds from whatever source they arose. Lawmakers recognized that state rights would have to be limited, and they limited them.[34]

The transformation of the amendment that Cooley made did not occur because of racism or because of a disbelief in the sovereignty of the national government. Cooley seems never to have displayed anti-Negro sentiment and he often displayed the contrary. He had vigorously supported the Union government during the war and had upheld the power of the national Congress over military Reconstruc-

---

[32]*Ibid.*, 657–59.

[33]*Ibid.*, 659; 16 *Wallace* 82.

[34]Analysis of the act reveals its intended impact on federalism. It declared that "any person [not just any state] who under color of any law, statute, ordinance, regulation or custom [the proscribed action need not be the passage of a state law] shall subject, or cause to be subjected, any inhabitant [not only citizens] of any State or Territory to the deprivation of any right secured or protected by this act" because of color or prior slavery, was deemed guilty of a misdemeanor and could be punished by a fine of $1000 and one year in jail, or both. Federal courts had exclusive jurisdiction over violations of this act. See *Statutes at Large* (1867), XIV, 27.

tion. He was much like Justice Miller in this regard. What led the
Michigan jurisprudent to strip from the Fourteenth Amendment its
intended potency was his passionate conviction that only abiding respect for constitutional traditions would provide the order necessary
for the realization of his Jacksonian dreams of equal liberty. As his
dreams envisioned an absence of excessive power, it is understandable
that he rejected a view of the amendment so permissive of the exercise of federal power. He believed that the war had saved the old
federal Union, not transformed it.[35]

The specific constitutional instrument whereby Cooley transformed the amendment from a call to action into a victory celebra-
tion was the venerable comity clause of the Constitution. Article IV
Section 2 declares "The citizens of each State shall be entitled to all
privileges and immunities of citizens in the several states." The common meaning of this clause was that a citizen of one state would not
be discriminated against in another state. As example, Georgia might
not pass a law which denied citizens of other states the access to
Georgia courts which her own citizens possessed. If such a discriminatory law were passed the injured party might appeal to the federal
courts for redress. But, for protection for exercising a right that he
shared equally in law with other citizens, a citizen was dependent on
the state. In short, unequal laws were appealable, unequal protection
was not.

This clause was an obvious referent for the Fourteenth Amendment. The words privileges and immunities appeared in both; the Supreme Court had rendered decisions which illuminated, albeit none
too clearly, the meaning of those words within the constitutional
system. It was the comity clause that was the subject of the 1823 case
of *Corfeld vs. Coryell* mentioned above. Clearly conservatives such as
Cooley could argue that the amendment was limited in its meaning to
what the federal system of the prewar years allowed.

This argument would have been untenable had the authors of the
amendment insisted that they intended to give the phrase new meaning
which would secure federal protection for important civil rights. Although this argument did appear occasionally in debates on the amendment it was not broadcast widely. It was not, because for thirty years
those abolitionists who advanced the amendment had been insisting,
despite court decisions to the contrary, that the comity clause already
secured that protection. Thus the amendment, in the eyes of most
of its proponents, was declaratory—it simply made a law out of a previously existing fact. It changed nothing. But this of course was

[35]Charles Fairman, *Mr. Justice Miller and the Supreme Court, 1862–1890* (Cambridge, 1939), 124–40.

Cooley's position too and those judges who studied the record for the true meaning of the amendment might conclude that both sides sought the same thing.[36]

What distinguished the two was their image of what the prewar constitutional world had been. And, in any argument where the weight of legal precedent mattered Cooley's opponents were on much weaker ground than he was. Guided by the belief that slavery must die because it violated the slaves' natural rights as human beings, abolitionists grabbed for arguments wherever they might find them to accomplish their goal. When they accepted the need to appease the pervasive constitutionalism of their fellow citizens they faced a difficult task. The Constitution had been written to secure the support of slaveowners; it did not yield antislavery arguments easily.

The comity clause was an especially weak reed. While it says that citizens of a state may claim its benefits, it does not confer them on non-citizens and, more importantly, it does not remove from the states the right to define who shall be citizens. The clause is not a grant of federal power to do anything; it is not even a prohibition of action by a state. It merely says that whatever a state decides to offer its citizens as benefits must be offered equally to citizens of other states. Further, the clause does not define what privileges and immunities are. For clarification of these points the decision of a court was required, and judges were unlikely to be moved deeply by arguments which rested basically on the sincere wish of abolitionists that the clause mean something that would advance their cause. Victory for the abolition view depended more on moral and humanitarian sentiment than on constitutional argument.[37]

But the war had generated a tremendous interest in legal and constitutional questions. Union troops had fought against what Lincoln called "the essence of anarchy" and for the rule of law. When victory for that viewpoint was assured, a society chastened by the consequences of excessive romanticism and individualism sought constitutional roots for its legislative efforts and as a foundation for reunion. Cooley, who had opposed slavery fundamentally because it endangered order, helped provide these roots by insisting on the continuity of past institutions with the war era's amendments.[38]

[36]Howard J. Graham, "Our 'Declaratory' Fourteenth Amendment," *Everyman's Constitution* (Madison, 1968), 295–336; Jacobus ten Broek, *Equal under Law* (New York, 1965), 94–108.

[37]Jacobus ten Broek, 97–103.

[38]Kenneth M. Stampp, *And the War Came: The North and the Secession Crisis, 1860–1861* (Baton Rouge, 1950), 221–39; George M. Fredrickson, *The Inner Civil War, Northern Intellectuals and the Crisis of the Union* (New York, 1965), 183–98; Abraham Lincoln, *Collected Works*, IV, 268 (March 4, 1861).

614                         PHILLIP S. PALUDAN

The Fourteenth Amendment, he insisted, was simply a restatement of the comity clause which changed the federal system not at all. the only concession to change that he made was to admit that now the question of Negro citizenship was no longer in doubt as it had been before the war. Blacks might now claim the protection of the comity clause without question. But they would do so within an unchanged institutional framework. The provisions of the amendment, he wrote, "have not been agreed upon for the purpose of enlarging the sphere of powers of the general government, or of taking from the States of any of those just powers of government which in the original adoption of the Constitution were 'reserved to the States respectively.' The existing division of sovereignty is not disturbed by it."[39]

The imperative preliminary to the protection of equal justice for all men was a significant alteration in the "existing division of sovereignty." But to Cooley such a change was intolerable. Although deeply worried about the condition of prewar society he had not considered the possibility that the Jacksonian dream of equal men exercising their freedom equally in a world where government played an essentially negative role might itself be a cause of failure. He did not ascribe the trouble to either the dream or the constitutional system. Rather, he hit upon slavery as the problem—as the corruptor of venerable institutions good in themselves and of ideals unquestionably worthy. He hit upon slavery with the same pathetic eagerness as earlier Jacksonians had hit upon the Bank of the United States as the source of all evils.

Cooley recognized that the war had produced an expanded national power, but he believed that only the necessity of destroying the great corruptor, slavery, justified such power. He hoped that with slavery and its most blatant vestiges gone, the *status quo antebellum* that he had dreamed of might be achieved. He therefore argued eloquently that the legal innovations of war and reconstruction were only temporary expedients and that the true fruit of victory was a restored prewar constitutional system. Given the respect of most Americans for the recently won union and the long-standing love affair of practically all of them with the Constitution, his argument was convincing. The nation accepted the prewar union as the prize of battle and rejected for almost one hundred years the much greater prize that had potentially been won.

University of Kansas.

[39]Story, 683–84; Cooley, *Constitutional Limitations* (Boston, 1878), 631, 497–98.

# 18

# THE CONSTITUTION IN THE GILDED AGE: THE BEGINNINGS OF CONSTITUTIONAL REALISM IN AMERICAN SCHOLARSHIP

*HERMAN BELZ*

# The Constitution in the Gilded Age: The Beginnings of Constitutional Realism in American Scholarship

*by* HERMAN BELZ*

Constitutional history was one of the first distinct fields to emerge when the writing of history became professionalized toward the end of the nineteenth century. Throughout the last century indeed the constitutional dimension was a natural focus for the analysis of political affairs, and the earliest academic historians and political scientists often wrote from that point of view. Because they began the modern study of history and politics, scholars in the constitutional field such as John W. Burgess and Herman Eduard von Holst have figured in accounts of general American historiography and political science.[1] Paradoxically, however, they have not been studied in a comprehensive way from the perspective of constitutional history.[2] One result has been the common assumption that modern constitutional studies began only during the progressive movement of the twentieth century, with scholars such as Charles A. Beard, and that in the previous era students of the constitution, in the words of Professor Paul Murphy, wrote " 'revealed' history to underwrite the virtue of established institutions."[3] While it is true that many constitutional writers reflected a reverential, uncritical attitude, the more important fact is that in the years after Reconstruction American scholars began the realistic study of the constitution, preparing the way for the more critical, reform-oriented scholarship of the early twentieth century.

*Associate Professor, Dept. of History, University of Maryland.

1. For example, in John Higham *et al., History* (Englewood Cliffs, N.J., 1965); Anna Hadow, *Political Science in American Colleges and Universities, 1636-1900* (New York, 1939); Bernard Crick, *The American Science of Politics: Its Origins and Conditions* (Berkeley, 1959).

2. Paul L. Murphy has adverted in a general way to the constitutional historians of the late nineteenth century, but without attempting to document his highly critical assertions about their accomplishments and methodology, which he described as "one of philosophic metaphysical analysis." See "Time to Reclaim: The Current Challenge to American Constitutional History," *American Historical Review*, vol. LXIX (Oct. 1963), 64-79. The quoted words are at p. 66.

3. *Ibid.,* 66.

The conception of the constitution as a formal legal instrument or code giving existence to government and prescribing and limiting the exercise of its powers, rather than as the basic structure of the polity, not consciously constructed but growing organically through history, was one of the distinctive achievements of the American Revolution, and oriented constitutional description and analysis in the early republic toward a legalistic approach. For most students of American government in the first half of the nineteenth century the chief fact about the American constitution was, in the words of Francis Lieber, that "It was the positive enactment of the whole at one time, and by distinct authority." This quality of being an "enacted or written constitution," said Lieber, "distinguishes it especially from the English polity with its accumulative constitution" consisting in "usages and branches of the common law, in decisions of fundamental importance, in self-grown and in enacted institutions, in compacts, and in statutes embodying principles of political magnitude." Writers in the ante-bellum period also generally held that America's constitution was a decisive guarantee of liberty because it effectively limited government. Without a written constitution, wrote Frederick Grimke, parties would do what the exigencies of the moment dictated, "for how would it be possible to argue upon the constitutionality of any measure, when there was no constitution in existence." The written constitution was furthermore regarded as definite and clear in its meaning. "Some of its provisions may be subject to dispute," Grimké said, "but in the great majority of instances, it will be a clear and most important guide in judging the actions of all the public functionaries." Generally to discuss the meaning of the constitution at this time meant to discuss the problem of the nature of the Union—whether it was a compact that could be withdrawn from or a binding political obligation. But however they answered this question, according to Alfred H. Kelly, almost all writers and commentators on constitutional matters maintained "the assumption of an ahistorical, static constitution." [4]

Yet there is evidence that at least some students of the constitution disagreed with the prevailing formalistic, static approach. As example, the *American Review* in 1847 carried an article, in-

4. Francis Lieber, *On Civil Liberty and Self-Government* (London, 1853), 131, 221; Joseph Story, *Commentaries on the Constitution of the United States*, second ed. (2 vols.; Boston, 1851), ix; Frederick Grimke, *Considerations upon the Nature and Tendency of Free Institutions* (Cincinnati, 1848), 123, 131; Alfred H. Kelly, "Clio and the Court," *The Supreme Court Review*, 1965 (Chicago, 1965), 122.

spired by opposition to President Polk's actions in the Mexican
War, which argued that the government's practical construction of
its own powers effectively altered the constitution and enlarged the
scope of its "real authority." Observing in English history how "an
unwritten or historical Constitution" could develop, the writer
warned, "We, in this country, deceive ourselves egregiously if we
suppose that, because we began with a written instrument, we are
therefore secure against any changes in its features or provisions,
except such as may be made according to the forms prescribed in
the terms of the written instrument itself, and plainly written down,
like the rest, as a part of it." [5] During the Civil War, Sidney
George Fisher criticized the conventional wisdom about the American constitution from a similarly realistic point of view. Fisher
attacked the "received theory" that the constitution was alterable
only by the people and not by the government. If Congress in an
emergency exceeded its usual powers and its action went unchallenged, he asked, "What power has the Constitution to protect itself?" The answer was, none. In time such governmental action
would become custom and organic law, he reasoned, so that "we
get at last to the English doctrine, that Parliament is omnipotent,
that is to say, it cannot be legally restrained." Rejecting the idea
that the constitution was "to be interpreted only by itself, and
[that] a thousand years hence it will be still the Constitution, un-
altered and supreme," Fisher asserted that in actuality "the construction put on the Constitution by the practice of the Government
and by judicial decisions [was] the supreme law." [6]

In the last quarter of the nineteenth century the writing of
constitutional history took its place alongside, indeed, began to
supersede in importance, the traditional legal commentary as an
established part of constitutional studies. What is more, much
general history was written from a constitutional perspective, a
fact which has struck some modern historians as strange or ironic,
since both federal and state governments had little direct contact
with the average citizen in his everyday life.[7] Yet against the

5. "The Constitution; Written and Unwritten," *The American Review: A Whig Journal of Politics, Literature, Art, and Science*, vol. VI
(July, 1847), 1-3.

6. Sidney George Fisher, *The Trial of the Constitution* (Philadelphia,
1862), 41, 56. Fisher's relationship to English political thought is discussed in William Riker, "Sidney George Fisher and the Separation of
Powers," *Journal of the History of Ideas* vol. XV (June, 1954), 397-412.

7. Cf. William T. Hutchinson, "The Significance of the Constitution
of the United States in the Teaching of American History," *The Historian*, vol. 13 (Autumn, 1950), 7, and Murphy, "Time to Reclaim," 65.

background of nationalism and constitution-making that characterized the nineteenth century, and in view of the great war fought
to determine the nature of the American Union, it was perfectly
understandable that constitutional history should become a popular field of study. The typical work in constitutional history, in any
event, usually described the formation of the constitution in 1787
and the growth of the nation through the crisis of civil war in the
mid-nineteenth century. This was the pattern in the works of
George Bancroft, George Ticknor Curtis, Herman E. von Holst,
John W. Burgess, and James Schouler, written from a Unionist
point of view, and the works of Alexander Stephens and Jefferson
Davis, written from a southern view. More interesting than the
theme of support or opposition to nationalism, however, are the
ideas about law, politics, government and constitutions that informed these and other works in the constitutional field.

The central themes or concerns in historical and analytical
writing about the constitution in the period 1875 to 1900 were the
historical origins of the American constitution, the role or place or
usefulness of the constitution in the conduct of public affairs, and
the nature of the constitution. Traditional formalistic concepts of
law and politics of course were present in this constitutional writing, as was idealism as represented by the old Jacksonian Democrat, George Bancroft, or the younger German-trained scholar John
Burgess. But prominent also were attempts to define and describe
the American constitution according to standards of critical historical realism which anticipated the point of view of progressive
historiography of the twentieth century.

In the years when historical study was being transformed into
a professional discipline which its practitioners likened to science,
and in a conservative era which valued stability in its political
institutions rather than precipitous change, it was natural that
historians, in dealing with the first of these problems, should be
concerned to repudiate the theory of the constitution as either a
divinely inspired or creative act of the founding fathers themselves,
or the sudden product of revolutionary upheaval. It seemed to von
Holst, writing in 1876, that Americans overlooked the struggle
waged over the constitution and preferred to see instead evidence
of "the 'divine inspiration' which guided the 'fathers' at Philadelphia." This was fine for Fourth-of-July addresses, he said, but it
had nothing to do with history. The American constitution, wrote
von Holst, like every constitution, was "a result of actual circumstances of the past and present, and not a product of abstract politi-

cal theorizing." [8] Even George Bancroft, whose quotation of William Gladstone's statement that the American constitution was the most wonderful work ever struck off at one time by the brain and purpose of man incurred criticism from a professional historian a short while later, held that the framers "followed the lead of no theoretical writer" and made "the least possible reference . . . to abstract doctrines." [9] A few years later Brooks Adams wrote an article to disprove the belief that Americans had suddenly invented the written constitution. Explaining that the charters of English trading companies were the embryo of American constitutions, Adams concluded, "Americans are subject to the same general laws that regulate the rest of mankind; and accordingly . . . they have worked out their destiny slowly and painfully, . . . and . . . far from cutting the knot of their difficulties by a stroke of inventive genius, they earned their success by clinging tenaciously to what they had." [10]

Around 1890, as though in response to the outpouring of uncritical patriotic sentiment a few years earlier on the centennial of the constitution, several of the emerging class of professional historians turned their attention to the problem of the origins of the constitution. J. Franklin Jameson, in the preface to a book of essays dealing with constitutional developments in the Confederation period, stated that many educated persons "think of our Constitution as having sprung full-armed from the heads of Olympian conventioners." With the progress of historical science, however, he explained, great national acts of settlement were being found to have been preceded by numerous tentative steps or by a long course of gradual development in the nation.[11] To refute the unhistorical implications of Gladstone's famous dictum about the constitution, Alexander Johnston, James Harvey Robinson, and W. C. Morey described the historical roots of the organic charter

8. Herman Eduard von Holst, *The Constitutional and Political History of the United States*, transl. by J.J. Lalor and A.B. Mason (7 vols.; Chicago, 1877-1892), I, 62-63; *The Constitutional Law of the United States of America*, transl. by A.B. Mason (Chicago, 1887), 2.

9. George Bancroft, *History of the Constitution of the United States*, 6th ed. (2 vols.; New York, 1900), II, 322. The criticism of Bancroft was made by William C. Morey, "The Genesis of a Written Constitution," *The Annals of the American Academy of Political and Social Science*, vol. I (April, 1891), 530.

10. Brooks Adams, "The Embryo of a Commonwealth," *The Atlantic Monthly*, vol. LIV (Nov. 1884), 610.

11. J. Franklin Jameson, ed., *Essays in the Constitutional History of the United States in the Formative Period, 1775-1789* (Boston, 1889), viii.

written in 1787. Writing in a frame of mind that is difficult to appreciate, so obvious does the matter appear to us today, Johnston, a professor of history at Princeton, argued that it was not possible to create _de novo_ a scheme of government such as the Philadelphia convention produced. According to Johnston, the framers selected from provisions of state constitutions that had been tested by experience, so that the constitution "was no empty product of political theory," but rather "a growth, or . . . a selection from a great number of growths then before the Convention." [12] James Harvey Robinson, a young instructor at the University of Pennsylvania, raised the same issue in asking: "Did they [the founding fathers], left without guide or precedent, by a simple effort of the intellect, draw up a form of government hitherto unknown, . . . Or did they rely on the experience of others, and find in the history of government . . . materials for the new structure?" Of course they did the latter, said Robinson, and their chief model was "their home experience" in the several state constitutions and governments. [13] A third scholar, William C. Morey of the University of Rochester, seeking to prove that the laws of historical development applied as well to a written as to an unwritten constitution, insisted that the American constitution was "not a fiat-constitution projected from the brain of the Fathers, nor a copy of the contemporary constitution of England." Morey stressed as the historical basis of the American constitution the royal charters to English trading companies, which became the first written constitutions. [14] Thus constitutional historians disposed of the creative- or divine-inspiration as well as the revolutionary theory of the origins of the constitution. By 1897 James Schouler could fairly disregard the problem as a serious matter for investigation in writing, almost as afterthought following an account of the formation of the Union, "Any notion that our Federal constitution of 1787 was a spontaneous birth must be a false and fanciful one. . . . Our brief exposition of the facts has shown that it was a gradual conception; . . . that it ripened as the matured fruit of political experience." [15]

12. Alexander Johnston, "The First Century of the Constitution," _New Princeton Review_, vol. IV (Sept. 1887), 176-178, 186-187.

13. James Harvey Robinson, "Original and Derived Features of the Constitution," _The Annals of the American Academy of Political and Social Science_, vol. I (Oct. 1890), 203-207.

14. William C. Morey, "The Genesis of a Written Constitution," _ibid._, (April, 1891), 530, 533-535.

15. James Schouler, _Constitutional Studies_ (New York, 1897), 95-96.

The attitudes of constitutional historians and other scholars toward the constitution as an instrument of government and their conceptions of its usefulness and value varied more than did their views of its origins. The prevailing attitude in the conservative years following Reconstruction was, predictably, one of considerable satisfaction with the constitution as a source of political stability. It is apparent that one of the main conclusions drawn from researches into the origins of the constitution, and one that was not reached reluctantly, was that American political institutions were conservative. Brooks Adams drew the moral with unmistakable clarity: "Their [the American people's] political genius did not lie in sudden inspiration, but in the conservative and at the same time flexible habit of mind which enabled them to adapt the institutions they had known and tested as colonists to their new position as an independent people. . . ." American governmental institutions, he added, "are not the ephemeral growth of a moment of revolution, but . . . are the offspring of a history and tradition as ancient as those which have moulded the common law." [16] Similarly Alexander Johnston held that the secret of success in American politics was to allow institutions to develop simply and naturally, then when they reached maturity to fix them permanently in legislation or in constitutions.[17]

That the constitution ensured social and political stability and best solved the ancient problem of the conflict between governmental power and individual liberty has been a favored notion throughout American history, but it had a special currency in the last quarter of the nineteenth century. George Bancroft, concluding a long life of scholarship and public service, wrote in 1882 that in America the gates of revolution were bolted down, for the constitution provided a legal and peaceful way to bring about change. In his best romantic style Bancroft rhapsodized: "The constitution establishes nothing that interferes with equality and individuality. It knows nothing of differences by descent, or opinions, of favored classes, or legalized religion, or the political power of property. . . . Each one of the three departments [of government] proceeded from the people, and each is endowed with all the authority needed for its just activity." [18] Almost equally uncritically Thomas M. Cooley, the prominent jurist and legal commentator,

16. Adams, "Embryo of a Commonwealth," 619.
17. Johnston, "First Century of the Constitution," 187.
18. Bancroft, *History of the Formation of the Constitution*, II, 334, 324, 327.

pointed out some of the conservative benefits of America's constitution. By it the political authority of the national government was conferred and measured exclusively, he said, and could not be enlarged merely by precedent as in other countries. Comparing the value of written and unwritten constitutions, Cooley wrote that in America written constitutions prescribed the extent to which power was exercised and were the "absolute rule of action and decision for all departments and offices of the government." [19] The British writer James Bryce discerned the same conservative effect of the American constitution. Though it was not a magic tool that of itself could restrain passions and cause reason to prevail, Bryce held that it blocked rash and hasty change and tended "to render the inevitable process of modification gradual and tentative, the result of admitted and growing necessities rather than of restless impatience." Moreover, the constitution trained Americans "to habits of legality" and strengthened "their conservative instincts, their sense of the value of stability and permanence in political arrangements." [20] Christopher Tiedeman, another leading jurist and constitutional commentator, felt that the operation of democracy had eroded many limitations placed on government officials by written constitutions. Nevertheless, he regarded the written constitution as an important "check upon the popular will in the interest of the minority." Making the same point that progressive critics of American government would emphasize but without any misgivings, Tiedeman wrote: "It [the constitution] legalizes, and therefore makes possible and successful, the opposition to the popular will," thereby enabling the United States to prevent the development of "democratic absolutism." [21]

Although criticism of the politically conservative nature of the constitutional system did not emerge among constitutional scholars until the early twentieth century, in the years 1875 to 1900 there were some dissenters to the general approval of the constitution as an instrument of government and its effect on American political life. Von Holst, for example, railed against the veneration of the constitution among Americans, which prevented them from seeing

---

19. Thomas M. Cooley, ed., *Constitutional History of the United States as Seen in the Development of American Law* (New York, 1889), 31; T.M. Cooley, *The General Principles of Constitutional Law in the United States of America*, 3rd ed. (Boston, 1898), 22.

20. James Bryce, *The American Commonwealth* (3 vols.; London, 1888), I, 536-538.

21. Christopher Tiedeman, *The Unwritten Constitution of the United States* (New York, 1890), 163-165.

the realities underlying their government. Thus he called it "a happy sign of progress towards a clearer judgment among thinking people" when a writer in *The Nation* declared that the constitution, in spite of its supposed precision and subjection to judicial construction, had through the theory of "latent powers" been made to serve party demands "quite as effectively as though congress had the omnipotence of parliament." Here was the same insight that had informed Sidney George Fisher's criticism of the constitution during the Civil War: the formal legal instrument did not prevent the national government from acting as any other sovereign government would have acted under similar circumstances. Furthermore, it was a "fundamental defect in the constitution itself," von Holst reasoned, that led to the undesirable situation so common in American politics in which discussion of the expediency of a measure was subordinated to discussion of so insubstantial a thing as its constitutionality.[22]

A few years later Woodrow Wilson continued the criticism of "an undiscriminating and almost blind worship" of the constitution which on the one hand had not prevented congressional control of the federal government from being established, overriding "all niceties of constitutional restrictions and even many broad principles of constitutional limitation," but on the other hand did prevent a clear and general understanding that the practices of American government were very different from what they ought to be according to the "literary theory" of the constitution. In seeking reforms along the lines of a strengthened executive branch and new forms of responsibility imposed on Congress, Wilson said he was asking "whether the Constitution [was] still adapted to serve the purposes for which it was intended.[23] Henry Jones Ford, like Wilson a political scientist, also was concerned with the effect of giving excessive attention to the formal constitution and thus obscuring the realities of the political system. In popular belief, Ford wrote, "The constitutional ideal is noble; but the politicians are vile. If only the checks could be made more effective, if only a just balance of power could be established beyond the strength of the politicians to disarrange,— . . . the constitution would work perfectly." But according to Ford it was precisely the checks and balances of the constitution and its failure to provide clear and direct responsibility for running the government which was the source of the

---

22. von Holst, *Constitutional and Political History*, I, 71, 78-79.
23. Woodrow Wilson, *Congressional Government: A Study in American Politics*, Meridian Books ed. (New York, 1956), 31, 27.

political troubles symbolized by party machines and boss rule. Political parties, even the party machines, were "a necessary intermediary between the people and their government," Ford concluded, and if the constitution did not operate well in practice the defect lay in the constitution itself.[24]

The third major concern of constitutional historians and scholars in the last quarter of the nineteenth century, implicit in the criticisms of writers such as Wilson and Ford, was the very problem of defining the American constitution and the nature of the constitutional process. Here the conflict between law and politics, or legal formalism and political reality, stood out most prominently. The usual view was to regard the constitution as formal, positive law. As noted earlier, throughout most of the nineteenth century when writers dealt with this issue they referred to the question of the nature of the Union, asking what kind of compact or contract, involving what kind of legal obligations, the constitution was. This was the approach of George Bancroft, George Ticknor Curtis, John W. Burgess, Jefferson Davis, and others whose thinking was shaped by the Civil War. That such writers conceived of the constitution in a legalistic way did not, it should be pointed out, mean that they wrote narrow legal history; their works were typically broad, general political histories, as we would describe them today, which gave a prominent place to constitutional disputes and interpretation. They understood, moreover, that answers to legal questions depended on non-legal ideas and events. George Ticknor Curtis, for example, distinguished constitutional history from constitutional law by pointing out that the former consisted of "those events and that public section which have shaped the text of a written Constitution, or which should be regarded in its interpretation." Constitutional law was the body of jurisprudence which included the text of the constitution and the constructions it had received from those whose duty it was to interpret its meaning. In the period with which Curtis was concerned, before the era of judicial supremacy, the President and Congress construed the constitution authoritatively, but the constitution was always the formal, written legal document or code; it was not legislation and governmental action, as in England, which there determined the powers of government and the rights of individuals.[25]

24. Henry Jones Ford, *The Rise and Growth of American Politics: A Sketch of Constitutional Development* (New York, 1898), 334-335, 352-353.

25. George Ticknor Curtis, *Constitutional History of the United States* (2 vols.; New York, 1903), I, iv. This work was first published in 1889.

Typical of the orthodox formalistic conception of the constitution that prevailed once the question of the nature of the Union
was settled was a volume edited and in part written by Thomas M.
Cooley, *Constitutional History of the United States as Seen in the
Development of American Law* (1889). Henry Wade Rogers, a professor at the University of Michigan Law School, contributed a
preface to this volume praising constitutional law as a distinctively
American contribution to jurisprudence and calling it "peculiarly
the pride and glory" of the country. "Written constitutions," asserted Rogers, "have been the distinguishing feature of American
institutions."[26] Constitutional history written under these assumptions concentrated almost entirely on the Supreme Court, which
Rogers said was "in reality . . . more powerful in its influence on
the character of the government than [were] the President or
Congress." The result was the history of constitutional law, but according to Rogers and Cooley, addressing themselves to the student
of history, the study of this subject was the best way "to understand
the nature of the [American] government."[27]

Other writers, however, especially historians, conceived of the
constitution more in political terms, with emphasis on the actual
practices of government, than in formalistic, juristic terms. Simon
Sterne, a reformer of the 1870's and 1880's, anticipated this more
realistic—as its exponents saw it—point of view in stating that an
account of the American constitution ought to consider, in addition
to the formal text and its interpretation by the Supreme Court, the
political controversies that led to changes in the instrument as well
as the situation of political parties. A constitutional history, he
thought, should be tantamount to "a view of the institutional condition" of the United States. Frankly approving of the interaction
of law and politics in the American constitution, Stern wrote:
"There is an unconscious influence exercised by public opinion

26. Cooley, ed., *Constitutional History of the United States*, 5-6.
27. *Ibid.*, 13, 23-24. By the 1890's a body of literature on the Supreme
Court and judicial review was beginning to develop which assumed the
proportions of a major political as well as scholarly controversy during
the early twentieth century. Generally the focus of such studies were the
questions of when judicial review began and whether the framers of the
constitution supported it, and the issue of its legitimate scope and place
in American politics. Whether for or against judicial review, students of
this problem tended to think in terms of the juristic conception of the
constitution at this time. For a discussion of this literature see Alan F.
Westin's essay, "Charles Beard and American Debate over Judicial Review, 1790-1961," in Charles A. Beard, *The Supreme Court and the Constitution*, Spectrum ed. (Englewood Cliffs, N.J., 1960), 1-34.

upon the minds of those who are called upon to decide finally constitutional questions, which is neither corrupt nor sinister, but
which causes a written constitution to approximate more closely to
an unwritten one."[28] The idea of the constitution as political institutions was more naturally conceivable to an Englishman and in
part informed Bryce's *The American Commonwealth*. Disavowing
concern with the legal aspects of the constitution and seeking to
explain the "framework and constitutional machinery," Bryce described the system of electing presidents, the powers of Congress,
the spoils system, and other political institutions and practices
which had "sprung up round the Constitution and profoundly affected its working." Similarly, legislation of Congress had "become
practically incorporated" with the original text of the constitution
and had given to its working a decisive character and direction.[29]

Around the time Bryce offered to the American public his
study of the constitution seen partly as institutional rather than
legal development, three young American scholars—J. Franklin
Jameson, Woodrow Wilson, and Henry Jones Ford—produced
works subscribing to and encouraging a similar broad, political, and
to their way of thinking more realistic conception of the American
constitution. Jameson, introducing a series of essays dealing with
the development of executive and judicial institutions under the
Articles of Confederation as well as with constitution-making in
American churches and the status of slaves, said that people who
lived under a written constitution were inclined to take too narrow
a view of constitutional history, confining their interest alone to
the document and its formation, adoption, amendment, and interpretation. The chief purpose of the volume, therefore, he explained, was to broaden the conception of the constitutional history. The American constitution included elements not embodied
in the written document, such as the "systems of party organization
. . . , democracy, . . . the Speaker of the House, [and] . . . its
committees, . . . federal statutes, . . . the constitutions and laws
of the states, and . . . the practices and usages of the government
and the people." Jameson believed that his view of constitutional
history was not simply a difference of opinion in the use of terms,

28. Simon Sterne, *Constitutional History and Political Development
of the United States* (New York, 1882), iii, 145-146.

29. Bryce, *The American Commonwealth*, I, 6-7, 521-522, 517-518.
When discussing judicial interpretation of the constitutional document,
however, Bryce was very formalistic, subscribing to the view that judges
had no will of their own and simply discovered and declared the law,
rather than shaped or made it themselves.

and that too narrow a conception of the field would lead to the neglect of the history of aspects of American political life which went as far toward determining "our form of government as anything set down in the Federal Constitution itself."[30]

What was necessary in Jameson's point of view was to understand that as law and politics are constantly interacting, the study of the constitution must go beyond merely formal, legal elements to include things political. This idea informed the work of Woodrow Wilson and Henry Jones Ford, who described essential elements of the constitutional system in terms similar to those of Jameson. The Civil War and Reconstruction according to Wilson had made clear "that there has been a vast alteration in the conditions of government; . . . and that we are really living under a constitution essentially different from that which we have been so long worshiping as our peculiar and incomparable possession." The constitution of 1787 was "now our *form of government* rather in name than in reality;" it was a "tap-root," he explained, and "the chief fact . . . of our national history is that from [it] has grown a vast constitutional system,—a system branching and expanding in statutes and judicial decisions, as well in unwritten precedent." Stressing the need in describing this system to "escape from theories and attach himself to facts," Wilson said the main inquiry must concern "the real depositories and the essential machinery of power." He concluded from a study of the "actual practices of the Constitution" that the balance inherent in the formal written instrument, or in what Wilson called the "literary theory" of the constitution, was ideal only, and that congressional government was "the real government of the Union."[31] Henry Jones Ford, whom Wilson brought to a teaching position at Princeton, studied political parties as an element in the American constitution. Ford's conception of the constitution was evident in the title of his great work, *The Rise and Growth of American Politics: A Sketch of Constitutional Development*, and in the fact that nowhere in it did he discuss John Marshall and the Supreme Court. His purpose was to describe the "political structure" or "the actual constitution of the government." Relying in large part on historical analysis, Ford said that party organization in the early nineteenth century stimulated democratic tendencies which made the electoral college a party agency and transformed the presidency into an instrument of popular control. By the end of Jackson's second term, Ford wrote, this transforma-

---

30. Jameson, ed., *Essays in the Constitutional History of the United States*, ix-xi.

31. Wilson, *Congressional Government*, 28-30, 53.

tion had marked a "profound change in the nature of the constitution." As politics became democratized, party organization took the place of class interests and social connections in providing unity of control between the legislative and executive branches, and became "virtually a part of the apparatus of government itself."[32]

By the start of the twentieth century this realistic approach to constitutional studies, defining the constitution in essentially political terms and positing an unwritten constitution, was fairly established, at least in academic circles. The historian and political scientist Albert Bushnell Hart epitomized the new learning in his well known college textbook, *Actual Government as Applied under American Conditions*, first published in 1903. Asserting that the formal constitution and statutes were merely an enveloping husk and that "the real kernel [was] that personal interest and personal action which vitalizes [sic] government," Hart took as his task to describe "the purpose, extent, division, exercise, and limitations of governing power." In an encyclopaedic survey of American legal and political institutions that was historical in scope though not in organization, he attempted to explain how government operated "not simply by what constitutions and statutes say ought to be done, but by the experience of what is done."[33] The constitutional historian Francis Newton Thorpe, though inclined to see the genius of American political science in written constitutions, nevertheless recognized the existence of an unwritten constitution in governmental actions, political parties, and, in general, "the manner of doing the public business." The constitutional historian must explain as his foremost duty the nature and growth of the principles or "civil notions" underlying the governmental system, Thorpe said, reflecting an older idealism; but he conceded that "whatsoever in the history of the unwritten constitution will make clearer the origin and development of civil notions has a just demand on the historian." In a practical sense Thorpe defined the constitution broadly and politically, including in his two volume constitutional history, which he described as a record of the evolution of government in America, accounts of democracy in the eighteenth century, the organization of state governments, suffrage requirements, west-

32. Ford, *The Rise and Growth of American Politics*, v, 217-220.
33. Albert Bushnell Hart, *Actual Government as Applied under American Conditions* (New York, 1908), vii, ix. Other textbooks employing the new realistic approach to constitutional studies were B.A. Hinsdale, *The American Government: National and State* (Chicago, 1891), and Roscoe J. Ashley, *The American Federal State* (New York, 1902).

ward migration, slavery and the free Negro, legislative apportionment, banking and finance, and the judicial system.[34]

Though lawyers naturally were critical of the definition of the constitution in terms of "actual government" and the conception of an unwritten constitution, some were attracted to the new realistic approach.[35] Christopher Tiedeman, for example, defined the constitution as "the order and structure of the body politic" and, anticipating the point of view of progressive historians such as Charles Beard, saw constitutional law as "the resultant of all the social and other forces which . . . make up the civilization of the people." He described among other things the electoral college, the two-term tradition concerning the presidency, and corporation and charter rights as aspects of the unwritten constitution. Expressing a kind of conservative sociological jurisprudence and asserting that judges make law rather than declare it, Tiedeman reserved his praise for what he considered the most important element in the unwritten constitution: "the disposition of the courts to seize hold of these general declarations of rights as an authority for them to lay their interdict upon all legislative acts which interfere with the individual's natural rights, even though these acts do not violate any specific or special provision of the Constitution."[36]

In the late nineteenth century, then, an attitude of critical realism became an important attribute of constitutional scholarship. Research into the origins of the constitution, refuting the divine-inspiration theory about the founding fathers and showing that the laws of historical development applied as well to Americans as to any other people, reflected this attitude in part, as historians tried to establish the credentials of their discipline as a true science. The critical evaluation of the constitutional system and the attempt to go beyond the façade of the formal written document in describing the constitution were a clearer manifestation of this

---

34. Francis Newton Thorpe, "What Is a Constitutional History of the United States?" *The Annals of the American Academy of Political and Social Science*, vol. XIX (March, 1902), 96-97; *A Constitutional History of the American People, 1776-1850* (2 vols.; New York, 1898).

35. For a critique of the idea of an unwritten American constitution see Emlin McClain, "Unwritten Constitutions in the United States," *Harvard Law Review*, vol. XV (March, 1902), 531-540. McClain begged the question of whether there was an unwritten constitution by asserting that institutions, practices, traditions are not part of the law, and since the constitution was "a part of the positive law," there could be no unwritten constitution in the United States.

36. Tiedeman, *The Unwritten Constitution of the United States*, 16, 40, 44, 81.

realistic approach. The evidence is insufficient as to a correlation
between this constitutional realism and the advocacy of political
reform, but it is at least suggestive that Wilson's and Ford's realistic
studies were related to specific reformist purposes. A conservative,
reverential attitude relying on the traditional legalistic or juristic
approach to the constitution persisted alongside this politically
oriented constitutional realism. But the more important fact was
that several constitutional scholars conceived of their subject in
realistic, political terms, thus preparing the way for the broader,
more vigorous reformist campaigns of constitutional history and
political science in the twentieth century, and raising fundamental
issues about politics, law, and the constitution which have remained central to the present day.

# E.  THE PROFESSION

# 19
# THE PATH OF THE LAW

*OLIVER WENDELL HOLMES*

# HARVARD
# LAW REVIEW.

| VOL. X. | MARCH 25, 1897. | No. 8. |

## THE PATH OF THE LAW.[1]

WHEN we study law we are not studying a mystery but a
well known profession. We are studying what we shall
want in order to appear before judges, or to advise people in such
a way as to keep them out of court. The reason why it is a profession, why people will pay lawyers to argue for them or to advise
them, is that in societies like ours the command of the public force
is intrusted to the judges in certain cases, and the whole power of
the state will be put forth, if necessary, to carry out their judgments and decrees. People want to know under what circumstances and how far they will run the risk of coming against what
is so much stronger than themselves, and hence it becomes a business to find out when this danger is to be feared. The object of
our study, then, is prediction, the prediction of the incidence of
the public force through the instrumentality of the courts.

The means of the study are a body of reports, of treatises, and
of statutes, in this country and in England, extending back for six
hundred years, and now increasing annually by hundreds. In
these sibylline leaves are gathered the scattered prophecies of the
past upon the cases in which the axe will fall. These are what
properly have been called the oracles of the law. Far the most
important and pretty nearly the whole meaning of every new effort
of legal thought is to make these prophecies more precise, and to

---

[1] An Address delivered by Mr. Justice Holmes, of the Supreme Judicial Court of
Massachusetts, at the dedication of the new hall of the Boston University School of
Law, on January 8, 1897. Copyrighted by O. W. Holmes, 1897.

generalize them into a thoroughly connected system.  The process is one, from a lawyer's statement of a case, eliminating as it does all the dramatic elements with which his client's story has clothed it, and retaining only the facts of legal import, up to the final analyses and abstract universals of theoretic jurisprudence.  The reason why a lawyer does not mention that his client wore a white hat when he made a contract, while Mrs. Quickly would be sure to dwell upon it along with the parcel gilt goblet and the sea-coal fire, is that he forsees that the public force will act in the same way whatever his client had upon his head.   It is to make the prophecies easier to be remembered and to be understood that the teachings of the decisions of the past are put into general propositions and gathered into text-books, or that statutes are passed in a general form.   The primary rights and duties with which jurisprudence busies itself again are nothing but prophecies.   One of the many evil effects of the confusion between legal and moral ideas, about which I shall have something to say in a moment, is that theory is apt to get the cart before the horse, and to consider the right or the duty as something existing apart from and independent of the con-sequences of its breach, to which certain sanctions are added after-ward.   But, as I shall try to show, a legal duty so called is nothing but a prediction that if a man does or omits certain things he will be made to suffer in this or that way by judgment of the court ; — and so of a legal right.

The number of our predictions when generalized and reduced to a system is not unmanageably large.   They present themselves as a finite body of dogma which may be mastered within a reasonable time.   It is a great mistake to be frightened by the ever increasing number of reports.   The reports of a given jurisdiction in the course of a generation take up pretty much the whole body of the law, and restate it from the present point of view.   We could re-construct the corpus from them if all that went before were burned.  The use of the earlier reports is mainly historical, a use about which I shall have something to say before I have finished.

I wish, if I can, to lay down some first principles for the study of this body of dogma or systematized prediction which we call the law, for men who want to use it as the instrument of their business to enable them to prophesy in their turn, and, as bearing upon the study, I wish to point out an ideal which as yet our law has not attained.

## THE PATH OF THE LAW.

The first thing for a business-like understanding of the matter is to understand its limits, and therefore I think it desirable at once to point out and dispel a confusion between morality and law, which sometimes rises to the height of conscious theory, and more often and indeed constantly is making trouble in detail without reaching the point of consciousness. You can see very plainly that a bad man has as much reason as a good one for wishing to avoid an encounter with the public force, and therefore you can see the practical importance of the distinction between morality and law. A man who cares nothing for an ethical rule which is believed and practised by his neighbors is likely nevertheless to care a good deal to avoid being made to pay money, and will want to keep out of jail if he can.

I take it for granted that no hearer of mine will misinterpret what I have to say as the language of cynicism. The law is the witness and external deposit of our moral life. Its history is the history of the moral development of the race. The practice of it, in spite of popular jests, tends to make good citizens and good men. When I emphasize the difference between law and morals I do so with reference to a single end, that of learning and understanding the law. For that purpose you must definitely master its specific marks, and it is for that that I ask you for the moment to imagine yourselves indifferent to other and greater things.

I do not say that there is not a wider point of view from which the distinction between law and morals becomes of secondary or no importance, as all mathematical distinctions vanish in presence of the infinite. But I do say that that distinction is of the first importance for the object which we are here to consider, — a right study and mastery of the law as a business with well understood limits, a body of dogma enclosed within definite lines. I have just shown the practical reason for saying so. If you want to know the law and nothing else, you must look at it as a bad man, who cares only for the material consequences which such knowledge enables him to predict, not as a good one, who finds his reasons for conduct, whether inside the law or outside of it, in the vaguer sanctions of conscience. The theoretical importance of the distinction is no less, if you would reason on your subject aright. The law is full of phraseology drawn from morals, and by the mere force of language continually invites us to pass from one domain to the other without perceiving it, as we are sure to do unless we have the boundary constantly before our minds. The law talks about rights, and duties, and malice, and intent, and negligence, and so forth, and nothing is easier, or, I may say, more common in legal reasoning, than to take these words in their moral sense, at some stage of the argument, and so to drop into fallacy. For instance, when we speak of the rights of man in a moral sense, we mean to mark the limits of interference with individual freedom which we think are prescribed by conscience, or by our ideal, however reached. Yet it is certain that many laws have been enforced in the past, and it is likely that some are enforced now, which are condemned by the most enlightened opinion of the time, or which at all events pass the limit of interference as many consciences would draw it. Manifestly, therefore, nothing but confusion of thought can result from assuming that the rights of man in a moral sense are equally rights in the sense of the Constitution and the law. No doubt simple and extreme cases can be put of imaginable laws which the statute-making power would not dare to enact, even in the absence of written constitutional prohibitions, because the community would rise in rebellion and fight ; and this gives some plausibility to the proposition that the law, if not a part of morality, is limited by it. But this limit of power is not coextensive with any system of morals. For the most part it falls far within the lines of any such system, and in some cases may extend beyond them, for reasons drawn from the habits of a particular people at a particular time. I once heard the late Professor Agassiz say that a German population would rise if you added two cents to the price of a glass of beer. A statute in such a case would be empty words, not because it was wrong, but because it could not be enforced. No one will deny that wrong statutes can be and are enforced, and we should not all agree as to which were the wrong ones.

The confusion with which I am dealing besets confessedly legal conceptions. Take the fundamental question, What constitutes the law ? You will find some text writers telling you that it is something different from what is decided by the courts of Massachusetts or England, that it is a system of reason, that it is a deduction from principles of ethics or admitted axioms or what not, which may or may not coincide with the decisions. But if we take the view of our friend the bad man we shall find that he does not care two straws for the axioms or deductions, but that he does want to know what the Massachusetts or English courts are likely to do in fact. I am much of his mind. The prophecies of what the courts will do in fact, and nothing more pretentious, are what I mean by the law.

Take again a notion which as popularly understood is the widest conception which the law contains ; — the notion of legal duty, to which already I have referred. We fill the word with all the content which we draw from morals. But what does it mean to a bad man ? Mainly, and in the first place, a prophecy that if he does certain things he will be subjected to disagreeable consequences by way of imprisonment or compulsory payment of money. But from his point of view, what is the difference between being fined and being taxed a certain sum for doing a certain thing ? That his point of view is the test of legal principles is shown by the many discussions which have arisen in the courts on the very question whether a given statutory liability is a penalty or a tax. On the answer to this question depends the decision whether conduct is legally wrong or right, and also whether a man is under compulsion or free. Leaving the criminal law on one side, what is the difference between the liability under the mill acts or statutes authorizing a taking by eminent domain and the liability for what we call a wrongful conversion of property where restoration is out of the question ? In both cases the party taking another man's property has to pay its fair value as assessed by a jury, and no more. What significance is there in calling one taking right and another wrong from the point of view of the law? It does not matter, so far as the given consequence, the compulsory payment, is concerned, whether the act to which it is attached is described in terms of praise or in terms of blame, or whether the law purports to prohibit it or to allow it. If it matters at all, still speaking from the bad man's point of view, it must be because in one case and not in the other some further disadvantages, or at least some further consequences, are attached to the act by the law. The only other disadvantages thus attached to it which I ever have been able to think of are to be found in two somewhat insignificant legal doctrines, both of which might be abolished without much disturbance. One is, that a contract to do a prohibited act is unlawful, and the other, that, if one of two or more joint wrongdoers has to pay all the damages, he cannot recover contribution from his fellows. And that I believe is all. You see how the vague circumference of the notion of duty shrinks and at the same time grows more precise when we wash it with cynical acid and expel everything except the object of our study, the operations of the law.

Nowhere is the confusion between legal and moral ideas more manifest than in the law of contract. Among other things, here again the so called primary rights and duties are invested with a mystic significance beyond what can be assigned and explained. The duty to keep a contract at common law means a prediction that you must pay damages if you do not keep it, — and nothing else. If you commit a tort, you are liable to pay a compensatory sum. If you commit a contract, you are liable to pay a compensatory sum unless the promised event comes to pass, and that is all the difference. But such a mode of looking at the matter stinks in the nostrils of those who think it advantageous to get as much ethics into the law as they can. It was good enough for Lord Coke, however, and here, as in many other cases, I am content to abide with him. In Bromage *v.* Genning,[1] a prohibition was sought in the King's Bench against a suit in the marches of Wales for the specific performance of a covenant to grant a lease, and Coke said that it would subvert the intention of the covenantor, since he intends it to be at his election either to lose the damages or to make the lease. Sergeant Harris for the plaintiff confessed that he moved the matter against his conscience, and a prohibition was granted. This goes further than we should go now, but it shows what I venture to say has been the common law point of view from the beginning, although Mr. Harriman, in his very able little book upon Contracts has been misled, as I humbly think, to a different conclusion.

I have spoken only of the common law, because there are some cases in which a logical justification can be found for speaking of civil liabilities as imposing duties in an intelligible sense. These are the relatively few in which equity will grant an injunction, and will enforce it by putting the defendant in prison or otherwise punishing him unless he complies with the order of the court. But I hardly think it advisable to shape general theory from the exception, and I think it would be better to cease troubling ourselves about primary rights and sanctions altogether, than to

---

[1] 1 Roll. Rep. 368.

describe our prophecies concerning the liabilities commonly imposed by the law in those inappropriate terms.

I mentioned, as other examples of the use by the law of words drawn from morals, malice, intent, and negligence. It is enough to take malice as it is used in the law of civil liability for wrongs, — what we lawyers call the law of torts, — to show you that it means something different in law from what it means in morals, and also to show how the difference has been obscured by giving to principles which have little or nothing to do with each other the same name. Three hundred years ago a parson preached a sermon and told a story out of Fox's Book of Martyrs of a man who had assisted at the torture of one of the saints, and afterward died, suffering compensatory inward torment. It happened that Fox was wrong. The man was alive and chanced to hear the sermon, and thereupon he sued the parson. Chief Justice Wray instructed the jury that the defendant was not liable, because the story was told innocently, without malice. He took malice in the moral sense, as importing a malevolent motive. But nowadays no one doubts that a man may be liable, without any malevolent motive at all, for false statements manifestly calculated to inflict temporal damage. In stating the case in pleading, we still should call the defendant's conduct malicious; but, in my opinion at least, the word means nothing about motives, or even about the defendant's attitude toward the future, but only signifies that the tendency of his conduct under the known circumstances was very plainly to cause the plaintiff temporal harm.[1]

In the law of contract the use of moral phraseology has led to equal confusion, as I have shown in part already, but only in part. Morals deal with the actual internal state of the individual's mind, what he actually intends. From the time of the Romans down to now, this mode of dealing has affected the language of the law as to contract, and the language used has reacted upon the thought. We talk about a contract as a meeting of the minds of the parties, and thence it is inferred in various cases that there is no contract because their minds have not met; that is, because they have intended different things or because one party has not known of the assent of the other. Yet nothing is more certain than that parties may be bound by a contract to things which neither of them intended, and when one does not know of the other's assent. Sup-

---

[1] See Hanson v. Globe Newspaper Co., 159 Mass. 293, 302.

pose a contract is executed in due form and in writing to deliver a
lecture, mentioning no time. One of the parties thinks that the
promise will be construed to mean at once, within a week. The
other thinks that it means when he is ready. The court says
that it means within a reasonable time. The parties are bound
by the contract as it is interpreted by the court, yet neither
of them meant what the court declares that they have said. In
my opinion no one will understand the true theory of contract
or be able even to discuss some fundamental questions intelligently
until he has understood that all contracts are formal, that the
making of a contract depends not on the agreement of two minds
in one intention, but on the agreement of two sets of external
signs, — not on the parties' having *meant* the same thing but on
their having *said* the same thing. Furthermore, as the signs may
be addressed to one sense or another, — to sight or to hearing, —
on the nature of the sign will depend the moment when the contract is made. If the sign is tangible, for instance, a letter, the
contract is made when the letter of acceptance is delivered. If it is
necessary that the minds of the parties meet, there will be no contract until the acceptance can be read, — none, for example, if the acceptance be snatched from the hand of the offerer by a third person.

This is not the time to work out a theory in detail, or to answer
many obvious doubts and questions which are suggested by these
general views. I know of none which are not easy to answer, but
what I am trying to do now is only by a series of hints to throw
some light on the narrow path of legal doctrine, and upon two pit-
falls which, as it seems to me, lie perilously near to it. Of the
first of these I have said enough. I hope that my illustrations
have shown the danger, both to speculation and to practice, of con-
founding morality with law, and the trap which legal language lays
for us on that side of our way. For my own part, I often doubt
whether it would not be a gain if every word of moral significance
could be banished from the law altogether, and other words
adopted which should convey legal ideas uncolored by anything
outside the law. We should lose the fossil records of a good deal
of history and the majesty got from ethical associations, but by
ridding ourselves of an unnecessary confusion we should gain very
much in the clearness of our thought.

So much for the limits of the law. The next thing which I
wish to consider is what are the forces which determine its content

and its growth.    You may assume, with Hobbes and Bentham and Austin, that all law emanates from the sovereign, even when the first human beings to enunciate it are the judges, or you may think that law is the voice of the Zeitgeist, or what you like.    It is all one to my present purpose.    Even if every decision required the sanction of an emperor with despotic power and a whimsical turn of mind, we should be interested none the less, still with a view to prediction, in discovering some order, some rational explanation, and some principle of growth for the rules which he laid down.    In every system there are such explanations and principles to be found.    It is with regard to them that a second fallacy comes in, which I think it important to expose.

The fallacy to which I refer is the notion that the only force at work in the development of the law is logic.    In the broadest sense, indeed, that notion would be true.    The postulate on which we think about the universe is that there is a fixed quantitative relation between every phenomenon and its antecedents and consequents.    If there is such a thing as a phenomenon without these fixed quantitative relations, it is a miracle.    It is outside the law of cause and effect, and as such transcends our power of thought, or at least is something to or from which we cannot reason.    The condition of our thinking about the universe is that it is capable of being thought about rationally, or, in other words, that every part of it is effect and cause in the same sense in which those parts are with which we are most familiar.    So in the broadest sense it is true that the law is a logical development, like everything else. The danger of which I speak is not the admission that the principles governing other phenomena also govern the law, but the notion that a given system, ours, for instance, can be worked out like mathematics from some general axioms of conduct.    This is the natural error of the schools, but it is not confined to them.    I once heard a very eminent judge say that he never let a decision go until he was absolutely sure that it was right.    So judicial dissent often is blamed, as if it meant simply that one side or the other were not doing their sums right, and, if they would take more trouble, agreement inevitably would come.

This mode of thinking is entirely natural.    The training of lawyers is a training in logic.    The processes of analogy, discrimination, and deduction are those in which they are most at home. The language of judicial decision is mainly the language of logic.

And the logical method and form flatter that longing for certainty and for repose which is in every human mind. But certainty generally is illusion, and repose is not the destiny of man. Behind the logical form lies a judgment as to the relative worth and importance of competing legislative grounds, often an inarticulate and unconscious judgment, it is true, and yet the very root and nerve of the whole proceeding. You can give any conclusion a logical form. You always can imply a condition in a contract. But why do you imply it? It is because of some belief as to the practice of the community or of a class, or because of some opinion as to policy, or, in short, because of some attitude of yours upon a matter not capable of exact quantitative measurement, and therefore not capable of founding exact logical conclusions. Such matters really are battle grounds where the means do not exist for determinations that shall be good for all time, and where the decision can do no more than embody the preference of a given body in a given time and place. We do not realize how large a part of our law is open to reconsideration upon a slight change in the habit of the public mind. No concrete proposition is self-evident, no matter how ready we may be to accept it, not even Mr. Herbert Spencer's Every man has a right to do what he wills, provided he interferes not with a like right on the part of his neighbors.

Why is a false and injurious statement privileged, if it is made honestly in giving information about a servant? It is because it has been thought more important that information should be given freely, than that a man should be protected from what under other circumstances would be an actionable wrong. Why is a man at liberty to set up a business which he knows will ruin his neighbor? It is because the public good is supposed to be best subserved by free competition. Obviously such judgments of relative importance may vary in different times and places. Why does a judge instruct a jury that an employer is not liable to an employee for an injury received in the course of his employment unless he is negligent, and why do the jury generally find for the plaintiff if the case is allowed to go to them? It is because the traditional policy of our law is to confine liability to cases where a prudent man might have foreseen the injury, or at least the danger, while the inclination of a very large part of the community is to make certain classes of persons insure the safety of those with whom they deal. Since the last words were written, I have seen the requirement of such insurance put forth as part of the programme of one of the best known labor organizations. There is a concealed, half conscious battle on the question of legislative policy, and if any one thinks that it can be settled deductively, or once for all, I only can say that I think he is theoretically wrong, and that I am certain that his conclusion will not be accepted in practice *semper ubique et ab omnibus.*

Indeed, I think that even now our theory upon this matter is open to reconsideration, although I am not prepared to say how I should decide if a reconsideration were proposed. Our law of torts comes from the old days of isolated, ungeneralized wrongs, assaults, slanders, and the like, where the damages might be taken to lie where they fell by legal judgment. But the torts with which our courts are kept busy to-day are mainly the incidents of certain well known businesses. They are injuries to person or property by railroads, factories, and the like. The liability for them is estimated, and sooner or later goes into the price paid by the public. The public really pays the damages, and the question of liability, if pressed far enough, is really the question how far it is desirable that the public should insure the safety of those whose work it uses. It might be said that in such cases the chance of a jury finding for the defendant is merely a chance, once in a while rather arbitrarily interrupting the regular course of recovery, most likely in the case of an unusually conscientious plaintiff, and therefore better done away with. On the other hand, the economic value even of a life to the community can be estimated, and no recovery, it may be said, ought to go beyond that amount. It is conceivable that some day in certain cases we may find ourselves imitating, on a higher plane, the tariff for life and limb which we see in the Leges Barbarorum.

I think that the judges themselves have failed adequately to recognize their duty of weighing considerations of social advantage. The duty is inevitable, and the result of the often proclaimed judicial aversion to deal with such considerations is simply to leave the very ground and foundation of judgments inarticulate, and often unconscious, as I have said. When socialism first began to be talked about, the comfortable classes of the community were a good deal frightened. I suspect that this fear has influenced judicial action both here and in England, yet it is certain that it is not a conscious factor in the decisions to which I refer. I think that something similar has led people who no longer hope to control the legislatures to look to the courts as expounders of the Constitutions, and that in some courts new principles have been discovered outside the bodies of those instruments, which may be generalized into acceptance of the economic doctrines which prevailed about fifty years ago, and a wholesale prohibition of what a tribunal of lawyers does not think about right. I cannot but believe that if the training of lawyers led them habitually to consider more definitely and explicitly the social advantage on which the rule they lay down must be justified, they sometimes would hesitate where now they are confident, and see that really they were taking sides upon debatable and often burning questions.

So much for the fallacy of logical form. Now let us consider the present condition of the law as a subject for study, and the ideal toward which it tends. We still are far from the point of view which I desire to see reached. No one has reached it or can reach it as yet. We are only at the beginning of a philosophical reaction, and of a reconsideration of the worth of doctrines which for the most part still are taken for granted without any deliberate, conscious, and systematic questioning of their grounds. The development of our law has gone on for nearly a thousand years, like the development of a plant, each generation taking the inevitable next step, mind, like matter, simply obeying a law of spontaneous growth. It is perfectly natural and right that it should have been so. Imitation is a necessity of human nature, as has been illustrated by a remarkable French writer, M. Tarde, in an admirable book, "Les Lois de l'Imitation." Most of the things we do, we do for no better reason than that our fathers have done them or that our neighbors do them, and the same is true of a larger part than we suspect of what we think. The reason is a good one, because our short life gives us no time for a better, but it is not the best. It does not follow, because we all are compelled to take on faith at second hand most of the rules on which we base our action and our thought, that each of us may not try to set some corner of his world in the order of reason, or that all of us collectively should not aspire to carry reason as far as it will go throughout the whole domain. In regard to the law, it is true, no doubt, that an evolutionist will hesitate to affirm universal validity for his social ideals, or for the principles which he thinks should be embodied in legislation. He is content if he can prove them best for here and now. He may be ready to admit that he knows nothing about an absolute best in the cosmos, and even that he knows next to nothing

## THE PATH OF THE LAW.                      469

about a permanent best for men.    Still it is true that a body of law is more rational and more civilized when every rule it contains is referred articulately and definitely to an end which it subserves, and when the grounds for desiring that end are stated or are ready to be stated in words.

At present, in very many cases, if we want to know why a rule of law has taken its particular shape, and more or less if we want to know why it exists at all, we go to tradition.    We follow it into the Year Books, and perhaps beyond them to the customs of the Salian Franks, and somewhere in the past, in the German forests, in the needs of Norman kings, in the assumptions of a dominant class, in the absence of generalized ideas, we find out the practical motive for what now best is justified by the mere fact of its acceptance and that men are accustomed to it.    The rational study of law is still to a large extent the study of history.    History must be a part of the study, because without it we cannot know the precise scope of rules which it is our business to know.    It is a part of the rational study, because it is the first step toward an enlightened scepticism, that is, toward a deliberate reconsideration of the worth of those rules.    When you get the dragon out of his cave on to the plain and in the daylight, you can count his teeth and claws, and see just what is his strength.    But to get him out is only the first step.    The next is either to kill him, or to tame him and make him a useful animal.    For the rational study of the law the black-letter man may be the man of the present, but the man of the future is the man of statistics and the master of economics.    It is revolting to have no better reason for a rule of law than that so it was laid down in the time of Henry IV.    It is still more revolting if the grounds upon which it was laid down have vanished long since, and the rule simply persists from blind imitation of the past.    I am thinking of the technical rule as to trespass *ab initio*, as it is called, which I attempted to explain in a recent Massachusetts case.[1]

Let me take an illustration, which can be stated in a few words, to show how the social end which is aimed at by a rule of law is obscured and only partially attained in consequence of the fact that the rule owes its form to a gradual historical development, instead of being reshaped as a whole, with conscious articulate reference to the end in view.    We think it desirable to prevent one man's property being misappropriated by another, and so we

---

[1] Commonwealth *v.* Rubin, 165 Mass. 453.

make larceny a crime.  The evil is the same whether the misap-
propriation is made by a man into whose hands the owner has put
the property, or by one who wrongfully takes it away.  But primitive law in its weakness did not get much beyond an effort to
prevent violence, and very naturally made a wrongful taking, a
trespass, part of its definition of the crime.  In modern times the
judges enlarged the definition a little by holding that, if the wrong-
doer gets possession by a trick or device, the crime is committed.
This really was giving up the requirement of a trespass, and it
would have been more logical, as well as truer to the present object
of the law, to abandon the requirement altogether.  That, however,
would have seemed too bold, and was left to statute.  Statutes
were passed making embezzlement a crime.  But the force of tradition caused the crime of embezzlement to be regarded as so far
distinct from larceny that to this day, in some jurisdictions at least,
a slip corner is kept open for thieves to contend, if indicted for
larceny, that they should have been indicted for embezzlement, and
if indicted for embezzlement, that they should have been indicted
for larceny, and to escape on that ground.

Far more fundamental questions still await a better answer than
that we do as our fathers have done.  What have we better than a
blind guess to show that the criminal law in its present form does
more good than harm?  I do not stop to refer to the effect which
it has had in degrading prisoners and in plunging them further
into crime, or to the question whether fine and imprisonment do
not fall more heavily on a criminal's wife and children than on
himself.  I have in mind more far-reaching questions.  Does punishment deter?  Do we deal with criminals on proper principles?
A modern school of Continental criminalists plumes itself on the
formula, first suggested, it is said, by Gall, that we must consider the criminal rather than the crime.  The formula does not
carry us very far, but the inquiries which have been started look
toward an answer of my questions based on science for the first
time.  If the typical criminal is a degenerate, bound to swindle
or to murder by as deep seated an organic necessity as that which
makes the rattlesnake bite, it is idle to talk of deterring him
by the classical method of imprisonment.  He must be got rid
of ; he cannot be improved, or frightened out of his structural
reaction.  If, on the other hand, crime, like normal human conduct, is mainly a matter of imitation, punishment fairly may be

expected to help to keep it out of fashion. The study of criminals has been thought by some well known men of science to sustain the former hypothesis. The statistics of the relative increase of crime in crowded places like large cities, where example has the greatest chance to work, and in less populated parts, where the contagion spreads more slowly, have been used with great force in favor of the latter view. But there is weighty authority for the belief that, however this may be, "not the nature of the crime, but the dangerousness of the criminal, constitutes the only reasonable legal criterion to guide the inevitable social reaction against the criminal." [1]

The impediments to rational generalization, which I illustrated from the law of larceny, are shown in the other branches of the law, as well as in that of crime. Take the law of tort or civil liability for damages apart from contract and the like. Is there any general theory of such liability, or are the cases in which it exists simply to be enumerated, and to be explained each on its special ground, as is easy to believe from the fact that the right of action for certain well known classes of wrongs like trespass or slander has its special history for each class? I think that there is a general theory to be discovered, although resting in tendency rather than established and accepted. I think that the law regards the infliction of temporal damage by a responsible person as actionable, if under the circumstances known to him the danger of his act is manifest according to common experience, or according to his own experience if it is more than common, except in cases where upon special grounds of policy the law refuses to protect the plaintiff or grants a privilege to the defendant.[2] I think that commonly malice, intent, and negligence mean only that the danger was manifest to a greater or less degree, under the circumstances known to the actor, although in some cases of privilege malice may mean an actual malevolent motive, and such a motive may take away a permission knowingly to inflict harm, which otherwise would be granted on this or that ground of dominant public good. But when I stated my view to a very eminent English judge the

---

[1] Havelock Ellis, "The Criminal," 41, citing Garofalo. See also Ferri, "Sociologie Criminelle," *passim*. Compare Tarde, "La Philosophie Pénale."

[2] An example of the law's refusing to protect the plaintiff is when he is interrupted by a stranger in the use of a valuable way, which he has travelled adversely for a week less than the period of prescription. A week later he will have gained a right, but now he is only a trespasser. Examples of privilege I have given already. One of the best is competition in business.

other day, he said : " You are discussing what the law ought to be ; as the law is, you must show a right.  A man is not liable for negligence unless he is subject to a duty."  If our difference was more than a difference in words, or with regard to the proportion between the exceptions and the rule, then, in his opinion, liability for an act cannot be referred to the manifest tendency of the act to cause temporal damage in general as a sufficient explanation, but must be referred to the special nature of the damage, or must be derived from some special circumstances outside of the tendency of the act, for which no generalized explanation exists.  I think that such a view is wrong, but it is familiar, and I dare say generally is accepted in England.

Everywhere the basis of principle is tradition, to such an extent that we even are in danger of making the rôle of history more important than it is.  The other day Professor Ames wrote a learned article to show, among other things, that the common law did not recognize the defence of fraud in actions upon specialties, and the moral might seem to be that the personal character of that defence is due to its equitable origin.  But if, as I have said, all contracts are formal, the difference is not merely historical, but theoretic, between defects of form which prevent a contract from being made, and mistaken motives which manifestly could not be considered in any system that we should call rational except against one who was privy to those motives.  It is not confined to specialties, but is of universal application.  I ought to add that I do not suppose that Mr. Ames would disagree with what I suggest.

However, if we consider the law of contract, we find it full of history.  The distinctions between debt, covenant, and assumpsit are merely historical.  The classification of certain obligations to pay money, imposed by the law irrespective of any bargain as quasi contracts, is merely historical.  The doctrine of consideration is merely historical.  The effect given to a seal is to be explained by history alone. — Consideration is a mere form.  Is it a useful form ?  If so, why should it not be required in all contracts ?  A seal is a mere form, and is vanishing in the scroll and in enactments that a consideration must be given, seal or no seal. — Why should any merely historical distinction be allowed to affect the rights and obligations of business men ?

Since I wrote this discourse I have come on a very good example of the way in which tradition not only overrides rational policy, but

*THE PATH OF THE LAW.*                    473

overrides it after first having been misunderstood and having been given a new and broader scope than it had when it had a meaning. It is the settled law of England that a material alteration of a written contract by a party avoids it as against him. The doctrine is contrary to the general tendency of the law. We do not tell a jury that if a man ever has lied in one particular he is to be presumed to lie in all. Even if a man has tried to defraud, it seems no sufficient reason for preventing him from proving the truth. Objections of like nature in general go to the weight, not to the admissibility, of evidence. Moreover, this rule is irrespective of fraud, and is not confined to evidence. It is not merely that you cannot use the writing, but that the contract is at an end. What does this mean ? The existence of a written contract depends on the fact that the offerer and offeree have interchanged their written expressions, not on the continued existence of those expressions. But in the case of a bond the primitive notion was different. The contract was inseparable from the parchment. If a stranger destroyed it, or tore off the seal, or altered it, the obligee could not recover, however free from fault, because the defendant's contract, that is, the actual tangible bond which he had sealed, could not be produced in the form in which it bound him. About a hundred years ago Lord Kenyon undertook to use his reason on this tradition, as he sometimes did to the detriment of the law, and, not understanding it, said he could see no reason why what was true of a bond should not be true of other contracts. His decision happened to be right, as it concerned a promissory note, where again the common law regarded the contract as inseparable from the paper on which it was written, but the reasoning was general, and soon was extended to other written contracts, and various absurd and unreal grounds of policy were invented to account for the enlarged rule.

I trust that no one will understand me to be speaking with disrespect of the law, because I criticise it so freely. I venerate the law, and especially our system of law, as one of the vastest products of the human mind. No one knows better than I do the countless number of great intellects that have spent themselves in making some addition or improvement, the greatest of which is trifling when compared with the mighty whole. It has the final title to respect that it exists, that it is not a Hegelian dream, but a part of the lives of men. But one may criticise even what one reveres. Law is the business to which my life is devoted, and I should show less than devotion if I did not do what in me lies to improve it, and, when I perceive what seems to me the ideal of its future, if I hesitated to point it out and to press toward it with all my heart.

Perhaps I have said enough to show the part which the study of history necessarily plays in the intelligent study of the law as it is to-day. In the teaching of this school and at Cambridge it is in no danger of being undervalued. Mr. Bigelow here and Mr. Ames and Mr. Thayer there have made important contributions which will not be forgotten, and in England the recent history of early English law by Sir Frederick Pollock and Mr. Maitland has lent the subject an almost deceptive charm. We must beware of the pitfall of antiquarianism, and must remember that for our purposes our only interest in the past is for the light it throws upon the present. I look forward to a time when the part played by history in the explanation of dogma shall be very small, and instead of ingenious research we shall spend our energy on a study of the ends sought to be attained and the reasons for desiring them. As a step toward that ideal it seems to me that every lawyer ought to seek an understanding of economics. The present divorce between the schools of political economy and law seems to me an evidence of how much progress in philosophical study still remains to be made. In the present state of political economy, indeed, we come again upon history on a larger scale, but there we are called on to consider and weigh the ends of legislation, the means of attaining them, and the cost. We learn that for everything we have to give up something else, and we are taught to set the advantage we gain against the other advantage we lose, and to know what we are doing when we elect.

There is another study which sometimes is undervalued by the practical minded, for which I wish to say a good word, although I think a good deal of pretty poor stuff goes under that name. I mean the study of what is called jurisprudence. Jurisprudence, as I look at it, is simply law in its most generalized part. Every effort to reduce a case to a rule is an effort of jurisprudence, although the name as used in English is confined to the broadest rules and most fundamental conceptions. One mark of a great lawyer is that he sees the application of the broadest rules. There is a story of a Vermont justice of the peace before whom a suit was brought by one farmer against another for breaking a churn. The justice took time to consider, and then said that he had looked through the statutes and could find nothing about churns, and gave judgment for the defendant.   The same state of mind is shown in all our common digests and text-books.   Applications of rudimentary rules of contract or tort are tucked away under the head of Railroads or Telegraphs or go to swell treatises on historical subdivisions, such as Shipping or Equity, or are gathered under an arbitrary title which is thought likely to appeal to the practical mind, such as Mercantile Law.   If a man goes into law it pays to be a master of it, and to be a master of it means to look straight through all the dramatic incidents and to discern the true basis for prophecy.   Therefore, it is well to have an accurate notion of what you mean by law, by a right, by a duty, by malice, intent, and negligence, by ownership, by possession, and so forth. I have in my mind cases in which the highest courts seem to me to have floundered because they had no clear ideas on some of these themes.   I have illustrated their importance already.   If a further illustration is wished, it may be found by reading the Appendix to Sir James Stephen's Criminal Law on the subject of possession, and then turning to Pollock and Wright's enlightened book.   Sir James Stephen is not the only writer whose attempts to analyze legal ideas have been confused by striving for a useless quintessence of all systems, instead of an accurate anatomy of one. The trouble with Austin was that he did not know enough English law.   But still it is a practical advantage to master Austin, and his predecessors, Hobbes and Bentham, and his worthy successors, Holland and Pollock.   Sir Frederick Pollock's recent little book is touched with the felicity which marks all his works, and is wholly free from the perverting influence of Roman models.

The advice of the elders to young men is very apt to be as unreal as a list of the hundred best books.   At least in my day I had my share of such counsels, and high among the unrealities I place the recommendation to study the Roman law.   I assume that such advice means more than collecting a few Latin maxims with which to ornament the discourse, — the purpose for which Lord Coke recommended Bracton.   If that is all that is wanted, the title " De Regulis Juris Antiqui " can be read in an hour.   I assume that, if it is well to study the Roman law, it is well to study it as a working system.   That means mastering a set of technicalities more difficult and less understood than our own, and studying another course of history by which even more than our own the Roman law must be explained. If any one doubts me, let him read Keller's "Der Römische Civil Process und die Actionen," a treatise on the prae-tor's edict, Muirhead's most interesting "Historical Introduction to the Private Law of Rome," and, to give him the best chance possible, Sohm's admirable Institutes. No. The way to gain a liberal view of your subject is not to read something else, but to get to the bottom of the subject itself. The means of doing that are, in the first place, to follow the existing body of dogma into its highest generalizations by the help of jurisprudence; next, to dis-cover from history how it has come to be what it is; and, finally, so far as you can, to consider the ends which the several rules seek to accomplish, the reasons why those ends are desired, what is given up to gain them, and whether they are worth the price.

We have too little theory in the law rather than too much, espe-cially on this final branch of study. When I was speaking of his-tory, I mentioned larceny as an example to show how the law suffered from not having embodied in a clear form a rule which will accomplish its manifest purpose. In that case the trouble was due to the survival of forms coming from a time when a more limited purpose was entertained. Let me now give an example to show the practical importance, for the decision of actual cases, of understanding the reasons of the law, by taking an example from rules which, so far as I know, never have been explained or theo-rized about in any adequate way. I refer to statutes of limitation and the law of prescription. The end of such rules is obvious, but what is the justification for depriving a man of his rights, a pure evil as far as it goes, in consequence of the lapse of time? Some-times the loss of evidence is referred to, but that is a secondary matter. Sometimes the desirability of peace, but why is peace more desirable after twenty years than before? It is increasingly likely to come without the aid of legislation. Sometimes it is said that, if a man neglects to enforce his rights, he cannot complain if, after a while, the law follows his example. Now if this is all that can be said about it, you probably will decide a case I am going to put, for the plaintiff; if you take the view which I shall suggest, you possibly will decide it for the defendant. A man is sued for trespass upon land, and justifies under a right of way. He proves that he has used the way openly and adversely for twenty years, but it turns out that the plaintiff had granted a license to a person whom he reasonably supposed to be the defendant's agent, although

*THE PATH OF THE LAW.*                    477

not so in fact, and therefore had assumed that the use of the way was permissive, in which case no right would be gained. Has the defendant gained a right or not? If his gaining it stands on the fault and neglect of the landowner in the ordinary sense, as seems commonly to be supposed, there has been no such neglect, and the right of way has not been acquired. But if I were the defendant's counsel, I should suggest that the foundation of the acquisition of rights by lapse of time is to be looked for in the position of the person who gains them, not in that of the loser. Sir Henry Maine has made it fashionable to connect the archaic notion of property with prescription. But the connection is further back than the first recorded history. It is in the nature of man's mind. A thing which you have enjoyed and used as your own for a long time, whether property or an opinion, takes root in your being and cannot be torn away without your resenting the act and trying to defend yourself, however you came by it. The law can ask no better justification than the deepest instincts of man. It is only by way of reply to the suggestion that you are disappointing the former owner, that you refer to his neglect having allowed the gradual dissociation between himself and what he claims, and the gradual association of it with another. If he knows that another is doing acts which on their face show that he is on the way toward establishing such an association, I should argue that in justice to that other he was bound at his peril to find out whether the other was acting under his permission, to see that he was warned, and, if necessary, stopped.

I have been speaking about the study of the law, and I have said next to nothing of what commonly is talked about in that connection, — text-books and the case system, and all the machinery with which a student comes most immediately in contact. Nor shall I say anything about them   Theory is my subject, not practical details. The modes of teaching have been improved since my time, no doubt, but ability and industry will master the raw material with any mode. Theory is the most important part of the dogma of the law, as the architect is the most important man who takes part in the building of a house. The most important improvements of the last twenty-five years are improvements in theory. It is not to be feared as unpractical, for, to the competent, it simply means going to the bottom of the subject. For the incompetent, it sometimes is true, as has been said, that an interest in general ideas means an

absence of particular knowledge. I remember in army days reading of a youth who, being examined for the lowest grade and being
asked a question about squadron drill, answered that he never
had considered the evolutions of less than ten thousand men.
But the weak and foolish must be left to their folly. The danger
is that the able and practical minded should look with indifference
or distrust upon ideas the connection of which with their business
is remote. I heard a story, the other day, of a man who had a
valet to whom he paid high wages, subject to deduction for faults.
One of his deductions was, " For lack of imagination, five dollars."
The lack is not confined to valets. The object of ambition, power,
generally presents itself nowadays in the form of money alone.
Money is the most immediate form, and is a proper object of
desire. " The fortune," said Rachel, " is the measure of the intelligence." That is a good text to waken people out of a fool's para-
dise. But, as Hegel says,[1] " It is in the end not the appetite, but
the opinion, which has to be satisfied." To an imagination of any
scope the most far-reaching form of power is not money, it is the
command of ideas. If you want great examples read Mr. Leslie
Stephen's "History of English Thought in the Eighteenth Century," and see how a hundred years after his death the abstract
speculations of Descartes had become a practical force controlling
the conduct of men. Read the works of the great German jurists,
and see how much more the world is governed to-day by Kant than
by Bonaparte. We cannot all be Descartes or Kant, but we all
want happiness. And happiness, I am sure from having known
many successful men, cannot be won simply by being counsel for
great corporations and having an income of fifty thousand dollars.
An intellect great enough to win the prize needs other food beside
success. The remoter and more general aspects of the law are
those which give it universal interest. It is through them that
you not only become a great master in your calling, but connect
your subject with the universe and catch an echo of the infinite, a
glimpse of its unfathomable process, a hint of the universal law.

---

[1] Phil. des Rechts, § 190.

# 20

# SOURCES OF ANTI-LAWYER SENTIMENT IN MASSACHUSETTS, 1740-1840

*GERARD W. GAWALT*

# Sources of Anti-Lawyer Sentiment in Massachusetts, 1740-1840

*by* GERARD W. GAWALT*

For a half-century after the Revolution, critics of the emerging legal profession expounded their fear of a "lawyer class" in American society. Wary of directing their attacks against individual members of the profession, opponents castigated lawyers for dominating political and judicial offices, and establishing and perpetuating an exclusive monopoly by excluding practitioners, who were not formally trained, from legal business.

Careful study of the development of the Massachusetts legal profession during the century, 1740-1840, indicates that a lawyer class based on education, marriage alliances, economic prosperity, and paternal occupations certainly did exist and did dominate the most prestigious and lucrative political and judicial positions after the Revolutionary War.

Legal historians, passing over these broader criticisms by the lawyers opponents, which reflected dissatisfaction with the actual structure of society, have focused merely on specific issues raised by critics of the profession.[1] High fees and the regulatory powers of the bar associations, for example, have been identified as important problems. But general dissatisfaction with the restrictive nature of a professional elite—an anomalus development during an era characterized by rising expectations for social, economic, and political democracy—has been ignored. In fact, increased social and eco-

---

*American Revolution Bicentennial Committee, Library of Congress.

1. 2 Anton-Hermann Chroust, *The Rise of the Legal Profession in America* 11-18 (1965); Albert Farnsworth, "Shays' Rebellion," 12 *Mass. L.Q.* 29-43 (1927); Frank W. Grinnell, "The Judicial System and the Bar," 4 Albert Hart, ed., *Commonwealth History of Massachusetts* 38-39 (1928); Alfred Z. Reed, *Training for the Public Profession of the Law* 68-73 (1921); W. R. Blackard, "The Demoralization of the Legal Profession in Nineteenth Century America," 16 *Tennessee L. Rev.* 314-315 (1940); James W. Hurst, *The Growth of American Law* 278 (1950); Roscoe Pound, "The Lay Tradition as to the Lawyers," 12 *Michigan L. Rev.* 631 (1914); Charles Warren, *A History of the American Bar* 212-239, 510-512 (1st ed. 1912); 1 Charles Warren, *History of the Harvard Law School and of Early Legal Conditions in America* 186-202 (1908).

nomic stratification may have been the fundamental cause of attacks on not only the legal profession, but medicine and the ministry as well at this time.

The purpose of this article is not to prove that such stratification was the underlying cause of unrest, but rather to identify the existence of a closely restricted and interrelated lawyer class. The presence of such a new element in society can be sufficiently established to suggest that there was indeed a basis for the denunciation of the "lawyer class"—if class is defined as a group of people with similar education and training; occupations that are closely associated if not identical; similar economic and social goals; intermarriage; and are recognized by the rest of society as a distinct element in that society.

Although there were some self-appointed, part-time legal practitioners, trained lawyers were *scarce* in Massachusetts Bay Colony during the seventeenth century and most men handled their own legal affairs—as they did in the other English colonies. Not only was popular prejudice against the lawyer class an English tradition, but most Puritans held the religious view that the administration of justice should be based on individual conscience and the word of God rather than legal precedents. Questions of law, therefore, were considered as being theological not legal in nature and not requiring the counsel of common law lawyers.[2]

When Massachusetts Bay became a royal colony in 1691, a common law court system was organized that created the first real demand for men trained in the law. The need for lawyers was first formally recognized in 1701 when the legislature established an oath of office for attorneys and set maximum fees for court cases that only regularly admitted attorneys could collect. Trained lawyers, however, remained *scarce*. This was evident in the law of 1715 that forbade any party in a suit from retaining more than two lawyers in order to allow his adversary to avail himself of legal counsel.[3]

Several factors stimulated a rise in the number of trained lawyers. Business expansion in New England led to a greater demand for knowledge of commercial law; and the complexity of business arrangements provided for increased litigation. The transformation of the judicial system after 1691 simultaneously led to a greater stress on the technicalities of common law which made the law so

---

2. Warren, *American Bar*, 68-71; Pound, *op. cit. supra* note 1, at pp. 634-635; 1 Lyman H. Butterfield *et al.*, eds., *Diary and Autobiography of John Adams* 184 (1964).

3. *Acts and Resolves, Public and Private of the Province of Massachusetts . . . 1692-1714*, v. 1, Chap. 7, 1701, 467 (1869); Warren, *American Bar*, 78.

much more disciplined and specialized that laymen could no longer effectively practice it without some professional training. As financial opportunities for lawyers increased, men of greater ability and education began to enter legal practice. The self-interest of lawyers, who taught as well as practiced law, added force to the growth of the profession.[4] As a result, as can be seen in Tables I and II, the numerical strength of trained lawyers increased steadily from 15 in 1740 to 640 in 1840, dramatically lowering the ratio of lawyers to the general population from 1 to 10,108 to 1 in 1,153.

Despite the increase of the legal profession it remained a numerically minor occupation in society. Yet the profession's growth had major ramifications. Strategically placed through their monopoly of legal expertise, when changes in government and business demanded men who were immersed in law and willing to apply their knowledge, the legal profession had a far greater im-

*Table I*

NUMERICAL STRENGTH OF LAWYERS: 1740-1840[1]

| Year | Number | Ratio of Lawyers to Total Population |
|------|--------|--------------------------------------|
| 1740 | 15 | 1 to 10,108 |
| 1775 | 71 | _____ |
| 1780 | 34[2] | 1 to 9,349 |
| 1785 | 92 | _____ |
| 1790 | 112 | 1 to 4,244 |
| 1800 | 200 | 1 to 2,872 |
| 1810 | 492 | 1 to 1,424 |
| 1820 | 710 | 1 to 1,159 |
| 1830 | 582[3] | 1 to 1,049 |
| 1840 | 640 | 1 to 1,153 |

1. Docket Books, Massachusetts Superior Court of Judicature, 1740-1774 (microfilm, reels 4, 5, 6, 7), Massachusetts Historical Society, Boston, Mass. *Mein and Fleeming's Register for New England . . .* (Boston, 1773-1775); From 1780 to 1840 these figures were taken from the listing of attorneys and counsellors in the *Massachusetts Register* for these years: U.S. Bureau of the Census, *Historical Statistics of the United States, Colonial Times to 1957* (Washington, D.C., 1960), 13, 756.

2. Decline due to 29 lawyers remaining loyalists.

3. Decline due to loss of 9 counties with formation of the state of Maine.

4. Gerard W. Gawalt, Massachusetts Lawyers: A Historical Analysis of the Process of Professionalization, 1760-1840, 6-128 (unpubl. Ph.D. diss., Clark U., 1969).

pact than lawyers originally anticipated and laymen were willing to accept. New governments, improved judicial systems, and the rise of banking and business corporations propelled lawyers from the background of society to positions of leadership.

The emergence of large banking, manufacturing, commercial, and transportation corporations in the state during the last decade of the eighteenth century and the nineteenth century created a demand for lawyers that far exceeded the needs of the previously dominant farmer-merchant economy of the colonial period. Many lawyers risked their income or their time as investors, counselors,

### Table II[1]

### INCREASE IN NUMBER OF LAWYERS BY COUNTY

|              | 1800 | 1805 | 1810 | 1815 | 1820 | 1825 | 1830 | 1835 | 1840 |
|--------------|------|------|------|------|------|------|------|------|------|
| Barnstable   | 3    | 2    | 5    | 9    | 7    | 11   | 8    | 8    | 8    |
| Berkshire    | 20   | 21   | 31   | 34   | 35   | 38   | 36   | 36   | 40   |
| Bristol      | 10   | 12   | 18   | 24   | 25   | 25   | 34   | 34   | 38   |
| Dukes        | —    | 3    | 4    | 3    | 3    | 3    | 3    | 4    | —    |
| Essex        | 14   | 20   | 33   | 42   | 41   | 47   | 55   | 47   | 57   |
| Franklin[2]  | —    | —    | —    | 16   | 23   | 26   | 26   | 27   | 23   |
| Hampden[2]   | —    | —    | —    | 22   | 31   | 35   | 37   | 34   | 28   |
| Hampshire    | 32   | 40   | 48   | 21   | 31   | 29   | 34   | 30   | 30   |
| Middlesex    | 20   | 25   | 42   | 49   | 47   | 56   | 65   | 71   | 82   |
| Nantucket    | —    | —    | 5    | 2    | 2    | 2    | 4    | 5    | 6    |
| Norfolk      | 9    | 14   | 18   | 24   | 26   | 32   | 31   | 31   | 26   |
| Plymouth     | 6    | 10   | 17   | 19   | 20   | 24   | 26   | 28   | 25   |
| Suffolk      | 33   | 58   | 83   | 115  | 135  | 136  | 146  | 196  | 215  |
| Worcester    | 18   | 33   | 44   | 56   | 63   | 65   | 77   | 74   | 62   |
| Cumberland[3]| 9    | 26   | 41   | 37   | 45   |      |      |      |      |
| Hancock      | 4    | 13   | 23   | 30   | 17   |      |      |      |      |
| Kennebeck    | 12   | 26   | 33   | 31   | 43   |      |      |      |      |
| Lincoln      | 5    | 12   | 20   | 26   | 28   |      |      |      |      |
| Oxford[2]    | —    | —    | 5    | 7    | 13   |      |      |      |      |
| Penobscot[2] | —    | —    | —    | —    | 13   |      |      |      |      |
| Somerset[2]  | —    | —    | 4    | 5    | 11   |      |      |      |      |
| Washington   | 1    | 4    | 4    | 3    | 7    |      |      |      |      |
| York         | 4    | 17   | 14   | 25   | 24   |      |      |      |      |

1. Composed from listing of attorneys and counsellors in *Massachusetts Register* for these years. Although the lists in the *Register* are occasionally incomplete, they do provide evidence of the great increase in lawyers throughout the state.

2. Indicates that this county did not exist before the date shown.

3. This and the following counties became the state of Maine in 1820.

and directors in such new economic ventures as canals, banks, and railroads. Neither lawyers nor the members of any other profession, however, provided the chief source of capital for the rising corporations. [5]

A few lawyers, such as James Sullivan, a Boston barrister, judge, and politician, were, however, deeply involved in corporations. While president of the Middlesex Canal Company and of the Boston Aqueduct Corporation, Sullivan also invested in the Massachusetts Mutual Fire Inc. and the West Boston Bridge Company. [6] Isaac Davis, a Worcester counsellor, was president of the Quinsigamond Bank, 1835-1845, 1854-1878; president of the Mechanic Savings Bank, 1851-1855; a director of the Providence and Worcester Railroad, 1857-1878; and president of the Worcester and Nashua Railroad, 1848-1853, 1874-1879.[7] A survey of the directors and officers of banks and other corporations in Massachusetts from 1800 to 1840, however, showed that although lawyers held many of these positions, a majority of the officers were not lawyers, and most lawyers did not reach positions of such economic power.[8]

The attraction that finance and industry held for lawyers can be more fully understood by studying the number of lawyers who left the profession for other occupations: i.e. ceased to practice law in the traditional manner of a general court attorney. Banks, railroads, and industries increasingly drew lawyers from office practice into the corporate structure as counsellors, directors, cashiers, and other officers, as can be seen in Table III.[9] While only 20 trained lawyers (4 per cent of a sampling of 498), who were college graduates, left the profession in Massachusetts prior to 1810, 136 college-educated lawyers (19.7 per cent of the 690 lawyers in this segment of the study), left the profession between 1810 and 1840.

---

5. Joseph S. Davis, *Eighteenth Century Business Corporations in the United States* 298 (1917).

6. Davis, *op. cit. supra* note 5, at p. 299.

7. William Lincoln, *History of Worcester, Massachusetts* 209 (1862); Mary D. Vaughan, ed., *Historical Catalogue of Brown University* 134 (1905).

8. *The Massachusetts Register and United States Calendar* (Boston, 1800-1840).

9. Based on biographical studies of 2,018 lawyers in Massachusetts proper and 600 lawyers in the district of Maine these statistical studies are divided into four basic categories: college and non-college graduates, because of the emphasis on a college degree by the bar associations; lawyers from the present state of Massachusetts and from the district that became Maine. These categories were then sub-divided into the periods 1740-1809 and 1810-1840 because 1810 was the year that the autonomy of the profession was formally recognized by the Supreme Court.

288          THE AMERICAN JOURNAL OF LEGAL HISTORY     Vol. XIV

Banking, railroads, and manufacturing held the greatest attraction
for former office lawyers. In the eastern district of Massachusetts—
Maine—only one college-educated lawyer out of 127 abandoned the
profession before 1810, but between 1810 and 1840, 13.3 per
cent (40 of 300) left for other occupations. As in the main part of
Massachusetts the most attractive alternatives were banks, railroads, and manufacturing.

Many lawyers entered the emerging business opportunities,
but most lawyers remained traditional office practitioners. Their
relative economic status in the communities where they resided
presents a more balanced view of the economic position of the legal
profession in society. Utilizing a tax valuation list, compiled for
the Federal Government in 1815 (Table IV), an analysis of the economic status of lawyers was made. Worcester County's mixed economy of farming, manufacturing, and transportation business
dictated its selection.

Using property values, which put lawyers at a disadvantage
because much of their personal value was in intangibles such as
training, skill, clientele etc., the legal profession still emerged as a
strong economic force in the communities. Two of the fifty-eight
lawyers in the county were the largest landowners in their towns.
Four (6.9%) owned property valued at more than $5000, but twenty-
three (46%) lawyers owned property worth between $1000 and
$5000. When the fact that five of the twenty-nine towns where law-
yers resided contained a maximum property valuation of less than
$5000 is considered, these figures indicate that a majority of law-

*Table III[1]*

## LAWYERS LEAVING THE PROFESSION

|  | Ministry | Farming | Banking | Railroads | Commerce Manufacture | Others |
|---|---|---|---|---|---|---|
| **Massachusetts College Graduates** | | | | | | |
| 1740 to 1810 | 2 | 5 | 0 | 0 | 7 | 6 |
| 1810 to 1840 | 7 | 16 | 18 | 9 | 40 | 46[2] |
| **Maine College Graduates** | | | | | | |
| 1740 to 1810 | 0 | 0 | 0 | 0 | 0 | 0 |
| 1810 to 1840 | 8 | 5 | 5 | 4 | 10 | 7 |
| **Massachusetts Non-College Graduates** | | | | | | |
| 1740 to 1810 | 1 | 1 | 0 | 0 | 0 | 0 |
| 1810 to 1840 | 2 | 1 | 1 | 1 | 5 | 2 |

Table III[1]—(Continued)

| | Ministry | Farming | Banking | Railroads | Commerce Manufacture | Others |
|---|---|---|---|---|---|---|
| Maine Non-College Graduates | | | | | | |
| 1740 to 1810 | 0 | 0 | 0 | 0 | 1 | 1 |
| 1810 to 1840 | 2 | 1 | 0 | 2 | 4 | 1 |

1. See footnote 22. The sampling for this study was 1188 out of 2018 lawyers in Massachusetts and 427 of 600 lawyers in the district of Maine.

2. Includes insurance agents, editors, teachers, and land speculators.

Table IV[1]

## VALUE OF LAND, LOTS, AND DWELLINGS OWNED BY WORCESTER COUNTY LAWYERS—1815

| Name | Town | $ Value | Highest Value in Town |
|---|---|---|---|
| Samuel Eastman | Hardwick | 577 | 7300 |
| Ephraim Hinds | Barre | 0 | 4443 |
| Eleazar James | Barre | 3370 | 4443 |
| Nath'l Houghton | Barre | 0 | 4443 |
| Lewis Bigelow | Petersham | 1602 | 4698 |
| Joseph Proctor | Athol | 1243 | 10362 |
| Samuel Swan | Hubbardston | 691 | 4616 |
| Alexander Dustin | Westminster | 2512 | 5773 |
| Solomon Strong | Westminster | 1539 | 5773 |
| Samuel Cutting | Templeton | 1036 | 3627 |
| Lovell Walker | Templeton | 1295 | 3627 |
| Isaac Goodwin | Sterling | 756 | 5997 |
| John Davis Jr. | Lancaster | 0 | 6188 |
| William Stedman | Lancaster | 5417 | 6188 |
| William Stedman | Worcester | 2591 | 18628 |
| Moses Smith | Lancaster | 1103 | 6188 |
| Joel Harris | Harvard | 0 | — |
| Abijah Bigelow | Leominster | 1413 | 7756 |
| Asa Johnson | Leominster | 2057 | 7756 |
| John Shepley | Fitchburg | 196 | 6296 |
| Calvin Willard | Fitchburg | 0 | 6296 |
| Zabdiel Adams | Lunenburg | 2889 | 3807 |
| Daniel Henshaw | Winchendon | 991 | 5809 |
| Seth Hastings | Mendon | 4694 | 10597 |
| Warren Rawson | Mendon | 2473 | 10597 |
| Benjamin Adams | Uxbridge | 2649 | 12364 |
| Bezaleel Taft Jr. | Uxbridge | 3179 | 12364 |
| Sumner Bastow | Sutton | 518 | 9190 |
| Samuel M. Crocker | Douglas | 0 | 9190 |
| Francis Blake | Worcester | 0 | 18628 |
| Levi Lincoln | Worcester | 18628 | 18628 |

*Table IV*[1]—*(Continued)*

| Name | Town | $ Value | Highest Value in Town |
|---|---|---|---|
| Levi Lincoln Jr. | Worcester | 8478 | 18628 |
| Nathaniel Paine | Worcester | 4710 | 18628 |
| Wm. E. Green | Worcester | 7348 | 18628 |
| Benjamin Heywood | Worcester | 3925 | 18628 |
| Estes Howe | Worcester | 0 | 18628 |
| Wm. C. White | Worcester | 0 | 18628 |
| Rejoice Newton | Worcester | 0 | 18628 |
| Edward Bangs | Worcester | 2198 | 18628 |
| Samuel Burnside | Worcester | 0 | 18628 |
| Levi Heywood | Worcester | 1177 | 18628 |
| Enoch Lincoln | Worcester | 0 | 18628 |
| Gardner Burbank | Worcester | 0 | 18628 |
| Nathaniel P. Denny | Leicester | 3666 | 5731 |
| Liberty Bates | Charlton | 1189 | 9420 |
| Frederic Bottom | Charlton | 0 | 9420 |
| George Davis | Sturbridge | 471 | 7222 |
| Daniel Gilbert | No. Brookfield | 2747 | 5652 |
| Jesse Bliss | Brookfield | 353 | 7458 |
| Dwight Foster | Brookfield | 7458 | 7458 |
| Pliny Merrick | Brookfield | 0 | 7458 |
| Elisha Hammond | Brookfield | 3729 | 7458 |
| Amos Crosby | Brookfield | 549 | 7458 |
| Jacob Mansfield | Western | 254 | 9067 |
| Rufus Putnam | Rutland | 981 | 5883 |
| Jonathan Morgan | Shrewsbury | 0 | 6319 |
| Andrew A. Ward | Shrewsbury | 0 | 6319 |
| Wm. J. Wipple | Dudley | 0 | 5966 |
| Nahum Harrington | Westboro | 0 | 5180 |

1. United States Tax Valuation, 1815, Worcester County Collection, I & II, American Antiquarian Society, Worcester, Mass.

yers in the county were moderately, prosperous landowners, in addition to the value of their office practice and other investments. Psychologically more important, perhaps, was that they represented a relatively new major, economic grouping within Massachusetts society.[10]

Even though lawyers had become an important factor in the state's economy, they were not the dominant force. The total wealth of $38,800 of Levi Lincoln, the richest lawyer in the county in 1834, does not compare very favorably with the $317,250 attributed to Stephen Salisbury, a Worcester financier.[11] The emergence of a

10. Gawalt, *op. cit. supra* note 4, at pp. 206-224.
11. Worcester Valuation and Assessment List, 1834 in William Lincoln Papers, Worcester County Collection, American Antiquarian Society, Worcester, Mass.

strong legal profession, in short, did not substantially alter the economic structure of society, but was in part a response to the demand of corporations for legal expertise.

Psychologically the economic achievements of lawyers had a much greater effect than statistics would indicate. Laymen, for example, resented the fact that lawyers made a livelihood from misfortune and became prosperous during periods of economic hardship. A combination of these two factors contributed substantially to the hostility displayed towards the legal profession in Massachusetts, particularly during the depression following the Revolutionary War.

During 1785 verbal attacks on the legal profession escalated in intensity until by the summer of 1786 the protests of the rural residents had shifted from the newspapers to town meetings and county conventions. Even relatively quiet eastern towns, such as Braintree, recommended

> that there may be such laws compiled as may crush or at least put a proper check or restraint on that order of Gentlemen denominated Lawyers the completion of whose modern conduct appears to us to tend rather to the destruction than the preservation of this Commonwealth.[12]

The lawyers' virtual monopoly of legal business, one element of the state's economic, political, and social systems, added to the animosity. Frederick Robinson, an ardent Jacksonian reformer, summarized the anti-monopolists' attack on the legal profession, when he wrote:

> And although you have left no means unattempted to give you the appearance of *Officers*, you are still nothing more than followers of a trade or calling like other men, to get a living, and your trade like other employments, ought to be left open to competition.[13]

---

12. Petition of the Braintree Town Meeting, Sept., 1786 in 2 Charles F. Adams, *Three Episodes of Massachusetts History* 895-897 (1903); Among other attacks on the legal profession were: *Massachusetts Centinel* (Boston), Sept. 24, Oct. 8, Nov. 2, 16, 1785, April 5, 12, 15, 22, 26, 29, May 6, 10, 17, 27, June 17, 24, July 12, 1786; *Independent Chronicle* (Boston), Mar. 23, April 20, 1786; *Boston Gazette*, June 19, 26, April 17, 1786; *Hampshire Gazette* (Northampton) Oct. 4, 25, Dec. 27, 1786, Feb. 14, 1787; George Watterston, *The Lawyer, Or Man as He Ought Not To Be* (1829); *Berkshire American* (North Adams) Jan. 23, 1828; *Essex Register* (Salem), Mar. 16, 1835.

13. Frederick Robinson, *Letter to the Hon. Rufus Choate Containing a Brief Exposure of Law Craft, and Some of the Encroachments of the Bar Upon the Rights and Liberties of the People* 14-15 (1832).

The economic impact of the legal profession was emotional but none the less real.

Lawyers had a more direct impact on the political and judicial life of the state. Rising from a point of relative political obscurity early in the eighteenth century, political participation by lawyers became so pronounced during and after the Revolution that many people came to consider politics and patronage as subsidiaries of legal business. One of the benefits of membership in a profession was the opportunity to arrange business affairs in order to provide for greater leisure time. Politics provided attorneys the means to use their available time to enhance their own personal status and power.

Until the Revolutionary era, lawyers were barely involved in the political system of the colony. Lacking the connections with the mother country that many merchants possessed, they were estranged from many of the competitive positions for royal patronage. Their role within the elected lower house of the General Court was limited, in part, by the paucity of lawyers. Until 1691, in fact, lawyers were forbidden to sit in the legislature because it acted as the court of appeals. The first practicing lawyer to be elected to the General Court was John Reed in 1738. He was followed by Benjamin Pratt in 1758.[14] Only after the French and Indian War did lawyers become a major voice in colonial politics.

Lawyers, such as James Otis Jr., John Adams, and Josiah Quincy Jr., played leading roles in the political life of the colony prior to the Revolution, but the fluid situation and the demand for men knowledgeable in the law created by the formation of a new government presented the opportunities for many lawyers to enter the political circle. The political influence of lawyers increased more rapidly than their numerical strength, and greatly exceeded their quantitative importance in society. This trend can be seen by comparing Tables I and II with Tables V and VI. Lawyers not only became a powerful voice in the state legislature, but they became the dominant element in the state's delegation to the United States Congress as Tables V and VI demonstrate.

Indicative of the important political role of lawyers was the high degree of participation by members of the legal profession. The commitment of lawyers to political action is revealed by a study of the political involvement of 764 professional lawyers between 1760 and 1810, and of 1222 trained lawyers from 1810 to 1840. Of the 764 lawyers before 1810, 338 (44.2 per cent) were elected to a public office on the local, state, or national level. After 1810, 403 lawyers (32.9 per cent) were chosen for an elected position. Many

14. Thomas Hutchinson, *The History of the Province of Massachusetts Bay*, v. 3, p. 104n (2nd ed. 1828).

more members of the legal profession tried their political fortunes at the polls, but were defeated and therefore remained unnoticed by historians. There were also many lawyers, not included in this study, who held appointive government posts.[15]

Lawyers not only participated in politics in large numbers, but they joined all political parties. An examination of the political affiliation of 304 lawyers between 1790 and 1860 (Table VII), shows the division of members of the legal profession among the major political parties. It is not accurate to say that lawyers tended to belong to the presumably more conservative parties, even though a majority of the lawyers in the sampling were associated with either the Federalist or Whig parties; historians themselves are still ambivalent about identifying these parties as either liberal or conservative. In Massachusetts, for example, many of the legal reforms were accomplished under Whig administrations.[16] The small number of lawyers appearing in the Republican Party probably can be attributed to the fact that only lawyers admitted to the Bar before 1840 were included in this analysis and because primary sources after 1840 were not consulted. What is important is that trained lawyers were members of all major parties.

Many trained lawyers entered politics because of sincere political beliefs and the desire for the prestige and power of elective office, but others entered the forum to obtain appointed posts, which were available at all levels of government. Patronage,

*Table V[1]*

## LAWYERS ELECTED TO THE GENERAL COURT

| Year | Senators | Representatives |
|------|----------|-----------------|
| 1760 | –        | 4               |
| 1770 | –        | 10              |
| 1780 | 3        | 3               |
| 1784[2] | 6     | 13              |
| 1785 | 5        | 15              |
| 1786 | 3        | 8               |
| 1787 | 2        | 11              |

15. Biographical data for the statistical studies in this article was found in historical catalogues of colleges, biographical studies, local histories, almanacs, diaries; and historical journals. To list individual works would require more space than is available for this article, but complete citations may be found in Gawalt, *op. cit. supra* note 4, at Appendix I, 261-277.

16. Gawalt, *op. cit. supra* note 4, at pp. 112-126.

294          THE AMERICAN JOURNAL OF LEGAL HISTORY     Vol. XIV

### Table V[1]—(Continued)

| Year | Senators | Representatives |
|------|----------|-----------------|
| 1788 | 3 | 16 |
| 1790 | 4 | 19 |
| 1800 | 6 | 20 |

1. *Acts and Resolves . . . of the Province of Massachusetts Bay* (Boston, 1909, 1912), XVI, 1757-1760, 563-565, XVIII, 1765-1774, 463-466; *Acts and Laws of the Commonwealth of Massachusetts, 1784-1787* (Boston, 1893), 197-201, 265-270, 621-626, 663-667; *Acts and Laws of . . . Massachusetts, 1788-1789* (Boston, 1890), 171-176; *Acts and Laws of . . . Massachusetts, 1780-1781* (Boston, 1890), 129-133; *Acts and Laws of . . . Massachusetts, 1790-1791* (Boston, 1895), 91-95; *Acts and Laws of . . . Massachusetts, 1800-1801* (Boston, 1897), 129-134.

2. The years 1784-1788 were during a period of high public animosity to the legal profession. Demands were made to exclude lawyers from public office and even to abolish the profession. These figures indicate the minor effect of this verbal campaign on the political fortunes of lawyers.

### Table VI[1]

### LAWYERS IN CONGRESS

| Year[2] | Number of Congressmen | | Lawyers in House | | Lawyers in Senate | |
|---------|-----------------------|---|------------------|---|-------------------|---|
| 1789 | 7 | | 4 | | 1 | |
| 1791 | 7 | | 5 | | 1 | |
| 1793 | 14 | | 7 | | 1 | |
| 1795 | 16 | | 8 | | 2 | |
| 1797 | 16 | | 9 | | 1 | |
| 1799 | 17 | | 10 | | 2 | |
| 1801 | 16 | | 8 | | 2 | |
| 1803 | 18 | | 8 | | 2 | |
| 1805 | 17 | | 7 | | 2 | |
| 1807 | 19 | | 9 | | 2 | |
| 1809 | 20 | | 11 | | 1 | |
| 1811 | 19 | | 8 | | 0 | |
| 1813 | 20 | | 14 | | 1 | |
| 1815 | 19 | | 14 | | 2 | |
| 1817 | 20 | | 17 | | 2 | |
| 1819 | 23 | Maine | 12 | Maine | 2 | Maine |
| 1821 | 13 | 8 | 9 | 5 | 2 | 1 |
| 1823 | 13 | 7 | 9 | 5 | 1 | 1 |
| 1825 | 13 | 8 | 9 | 6 | 1 | 1 |
| 1827 | 14 | 8 | 10 | 5 | 1 | 2 |
| 1829 | 13 | 8 | 9 | 3 | 1 | 2 |
| 1831 | 13 | 7 | 10 | 4 | 1 | 2 |
| 1833 | 14 | 8 | 11 | 5 | 1 | 2 |

*Table VI[1]—(Continued)*

| Year[2] | Number of Congressmen | Maine | Lawyers in House | Maine | Lawyers in Senate | Maine |
|---|---|---|---|---|---|---|
| 1835 | 11 | 8 | 7 | 4 | 2 | 2 |
| 1837 | 13 | 10 | 10 | 5 | 2 | 2 |
| 1839 | 14 | 8 | 12 | 6 | 2 | 2 |

1. The information for this table was gathered from the *Biographical Directory of the American Congress, 1774-1961* (USGPO, 1961).

2. The number of congressmen varies because members died or resigned during the two years between elections, as well as from reapportioning of congressional seats.

*Table VII[1]*

## PARTY AFFILIATION OF LAWYERS, 1790-1860

| Party | Number | Percentage of Total |
|---|---|---|
| Jeffersonian Republicans | 40 | 13.1 |
| National Republicans | 29 | 9.3 |
| Whigs | 74 | 24.4 |
| Democrats | 49 | 16.1 |
| Free Soil | 7 | 2.3 |
| Republican | 11 | 3.6 |
| Federalist | 94 | 30.9 |

1. The political affiliation was determined by a study and comparison of numerous sources, particularly nomination lists in newspapers, the *Biographical Directory of the American Congress . . .* (USGPO, 1961), and political and biographical studies of the period. *The Essex Register* (Salem), Nov. 5, 1835, March 14, Oct. 20, 1836; *Massachusetts Spy* (Worcester), March 18, Sept. 30, 1818, March 31, 1819; *Independent Chronicle* (Boston), March 30, 1801, March 31, 1803; March 28, 1808; *Greenfield Gazette and Franklin Herald*, Sept. 17, Oct. 8, 29, 1833; *The Hampshire Gazette* (Northampton), Oct. 13, 1824; *The Massachusetts Eagle* (Lenox), Oct. 23, Nov. 6, 1834; *Columbia Centinel* (Boston), April 5, 9, 16, 1800, March 27, 31, April 3, 7, May 12, 1819, Nov. 12, 1836; *The Boston Advertiser*, April 16, Oct. 20, 1836; *The Eastern Argus* (Portland), Oct. 4, 1804; March 8, 1805, March 18, April 8, 1823; *Salem Gazette*, Oct. 24, 1800; Samuel E. Morison, *The Life and Letters of Harrison Gray Otis: Federalist 1765-1848* (Boston, 1913), I, 42, 224, II, 94-95, 131-133; David H. Fischer, *The Revolution of American Conservatism . . .* (New York, 1965), 245 ffl; Paul Goodman, *The Democratic-Republicans of Massachusetts, Politics in a Young Republic* (Cambridge, 1964), 61, 80-82, 84, 99, 100, 107, 121-122, 125; Edward Everett, Letter of Acceptance of Whig Gubernatorial Nomination, to Whig Central Committee, April 12, 1836, Everett Papers, 1835-1836, Massachusetts Historical Society, Boston, Mass.; Robert C. Winthrop, Jr., *A Memoir of*

particularly in the judicial branch of government, was a lucrative plum to be dispensed on the basis of political strength. One measure of the political power of the legal profession was the degree to which lawyers were able to obtain political patronage.

Prior to the political debut of the legal profession within Massachusetts during the Revolutionary era, there were few lawyers within the judicial establishment. Of the thirty-three members of the Superior Court between 1692 and 1775, for example, only seven had been trained in the law. Their best qualification for presiding on the bench was usually some connection with the government.[17]

When lawyers achieved political power, they were able to secure much of the patronage that had previously fallen to other political participants, such as farmers or merchants. Lawyers stressed the importance of legally-trained judges and quasi-judicial officials.[18] Although lawyers were not able to gain complete control of the judiciary, they made considerable progress toward that end, as can be seen in Table VIII. Only the judges of the Supreme Judicial Court were required by state law to be "trained in the law." [19] This study of the judiciary and court-oriented offices, however, demonstrates that lawyers monopolized not only the Supreme Court but also the Court of Common Pleas (1821-1840) and the office of county attorney. They also held a majority of positions on the Circuit Court of Common Pleas and the probate

---

*Robert C. Winthrop* (Boston, 1897), 21-22; Arthur B. Darling, *Political Changes in Massachusetts 1824-1848* . . . (New Haven, 1925), 39, 41-42, 47, 65-66, 68, 270-271; J. W. Osgood to William Lincoln, Jonas H. Kendall to Thomas Kinnicutt, June 1, 1832, William Lincoln Papers, Worcester County Collection, American Antiquarian Society, Worcester, Mass. See note 20.

---

17. Emory Washburn, *Sketches of the Judicial History of Massachusetts from 1630 to* . . . *1775,* 241-317 (1840); John D. Cushing, A Revolutionary Conservative: The Public Life of William Cushing, 1732-1810 32 (unpub. Ph.D. diss. Clark U., 1960).

18. *Western Star* (Stockbridge) April 14, 28, May 5, 1795; James Sullivan to Elbridge Gerry, March 22, July 30, 1789 in Elbridge Gerry Papers, 1770-1848, Mass. Hist. Soc., Boston, Mass.; Theodore Sedgwick to Harrison G. Otis, Feb. 7, 1803, Jan. 7, 1804 in Harrison G. Otis Papers, 1800-1805, Mass. Hist. Soc., Boston, Mass.; Abraham Holmes, *Address Before the Bar of the County of Bristol* . . . *1834,* 15-16 (1834); Editorial, *The Jurisprudent* (Boston) Nov. 27, 1830, p. 139; Editorial, 2 *The Law Reporter* 318-319 (1840).

19. *Acts and Laws of the Commonwealth of Massachusetts, 1782-1783* Chap. 9, 28-29 (1890).

court. More than forty per cent of the judges of the County Court of Common Pleas, registers of probate, and clerks of court were lawyers. By monopolizing legal practice and dominating the judicial structure through political power, lawyers were certainly open to the charge of controlling the process of law.

Critics of the legal profession were not slow to point out the inherent danger of concentrated political power in a special interest group. Opposition to the profession's growing political and judicial power and the way to correct the imbalance was not kept a secret by angry laymen. One critic wrote bluntly that:

> It is scarcely necessary to caution the voters at the approaching election against giving their suffrage to a class of citizens, whose only aim is publick ruin.[20]

*Table VIII*[1]

## OFFICES HELD BY LAWYERS: 1780-1840[2]

| Position | Number of Lawyers | Number of Vacancies Filled | Percentage |
|---|---|---|---|
| Judges of Circuit Court of Common Pleas, 1811-21 | 14 | 21 | 66.6 |
| Mass. Court of Common Pleas, 1821-1840 | 6 | 6 | 100. |
| County Judges of General Sessions of the Peace 1807-1828 | 46 | 176 | 26. |
| County Court of Common Pleas, 1782-1811 | 37 | 89 | 41.5 |
| Judge of Probate, County | 36 | 59 | 61. |
| Register of Probate | 22 | 50 | 44. |
| Clerks of Court | 29 | 61 | 47.5 |

20. *Massachusetts Centinel* (Boston) Apr. 26, 1786; Other attacks on the lawyers' political power were: *Western Star* (Stockbridge), Oct. 17, 24, 31, 1796, Oct. 27, 1800; *Massachusetts Centinel* Apr. 29, 1796; *Hampshire Gazette* (Northampton) Nov. 8, 1786, Feb. 14, 1787; *Independent Chronicle* (Boston) Jan. 8, Mar. 19, 1795, Mar. 2, 30, 1797; William Manning, *The Key of Liberty . . . 1798* (2nd ed. 1928); "Report of the Committee of Agriculture in the Massachusetts House," 1 *The Law Reporter* 341-342 (1839).

*Table  VIII¹—(Continued)*

| Position | Number of Lawyers | Number of Vacancies Filled | Percentage |
|---|---|---|---|
| Register of Deeds | 9 | 48 | 18.7 |
| Sheriffs | 21 | 73 | 28.7 |
| County Attorney | 54 | 55 | 98.1 |
| Supreme Court | 20 | 21 | 95.2 |

1. This table was compiled by comparing the listings of public officials in *Fleet's Pocket Almanack,* and *The Massachusetts Register* for these years with the author's biographical file of 2,618 lawyers in the state.

2. Includes the counties of Barnstable, Berkshire, Bristol, Dukes, Essex, Franklin, Hampden, Hampshire, Middlesex, Nantucket, Norfolk, Plymouth, Suffolk, and Worcester.

Laymen not only objected to the economic, political, and judicial power of the legal profession, they fiercely resented the exclusive nature of the lawyer class. Placed within the context of the emergence of a professional elite within society, the hostility of laymen toward the restrictive nature of the professions can be better understood. Did lawyers engender animosity because many reached their privileged positions through the aid of their fathers who were professional men with the wealth and influence to provide their sons with the college education and long years of training that were a prerequisite for entry into the field? Did marriage alliances between professionally oriented families make it possible for candidates to gain an easy access into a given field? Did extended educational requirements exclude those whose families depended on manual labor? The statistical analysis that follows would indicate that a professional elite based on extended education, paternal occupation, and marriage alliances was well-established in nineteenth-century Massachusetts.

The high educational level of members of the legal profession can be readily established. Of the 2,618 trained lawyers[21] practicing in Massachusetts and Maine from 1740 to 1840, 71.4 per cent or 1,859 lawyers had received a college education. Surprisingly the percentage was highest in the district that became Maine in 1820, a frontier area for most of the period. This situation may have resulted from the greater opportunities available in an under-developed region. Of 600 trained lawyers practicing from 1740 to 1840, 450 or 75 per cent were college graduates. In Massachusetts

21. This sampling is about 95 per cent of the lawyers during this period.

proper, out of 2,018 trained practitioners, 1,409 or nearly 70 per cent were college graduates.[22] These educational qualities reflect the high measure of success that members of the legal profession had in recruiting the products of colleges.

The majority of the college graduates in Massachusetts and New England did enter the learned professions—law, medicine, and the ministry. An increasingly large percentage were attracted to the legal profession. These trends can be seen from a study of the graduates of Yale College, where many residents of Massachusetts secured their college degrees. The statistical breakdown of Yale graduates, 1701-1815, in Table IX indicates the continuous attraction of the professions, and particularly the growing number of college graduates entering the legal profession.

Education, then as now, provided opportunities for some members of lower economic strata to enter the professional class, but most members appear to have been born into it. Lawyers, for the most part, were the sons of professional men. During the period from 1740 to 1840 they increasingly represented the sons of lawyers or judges. The majority of college-educated lawyers in Massachusetts and the counties of Maine were the children of lawyers, judges, doctors, or ministers, as can be seen in Table X. Of the non-college graduates a majority of the paternal occupations were in this category in Massachusetts, but this fell to less than 50 per cent for the district of Maine.

A more detailed examination of the paternal occupations of lawyers makes the emergence of an interwoven professional class even more vivid. In order to provide a point of reference and to determine whether there was any progression from the eighteenth to the nineteenth century, the statistics that follow have been divided at the year 1810—the year when the autonomy of the legal profession was formally recognized by the Supreme Judicial Court. Lawyers who entered practice between 1740 and 1809 comprise one group; those who entered between 1810 and 1840 form the other. The groupings are further broken down into the categories of college and non-college graduates in the Maine counties and the same groups in Massachusetts proper. The factors determining into which group a particular lawyer would be placed were his education, geographic residence, and the year that he was admitted to practice in the Court of Common Pleas.

Statistics for lawyers who were college graduates in Massachusetts, exclusive of the Maine counties, indicate that their fathers increasingly tended to be either judges and/or lawyers. Of the 185 lawyers who represent the sample for this aspect of the

---

22. See footnote 15.

300          THE AMERICAN JOURNAL OF LEGAL HISTORY          Vol. XIV

*Table IX*[1]

OCCUPATIONAL DISTRIBUTION OF YALE
GRADUATES: 1701-1815

| Years | Total | Lawyers | Ministers | Doctors | Others |
|-------|-------|---------|-----------|---------|--------|
| 1701-1745 | 483 | 33 | 242 | 30 | 178 |
| 1746-1763 | 505 | 56 | 186 | 64 | 199 |
| 1764-1778 | 484 | 52 | 154 | 59 | 219 |
| 1779-1792 | 543 | 168 | 129 | 57 | 189 |
| 1793-1805 | 540 | 182 | 109 | 37 | 212 |
| 1806-1815 | 601 | 191 | 108 | 71 | 231 |

---

1. Franklin B. Dexter, *Biographical Sketches of the Graduates of Yale College* . . . (New York, 1885-1912), I-773, II-786, III-715, IV-810, VI-836.

*Table X*[1]

PERCENTAGE OF LAWYERS WHOSE
FATHERS WERE LAWYERS, JUDGES,
DOCTORS, MINISTERS

| Geographic Residence | Level of Education | 1740-1809 | 1810-1840 |
|----------------------|--------------------|-----------|-----------|
| District of Maine | College Graduate | 63.6 | 80.7 |
| District of Maine | Non-College Graduate | 44.4 | 41. |
| Massachusetts | College Graduate | 73.3 | 75.4 |
| Massachusetts | Non-College Graduate | 66.5 | 73. |

---

1. See footnote 22.

study, and who were admitted to the bar before 1810, only 71 (38.3%) were the sons of lawyers and judges. After 1810, however, 109 (54.8%) of the 199 lawyers examined were the offspring of lawyers or judges. Conversely, the descendants of members of other professions such as medicine and the ministry showed a declining tendency to enter the legal profession. Before 1810, 35 per cent (sixty-five) of the lawyers were the sons of doctors and ministers; after that date, only 20.6 per cent (forty-one) of the trained practitioners were the children of such professional men.[23]

---

23. Figures for this sampling: 457 of 2018 Mass. lawyers, 126 of 600 Maine lawyers.

Over this same period the sons of merchants, manufacturers, and sea captains entered the profession in increasing numbers, while those of farmers and tradesmen declined. The sons of merchants in the legal profession increased from fifteen (8.1%) before 1810 to nineteen (9.5%) after 1810. The progeny of sea captains grew from none admitted before 1810 to nine (4.5%) after 1810. Although there were three sons of manufacturers admitted to the bar after 1810, there were none before 1810. One sign that the legal profession declined as a vehicle for upward mobility in Massachusetts except for the district of Maine, was the decline in the number of farmers' sons entering the profession. The number dropped from eighteen (9.7%) before 1810 to twelve (6%) after 1810. Moreover, the sons of prosperous farmers entering the practice of law fell even more sharply from thirteen (7%) before 1810 to two (1%) after 1810. The sons of tradesmen declined from three to one after 1810.

Although there was some decline in the number of sons of fathers from non-professional groups entering the legal profession after 1810, this in itself does not indicate that the legal profession discriminated against lower class elements. We do not know, for example, whether the colleges excluded such groups from higher education at this time. Statistics do indicate, however, that after 1810 college-educated lawyers in the present geographic area of Massachusetts tended to be second-generation lawyers, sons of professionals, and, increasingly, the sons of members of the upper economic status—merchants, manufacturers, and sea captains.

A study of the college-educated lawyers who practiced in the eastern district of Massachusetts, which became the state of Maine in 1820, reveals the same trends. This sampling included forty-four lawyers who entered legal practice before 1810 and forty-seven who became lawyers between 1810 and 1840. Of the lawyers admitted to practice before 1810, eleven (25%) were the sons of lawyers or judges. Of those admitted to the Bar in 1810 or after, thirty-two (68%) were the sons of judges or lawyers. The number whose fathers were doctors or ministers declined just as in the developed part of Massachusetts from seventeen (38.6%) before 1810 to six (12.7%) after that date. The percentage of lawyers whose fathers were farmers, however, shifted even more dramatically in the eastern district than in Massachusetts. Nine (20.4%) were descended from farmers before 1810, but only five (10.6%) were the sons of husbandmen after 1810. Children of tradesmen did not appear in the sampling.

Separate studies of non-college graduates in Massachusetts and the eastern district of Maine indicate that the same developments occurred with the notable exception of an increasing percentage of the sons of farmers entering the legal profession after 1810.[24] Once again statistics show that a person who was the son of a lawyer or judge was most likely to become a lawyer.

In Massachusetts, the percentage of lawyers,[25] who were not college graduates, whose fathers were lawyers or judges, increased from 52.3 per cent (eleven) before 1810 to 6.5 per cent (thirty-two) after 1810. The sons of doctors or ministers decreased from 14.2 per cent (three) to 11.5 per cent (six). Lawyers whose fathers were merchants also declined from 14.2 per cent (three) to 3.8 per cent (two), after 1810. Unlike the sampling of Massachusetts lawyers who were college graduates, the lawyers who had not received a college degree came increasingly from the ranks of farmers—9.5% (two) to 1810 and 13.4% (seven) after 1810. The distribution of lawyers whose fathers did not belong to the above categories was one son of a prosperous farmer, a teacher, a sea captain, and a wagon maker.

A similar study of non-college graduates in the eastern district, a frontier area, shows much the same trends. The only significant change was a much lower percentage of lawyers whose fathers were lawyers or judges. Of the lawyers admitted to the Bar before 1810,[26] in this sampling, only four (22.2%) were the sons of lawyers or judges. Although this percentage increased after 1810 to 35.2 per cent (six), it remained much lower than in the settled district of Massachusetts. The sons of doctors and ministers declined from 22.2 per cent (four) before 1810 to 5.8 per cent (one) after 1810. Sons of merchants appearing in this study declined from four (22.2%) before 1810 to zero after 1810. There were two sons of school teachers (11%) before 1810 and one (5.8%) after 1810. Just as in Massachusetts the percentage of sons of farmers increased significantly from 11 per cent (two) before 1810 to 35.2 per cent (six) after 1810.

An examination of the marriage patterns of lawyers indicates the same continued development of a professional class in society as the study of paternal occupations. Lawyers increasingly married the daughters of lawyers, doctors, and ministers. The major

---

24. This might indicate that the cost and long period of preparation tended to exclude some elements of society from college. That college scholarships virtually ceased to exist during the 18th century is a basic premise of David Allmendenger, Jr., Indigent Students and Their Institutions, 1800-1860 (Unpub. Ph.D. diss. U. of Wisconsin, 1968).

25. Twenty-one lawyers were in the sampling 1740-1809 and 52 for 1810-1840.

26. Eighteen lawyers in the sampling before 1810 and 17 from 1810 to 1840.

effect of this development for the social status of lawyers was that their social position relative to other occupational groups remained static. Not only does this point to an arrested development, but it also indicates the increasingly isolated nature of not only the legal profession but the other learned professions as well.

This interpretation is supported by an examination of the family background of lawyers' wives. The occupations of the fathers-in-law of 113 college-educated lawyers admitted to the Bar in Massachusetts before 1810, and of 91 for the years 1810 to 1840 were examined. It was found that seventy-three (64.6%) of the wives were the daughters of lawyers, doctors, and ministers before 1810. After 1810, sixty-one (67%) were the daughters of members of these learned professions. Other classifications showed a corresponding decline. The daughters of merchants married by lawyers fell from 14 per cent (sixteen) before 1810 to 12 per cent (eleven) after 1810. The number of wives whose fathers were farmers dropped precipitously from 14.1 per cent (sixteen) before 1810 to 8.7 per cent (eight) after 1810. Other categories of paternal occupations were not statistically important, but they included artisans, sea captains, bankers, and a plantation owner.

A similar pattern emerged for the district of Maine. The only exception was that a higher percentage of wives were the daughters of lawyers, doctors, or ministers—86.6 per cent (thirteen) to 1810 and 72 per cent (thirteen) after 1810. Significantly, more lawyers in the eastern district tended to move up in economic status for wives after 1810 than before. While no daughter of merchants appeared in the sampling before 1810, four (21 per cent) wives were from mercantile families after 1810. The breakdown for other occupational categories was: one farmer and one wealthy landowner before 1810; one publisher and one soldier after 1810.

The studies of non-college educated lawyers proved inconclusive because of the lack of necessary information. For Massachusetts relevant data for non-college graduates was found for only seven wives before 1810 and ten wives after 1810. The occupations of their fathers followed the same inward pattern. One lawyer, three merchants, and three farmers were the fathers of wives of lawyers before 1810. For the period after 1810 their occupations were six professionals—doctors, lawyers, and ministers—one merchant, one farmer, one prosperous farmer, and one sea captain. Non-college graduates in the district of Maine before 1810 married wives whose fathers were four professionals, three farmers, and one sea captain. After 1810 they chose the daughters of six professionals, one merchant, and one gentleman farmer. Even with this small sampling the trends revealed for the marriage patterns of college graduates remained basically the same for non-college graduates.

The importance of these statistical studies lies not only in the demonstration of the static, inbred status of the legal profession, but also in the growing exclusive nature of the legal class and other professional occupations. As a result, while American society in the view of some historians presumably was moving toward an attitude of an open and democratic society of equal opportunity for equal talent during this period—with the notable exceptions of women and Negroes—the legal class in Massachusetts, at least, was becoming an increasingly closed profession. The result was that the legal profession became more and more isolated from the rest of society at the same time that it was becoming more economically and politically important.

This combination of social isolation and growing political and economic importance may well have been a major underlying cause for the hostility of laymen towards not only lawyers but doctors, ministers, and educators, as well. This alienation became politically important during Shays' Rebellion in Massachusetts and rose to national prominence during the period of Jacksonian democracy, when restrictive professional institutions and requirements came under attack.[27]

But while all professions came in for popular attack in Jacksonian America, the lawyer class was a special target for more specific reasons. At the same time that family tradition and influence, marriage, and education were informally creating an exclusive legal profession, the lawyers were erecting further restrictions through the rules of the county bar associations and the lawyer-dominated courts. After 1760 trained lawyers in Massachusetts organized themselves into county bar associations in order to raise their status by requiring long periods of education and training, and eliminating untrained attorneys from the practice of law. By the end of the 18th century the trained lawyers had created a system that required college graduates to study law for three years as apprentices to a trained lawyer and non-college graduates to serve as apprentices for five years. Full court practice—the right to argue issues of law or fact before the Supreme Court—was open only to trained lawyers who had practiced as attorneys for two years at the lower court of Common Pleas and two more years as attorneys at the Supreme Court. A profession

---

27. Chroust, *op. cit. supra* note 1, at 231-232; Blackard, *op. cit. supra* note 1, at pp. 314-315; Hurst, *op. cit. supra* note 1 at p. 278; Pound, *op. cit. supra* note 1 at p. 631; Donald P. Kommers, "Reflections on Professor Chroust's the Rise of the Legal Profession in America," 10 *Amer. J. Leg. Hist.* 209 (1966).

that demanded nine to eleven years of study, apprenticeship, and minor practice before allowing entrance to full membership was certain to be viewed as restrictive by those denied access to the fruits of legal business.[28]

Until 1806 this system was enforced by the bar associations with the informal collusion of the courts by refusing to recommend a candidate for admission to court practice unless he adhered to their requirements. Thereafter they were accepted by the Supreme Court and incorporated into the legal system through the rules of the court governing court officers. The bar associations were installed as the formal review board for all candidates to the practice of law.[29] With the lawyers controlling entrance into the profession, the danger of crossing the thin line between restrictions necessary to maintain qualified, skilled lawyers and those designed to insure a profitable monopoly for the benefit of an exclusive few greatly increased. Efforts by lawyers to erect a minimum fee schedule, and to nullify a 1785 state law—a law that allowed any one to act as his own attorney or to appoint any person to act as his lawyer—served as proof to many laymen that the designs of trained lawyers were based on pure self-interest at the expense of their clients.

The spirit of the statute opening legal practice to laymen was quickly tested and broken by the trained lawyers. Challenging the law in western Massachusetts—the center of anti-lawyer sentiment in the years 1784-1786—trained lawyers in 1789 harassed William Lyman, an irregular practitioner in Berkshire County, when he attempted to argue a case. Then they convinced the judges of the Court of Common Pleas to rule that he did not have legal power to act as attorney for these clients.[30] With a test case won, trained lawyers had reversed the legislative will. The support of legally-trained judges and bar association rules forbidding any trained attorney to argue any cause involving an irregular practitioner were sufficient to maintain the monopoly of trained lawyers for nearly fifty years.[31]

---

28. Gawalt, *op. cit. supra* note 4, at pp. 6-90. The evolution of this system is too complex to be detailed in this brief article.

29. Gawalt, *op. cit. supra* note 4, at pp. 6-90.

30. *Hampshire Gazette* (Northampton) March 31, April 7, May 5, 12, 1790.

31. Suffolk County Bar, *Rules . . . 1805* 7 (1805); Essex County Bar, *Rules . . . 1806* 8 (1806); Worcester County Bar Rules, 1809 in William Lincoln Papers, American Antiquarian Society, Worcester, Mass.; Worcester County Supreme Court Docket Books, 1786-1830, at Court House, Worcester, Mass.; Docket Books of the Massachusetts Supreme Court, microfilm reel 4, Mass. Hist. Soc., Boston, Mass.; Kennebec County Su-

Fees charged by lawyers were one of the chronic complaints of laymen. Despite sporadic efforts by the state legislature to establish maximum legal fees, trained lawyers by 1800 had erected a complex system of minimum fees that more than doubled the state rates and continued to rise. Enforced through the bar associations by threat of disbarment, the minimum fee schedules became another grievance against the legal profession.[32]

After more than a half-century of attempts to destroy the power of the bar associations and the stiff entrance requirements into the profession, the movement reached its climax during the period of Jacksonian Democracy. The Revised Statutes of Massachusetts as passed on November 4, 1835 completely overturned the power of the lawyers and their bar associations to control the admissions to the practice of law through the courts. Rather than allow the courts or lawyers to establish the rules and regulations, the laws set new rules to control the professional standards. Any candidate who had studied law in the office of any attorney of the state for three years was to be automatically admitted to the bar upon his application to the Supreme Court or the Court of Common Pleas. If a person had not studied for three years, he could apply to the Supreme Court or the Court of Common Pleas for an examination by the judges. Every attorney admitted to practice in any court could practice in every court in the state without difference or distinction. The various ranks of attorney and counsellor were abolished outright.[33]

These laws meant that the bar associations would no longer have the right to control admission to the practice of law. It meant also the disestablishment of the graded and restricted legal pro-

---

preme Court Docket Books, 1799-1836, at **Court House,** Augusta, Maine; Ephraim Williams, *Reports of Cases . . . in the Supreme Judicial Court of Massachusetts, 1804-1805* (1805); 1-17 Dudley A. Tyng, *Reports of Cases . . . in the Supreme Judicial Court of Massachusetts 1806-1822* (1807-1823); 1-23 Octavius Pickering, *Reports of Cases Argued . . . 1822-1839* (1824-1864); 1-9 Simon Greenleaf, *Reports of Cases . . . in the Supreme Judicial Court of Maine, 1820-1832* (1822-1835); 1-6 John Shepley, *Reports of Cases . . . in the State of Maine, 1836-1839* (1836-1840).

32. George Dexter, ed., "Record Book of the Suffolk Bar," 19 Mass. Hist. Soc., *Proceedings* 149, 167-169 (1881-1882); Rules of the Berkshire County Bar, 1792 in Sedgwick Papers, 1767-1798, at Mass. Hist. Soc., Boston, Mass.; Suffolk County Bar, *Rules . . . 1805* 7-8 (1805); Suffolk County Bar, *Rules . . . 1810* 11-13 (1810); Essex County Bar, *Rules . . . 1806* 9 (1809); Bristol County Bar, *Rules . . . 1817* 7-11 (1817); Hampden County Bar, *Rules . . . 1816* 5-6 (1816); Worcester County Bar, *Rules . . . 1816* 5-6 (1816); Suffolk County Bar, *Rules . . . 1819* 10-16 (1819).

33. *The Revised Statutes of Massachusetts,* Part III, Title I, Chap. 88, 541-542 (1836).

fession that had existed for eighty years. Furthermore, the educational standards for the profession developed by lawyers were unenforceable because there was no longer any distinction between applicants who were college graduates and those who were not. Legal study became more a matter of "putting in time" rather than acquiring knowledge. State law had made entrance into the legal profession, at least superficially, more attainable for people without family wealth or connection.

The use of the state government by the opponents of professional monopolies raises serious questions. Why did the critics of artificial restrictions and institutions turn to the state governments to legislate reforms? Did the need to turn to government in order to break down artificial barriers and maintain social and economic mobility symbolize a decline of vertical mobility and a hardening of occupational class structures in American society? Placed within this context of the emergence of a lawyer class, the hostility of laymen toward any entrance requirements into the profession can be better understood.

# 21
# MASSACHUSETTS LEGAL EDUCATION IN TRANSITION, 1766-1840

*GERARD W. GAWALT*

# Massachusetts Legal Education In Transition, 1766-1840

*by* GERARD W. GAWALT*

Although a highly trained and organized legal profession existed in Massachusetts before the American Revolution, apprenticeship remained the sole means of legal education in the state until Harvard College named its first professor of law in 1815. Despite successful experiments with college law lectures and independent law schools in other states before 1800, the lack of interest in systematic, centralized legal instruction among Massachusetts lawyers was so profound that even Isaac Royall's endowment of a law professorship at Harvard produced no action for more than thirty years. Private law schools, moreover, did not even make an appearance in Massachusetts until 1823.

This reluctance to supplement or replace the apprenticeship system of legal education with lecture courses in a state that contained an ambitious, educated, and cohesive legal profession poses a serious problem for legal historians. Arthur Sutherland, a recent historian of Harvard Law School, disputed the traditional argument of Charles Warren that the delay was due to conflict with England, the embargo and the resulting economic disruption, which depressed legal business and discouraged the Harvard Corporation from starting instruction in the law.[1] The major reason for Harvard's reticence, in Sutherland's opinion, was the conviction at the Cambridge school that legal training was not a respectable endeavor for a college. The college's dilemma, Sutherland wrote, was that "if education was to be practical, it would not be academically respectable; if it was to be respectably academic, it must be professionally unprofitable."[2] These and other historical explana-

---

*American Revolution Bicentennial Office, Library of Congress, Washington, D.C.

1. Arthur E. Sutherland, *The Law at Harvard: A History of Ideas and Men, 1817-1967* 43-45 (1967); 1 Charles Warren, *History of the Harvard Law School and of Early Legal Conditions in America* 285 (1st ed. 1908).
2. Sutherland, *op. cit. supra* note 1 at p. 45.

28              THE AMERICAN JOURNAL OF LEGAL HISTORY      Vol. XVII

tions[3] deal with contributing factors, but they are too limited to explain satisfactorily the fundamental reasons for the slow shift from experience to classroom as the preferred way to educate lawyers.

Massachusetts lawyers, themselves, were responsible for delaying the appearance of law schools. Apprenticeship meant more than a manner of training for the legal profession. By the revolutionary era, apprenticeship had become a method of regulating and restricting membership in the profession, as skilled lawyers sought to impose higher standards for admission. Bar associations served as the vehicles to achieve the goals of a highly trained and educated membership, and they restricted entrance into the profession to maintain high quality and reduce competition.

This dual role of education and regulation led to the failure of both. Although lawyers sincerely felt that each function would improve the quality of the profession, this ideal often became mixed with powerful desires to improve the economic status of the bar by restricting the number of lawyers, establishing fee systems, and inflating the cost of legal education. Clashing local regulations of county bar associations mingled with these conflicting aims to produce administrative chaos. Under the weight of these conflicting demands, the bar associations collapsed in the early nineteenth century. The state assumed their regulatory role in 1836, and law schools absorbed their educational function. How lawyers and their agency, the bar association, lost control of legal education is the subject of this paper.

*        *        *

Regulation became coupled with legal education during the middle of the eighteenth century. When lawyers began organizing and structuring an autonomous profession, apprenticeship was considered the only adequate method of preparing students for the law. Lawyers did not view the student's term of study in the

---

3. Samuel E. Morison in *Three Centuries of Harvard, 1636-1936* 238-239 (1936) offers the defense that Harvard could not obtain the legacy of Isaac Royall for thirty years. Josiah Quincy in 2 *The History of Harvard University* 317-19 (1860) offers no explanation for the delay in the appearance of the law school. Alfred Z. Reed, *Training for the Public Profession of the Law*, Carnegie Foundation for the Advancement of Training, 15 *Bulletin* 128, 134-135 (1925) touches on the basic reason when he argues that English tradition and the Suffolk County Bar rule of 1783 prohibiting barristers from training more than three apprentices at a time stiffled the growth of law schools, but his view is too narrow. 2 Anton-Hermann Chroust, *The Rise of the Legal Profession in America* 191-202 (1965) offers no explanation for the delay.

office of a barrister or attorney as a substitute or an alternative to
a college education. Attainment of a general education had to
come before apprenticeship. The period of instruction became a
time when the student not only acquired the technicalities of the
law but also identified with his prospective profession and learned
the role expected of him by clients and future colleagues.[4] These
requirements necessitated a long period of close association with
members of the profession. Apprenticeship filled all these needs.

What educational model did the lawyers seek to emulate?
For the most part, they looked upon the medical and ministerial
professions in the colony and the English legal profession as guides.
All examples led the lawyers to the same course of action. Apprenticeship, in short, was the accepted, sound means of professional
training. In the colony, doctors and ministers received instruction
by the apprenticeship method throughout the seventeenth and
eighteenth centuries. Leading ministerial candidates could become
resident graduates at college—studying theology while they were
supported by scholarships and occasional preaching positions—
but most read theology with a minister while they taught school or
worked the minister's farm. Samuel Haven, a theological apprentice, claimed that he not only enjoyed "the advantages of his [the
minister] most Learned as well as Christian Conversation, but
also the pleasure and profit of perusing a Collection of Books not
inferiour to the best in the hands of Any Country Minister nor
do I imagine my privilege less noble than those to be enjoyed at
College."[5] Not until 1812 were ministerial candidates provided
special graduate classes at Harvard College.[6] Only later  would
proponents of educational institutions discover the "limited" training opportunities in the apprenticeship system.

Professional instruction in colonial Massachusetts was not
outmoded because of its reliance on apprenticeship. Even in England the primary means of legal education remained clerkship,
despite William Blackstone's law lectures at Oxford for thirteen
years after 1753. Candidates for admission as attorneys, solicitors,
or proctors as a rule obtained their legal education while serving

4. Two of the best discussions of the role of professional education are
found in Everett Hughes, *Men and Their Work* (1958), and Roy Lubove,
*The Professional Altruist: The Emergence of Social Work as a Career
1880-1930* (1965). Paul M. Hamlin's *Legal Education in Colonial New
York* (1939) is a good study of legal education itself.

5. Samuel Haven to Robert T. Paine, June 21, 1750, Paine Papers,
Massachusetts Historical Society, hereafter cited as MHi; Mary L. Gam-
brell, *Ministerial Training in Eighteenth Century New England* 101-139
(1937).

6. Morison, *op. cit. supra* note 3 at p. 241.

as articled clerks to their professional masters. Reading in the office of an established practitioner and attendance at court sessions was the normal means of instruction—producing a student with a practical knowledge of the law, but, critics would argue, without an appreciation for the broad underlying principles. By the eighteenth century, legal education at the Inns of Court had declined to the point where candidates for the rank of barrister were left to do undirected reading and to attend sessions in chambers, a law office, or in the courts, if they wanted to acquire a knowledge of the law. The Inns of Court no longer functioned as legal universities with prescribed courses of study, lectures, and moot courts.[7]

With professional education in both the colony and in the mother country revolving around the apprenticeship system, it should be no surprise that the lawyers in Massachusetts considered it the best educational method. Suffolk County lawyers—the first to organize a formal county bar association in Massachusetts—also assumed the lead in establishing the pattern of training for law students. Before lawyers organized, no specific standards of legal education existed for attorneys trained in the colony, leading to the emergence of a large number of untrained pettifoggers. Their efforts to eliminate self-trained lawyers led the colony's leading lawyers to the apprenticeship system. In 1766 and in 1771 the barristers and attorneys of the Suffolk County Bar Association agreed to require a three-year residency with a barrister beyond a college or liberal education. But no requirements existed for an examination by either the court or the bar before a law student would be recommended for admission to the practice of law by the bar association. As in England, the emphasis fell on fulfilling the term of residency, not on knowledge. Faith in the barrister's efforts to instill competence in his clerk apparently guaranteed the acquisition of skills.[8]

---

7. 12 William Holdsworth, *A History of English Law* 15-18, 22-27, 77-88, 100 (6th ed. 1938). For a detailed view of English legal education, see Edwin Freshfield, ed., *The Records of the Society of Gentlemen Practisers in the Courts of Law and Equity Called the Law Society* (1897); William J. Reader, *Professional Men: The Rise of the Professional Classes in Nineteenth Century England* (1966); Robert Robson, *The Attorney in Eighteenth Century England* (1959).

8. George Dexter, ed., "Record Book of the Suffolk Bar," 29 *Mass. Hist. Soc. Proceedings* 149 (1881-1882); Holdsworth, *op. cit. supra* note 7 at pp. 77-82, 100; July 28, 1766 entry in Lyman H. Butterfield et al. eds., 1 *Diary and Autobiography of John Adams* 316 (1964). Attorneys of the Inferior Court of Common Pleas could prepare, enter and argue cases before the lower courts. Attorneys of the Superior Court could prepare and enter cases in the highest court, but only barristers

At the end of the century, the program of legal education established by the lawyers of Suffolk County had become accepted, with
only slight modifications, throughout the state. Although educational
prerequisites, length of study, and reading assignments varied
from county to county and lawyer to lawyer, all attorneys accepted
a prescribed term of apprenticeship as a requirement for admission to the profession. A three-year term of study for college graduates was general; terms of apprenticeship for non-college graduates varied between four and seven years. Some counties, such as
Essex, Suffolk and Worcester, even required examinations for law
students. This step was remarkable in an age that produced a 1791
riot at Harvard over the institution of year-end exams. The basic
concept that members of a learned profession required a long
period of education was, however, firmly established in principle.[9]

Dissatisfaction with the apprenticeship system arose con-
currently with its development. The legal education provided under
apprenticeship was undoubtedly monotonous, arduous, and often
unedifying. Spending most of his time copying wills, pleadings,
briefs, and other documents needed by his master, the law student
often had little time left to absorb any knowledge from the few law
books available to the practicing lawyer in the eighteenth century.
John Adams, for example, who studied law from 1756 to 1758 under
a Worcester attorney, James Putnam, complained to his friends
that his legal studies were tiring and that the subject matter consisted of "Old Roman Lawyers and Dutch Commentators."[10]

Law books continued to bore legal clerks throughout the
period, and an English text prompted Alexander Hamilton, a
Massachusetts law student, to remark in 1830 that Old Chitty lies
before me, "looking for all the world as inviting as a shrivelled old
maid."[11] If legal education had only been dull, then lawyers

---

could argue cases in the Superior Court. Because barristers were considered the most highly qualified lawyers, only they were to be allowed to
train law clerks. Not all of the county bar associations adopted this rule.

9. The development of this system was erratic and is fully explored in
Gerard W. Gawalt, "Massachusetts Lawyers: A Historical Analysis of
the Process of Professionalization, 1760-1840" (Unpubl. Ph.D. Diss.,
Clark U., 1969), 6-128; Oscar and Mary Handlin, *Facing Life: Youth
and the Family in American History* 127-128 (1971).

10. Probably Johannes Van Muyden (1652-1729), *Compendium Insti-
tutionum Justani Tractatio in Usum Collegiorum*, an abridgment of *Jus-
tinian's Institutes* published in 1694. John Adams to John Wentworth,
John Adams to Tristram Dalton, John Adams to Samuel Quincy, Oct.-
Nov., 1758 in Lyman H. Butterfield ed., *The Earliest Diary of John
Adams* 62-63 (1964).

11. Alexander Hamilton to Edwin Conant, Oct. 19, 1830, Edwin Conant
Papers, American Antiquarian Society, hereafter cited as MWA.

and interested laymen would not have needed to vitalize it. But often legal training depended to such a degree on the interest of a young man and a harried practitioner that it lacked the serious application necessary to produce lawyers rather than pettifoggers.

Adams' legal study was so unstructured that after two years of clerkship, he commented bitterly after struggling to write his first writ: "Now I feel the Disadvantages of Putnam's Insociability and neglect of me." "Had he given me now and then a few Hints concerning Practice," Adams continued, "I should be able to judge better at this Hour than I can now."[12] If Adams had the best professional legal education available in English America in the 1750's as Arthur Sutherland argues,[13] then it is no surprise that educational reform should have become one of the main objects of the organized lawyers.

A scarcity of law books undoubtedly presented a serious problem for law students and lawyers, but the system of legal study, not the unavailability of books, made law students react against their training. John Quincy Adams, who had a much wider selection of law books while studying with Theophilous Parsons than his father had possessed under Putnam, voiced a common complaint of law students when he reported that Parson's office was so busy and noisy that he couldn't study. At the same time, James Bridge, an apprentice under Pownalboro's John Gardiner, who himself was trained at the English Inns of Court, complained that his mentor gave him no guidance at all. Bridge claimed that Gardiner allowed him to study at home and that his only source for study was a set of Blackstone. "About once a fortnight I spend an afternoon in the family in the mode of chit-chat, cards, back-gammon etc.," Bridge wrote. "This is the only kind of instruction I am here acquainted with," he stated. John M. Forbes, a student of John Sprague at Lancaster, echoed Bridge's cries of lack of guidance with the terse comment that "as to talking with him there is no such thing!"[14] Despite private complaints by law students, no serious consideration was given to changing the basic method of professional preparation until well into the nineteenth century.

---

12. Dec. 18, 1758 in Butterfield *op. cit. supra* note 8, v. 1, p. 63.

13. Sutherland, *op. cit. supra* note 1 at p. 15.

14. Charles Warren, *A History of the American Bar* 172 (3rd ed. 1966); Benjamin Brown to George Thatcher, June 4, 1789, Charles P. Greenough Papers, MHi; journal of Dwight Foster, Jan. 11, 1777-Sept. 23, 1778, MWA; March 25, 1788 entry in "John Q. Adams Diary," 2nd ser. 16 *Mass. Hist. Soc. Proceedings* 399 (1902); James Bridge to John Q. Adams Sept. 28, 1787 in "John Q. Adams," *ibid.* 435; John M. Forbes to Dorothy Forbes, Feb. 14, 1788 in Forbes Papers, MHi.

Lawyers believed adjustments might be needed but that the system provided the best all-round legal instruction.

As the apprenticeship system developed in Massachusetts, however, there was much more involved in the process of training than merely schooling. Plans to eliminate untrained practitioners for economic reasons and to regulate competition among members of the profession became woven into the fabric of the clerkship system. The institution was forced to assume burdens it could not handle. It restricted the number of law students; it provided lawyers with an inexpensive source of office labor, as well as an additional means of income; and it presented a rationale for excluding lawyers trained in other states and even in other counties. Apprenticeship may have given the law student a practical knowledge of the law, but it also produced security and stability for veteran members of the profession.

Institutions and individuals in other states at least gestured toward formal legal instruction outside of office clerkships in the eighteenth century. None occurred in Massachusetts. Litchfield Law School, founded in 1784 by Tapping Reeve in neighboring Connecticut, provided the only place in New England where law was taught in a systematic, lecture-oriented manner. Yet, William and Mary College, the University of Pennsylvania, Transylvania University, and Columbia College offered law lectures before 1800.[15] With an active, prosperous, and highly organized legal profession, Massachusetts might have been expected to foster at least one college-connected or independent institution for legal instruction, but no one even attempted to present law lectures until 1815.

Law schools undoubtedly lost some of their luster and attraction as a model for Massachusetts because of mixed success with the lecture system and limited acceptance by students and lawyers. Reeve's Litchfield Law School attracted about 100 Massachusetts men among more than 800 students over a fifty-year existence. Samuel Howe and Theron Metcalf utilized their Litchfield experience to form their own law schools in Massachusetts. On the other hand, James Kent's law lectures at Columbia fared badly. His course's popularity dwindled from seven students and thirty-six auditors in 1794-95 to two students in 1795-96 and then to no students the next year.[16] Desires for a Blackstone-like lecture system lacked demonstrable conviction among many lawyers.

---

15. 4 Timothy Dwight, *Travels in New England and New York: 1801-1802* 306 (1822); James Thayer, "The Teaching of English Law at Universities," 9 *Harv. L. Rev.* 170-171 (1895); Reed, *op. cit. supra* note 3 at pp. 118, 128-130.

16. Samuel H. Fisher, *The Litchfield Law School, 1775-1833* (1933);

Most lawyers believed that apprenticeship supplied the best training. Other factors, however, contributed to their reticence in supporting large-scale systems of training outside an office. One of the principal reasons for the delayed appearance of a non-apprenticeship program of legal education in Massachusetts was the lawyers' attempts to use education as a means of limiting professional competition. Long periods of clerkship promised better-trained lawyers but also helped to restrict the number of lawyers. Seven years served as the standard term of apprenticeship for the legal profession before a candidate could be recommended by the county bar associations for admission to the lowest court, the county Court of Common Pleas. Bar associations, moreover, with the support of the Supreme Judicial Court, insisted that four years of practice as an attorney in the Court of Common Pleas and the Supreme Judicial Court were prerequisites for full practice in the state's courts. Even though the lawyers were concerned about the quality of legal knowledge, they also saw the graded system of full admission and the lengthy term of apprenticeship as added guarantees of high incomes.[17]

The fees paid by law students while clerks may also have influenced bar-leaders to keep a few members of the profession or outside institutions from monopolizing legal education. When the average professional lawyer's earnings hovered around $500,[18] the income from law students, not to mention their free labor, was very important. Most county bar associations established standard fees for apprenticeships, not only to protect the law student, but to prevent competition for students and to spread the available clerks among the leading lawyers. Law students had paid as little as £10 per annum before the growth of bar associations, but these rates changed radically. After 1783, for example, the lawyers of Suffolk, Essex, and Middlesex counties charged £100 sterling for a three-year term of study. Suffolk lawyers raised their rates to $150 per year in 1805 and to $500 for three years in 1810. Lawyers in Essex County charged $150 per year after 1806. Apprentices in the Maine counties paid only $150 for three years; Hampshire County practitioners required only $250 for a three-year term; and students in Bristol, Worcester, and Hampden counties were required to pay $100 per year. Occasionally a clerk, such as George N. Briggs, could arrange to pay only $40 per year in a rural section of the

---

Frederick C. Hicks, "James Kent" Allen Johnson and Dumas Malone, eds., 10 *Dictionary of American Biography* 345 (1933).

17. Gawalt, *op. cit. supra* note 9 at pp. 6-128.

18. *Ibid.*, 206-221.

state in the nineteenth century, but this was a rare occurrence.[19]
Very few lawyers were willing to sacrifice that much money for an
experiment in legal education that had yet to prove itself capable
of preparing qualified attorneys.

In the two counties where lawyers were the most prosperous
and numerous a decision to limit the number of students permitted
in a law office to three guaranteed a division of clerk's fees and
served to insure the long delay in establishing private law schools
in Massachusetts until the 1820's. This move was made by the
barristers and attorneys of Suffolk County in 1783 and was imitated
by Essex County practitioners in 1806. Hopes to promote better
training by allowing a master lawyer more time for each clerk, to
limit the number of prospective lawyers, and to spread the fees of
law clerks among a wide selection of practitioners provided the
motivation.[20] Lawyers in less commercially developed and less
populous counties made no move to formally emulate their eastern
brethren. Their chances of attracting more than three clerks in
one office were probably slim, and their actions reflect this situation. The absence of this regulation allowed office law schools to be
launched in such counties during the 1820's. Even though the bar
associations in other counties did not follow the leadership of Suffolk and Essex counties with formal regulations, such action by the
leading lawyers in the state inhibited the development of private
law schools.

Another possible cause for the delay in the founding of law
schools arose from the requirement that students must study law
in the office of a barrister, counsellor, or attorney. Although this

---

19. Clifford K. Shipton, "Daniel Oliver," 15 *Biographies of Those Who
Attended Harvard* 278-281 (1970); Dexter, *op. cit. supra* note 8
at pp. 152-155; Suffolk County Bar Association, *Rules, 1805* 8 (1805);
Suffolk County Bar Association, *Rules . . . 1810* 14 (1810); Essex County
Bar Association, *Rules . . . 1806* 9 (1806); Essex County Bar Association,
*Rules . . . 1819* 17 (1819); James D. Hopkins, *An Address to the Members
of the Cumberland Bar . . . 1833* 30 (1833); Hollis R. Bailey, *Attorneys
and Their Admission to the Bar in Massachusetts* 36-37 (1907); Bristol
County Bar Association, *Rules . . . 1817* 12 (1817); Worcester County
Bar Association Rules, 1809, MS in William Lincoln Papers, MWA;
Hampden County Bar Association, *Rules . . . 1816*, 4 (1816); George N.
Briggs to Rufus Briggs, Oct. 15, 1831 in William C. Richards, *A Memoir
of George N. Briggs* 40-41 (1866).

20. Gawalt, *op, cit. supra* note 9 at p. 225; Dexter, *op. cit. supra* note
8 at p. 157; Suffolk County Bar Association, *Rules . . . 1805*, 11; Essex
County Bar Association, *Rules . . . 1806*, 11-12; Suffolk County Bar Association, *Rules . . . 1819*, 20 (1819); Essex County Bar Association, *Rules
. . . 1819*, 20.

rule could be interpreted broadly enough to encompass private law schools or even college-connected law schools, the intent of the regulation discouraged candidates from studying outside of apprenticeship. Framed originally by the county bar associations to enhance the quality of legal preparations, the rule received the sanction of the state Supreme Judicial Court in 1806.[21] This rule appears to have been a laudatory and successful attempt to require a minimum of instruction for law students. When combined with later demands that prospective lawyers study in the state and county in which they sought to be admitted to practice, it proved to be a major barrier to the growth of law schools.

Stimulated by an increase in the number of active practitioners, the parochial pride of members of the county bar associations, and an influx of lawyers from other states, each county bar association erected barriers against out-of-state lawyers and against law students who were trained in another state or even in another county within Massachusetts. Migration of lawyers trained at the Litchfield Law School in nearby Connecticut to western counties, for example, motivated the practitioners of Berkshire County to initiate protective measures in 1792 by refusing to recommend for admission to practice any law student not trained by an attorney of the Massachusetts Supreme Judicial Court. New rules agreed to in 1800 by lawyers of Suffolk County showed a marked disdain for out-of-state attorneys by providing that candidates who had studied law in other states would not be recommended for admission until they had studied law for one year in Suffolk or had practiced in the highest court of their state for four years. Lawyers in Essex and Worcester counties sought to recommend only attorneys who had met the same qualifications as local candidates. The general rules for governing the admission of attorneys established by the Supreme Judicial Court in 1810 provided that out-of-state candidates for the bar must have studied at least two years in the office of a Massachusetts counsellor. Within a few years, most county bar associations had passed similar resolutions discriminating against lawyers from other states. These regulations kept the immigration of outside lawyers to a minimum, but increasing demands for legal talent could not be met by locally trained law-

---

21. July 28, 1766 entry in Butterfield, *op. cit. supra* note 8 at p. 316; Dexter, *op cit. supra* note 8 at p. 149; Bailey, *op. cit. supra* note 19 at pp. 32-33; Rules of the Berkshire Bar, 1792 in Sedgwick Papers, 1767-1798, MHi; Suffolk County Bar Association, *Rules . . . 1805*, 11; Essex County Bar Association, *Rules . . . 1806*, 11-12; "Rules of the Supreme Judicial Court, 1810" in Dudley A. Tyng, *Reports . . . 1809-1810* 382 (1811).

yers. Nearly 15 percent of Massachusetts lawyers between 1810 and 1840 were born outside the state.[22] This demand for legal talent helped lead to an influx of "foreign" lawyers and also led the way to law schools.

Growth of a law school in Massachusetts was probably delayed by demands from most bar associations members that before they would even vote to recommend a candidate for admission to practice, each student should have sutdied for his last year in a law office in that county. A law student, for example, who spent a three-year apprenticeship in Essex County would not be eligible for a Suffolk County Bar recommendation. This parochial attitude appeared during the 1790's and remained a dominant element of control during the first twenty-five years of the nineteenth century. Members of the Suffolk County Bar Association even went so far as to refuse their recommendation to practice in Suffolk County to a lawyer from another county unless he provided proof of at least two years prior practice and the recommendation of the county bar in which he practiced.[23] When attempts were made to establish law schools in the 1820's, this inter-county jealousy contributed to their failure.

The concern of some lawyers to improve the quality of legal studies by broadening their scope led to questioning of the apprenticeship system. Both substitutes and ways to buttress this traditional means of training attracted attention. Massachusetts lawyers found little encouragement toward establishing law schools in their favorite model, the English legal profession. Not until 1833 did the London Law Society offer a program of law lectures to candidates for the rank of attorney. Gray's Inn had abandoned law lectures in 1769 after a fifteen-year trial. Lincoln's Inn offered law lectures after 1799, but they were poorly attended. Establishment of three medical professorships at Harvard in 1782 might have been expected to spark a demand for equal attention to law. But only after the dissatisfaction of law students was joined with a growing view

---

22. Gawalt, *op. cit. supra* note 9 at pp. 189-229; Berkshire County Bar Rules, 1792 in Sedgwick Papers, MHi; Dexter, *op. cit. supra* note 8 at p. 174; Essex County Bar Association, *Rules, 1806,* 13; Worcester County Bar Rules, 1809 MS in William Lincoln Papers, MWA; Tyng, *op. cit. supra* note 21 at p. 383; Gerard W. Gawalt, "Sources of Anti-Lawyer Sentiment in Massachusetts, 1740-1840," 14 *Am. Journal of Legal Hist.* 285-286 (1970).

23. Dexter, *op. cit. supra* note 8 at p. 167; Worcester County Bar Rules, 1809 in William Lincoln Papers, MWA; Suffolk County Bar Association, *Rules, 1805,* 11-12; Essex County Bar Association, *Rules . . . 1816,* 2-3; Suffolk County Bar Association, *Rules . . . 1814* 16 (1814).

of law as a science did alternatives to the apprenticeship system become attractive to the legal profession.[24]

By 1800, sentiment for treating the law as a science among younger practitioners merged with a growing demand among older leaders of the profession for making a college degree a prerequisite for admittance to the bar. Bar associations began prescribing longer apprenticeships for clerks without collegiate training; and the law, in turn, began attracting an increasing number of college graduates.[25] By 1835, the law rivaled the ministry as the professional choice of Yale, Bowdoin, Brown and Dartmouth students (Tables I, II, and III).

In Massachusetts and Maine, seventy-one percent or 1859 of the 2618 trained lawyers practicing from 1760 to 1840 held college degrees. Surprisingly the percentage for the Eastern District—a largely frontier area that became the state of Maine in 1820— topped that for the old Massachusetts Bay region. This development might have stemmed from the attraction of expected opportunities in a newly developed region. Of 600 trained lawyers practicing from 1760 to 1840, 450 or seventy-five percent graduated from college. In Massachusetts itself, out of 2018 practitioners, 1409, or nearly seventy percent, held college degrees. A 1963 study of American lawyers reveals that only 62.6 percent had college degrees, but 86.5 percent had attended college.[26]

The educational level of lawyers in the perspective of the times ranked between ministers and doctors and above the average for the three learned professions in Massachusetts during 1740-1840. A study of 3503 ministers and doctors indicates that 62.9 percent of these groups were college graduates—84.5 percent of 1917 ministers and 35.3 percent of 1576 doctors. In Maine, ministers and doctors showed a lower educational index than lawyers: for ministers, 72.9 percent college graduates in Maine and 88.5 percent in Massachusetts; for doctors, 16.9 percent in the Eastern District and 42.9 percent in Massachusetts.[27] Ministers and lawyers empha-

---

24. Holdsworth, *op. cit. supra* note 7 at pp. 77-100; Quincy, *op. cit. supra* note 3 at pp. 266-267; John Davis, "Discourse to Suffolk Bar, 1801," in Davis Papers, MWA; Joseph Story to Thomas Welch, Oct. 19, 1799, Joseph Story to Gabriel Duvall, March 30, 1803 in 1 William Story, ed., *Life and Letters of Joseph Story* 83, 103 (1851).

25. Reader, *op. cit. supra* note 7 at pp. 9-11, 45-47; Suffolk County Bar Association, *Rules . . . 1805*, 11-12; Bristol County Bar Association, *Rules . . . 1817*, 12; Essex County Bar Association, *Rules . . . 1806*, 13.

26. Gawalt, *op. cit. supra* note 22 at pp. 298-299; Quintin Johnstone and Dan Hopson, Jr., *Lawyers and Their Work: An Analysis of the Legal Profession in the United States and England* 20n (1967).

27. These statistics were developed in a study of ministers and doctors

sized the need for a college education and physicians did not. The statistics reflect these values.

The shift from the college atmosphere to a law office was sometimes a traumatic experience for students and sometimes merely a boring one. Willard Phillips, who later edited *The American Jurist and Law Magazine,* satirized his lack of interest in legal training by claiming that he was so "diligent" in his attendance at the law office where he clerked that "I am under the necessity of inquiring my way when I visit it." Phillips' interest certainly was not fixed by his law studies. Peter C. Bacon, a law student in Oxford, studied law for only thirteen months during the three years he was entered as a clerk in the office of Ira M. Barton. Essex County practitioners tried to control the education of students even to the point of prescribing legal work or study for six hours a day, six days a week.[28] Such emphasis on time serving turned some law students against the apprenticeship system.

*Table I[1]*

OCCUPATIONAL DISTRIBUTION OF YALE GRADUATES:
1701-1815

| Years | Lawyers | Ministers | Doctors | Others | Total |
|---|---|---|---|---|---|
| 1701-1745 | 33 | 242 | 30 | 178 | 483 |
| 1746-1763 | 56 | 186 | 64 | 199 | 505 |
| 1764-1778 | 52 | 154 | 59 | 219 | 484 |
| 1779-1792 | 168 | 129 | 57 | 189 | 543 |
| 1793-1805 | 182 | 109 | 37 | 212 | 540 |
| 1806-1815 | 191 | 108 | 71 | 231 | 601 |

*Table II[2]*

OCCUPATIONAL DISTRIBUTION OF BOWDOIN GRADUATES:
1806-1835

| Years | Lawyers | Ministers | Doctors | Merchants | Others[3] | Total |
|---|---|---|---|---|---|---|
| 1806-1815 | 40 | 11 | 4 | 8 | 12 | 75 |
| 1816-1825 | 85 | 32 | 27 | 8 | 31 | 183 |
| 1826-1835 | 89 | 62 | 29 | 7 | 61 | 248 |

1. Franklin B. Dexter, *Biographical Sketches of the Graduates of Yale College* I-773, II-773, III-715, IV-810, VI-836 (1885-1919).

2. H. Hall, *General Catalogue of Bowdoin College and the Medical School of Maine 1794-1912* 55-96 (1912).

3. Includes teachers, editors, farmers, and manufacturers.

that will be published in a forthcoming article entitled, "Professions as a Means of Mobility in Massachusetts, 1740-1840."

28. Willard Phillips to Edmund Story, Jan. 24, 1811 in Willard Phillips

*Table III*

## OCCUPATIONAL DISTRIBUTION OF BROWN AND DARTMOUTH STUDENTS[1]

| Year | Ministers | Doctors | Lawyers | Farmers | Commerce | Others | Total |
|------|-----------|---------|---------|---------|----------|--------|-------|
| 1770[2]B | 4 | 1 | 3 | 0 | 0 | 3 | 11 |
| 1780 B | 17 | 9 | 4 | 1 | 2 | 16 | 49 |
| D | 48 | 4 | 5 | 12 | 5 | 20 | 94 |
| 1790 B | 20 | 8 | 19 | 2 | 10 | 27 | 86 |
| D | 83 | 9 | 38 | 7 | 16 | 27 | 180 |
| 1800 B | 49 | 21 | 53 | 3 | 14 | 56 | 196 |
| D | 95 | 31 | 137 | 8 | 22 | 56 | 348 |
| 1810 B | 56 | 26 | 78 | 6 | 11 | 73 | 250 |
| D | 69 | 39 | 173 | 0 | 6 | 48 | 335 |
| 1820 B | 72 | 26 | 83 | 4 | 12 | 77 | 274 |
| D | 116 | 37 | 138 | 0 | 6 | 37 | 334 |
| 1830 B | 95 | 48 | 85 | 4 | 16 | 57 | 305 |
| D | 134 | 34 | 114 | 0 | 4 | 49 | 335 |
| 1835 B | 35 | 12 | 24 | 3 | 9 | 22 | 105 |
| D | 60 | 15 | 57 | 1 | 9 | 25 | 167 |
| TOTALS | | | | | | | |
| To 1800 | | | | | | | |
| B | 90 | 39 | 79 | 6 | 26 | 102 | 342 |
| Percent | 26.3 | 11.4 | 23.1 | 1.7 | 7.9 | 29.6 | 100 |
| D | 206 | 44 | 180 | 27 | 43 | 103 | 603 |
| Percent | 34.2 | 7.3 | 29.9 | 4.5 | 7.1 | 17.0 | 100 |
| 1800-1835 | | | | | | | |
| B | 258 | 112 | 270 | 17 | 48 | 239 | 944 |
| Percent | 27.3 | 11.8 | 28.6 | 1.8 | 5.1 | 25.3 | 100 |
| D | 399 | 125 | 482 | 1 | 31 | 59 | 1097 |
| Percent | 36.4 | 11.4 | 43.9 | 0.1 | 2.8 | 5.4 | 100 |

---

1. George T. Chapman, *Sketches of the Alumni of Dartmouth College from 1771* . . . 13-281 (1867). Mary D. Vaughan, *Historical Catalogue of Brown University, 1764-1904*, 67-169 (1905).

2. Brown is signified by B and Dartmouth is signified by D; Brown graduated a class in 1769 but did not graduate a class 1778-1781; Dartmouth's first graduating class was 1771 but did not miss any years because of the war.

---

Papers, 1803-1811, MHi; Memorandum in Lawyers Ledger, 1823-1833, of Sumner Bastow and Ira M. Barton, MWA; Essex County Bar Association, *Rules . . . 1819*, 16 as agreed to November Term, 1814.

Other law students felt that they were merely fulfilling a residence requirement and not acquiring an education. Joseph G. Kendall, who later became a congressman and the Worcester County clerk of courts, wrote to Phillips that he was thoroughly unhappy with his situation in the Leominster office of Abijah Bigelow because of the non-literary atmosphere of the town and the absence of Bigelow in Washington. "I am not so much in love with law," Kendall complained, "that I am willing to spend 12 hours a day in reading it." Other students, such as Benjamin Brown of Kennebunk, hoped to avoid a law office altogether. At least he proposed that plan to Congressman George Thatcher with the proviso that "there would be no doubt of my being admitted by the Gentlemen of the Bar after Studying the usuall time and making the usual proficiency."[29]

A law school in Litchfield, Connecticut, grew as an alternative to a full term of apprenticeship in Massachusetts. Despite discouraging regulations of the Massachusetts courts and bar associations, a growing number of students flocked to the Connecticut law school until the depressing aftermath of the War of 1812 shut off the flow. Ninety-four lawyers from Massachusetts attended the law school in the years 1798-1833 and comprised about one-ninth of the 805 students. Attendance from Massachusetts peaked at 11 in 1812; there were nine students in 1813, eight in 1814, and only one in 1815.[30] Samuel Fischer offered the students' view of why the school had become a favorite of legal aspirants in the early nineteenth century. "With respect to the law school here, I have the satisfaction of being able to assure you that it answers my expectations fully." Fischer continued, that "The lectures by Judge Reeve, and his associate Mr. Gould are highly valuable, & afford important assistance to a student. . . ." "Generally speaking the advantages here for the study of law are certainly favorable," he added. "I have no doubt much better for at least the first half of the time usually spent in the study before pretending to practice, than the best private office in New England," Fischer stated.[31] Returning law school graduates provided support for those lawyers and laymen who were advocating the founding of a similar system of instruction in the Bay state.

---

29. Joseph G. Kendall to Willard Phillips, Feb. 10, 1811 in Willard Phillips Papers, 1803-1811, MHi.

30. Dwight C. Kilbourn, *The Bench and Bar of Litchfield County, Connecticut 1709-1909 . . . History and Catalogue of the Litchfield Law School . . . .* 195-214 (1909).

31. Samuel Fischer to Willard Phillips, Feb. 3, 1811 in Willard Phillips Papers, 1803-1811, MHi; see also Joseph Willard To Theodora Willard, Oct. 12, 1819 in Susan Willard, ed., "Letters of Rev. Joseph Willard," 11 *Cambridge Historical Soc., Proceedings* 21 (1916).

A number of factors bolstered their efforts. Dissatisfaction with the apprenticeship system joined with the increasing complexity of commercial and civil law to demand a more analytical approach to law. A scarcity of lawyers for the newly emerging industrial society called for the training of more attorneys than the old system produced. A new view of law—a concept of law as a science—began to bring these variant factors together and suggested that a lecture-oriented law school might be the best approach for Massachusetts legal education. The decision of the Harvard Corporation in 1817 to establish a law school came in the midst of this atmosphere.[32]

Vocal support for the new law school came from leading lawyers, law school graduates, and those attorneys who believed law should be systematized. To them the scientific study of jurisprudence was "the consideration of its origin and purposes of this particular laws philosophically and historically, so as to determine whether any case is within the scope of its authority, and if not, to be able to form a new rule by the same process and from the same elements from which, by the theory of the functions of society, all laws must necessarily have originated." The fulfillment of this objective required a more complex educational system than a law office. As law professor Asahel Stearns said: "It was thought that the time had arrived, when the demands of the public for the means of thorough and methodical education of all engaged in the study of liberal professions, should be complied." Especially, argued Stearns, was this important for "those who are to administer the laws defend the rights of their fellow citizens, and become in no inconsiderable degree the directors of public opinion, and the guardians of the public liberty and welfare."[33] Law would have to join the general movement of educational reform—high school and commercial schools would replace business clerkship, and law schools would replace law apprenticeship.

Leading proponents of law as a science and a fit subject for the university included some of the leading lawyers in the state. Both Joseph Story, a justice of the United States Supreme Court and later a law professor at Harvard, and Theron Metcalf, founder of an office law school and a noted legal scholar, believed that the science of law could best be understood in the forum of a law school.[34] Story summarized the choice between a law school and

---

32. The details of Harvard Law School, which are too intricate for explanation here, can best be found in 1 Warren, *op cit. supra* note 1; or the more recent work of Sutherland, *op. cit. supra* note 1, at pp. 1-139.

33. Anonymous, "Origins of Customary Law," 7 *Am. Jurist and Law Mag.* 33 (1830); Asahel Stearns, Report to the Corporation, 1825 in 1 Warren, *op. cit. supra* note 1, 304.

34. Theron Metcalf, "Notice of James Kent's Commentaries on Amer-

the traditional method in an article for the *North American Review* in 1817. Reviewing David Hoffman's *A Course of Legal Study Addressed to Students of Law in the United States*, Story argued that this work would demonstrate the necessity of the law school at Harvard. "No work can sooner dissipate the common delusion, that the law may be thoroughly acquired in the immethodical, interrupted and desultory studies of the office of a practicing counsellor," he said.[35] A complete commitment to a law school education remained rare.

Many lawyers, including some supporters of the law school idea, maintained an ambivalent attitude toward the Harvard Law School for many years. The belief remained among attorneys that at least a year of study in the office of a counsellor beyond attendance at a law school was still needed to acquire the practical knowledge of an attorney. Isaac Parker, the first Royall Professor of Law at Harvard, even expressed such a view at his inauguration in 1816. Parker, who also served as Chief Justice of the Massachusetts Supreme Court, endorsed the establishment of a law school with this qualification: "one or two years devoted to *study only*, under a capable instructor, before they shall enter into the office of a counsellor, to obtain a knowledge of practice, will tend greatly to improve the character of the bar of our state." Story recommended studying one year out of the three-year term required by the bar association at a law school.[36]

Just as lawyers affected the development of law schools, the establishment of Harvard Law School had a subtle but important effect on the lawyers and the autonomy of the legal profession. Although lawyers would be instructors in the new law school, the precedent, and later the reality, of university control of legal education had been established. Ultimately the power of lawyers as a professional group to determine the qualifications of candidates for admission to the legal profession declined. The directors of the law school never felt constrained by the bar association regulations and immediately challenged the residency requirements. Ultimately, lawyers suffered a further loss of power to an institution

---

ican Law," 2 *U.S. Rev. and Lit. Gaz.* 81-83 (1827); Joseph Story, "Review of David Hoffman's *A Course of Legal Study . . . ,*" 6 *North Am. Rev.* 77 (1817). The same view was expressed in Isaac Parker, "Inaugural Address Delivered in the Chapel of Harvard University . . . ," 3 *North Am. Rev.* 15-19 (1816).

35. Story, *op. cit. supra* note 34 at p. 77.

36. Parker, *op. cit. supra* note 34 at p. 25; Story, *op. cit. supra* note 34 at p. 77. Asahel Stearns, Harvard Law Professor, recommended the same course of action to Ira Barton in a letter, Feb. 6, 1828 in Ira M. Barton Papers, II, MWA.

beyond their control, but for twenty years the question of who and what institution would control legal education remained very much unanswered.

Requirements for admission and for the granting of the degree of bachelor of laws fully reflected the rules of the Massachusetts Supreme Court and the regulations of county bar associations. Only an eighteen-month course was planned, similar to that of the Litchfield Law School. Sufficient time remained within the normal three-year clerkship for an office stint. Students who spent at least eighteen months at the university school and who then passed the remainder of their three-year or five-year term of study in the office of a counsellor of the Supreme Court of Massachusetts received a bachelor of laws degree. If students had graduated from college, they could spend three years at the law school; and if non-graduates, they could attend law school for five years and receive the same degree, provided that the professor continued to be a practitioner in the Supreme Court. At first, the college restricted entrance to graduates of a college or students who had studied five years in the office of a counsellor. Admission standards, however, shifted in 1829 to allow the admittance of any student producing a recommendation of good moral character and a statement of his education. As a further incentive, tuition fees remained at $100 per year, less than the average fee required by bar associations for practicing counsellors.[37] Even though college officials shaped the structure of the law school to fit many of the traditional regulations of the legal profession, this challenge to apprenticeship and local control of education aroused many lawyers.

Lawyers of Suffolk County in 1819 specifically excluded graduates of the school from admission to the county court unless they had spent the last year of their term of study in the office of a counsellor in Suffolk County. The professor of law at Harvard Law School was considered to be just another counsellor in the Supreme Judicial Court of the state and a resident of Middlesex County. His students received no preferential treatment. Lawyers in Essex County adopted the same rule in 1819. Lawyers in other counties, not so directly affected, gradually excused Harvard Law School graduates from this residency requirement, but those of Suffolk County, which contained the largest port, the state capitol and the greatest number of lawyers remained opposed.[38] Obstructionist

37. *Boston Daily Advertiser*, July 28, 1817; Sutherland, *op. cit. supra* note 1 at pp. 54, 57, 123-124; Harvard College Catalogue, 1825-1839; Essex County Bar Association, *Rules . . . 1806*, 9; Suffolk County Bar Association, *Rules . . . 1805*, 8; Worcester County Bar Association, *Rules . . . 1816*, 5; William Lincoln Notes, Sept. 17, 1827 in Lincoln Papers, MWA.

38. Suffolk County Bar Association, *Rules . . . 1819*, 18; Essex County

tactics of the Suffolk lawyers could not by themselves deter law school proponents.

Once Harvard College had taken the initiative and evaded the rulings of the bar associations against any counsellor having more than three clerks, several law schools, modeled on the Litchfield Law School and the New Haven Law School in Connecticut, opened in the Bay State. Judge Samuel Howe, a graduate of the Litchfield Law School, and Elijah H. Mills, his law partner, established such a law school in Northampton in 1823. With the assistance of John H. Ashmun, the school flourished with between ten and fifteen law students a year until 1829. Then Howe died, Ashmun was hired as a law professor by Harvard, and the office school dissolved.[39]

The influence that the concept of law as a science had on legal education and the establishment of law schools is revealed, in part, by the emphasis on science in efforts of the Northampton Law School to attract students. *The Hampshire Gazette* in mid-1823 carried a notice that boosted the law school. The advertisement concluded that "considering the progress which has been made in modern times in the science of jurisprudence, and the varied attainments necessary for distinction at the bar, the advantages of a regular system of instruction over the desultory course usually pursued, must be obvious to all who have turned their attention to the subject."[40]

Howe and Mills delivered three one-hour lectures per week in a plan of study that included recitations three times a week and a discussion on current cases once a week. One observer conluded that such a course "combines every advantage which can arise from a term of study in the office of a counsellor, with all those of an academic institution." Theron Metcalf, a Dedham counsellor, argued that the emergence of private law schools and university law professorships would be great aids to young men in understanding the more intricate laws of the United States. He felt con-

---

Bar Association, *Rules . . . 1819*, 11; Joseph Story to Suffolk Law Association, 1830 in Warren, *op. cit. supra* note 1, v. 2, p. 181.

39. *The Hampshire Gazette* (Northampton), July 2, 1823, June 17, Sept. 9, 1829; Lawrence E. Wikander *et al.*, eds. *The Northampton Book . . . 1654-1954* 290 (1954); 2 Chroust, *op. cit. supra* note 3, 217-218; William Lincoln, *History of Worcester . . . 211* (1862); Joel Parker, *The Law School at Harvard College* 10-11, 13 (1871); Sutherland, *op. cit. supra* note 1 at p. 99.

40. *The Hampshire Gazette*, July 2, 1823. The emphasis on a systematic course of study can be seen in the lectures of Howe published in 1834 as: Samuel Howe, *The Practice on Civil Actions and Proceedings at Law in Massachusetts* (1834).

fident that the law schools, such as at Northampton, would produce a more erudite bar.[41] Advocates of classroom instruction as a substitute for experience began to gain ground. A surge of institutional activity appeared with their optimism.

The success of the Northampton Law School and the Harvard Law School encouraged three other Massachusetts counsellors to establish private law schools. The efforts of Samuel Burnside in Worcester and Samuel F. Dickinson in Amherst never survived the openings in 1828. Theron Metcalf, a graduate of Litchfield Law School, managed to establish a law school in Dedham in 1828, but it survived less than two years.[42]

The failure of these law schools must be attributed, at least in part, to the predicament of the students who attended them rather than to competition from Harvard Law School or the Connecticut schools. Harvard Law, for example, had declined to two students in 1829, while Litchfield had but one in 1828 and none in 1827, 1829, and 1830. Rather their downfall stemmed, in part, from the problems of students who attended these law schools. In Connecticut, a college graduate could be admitted to the bar after only two years of study, the length of the course of study at a law school. But in Massachusetts, students found themselves trapped by the requirements of the bar associations and the Supreme Judicial Court, which called for a minimum of three years of study for college graduates and five years for non-college graduates. This meant that a law student would have to eventually study for at least one year in the office of a counsellor, because the courses of study at the law schools ran for two years or less. Where a candidate for the bar could be admitted after only two years of study, as in Kentucky and Connecticut, the law schools generally flourished. In Massachusetts both lawyers and students found it more convenient to enter an office for a full term rather than one year, thus making it potentially difficult for law school graduates to find a proper office apprenticeship for one year. Some county bar associations, moreover, required that before a candidate could be recommended for admission he must have studied the last year in the county in which he sought admission.[43] Therefore, even if a student studied the full three-year

41. "The Law School at Northampton," 1 *N.Y. Rev. and Atheneum* 322-324 (1825); Metcalf, *op. cit. supra* note 34 at pp. 81-83.

42. Peter C. Bacon to Ira M. Barton, Mar. 19, 1828 in Ira M. Barton Papers, I, MWA; "Prospectus of Samuel F. Dickinson's Law School," 2 *Am. Jurist and Law Mag.* 192-193 (1829); Reed, *op. cit. supra* note 3 at p. 431; 2 Chroust, *op. cit. supra* note 3, pp. 219-220; "Metcalf's Law School at Dedham," 1 *Am. Jurist and Law Mag.* 378-380 (1829); Anonymous, "The Litchfield Law School," 20 *Albany Law Jour.* 73 (1879).

43. Sutherland, *op. cit. supra* note 1 at p. 79; Frederick C. Hicks, *Yale*

term in Northampton, for example, he could not be readily admitted to practice in Suffolk County. These attempts at maintaining educational standards and restricting competition through local and court regulations undoubtedly contributed to the collapse of the weaker law schools.

Experience had not yet yielded to books and lectures as the best means of training, and many lawyers and law students simply preferred the apprenticeship system over law schools. Such was the view expressed by William Lincoln, son of a wealthy and influential Worcester counsellor. In a letter to a friend, Christopher Baldwin, while both were students, Lincoln outlined the advantanges of an office apprenticeship in these words. "If you would root out elementary principles," he said, "there are the researches of legal sages and the long series of reporters." On the other hand he added, "if you would attend to the practical details of business, there are the inquiring clients and the responding counsellors."[44] To prospective lawyers like Lincoln, the new law schools were just not attractive enough to outweigh the uncertainty of innovation.

Another factor in the law schools' limited drawing power might have been the course of study. Although lectures provided students with a systematic analysis of some phases of the law, much of the learning process did not differ very much from the studies of the average apprentice. At Dedham, Metcalf insisted that he would stress only the elementary principles of the law. The lectures of Howe at Northampton and Asahel Stearns at Harvard stressed the practical rather than the broad scientific aspects of the law. Both schools relied heavily on Blackstone, Littleton, Coke, Sugden, and Saunders—all standard English authorities.[45] Stearns' comment in 1826 on the use of Blackstone reflects the conservatism of the course of study at that time. Stearns first assigned the student a reading of the whole of Blackstone, which "aids the student in fixing his attention, enables him more readily to acquaintance with the technical terms and language of the law, and at the same time to obtain a more distant view of that admiral outline of the science."[46]

---

*Law School* 2-3, 20-21 (1936); Kilbourn, *op. cit. supra* note 30 at pp. 195-214; Reed, *op. cit. supra* note 3 at pp. 83-84, 450.

44. William Lincoln to Christopher Baldwin, June 1, 1823, in William Lincoln Papers, Letters, MWA.

45. Reading lists of Harvard Law School students in 1 Warren, *op. cit. supra* note 1 at pp. 333-334, 355-356; Howe, *op. cit. supra* note 40; "Metcalf's Law School at Dedham," *op. cit. supra* note 42 at pp. 378-380; Harvard College Catalogues, 1829-30; Asahel Stearns to the Board of Overseers, Jan. 9, 1826 in Warren, *op. cit. supra* note 1, v. 1, p. 334; Joseph Story to John H. Ashmun, May 14, 17, Dec. 2, 1831, Story Papers, MHi.

46. Asahel Stearns to Board of Overseers, 1826 in Warren, *op. cit. supra* note 1, v. 1, p. 333.

48          THE AMERICAN JOURNAL OF LEGAL HISTORY     Vol. XVII

Harvard, like Northampton Law School, did offer students moot courts, debating clubs, regular examinations and written disputations. Yet the law schools did not appear to offer enough advantages over apprenticeship to warrant substituting themselves for the latter.

Harvard Law School's revival can be traced to the passage of the Revised Statutes in 1835. One section of these laws transferred control over attorneys' admissions from the bar associations and courts to the state. Candidates for the legal profession who had studied law less than three years could be admitted to the practice of law after an examination by a member of the judiciary. Students who had studied law less than three years could be admitted to the practice of law after an examination by a member of the judiciary. Students who had studied three years regardless of prior education or manner of law study automatically were admitted to law practice upon application.[47] This law allowed students who had completed the eighteen-month course at Harvard Law School to be admitted directly to practice in any court in the state after an examination.

Leading historians of Harvard Law School, Warren and Sutherland, attribute major credit for the temporary revival of Harvard Law School to the methods and reputations of Professors Joseph Story and John Ashmun. In fact, just three years after their appointment as Harvard law professors, Story expressed his surprise to Ashmun at the decline of students at Harvard Law and the hope that a new revision of the courses and the introduction of moot courts would attract more students.[48] Additional evidence indicates that the effects of the 1835 law on the fortunes of the law school were, perhaps, decisive.

Passage of the Revised Statutes as applied to attorneys affected both the geographic areas from which students were drawn and the quality of the students' prior education. In 1836 there were twenty-three students from Massachusetts and Maine at the law school, all of whom had a college education. In 1838, only two years after the law went into effect, there were forty-one law students from the same area, an increase of seventy-eight percent. Five of the latter lacked college degrees, compared to none in 1836. At the same time the total enrollment of the school increased fifty-six percent and the number of students from outside Massachusetts and Maine increased from twenty-nine to thirty-seven students, a rise of twenty-

---

47. The many reasons for the state's assumption of control of the educational standards of the legal profession and its concurrent lowering of standards are treated in Gawalt, *op. cit. supra* note 9 at pp. 91-128.

48. Warren, *op. cit. supra* note 14 at p. 365; Sutherland, *op. cit. supra* note 1, pp. 92-139; Joseph Story to John H. Ashmun, Jan. 19, 1832, Story Papers, 1808-1845, MHi.

seven percent.[49] As a result, Harvard Law School became more provincially oriented, but its program had gained support in its home state.

Significant changes, particularly quantitative, occurred in the degree-granting program. The number of degrees awarded increased from thirty-six in 1836 to sixty-eight in 1838. While Harvard granted only twenty degrees to non-college graduates between 1820 and 1837, seventeen law degrees went to candidates without a college education in the two years, 1838 and 1839, alone. Harvard Corporation formally recognized the end of the three-year term of study in 1839 by authorizing the degree of bachelor of laws for a person who completed only eighteen months of study or one year of study if the student had already been admitted to the practice of law. By 1845 the number of law students at Harvard had increased to 145, and the permanence of a systematic course of instruction at a Massachusetts law school was assured.[50]

Added impetus for law school education came from the destruction of the county bar associations' control over entrance into the legal profession.[51] After 1836 law students could no longer be refused admittance to practice in a county because they had not studied at least one year within its geographic confines. This freed the law school student of the need to seek a one-year apprenticeship in the county in which he wanted to practice, making education at a law school more attractive. Because candidates no longer needed the approval of the bar associations, they did not even have to clerk with a lawyer but could study alone. Legal knowledge demonstrated to a state judge would guarantee admission to law practice.

Advocates of the classroom over the counsellor's office were well on their way to downgrading the value of apprenticeship as a means of training lawyers. Writing to a friend in 1832, Joseph Story voiced the position of law school supporters. "In America it requires no argument to establish the importance nay necessity of a systematical and scientific study of the law," he observed. "No lawyer in this country would, in the present time, deem his education at all complete without availing himself of the lectures of some Law Insti-

---

49. Both Maine and Massachusetts are used because many law students from Maine settled in Massachusetts. Harvard College Catalogues, 1836, 1838; *Harvard University: Quinquenial Catalogue of the Officers and Graduates: 1636-1925* 813-15 (1925); Parker, *op. cit. supra* note 3 at p. 14; 2 Warren *op. cit. supra* note 1, p. 91.

50. Harvard College Catalogues, 1836-1845; Harvard University, *op. cit. supra* note 49 at pp. 813-816.

51. *Rev. Stat. Mass.* (1836), c. 88, pp. 541-542.

tution."[52] His statement had come prematurely, but within a few years his views were fact.

With Harvard Law School firmly established, the study of law through formal courses of instruction became the accepted pattern of legal education in Massachusetts. The apprenticeship system did not die immediately, but it was gradually replaced. The idea that experience in a law office could prepare a student for his profession was the creation of the bar association. Both apprenticeship and the power of the bar associations waxed together; the two also fell into disrepute together.

---

52. Joseph Story to James Wilkinson, August 25, 1832 in 2 Story, *op. cit. supra* note 24 at p. 108.

# 22
## FRONTIER JUSTICE: WAYNE COUNTY 1796-1836

*ELIZABETH GASPAR BROWN*

# Frontier Justice: Wayne County 1796-1836

by ELIZABETH GASPAR BROWN*

## INTRODUCTION

. . . they had obtained their information exclusively
from books, and never from actual observation. If they wanted
to lecture on the sturgeon or on caterpillars, they read the
Old and New Testaments and Aristotle, and told their students
everything these good books had to say upon the subject of
caterpillars and sturgeons. They did not leave their libraries
and repair to the backyard to catch a few caterpillars and
look at these animals and study them in their native haunts.
Even such famous scholars as Albertus Magnus and Thomas
Aquinas did not inquire whether the sturgeons in the land of
Palestine and the caterpillars of Macedonia might not have
been different from the sturgeons and the caterpillars of
western Europe.[1]

According to American folklore—widely disseminated by
western movies and television—American frontier justice at all
times and in all places was a rough and ready matter, presided
over by popularly elected judges, impatient with legal niceties.
Lawyers were either inadequately trained advocates with hearts
of gold or well-trained skillful shysters. Local mores and Blackstone
were the chief sources of law. Legal practice and court procedures
were uniform from Daniel Boone's Kentucky to the Cimarron
Country of Oklahoma northward to the Dakota Badlands and
westward to the Golden Gate.

Where historians have not ignored the administration of
justice, they have tended to reinforce the myth.[2] Describing the
United States in 1830, Frederick Jackson Turner stated:

. . . men readily took the law into their own hands. A
crime was more a personal affront to the victim than an outrage upon the law of the land. Substantial justice secured in
the most direct way was . . . [this society's] aim. It had

---

* Research Associate in Law, The University of Michigan.
1. Van Loon, *The Story of Mankind* 185 (1921).
2. See, for example, the indices to two highly respected histories of
the United States: Beard, *Rise of American Civilization* (1927) and Morison, *Oxford History of the American People* (1965).

126

little patience with fine-drawn legal or constitutional distinctions, or even scruples of method. If the thing itself was proper to be done, then the most immediate, rough-and-ready, effective way was the best way.[3]

Facilitating the persistence of the myth has been the unfortunate fact that few legal historians have been willing or able to engage in the detailed research necessary to build a causeway out of the attractive mists of ignorant generalizations on to the firm ground of truth.[4] Materials for such a causeway are plentiful. Despite advertent and inadvertent destruction,[5] the county courthouses of the United States contain volume after volume and file after file of cases in the lower courts of record, dating in many cases back to the year of each particular county's founding. Access is relatively easy. But even where these records are arranged properly, reasonably clean, and located in well-lighted rooms, their effective use is incredibly demanding. An exhaustive knowledge of superseded forms of practice and procedure is an absolute prerequisite for any researcher who plans to extract information from these records antedating the introduction of code pleading. Good eyesight, incredible patience, and adequate financing are added essentials. Given these conditions, the non-use of these records is not surprising. Yet they constitute the prime if not the only source for determining how justice was administered in fact. They alone can show the manner in which judges and lawyers carried out the routine daily work of the courts, how statutory and decisional law was applied at a specific time in a particular place by a judge or bank of judges to the parties in a single case.

However understandable is the non-use of these records, the widespread non-recognition of their importance is not. There is a frequent willingness to rely on what is said to have been done and a corresponding unwillingness to discover what was done. The unfortunate consequences of this uncritical utilization of hearsay evidence have been aggravated by the erection of generalizations upon truths of limited application. If a condition did exist at one time in one place, the assumption often is made that that same

---

3. Turner, *The United States 1830-1850*, 20 (1935).

4. Like every generalization, this is subject to exceptions. In addition to the work, published and unpublished, of William Wirt Blume, see Goebel, *Law Enforcement in Colonial New York: A Study in Criminal Procedure, 1664-1776* (1944) and Goebel, ed., *The Law Practice of Alexander Hamilton: Documents and Commentary* (1964).

5. Fire, dirt, and mice have been the prime inadvertent destroyers, although on occasion custodians have prized neatness over record retention. Illustratively, see Brown, *Doty's Notes of Trials and Opinions 1823-1832*, 9 *Amer. J. Leg. Hist.* 17, 24-25 (1965).

condition existed at other times and in other places, though it may not have existed at another time in the place where it did at one time exist.[6] Roscoe Pound made this assumption in 1920. Anton-Hermann Chroust made it in 1965.[7] Largely overlooked has been Joseph Beale's 1933 observation:

> . . . The development of our legal history was not in one line but in fifty; and while in some respects there has been a similar development in different states, each state has had its own individual experiences, political, economic and social. These varied experiences have led to differences in legal history which must be separately mastered before we can understand what we are in the habit of calling "The History of American Law". . . .[8]

Stemming from this assumption has come the conclusion that, because at certain times and in certain places on the American frontier there were inadequate jurists, *ad hoc* decisions, and ill-trained lawyers, always and everywhere American frontier justice was crude and makeshift.

The general historian cannot be criticized for relying upon legal historians. But when legal historians use uncritically as prime source material nineteenth century reminiscences of bench and bar or accounts of trials written years later and printed in local historical collections, it is difficult not to suspect that the first six weeks of *Evidence I* have been conveniently overlooked. Heartbreakingly slow as it is to read through the files of cases for the Wayne County Court of Common Pleas commencing in 1796 or the records of the Supreme Court of the Territory of Michigan commencing in 1805, there is no other reliable method for determining what happened in those particular courts in those particular years.

This study deals with what did happen. What business came before certain courts in a certain territory within a certain time span under the jurisdiction conferred upon those particular courts. How that business was transacted within an existing frame of reference.[9] What were the sources of law used by the men presiding over and practicing in those courts.

---

6. For an admirable discussion of the consequences of this fallacious assumption, see Goebel, "Introduction," *Law Enforcement in Colonial New York: A Study in Criminal Procedure 1664-1776*, xvii (1944).

7. Pound, "The Pioneers and the Common Law," 27 *W. Va. L. Q.* 1 (1920); Chroust, "The Legal Profession on the Frontier," *Rise of the Legal Profession in America* v. 2, p. 92 (1965).

8. Beale, *The Study of American Legal History*, 39 *W. Va. L. Q.* 95 (1933).

9. For a discussion of the conditions under which men were admit-

## I. The Framework for the Administration of Justice

The Ordinance, enacted by the Continental Congress in 1787 for the "Territory of the United States northwest of the river Ohio," extended sovereignty over wide areas of land in fact occupied by the British. Not until the proclamation of Jay's Treaty in 1796 did Great Britain relinquish her forts at Detroit and Michilimackinac. In the intervening years between 1787 and 1796, however, the provisions of the Ordinance were being implemented in those portions of the territory which the Americans did control. Consequently, when civil authority was extended into the newly-relinquished area, its form already was shaped.

The Contental Congress had not given its "Territory northwest of the river Ohio" leave to experiment or improvise. Rather, the Ordinance specified the appointment of a governor and three judges who were to exercise the legislative power but *only* to the extent of adopting "such laws of the original states criminal and civil as may be necessary and best suited to the circumstances of the district." The same three judges were to constitute a court which, stated the Ordinance, was to have "a common law jurisdiction"[10] with the inhabitants "entitled to the benefits . . . of judicial proceedings according to the course of the common law."[11]

The single general court provided by the Ordinance was supplemented by the courts created under statutes "adopted" by the governor and judges in August 1788. Each county was to have separate courts for Common Pleas, Quarter Sessions of the Peace,[12] and Probate,[13] with the jurisdiction for each set out precisely.

Only three days after the proclamation of August 15, 1796,[14]

---

ted to the practice of law and their professional qualifications, see Brown, "The Bar on a Frontier: Wayne County 1796-1836," 14 *Amer. J. Leg. Hist.* 136 (1970).

10. The "adoption of laws" by the governor and judges in the Northwest, Indiana, and Michigan territories between 1788 and 1823 is discussed by Blume, "Legislation on the American Frontier," 60 *Mich. L. Rev.* 317 (1962).

11. The Northwest Ordinance, §4 provided for a general court. No appeal or writ of error from this court was authorized. *Clarke v. Bazadone,* 1 Cranch (5 U.S. 212) (1803).

12. *Laws of the Territory Northwest of the River Ohio 1787-1802,* 295 (1933).

13. Pease, ed., *Laws of the Northwest Territory 1788-1800,* 9 (1925).

14. "Proclamation Organizing Wayne County," Carter, ed., *Territorial Papers of the United States: The Territory Northwest of the River Ohio, 1787-1803,* v. 2, p. 567 (1934).

extending civil authority to Wayne County—then, like the rest of the Northwest Territory, lying well beyond the frontier line[15]— Acting Governor Winthrop Sargent proceeded to the implementation of the 1788 territorial statutes. He established the Wayne County Court of Quarter Sessions on August 18, 1796, and the Wayne County Court of Common Pleas on September 29.[16] The latter held at Detroit its first session in December of that same year.

Theoretically, appeal lay from a decision of the Wayne County Court of Common Pleas to the General Court for the entire territory, but difficulties of time and place constituted effective deterrents. As a practical matter, from 1796 to 1805 the Wayne County Court of Common Pleas was the court of last resort for the great majority of all civil cases within its jurisdiction.

With the organization of Michigan Territory in 1805,[17] the existing court organization ceased to function and a new system came into being, headed by the Supreme Court of the Territory of Michigan. While a number of lower court systems was in effect during the Michigan territorial period,[18] the Supreme Court continued to function as the apex from 1805 to 1836. Thus in fact the Wayne County Court of Common Pleas and the territorial Supreme Court exercised final jurisdiction for a forty-year period within the area of Wayne County. During these four decades, whatever the changes in territorial government, Detroit remained the county seat of Wayne County and the only place of sitting for these two courts. Further, Detroit was the territorial capital of Michigan.

The records of these two "apex" courts have survived in remarkable numbers. Over 1100 case-files of the Wayne County Court of Common Pleas exist.[19] The Calendar of Cases for the

---

15. Inhabited Area in United States in 1790, Bureau of the Census, *A Century of Population Growth: 1790-1900*, 18 (1909).

16. "Judicial Organization of Wayne County," Carter, ed., *op. cit.* note 14 *supra* at 568. For a discussion of the personnel appointed to these two courts see Bald, *Detroit's First American Decade 1796 to 1805*, p. 55-58 (1948).

17. "An Act for the division of Indiana Territory," approved January 11, 1805. 2 *Stat.* 309-310.

18. The organization of lower courts in Michigan Territory was changed on several occasions. A series of diagrams showing the several courts in the territory, account being taken of all the changes, appears in Blume, *Transactions of the Supreme Court of the Territory of Michigan* [hereinafter cited as *Transactions*] *1805-1814*, I:9-13 (1935), *id. 1814-1824*, I:3-7 (1938), *id. 1825-1836*, I:3-8 (1940).

19. The files of the Wayne County Court of Common Pleas survived the devastating Detroit fire of 1805. Persistent legend credits Peter Audrain with their rescue, alleging that he dragged them to the Common and

territorial Supreme Court lists over 1500 cases, excluding three supplementary calendars with over 500 cases. From the records of these 300-odd cases, it is possible to draw fact-based conclusions pertaining to the courts and their business for the years of their existence.

During the forty years of those two courts' existence, marked changes took place in Wayne County, not limited to the shifts in territorial organization. Population increased and changed its composition. The number of Indians and soldiers seen on the Detroit streets decreased but the mud was as sticky and dust as thick as ever. Commercial enterprise came more and more into American hands, though accounts were figured impartially in dollars and shillings. Trading with Indians remained lucrative enough for respectable citizens to make a considerable effort to smuggle in "trade goods," as well as whiskey, cider, assorted yard goods, and several cows. Plaintiffs ceased to be identified as "soldier," "carpenter," "yeoman," or "merchant," but Judge Woodward wrote his opinions on a bale of straw to preserve body heat. Perched on the Detroit River, its back to the wilderness or to farms recently wrested from that wilderness, Detroit, until its last decade of territorial existence, was an outpost of the frontier. It was at no time the settled east. If the assertions of legal historians pertaining to the influence of the frontier upon American legal developments have uniform validity, some evidence of such influence should be reflected in the *manner* whereby these two courts conducted their business.

It is not.

This assertion does not mean that the frontier was not reflected in the *nature* of the business which came before those courts. It was. There were cases involving Indians and soldiers posted to frontier forts. A libel was brought to condemn property seized by the collector of customs, namely 550 pairs of "silver wrought Indian earbobs and four pairs silver wrought arm-bands." The change in sovereignty gave rise to actions over land titles and slave ownership. Yet the surviving records show that the procedures used by the courts and the lawyers who practiced before them were those used along the eastern seaboard.

Before looking briefly at the nature of the business which

---

watched over them. Sargent had appointed Audrain as clerk of the Court of Quarter Sessions, judge of Probate, prothonotary of the Court of Common Pleas, and recorder. Later he served as clerk of the Supreme Court of the Territory of Michigan from 1805 until a forced retirement in 1819. Probably he is responsible for preserving all existing court records during the British occupation during the War of 1812. Any user of those records in his handwriting is grateful for his clear and precise penmanship.

came before these courts and the manner in which the attorneys handled it, reference must be made to the framework within which each court operated.

The enactment by the Continental Congress of the Ordinance for the "Territory of the United States northwest of the river Ohio" established the fundamental law for that area. Subsequently the Congress of the United States adapted the Ordinance to the United States Constitution.[20] The law in force in the Northwest Territory was bottomed on these two documents. Also Congress enacted statutes pertaining to territories, sometimes applicable to only one, sometimes to all.[21] Predictably, the grant of the legislative power by Congress to the several territories produced the enactment of territorial statutes. The body of law, which the courts of any given territory were bound to apply, grew.[22]

In 1795 the Northwest Territory governor and judges, previously employing the statute-by-statute adoption-enactment process, enormously enlarged the framework of operations for the territorial courts by their adoption of a Virginia statute. As adopted, the new territorial statute stated:

> The common law of England, all statutes or acts of the British parliament made in aid of the common law, prior to the fourth year of the reign of King James the first (and which are of a general nature, not local to that kingdom) and also the several laws in force in this Territory, shall be the rule of decision, and shall be considered, as of full force, until repealed by legislative authority, or disapproved of by Congress.[23]

Under this statute, when the Wayne County Court of Common Pleas commenced to function in 1796, the judges—required by territorial statute to exercise their jurisdiction "according to the

---

20. "An Act to provide for the Government of the Territory Northwest of the river Ohio," approved August 7, 1789. 1 *Stat.* 50.

21. See Farrand, *Legislation of Congress for the Government of the Organized Territory of the United States: 1789-1895*, 57 (1896). See also Brown, "Acts of Congress Relating to the Government of the Territories of the United States, Organized and Unorganized, 1789-1955," Blume & Brown, *Digests and Lists Pertaining to the Development of Law and Legal Institutions in the Territories of the United States: 1787-1954* (6 vols. in 3, 1960).

22. For the laws declared to be in force, as distinct from specific enactments, see Brown, "Laws in Force of the Territories of the United States 1787-1912. Part II. Territorial Provisions," Blume & Brown, *op. cit. supra*, note 21.

23. Pease, ed., *op. cit. supra*, note 13, p. 253.

constitution and laws of this terrotory"[24]—possessed as such "constitution and laws," in addition to the Northwest Ordinance, the acts of Congress applicable to the territory, and the specifically adopted territorial enactments, the common law of England and the English statutes prior to 1607. Like all other judges in the Northwest Territory, these Wayne County judges were not given any freedom to improvise or follow their own notions of justice.

Beyond these specific statements of the laws in force, the territorial judges had further constraints. By Ordinance and territorial statute, the business of the Court of Common Pleas—the civil cases of the locality—was to be conducted in accordance with long-standing rules of practice and procedure.

The Northwest Ordinance gave the judges of the general court a "common law jurisdiction." In 1792 the governor and judges adopted *inter alia* two statutes, one prescribing the forms of writs in civil cases and the other setting out a detailed schedule of fees applicable to actions in the several courts.[25] Other statutes, taken in conjunction with the foregoing, make it clear that the legislators intended to continue the use of the English forms of action.[26] The files of papers for the 1100-odd surviving cases from the Wayne County Court of Common Pleas revealing as they do "a striking familiarity with the common law practice," with the

---

24. "A Law for establishing . . . County Courts of Common Pleas . . . ," published August 23, 1788, Pease, ed., *op. cit. supra*, note 13, p. 4, 7.

25. Pease, ed., *op. cit. supra*, note 13, p. 93, 102.

26. Note the following extract from Blume, "Civil Procedure on the American Frontier," 56 *Mich. L. Rev.* 161 at 181-182 (1957):

"Although . . . 'original writs' of the type used by the English Chancery were not in use in the Northwest Territory, the practice of classifying actions as they were classified under the old system of writs was regularly employed. In the statutes of the Territory provisions will be found regulating to some extent actions of:

| | | |
|---|---|---|
| Account | Detinue | Trespass |
| Case | Dower | Trespass on the case |
| Covenant | Ejectment | Trover |
| Debt | Replevin | Waste |

Some statutory attention is given to assumpsit (a type of case or trespass on the case), and to trespass on the case for slander; also to common counts in assumpsit: money had and received, quantum meruit, and quantum valebant. But nowhere in the statutes do we find express authority for using or not using particular forms of action, other than replevin and dower, and no provision is found modifying the scope of the English forms."

"English common law [being] followed with unusual fidelity," show no disposition to deviate from the legislative guidelines.[27]

The Supreme Court of the Territory of Michigan showed a similar adherence to its specified frame of operations. Its jurisdiction stemmed initially from the "common law jurisdiction" conferred on the general court by the Ordinance but had been broadened by a March 3, 1805 Act of Congress[28] and by Michigan territorial statute of July 24, 1805[29] to include federal crimes, admiralty, divorce, and equity cases. The court, in exercising its conferred jurisdiction, was bound to take account of the 1787 ordinance, the United States Constitution, the Michigan organic act, and the Michigan territorial statutes. Precedents were drawn from prior judicial decisions: there was no disposition to alter the rule of *stare decisis*. Between 1805 and 1810, the framework also included the statutes of the Northwest and Indiana territories in effect in 1805.[30] This included the Northwest statute which had adopted the Virginia act declaring pre-1607 British statutes and the common law to be in force. In 1810, however, a Michigan territorial act declared that all acts of prior territories, all British statutes, and the *coutume de Paris* were without force and effect in the territory. Unmentioned was the common law of England.[31] Despite alterations in the structure of the framework, a framework existed.

The business of the territorial Supreme Court is best revealed by an examination of its unusually complete surviving records, which include 2,098 cases and "matters."[32] Setting aside the thirty-nine "matters" heard by one or more of the judges, there were 309 cases on the court's "Admiralty Side," 249 on the "Equity Side," and 1501 on the "Common Law Side." Within the "Common Law Side" category, there were 1022 "Ordinary Civil Actions at Law,"

27.  Blume, *op. cit. supra*, note 26, p. 182.
28.  "An Act to extend jurisdiction in certain cases, to the Territorial Courts," approved March 3, 1805. 2 *Stat.* 338.
29.  "An Act concerning the supreme court of the territory of Michigan, signed July 24, 1805. 1 *Laws of the Territory of Michigan* 9 (1871).
30.  It was assumed that the laws of the prior territories, Northwest and Indiana, had not continued in force in Michigan Territory, until the territorial supreme court held otherwise. *United States v. Muir*, 1806, Blume, *Transactions 1805-1814*, I:58 (1935).
31.  "An Act to repeal all acts of the Parliament of England, and of the Parliament of Great Britain, within the Territory of Michigan . . . and for other purposes," signed September 16, 1810. 1 *Laws of the Territory of Michigan* 900 (1871). This act *inter alia* declared the laws of the Indiana and Northwest territories to be without effect in Michigan.
32.  Blume edited the records of the territorial supreme court in the six volumes of the *Transactions*. See note 18.

less than ten percent of which set out a cause of action trespass *vi et armis,* about fifteen percent declared in debt and sixty-five percent in trespass on the case. Criminal matters accounted for something over ten percent of the total business coming before the court.

Reading through the journals of the territorial Supreme Court is the easiest and certainly the most vivid method of gaining an understanding of the manner in which the court conducted its daily business. The journals speak for themselves. They demonstrate that the court conducted its work "in a careful and orderly manner according to the orthodox procedures of the time."[33] Slapdash methods and short cuts were not utilized. This conclusion is reinforced by examining the papers in the files of the several cases. These documents were not produced by illiterate frontiersmen but by craft-conscious practitioners following accepted norms of common law pleading and practice. Although the following court rule was not adopted until 1819, it confirmed an existing practice. Significantly, it was not rescinded in 1821 when the great majority of court rules heretofore issued was revoked:

> ORDERED, That it be a rule of the Court; That in all cases where no particular form is prescribed, the clerk shall pursue, according to the best of his discretion, the forms used in the Courts of England, or other approved precedents; adapting the same to the circumstances of the Territory of Michigan, and to the usages and practice of this Court.[34]

## II. The Sources of Law

Granting the existence of a framework within which the judges and lawyers were bound, in theory, to operate, and given proper utilization of long-established procedural patterns, a final question remains: Did the lawyers and the judges consider themselves to be operating within the traditional framework composed of statutory enactments and of prior decisions, or did they believe themselves free to plead and adjudicate in accordance with their own concepts of right and wrong? Was there reliance upon legal authorities or did lawyers and judges alike prefer to ignore precedent and to rely upon their own appraisals of the merits?

Two prime pieces of evidence exist which show that the law which filled the earthen vessels of procedure was drawn from the Ordinance, the Constitution, the common law, statutes in force, and precedents. There is no indication that the law, so drawn, was diluted by abstract conceptions.

---

33. *Transactions 1805-1814,* v. 1, p. liv (1935).
34. *Transactions 1814-1824,* v. 1, p. 207 (1938).

The first evidence lies in the use made of legal authorities by lawyers and judges alike in their briefs, memoranda, and opinions. The second lies in the number and variety of law books known to have been physically present in the territory.

Even a cursory examination of the existing records shows how lavishly legal citations were used by attorneys and jurists. The sheer bulk of their references to legal authorities deterred preparation of a definitive list on the ground of the time which would be required. Citation, however extensive, nevertheless in itself suggests only an awareness on the part of the citing individual that precedent was important and that there was a need to rely upon it. Mere reference to a particular source *could* mean little more than that a particular judge or attorney possessed one or more of the compendiums or digests so popular at that period. But where citation is coupled with unimpeachable evidence of the existence in the territory of specific law books, it becomes difficult to overcome the conclusion that men of the law in the Territory of Michigan not only *cited* law books but that they *used* and *relied* upon law books as customary and indispensable tools in their daily work.[35]

Illustrative of an attorney's use of legal authorities is a memorandum, prepared by Solomon Sibley for his own use as an outline for oral argument in an action in debt commenced in 1808. Ten cases and three secondary authorities—all English—were cited.[36] Solomon Sibley was an American by birth, yet in 1808 he relied entirely upon non-American authorities. About twenty years later, the briefs filed by opposing counsel in a single case evidence the transition from almost total dependence on British sources to an increased use of American citations.[37] Alexander Fraser, who had received his legal training in Edinburgh before coming to the United States, filed a brief which, with the exception of two references to the laws of Michigan, relied entirely on British authorities.[38] John Leib, born before the American Revolution, had come to Michigan Territory from Philadelphia. In his brief, opposing Fraser's arguments, both British and American authorities were cited.[39] Neither brief contained the slightest indication

---

35. Citations in chancery cases in the Michigan territorial supreme court are listed in Blume, "Chancery Practice on the American Frontier," 59 *Mich. L. Rev.* 49 at 89 (1960).

36. *Pattinson v. Dodemead*, Wilkinson, Jr., and Dodemead, 1808, Blume, *Transactions 1805-1814*, v. 1, p. 118; v. 2, p. 127 (1935).

37. *Lariviere v. Campau*, Blume, *Transactions 1825-1836*, v. 1 p. 82 (1940).

38. Blume, *Transactions 1825-1836*, v. 1, p. 306.

39. Blume, *Transactions, 1825-1836*, v. 1, p. 307.

of any interest in abstract concepts. Both attorneys presented their arguments and bottomed them on precedents.

The judges likewise based their decisions on cited authority. Their opinions show no disposition to break with the past whether the case before the court was an action of trespass on the case (slander)[40] or a petition for *habeas corpus ad subjiciendum.*[41] In the latter case, Chief Judge James Witherell discussed the issuance of a *capias ad satisfaciendum* on a judgment in a civil case, taking account of the "Ancient common Law of England" as modified by the "Statute of Edward the 3rd" and the existing territorial statutes. An opinion in the handwriting of Judge Solomon Sibley, filed in an action of trespass on the case (trover) commenced in 1827, discusses the meaning of the term "common law" as used in the Ordinance of 1787.[42]

The totality of the documents—whether the official court records or the private papers of judges and attorneys—argues strongly for genuine reliance upon legal authorities. The argument is reinforced by contemporary evidence of the high value accorded law books.[43] The notebook of Solomon Sibley, then an attorney and later a judge of the territorial supreme court, shows that in either 1798 or 1799 he prepared a list of "Law Books necessary for a Practicing attorney."[44] Thirty-four separate titles with a total of eighty volumes were listed, including English reports, treatises, Grotius on "law and peace" and "Hawkins abdt of Coke's Littleton." This list does not, of course, show what books were present in the Northwest Territory. It does show what tools Solomon Sibley considered necessary for the practice of law in an area which lay well beyond the line of continuous settlement.

When to extensive citation of legal authorities and the high value placed upon legal writings is added the demonstrable physical presence of particular law books in Wayne County during the

---

40. *Labady v. Richard,* Blume, *Transactions 1814-1824,* v. 1, p. 119, 452 (1938).

41. *In the matter of Fulton,* Blume, *Transactions 1814-1824,* v. 1, p. 364, 454 (1938).

42. *Lariviere v. Campau,* Blume, *Transactions 1825-1836,* v. 1, p. 82, 309 (1940).

43. The importance accorded law books by attorneys practicing in Detroit during the territorial period is illustrated by a comment relating to George Porter, one of Detroit's prominent attorneys. When Porter first came to Detroit, he was said to have been unable to practice law "being too poor to purchase law books." Ross, *Early Bench and Bar of Detroit* 161 (1907).

44. Sibley Papers, MS pp. 179-180, Burton Historical Collection, Public Library, Detroit.

territorial period, only one conclusion seems possible: Legal precedents and legal authorities were important to and were used routinely by the territorial bench and bar.

Proof of the physical presence of specific law books in the Detroit area between 1796 and 1836 is drawn solely from contemporary sources. Inventories filed in the course of probating the estates of deceased lawyers and judges list the books owned by the decedents.[45] These lists were extremely productive. Additional titles were found in the evidence of book purchases, such as invoices,[46] in references to the presence of books in contemporary sources,[47] and in extant books containing the signature of a territorial attorney or judge.[48]

With the exception of those law books which contained the signature of an owner, the contemporary sources lacked complete bibliographical information. The original references were not prepared with any thought of century-later use. However, those same references were sufficiently explicit to enable identification of approximately ninety-eight percent of the titles located.

Lists were prepared from the several sources. The total number of references—not law *books*, as some particular treatises or reports were owned by more than one individual—is impressive. Yet the titles accumulated should *not* be equated with those law books actually in Wayne County during this period. The lists were prepared from volumes whose physical presence can be established. A contemporary inventory of the law library of either Alexander Fraser or Solomon Sibley would very probably add further titles.

---

45. The probate files for Wayne County show that prior to 1840 the inventories filed for decedents' estates were extremely detailed, containing, *inter alia*, the titles of individual books. Elijah Brush, an attorney, died in 1813. Probate File 108 includes the customary inventory with "School & other Books appertaining to the profession of the deceased" valued at $452.00. The list included 113 law books, with 50 English reports, 33 texts, 17 digests and abridgments, 11 volumes of statutes, and 2 dictionaries.

46. For an invoice for law books, signed by Elijah Brush in 1803, see the Sibley Papers, note 44.

47. In a notebook kept by Solomon Sibley, Sibley Papers, note 44, MS pp. 179-182, the attorney noted the borrowing of specified law books in 1798 and 1799. For a letter, dated at Monroe, Michigan, December 14, 1827, setting out a list of the "elementary works in ordinary use" then "in town," see Woodbridge Papers, Burton Historical Collection, note 44.

48. The University of Michigan Law Library maintains a fairly complete card file of books catalogued or recatalogued after 1927, which makes it possible to identify those books in the Library containing autographs of previous owners. The Library possesses several books owned by territorial lawyers.

The lists were broken down as follows:

Primary Sources
    Reports
    Statutory Materials

Secondary Sources
    Law Dictionaries
    Digests and Abridgments
    Treatises

The purpose of these lists was to show the sources of law, *i.e.*, the legal authorities, available in printed form to the attorneys of Wayne County during the territorial period. They were not designed as an exercise in bibliographical techniques. Each of the two primary sources—reports and statutory materials—was treated differently. The three secondary sources were treated alike. Each of these five categories is discussed separately in the following paragraphs.

*Primary Sources*

    *Reports*—Reports of cases are more significant for the years covered by the cases reported therein than for the year of publication. Hence, no attempt was made to determine the identity of the probable edition of a particular report determined to have been in the territory. For purposes of convenience, the reports are divided between the two prime categories of British and American and then subdivided by court.

    The British reports included a total of 106 volumes. Twenty-four were chancery reports, covering these years: 1667-1755, 1783-1806, 1815, 1818-1819.[49] Sixty-five were King's (Queen's) Bench reports of these years: 1550-1580, 1582-1641, 1666-1749, 1757-1771, 1774-1781, 1785-1812.[50] Eight were Common Pleas

---

49. British Chancery reports. The years covered by the reports appear in brackets.
    Atkyns 3 v. [1736-1755]
    Cooper 1 v. [1815]
    Cox 2 v. [1783-1796]
    General abridgment of cases in equity 2 v. [1667-1774]
    Peere Williams 3 v. [1695-1736]
    Schoales & Lefroy 2 v. [1802-1806]
    Vernon 2 v. [1681-1720]
    Vesey Jr. [1789-1801] v. 1-5
    Vesey Sr. 2 v. [1747-1755]
    Wilson 2 v. [1818-1819]
50. British King's (or Queen's) Bench reports. The years covered by such reports appear in brackets.

reports for 1732-1760 and 1789-1807.[51] Six volumes of Nisi Prius
reports covered 1793-1807.[52] The single volume of House of
Lords reports covered the twenty years between 1729 and 1749.[53]
Two volumes of Crown Cases, Criminal, covered the years 1730-
1815.[54]

American reports totalled seventy-seven volumes, forty-four
covering federal decisions, thirty-three state decisions. Of the
forty-four federal volumes, thirty-two were Supreme Court reports
for 1790-1827.[55] There were nine volumes of circuit court
reports, seven for the First Circuit, 1812-1830, and two for the
Third Circuit, 1803-1811,[56] and three volumes of federal district court reports.[57]

---

Burrow 5 v. [1757-1771]
Cowper 2 v. [1774-1778]
Croke 4 v. [1582-1641]
Douglas 2 v. [1778-1781]
Durnford & East 8 v. [1785-1800]
East 16 v. [1801-1812]
Latch, Plusieurs tres-bons Cases 1 v. [1625-1628]
Modern reports 12 v. [1669-1732]
Plowden 2 v. [1550-1580]
Raymond 3 v. [1694-1732]
Salkeld 3 v. [1689-1712]
Saunders 3 v. [1666-1673]
Shower 2 v. [1678-1694]
Strange 2 v. [1716-1749]
51. British common pleas reports. The years covered by these reports
appear in brackets.
Barnes 1 v. [1732-1760]
Blackstone, H. 2 v. [1789-1796]
Bosanquet & Puller 3 v. [1796-1804]
Bosanquet & Puller 2 v. [1804-1807]
52. Espinasse, *Reports of cases argued and ruled at Nisi Prius* 6 v.
[1793-1807]
53. Brown's *Parliamentary cases* [1729-1749] v. 4
54. Leach, *Cases in crown law* 2 v. [1730-1815]
55. Reports of the Supreme Court of the United States. The years
covered by these reports appear in brackets.
Cranch 9 v. [1801-1815]
Dallas 4 v. [1794-1800]
Peters [1828-1833] v. 1-7
Wheaton 12 v. [1816-1827]
56. Reports of the circuit courts of the United States. The years
covered by these reports appear in brackets.
Gallison 2 v. [1812-1815]
Mason 5 v. [1816-1830]
Washington [1803-1811] v. 1-2
57. Reports of the district courts of the United States. The years cov-

Out of the thirty-three state reports, twenty-six contained New York cases decided in various courts between 1794 and 1825. The remaining seven volumes were scattered between Connecticut, Massachusetts, and Vermont.[58]

*Statutory Materials*—The statutory materials presented substantial problems of identification. The references gave no clue to the years covered. Consequently, the only dates which could be established were terminal dates—that is, the dates of the documents which contained the references, after which the several volumes could not have been acquired.

These materials fall into three categories: federal, state, and foreign.

References to federal statutory materials appear in five estate inventories between 1813 and 1830. These items can be grouped as follows: Constitution of the United States,[59] Laws of the United States,[60] Acts of Congress,[61] and "State Papers, Journals,

ered by these reports appear in brackets.

Bee 1 v. [1792-1809]

Peters 2 v. [1780-1807]

58. State reports. The years covered by these reports appear in brackets.

*Connecticut*
Day [1802-1810] v. 1-4
Kirby 1 v. [1785-1788]
*Massachusetts*
    One volume of Massachusetts reports, not further identified.
*New York*
Anthon, Law of Nisi Prius 1 v. [1808-1818]
Caines 3 v. [1803-1805]
Coleman 1 v. [1794-1800]
Johnson 3 v. [1799-1803]
Johnson [1806-1818] v. 1-15
Wheeler Reports of criminal cases 3 v. [1791-1825]
*Vermont*
Chipman, N. 1 v. [1789-1791]

59. The inventory of the estate of Andrew G. Whitney, 1826, listed the Constitution of the United States.

60. The following table provides information concerning the volumes of Laws of the United States:

| Date of inventory | Name of decedent | Volumes of Laws of the United States listed |
|---|---|---|
| 1813 | Elijah Brush | 1 vol., 5 vols., 5 pamphlets |
| 1827 | Augustus B. Woodward | 1 vol., 10 vols. |
| 1827 | John Hunt | 7 vols. |
| 1830 | Cyprian Stevens | 2 vols. |

61. The inventory of the estate of Andrew G. Whitney, 1826, listed "1 number, 4 numbers," suggesting the possibility of unbound material.

Reports of Committees."[62] The inability to establish the actual years covered by the volumes containing laws of the United States raises the possibility that a volume appearing in the inventory of one estate later became the property of another and ultimately was listed in his estate. However, the 1827 inventory of the estate of former Chief Judge Augustus Woodward listed eleven volumes of the Laws of the United States and thirty-seven volumes of "State Papers, Journals, Reports of Committees." It is safe to conclude that at the least these volumes, in addition to the Constitution of the United States, actually were in the territory.

In addition to Michigan, estate inventories from 1823 to 1836 refer to statutory material for the following seven American jurisdictions: Connecticut, Louisiana, Massachusetts, New York, Northwest Territory, Rhode Island, and Vermont.[63] References

---

62. These items, totalling 37 volumes, were listed in the estate inventory of former Chief Judge Woodward in 1827.

63. Statutory materials. Note the following table:

| Jurisdiction | Date of Source | Original Identification | Name of Decedent |
|---|---|---|---|
| Conn. | 1826 | *Statutes of Connecticut* | Andrew G. Whitney |
| La. | 1826 | *Civil Code of Louisiana* | Andrew G. Whitney |
| Mass. | 1827 | *Digest of the Laws of Massachusetts* | John Hunt |
| Mich. | 1826 | *Laws of Michigan* (2 v.) | Andrew G. Whitney |
| | 1827 | *Laws of Michigan* (1 v., pamphlets) | John Hunt |
| | 1827 | *Laws of Michigan* (2 v.) | Augustus B. Woodward |
| | 1830 | *Michigan Laws and Journals* (13 v.) | Cyprian Stevens |
| | 1832 | *Laws of Michigan* (2 v., 6 v.) | Gabriel Richard |
| | 1836 | *Laws of Michigan* (1 v.) Woodward Code | Henry S. Cole |
| N. Y. | 1823 | *Laws of New York* (6 v.), *Rules of the Supreme Court of New York* | Spencer Coleman |
| | 1826 | *Laws of New York* (1 v., 2 v.), New York State Convention | Andrew G. Whitney |
| | 1827 | *Laws of New York* (3 v., additional vols.), Rules of the Supreme Court of New York | John Hunt |

\* While not an attorney, Fr. Gabriel Richard's library was so accessible to Detroit residents that the inclusion of items listed in the inventory of his estate appears permissible. For a recent biography, see Woodford & Hyma, *Gabriel Richard* (1958).

to Michigan materials appear in seven inventories. The estate of Cyprian Stevens (1830) had thirteen volumes of Michigan Laws and Journals. Father Gabriel Richard's estate inventory (1832) listed eight volumes of the Laws of Michigan. Henry S. Cole's estate (1836) had the Woodward Code and one volume of the Laws of Michigan. References to New York materials appear in four inventories. Andrew G. Whitney's estate (1826) had two volumes of Vermont statutes.

Three volumes of foreign statutory materials were listed. Gabriel Richard's estate (1832) had two volumes of the constitution of Colombia and Andrew Whitney (1826) had a copy of *Les Cinque Codes*. No estate inventory listed a copy of any British statutes.

*Secondary Sources*

The original references to the three classes of secondary sources—law dictionaries, digests and abridgments, and treatises—typically supplied enough information to establish the title and author. Where a title had only one edition, there was no question but that the volume listed could be given the date of original publication. Where, however, a particular work went through more than one edition, it would have been an exercise in futility to try to determine which edition supplied the copy in Wayne County—except for the relatively small number of volumes in the Michigan Law Library. To avoid this dilemma, the date of initial publication was used, unless one set of circumstances existed: Where the contemporary source gave a number of volumes for a single title and bibliographical sources established that an edition other than the first was the earliest with that particular number, the date of publication for that edition was used.

This unorthodox system of dating is justified by the purpose of the inquiry: to show the sources of law available to the lawyers of Wayne County. The dates on which these volumes first appeared indicate far more satisfactorily the nature of the sources and the state of the law when they were written than would precise dates for the editions actually used—which, at best, would have been a

| Jurisdiction | Date of Source | Original Identification | Name of Decedent |
| --- | --- | --- | --- |
| | 1836 | *Abstract of New York Revised Laws* | Henry S. Cole |
| Nw. Terr. | 1826 | *Laws of the Northwest Territory* | Andrew G. Whitney |
| R. I. | 1830 | *Laws of Rhode Island* | Cyprian Stevens |
| Vt. | 1826 | *Laws of Vermont, Acts of Vermont Legislature* (1 number) | Andrew G. Whitney |

matter of informed guessing. This state of affairs is particularly pertinent for the treatises.

*Law Dictionaries*—Only two titles of law dictionaries were listed in estate inventories. Both were English publications: Burn, *New law dictionary: intended for general use as well as for gentlemen of the profession* (1792) and Jacob, *New law-dictionary* . . . (1729), an extremely popular work republished in many subsequent editions. Jacob's *Dictionary* appeared in three estate inventorieś, each listing a different number of volumes.[64]

*Digests and Abridgments*—This class of legal reference was understandably popular and widely used, providing at a time of limited book-access a handy reference tool. Both English and American works were owned by Wayne County lawyers, with ten titles of American and seven of English origin.

Of the ten American works (twenty-one volumes) listed, five dealt with a particular state (Connecticut, Massachusetts, New York)[65] and one with the United States Supreme Court.[66] The other four were wider-ranging and included Dane's eight-volume *Abridgment and Digest of American Law* (1823-1824).[67]

The seven English titles (forty volumes) included the seven volumes of the fifth edition of Bacon's *A New Abridgment of the Law* (1798), six volumes of the fourth edition of Comyns' *Digest of the Laws of England* (1793), and apparently a complete set of Pe-

---

64. The estate inventory for Elijah Brush (1813) listed one volume of Jacob's *Dictionary*, that of Andrew G. Whitney (1826) four volumes, that of John Hunt (1827) six volumes.

65. *Connecticut:* Swift, *System of the laws of Connecticut* (2 v., 1795-1796).

*Massachusetts:* Bigelow, *Digest of the cases argued and determined in the Supreme Judicial Court . . . of Massachusetts . . .* (1818).

*New York:* Church, *Digested index to the reports . . . in the state of New York . . .* (2 v., 1822). Cowen, *General digested index to the nine volumes of his reports of cases in the Supreme Court and Court of Errors in New York* (1831). Johnson, *Digest of cases in the Supreme Court, the Court of Chancery, and the Court of Errors of New York, from 1799 to 1823* (2 v., 1825).

66. Wheaton, *Digest of decisions of the United States Supreme Court . . .* (1821).

67. Anthon, *Digested index to the reported decisions of the several courts of law in the United States* (1 v., 1813). Dane, *Abridgment and digest of American law* (8 v., 1823-1824). Gordon, *Digest of the laws of the United States . . .* (1827). Griffith, *Annual register of the United States* (v. 3-4, 1821-1823).

*Note:* the first two volumes never were published.

tersdorf's *Abridgment* (1825-1830) which covered the years from 1660 to 1824.[68]

*Treatises*—This is the largest single category of titles owned by the early lawyers of Wayne County. Its importance in assessing the sources of law available to these men cannot be overestimated. The 125 titles were published over a century and a quarter, ranging from the beginning of the eighteenth century[69] to 1834. Roughly one-third was published before 1800, one-third between 1800 and 1814, and the remainder in 1815 and thereafter.

Slightly less than ten percent of the titles can be classed as general works. This group includes multi-volume sets of Blackstone as well as one-volume summaries. The quality range probably was equally wide.[70]

---

68. The titles in this category follow.*

Bacon, *A new abridgment of the law* (7 v., 5th ed, 1798).

*Note:* The fifth edition was the earliest edition with seven volumes.

Baylies, *Digested index to the modern reports of common law in England and in the United States* (v. 1-3, 1814).

Comyns, *Digest of the laws of England* (6 v., 4th ed, 1793).

*Note:* The fourth edition was the earliest edition with six volumes.

Manning, *Digested index to nisi prius reports* (2d ed. 1820).

Petersdorf, *Practical and elementary abridgment of the cases determined in the courts of K.B., C.P., Ex., and at Nisi Prius, and of the rules of court, from 1660, to M.T., 4 Geo. IV* . . . (15 v., 1825-1830).

Viner, *General abridgment of law and equity* (3 odd volumes from a set of 23, 1742-1753).

Williams, *Abridgment of cases argued and determined in the courts of law during the reign of Geo. III, to 1803.* . . (5 v., 1798-1803).

* It is possible that Fitzherbert, *Le Graunde Abridgment* (1514) should be added to the foregoing list of titles. Solomon Sibley recorded in his notebook in 1799 that he had borrowed a copy of "Fitz Herbert" but gave no further identification. See note 69 *infra.*

69. Booth, *Nature and practice of real actions* . . . (London, 1701). While Sibley is known to have borrowed "Fitz Herbert" in 1799, his notes do not show the title of tne work. If it was the *New Natura Brevium* (1534), it properly belongs with the procedure treatises. However, Booth is the next earliest treatise in point of time.

70. Titles in this category follow. Those with an English origin are marked with an asterisk.

* Attorney's complete pocket book (v. 1, 7th ed. 1772).

Attorney's manual.

*Note:* No bibliographical indicators have been located.

* Blackstone, *Commentaries on the laws of England* (4 v., 1765-1769).

Brackenridge, *Law miscellanies* . . . (1814).

* Chitty, *Practice of the law in all its departments* . . . (1833).

* Curry, ed., *Commentaries of Sir William Blackstone* . . . *careful-*

The largest single group within the treatise category pertains to procedure, treating one or more of its several aspects.[71] Approx-

ly abridged, in a new manner . . . (2d ed. 1809).
    * Every man his own lawyer; or, a summary of the laws of England . . . (1787).
    Kent, Commentaries on American law (4 v., 1826-1830).
    Lawyer's guide.
    Note: No bibliographical indicators have been located.
    * Treatise on the study of the law . . . (1797).
    Tucker, Blackstone's Commentaries . . . (5 v., 1803)
    71. The following treatises deal with one or more aspects of pleading, practice, or procedure. Titles originally published in England are identified with an asterisk. A substantial number of these works, written in England for English lawyers, later was published in the United States and identified as American editions. Occasionally, an American publication would state on the title page that this was the first, or second, or third, American edition, based on the third, or fourth, or sixth, English edition. It should be recalled that at this period, there was no copyright protection for a foreign author in the United States.
    Anthon, American precedents of declarations (1810).
    * Archbold, A collection of the forms and entries, which occur in practice in the courts of King's Bench and Common Pleas, in personal actions and ejectment (1828).
    * Archbold, Practice (2 v., 1819).
    Blake, Practice of the court of chancery of New York (1824).
    * Booth, Nature and practice of real actions . . . (1701).
    * Buller, Introduction to the law relative to trials at nisi prius (5th ed. 1785).
    Caines, Summary of practice in the supreme court of the state of New York (1808).
    * Chitty, Practical treatise on pleading . . . (2 v., 1809).
    Complete index to Wentworth's System of pleading . . . (1822).
    Note: While the Complete index . . . was published in the United States, Wentworth, A complete system of pleading: comprehending the most approved precedents and forms of practice . . . was published in London (10 v. 1797-1799).
    * Cooper, Treatise of pleading on the equity side of the High Court of Chancery (1809).
    * Crompton, Practice common-placed: or, The rules and cases of practice in the courts of King's Bench and Common Pleas, methodically arranged (2 v., 2d ed. 1783).
    Dunlap, Practice of the Supreme Court of New York in civil actions; together with the proceedings in error (2 v., 1821-1823).
    Duponceau, Dissertation on the nature and extent of the jurisdiction of the courts of the United States . . . (1824).
    * Eden, Treatise on the law of injunctions (1821).
    * 'Espinasse, Digest of the law of actions at nisi prius (2 v., 1789).
    Evans, Essay on pleading, with a view to an improved system (1827).

imately one-quarter of all the titles deal with this area of the law. The earliest is Harrison's *Accomplish'd Practiser in the High Court of Chancery, showing the whole method of proceedings . . .* (1741), the latest is Graham's *Essay on New Trials* (1834). The number of these treatises with an English origin further evidences the adherence of these "frontier" attorneys to accustomed methods and forms of pleading and practice.

The importance of Detroit as a commercial center at the head of the water route from New York State is underscored by the number of treatises dealing with some aspect of mercantile or maritime

---

* Fitzherbert, *New Natura Brevium* (1534).

*Note:* See note 69 *supra.*

* Gilbert, *Law of evidence* . . . (1717).

Gould, *Treatise on the principles of pleading in civil actions* (1832).

Graham, *Essay on new trials* (1834).

Harrison, *Accomplish'd practiser in the High court of chancery, showing the whole method of proceedings* . . . (1741).

Hoffman, *Office and duties of masters in chancery, and practice in the master's office* . . . (1824).

* Impey, "Practice"

*Note:* The entry was "Impey's Practice." It probably referred to the following title: *The new instructor clericalis, stating the authority, jurisdiction, and modern practice of the Court of common pleas. . . .* (1784). Alternatively, it might have referred to this later work: *The modern pleader, containing the several forms of declarations in all actions, with notes thereon* . . . (1795).

* MacNally, *Rules of evidence on pleas of the crown* (v. 1-2, 1802).

* Maddock, *Treatise on the principles and practice of the High court of chancery* . . . (2 v., 1817).

* Mitford (Redesdale), *Treatise on the pleadings in suits in the court of chancery, by English bill* (2d ed. 1815).

* Morgan, *Attorney's vade mecum, and client's instructor, treating of actions* (Such as are now most in use) . . . (3 v. in 2, 1792).

* Morgan, *Law essays* (v. 2, 1789).

* Peake, *Compendium of the law of evidence* (1801).

* Phillips, *Treatise on the law of evidence* (2 v., 1814).

* Saunders, *Law of pleading and evidence* (2 v., 1828).

* Sellon, *Practice of the courts of K.B., and C.P.* (2 v., 1798).

* Starkie, *Practical treatise on the law of evidence* (2 v., 2d ed. 1833).

Story, *Selection of pleadings in civil actions* . . . (1805).

* Tidd, *Practice of the court of King's bench, in personal actions* . . . (v. 1, 2, 2d Am. ed. 1807).

* Van Heythuysen, *Equity draftsman* . . . (1st Am. ed. 1819).

White, *View of the jurisdiction and proceedings of the courts of probate, in Massachusetts* (1822).

law.[72] If the four contracts titles are included,[73] this category accounts for over one-fifth of all titles located. Three groups make up two-thirds of the remaining works: real property (twelve titles),[74]

---

72. Titles in this category follow. Those with an English origin are marked with an asterisk.

    * Annesley, *Compendium of the law of marine insurance* . . . (1808).

    * Caldwell, *Treatise on the law of arbitration; with an appendix of precedents* (1st Am. ed. 1822).

    * Chitty, *Treatise on the law of bills of exchange, checks on bankers, promissory notes, bankers' cash notes, and bank-notes* (1807).

    *Clerk's assistant*, in two parts. *Part I. Containing the most useful and necessary forms of writings, which occur in the ordinary transactions of business* . . . *Part II. Containing, selections of various useful and practical forms, proceedings in the partition of lands, &c &c. To which is added, an appendix containing a variety of precedents for the use of . . . town officers* . . . (1805).

    * Fell, *Treatise on the law of mercantile guarantees, and of principle and surety in general* (1st Am. ed. from 2d Eng. 1825).

    Fessenden, *Essay on the law of patents for new inventions. With an appendix, containing the French patent law, forms, &c* (1810).

    Ingersoll, ed., trans., *Roccus' Maritime law and insurance* (1800).

    Jacobson, *Laws of the sea* . . . (trans. 1818).

    Jeremy, *Law of carriers* . . . (1815).

    * Jones, *Essay on the law of bailments* (1781).

    * Kyd, *Treatise on the law of awards* (1791).

    * Kyd, *Treatise on the law of bills of exchange and promissory notes* (1790).

    Livermore, *Treatise on the law relative to principals, agents, factors, auctioneers, and brokers* (1811).

    * Montagu, *Digest of the law of partnership* . . . (2 v. 1815).

    * Montagu, *Summary of the law of lien* (1821).

    * Montagu, *Summary of the law of set-off* . . . (1806).

    Montefiore, *Commercial and notarial precedents* . . . (1803).

    Montefiore, *Commercial dictionary* (v. 1-3, 1804).

    Story, ed., *Chitty's Practical treatise on bills of exchange* . . . (1809).

    * Watson, *Treatise on the law of partnership* (1795).

73. Titles in this category follow. Those with an English origin are marked with an asterisk.

    Chipman, D., *Essay on the law of contracts* . . . (1822).

    * Comyn, *Treatise on the law of contracts and promises* . . . (2 v., 1807).

    * Newland, *Treatise on contracts* . . . (1806).

    * Powell, *Essay on the law of contracts and agreements* (2 v., 1790).

74. Titles in this category follow. Those with an English origin are marked with an asterisk.

    * Adams, *Treatise on the principles and practice of the action of*

criminal law, including the accounts of two political trials (eight titles),[75] and practical aspects of local government (eight titles, all but one an American work).[76]

---

*ejectment, and the resulting action for mesne profits* . . . (1812).

Angell, *Treatise on the common law in relation to water courses* (1824).

    * Booth, *Nature and practice of real actions* . . . (1701).

    Clerk's *assistant, in two parts.* See note 72.

    ° Cruise, *Digest of the laws of England, respecting real property* (v. 1-6, 1804-1807).

    Oliver, *Practical conveyancing* (2d ed. 1827).

    * Powell, *Essay upon the learning of devises, from their inception by writing, to their consummation by the death of the devisor* (1788).

    * Powell, *Treatise on the law of mortgages* (v. 1-2, 4th ed. 1799).

    ° Roberts, *Treatise on the construction of the statutes 13 Eliz. c. 5, and 27 Eliz. c. 4, relating to voluntary or fraudulent conveyances* . . . (1800).

    * Roberts, *Treatise on the statute of frauds* . . . (1805).

    * Runnington, *History, principles and practice . . . of the legal remedy by ejectment* . . . (1795).

    * Woodfall, *Practical treatise on the law of landlord and tenant* . . . (1802).

    75. Titles in this category follow. Those with an English origin are marked with an asterisk.

    Carpenter, ed., *Report of the trial of Col. Aaron Burr* . . . (3 v. 1807).

    ° Chitty, *Practical treatise on the criminal law* (3 v., in 2, 1819).

    ° Dogherty, *Crown circuit assistant* . . . (1787).

    ° Hale, *History of the pleas of the crown* (2 v., 1736-1739).

    * Hawkins, *Treatise on pleas of the crown* (6th ed., 2 v., 1788).

    ° Highmore, *Digest on the doctrine of bail* . . . (1783).

    Hull's Trial

    *Note:* The entry was "Hull's Trial." In 1814 three works dealing with the trial of General William Hull were published. The following title most closely resembles the entry: Trial of Brig. Gen. William Hull, for neglect of duty and un-officer like conduct.

    * Russell, *Treatise on crimes and misdemeanors* . . . (2 v., 1819).

    76. Titles in this category follow. Those with an English origin are marked with an asterisk.

    Bache, *Manual of a Pennsylvania justice of the peace* . . . (2 v., 1810-1814).

    Backus, *Digest of laws relating to the affairs and duties of sheriff, coroner, and constable, in Connecticut* (2 v., 1812).

    *Clerk's assistant, in two parts.* (See note 72).

    ° *Conductor generalis* . . . (1722).

    Cowen, *Civil jurisdiction of New York justice of peace* (1821).

    Dunlap, *New-York justice; or, A digest of the law relative to justices of the peace in the state of New-York* (1815).

The works heretofore unclassified are scattered over diverse areas: constitutional law (three American and two English titles),[77] ecclesiastical law,[78] equity, [79] inheritances,[80] married women,[81] martial law,[82] medical jurisprudence,[83] powers,[84] principles of Scottish law,[85] the Irish exchequer.[86]

Aside from treatises dealing with procedural and substantive areas of the law, the lawyers of Wayne County were willing to buy additional legal works. Burlamaqui, Justinian's Institutes, Montesquieu, Thomas Paine, and Vattel were represented, as well as some historical works.[87]

---

Jefferson, *Manual of parliamentary practice* (1822).

Waterman, *Justice's manual: or, A summary of the powers and duties of justices of the peace in the state of New-York* . . . (1825).

77. Titles in this category follow. Those with an English origin are marked with an asterisk.

Adams, *Defence of the constitutions of government of the United States of America* (3 v., 1787).

Chipman, N., *Principles of government* . . . (1833).

Sergent, *Constitutional law. Being a collection of points arising upon the Constitution and jurisprudence of the United States* . . . (1822).

* Sidney, *Discourses concerning government* . . . (v. 1-2, 1750).

* Sullivan, *Lectures on the constitution and laws of England* (2 v., 1st Am. ed. 1805).

78. Burn, *Ecclesiastical law* (London, 1760).

79. Fonblanque, ed., *Treatise on equity* (by Henry Ballow) (vols. 1-2, London, 1793-1795).

80. Roper, *Treatise on the law of legacies* (v. 1-2, 3d ed., London, 1828); Toller, *Law of executors and administrators* (London, 1800).

81. Clancy, *Essay on equitable rights of married women* (Dublin, 1819); Reeve, *Baron and femme* . . . *powers of courts of chancery* (New Haven, Connecticut, 1816).

82. Macomb, *Treatise on martial law and courts martial* (Charleston, South Carolina, 1809).

83. Beck, *Elements of medical jurisprudence* (London, 1823).

84. Sugden, *Practical treatise of powers* . . . (1st Am. ed. 1805).

85. Erskine, *Principles of the law of Scotland* . . . (Edinburgh, 1827).

86. Howard, *Treatise on the exchequer and revenue of Ireland* . . . (2 v., Dublin, 1776).

87. Titles in this category follow. Those with a British origin are marked with an asterisk.

Burlamaqui

Note: Probably one of the many editions of this author's treatises dealing with natural law.

Cooper, T., ed., *Justinian's Institutes* (1812).

* Curran, *Speeches of J. P.* (2 v., 1811).

* Erskine, *Speeches when at the bar, connected with the liberty of the press, and against constructive treasons* (5 v., 1810).

Considering the titles and authors of all of the treatises, it is proper to inquire if the preponderance of British works resulted primarily from a preference for British sources or from the relative scarcity of American titles. Undoubtedly the latter factor influenced markedly the book purchases of attorneys. As American treatises became available, they were acquired: Chipman on *Contracts*, Caines' *New York Practice*, Kent's *Commentaries*. Nevertheless, the British treatises—as well as the British reports, the British digests and abridgments—must have been *useful to* and *usable by* these frontier lawyers in Wayne County. Otherwise, these British-oriented volumes (for some were reprinted in the United States), dealing with specific areas of the law in the British Isles or with methods of pleading and practice in the several British courts, written as they were for British buyers, would not have been bought.

Money was scarce on the frontier. Law books were paid for in cash, not by services or with goods. They were not produced locally. It is doubtful if John Askin, Joseph Campau, or any other Detroit merchant stocked law books among the bolts of book muslin, cambric, or molton, pounds of thread, barrels of flour, brittania spoons, beaver traps, piggins of maple sugar, red pepper, scalping knives, and toilette glasses. An attorney, if he had not brought his law books with him from the east, would have had to order specific titles. Until the *Walk-in-the-Water* inaugurated the era of steam on the lakes in 1818, goods—and people—came into Detroit on a sailing vessel or over the bone-breaking land route. Transportation costs alone were significant. Law books were acquired for use, not as status symbols. Contemporary evidence shows these books were in fact used and relied upon daily and matter-of-factly in the routine transaction of legal business.

## Comment

The totality of the foregoing titles should demolish effectively the romantic notion that the frontier lawyers of Wayne County shed the law of the past and created all things new. If this notion had any

---

* Hale, *History of the common law of England* (v. 1-2, 1739).

* Kames, *Historical law tracts* (2d ed. 1761).

Montesquieu, *Spirit of Laws* (v. 1-2, 1748).

Necker, *Essay on the true principles of executive power in great states* (trans., London, 2 v. 1792).

Paine, *Writings.*

*Note:* A two-volume edition of Paine's work, *Political Writings of Thomas Paine* . . . , was published at Charlestown, Massachusetts, in 1824.

* Reeves, *History of the English law* (4 v., 2d ed. 1787).

Vattel, *Law of nations; or, Principles of the law of nature.*

*Note:* A translation was published in London in 1760.

semblance of truth in it, why should any attorney have acquired reports of the states on the eastern seaboard as well as those of the
King's Bench for the seventeenth century? On the titles of the reports alone—ignoring the treatises, the digests and abridgments—
the Turner-spawned thesis is shattered irrevocably.

The cumulative impact of these books demonstrates that the
practising lawyer in Wayne County did not find his sources of law
in theoretical abstractions of justice or local conceptions of right
and wrong. Rather, he possessed and used the same sources of law
as his contemporaries in Philadelphia or New York. Excluding the
purely American materials, he drew his water from the same well
used by his British counterpart.

With the statutes throughout the greater part of the territorial
period "adopted" from the laws of the original states, with the citation of and reliance upon published reports of cases in British and
American courts, with the unquestioned use of accepted and customary procedural patterns, the early nineteenth century lawyer in
Wayne County had scant opportunity for experimentation—and
there is not a scintilla of evidence that any was attempted.

*Conclusion*

When all the evidence—the existence of a statutory framework
establishing both the laws in force and the jurisdiction within
which the courts of Wayne County were bound to operate, the adherence by courts and lawyers alike to the traditional methods of
conducting their business, the routinely careful use of precedent
and citation of authority—has been laid out and when it all has
been examined, it is difficult indeed to sustain the long-continued
allegations of frontier informality and ad hoc justice. On the contrary, there is much to buttress the assertion that judges and attorneys alike took seriously their responsibilities and made no effort
to overturn the shape of the laws or the methods of pleading and
practice. Challengers of this assertion should examine the surviving
court records. To do otherwise is to deny the relevance of the prime
evidence.

On March 5, 1829, Judge William Woodbridge, in an opinion
filed in an action brought by the United States against the publisher
of a newspaper article alleged to be "scandalous and contemptuous
against" the territorial supreme court, stated as follows:

> The decisions, &c all the proceedings of this Court, are
> of record: —They there exhibit true & imperishable evidence
> of the quantity of business done by the Court, & of the manner
> of doing it; —of the degree of skill therefore, & capacity pos-
> sessed by this Court, or of its ignorance, incapacity & arro-
> gance. Upon *this* basis, our reputation must rest: —By this

test we expect,—we wish to be judged. —If our decisions be legal & just, we shall receive the highest reward which can be conferred by men,—the approbation of this & future time: —If our decisions exhibit ignorance of our duties—arrogance, or any unfitness, obloquy & shame will meet us:[88]

On the record, that court—and its lawyers and judges—well may rest.

---

88. *United States v. Sheldon,* Case 1315, Blume, *Transactions* 1825-1836, I:107, 336 at 363 (1940).

# 23
# LAW VS. POLITICS: THE SELF-IMAGE OF THE AMERICAN BAR (1830-1860)

*MAXWELL BLOOMFIELD*

# Law vs. Politics: The Self-Image
# of the American Bar (1830-1860)

*by* MAXWELL BLOOMFIELD *

THE ADVENT OF JACKSONIAN DEMOCRACY in American politics coincided with a vigorous levelling movement in American law. In
one sense the latter crusade was nothing new: hostility toward the
elitism of the legal fraternity had been rife since the days of the
Revolution. But whereas earlier critics had worked to simplify the
content of the law, reformers in the 1830's and 1840's attacked the
problem from a different angle. Eschewing substantive changes,
they sought instead to bring the administrators of the law under
more direct popular control. Their program embraced a wide range
of legislative measures in which worried conservatives read portents
of mob rule.

Mississippi inaugurated one important trend in 1832 by
adopting a constitutional provision which called for the popular
election of all state judges for a term of years. By 1852 fifteen
other states were following her example; of the remaining sixteen
states, ten endorsed the principle of indirect election of judges by
the legislature, while only six adhered to the older system of executive appointment during good behavior. Complementing this
extension of the spoils system to the bench went a curtailment of
judicial power over jury trials. Many states witnessed the enactment of procedural rules which made the judge little more than a
passive moderator in his own court, forbidden to comment on the
evidence or otherwise to assist the jury in reaching a verdict.

Nor did the ordinary lawyer escape the ken of the reformers
in these years. Legislatures redefined professional standards in
many states, scaling down educational requirements for admission
to the bar or eliminating them altogether in such areas as New
Hampshire, Wisconsin, and Indiana. Champions of the common
man likewise found the local bar association as vulnerable a target
as the "monster" Bank of the United States. Both these institu-

* Department of History, Catholic University of America, Washington, D. C.

tions shared the same defects in the eyes of a militant democracy: they impaired economic competition and they threatened to become dangerous political pressure groups, isolated from the masses behind a wall of corporate solidarity.

"The tendency of the age is clearly marked," lamented a legal writer in 1847.

> The voice of the multitude is against the legal community. Leveling begins with the mount of justice. In a sister State, systems are tottering to their downfall, and innovation and experiment walk about the ruins. The day is past when the lawyer can call upon the legislature to assert his rights. The bar finds no favour at the ballot box. The influence which impresses the stranger, arises from individual energy and not from association. A cry is going out over the land. Radicalism is infectious as the pestilence. The tide of popular will must soon sweep away our prerogative, unless we stay its waters.[1]

Aside from the admission that lawyers *had* a prerogative worth defending, this was a standard complaint which later historians have tended to accept at face value. It enables them to fit the second third of the nineteenth century neatly into a dramatic triptych illustrating "The Lawyer's Progress." On one side appears the Golden Age of revolutionary jurisprudence; on the other, the dawn of modern professionalism with the formation of the American Bar Association (1878) and similar agencies. In between sprawls a scene of darkness and confusion—the lower depths of the American bar, whose earlier attainments and esprit de corps are alike submerged beneath a wave of barbarian invasions. "Demoralization" and "deprofessionalization" are the terms most often used to describe the condition of the lawyer in the 1840's and 1850's.[2]

Appealing to the imagination through its vivid contrasts, this interpretation satisfies the demands of common sense as well. It even adds another link to the chain of causation leading to the Civil War, insofar as popular contempt for legal authority may have contributed to the ultimate recourse to armed violence. But for all its

---

[1] "New Publications: *Règles sur la Profession d'Avocat, par Mallot,*" 7 *Penn. L. J.* 99 (1847).

[2] Standard surveys include: Roscoe Pound, *The Lawyer from Antiquity to Modern Times* (St. Paul, 1953), 232 ff.; and Blackard, "The Demoralization of the Legal Profession in Nineteenth Century America," 16 *Tenn. L. Rev.* 314 (1940).

plausibility, it rests upon a very shaky foundation. The closing with eclat of several small bar associations; the jeremiads of conservative academics such as James Kent and Joseph Story; the presumed incompetence of elected judges and self-taught lawyers—these are the meager sources from which elaborate, and often unwarranted, inferences have been drawn.

Wherever one turns, the details of the picture cry out for reappraisal. Did the caliber of state judges deteriorate as a result of popular election? Basic to such an inquiry should be a clear understanding of the nature and rate of turnover among judicial personnel both before and after the elective system went into effect. The materials for a thorough study are abundant, but to date no scholar has undertaken the task, even at the superior court level. Yet the results might well prove shattering to conventional assumptions regarding the vagaries of mass political behavior. To cite only one example: Isaac F. Redfield, chief justice of the Vermont Supreme Court and a distinguished jurist, was re-elected to his post annually for twenty-five years, from 1835 to his retirement in 1860, although he was a rather stiff-necked character who opposed the dominant political forces of his state. Except for his unusually long period of service, his case typified a general trend in Vermont, where judges were regularly returned to office from year to year during good behavior.

Was the Vermont pattern repeated in other states? Did the elective principle offer greater security of tenure to frontier judges than to their counterparts in more sophisticated urban environments? These questions still await serious investigation, as does the role of bar associations in the middle years of the nineteenth century.

The statistical incidence of these associations has never been computed. To do so would involve an exhaustive search through local newspapers, since state and national organizations did not exist. But a careful study of even one key area, such as Massachusetts, would do much to test the validity of the accepted hypothesis that institutional ties crumbled before an aroused public opinion.[3]

Meanwhile some new perspectives on the alleged demoralization of the bar may be gleaned from a study of legal periodicals. These publications have been strangely neglected by historians,

---

[3] Anton-Hermann Chroust has verified the existence of some seventeen bar associations in various states during the post-1830 period, but his fragmentary researches leave many important questions unanswered and serve chiefly as a useful introduction to the problem. See Chroust, *The Rise of the Legal Profession in America* (2 vols., Norman, 1965), II, 129-154.

although in volume alone they form a striking feature of the post-1830 years, as the following chart attests:

| Date | New Law Magazines |
|------|-------------------|
| Pre-1830 | 12 |
| 1830-1839 | 5 |
| 1840-1849 | 13 |
| 1850-1859 | 19 |
| 1860-1869 | 15[4] |

To be sure, these figures are somewhat misleading, since most fledgling journals failed to survive more than a few years A tabulation of all law magazines in existence at the beginning of each decade reveals a more conservative picture:

| Date | Law Magazines |
|------|---------------|
| 1810 | 1 |
| 1820 | 1 |
| 1830 | 5 |
| 1840 | 2 |
| 1850 | 10 |
| 1860 | 9 |
| 1870 | 17 |

Nor should it be forgotten that magazine publishing generally experienced a boom during these years, due to low postage rates, typographical innovations, and improved transportation and distribution facilities.

Yet with due allowance for these caveats, the rate of growth for such specialized publications remains impressive, and suggests that the legal journal may have filled a peculiar need among American lawyers sensitive to popular distrust of more formal professional agencies.

The changing format of the law magazine itself supports this impression. Whereas earlier journals (of which Hall's *American Law Journal* (1808-1817) was both pioneer and prototype) tended to be speculative and treated many subjects of general interest to the educated community, the typical magazine of the post-1830 years conceived its function in rigorously utilitarian terms. De-

---

[4] This statistical table, and the one below, have been compiled from lists found in Frederick C. Hicks, *Materials and Methods of Legal Research* (2d ed., Rochester, 1933), 147-148, supplemented by material from Leonard A. Jones, ed., *An Index to Legal Periodical Literature* (Boston, 1888).

signed to serve the *"workingmen* of the profession," such journals
as the *Monthly Law Reporter* (1838-1866), *New York Legal Observer* (1842-1854), *Pennsylvania Law Journal* (1842-1848), and
*Western Law Journal* (1843-1853) disdained theorizing and offered
their readers a "medium of communication concerning legal matters of fact useful and interesting to gentlemen of the bar."[5] A
major portion of every issue was devoted to a reporting of recent
court decisions, in advance of their appearance in official volumes
of reports. Reviews of new law books, hints for the improvement
of office habits or courtroom techniques, summaries of new state
laws, and memoirs of practitioners living and dead completed the
contents. Behind these diverse features and pervading them all lay
a further objective which was seldom openly avowed: to create for
lawyers an effective counterimage to the popular stereotype of the
crafty despoiler of the poor.[6]

In this quest for a usable symbolism the obituary notice
played a conspicuous part. Perhaps, as Herbert Butterfield has suggested in regard to seventeenth-century science,[7] every great movement sooner or later enters a myth-making phase, in which earlier
achievements and personalities are reappraised and idealized as
guides for the future. The traits of the departed pioneer then become an imaginary yardstick by which to measure the progress of
his successors.

American law was clearly ripe for such a retrospective critique
by 1830. A juristic revolution had long been completed; new institutions and techniques were in successful operation; and the old
actors were fast passing from the stage. For beleaguered law
writers necrology held both the seeds of corporate identity and a
possible answer to the egalitarian challenge.

A few simple themes recur from obituary to obituary, from
journal to journal. The American lawyer was invariably a man of
indomitable industry and perseverance. Lamenting the early death
of a promising young Massachusetts attorney, his biographer
struck a familiar chord when he informed his readers:

> He was a born lawyer. His mind had a native affinity for the
> study of legal rules and principles . . . His taste for the law
> was natural and instinctive, and the study of it was a labor of

---

[5] "Miscellany," 1 *Monthly L. Rep.* 55 (1838).

[6] The generalizations which follow are based upon a survey of sixteen law magazines, selected with a view to geographical distribution
and representing the least as well as the most successful publications.

[7] Herbert Butterfield, *The Origins of Modern Science: 1300-1800*
(rev. ed., N.Y., 1958), 161-174.

love. He would have been a good lawyer with very little study, for the legal character of his mind would have supplied the deficiencies of book knowledge, and led him by a sort of *"rusticum judicium"* to the same results to which others had arrived by the laborious processes of study. . . . Many men would have been contented with this original turn for the law, this legal mother-wit, and have preferred to solve the questions which came before them by a sort of Zerah Colburn process, rather than avail themselves of the borrowed aid of the learning of others. But his ambition was of a nobler and higher kind, and he studied the law as zealously and conscientiously as if his books had been his only guides and dependence. He had that invaluable property in a lawyer—one not often found in combination with a mind so rapid in its movements and powerful in its grasp as his—unwearied patience in legal investigation.[8]

The need for constant application scarcely diminished as one moved upward in the profession. The example of Reuben Saffold (1788-1847), chief justice of the Supreme Court of Alabama, could serve as a text for many another early jurist: "Endowed by nature with sound judgment and an accurate and discriminating mind, he never feared that laborious attention which enabled him to master the subjects he was to decide."[9]

A stress on the laborious pursuit of legal knowledge acquitted the lawyer of quackery but opened the door to a paradox. For if the path to success was indeed so arduous, how could the average man hope to achieve it? And was this not the chief complaint against the bar of the 1830's—that its members formed an exclusive clique sustained by esoteric rules which the masses could not understand? To reconcile the technicalities of the law with the demands of an open society required no little skill; but the publicists of the day measured up to the challenge.

They were careful to dissociate the practice of their craft from mere dilettantism or an undue reliance on book learning. Since law was a rational science, they argued, its basic principles could be easily grasped by all men. Uncertainties arose only when one sought to apply these principles to varying fact situations. Success in this context depended upon common sense and a firsthand knowledge of everyday life, two qualities in which most early lawyers had excelled.

---

[8] Hillard, "Biographical Sketch of James C. Alvord," 2 *Am. Jurist and L. Mag.* 377-378 (1840).

[9] "Obituary Notices," 10 *Monthly L. Rep.* 383 (1847).

Plain-spoken Oliver Ellsworth, Chief Justice of the United States Supreme Court (1796-1800), demonstrated the "active virtue" of an entire generation of legal types who solved their problems with rule-of-thumb practicality: "He satisfied or subdued the reason, with little endeavour either to excite the feelings or to gratify the fancy."[10] And a grass-roots realism characterized the successful practitioner of later days as well. When the brilliant Massachusetts jurist Lemuel Shaw died in 1861, his eulogists found that his most advantageous trait had been "good, sound, Anglo-Saxon common sense:"

> This it was which gave him such mastery over the rules and principles of the common law, that "ample and boundless jurisprudence" which the experience and common sense of successive generations of men have gradually built up, and which came to us from our English ancestors, a precious inheritance of freedom and of the great principles of justice and right.[11]

As a paragon of industry, fortitude, and shrewdness, the American lawyer shared several of the attributes ascribed to the "self-made man" by contemporary writers of success manuals and didactic novels. Nor does the analogy end here. Both ideals embodied the "work and win" formula of the Protestant ethic, according to which rewards invariably followed well directed effort. "I have often thought that if other men could have been as diligent and assiduous as Mr. Webster, they might have equalled him in achievement," declared a member of the New York Bar in a characteristic vein.[12] Success for the lawyer, as for the self-made man, did not necessarily imply large financial returns, however; the true measure of accomplishement lay in the moral satisfaction afforded by a life well spent in the service of others.

Striking in their parallelism, the two mythologies diverged in equally important ways that point up the limits within which law writers had to operate. As John G. Cawelti has shown, the self-help advocates of the antebellum period spoke for a status-oriented, preindustrial America that no longer existed in fact. Fearful of violent social change, they continued to preach the gospel of improvement within one's God-given calling; hostile to big business

---

[10] "Biographical Sketch of Chief Justice Ellsworth," 3 *Am. L. Mag.* 271 (1844).

[11] "The Death of Chief Justice Shaw," 24 *Monthly L. Rep.* 10 (1861).

[12] "Proceedings of the Bar upon the Occasion of the Death of Daniel Webster," 15 *Monthly L. Rep.* 585 (1853).

and immigrant labor, they reaffirmed the standards of the independent craftsman as a guide to success in the age of the corporation. Self-made men, by definition, were conservative Christians who aspired only to a modest respectability that posed no threat to established power structures.[13]

This formula did not meet the needs of law writers. Since the bar was already under attack for its alleged exclusiveness, any talk of stabilizing vocational lines would mean a gain for the enemy. Instead, publicists sought to show that the law had always been a wide-open field, inviting ambitious men from other walks of life to abandon their previous pursuits in order to join the ranks of its leaders. This was a far cry from the static society envisaged by the self-help school; in its fully developed form it amounted to an endorsement of continuing social upheaval within the profession:

> It is as hard for a rich man's son to obtain the honors of the bar, as it is for the rich man himself to enter the kingdom of heaven. They come from the farm and the workshop, from that condition of life to which the great majority belong. They are counted by the multitude as one of themselves, and they hail their elevation as a triumph of their own over all that looked like aristocracy. With enthusiastic pride they push them on from honor to honor, until a new generation arises that knew not their origin and see them only in their exaltation. They see them lifted above the common level; their jealousy is awakened; the order of aristocracy is scented in the atmosphere that surrounds them, and they receive no cordial support except for those august stations to which only advanced age and extensive renown can aspire. A new set is brought up from the same origin to run the same career. And thus it happens that the children of the cabins come up and occupy the palaces of the Republic.[14]

This mobility received specific documentation in the obituary columns. A random sampling of forty-eight death notices carried in the *Monthly Law Reporter* (which made a point of listing obscure practitioners as well as celebrities) reveals the following family backgrounds:

---

[13] John G. Cawelti, *Apostles of the Self-made Man* (Chicago, 1965), 39-75.

[14] "Inaugural Address of Hon. A. Caruthers, Professor of Law in Cumberland University, Lebanon, Tennessee," 3 *U.S. Monthly L. Mag.* 542 (1851).

Doctor    - 3
Merchant - 5
Minister -11
Farmer   -10
Mechanic- 2
Soldier   - 2
Lawyer   -11
Judge    - 4
-------
48

Several foreign-born lawyers figure in the list, as a further indication of the varied sources of legal recruitment. While spokesmen for the self-made man might draw invidious comparisons between the mores of the immigrant and the old-stock native, law writers could not ignore the contributions to their science made by men of the stamp of Peter S. Du Ponceau of France, Thomas Addis Emmet of Ireland, and Francis Lieber of Germany.

Similarly, lawyers were more realistic in acknowledging pecuniary motives as a major factor in their choice of a career. If they insisted that the average practitioner "lived well and died poor," this was hardly a counsel of Christian moderation. A surplus of riches enhanced one's legal reputation. "It is understood, that he was as eminently successful in the accumulation of wealth, as in the prosecution of his professional pursuits," observed the biographer of one minor figure, with obvious satisfaction.[15]

Having entered the law to improve their economic status, young men could not be expected to conform to the strict vocational limitations imposed by the self-help manuals. Law was accordingly defined as a primary, but not exclusive, pursuit. Since an attorney's practice so often revolved about business questions, a personal involvement in the world of affairs could prove beneficial both to his pocketbook and to his standing at the bar. He might safely engage in real estate ventures, railroad promotion, or banking, so long as he continued to give his paramount allegiance to the law. For there was no way to move *up* from the legal profession, which alone offered a satisfying blend of material reward, intellectual challenge, and social utility. Attorneys who abandoned their practice to pursue other callings were like apostates from a true faith; and none deserved greater censure for their acts of heresy than lawyer-politicians.

The divorce of law from politics was the most significant contribution which publicists of the Jacksonian era made to legal

---

[15] "Obituary Notices: Lewis Bigelow," 1 *Monthly L. Rep.* 275 (1839).

mythology. Hitherto political service had always been regarded as a legitimate by-product of legal competence. Few of the practitioners whose deaths were recorded in the law journals of the 1840's had missed election to a state or national legislature at some point in their careers. Collectively they established a pattern of public leadership which had answered well the needs of the early Republic. Biographers described their conduct in office as "fearless," "manly," and "independent," and paid tribute to their statesmanlike vision and grasp of sound principles.

Yet their example, however useful in the days of Washington, Adams, and the Virginia Dynasty, had little relevance for a more democratic age. Latter-day lawyers were informed that they might learn more valuable lessons from studying the unworthy politicians of the past, such as the Maine legislator John Holmes, who "trimmed his sails to the prevailing wind of popular favor" during the first administration of James Madison:

> "The gladsome light of jurisprudence" was not bright and warm enough for him;—he loved law, but he loved politics more. . . . In reviewing the life of such a man, we may perhaps derive a useful reflection upon the danger, not to say folly, of leaving the broad highway of an honorable and profitable profession, for the fitful and the exciting pursuits, and the unsubstantial rewards of the mere politician. That Mr. Holmes had as much of popular favor and its fruits, as falls to the lot of men, none will deny; that they furnished him the satisfaction and the rewards which he would have acquired in the quiet progress of his profession, we do not believe.[16]

Though Holmes's political opportunism was exceptional for its time, according to law writers, since 1830 the exception had become the rule. "It is well known," declared one commentator in reference to the latter period, "that men of the highest eminence in our profession are seldom members of legislative assemblies in this country, and, when they are, their influence is comparatively small."[17] Political posts now went to party men—third or fourth-rate lawyers who acknowledged no higher principle than self-interest. To retain the support of a mass electorate, these legal turncoats placed themselves at the head of every popular movement, however unwise or dangerous its objectives. They even spearheaded legislative attacks upon the bar and the judiciary, and encouraged a rash of other ill-considered measures which purportedly reflected an ever changing popular will. Under such circumstances politics

---

[16] "The Hon. John Holmes," 6 *Monthly L. Rep.* 151, 154 (1843).
[17] "Codification," 7 *Monthly L. Rep.* 350 (1844).

no longer provided an attractive avocation for the responsible lawyer, who was advised by publicists to stick to his practice if he valued his self-respect.

Behind this warning lay no lament for the passing of the class-conscious "gentleman" in politics. Law writers of the 1830's denied that such a haughty personage had ever existed, at least among lawyers, who had always been simple, hardworking, democratic types. It was not pride or fastidiousness which kept the best attorneys out of politics in the Jacksonian era, but the fact that politics had developed into a full-fledged profession with specialized rules of its own—several of which ran counter to deeply cherished legal attitudes and practices.

Representation, for example, no longer meant what it once did. When biographers praised the manly independence of an early legislator, they were reading political history through legal spectacles. A good politician, by their criteria, represented his constituents as an attorney represented his clients. That is, he acted to promote their best interests as he understood them; and in case of disagreement, his judgment ultimately prevailed. This view of political responsibility could not be reconciled with the more democratic notion that a representative was bound in all cases to carry out the wishes of his constituents. While few successful law-makers ever disregarded the majority will in practice, law writers continued to promote the theory of legal representation until the perfecting of party organization and party discipline in the 1830's demonstrated its obsolescence for all purposes save that of myth.

A similar conflict between legal attitudes and political realities occurred in connection with the problem of electioneering. Lawyers were trained to believe that the job must seek the man. A mass of literature stretching back to the Middle Ages condemned the improper solicitation of legal business and required that the lawyer wait patiently in his office for clients to appear (which they were certain to do, by a process of legal legerdemain, if the would-be practitioner had worked sufficiently hard to prepare himself for the duties of the profession). Publicists incorporated this trait into their image of the early American lawyer, who allegedly looked upon public office as a temporary employment, to be secured like any other retainer. Typical were the circumstances surrounding the election of Charles Marsh, a Vermont attorney, to the House of Representatives in 1814: "He was always averse to holding elective offices, and in this instance, was forced into Congress against his will."[18]

---

[18] "Obituary Notice," 11 *Monthly L. Rep.* 527 (1849).

Twenty years later the reluctant candidate stood little chance of winning an election, even in fiction. Political campaigning had become an art in itself, demanding catchy slogans, colorful personalities, and a degree of ballyhoo foreign to the thinking of earlier generations. No lawyer could now be a successful politician, writers cautioned, unless he abandoned his professional integrity and became a hireling of the masses. Perhaps the insistent appeal to the tradition of the independent practitioner betrayed some uneasiness over current values within the profession itself, where many an attorney had already shown an unseemly willingness to exchange his independence for a secure job with a law firm or corporation.

From a tactical standpoint, of course, the separation of the "real" lawyer from politics offered several advantages to propagandists. It enabled them to class as unprincipled demagogues all members of the bar who spoke up for legislative reform of the law; it suggested that most statutes were either unwise or unnecessary additions to an existing body of basic principles; and it reaffirmed the image of the lawyer as a hardworking technician whose services were as necessary to society as those of any other skilled craftsman:

> To the mass of practitioners, the law is not, except on some rare occasions, an intellectual pursuit. Truth compels us to own, with Wordsworth, that "the demands of life and action," with us, as with men of other pursuits, "but rarely correspond to the dignity and intensity of human desires." We are clever men of business, as a mass, and no more. It is our BUSINESS TALENTS, our PROMPTNESS, ACCURACY, and DILIGENCE, that commands success, respect and influence.[19]

Much the same utilitarian and antipolitical line was taken by apologists for another unpopular occupational group—the officer corps of the United States Army and Navy—during these years, and for similar reasons. Military journalists argued that a permanent cadre of trained professionals posed no threat to democratic institutions, because their energies were wholly absorbed by the technical demands of their science, which gave them neither the time nor the inclination for political intrigues.[20]

---

[19] "Office Duties," 4 *Am. L. Reg.* 193 (1856).

[20] See, for example: Sydney, "Thoughts on the Organization of the Army," *The Military and Naval Magazine of the United States,* II (December, 1833), 193-198; and "The Wants of the Navy," *Army and Navy Chronicle,* XI (December 17, 1840), 398-399. William B. Skelton of Ohio State University, who brought this analogy to my attention, is planning a major study of the military mind in nineteenth century America.

The defense of professional groups in terms of their practical usefulness to society deserves special emphasis, since Perry Miller, in a recent important study of the legal mind in nineteenth-century America, has suggested that the antebellum lawyers were trying to establish themselves as an intellectual elite in the eyes of the public.[21] While this may have been the objective of certain academic jurists such as Kent, Story, and David Hoffman, a different view prevailed among the rank and file who patronized the law magazines. For them legal practice was a bread-and-butter concern, a daily business in which intellectual refinements found little place. "The most learned lawyer in the world would not get business, if he did not attend to it," warned Timothy Walker to the graduating class of the Cincinnati Law School in 1839. "The question with the client is, not who knows the most law, but who will manage a cause the best; and, all other things being equal, he will manage a cause the best, who devotes most attention to it."[22]

Practitioners could not afford to waste time on frivolous cultural pursuits, when it took constant effort just to keep abreast of the increasing volume of new court decisions. If they turned to polite literature for occasional relaxation, they were likely to choose an established classic whose familiarity with the public could be put to good use in courtroom debate. The Bible and Shakespeare were particular favorites for, as one commentator explained, quite apart from their aesthetic qualities, "they may also, sometimes, be quoted to great advantage; the former never but with reverence; the latter, never pedantically."[23] At a time when legal reputations still owed much to oratorical skills, an acquaintance with "good" literature could further aid an attorney to develop a graceful speaking style. On the death of Rufus Choate (1799-1859), perhaps the most cultivated orator of his time, an attempt was made to place the whole matter of nonlegal learning in proper perspective: "True, he laid his foundations deep and broad, by no means confined to legal acquirements, but embracing a rich classic culture, and what we believe aided him more than all, the devoted reading of the Bible: yet these other studies were only episodes, or rather recreations, renewing his professional energies."[24]

---

[21] Perry Miller, *The Life of the Mind in America from the Revolution to the Civil War* (New York, 1965), 99-265.

[22] "Ways and Means of Professional Success; being the substance of a Valedictory Address to the Graduates of the Law Class, in the Cincinnati College, by T. Walker, Professor of Law in that Institution: delivered March 2, 1839," 1 *Western L. J.* 545 (1844).

[23] "A Letter of Judge Daggett," 8 *Monthly L. Rep.* 94 (1845).

[24] Fuller, "Rufus Choate," 25 *Monthly L. Rep.* 266-267 (1863).

To picture the lawyer as detached from all interests which did not relate to his professional life suited the needs of myth-makers; but they found it difficult to reconcile their antipolitical attitudes with the demands of public order. For if legislatures were corrupt and the laws they passed unwise, why should citizens obey? A mounting wave of lawlessness throughout the Union made the question far from academic, as journalists pointed with concern to lynchings in Mississippi, riots in Pennsylvania and Massachusetts, duels in Louisiana, and vigilante justice in the goldfields of California. Nor were these symptoms of social disintegration confined to the local level; even Federal authorities met with popular resistance in their efforts to enforce fugitive slave laws. Some anti-slavery agitators openly professed adherence to a "higher law" than that found in the Constitution of the United States, making the individual conscience the determining guide to political, as well as religious, behavior. Such subjectivity impressed legal writers as the ultimate democratic heresy, and they denounced the use of moralistic arguments to justify the overthrow of existing institutions:

> It is among the strange signs of the times, that individuals are found saying and doing the most violent, unjust and dangerous things, without rebuke, *because they say and do them in the cause of anti-slavery*. Scarcely a voice is raised against these excesses, because, if raised, it would be answered with the charge of enmity to the slave. This should not be. . . . If we would resist the extension of slavery, we must equally resist the spirit of rebellion against the constitution.[25]

But counsels of moderation and proposals to strengthen the police forces in major urban centers provided no adequate solution to the problem of bad laws. Acknowledging that the public had reason to distrust its legislators, spokesmen for the "workingmen of the profession" sought a technique by which the bar might assume responsibility for a reform program without becoming embroiled in partisan politics. Their strategy called for the creation of a new institution which did not take practical shape until the next generation: the independent administrative commission.

In its most rudimentary form, the commission idea suggested a small permanent body of trained specialists appointed by the governor of a state to scrutinize the final draft of all legislative measures. They would act primarily as stylistic critics, correcting the language of a law to make it more intelligible to the general

---

[25] "The Latimer Case," 5 *Monthly L. Rep.* 497 (1843).

public as well as consistent with professional norms. Some writers
went further and argued for a true board of censors, with power
to weed out in advance all doubtful bills, including any which con-
tradicted previous enactments. Through their expert guidance a
haphazard mass of state legislation might in time be reduced to an
orderly system of harmonious rules.

But it was as a potential planning agency that the commission
made its strongest appeal to the legal imagination. Publicists
dreamed of interstate boards of lawyers and jurists entrusted with
the duty of framing national laws to cover such matters as commerce, land tenures, education, and crimes. Unlike "tinkering legislatures," these professional bodies would engage in comprehensive social planning, working from basic principles to their most
far-reaching ramifications:

> . . . and this process seems to be most in harmony with the
> spirit of the time, which is inquiring, philosophical and theo-
> rizing. . . . What would be said of the architect, who, to
> build his arch, should try, one after another, all possible shapes,
> till at last he hit the one which would stand, when he had a
> slate, and in his head principles, on which he could in a little
> while reckon just what must be built to form a true and perfect
> structure?[26]

For the first time since the early Republic the interests of the
technician could also be reconciled with those of the statesman,
as lawyers proposed to bury sectional differences within a network
of uniform economic and cultural regulations coextensive with the
Union.

Their visions remained unfulfilled, however, for reasons which
should have been apparent to every realistic member of the bar.
Apart from their elitist pretensions, all of these schemes depended
in greater or less degree upon the support of those very legislative bodies whose alleged irresponsibility had created the nation's
lawless temper. Furthermore, the commission idea, for all its
apolitical tone, pointed to the development of a fourth branch of
the government—an administrative wing whose personnel would
enjoy the substance of political power without its attendant risks.

---

[26] "Advancement of the Law by Lawyers," 11 *Monthly L. Rep.* 150-
151 (1848). For the details of several projects, see: Tellkampf, "On
Codification, or the Systematizing of the Law," 8 *Am. Jurist and L. Mag.*
283 (1842); "National Jurisprudence," 3 *U.S. Monthly L. Mag.* 125
(1851); "Legislation," 5 *U.S. Monthly L. Mag.* 125 (1852); Bishop, "Law
in the United States," 3 *Am. L. Reg.* 60 (1854).

And it would take a Civil War to demonstrate the merits of bureaucratic planning to a public still wedded to theories of laissez faire.

Meanwhile the idealism of the antebellum bar found a practical outlet closer to home. In 1849 the American Legal Association was established

> for the purpose of insuring safety and facility in the collection of claims and the transaction of legal business throughout the United States. Its design is to furnish professional and business men with the name of at least one prompt, efficient and trustworthy Lawyer in every shire-town and in each of the principal cities and villages in the Union, who will transact with despatch and for a reasonable compensation, such professional business as may be entrusted to him.[27]

Promoted largely through the efforts of John Livingston, a law writer and editor, the Association was both broader and narrower than any previous legal organization in the nation's history. While it claimed members in every state of the Union (as well as two in England), its objectives were rigorously limited. As a lawyer referral service, it disclaimed all interest in politics, community welfare, or even the encouragement of a general spirit of fraternalism among practitioners. Instead, it appealed to the technician's desire for more rational procedures, as it focused attention upon the lawyer as a competitive businessman.

Every practicing attorney who subscribed five dollars and furnished "satisfactory evidence of professional integrity and capacity" could join the A.L.A. on a two-year basis. He thereupon received an official Manual, complete with constitution, by-laws, and a list of the names and addresses of all members (including one director in each state). The Association undertook to distribute additional copies of the Manual to the "business public," and also to place advertisements from time to time in major newspapers across the country. The advantages of such a centralized reference bureau were sufficiently alluring to keep the A.L.A. in existence for some five years, after which it quietly expired.

As a stimulus to professional unity, the Association served a useful purpose; but even more important was the work of its Secretary, John Livingston. Drawing upon a voluminous legal correspondence, Livingston compiled in 1850 an authoritative list of the names and addresses of all practicing lawyers and judges in the United States. His *United States Lawyer's Directory and Official*

---

[27] "The American Legal Association," 3 *U.S. Monthly L. Mag. Advertiser* (1851).

*Bulletin* incorporated data supplied by state and local officials down to the level of county sheriffs, and formed the first accurate legal census ever taken in America. Its publication testified both to the coming-of-age of the American bar and to its growing preoccupation with intramural matters. Livingston revised his register annually until the collapse of the A.L.A. in 1854; thereafter he continued to bring out new editions at irregular intervals through 1868.[28]

The approach of civil war did little to change the introspective bias of most legal writers. Characteristically they tended to view the slavery crisis as a contrivance of partisan politicians, useful in campaign years but of no real concern to the general public. As late as October, 1860, one commentator predicted that if "these contending dogmas be pressed to the practical result of deranging trade, augmenting prices, and curtailing commerce, a spirit will be roused which will put an end to all further disturbance from this source."[29]

One may deprecate these attitudes of olympian detachment as a cowardly flight from responsibility, but they may likewise have represented an inevitable stage in the professionalization of the American lawyer. This much at least is certain: in the developing pattern of nineteenth-century legal thought they played no inconsiderable role. Emory Washburn illustrated the ease with which they were transmitted to the postwar generation when he told a graduating class at Harvard Law School in July, 1864, of the destiny that awaited the legal expert in the reconstruction era to come:

> You have only to wait a brief time, when the business of reorganization must be resumed; and the people will look to the aid and counsel of others than the mad or selfish politicians, whose evil counsels or rash judgments first involved them in the disastrous consequences of alienated affections and civil discord. Such a violence has been done to our institutions, such a strain has been made upon the strength of the common bond that bound us together as a nation, that it will require the wisest counsel, the calmest judgment, and the most devoted patriotism to restore the government again to anything like

---

[28] The Library of Congress records list ten separate publications between 1850 and 1868. As editor of the *United States Monthly Law Magazine,* Livingston also devoted one composite issue (Oct.-Dec., 1851) to a reprinting of his complete *Law Register* for that year.

[29] "Slavery in the States and Territories," 23 *Monthly L. Rep.* 458 (1860).

harmonious action. And these, I repeat, are not to be found in the political leaders who caused the mischief to begin with. Nor is it to the mere man of business that we are to look, nor to the scholar, or man of letters, however speculative he may have shown himself in his study into causes which be hid beyond the reach of his unpractised vision. In the restoration of peace to our distracted country under the dominion of well administered law, such as she had enjoyed for three quarters of a century, I am sure that our profession are to take a most important part.[30]

Indeed, in the postwar world of regulatory commissions, scientific planning, and patrician politics, the elitist ideals of the antebellum bar became practical realities for the first time. But the growth of administrative agencies, far from settling the conflict between political and legal values, merely added a new dimension to the American lawyer's continuing quest for acceptance in a democratic society.

---

[30] Washburn, "Reconstruction: The Duty of the Profession to the Times," 26 *Monthly L. Rep.* 278 (1864).

# INDEX

Abinger, Lord, 306

Absolute (strict) liability, 274

Adams, Brooks, 584, 586

Adams, John, 109, 211, 217, 222, 633, 654, 655

Adams, John Quincy, 160-61, 166, 470, 665

Admiralty jurisdiction, federal: advantages to plaintiffs under, 419-20; and commerce clause powers, 420, 422-23, 427; compared with England's admiralty jurisdiction, 414; constitutional source of, 429, 431, 432; effect of states' rights doctrine on, 424-25; extensions of, 421, 422-24, 434; interstate limitations on, 425-27; resentment against extension of, 416-18; separation from state jurisdiction, 425-26; and steamboards, 418-19; tidewater limitations on, 413, 415, 419-20

Admiralty jurisdiction, states, 423-24, 425-26, 432

Admiralty law, 123-24, 139-40, 428; developed independently from commerce clause regulation, 434; effect of Civil War on, 426-27; limited by Eng-lish tidewater precedents, 412, 413, 416, 418, 422, 429; origins, 428; subject to Congressional control, 434. *See also* Admiralty jurisdiction, federal; Admiralty jurisdiction, states

Adoption: by deed, 391-92, 393; effect on testate succession, 397-403; and expansion of the family, 352-53; forms of, 338, 346, 407-8; and hereditary traits, 360, 404; need for regulation of, in America, 353-54; in New England Puritan society, 349-52; pragmatic versus philanthropic views of, 375-76, 404; in primitive cultures, 338, 339; problems with blood relatives, 389-91; in Roman society, 339-41, 407; as source of child labor, 351-52; under Roman law, 339-40; unrecognized in England, 341-43, 345, 407-8; by will, 350

Adoption, law of, American: chronology of, 336-37; and contractual arrangements, 387-89; purpose, 401-2; recognition by, of Spanish adoptions, 383-84; religious purposes of, in Puritan New England, 349; response to Hawaiian customs, 383; response to Indian

**About the Editor**

Wythe Holt, professor of law at the University of Alabama, has specialized in American legal history. His essays have appeared in such journals as the *Indiana Law Review,* the *Virginia Law Review,* and the *Virginia Magazine of History and Biography.*